W0373375

UTB

UTB **8432**

Eine Arbeitsgemeinschaft der Verlage

Böhlau Verlag · Köln · Weimar · Wien
Verlag Barbara Budrich · Opladen · Farmington Hills
facultas.wuv · Wien
Wilhelm Fink · München
A. Francke Verlag · Tübingen und Basel
Haupt Verlag · Bern · Stuttgart · Wien
Julius Klinkhardt Verlagsbuchhandlung · Bad Heilbrunn
Lucius & Lucius Verlagsgesellschaft · Stuttgart
Mohr Siebeck · Tübingen
Orell Füssli Verlag · Zürich
Ernst Reinhardt Verlag · München · Basel
Ferdinand Schöningh · Paderborn · München · Wien · Zürich
Eugen Ulmer Verlag · Stuttgart
UVK Verlagsgesellschaft · Konstanz
Vandenhoeck & Ruprecht · Göttingen
vdf Hochschulverlag AG an der ETH Zürich

Peter Fenn

A Student's Advanced Grammar of English (SAGE)

francke
VERLAG

Dr. Peter Fenn lehrt Englisch an der Pädagogischen Hochschule Ludwigsburg.

Bibliografische Information der Deutschen Nationalbibliothek

Die Deutsche Nationalbibliothek verzeichnet diese Publikation in der Deutschen Nationalbibliografie; detaillierte bibliografische Daten sind im Internet über <http://dnb.d-nb.de> abrufbar.

Dischingerweg 5 · D-72070 Tübingen
ISBN 978-3-7720-8344-0

Gedruckt auf chlorfrei gebleichtem und säurefreiem Werkdruckpapier.

Internet: http://www.francke.de
E-Mail: info@francke.de

Einbandgestaltung: Atelier Reichert, Stuttgart
Satz: Informationsdesign D. Fratzke, Kirchentellinsfurt
Druck und Bindung: fgb – freiburger graphische betriebe
Printed in Germany

ISBN 978-3-8252-8432-9 (UTB-Bestellnummer)

To the memory of Albrecht Metzger

Foreword

This book has evolved from a professional lifetime of teaching English language and linguistics in German higher education. Among target audiences, over time, a wide variety of native languages have been represented: French, Italian, Russian, Chinese, Greek, Turkish, Norwegian, Hungarian, to name just a few. Not surprisingly, however, the principal group has consisted of native speakers of German, largely pre-service teacher trainees pursuing university-type English studies at the immediate post-school stage, but including also serving teachers in a variety of contexts: within the framework of student school practice, for example, on in-service or further training programmes, as instructors in the university or postgraduate training fields, and in numerous other professional and personal environments. It is therefore specifically the needs and experiences of the German-speaking language-user that have gone into the shaping of this advanced English reference grammar.

I take this opportunity of thanking the multi-generations of students that I have taught for demonstrating to me what a complex matter the English language is, and for challenging me to provide them with appropriate instruction and explanation.

My interest and involvement in various language research projects also received particular stimulation from fruitful association over many years with colleagues in the English department of Ludwigsburg Pedagogical University. Among these I would firstly like to name Dr. Peter Dines and Professor Günter Nold, both pioneers and field-workers in diverse areas of applied language study.

My closest and longest association was with the late Professor Albrecht Metzger, with whom I held seminars and conducted research not only during the latter years of his normal staff tenure, but also for no fewer than thirteen years after his official retirement from the department. Albrecht Metzger was effectively the founding father of applied linguistic research in Ludwigsburg. For many, many hours of stimulating discussion, professional encouragement and personal companionship, as well as for numerous insights into the English language, I will always remain in his debt.

Peter Fenn, Ludwigsburg, April 2010

Contents

Chapter 1 Introduction – Elements of English

On grammar 001

In certain corners of language teaching methodology, *grammar* has recently become rather a dirty word, associated with a whole range of negatives. Most of these, with some basis in fact, have hardened into a string of prejudices: skill in grammatical explanation is not the same as command of the language; grammar consists of learning rules by heart; 'communicating' is the natural way to learn language, whereas learning cognitively is artificial; learning is more effective if learners are allowed to express themselves freely, with no onus upon them to produce what the teacher feels is correct; grammar rules are difficult to define anyway, and native speakers do not know them consciously, so why demand this of foreign learners? And so on.

In defence of the anti-grammar lobby it must be said that grammar in its traditional sense conjures up visions of heavily cognitive approaches to language teaching. These assume an educated older learner of secondary school age and beyond. Emphasis on early learning, plus critical reflection on how to teach beginners in general, has naturally led to a search for alternatives. In this respect it is understandable and desirable that 'communication' should be given a forefront position in the modern language classroom. Approaches that require intensive rote-learning before communication takes place at all are clearly not suitable for learners at elementary and pre-elementary educational stages. Furthermore, informal observation suggests that learners at all stages have benefitted, and continue to benefit, from the more prominent position that communicative interaction has generally begun to occupy in classroom procedure (at least in Germany) over the last thirty years.

However, didactic theories tend to overgeneralize their position. They present themselves, firstly, as exclusive, and deny the pluralism and eclecticism which exist in teachers' professional practice. Secondly, and connected with this, they often presuppose that all learners learn in the same way. Thirdly, and more gravely, their validity is often asserted for all ages of learners, although their focus is demonstrably limited to a particular sector or phase of the learning process.

In Germany, for instance, 'no-grammar' attitudes persist far beyond the initial stages of teaching. Paradoxically, they seem to be especially widespread in pre-university phases of education, precisely when, among advanced learners, cognitive strategies are necessary, and require particular attention and development. In grammar there is the need not only to counteract fossilization ('pet mistakes'), but to exploit more complex structural domains of the language (for instance in syntax) to achieve a higher level of proficiency in connected speech and writing. Evidence shows that advanced learners who wish to improve must develop habits of ***targeted language observation***. This applies as much to sentence-structure as it does to vocabulary. Apart from that, it is often impossible to separate the two in the learning task. All forms of contextual and co-textual learning (e.g. what is known nowadays in some quarters as 'chunk-learning') require a cognitive grasp of the syntax involved.

Finally, extensive areas that are regarded as belonging to the 'grammar' of the language (because they are part of the structural system) involve semantic criteria of application, e.g. tense forms, modal verbs, prepositions, etc. Meaning, usage and the formal system coalesce here, and strict division of learning material into the separate categories of grammar and semantics would be a delusion. Precisely holistic learning, as necessary at the latest from the intermediate stage onwards, requires a sturdy portion of grammatical cognition to be successful. Ideological enshrinement of early learning principles is especially unhelpful here.

As with human dress, fashions in teaching methodology come and go, but the anatomy of the object remains: in this case the body of the language – one that requires continual exploration and explication.

This brings us to the next point concerning grammar and directly affecting the aim of this book. Why yet another English grammar? There are several answers to this question. Firstly, although English is one of the most thoroughly documented languages in the world, it is wrong to assume that the process of describing it has been exhausted and the final judgement spoken. English language research is an alive and ongoing field, and English grammar a broad discipline where controversies continue in many an unsuspected corner. Even the wider avenues have dark spots and sudden bends. One need only take the body of research on tense and modality in the last fifty years, for instance, to realize how arduous the quest for an understanding of certain language phenomena can be. And the findings then have to be translated into manageable guidelines for the learner. This book attempts to contribute to that process, and bridge the gap between language research and language user.

Secondly, there is an obvious need in Germany for an applied linguistic approach to grammar explanation which is aimed at specific groups of students and scholars: in the case of this book, students of upper-school and university levels, as well as language professionals in teaching, translating, publishing and numerous other fields of advanced language practice and linguistic enquiry.

Thirdly, this book is intended to answer several purposes at the same time:

- to give systematic insights into the fine mechanics of English
- to support and further practical command of the language at both basic and advanced levels
- to present a readable and structured text with a top-down approach to the data
- to provide an authoritative reference work on individual phenomena
- to equip teachers of English with viable modes of explanation and communicable rule guides
- to account especially for the German-speaking learner, and where appropriate to point out contrasts and similarities with the German language

- to act as a basis for linguistic discussion of various areas of English (e.g. aspects of syntax, semantics of tense usage, the noun phrase, etc.) in a university seminar or research setting.

The character of English 002

002/1 Who speaks English?
002/2 Where English comes from
002/3 Language varieties
002/4 Regional variants of English and standard languages

002/1 Who speaks English?

English is quite literally a world language. It is the dominant mother tongue in Britain and Ireland, the USA, Canada, Australia and New Zealand. In South Africa, although native to only 9% of the population, English is a joint official language along with several local ones, such as Xhosa, Zulu and Afrikaans. In India it is also an official national language, together with Hindi and seventeen other regional languages.

In these and other former British colonies and administrative areas, including several Caribbean, African and Far Eastern states, English has a central position in education and other walks of public life, and is learnt by non-natives as a strong second language. Altogether, it is spoken in a prominent cultural or official capacity in more than 60 countries or territories around the globe. In quite a few more it has some kind of special status as a general and traditional means of communication. All these regions taken together have a population of something like 2,000,000,000, or about one-third of all the world's people. Of these, about 337 million speak it as a first language, and roughly 235 million as a second language. In addition to this, it is the world's most learned foreign language, i.e. the first foreign language in about 50% of all countries. And it is the most used international language in diplomacy, politics and the law, in all fields of industry and commerce, including media communication, transport, tourism and sport, and, of course in the scientific and academic world.

002/2 Where English comes from

Within the Indo-European super-clan, English belongs to the Germanic family. Its modern siblings are Low German and Dutch, with the Scandinavian languages as slightly more distant cousins. English originally came to the British Isles in the 5th century A.D. in the form of several old Low German dialects. These were brought by North German tribes known collectively as ***Anglo-Saxons***, who invaded lowland Britain and settled there permanently after the fall of the Roman Empire. (English children learn that the Romans 'went home' in 410 A.D., leaving England at the mercy of 'barbarian' Germanic tribes.) Over the next three centuries the Anglo-Saxon parts of Britain became ***'Engla-land'***, and the Anglo-Saxons grew into the ***'Englisc'***. (They did not learn to spell their new name properly until the French taught them later to write the ***c*** as an ***h***.)

The Anglo-Saxon (or ***Old English***) language in the 8th century was still similar in grammar and a lot of its vocabulary to Old High German, with a complex case system and verb conjugation. By this time, Anglo-Saxon society had become stabilized and orderly, formed into kingdoms and settled communities with established administrative and legal procedures. A flourishing Christian culture had developed, influenced mainly by Rome and the Continent (though in the north also by Irish monastery traditions and learning). The 9th century reign of the famous ***King Alfred*** of ***Wessex*** (the 'kingdom of the West Saxons'), a devout Christian ruler and also a writer and scholar, saw the beginnings of public education and English literature.

Meanwhile, however, the peace and tranquillity of 'Old England' was being threatened by new invaders, the ***Danes*** (or ***'Vikings'***) of Scandinavia. These fresh waves of migrants had begun to settle in the east and north of England, where their language, ***Old Norse***, and their own tribal customs took root. England in Alfred's time was divided into two parts, one Danish, the other Anglo-Saxon. Re-conquest followed, but Viking attacks renewed, and in the early 1000s Britain became entirely Danish. ***Old Norse*** had a considerable impact on Old English. The plosive consonants [k] and [g], as in *kid, dyke, get* and *give* and the combination [sk], as in *sky, skin, skill,* etc., are of Norse origin. The surname ending *-son,* as in *Robertson* or *Gibson,* final syllables like *-by* and *-thorpe* in place-names (*Grimsby, Scunthorpe*), and above all the pronouns *they/them/their,* are all parts of England's Scandinavian legacy.

Despite these changes, however, the basic character of Old English remained as it was, as the two languages were similar. A far greater upheaval, not just socially and politically, but also in language, took place as a result of the ***Norman Conquest*** a little later. The ***Normans*** were also originally Vikings, but had settled in the northwest coastal region of France permanently, and were now a powerful French-speaking territorial people. When they invaded the south of Britain in 1066, they were to change the face and tongue of Old England for ever. Great castles and fortresses were built (including the Tower of London), the feudal system was introduced and the language of a foreign aristocracy for 200 years was French. The Middle Ages had begun (though presumably nobody knew this at the time)! Slowly, native English people started to infiltrate the aristocracy and the Norman rulers began to develop a kind of 'French English' to communicate with them. By about 1200, this had become the general tongue among most social groups. Norman French and Anglo-Saxon died out, and French English became what was later called Middle English, i.e. the ordinary English of the Middle Ages and the forerunner of the modern language.

Middle English was quite different from Old English, not just in vocabulary, but also in pronunciation and grammar. Most of the old grammatical inflections were lost, verbs became simplified and grammatical case and gender disappeared. By about the middle of the 14th century, English had taken on a lot of the general character that it has today. With a bit of effort and a little learning, a present-day speaker can come to understand Middle English fairly easily. Old English, by comparison, has to be learnt more or less like a foreign language.

The development of printing in the later 15th century made an important contribution to stabilizing and spreading written forms of Middle English. Printing was centred on London, the capital, the seat of government and the commercial hub of England. This helped to establish London administrative English as a standard language. It was around this time, however, that English started to undergo further changes, focused now on the pronunciation of vowels. The ***Great Vowel Shift***, completed mainly in the first decades of the 16th century (i.e. during the early reign of Henry VIII), marks the transition from Middle English to Modern English. It involved changes in the long vowel system: generally speaking, long open vowels became closer and long close vowels became diphthongs. For example, the word *loud* was spelt *loude* in Middle English and pronounced [lu:də]. By Shakespeare's time the long [u:] had become a diphthong [oʊ], paving the way for its further development into its present form [aʊ] in the early 18th century. (Some vowels, particularly diphthongs, changed in several stages and took a little longer to reach their final modern form.)

It is the ***Vowel Shift*** which is mainly responsible for the irregularities of modern English spelling. Printing fixed the spelling of many words before the vowels had shifted into their modern form. In other words, we still have Middle English spelling, but with Modern English pronunciation. The discrepancy can drive schoolchildren and teachers to desperation.

In summary, the general stages in the historical development of English are as follows:

- 450–1150: Old English (Anglo-Saxon)
- 1150–1500: Middle English
- 1500 – ***present-day***: Modern English

Additionally, the modern period is sometimes divided into:

- 1500–1700: Early Modern English
- 1700 – ***present-day***: Late Modern English

This takes account of two things: firstly, some elements in the vowel shift did not find their true modern form until the beginning of the 18th century; and secondly, some 16th and early 17th century English (e.g. from Shakespeare and his contemporaries) is not easy for modern readers to understand without considerable guidance and practice.

002/3 Language varieties

Varieties are certain types of language used in certain contexts. Where context and language have a close relationship, the language usually shows highly ***conventionalized*** features, i.e. stereotyped and rule-governed characteristics. For instance, I was once in a pub paying for food at the bar, and offered a credit card to the barmaid, who responded with (1)a. The meaning of this, expressed in more neutral terms, is (1)b.:

(1) a. Sorry, love, can't swipe it, electro's up the spout.
b. I'm sorry, but the machine won't register the card, as the electronics aren't working.

The most general ***variety*** characteristic we can see in (1)a. is that this is ***informal*** language typical of ***casual speech*** (though not necessarily exclusive to it): ***weak*** or ***contracted***

forms are used (*can't, electro's*), the personal pronoun *I* is missing (***pronoun ellipsis***), and there is an ***informal vocative***, *love*, which, though addressed to a stranger (myself in this case), suggests in many parts of Britain a certain familiarity and social equality (the formal alternative in this case would have been *sir*). The phrase *up the spout* for 'broken/out of order' is one example of ***slang***. This means the conscious replacement of a standard expression by one that creates a coarser, and usually more trivial image. The effect is often humorous or ironic, especially when, as in this case, the slang term is a ***metaphor*** from a completely different (and usually more concrete) area of meaning. Another example of slang is the ***abbreviation*** of *electronic equipment* to *electro*, again tending to trivialize, by making something complex into something familiar (almost personal), and 'easy to handle'.

All this adds up to the variety that we call ***colloquial***, i.e. relating to the ***spoken*** rather than the written language, and a ***casual*** rather than a formal tone. In addition, the informality here, particularly the use of the vocative *love*, suggests friendliness (which in fact was underlined by the barmaid's tone of voice and facial expression, conveying sympathy). This kind of ***variety*** can be regarded as 'style' (or as it is often called linguistically, ***register***), and conveys ***attitude***. Apart from this example of ***general register***, we have a more specific kind in *electro* and *swipe*. In addition to being slang, *electro* is also a technical term connected with a specialized sphere of activity, i.e. the world of computerized pay-machines. *Swipe* is the same. This is ***special register***, and immediately tells us what subject field we are in. Similarly, when we read or hear expressions like *cross, shot, header, long ball,* or *opposition party, speech, table a motion, backbencher,* or *add spices and onions to pan and fry gently,* then we recognize certain topic areas or ***fields of discourse*** (here, respectively, soccer, politics and cookery).

The following two ***register*** samples, which refer to the same thing, show a striking contrast. The first is a diary description by a woman called Dorothy Wordsworth of a particular view of the Thames and London as she left the capital by coach on a summer morning at the beginning of the 18th century. The second is by her brother William, the popular Romantic poet, who was with her on the same occasion and later wrote a sonnet about how the scene had struck him:

(2) a. We mounted the Dover coach at Charing Cross. It was a beautiful morning. The city, St. Paul's, with the river and a multitude of little boats, made a most beautiful sight as we crossed Westminster bridge.
b. Earth has not anything to show more fair:/Dull would he be of soul who could pass by/A sight so touching in its majesty:/This City now doth, like a garment, wear/The beauty of the morning …

There are several obvious ***register signals*** in (2)a. These show, firstly, the topic of discourse (leaving London on a journey): *Dover coach, Charing Cross, the city, St.Paul's, the river,* etc. Other features indicate to us the type of text that this is, i.e. a personal report in prose, giving personal impressions: … *made a most beautiful sight as we crossed Westminster bridge*. Though we can sense the experience and mood of the writer, the style has a neutral, factual quality to it, firstly through the ordinary sentence structure, and secondly because of the names. (2)b., on the other hand, has a rhythm and a lyrical intensity that are typical of a consciously chosen ***poetic register***. Names are unimportant here. It is the depth of feeling experienced by the poet-observer that attention is focused on.

Returning to pub-talk, we must consider other features in (1)a. that cannot be seen on the page, but which were very obvious in the spoken message. The barmaid had an ***accent*** showing that she was a Londoner: *swipe*, for example, was pronounced [swɒɪp], and *spout* [spæʊʔ] with a 'swallowed' [t] at the end, i.e. a glottal stop. A particular ***accent*** is one important mark of a ***regional variety***. Pronunciation, that is, can show geographical area of origin. A further indication can be ***local forms*** of ***grammar*** and ***vocabulary***. (3)a. gives examples, again from London, and (3)b. the translation:

(3) a. No good asting me bruvver. He don't know nuffin, do 'e?
b. It's no good asking my brother. He doesn't know anything, does he?

Here, instead of *my* the possessive is *me*. And in the second part of the sentence we have the famous ***double negative*** found in many spoken varieties of English, not only in Britain but in most other parts of the English-speaking world, including, prominently, America. Londoners also switch certain individual singular and plural verb forms (e.g. *he do, he were*, but *they was*). Again, this is also found in other regional varieties. When, in addition to ***accent***, there are other noticeable local characteristics like this, we speak of a ***dialect***. Note that in (3)a. the spelling represents the pronunciation: here we can see the pronunciation of [k] as [t] in some words, and the widespread use of [f] for ***th*** [θ]. This is not 'official' spelling, of course, as the written language is entirely standardized, and spoken variants have no written form. Nevertheless, writers have often created special 'phonetic' spellings for regional speech in order to represent it authentically in texts. This has led to certain generally accepted ways of putting some regional varieties on paper.

To come back to 3(a), the kind of London speech represented here, known traditionally as ***Cockney***, is regarded as ***low-class*** speech and a taboo in all more educated circles. That is, we have an example here of not just a ***regional*** but also a ***social variety***. Among British dialects, Cockney is literally in a class of its own, and is not used by higher class groups at all, even in London. To a certain extent, however, this trend applies to most regional variants in their more 'extreme' forms: the more local they are (one could also say the more broadly they are spoken), the more they are regarded as having low social prestige. That is, ***broad dialect*** (or even just ***accent***) is generally a ***social marker***, and to a certain extent is therefore also a ***social variety***. On the other hand, the prestige of a particular variety may be high among the people who speak it, even if it is low outside. This can lead to the kind of 'inverted snobbery' which many Cockney speakers, for example, used to be notorious for, with their traditional disdain for the 'upper-classes'. In the past, country dialect speakers also used their insular speech patterns chauvinistically, in order to emphasize their own insular identity and solidarity, and to exclude unwanted outsiders.

002/4 Regional variants of English and standard languages

Of anywhere in the English-speaking world, regional variation is greatest in Britain. This may surprise many who like to think of Britain as the 'mother of good English'. But this is actually a myth. It is true that for a long time in history the accent of the English aristocracy ('Queen's English') enjoyed great prestige in the power structures of the English-speaking world. It was the educated cultural ideal. But it was not naturally spoken by many outside the power élites. The class system and the very traditional regional divisions dating back at least to later Anglo-Saxon times made Britain a land of many 'Englishes'. The differences have now been levelled to some extent by general education, mass communications and resulting social mobility. But they are still very noticeable in certain sections of the more static regional populations. This also applies to immigrant communities, which have given some of their own specific features to the native varieties, especially in London, for instance, or in the large cities of the Midlands and the North. The following overview of regional varieties is based on ***accent***. The prominent features are generally in the ***vowel*** sounds. We can give here only a few examples of each variety. They are intended as a ***selection*** of pronunciation features from a particular region: but this does not necessarily mean that all speakers in that region share them. Scottish, Welsh and Irish English, for example, can be further sub-divided, and are more differentiated within their own individual internal regions than we can describe in this general overview.

002/4.1 England

There are three main divisions in ***England***: ***Southern English*** (Channel coast to southern border of West Midlands in the Birmingham area); ***Midlands English*** (from Birmingham to the northern borders of Cheshire, Derbyshire, Nottinghamshire, Lincolnshire); ***Northern English*** (from Manchester and Humberside to the Scottish border). Characteristic features of the main varieties are reflected in the two vowel sounds in *made up*. In ***Southern*** and Standard English these are [eɪ] and [ʌ]. In ***Northern***, they are [e:] and [ʊ], and in ***Midlands*** a mixture: *made* as in Southern and *up* as in Northern. A particular Northern feature is the use of [æ] for long [ɑ:], as in [bæθ] and [pæs] for *bath* and *pass*.

Within Southern, there are differences between East (London) and West (Devon, Cornwall, Somerset, Dorset). Two of the most significant are the tendency in the West to pronounce the ***o***-diphthong as in *no* as a long monophthong [o:] and the consonant ***r*** in the rhotic American way after vowels, so that *no car* comes out as [no: kar].

There are also distinct 'islands' in the ***Northern*** region: ***Merseyside*** English (around Liverpool), known popularly as 'Scouse', and ***Northeast***, centred on Newcastle, traditionally called 'Geordie'.

The three other general accent varieties in Britain are ***Scottish*** (or ***Scots***), ***Welsh*** and ***Irish***, all of which are also very distinctive.

002/4.2 Scotland

Scottish shares one or two vowel renderings with Northern English, e.g. the diphthong in *day* is a half-close monophthong [e:] as in German *leben*, although often shorter, as [e].

Most, however, are its own, such as the pronunciation of [aʊ] as in *house* as if it was Southern English [əʊ] in *road*. A further variant of this is like German short ***ü*** in *küssen*, i.e. *house* as [hys]. This is also used for long [u:] as in *truth*, pronounced in Scots [tryθ]. Open [ɒ] as in Southern *hot* is a long [ɔ:], as in Southern *ought*, but the *ought*-vowel itself is often shortened to [ɔ]. Southern [æ] is generally [a:], i.e. [ka:t] for *cat*.

002/4.3 Wales

Wales has its own traditional Celtic language, ***Welsh***, still spoken as a first language by nearly one-fifth of the population, and supported nowadays a great deal in education, the arts and the media. Welsh English is very much influenced by the Welsh language: the Welsh English accent is basically the 'foreign' accent of a Welsh speaker, even among the 80% who do not speak native Welsh. Particular features are: a certain lilt or ***sing-song*** in the rhythms of connected speech, especially emphasized by ***rising intonation*** at the ends of phrases and sentences; a general tendency in South Wales to lengthen all vowels; use of [ə] for [ʌ], so that the vowels in *the cut* are the same; use of a diphthong [ɪu] for [u:] in certain words like *drew* and *pew*: [drɪu], [pɪu], etc.; pronunciation of long [ɑ:] as [æ], as in ***Northern*** English (see above); the lengthening or 'drawing out' of consonants between vowels: [bɪz:i], *busy*, [məd:i], *muddy*.

002/4.4 Ireland

Ireland also has its own Celtic language, ***Gaelic***. Despite its status as an official co-national language (with English), it is spoken nowadays as a native language by a relatively small section of the population, mainly in the western parts of the country. Nevertheless, in Ireland, also, most of the English accent features derive from the old native language.

Characteristic of Irish English are the following: [ɑ:] or [a:] for [ɔ:], as in [kɑ:t], *caught*; [ɔ] for [ʌ], as in [bɔt], *but*; pronunciation of [r] after vowels, i.e. ***rhotic***, [kɑ:r] *car*; [a:] for [ə:] and sometimes [ɑ:], as in [ba:rd], *bird*, and [ka:rt], *cart*; [e:] for final long [i:], as in [te:], *tea*; use of a clear ***l***-sound instead of a dark or velarized [ɫ] at the ends of syllables, so that the two ***l***-sounds in *little* are the same; ***th***-sounds replaced by [t] and [d], as in [dɪs], *this*, and [tɪn], *thin*; on the other hand ***t***- and ***d***-sounds are often pronounced dentally, which makes them sound like a 'light' ***th***, especially in final position, e.g. [bet^h], *bet*.

Northern Irish is strongly influenced by Scottish, and is often referred to as ***Ulster Scots***. This goes back to the politically motivated settlement of Scottish Protestants in Ulster in the 17th century.

002/4.5 Standard British English

The British pronunciation standard is known as Received Pronunciation, RP for short. It is usually defined as the pronunciation used by educated speakers in London and southeast England. This role has developed from London's long historical tradition as the political, administrative, commercial and cultural centre of the nation, more or less uninterrupted since the Norman Conquest. The idea of a national and social standard in language is aristocratic in origin and has to do with social acceptance among the ruling classes. Educational institutions and public media promoted this top-down ideal, with the result that RP became enshrined as the desirable phonetic form of leadership behaviour long after the aristocracy had lost most of its political power. The old language transferred to the new rulers. As education and social mobility have spread, however, RP has itself changed from what used to be called 'Queen's English' or Oxford English, and has become more generalized. Conservative RP, as the old norms are called, has loosened its social stranglehold on public life and has given way to more generous, encompassing forms. RP with a slight Northern, Scottish or Irish flavour has been well regarded now for at least a generation. Even certain characteristics of lower-class London speech, formerly a source of suspicion to those at the top, have started to infiltrate the natural pronunciation of the younger generation in the more educated classes, even including, occasionally, their representatives in the Royal Family! What might be called a strongly modified Cockney pronunciation is now a generally accepted middle-class norm throughout the Southeast. Its unofficial new name, coined in the 1990s, is 'Estuary English' (*estuary* in this case meaning the London Thames as it widens downstream – a fitting metaphor, if ever there was one!).

It should be emphasized at this point that pronunciation (i.e. RP) is only one aspect of the standard language as a whole. The others are grammar and semantics, dimensions which in a book like this, of course, we are much more centrally involved with.

002/4.6 America

In America the equivalent of Standard British is ***General American***. Between these two norms there is some divergence, firstly and most obviously in pronunciation. The differences here are similar in kind and degree to many of those between Standard and regional British. What has to be remembered in this case, however, is that in contrast to regional varieties in Britain, General American has the status of a ***standard language***. In terms of international English and EFL, therefore, General American and Standard British are what one might call 'rival enterprises'. A selection of distinctions are the following:

		Standard British	General American
Pronunciation (individual sounds)	p*a*th	[ɑ:] [pɑ:θ]	[æ:] [pæ:θ]
	h*o*t	[ɒ] [hɒt]	[ɑ:] [hɑ:t]
	*ough*t	[ɔ:] [ɔ:t]	[ɒ:] [ɒ:t]
	r*oa*d	[əʊ] [rəʊd]	[oʊ] [roʊd]
	t*u*be	[ju:] [tju:b]	[u:] [tu:b]
	le*tt*er	[-t-] [letə] [-]	[-d-] [ledər] [-r]

For many it is the typical [r] that characterizes American pronunciation. This has two significant features: firstly, it is ***postvocalic***, or ***rhotic***, i.e. occurs, in contrast to the British

[r], after vowels. Secondly, it is produced in a special way called ***retroflexive***, with the tip of the tongue curled back.

Other points considered 'typically American' by non-American speakers are the voicing of ***t*** between vowels, making it more or less into a [d], and the long [æ:] for British [ɑ:].

There is also quite a lot of divergence in the pronunciation of individual words:

		Standard British	**General American**
Pronunciation (individual words)	clerk	[klɑ:k]	[klə:rk]
	leisure	[leʒə]	[li:ʒər]
	lieutenant	[leftenənt]	[lu:tenənt]
	missile	[mɪsaɪl]	[mɪsl]
	progress	[prəʊgres]	[prɑ:gres]
	schedule	[ʃedju:l]	[skedʒəl]
	tomato	[təmɑ:təʊ]	[təmeɪtəʊ]
	vase	[vɑ:z]	[veɪz]

American speakers also stress certain words differently:

	Standard British	**General American**
Pronunciation (different stress)	ad'dress	'address
	'ballet	ball'et
	'cafe	ca'fe
	cigar'ette	'cigarette
	'garage	ga'rage
	maga'zine	'magazine
	re'search	'research
	week'end	'weekend

There are also systematic, as well as individual differences between British and American spelling:

	British	**American**
Spelling (regular distinctions)	-our (colour)	-or (color)
	-re (centre)	-er (center)
	-ogue (dialogue)	-og (dialog)
	-gramme (programme)	-gram (program)
	-ll- (councillor)	-l- (councilor)
	-l (instil, wilful)	-ll (instill, willful)
	-ence (licence, *noun*)	-ense (license, *noun*)

	British	American
spelling (individual distinctions)	aeroplane	airplane
	axe	ax
	cheque	check
	draughty	drafty
	manoeuvre	maneuver
	plough	plow
	pyjamas	pajamas
	sceptical	skeptical
	tyre	tire

British English and American English frequently have different terms for the same thing, i.e. there are lexical distinctions between the two varieties:

	British	American
Lexical items	pants	underpants
	trousers	pants
	autumn	fall
	pavement	sidewalk
	petrol	gas
	lift	elevator
	nappy	diaper
	caravan	trailer
	chemist's	drugstore
	flat	apartment

Grammar distinctions are not as numerous as one might imagine. American speakers sometimes favour the past tense in contexts where British usage requires the present perfect (see chapter 10). They tend also to make greater use of the subjunctive (e.g. *She preferred that I go* instead of *She preferred me to go; If the dog were in the garden* … vs. *If the dog was in the garden* …). And there are one or two differences in past tense forms (e.g. American *burned* for British *burnt*, American *dove* for British *dived*).

Apart from this, divergence tends to be occasional rather than systematic: Americans use only *have* for informal British *have got, go see/come see* for British *go/come and see*, the definite article in the phrase *in the hospital* (British *in hospital*), etc. Prepositions differ in certain collocations: *different than* for *different from; through* for *to/till* and *after/before* for *past/to* in certain expressions of time (*Monday through Saturday, It's twenty minutes after nine*), etc.

There are far more American-British differences in the colloquial varieties of each language. But there is also greater exchange and mutual familiarity. The 'flow' is felt especially in the American-British direction, as America constantly exports its spoken culture, e.g. via film, music and IT media, to the rest of the world. An interesting cultural point in this connection is that in popular music since the 1940s British singers have tended mainly to use American accents, especially emphasized in the advent and development of rock music from the 1950s and 1960s onwards. Even the famous 'Liverpool Sound' of the 1960s (keyword *Beatles*) used largely American English.

Differences in the two standard languages can become an issue in educational settings. In German education both standards are accepted. However, only one is generally taken as the basis for teaching, and that is usually Standard British. School pupils are informed of the divergences in General American, and if they use these individually instead of the British variants, it is normally accepted. It should be pointed out, however, that British and American cultures themselves do not generally (with the exception of native accent) accept each other's language systems in public life. Using British spelling, for instance, would usually attract censure or correction in an American school, and vice versa.

002/4.7 Regional variation in America

The basis of ***General American*** is ***General Northern***. This is spoken, with certain local variations, from New England across the northernmost states (including most of Pennsylvania and the northern parts of Ohio, Indiana, Illinois, Iowa, and South Dakota) to the Pacific coast. Very distinctive areas within this belt are urban New York, and New England, which is famous for dropping postvocalic [r] (*'The cah is pahked in Hahv'd Yahd'*).

General Southern is typified by the 'southern drawl': [aɪ] becomes [ɑ:] (rhyming *I* with *ah*), [aʊ] becomes [eʊ] or [e:jə], making *loud* something like *'lay-ud'*, and the [ɑ:] of General American *dog* [dɑ:g] becomes an extended diphthong [ɑ:ɔ:] making *dog* sound like *'dah-awg'*. Postvocalic [r] becomes [a] or [ʌ], making *door* into *'do-uh'*. The General Southern area extends from Maryland southwards through the eastern half of Virginia and the Carolinas and then westwards across Georgia, Alabama and the Gulf states into Arkansas and eastern Texas, i.e. covers most of what was Confederate America in the Civil War.

Between these two regions is the area where ***Midland American*** is spoken. This comprises a southern half, from the Appalachian Mountains in the east to the Ozark mountains in the west; and a northern half comprising the central mid-west of America and running eastwards through most of Iowa, northern Missouri, central parts of Illinois, Indiana, Ohio and into Pennsylvania. The whole of the Midland region is regarded as a transition zone between Northern and Southern varieties.

002/4.8 Canada, Australia, New Zealand, South Africa

Canadian English is similar to American, sharing with it the rhotic [r] and many of the vowel sounds. Two distinctive features are the 'raising' of the two diphthongs [aɪ] and [aʊ], i.e. the first element is closer or higher. This happens before voiceless consonants, so that *writer*, for instance, is pronounced with a [ɜɪ], making it sound rather like *raider*, and *couch* with an [əʊ], making it the same as *coach* in RP. Canadians, as Americans sometimes joke, are always *oat'n aboat* (= *out and about*).

Australian and ***New Zealand*** English is much closer to British than American varieties. ***Australian*** is actually a descendant of London speech, and has vowel sounds similar to those of southeast England ('Estuary English'), e.g. in [æɪ] or even [aɪ] for RP [eɪ], as in *say*, [ɑə] or [ɒə] for RP [aɪ], as in *side*, and [æʊ] for RP [aʊ], as in *house*. This makes *say* rhyme (roughly) with RP *die*, and *side* with RP *toyed*; *house* sounds like *had us* without the ***d***-sound in the middle.

RP [əʊ], as in *so*, becomes [ɛʊ], i.e. with the first element more open and the tongue further forward. Some pure vowels tend to be pronounced in more closed form than their British equivalents, e.g. [æ] as in *hat* becomes [e], and [e] is raised in the direction of [ɪ], so that *bad* sounds a little like *bed*, and *bed* a little like *bid*. The long vowels [i:] and [u:] tend to turn into diphthongs, as in Australian *lean* [ləi:n] and *boot* [bəu:t]. Long RP [ɑ:] as in *dance*, is pronounced [æ:], i.e. [dæ:ns], as in America. In unstressed syllables [ɪ] drops to [ə], so that *it*, for instance, is pronounced [ət]. Between vowels [t] becomes [d] as in American, so that *metal* is the same as *medal*.

In ***New Zealand*** general pronunciation is very similar to Australian, but tends to be a little more RP-oriented.

In ***South Africa*** English is spoken as a native language by only about 9% of the population. Even among whites, it is second in place to Afrikaans, a dialect of Dutch, which has had considerable influence on the pronunciation and vocabulary of South African English. On the other hand, there are a lot of features that South African English has in common with the varieties of Australia and New Zealand. One general similarity is a strong orientation to British English. A more specific one is the raising of [æ] and [e] (see above). Diphthongs, however, tend to become pure vowels. *Care* and *hair*, for instance, are pronounced [ke:] and [he:], and RP [aʊ] and [aɪ] merge into [ɑ:], so that *I come from South Africa* sounds like *Ah come from Sahth Efrica*. RP [ɑ:], on the other hand is raised and rounded to the ***o***-sound [ɔ:], so that *car* is pronounced like *core*, and *dance* like *dawn* with a ***-ce*** on the end.

003 Some basic concepts in language study

003/1 Some general fields of language

In this section we discuss some general terms referring to component areas of language. Most of them originally meant fields of ***study*** or ***examination***, but several have also come to denote the particular field of language itself.

003/1.1 Morphology

Morphology is focused on ***word structure***, i.e. the grammatical components and the grammatical shapes of words. Because structure is related also to types or categories of words, like nouns, adjectives, verbs, etc. (called ***word classes*** or ***parts of speech***), morphology also deals with these classifications and the features that mark them.

For instance, an end-syllable (***suffix***) can be added to a noun to produce an adjective, e.g. *care* → *care**less***. Or if we replace *-less* by *-ful* we get the opposite meaning. This type of morphology has to do with ***word-formation***, and is called ***derivational morphology***, that is, creating one word from another.

A second type puts a word in a particular ***grammatical form***, like *-ed* for the past tense of a verb (*walk* → *walked*), *-er* for the comparative form of an adjective (*big* → *bigger*), or *-s* for the plural of a noun (*hand* → *hands*). Suffixes of this type are known as ***inflections***, and the branch of morphology concerned is ***inflectional morphology***. This does not create a new item of vocabulary, but fits the existing word into a particular grammatical context.

Grammatical operations like these do not always use inflections. Sometimes the change is made inside the word, e.g. *goose* → *geese*, *swim* → *swam*, etc. Or it is completely irregular and requires different words, e.g. *good* → *better*, *go* → *went*, etc. The functional grammatical character is nevertheless the same, and even irregular or internal forms are therefore regarded as variants within the framework of inflectional morphology.

003/1.2 Syntax

Syntax deals with the ***combination*** of words to form groups such as phrases, clauses and sentences. Here ***word class*** also plays a central role. Certain types of word can only occupy particular positions in a phrase or sentence, or may only combine with certain other types of word.

Adjectives, for instance, can occur before nouns or follow verbs of state like *be* and *feel*. An article such as *the* must precede not only a noun but also any adjectives belonging to that noun. Simple sentences as ***statements*** usually begin with the sequence noun phrase + verb phrase, but in ***questions*** the sequence is partly verb phrase + noun phrase, though with the verb phrase split into two: auxiliary verb + noun phrase + main verb. Such questions of combination and word-order are the domain of ***syntax***.

A particularly central ***syntactic factor*** in sentences is ***sentence function*** (or ***role***): that is, the general shape of a sentence is determined by categories such as ***subject***, ***predicator***, ***object***, etc. (see also section **003/3**). These are ***relational roles*** that are filled by specific word classes. Sentence function 'slots' are generally responsible for the larger architecture of the sentence, including, particularly, its word-order. ***Syntax***, then, has to do with the ***patterns*** of ***sentences*** and ***phrases***.

003/1.3 Semantics

Semantics is the study and/or property of ***meaning***: the meaning not only of individual words, but of words combined into groups, including phrases, clauses and whole sentences. The ***semantics*** of a sentence comes from various sources. In *I have broken my leg*, for example, there is first of all the meaning of the individual items *I*, *break*, and *leg*, known as ***lexical*** (or word) meaning. Then there is combined meaning in *break* and *leg* together, which signifies a particular type of injury, i.e. to a bone. This is ***collocational***

meaning. And finally there is the ***grammatical*** meaning of *my* (= 'possessed by me', 1st person singular possessive determiner), and the perfect form of the verb in *have broken* (= 'my leg is in a broken state now'). All this together produces the meaning of the sentence (its ***semantic*** content) as a whole.

003/1.4 Pragmatics

Let us suppose now that the person who says *I've broken my leg* is answering the question *Why aren't you playing in the team on Saturday?* In this communicational context, the speaker is giving a ***reason***, i.e. performing a particular kind of ***speech act***. This is ***pragmatic*** meaning, relating to the field of ***interaction between speakers***. Pragmatic meanings depend strongly on situational context. A different context for the statement *I've broken my leg*, for example, could be one in which the speaker ***protests***, e.g. *How am I supposed to sleep in a tent? I've broken my leg!* A third alternative (and there are of course many more) could simply be the ***telling of news*** (e.g. by letter, e-mail or in a telephone conversation): *By the way, I've broken my leg.*

003/1.5 The concept 'grammar'

The term ***grammar***, as used nowadays in the study of language, has several different meanings. It is useful to be aware of these when reading texts on language and linguistics. Compare for example:

(4) a. The grammar of Latin is difficult.
b. She has a reasonable vocabulary in English, but her grammar is weak.
c. I've got three English grammars at home.
d. It is bad grammar to end a sentence with a preposition.
e. His grammar is bad, as he speaks broad dialect.
f. Phrase-structure grammars use tree-diagrams.
g. Everyone knows grammar.

We will say first of all what ***grammar*** means in each of these sentences and then give one or two comments and explanations afterwards:

(4)a. refers to a ***characteristic*** or property of a particular language. In (4)b. ***grammar*** means a person's ***skill*** in speaking and writing English as a ***foreign language*** correctly. (4)c. uses the word in the sense of a ***book*** about English grammar. (4)d. means ***grammar*** in the sense of a ***language convention*** (a set of rules) for ***native speakers***. (4)e. is like b. in referring to a person's ***skill***; here, however, it means a ***native speaker's ability*** to use the standard version (as opposed to a regional/social variety) of his own language. (4)f. shows a modern linguistic use of the term. What is meant here is a theoretical ***model*** of grammar, i.e. an abstract schema representing a ***theory*** on the way in which language generally 'works' in some specified sense. (4)g. is also a statement associated with modern linguistics. Here ***grammar*** is also connected with ***ability***, but in the ***subconscious*** sense of being able to speak a language (for instance, one's native language) fluently.

In the sense of (4)a., this book explains the ***grammar of English***. Note that in its traditional sense, ***grammar*** means just morphology and syntax. However, the correct choice of an English grammatical form very often depends vitally on ***semantics***. Prime examples are tense forms, or 'function words' like prepositions or conjunctions. Semantic considerations therefore play a central role in our explanations here. This brings us to (4)b. and c. This book addresses the problems of ***grammar*** as meant in b. It is therefore also ***a grammar*** in the sense of c., and is furthermore a ***pedagogical grammar***: it aims, that is, to help the reader to improve skills in the use of English, and to avoid making mistakes.

(4)d. is an example of what modern linguists call ***prescriptive grammar***: rules intended for native speakers, to encourage them to use a variety of their language (the standard language) which is acceptable in particular social, occupational or political situations. This book is not prescriptive in any social sense. It focuses on a standard variety of English, i.e. Standard British English, but does so because this is a teaching convention in widespread EFL settings. Its recommendations follow a ***descriptive*** tradition, i.e. it tries to present British English as it is actually used. It does not support social or aesthetic value judgements as they are usually found in prescriptive grammars.

(4)e. is also a typically prescriptive statement. From a linguistic point of view, no particular native speaker variety of a language is superior or inferior to any other variety. ***'Dialect'*** is not 'bad'. Like the standard language, it is simply one language variety among others, and linguistically speaking, is quite neutral. Language norms are imposed by users and are related to particular purposes and intentions (e.g. wide or narrow acceptance, felt appropriateness in specific situations, aesthetic pleasure, as in certain forms of literature, and so on).

Grammar ***models***, as referred to in (4)f., follow some theoretical purpose. In the case, for instance, of 'phrase structure', the purpose is 'generative' and the model is intended to represent the way that speakers do something, i.e. produce sentences. Ultimately, that is, ***grammar*** in this sense is understood as a plan of the brain. (4)f. is connected with this view. To *know grammar* in this sense is to have the ability to communicate in language.

003/2 Basic grammatical categories

In this section we will briefly explain terms that grammars often do not define at all, but just expect readers and learners to know, so to speak, 'from experience'. One of the aims of this book is to *provide* experience in language, including basic experience. For that reason, importance is attached to definitions and explanations, even of rudimentary terms and concepts.

003/2.1 Structure

This is a general word used here to mean syntactic constructions and morphological forms. When we say that this or that verb takes the gerund after it, or is in the passive, or combines with an adverb particle or a preposition, we are speaking in ***structural*** terms. The same applies to morphological forms and word categories like parts of speech (or ***word classes***, to use a more modern expression). Descriptive terms such as *3rd person* *singular, participle, gerund, adjective, noun,* and so on, are ***structural*** terms. So also are the terms ***phrase, clause*** and ***sentence***, which are explained in the section following.

003/2.2 Phrase, clause and sentence

These terms refer to ***structural units***. A ***sentence*** is the largest unit of grammatical structure. (The smallest is the ***morpheme***, e.g. an inflection like *-**ing*** with verbs, or plural *-**s*** for nouns, see section **003/1.1**) This means, generally speaking, that sentences are ***grammatically independent*** of each other. The structure of a particular sentence (with one or two exceptions) is generally not linked to, or affected by, the grammar of any other sentence. Sentences, that is, are ***grammatically self-contained***.

A sentence may consist of smaller units which are rather like sentences themselves, i.e. 'mini-sentences', so to speak, inside it:

(5) a. Sarah left the cinema early, because she was bored by the film.
b. I'm hungry, but I can wait.
c. Tom didn't realize that Jerry was out.

These 'mini-sentences' are called ***clauses***. The three sentences in (5) each contain two ***clauses***: in (5)a. *Sarah left the cinema early,* and *because she was bored by the film;* in (5)b. *I'm hungry,* and *but I can wait;* and in (5)c. *Tom didn't realize* and *that Jerry was out.*

We could make separate sentences out of each clause, e.g.

(6) a. Sarah was bored by the film. She left the cinema early.
b. I'm hungry. I can wait, though.
c. Jerry was out. Tom didn't realize this.

And, of course, the other way around: separate sentences like those in (6) can be joined together to make one large sentence, as in (5). In that case, the former sentences become ***clauses*** in the new sentence.

The central feature of a clause is that it must have a ***verb*** (or, more exactly, a ***verb phrase***) of its own.

A ***phrase*** is a group of words which are grammatically dependent on one member of the group and are dominated by that member. For example, in *the small white plates* the words *the, small,* and *white* cannot exist without the main word, *plates.* The main word is called the ***head*** of the phrase. Grammatically we can leave out everything ***except*** the ***head***. That is, *plates* on its own would be grammatical, as in *Plates are necessary;* but *the small white* alone would not, i.e. we could not say **The small white are necessary.*

The ***head*** is a particular ***part of speech*** which determines the pattern of the phrase. Our phrases in these examples are ***noun phrases***, and have nouns as their heads. A phrase like *blue with cold* is an ***adjective phrase***, with an adjective as its head; one such as *on the table* is a ***prepositional phrase***, with a preposition as head; and a group of verbs belonging together, like *had been walking,* is a ***verb phrase***, with a ***lexical*** (or ***main***) ***verb*** as the head.

003/2.3 Functions

It was mentioned above that ***functions*** are ***relational roles***. More exactly, ***functions*** stand for ***relations*** between different parts of a sentence. For example, in *The little terrier was crunching some dog biscuits* we have the ***structures*** noun phrase (*the little terrier*) + verb phrase (*was crunching*) + noun phrase (*some dog biscuits*).

However, the structural facts alone do not tell us how these phrases are related to each other syntactically. Here we need to know the ***functions***: the first noun phrase is the ***subject*** of the sentence, the second is the ***direct object*** and the verb phrase has the role of ***predicator***. In functional terms the sentence has the shape ***subject + predicator + object***.

With another kind of verb we could add another noun phrase as a different kind of object: *The postman handed Mrs. Blaney's daughter a brown envelope*. Here the first object noun phrase (*Mrs. Blaney's daughter*) functions as an ***indirect object***, and the second as a ***direct object***.

If we abbreviate the ***subject*** as ***S***, ***indirect*** and ***direct objects*** as ***Oi*** and ***Od***, and the predicator as ***P***, we can say that the functional pattern of our two sentences is ***S + P + Od*** and ***S + P + Oi + Od***, respectively. The shape of sentences, that is, is generally given in ***functional*** terms.

003/3 Sentence functions

In our scheme of analysis there are seven sentence functions: ***subject (S)***, ***direct object (Od)***, ***indirect object (Oi)***, ***subject complement (Cs)***, ***object complement (Co)***, ***adverbial (A)***, and ***predicator (P)***.

003/3.1 Predicator (P)

This is the central function in a clause or sentence, and is filled by the ***verb phrase***. The verb phrase puts other phrases into a coherent relationship with one another, i.e. combines them into a message.

If, for example, with the sentence *Sylvia is writing a letter in her study* we remove the verb phrase *is writing*, the phrases *Sylvia*, *a letter* and *in her study* are no longer coherently connected. It is the verb which states, or as it is traditionally called, ***predicates***, something about the other elements. If it is left out, there is no longer a meaningful message, and the statement disintegrates. A clause therefore needs a ***verb phrase*** to function as the all-important ***predicator***. We can reverse this relationship, and say, as we did above, that a clause is part of a sentence with its ***own predicator***.

Generally speaking, the number of predicators in a sentence is equal to the number of clauses the sentence contains. The ***predicator*** function can be filled by a ***finite verb***, i.e. a ***conjugated*** one (= agreeing in form with its subject, such as *is writing*, in the example above), or by a ***non-finite verb*** such as an infinitive or gerund, e.g. *... to write a letter ...*, *... writing a letter ...*, etc.

A sentence must contain at least ***one predicator***. If it has only one, this must be filled by a ***finite verb phrase***. The sentence then consists of just ***one clause***, and is called a ***simple sentence*** (see also under section **003/4.1**).

003/3.2 Subject (S)

After the predicator, the most important function in the sentence is that of the ***subject (S)***. A finite verb always requires a subject, and must show ***grammatical agreement*** (or ***concord***, see also chapter 8) with it:

		S	*P*
(7)	a.	Sylvia	***is*** writing.
	b.	The children	***are*** playing.
	c.	Several dogs	***barked***.

English verbs have few differentiated person endings. In some forms (e.g. the simple forms of past tenses) they actually have none. Nevertheless, we still assume, in a sentence like (7)c., that there is ***potential concord***, because if we change the form to progressive, then this is clearly marked: *Several dogs* **were** *barking*.

Concord indicates that there is an especially close syntactic relation between ***subject*** and ***predicator***.

Other ***grammatical*** features of the ***subject*** are that it

- is always a ***noun phrase*** (including pronouns) in simple sentences,
- ***precedes*** the predicator in declarative sentences (= statements),
- ***follows*** the predicator in questions (except when it is a ***wh***-word itself),
- has a special ***case*** form with most ***personal pronouns***, the ***subject form*** (more traditionally the 'nominative' form), i.e. *I, he, she, we, they*, as opposed to the object forms *me, him, us*, etc. (see next section).

Semantically, there is no single feature that applies to all subjects. Nevertheless, there are certain typical meanings. When the verb refers to an action (and is in the ***active voice***), the subject noun denotes the person or thing that performs or causes the action. This 'acting' or 'doing' role is often called by the semantic term ***agent***. The examples in (7) all show the subject in this typical ***agent*** role.

Many verbs, on the other hand, refer to states or to involuntary acts that are not really 'performed' or carried out, but just happen, e.g.

		S	*P*	
(8)	a.	The wall	was	red.
	b.	We	heard	a noise.
	b.	The candidate	had	a mental blackout.

The semantic role in these cases is often called that of the ***experiencer***. A common variant of the ***experiencer*** role occurs in passive sentences, and is known as the role of ***patient***:

		S	*P-pass*
(9)	a.	The murder weapon	was not found.
	b.	The broken pipe	has been replaced.

003/3.3 Direct Object (Od)

Grammatically, the ***direct object***

- is always a ***noun phrase*** (including pronouns) in simple sentences,
- ***follows*** the predicator in declarative sentences (= statements),
- ***precedes*** the predicator as a ***wh***-word in questions (*Who did you see?*),
- with most ***personal pronouns*** has a special ***case*** form, the ***object form***: *me, him, her, us, them,*
- becomes the ***passive subject*** when a sentence is converted from ***active*** to ***passive*** voice (see under **003/3.4**, for an exception to this rule).

Direct objects vary in their occurrence. Verbs followed by direct objects are called ***transitive***. Those without direct objects are ***intransitive***. Some verbs are always ***transitive***, e.g. *repair*, as in *I repaired the vacuum cleaner*; others are always ***intransitive***, e.g. *bark*, as in *Dogs bark*; and many can be either, e.g. *sing*, as in *We sang* (***intransitive***), or as in *We sang songs* (***transitive***).

Semantically, the direct object typically denotes the 'sufferer' or ***patient*** of an action or experience, when the verb is in the active voice:

	S	*P*	*Od*
(10)	a. I	repaired	the vacuum cleaner.
	b. We	heard	a noise.
	c. She	had	a mental blackout.

003/3.4 Indirect Object (Oi)

Grammatically, the ***indirect object***

- is always a ***noun phrase*** (including pronouns),
- ***follows*** the predicator ***immediately*** in declarative sentences (= statements),
- always occurs ***together*** with a ***direct object***, which it always ***precedes***,
- requires the ***object form*** of a ***personal pronoun***, i.e. *me, him, her*, etc.
- can be paraphrased in simple sentences by a ***prepositional phrase*** (usually with *to* or *for*), converting its function to that of ***adverbial*** (see section **003/3.7**),
- cannot appear in questions, which require ***conversion to adverbial*** (*Who did you send the letter to?*, not **Who did you send the letter?*),
- can become ***passive subject*** when a sentence is converted from ***active*** to ***passive*** voice; in this case the ***direct object*** remains, see example below,
- cannot remain in passive sentences, i.e. if the active direct object becomes the passive subject, the ***active indirect object*** requires ***conversion to adverbial*** (*The letter was sent to Mary*, not **The letter was sent Mary*).

Semantically, the indirect object generally denotes the 'receiver' or ***recipient*** of an action or experience, when the verb is in the active voice. It usually refers to an animate object (person or animal):

	S	*P*	*Oi*	*Od*
(11)	a. I	lent	Tom	my vacuum cleaner.
	b. We	gave	the horses	water and hay.
	c. She	bought	herself	a new skirt.

003/3.5 Subject complement (Cs)

Subject complements follow ***intransitive*** verbs that grammatically and semantically require elements following them to complete the sentence (i.e. have ***compulsory complementation***). The subject complement

- ***follows*** the predicator in declarative sentences (= statements),
- ***precedes*** the predicator as a ***wh***-word in questions (*Who are you?*),
- can be a ***noun phrase*** (including pronouns), or an ***adjective phrase***,
- follows verbs with the meanings *be, seem* and *become* (*be, cost, feel, weigh, appear, seem, become, get, grow, turn,* etc.).

Semantically, the subject complement refers to a ***characteristic*** of the ***subject***:

	S	*P*	*Cs*
(12)	a. Charlie	is	my brother.
	b. Sharon	seems	tired.
	c. She	is getting	married.

Particularly with verbs of 'becoming' (*become, get, turn,* etc.), subject complements are sometimes mistaken for direct objects. Verbs like this might look transitive, but in fact they are ***intransitive***. An indication of this is that they can be complemented by ***adjectives*** and not just nouns.

003/3.6 Object complement (Co)

With certain verbs, ***object complements*** are grammatically necessary after direct objects. Semantically, too, they are needed to complete the sense of the verb-object relation. ***Object complements***

- ***follow*** the ***direct object*** in declarative sentences,
- ***precede*** the predicator as a ***wh***-word in questions (*What did he call you?*),
- can be a ***noun phrase*** (including pronouns), or an ***adjective phrase***,
- are linked to verbs of ***cause*** and denote their ***effect*** on what the direct object refers to.

	S	*P*	*Od*	*Co*
(13)	a. Good food	makes	me	happy.
	b. The board	elected	John	chairman.
	c. Events	proved	him	wrong.

Semantically, the direct object-object complement relation is similar to that between the subject and the subject complement. The object complement, that is, describes the direct object in the same way that the subject complement describes the subject. In fact we can often express similar meanings using subject and subject complement versions. As applied to (13), for example, this could be *I am happy* (*when I have good food*); *John became chairman* (*following the board's decision*), etc.

Verbs referring to thought and opinion also belong here (though their causative meaning is a little abstract compared with that of verbs like *make* and *elect*): *The police considered me a thief; We thought Jenny a little naïve; They found their guest charming and appreciative.*

003/3.7 Adverbial

This is a rather different function from the others. The others are usually compulsory when they occur. ***Adverbials***, however, are usually optional. Furthermore, there can be ***any number*** of ***adverbials*** in a sentence, whereas the other functions can only occur once per clause (except when joined by *and*). ***Adverbials*** have a broad range of meaning and generally provide information on the ***accompanying circumstances*** of an event or state. These, typically, are *where* (***place***), *when* (***time***), *how* (***manner***), *how often* (***frequency***) and *why* (***cause*** or ***reason***) it takes place. Adverbials are therefore a kind of functional extension of the word class ***adverb***. They

- can be ***noun phrases***, ***prepositional phrases***, or ***adverb phrases***,
- can vary in ***position***, but generally ***follow*** other complementation, i.e. objects and subject or object complements,
- although single adverbs (especially those expressing frequency) can occur before the main verb,
- and adverbials referring to the whole sentence, or given special prominence, can occur at the beginning of the clause (particularly ***connective*** and ***comment adverbials***).

		S	***P***	***Od***	***A***
(14)	a.	Brzinsky	spoke	the words	slowly.

	S	***P***	***Od***	***Co***	***A***
b.	The board	elected	John	chairman	last month.

	S	***P***	***A***	***A***
c.	She	spoke	to me	at the bus-stop.

	S	***A***	***P***	***A***	***A***
d.	We	sometimes	went	on long	hikes during the school holidays.

	A	***S***	***P***	***Od***	***A***
e.	By the way,	my wife	saw	Suzanne	at the butcher's.

	A	***S***	***P***	***Od***	***A***
f.	As a matter of fact,	Jeremy	doesn't like	Angela	at all.

Other quite common ***adverbial*** meanings are ***condition*** (*in that case*), ***degree*** (*at all*, as in (14)f.), ***concession*** (*in spite of …*), ***contradiction*** and ***contrast*** (*on the other hand, unlike …, apart from …*, etc.).

Adverbial meanings, and also sentence positions, are generally identical with those of ***adverbs***. It is important to realize, however, that ***adverbials*** and ***adverbs*** are ***not*** the same thing. The category ***adverbial*** is a ***functional*** one; the category ***adverb*** is a ***word class***, or ***part of speech***. All independent adverbs (or, to be more exact, ***adverb phrases***) function as ***adverbials***, but so do prepositional phrases and, occasionally, noun phrases, as the examples show.

003/4 Sentence types and sentence patterns

003/4.1 Simple sentences

We have already seen that these are sentences consisting of just one clause, i.e. they have only one predicator.

Sentences are formed according to certain functional patterns. The following are compulsory patterns for the simple sentence. The basic architecture or plan of a sentence depends to a great extent on the kind of complementation required by a particular verb. The type of verb functioning as predicator therefore has the major role in determining the sentence pattern in each case:

	S	***P***			
(15)	a. Celia	had been running.			[***S*** + ***P***]
	S	***P***	***Cs***		
	b. She	was	a teacher.		[***S*** + ***P*** + ***Cs***]
	S	***P***	***A***		
	c. She	went	into the class.		[***S*** + ***P*** + ***A***]
	S	***P***	***Od***		
	d. She	said	this.		[***S*** + ***P*** + ***Od***]
	S	***P***	***Od***	***Co***	
	e. She	called	her pupils	'her little team'.	[***S*** + ***P*** + ***Od*** + ***Co***]
	S	***P***	***Od***	***A***	
	f. She	put	her bag	on the desk.	[***S*** + ***P*** + ***Od*** + ***A***]
	S	***P***	***Oi***	***Od***	
	g. Joe	gave	his mother	a present.	[***S*** + ***P*** + ***Oi*** + ***Od***]

These seven functional patterns are the basic patterns of the English sentence. In each case, the pattern given is the ***compulsory minimum*** with each type of verb. The absolute minimum is the sequence ***S*** + ***P***, as in (15)a. This is not enough for the verbs in b., c., or d., however. We cannot say **She was*, **She went*, or **She said*. All these verbs require further complementation of the kind given. In (15)e.–f. the sequence ***S*** + ***P*** + ***Od*** is not enough either. This kind of verb requires a further function element before the sentence is grammatically complete.

Some of the patterns may represent optional sequences for other verbs. The verb *sing*, for instance, can take the pattern in (15)a., c., d., f., or g.:

(16) a. Brian sang.
b. Brian sang at a concert.
c. Brian sang three songs.
d. Brian sang three songs at a concert.
e. Brian sang his mother three songs.

Furthermore, for *give* there is an alternative to the pattern in (15)g., i.e. the one in (15) f.: *Joe gave a present to his mother*. The verb *be* is also not confined to the pattern (15)b. but can alternatively appear in thc (15)c. sequence, as in *She was in the classroom*.

003/4.2 Compound and complex sentences

Two or more simple sentences can be joined together grammatically to make one larger sentence. The two sentences *Fred fed the dog* and *Fred left the house*, for example, could be linked to produce *Fred fed the dog and left the house*. Each of the former sentences has now become a clause in a larger sentence, joined by the ***conjunction*** *and* (conjunction = 'grammatical joining word', see chapter 7 for details). This is the most common way of combining clauses (at least in speech), and is known as a ***compound sentence*** (= 'one clause added to another'). Apart from this simple addition, there is no special semantic or grammatical link between the clauses and they remain potentially independent. Because of their sovereignty as equal partners they are both referred to traditionally as 'main' clauses. This 'joining on the same level' is called ***co-ordination***, and *and* is called a ***co-ordinating*** conjunction. Other ***co-ordinating*** conjunctions are *or* and *but*.

If by contrast we take a different kind of conjunction, such as *after* or *before*, the clause that it links becomes grammatically ***dependent*** on the other one: *After he fed the dog, Fred left the house; Before he left the house, Fred fed the dog*.

Conjunctions of this kind give a specific meaning to the link; that is, they put their clause in a certain semantic relation to the other one (here a relation of ***time***).

But more than this, they also attach the dependent clause ***syntactically*** to the other one in terms of ***function***: in this case as an ***adverbial***. This process is called ***subordination***. The dependent clause is also known as the ***subordinate clause*** and the conjunction as the ***subordinating conjunction***.

Subordinate clause = A

(17) a. [After he fed the dog], Fred left the house.
b. [Before he left the house], Fred fed the dog.

Traditionally, the independent clause is called the 'main clause', but for reasons discussed later (see chapter 7), we will use the term ***matrix clause***. Apart from ***adverbial (A)***, subordinate clauses can function as ***subject (S)***, ***subject complement (Cs)***, and ***direct object (Od)***:

S

(18) a. [That Brian failed the test] is very unfortunate.

Cs

b. The fact is [that Brian failed the test].

Od

c. I think [that Brian failed the test].

Subordinate clauses can also be ***non-finite***, i.e. with verbs in infinitive, gerund or participle forms. These have no conjunctions (with one or two very occasional exceptions).

Non-finite clauses have the same kinds of functional relation to the matrix clause as those shown in (17) and (18). In addition, infinitive clauses can function as ***object complement (Co)***.

(19) a. [To fail/failing tests] (***S***) is usually very inconvenient.
b. My greatest triumph would be [to pass the test] (***Cs***).
c. I hate [failing tests] (***Od***).
d. She sat at the desk [writing a letter] (***A***).
e. We expected Brian [to pass the test] (***Co***).

003/4.3 A mixture of co-ordination and subordination

Sentences of more than one clause need not simply be either compound or complex: they can be a mixture of both. One subordinate clause may be co-ordinated with another, as in (20)a. and b., or a co-ordinated clause may have a subordinate one attached to it, as in (20)c.:

(20) a. I hate [(failing tests) and (having to re-take them)] (***Od***).
b. [(After he had washed the cups) and (fed the dog)] (***A***), Fred left the house.
c. (She just came into the office) and (announced [that she was leaving the firm] (***Od***)).

Chapter 2 Nouns

2.1 Basic features: introduction

Main grammatical features 004

004/1 Nouns and noun phrases

Nouns typically have certain kinds of words and structures associated with them. Before nouns, for example, there are often determiners (such as articles, numerals and quantifiers), or adjectives. After the noun there may be prepositional phrases, relative clauses, participle clauses, etc. The noun and any of these further elements form a grammatical group, a unit, that we call a ***noun phrase***. The noun itself is the main word, or ***head***, of the phrase. And in a sentence it is the whole phrase that functions together, for instance as ***subject*** or ***object***.

(1) a. The fat boy kissed the thin girl. (*the fat boy* = ***subject***; *the thin girl* = ***direct object***)
b. The thin girl kissed the fat boy. (*the thin girl* = ***subject***; *the fat boy* = ***direct object***)

Similarly, if a noun phrase is moved to another part of the sentence, it can only be moved as a whole unit. The words always belong together in that order. We cannot split them up, or put other parts of the sentence between them, e.g.

(2) a. Was it the fat boy who kissed the thin girl passionately?

And not

b. * Was the it fat who boy kissed the thin passionately girl?

However, a noun phrase may consist of just the head alone, without further accompaniment:

(3) Dogs eat meat. (*dogs* = ***subject***; *meat* = ***direct object***)

The following are examples of common noun phrase patterns:

• a single noun	(*dogs*)
• determiner + noun	(*the dogs*)
• adjective + noun	(*big dogs*)
• determiner + adjective + noun	(*the big dogs*)
• determiner + adjective + noun + prepositional phrase	(*the big dogs in the garden*)
• determiner + adjective + noun + relative clause	(*the big dogs which are barking next door*)

Any elements before the head noun form the ***premodification***, any following it form the ***postmodification***:

	Premodification	***Head***	***Postmodification***
(4)	The big	dogs	which are barking next door.

Other common forms of ***postmodification*** are participle clauses (a.), infinitive clauses (b.) and *of*-phrases (c.):

(5) a. The dogs barking next door belong to our neighbour's son.
b. The only way to win is to concentrate hard on the game.
c. The wheels of the car had been clamped.

004/2 Syntactic roles of noun phrases

Typical sentence functions of noun phrases are ***subject***, ***direct*** and ***indirect object***, ***subject complement*** and ***object complement***. Noun phrases also follow prepositions in prepositional phrases, in which they function as ***prepositional complement***:

(6)	a. The car-park is full.	(*the car-park* = ***subject***)
	b. The cat was drinking some milk.	(*some milk* = ***direct object***)
	c. A studio has given Lennie a contract.	(*Lennie* = ***indirect object***)
	d. Lennie is a singer.	(*a singer* = ***subject complement***)
	e. They made him their leader.	(*their leader* = ***object complement***)
	f. Runners in tracksuits were jogging through the park.	(*tracksuits* and *the park* = ***prepositional complements***)

004/3 Morphological invariance

English nouns have no grammatical gender and no case (unlike German nouns). The only inflections are for the genitive and the plural. Otherwise, as we can see from the examples in (6), nouns are ***morphologically invariant***, regardless of syntactic function. So, too, are the other members of a noun phrase, such as articles and adjectives. These do not change at all, even with genitive or plural nouns:

(7) a. *The young* woman's *heavy* cases were in *the large* hall.
b. The *little* postman gave two *old* ladies *huge* parcels.

The only exceptions to this principle are demonstrative pronouns, which have singular and plural forms, and certain distributives and quantifiers which are restricted to nouns of particular singular and plural types (see chapter 3).

004/4 Number: singular and plural

Singular and ***plural*** belong to the grammatical category of ***number***. In most cases noun plurals are formed in writing by adding *-s* to the singular. Pronunciation rules are a little more complex, as we will see further below. Apart from regular plurals in *-s*, there are also a few irregular plural forms, but these are unproblematic. A more important point is that many nouns can occur only in the singular or plural, but not in both. In addition, there are nouns with singular forms that are treated as plural, and others with plural forms that count as singular. These difficulties are discussed fully below.

Number affects verbs as well. Finite verbs must agree in number with their subject nouns: singular nouns require singular verb forms, and plural nouns require plural verb forms.

What do the terms ***singular*** and ***plural*** actually mean? The usual explanation is that singular forms refer to *one* entity, and plural forms to *more than one*:

(8) a. The thin ***girl*** (***singular*** = *one girl*)
b. The thin ***girls*** (***plural*** = *more than one girl*)

This is the basic distinction, but it is not the whole story. The grammatical use of forms sometimes goes beyond the limits of their basic meanings. This is the case with number. Grammatically, every noun is either singular or plural. But with some types of noun the semantic distinction between *one* and *more than one* does not really apply:

(9) a. Cheap accommodation was difficult to find. (accommodation = ***singular***)
b. The surroundings were completely unfamiliar. (surroundings = ***plural***)

Accommodation and *surroundings* are typical examples of what we will later call ***mass*** and ***collective*** nouns. These do not describe individual entities in single units. Semantically, therefore, they are neither singular nor plural, although grammatically their number status is clear. The form of the word, that is, shows grammatical number, but this does not really mean anything. One consequence is that such words have only one number form, i.e. there is no plural of *accommodation*, and no singular of *surroundings*. We will say that nouns like these have ***bound number status***: *accommodation* is a ***bound singular***; *surroundings* is a ***bound plural***. The noun *girl*, by contrast, has ***free number status***, i.e. it can occur in the singular or plural: *girl* is a ***free singular*** form, and *girls* a ***free plural*** form. Further examples are discussed in detail below.

There are many English words which do not correspond in ***number status*** to their counterparts in other languages. This can sometimes cause difficulty for speakers of those languages learning English. In German, for instance, *Unterkunft* (*accommodation*) and *Information* (*information*) both have ***free number status***, i.e. they can each be used in the singular and plural.

004/5 Countability

The numeral *one* (and also the indefinite article *a/an*) normally goes with singular nouns, and any numeral from *two* onwards (*two, three, ... forty-five*) with plural nouns. With our two examples *accommodation* and *surroundings*, however, this is not so.

We cannot say **an/one accommodation* or **three surroundings*. This is another consequence of the mass and collective meanings just mentioned. As nouns like these do not refer to individual units, ordinary ***counting expressions***, such as numerals, cannot be used to quantify them. They are "uncountable", or, as we will call them here, ***non-count*** nouns. Nouns like *girl*, which can be counted, are ***count*** nouns.

Countability and ***number status*** are not the same thing, but they are closely connected. All ***free*** nouns (like *girl*) are ***count*** nouns; all ***non-count*** nouns (like *accommodation* and *surroundings*) are ***bound***. However, some ***count*** nouns are also ***bound***. For instance, the noun *people* has no singular form, but we can still add plural numerals: *two people, three people*, etc. This is therefore a ***bound plural count*** noun. There are also many ***bound singular count*** nouns. Although they have no plural, they can be "counted" in the singular, i.e. they occur with *a/one*:

(10) a. Don't make such a fuss! (*fuss* = ***bound singular***)
Mach' doch nicht so ein Theater!
b. There was a terrible commotion upstairs. (*commotion* = ***bound singular***)
Oben war ein fürchterlicher Krach zu hören.

Nouns of this kind cannot be counted beyond *one*: we can say *a fuss* or *one fuss after another*, but not **two fusses*. ***Bound singular count*** nouns like this can be contrasted with ***bound singular non-count*** nouns, like *accommodation* or *information*, which can have no numeral or indefinite article before them at all.

In summary, then, plural-singular relations are described according to three criteria:

- ***singular*** or ***plural*** (***number form***)
- ***free*** or ***bound*** (***number status***)
- ***count*** or ***non-count*** (***countability***)

Further examples:

car (***free singular count***); *cars* (***free plural count***);
graces (***bound plural count***); *thanks* (***bound plural non-count***);
uproar (***bound singular count***); *sugar* (***bound singular non-count***).

Nouns with more than one meaning may vary in number orientation and countability accordingly, e.g.:

(11) a. He has many social graces. (*graces* = ***bound plural count***)
Er hat viele soziale Fertigkeiten.
b. She gave the speech with grace and dignity. (*grace* = ***bound singular non-count***)
Sie hielt die Rede mit Anmut und Würde.

Further specific examples are given below.

Number and countability factors in nouns are important criteria for the correct use of singular and plural forms. They also influence the use of certain types of determiner (such as the indefinite article, and various quantifiers). With one or two quantifiers it is necessary to distinguish not only singular and plural, but also ***dual plural*** ("only two") and ***non-dual plural*** ("more than two").

004/6 The genitive

The basic written genitive inflection is *apostrophe* + *s* (*'s*) for singular nouns and *-s* + *apostrophe* (*s'*) for plural nouns. Pronunciation rules are a little more complex and similar to those for plural forms. They are discussed in the appropriate section later (see **009/2**).

The ***genitive*** is used to signal ***possession***. The noun in the genitive has the role of "possessor", and the noun following it denotes what is "possessed". ***Possession*** here not only means "ownership", but also a relationship of ***belonging*** in a wider sense, such as *doing, creating,* or *being responsible for*:

(12) a. Sarah's bicycle (= the bicycle Sarah rides/owns/uses)
b. Shakespeare's plays (= the plays that Shakespeare wrote)
c. Beckham's goal (= the goal that Beckham scored)
d. Mother's apple pie (= the apple pie that she bakes)
e. Brian's greatest mistake (= the greatest mistake that he made)
f. Maria's class (= the one she belongs to as a pupil/the one she is responsible for as a teacher)

There are also other ways of showing a ***belonging*** relationship: firstly, by an *of*-phrase, secondly, by ***compound noun***, i.e. one noun plus another, or thirdly by ***possessive determiners*** (*my, his, her, your,* etc.):

(13) a. The plays of Shakespeare
b. The garage roof (= the roof of the garage)
c. Your Uncle Stan

The differences in usage between these alternatives are discussed fully later.

005 Main semantic features

005/1 Common and proper nouns
005/2 Common nouns: concrete or abstract
005/3 Common nouns: individual, mass, collective, and pair nouns

Nouns refer to things, or (more technically) to ***entities***. These can be:

- material objects (*cup, stone, building, air*)
- living things (people, plants, animals)
- other natural phenomena (e.g. deserts, winds, mountains, stars)
- locations (places, points, spaces)
- abstract objects (mental and emotional concepts, e.g *love, knowledge, curiosity*)
- actions and events seen as "things" (e.g. *activity, event, party, match,* etc.).

Traditionally, nouns are divided into the following broad categories of meaning: ***common*** or ***proper*** nouns; ***concrete*** or ***abstract*** nouns; ***individual, collective,*** or ***mass*** nouns. To the last three we will add the category of ***pair*** nouns.

It is important to emphasize that these categories are ***semantic*** in nature. Nevertheless, they also have certain ***grammatical*** consequences.

005/1 Common and proper nouns

All nouns fall into one of these 2 categories. ***Proper nouns*** are names and titles. ***Common nouns*** are all those that are not proper nouns, i.e. "the rest". ***Proper nouns*** are spelt with an initial capital letter: *Manchester, Jenny Holmes, the Thames, Dr. Jekyll, Mr. Hyde.*

Typical ***proper noun*** types are:

- Personal first names and surnames: *Bill, Fred, Ramona, McDuff, Churchill*
- Common nouns used as personal titles, names and forms of address: *Mrs. Brown, President Roosevelt, Dr. Watson, Uncle Joe, Mother Riley, Nurse Forbes, Mum, Dad, Sir Frank O'Phobe, the Rolling Stones, Grandma*
- Common nouns in the titles of buildings, institutions, business organisations and cultural and market products: *Buckingham Palace, The Garrick Theatre, Blackburn Rovers, Guy's Hospital, Orpington Grammar School, The London Brick Company, Warner Brothers, Patak's Lime Pickle, Harvey's Salad Cream*
- Geographical names and common nouns included in them: *the River Clyde, Europe, Japan, Shaftesbury Avenue, Times Square, Borough High Street, the Blue Ridge Mountains*
- Calendar names (months, days of the week, religious festivals) and historical periods: *Wednesday, Saturday, June, August, Christmas, Ramadan, Passover, Whitsun, the Jazz Age, the Renaissance*
- Media titles (films, print media, music, etc.): *Star Wars, The Daily Mirror, Pride and Prejudice, the Enigma Variations*

005/2 Common nouns: concrete or abstract

Common nouns can have concrete or abstract meanings. ***Concrete*** nouns refer to physical entities, i.e. things that can be experienced (directly or indirectly) through the senses: *cup, leg, person, car, air, water, whisky.*

Abstract nouns generally mean entities which have no physical form, and cannot be seen, smelt, touched, heard or tasted: they can only be experienced mentally or emotionally: *happiness, jealousy, politics, knowledge, idea, generosity, imagination, hate.* Many abstract nouns are ***bound singulars***, with a further tendency to be ***non-count***. However, these are tendencies only, and not fixed rules. Apart from this, the division into ***concrete*** and ***abstract*** has no further grammatical consequences. It is also difficult to apply clearly to many nouns. Words like *pollution, vacuum, sympathy, finance,* etc. could be classed as either, depending on the exact context. Although this traditional division may be useful in some cases, it is not really necessary, and we will use the terms here only in a general sense, if at all.

005/3 Common nouns: individual, mass, collective, and pair nouns

These are the ***semantic*** factors underlying grammatical ***number*** and ***countability***. All common nouns represent at least one of these four types (and some two or more, depending on different meanings).

- ***Individual*** nouns treat things as single and separate entities: *cup, leg, person, car, idea.* They are all ***count*** nouns. Most are ***free***, though some are ***bound***, e.g. *people* (***bound plural count***), *fuss, row, uproar* (***bound singular count***), etc.
- ***Mass*** nouns are the opposite. They treat entities as amorphous, i.e. without individual shape, form or limit. They refer to things like substances, characteristics, emotions, various fields of scientific and professional activity, types of belief and attitude, etc.: *sugar, generosity, anger, medicine, engineering, communism.*
  Mass nouns are all ***bound singular non-count***.
- ***Collective*** nouns refer to groups of individual entities. That is, they denote a quantity of separate things. They comprise singular and plural nouns, but all are ***bound non-count***, e.g. *information* (***bound singular non-count***), *surroundings* (***bound plural non-count***).
- ***Pair nouns refer to single objects with two "halves":*** *trousers, glasses.* Many of these are items of clothing for the lower half of the body.
  The two "halves" are the two legs. Others are tools with two interacting pieces joined together (e.g. *scissors, shears*). Pair nouns are ***bound plural non-count***.

Nouns with more than one meaning, or interpretation, can be variable regarding these categories. For example, in particular contexts ***mass*** and ***collective*** nouns can become ordinary ***individual*** nouns referring to single entities. Grammatical number status and countability then change, and the nouns concerned become ***free count nouns*** (see **008** below).

2.2 From singular to plural

006 Regular plural formation

Forming the plural of most nouns is not a grammatical problem. With the majority, as already mentioned, *-s* is simply added to the singular: *head – heads, toe – toes, hip – hips*. However, there are three pronunciation variants and two spelling distinctions involved. Furthermore, spelling and pronunciation do not entirely correspond.

006/1 Regular changes in spelling and pronunciation

- *-s* added and pronounced [s]: after the ***voiceless consonants*** [f], [k], [p], [t], [θ]: *cliffs* [klɪfs], *wrecks* [reks], *hips* [hɪps], *cats* [kæts], *myths* [mɪθs]
- *-s* added and pronounced [z]: after ***vowels*** and the ***voiced consonants*** [v], [g], [b], [d], [ð]: *toes* [təʊz], *hives* [haɪvz], *logs* [lɒgz], *sobs* [sɒbz], *lads* [lædz], *clothes* [kləʊðz]
- *-s* added to final *-e* and pronounced [ɪz]: after the ***voiced consonants*** [z] (spelt *-ze* or *-se*), and [dʒə] (spelt *-dge* or *-ge*), and the ***voiceless consonant*** [s] (spelt *-se* or *-ce*): *sizes* [saɪzɪz], *hoses* [həʊzɪz], *edges* [edʒɪz], *ages* [eɪdʒɪz], *cases* [keɪsɪz], *races* [reɪsɪz]
- *-es* added and pronounced [ɪz]: after the ***voiceless consonants*** [s] (spelt *-s*), [ks] (spelt *-x*), [ʃ] (spelt *-sh*), [tʃ] (spelt *-ch*): *kisses* [kɪsɪz], *foxes* [fɒksɪz], *crashes* [kræʃɪz], *torches* [tɔ:tʃɪz]

006/2 Special cases

- Final *-y* after a consonant is replaced by *-ies*: *baby – babies, lady – ladies, treaty – treaties* Pronunciation is not affected.
- Final *-f* or *-fe* is replaced by *-ves*, pronounced [vz], in the nouns: *calf, half, knife, leaf, life, loaf, self, sheaf, thief, wife, wolf*: *calves, halves, knives, leaves, loaves, selves, sheaves, thieves, wives, wolves*
  There is a choice of *-ves* or simple *-s* with the nouns: *hoof, roof, scarf, turf, wharf*: *hooves/hoofs, rooves/roofs, scarves/scarfs, turves/turfs, wharfs/wharves*
  All other nouns ending in *-f* and phonetic [f] add simple *-s*, e.g. *cliff – cliffs, cough – coughs* ([kɒfs]), *cuff – cuffs, laugh – laughs* ([lɑ:fs]), *safe – safes*, etc.
- With final *-th* the voiceless form [θ] is replaced by voiced [ð] + [z] after longvowels in certain words. Spelling is not affected: *baths* [bɑ:ðz], *paths* [pɑ:ðz], *mouths* [maʊðz], *oaths* [əʊðz].
  In other words of this type, however, there is no change, and the plural is pronounced [θs]: *faiths* [feɪθs], *heaths* [hi:θs].

The following are pronounced in either way: *truths* [tru:ðz/tru:θs], *wreaths* [ri:ðz/ri:θs], *youths* [ju:ðz/ju:θs].

- The voiceless [s] in *house* [haʊs] becomes voiced when the plural *-s* is added: *houses* [haʊzɪz]. Spelling is not affected. This is an absolute exception.
  All other nouns ending in long vowel + [s] retain the [s] when the plural ending is added, e.g.: *leases* [li:sɪz], *courses* [kɔ:sɪz], *curses* [kə:sɪz], etc., (see also under **006/1** above).
- Final *-o* has *-es* added: *echo – echoes, hero – heroes, potato – potatoes, tomato – tomatoes, veto – vetoes.*
  But this is not done with abbreviations or recently imported foreign words: *casinos, demos, dynamos, kilos, lilos, memos, photos, pianos, radios, studios,* etc. Pronunciation is not affected.

Irregular plural formation 007

007/1 Vowel change
007/2 Plurals in -en/-ence
007/3 Singular-plurals
007/4 Plural-singulars
007/5 Greek and Latin plurals
007/6 Modern loan-word plurals

There are a few nouns with no *-s*-plurals. Some are old Germanic plural forms which have survived into modern English. Others are original plurals of older loan-words from Greek or Latin. There are also one or two modern loan-word plurals which have been retained (particularly from Italian, but also from more "exotic" languages).

007/1 Vowel change

Most of the remaining older plurals concern vowel changes. Only a few words are affected, but there are regular patterns:

Singular	Plural	Vowel change (written)	Vowel change (spoken)
foot	*feet*	*-oo → -ee*	*[ʊ] → [i:]*
goose	*geese*	*-oo → -ee*	*[u:] → [i:]*
tooth	*teeth*	*-oo → -ee*	*[u:] → [i:]*
mouse	*mice*	*-ouse → -ice*	*[aʊ] → [aɪ]*
louse	*lice*	*-ouse → -ice*	*[aʊ] → [aɪ]*
man	*men*	*-a → -e*	*[æ] → [e]*
woman	*women*	*-a → -e*	*[ʊ] → [ɪ] + [ə] → [ɪ]*

The general phonetic rule here is: singular front vowels are raised; singular back vowels are fronted, and in most cases also raised.

007/2 Plurals in -en/-ence

Child (sing.) becomes *children* (plur.); *ox* (sing.) becomes *oxen* (plur.). There is also an *-en* plural of *brother, brethren,* used in a religious sense to mean members of a brotherhood or congregation. The plural of *penny* is *pence* in price references:

(14) The ice-creams cost fifty pence each.

007/3 Singular-plurals

A more common irregular type of plural is what we will call a ***singular-plural***: a word with a singular form but a plural meaning:

007/3.1 cattle, people, police

Number status and ***countability*** vary with nouns of this kind, and are dealt with further below. We will note now, though, that these three are all ***bound plurals***, i.e. they have no corresponding singular form.

The noun *people* is a ***free count singular*** when it means "nation, race" (*Volk*):

(15) In the course of history many different peoples have settled in South America.

007/3.2 crowd, family, etc.

Basically, nouns like this are ***individual***, i.e. ordinary ***free singulars*** with ***free plural*** forms. However, they are often used in a ***collective*** sense meaning "the members of …", and then become ***singular-plurals***:

(16) A family were having a picnic on the grass by their car.

In their ***collective*** meaning these are ***bound plurals***. As we will see later, the individual meaning is often preferred when the whole unit is thought of, e.g. when "one" is contrasted with "more than one":

(17) During the floods, one family was accommodated in the vicar's spare bedroom, and three other families were given beds in the church hall.

Here the noun is being used in its individual sense and has a ***free singular*** and a ***free plural*** form.

007/3.3 deer, fish, sheep

These nouns are ***individual*** in sense and ***free*** in number status, but simply have the same form for singular and plural:

(18) a. Four deer were grazing in the long grass by the wood.
b. One deer was being fed by the park-keeper.

With one or two exceptions, the common nouns in this group nearly all refer to animals and fish, Other examples are: *shrimp* (American), *cod, salmon, trout, herring, mackerel, bass, perch* (all fish); *grouse, snipe* (wild birds).

The nouns *herring, shrimp* and *mackerel* have alternative -*s*-plurals. *Fish* has an -*s*-plural *fishes,* rarely used nowadays except occasionally in the meaning "different species of fish".

Words from other lexical fields are *craft* and *aircraft,* and proper nouns referring to nationalities. These end in -*ese* or -*ss,* and are derived from adjectives: *Swiss, Chinese, Japanese, Vietnamese,* etc.

Native tribal names such as *Kikuyu, Bantu, Masai* (Africa), *Cheyenne, Blackfoot, Cree* (North America) are also ***singular-plurals*** of this type.

007/4 Plural-singulars

A ***plural-singular*** noun is the reverse of what we have just been discussing in **007/3**. It has a plural -*s,* but a singular meaning:

007/4.1 news, politics, etc.

These are ***collective*** nouns, but are used only in the singular, and grammatically are therefore ***bound singulars***:

(19) a. The news is good, I'm pleased to say.
b. Politics is a dirty business.

007/4.2 series, species, works, means, etc.

This type is the plural equivalent of nouns like *deer* and *fish* in **007/3.3**, i.e. ***individual*** in meaning and ***free*** in number status, but with the same form for singular and plural:

(20) a. Although there were fifty species of bird on the island, there was only one species of monkey.
b. The brick-works in Faraday Street is owned by the same company that runs the three engineering works in the town.
c. There are two means of getting there: by boat and on horseback.

007/5 Greek and Latin plurals

Some loan-words that originally came from Greek and Latin are still regarded as "foreign", and retain their original plural forms. Others have only English plurals. And some also have both: an English form and an old form. The old forms themselves are complex, and follow the grammar of the original language. Fortunately, there are not many of them!

007/5.1 Forms

Singular	Plural	Ending change	Other singular examples
phenomenon	*phenomena*	*-on* → *-a*	*criterion*
radius	*radii* [reɪdɪaɪ]	*-us* → *-i*	*stimulus, cactus, fungus, terminus, nucleus, focus, genius*
crisis	*crises* [kraɪsi:z]	*-is* → *-es*	*axis, oasis, analysis, thesis, basis*
index	*indices* [ɪndɪsi:z]	*-ix/-ex* → *-ices*	*appendix, codex*
stratum	*strata*	*-um* → *-a*	*medium, minimum erratum*
formula	*formulae* [fɔ:mjʊli:]	*-a* → *-ae*	

007/5.2 Original plural only

phenomena, criteria, stimuli, nuclei [nju:klɪaɪ], *radii, axes, crises, oases, analyses, theses, bases, codices, media, minima, errata, strata.*

007/5.3 English and original plurals with meaning difference

appendices (*Anhänge*), *appendixes* (*Blinddärme*); *foci* [fəʊkaɪ] (*physikalische Brennpunkte*), *focuses* (*Brennpunkte* im übertragenen Sinn); *formulae* (*wissenschaftliche Formeln*), *formulas* (*Phrasen*, bzw. bei Substanzen *Inhalte und Mischverhältnisse*); *genii* (*böse Geister*), *geniuses* (*Genies*); *indices* (*Indexziffern, Hinweiszeichen*), *indexes* (*Stichwortverzeichnisse, Register*).

007/5.4 English and original plurals with no meaning difference

cacti, cactuses (Kakteen); *termini, terminuses* (Endstationen); *fungi, funguses,* (*Pilze*); *gladioli, gladioluses* (*Gladiolen*); *rostra, rostrums* (*Podeste*); *referenda, referendums* (*Referenden*).

007/5.5 English plural only

apparatuses (*Apparate, Vorrichtungen*); *bonuses* (*Zulagen*); *choruses* (*Refrains, Chöre*); *crocuses* (*Krokusse*); *enigmas* (*Rätsel*); *rhododendrons* (*Rhododendren*); *prospectuses* (*Prospekte*); *forums* (*Foren*); *stadiums* (*Stadien*).

007/6 Modern loan-word plurals

Occasionally, "imported" modern foreign words keep their original plural forms: *kibbutzim* (*Kibbuze/Kibbuzim*), *mafiosi, muezzin* (*islamische Gebetsausrufer*), *paparazzi* (*Klatschjournalisten*), *tableaux* (*Bilder, Szenen*), etc.

Number, countability and meaning: details of use 008

008/1 Individual nouns

As we have seen, most of these are ***free count*** nouns, but a few are ***bound count***:

- ***bound plural count***: *people, graces;*
- ***bound singular count***: *fuss, row, uproar, commotion, spectacle, trial* (*Pein, Mühsal*), etc.

Many nouns usually thought of as individual take on ***mass*** meaning (and become ***bound singular non-count***) when the substance-type is stressed rather than the individual object. This is particularly common with types of food, but also with other materials:

(21) a. We had fish for lunch and apple-pie for dessert.
b. Would you like chicken or lamb?
c. The vegetables were wrapped in newspaper.
d. A piece of shoe was floating in the water.

008/2 Mass nouns

Mass nouns (***bound singular non-count***!) can be roughly divided into the following semantic categories:

008/2.1 Substances, materials, foodstuffs

beer, bread, chocolate, coal, coffee, gas, hair, liquid, meat, plastic, stone, sugar, wood.

Individualisation occurs here

- with general substances in the meaning *a type of*:
  Oxygen is a gas, water is a liquid, Guinness is a beer
  (***free singular count***)
- with foodstuffs in the meaning *a portion of*:
  A coffee with two sugars, please
  (***free singular count, free plural count***)
- with nouns that also have other ***individual*** meanings. These may be related to the mass meaning, or completely different from it:
  He threw stones/rocks at the police (= individual objects of that material, ***free plural count***)
  Behind the gardens there was a large wood (= an area of trees, ***free singular count***)

There were several hairs on her pillow (= individual strands, ***free plural count***).
Would you like a chocolate? (= *eine Praline, **free singular count***)

008/2.2 Elements

air, fire, rain, snow, water, wind.
The following also have different (or related) ***individual*** meanings:
air: *The man in the dark suit had an air of authority about him* (= appearance, manner, atmosphere: ***bound singular count***)
The pianist played an air from the Scottish isles (= old, traditional tune, melody: ***free singular count***)
fire: *There was a blazing open fire in the pub dining-room* (= a unit of burning material: ***free singular count***)
wind: *Strong winds were blowing on the coast* (= individual occurrences of the phenomenon: ***free plural count***)

008/2.3 Processes, activities and their consequences (-ion- and -age-endings are common here)

accommodation, action, activity, advice, care (*Pflege*), *communication, conversation, damage, education, footage, garbage, leisure, litter, permission, play, pollution, progress, recreation, rubbish, spillage, storage, talk, wastage, work* (also *homework, housework*).
Examples of other meanings with different count-status:
work (*künstlerisches Werk, wissenschaftliche Arbeit*), ***free count***; *works* (*Werk, Fabrik*), ***free plural-singular*** (!) ***count***: *There is a gasworks on the corner* (*An der Ecke ist ein Gaswerk*); *play* (*Schauspiel, Drama*), *care* (*Sorge*), ***free count***;
action, activity, conversation and *talk* (also in the sense of *Vortrag*) are all ***free count*** when they mean individual items of activity:
I had a short talk with Miriam and a long conversation with Bill yesterday (= *kurzes Gespräch/langes Gespräch*); *education* is individualised in quality references to specific schools or school biographies: *Few people had a good education in early Victorian England,* ***bound singular count***.

008/2.4 Finance, wealth

money, interest (*Zinsen,* also *Interesse*), *cash, income, wealth, poverty, luxury, finance*

In specific reference, *interest* (*Interesse*-meaning only!) and *income* are usually individualised: *a great interest in modern literature; an income from writing books* (***free count***).

008/2.5 Behaviour, attitudes, situation types (note also here the -ion-endings)

aggression, behaviour, confusion, derision, laughter, sympathy, violence, etc.

In specific reference, *sympathy* (*Mitgefühl*) is often individualised (***free count***).

008/2.6 Media, culture, science, beliefs

art, Buddhism, biology, gastronomy, literature, music, philosophy, television, theatre.

Common endings here denote areas of study, belief, and professional activity: *-ology, -onomy, -osophy, -ism.*

Also in this group are gerund references to pastimes and sports: *walking, rowing, jogging, cooking, sewing.* All gerunds are ***bound singular non-count.***

Examples of nouns with alternative individual meanings are: *television* (*Fernseher*), and *theatre* (= the building itself), both ***free count.***

008/2.7 Mind, emotion, character, experience (common here are the endings -ion, -ity, -ness)

creativity, emotion, experience, fear, generosity, happiness, imagination, information, knowledge, love, opportunity, personality, strength, etc.

Specification by adjectives, *of*-phrases and relative clauses can lead (optionally) to individualisation: *a knowledge of French or German, a profound happiness,* etc. (***bound singular count***).

And some distinct ***individual*** meanings: *love/fear* of particular things, e.g. *a love of cats, a fear of dogs, an emotion* (= a particular feeling), *a personality* (= an individual person, figure), *an experience* (= a single one, dt. *ein Erlebnis*), *an opportunity* (= a particular chance, dt. *eine Möglichkeit*), *a strength* (= a strong point or characteristic): *One of Dickens' great strengths as a writer was his vivid imagination.*

These are ***free count nouns.***

008/3 Collective nouns

008/3.1 Collective singulars

Many **collective singulars** also have characteristic end-syllables. One that they share with some mass nouns is the ending *-age*. In this case it stresses the idea of individual items unified in a functional whole: *baggage, luggage, foliage, plumage.*

Another, with a similar meaning, is *-ery/-ry,* denoting a collection of objects or tools designed for a single purpose: *crockery, cutlery, jewellery, machinery.*

A further typically collective ending is *-ing*; this usually means material, equipment, or the end-product of some action or operation: *clothing, washing (hängende Wäsche nach dem Waschvorgang), housing, decorating/painting* (*der Anstrich/die Bemalung/die Farben*), *wiring, plumbing* (*Wasseranschlüsse und -leitungen*).

Note: ***-ing-collectives*** are derived from gerunds, but function as full nouns, i.e. they mean things, not actions.

Other common collectives are *equipment, furniture, game, livestock, traffic,* etc.

All collective singulars are ***bound singular non-count*** nouns.

008/3.2 Collective plurals

Common **collective plurals** are: *clothes, belongings, goods, wages, savings, particulars, contents* (*Inhalt*), *arms* (*Waffen*), *outskirts, surroundings, steps/stairs* (*Treppe*), *damages* (*Schadenersatz*), *means* (*Mittel, Vermögen,* see also under **007/4.2** above).

Several topographical terms are collective plurals: *straits* (*Meeresstraße*), *flats* (*Ebene*), *heights* (*Anhöhe*).

Common abstract nouns in this category are: *riches, regards* (*Grüße*), *thanks, congratulations, manners* (*gutes Benehmen*).

Various colloquial expressions for physical and psychological conditions take the definite article:

the blues, the creeps, the dumps, the hiccups (*Schluckauf*).

All the nouns here are ***bound plural non-count***.

008/3.3 Singular-plural nouns as collective plurals

Collective plurals also include **singular plural** nouns *cattle, police, folk* (regional for *people*).

Among these are ***adjectival collectives***, referring (with the definite article) to particular sections of a population or society:

the rich, the poor, the young, the old, the sick, the handicapped. Here the adjective has been converted into a noun.

Further examples are nationality names, particularly those ending in *-sh*, and in one case *-ch*:

the Welsh, the Scottish, the Irish, the French, the Danish, the Swedish, etc.

All these are ***bound plural non-count*** nouns of essentially the same kind as in **008/3.2** The only difference is the singular form, and with ***adjectival collectives*** the use of the definite article.

A third kind of ***collective singular-plural*** noun can alternatively be regarded as ***individual***, with a ***free count*** character: *team, government, board, club, company, council, management, family, pair, couple, crowd, army, air-force, navy, pair, couple*, etc.

Although referring literally to single entities, these are usually regarded as meaning "a group of people", especially when the members of the group act, or experience things, together. In this case they are treated as ***collective singular-plurals***, grammatically, that is, as ***bound plural non-count*** nouns.

This also applies to proper nouns representing firms, clubs and other institutions:

(22) a. The management intend to change company policy.
b. The crowd were not happy with the way their team were playing.
c. The couple have been decorating their London home.
d. Arsenal are selling two of their defenders to Real Madrid.
e. British Telecom are increasing call rates in the new year.

It is not ungrammatical to treat such nouns as singular and to use singular verbs with them. But normal usage prefers the plural view. This changes, however, when the group is regarded impersonally, particularly if what it does, or experiences, applies only to the whole entity, and not to the individual members separately. The noun is then treated as ***free count***, and singular verb forms are used as for singular subjects:

(23) a. The management consists of the owner and his family.
b. The team includes three players under 21.
c. The company produces articles for use in the kitchen.
d. British Rail has been sold to a French company.
e. Manchester United has been bought by an American tycoon.

Other collective ***singular-plurals*** with an alternative ***individual*** interpretation are similar to the ***adjectival collectives***, as they refer to institutional, social, and professional groups and take the definite article: *the clergy, the laity, the military, the press, the aristocracy, the proletariat, the public*. Here, too, the normal form is plural when the group-idea is predominant:

(24) a. The general public were not in favour of the new measures.
b. The press are angry about the government's proposals.

008/3.4 Collective plural-singulars

These have a collective meaning and a plural form, but are grammatically singular. Most of them fall into three typical categories:

- nouns ending in *-ics* and referring to professional or scientific fields: *economics, politics, civics, mathematics, physics, linguistics*
- nouns (including one or two ending in *-ics*) referring to sports and games: *athletics, billiards, cards, charades, darts, draughts, gymnastics, marbles, skittles*
- certain words for illnesses: *measles, mumps, shingles, rabies, scabies*. And additionally the noun *news*.

All of these are ***bound singular non-count*** like those in **008/3.1** above.

008/4 Pair nouns

As already pointed out, a ***pair*** noun refers to what is really a single object. In other languages the equivalent words are often treated as individual nouns. English, however, sees here two joined "halves", rather than a single whole.

Items of clothing: *trousers, pants, underpants, knickers, braces, tights, flannels, overalls, jeans, shorts, swimming-trunks, pyjamas*.

Tools and functional objects: *scissors, glasses* (*Brille*), *spectacles* (*Brille*), *goggles, binoculars* (*Fernglas*), *shears, pliers, tweezers, scales* (*Waage*), *tongs, clippers, compasses, headphones*.

All are ***bound plural non-count***.

008/5 Quantifying non-count nouns

For use with numerals, non-count nouns need a "countable unit" placed before them. With ***mass*** and ***singular collective*** nouns this takes the form of an individual noun accompanied by the preposition *of* and known as a ***partitive expression***.

Partititive expressions usually refer to:

008/5.1 Types of container

a cup of tea, three bottles of milk, a glass of wine, two cans of soup, five sacks of rice, a mug of cocoa, a bar of chocolate, a carton of yoghurt, a jug of ale, a bowl of fruit, etc.

008/5.2 Small individual units of the material

a loaf of bread, four slices of cake, a piece of information, an item of news, two lumps of sugar, a leg of lamb, a bit of advice, a strip of plastic, three sheets of paper, a block of ice, a drop of water, etc.

008/5.3 Measured quantities

half a pound of butter, a pint of beer, four gallons of petrol, a litre of oil, a yard of cloth, four ounces of tobacco, two feet of snow, etc.
This also includes fractions (*Brüche*): *half* (*of*) *the coffee, two-thirds of the butter,* etc.

008/5.4 Indefinite quantities

a spoonful of sherry, a pinch of nutmeg, an amount of mud, large quantities of alcohol, etc.

Otherwise, they are used with quantifiers capable of singular reference, but not implying individuality: *some butter, a lot of snow, lots of wine, all the milk, no sugar,* (*not*) *any/much lamb.*

Pair nouns are quantified (not surprisingly!) using the noun *pair*:
four pairs of trousers, a pair of glasses, two pairs of scissors.

Regarding quantification, ***collective plural*** nouns are of two types:

- Some occur with indefinite plural quantifiers like (*a*) *few* and *many,* e.g. *a few clothes, many goods, few valuables.*
  Others like this are: *belongings, particulars, arms, regards, thanks, pains, attentions, congratulations, cattle, folk, clergy, savings, manners,* as well as all ***adjectival collectives,*** such as *the rich, the poor, the French, the Danish,* etc.
  Depending on meaning, many of these also combine with plural partitives like *a number of,* as well as other expressions suggesting the differentiation of individual members, such as *various, different,* etc.
  Other plural quantifiers possible here are those also used for mass singulars: *all, no, some, a lot of,* (*not*) *any.* (For details on quantifiers, see chapter 3).
- Other ***collective plurals*** focus on the whole entity alone. They can occur with *all, no,* and *not any,* but not with quantifiers having partitive or individual reference, i.e. we can say *no contents,* or *all surroundings,* but not **many contents,* or **some surroundings.* Despite their collective character, nouns like these focus more on the entire "mass" rather than on the individual members. To this group belong: *outskirts, customs, spirits, quarters, steps/stairs, damages, means, straits, falls, flats, heights, riches, studies, condolences.*

008/6 Mass, collective and pair nouns with different German equivalents

The following nouns have German equivalents with different countability or number status, and may therefore be a source of difficulty: ⚠

- ***Mass*** nouns: *abuse* (*Ausfälligkeiten*), *insolence* (*Unverschämtheiten*), *accommodation* (*Unterkunft*), *advice* (*Rat, Ratschlag*), *bread* (*Brot*), *toast* (*Toast*), *damage/harm* (*Schaden*), *evidence* (*Indiz, Beweisstück*), *proof* (*Beweis*), *help* (*Hilfe*), *information* (*Auskunft*), *news* (*Nachricht/-en*), *knowledge* (*Wissen/Kenntnisse*), *progress* (*Fortschritt/-e*), *pollution* (*Umweltverschmutzung*), *research* (*Forschung*), *scenery* (*Landschaft*), *thunder* (*Donner*), *lightning* (*Blitz*), *litter* (*Abfälle*), *work* (*Arbeit*)
- ***Collective singular*** noun: *furniture* (*Möbel*)
- ***Collective plural*** nouns: *clothes* (*Kleider*), *condolences* (Beileid), *congratulations* (*Glückwunsch/Glückwünsche*), *contents* (*Inhalt*), *customs* (Zoll), *damages* (*Schadensersatz*), *earnings/wages* (*Lohn*), *outskirts* (*Stadtrand*), *quarters* (*Quartier*), *riches* (*Reichtum*), *spirits,* (*Stimmung, Gemütslage*), *stairs/steps* (*Treppe*), *studies* (*Studium*), *surroundings* (*Umgebung*), *thanks* (*Dank*).
- ***Pair*** nouns: Nearly all ***pair*** nouns are expressed in German as individual nouns. This is therefore a group that need to be handled with care. This is a selection of the most common items from **008/4** above, with the German noun first:
  eine Hose/Unterhose/Badehose – (a pair of) trousers/underpants/panties/swimming-trunks
  eine Jeans/kurze Hose/Strumpfhose – (a pair of) jeans/shorts/tights
  ein Schlafanzug/Overal – (a pair of) pyjamas/overalls
  eine Schere/Pinzette/Zange – (a pair of) scissors/tweezers/pliers
  eine Brille/Schutzbrille – (a pair of) glasses/goggles

008/7 Summary: common nouns with different meanings in singular and plural

All singulars are ***free count***, and all plurals are ***bound non-count***, except where stated:

arm (*Arm*) – *arms* (*Waffen*); *compass* (*Kompass*) – *compasses* (*Zirkel*); *custom* (*Brauch*) – *customs* (*Zoll*); *flat* (*Etagenwohnung*) – *flats* (*Flachland/Watt*); *glass* (*Glas*) – *glasses* (*Brille*); *height* (*Höhe/Größe*, **bound singular count**) – *heights* (*Berg, Höhenzug*); *manner* (*Art/Auftreten*, **bound singular count**) – *manners* (*Benehmen*), *minute* (*Minute*) – *minutes* (*Sitzungsprotokoll*); *pain* (*Schmerz*) – *pains* (*Mühe/n*); *people* (*Volk*) – *people* (*Leute/Menschen*, ***bound singular-plural count***); *quarter* (*Viertel*) – *quarters* (*Quartier*); *scale* (*Skala/Dimension*) – *scales* (*Waage*); *spectacle* (*Spektakel/Schauspiel*, **bound singular count**) – *spectacles* (*Brille*); *spirit* (*Geist/Seele/Schnaps*) – *spirits* (*Stimmung*); *stair* (*Stufe*) – *stairs* (*Treppe*); *work* (*Arbeit*, ***bound singular non-count***, *künstlerisches/wissenschaftliches Werk*, ***free count***) – *works* (*Werk/Fabrik*, ***free plural-singular count***, *Uhrwerk*, ***bound plural non-count***).

2.3 The genitive

The genitive expresses a ***belonging-relation*** between one noun and another. Its most common forms are the ***s***-genitive and the ***of***-genitive.

The ***s***-genitive is attached to the *possessing* noun. The *belonging* noun follows it. With the ***of***-genitive, the order is reversed. The *belonging* noun comes first, and the *possessing* noun follows in the ***of***-phrase:

(25) a. Sarah's book = Sarah possesses the book/The book belongs to Sarah.
b. The roof of the garage = The garage "possesses" the roof/The roof belongs to the garage.

009 The s-genitive: form and syntax

009/1 Spelling

Singular nouns add apostrophe-*s* (*'s*): *the girl's family, the rabbit's foot, the boy's ball.*

Regular plural nouns simply add an apostrophe ('): *the girls' family, the rabbits' feet, the boys' ball.*

In terms of endings we can therefore say that the genitive singular is apostrophe-*s* (*'s*), and the genitive plural *s*-apostrophe (*s'*).

Irregular plural nouns take the singular form, i.e. they add apostrophe-*s* (*'s*): *the children's bedroom, the women's husbands, the people's votes.*

Proper nouns behave in the same way as common nouns, i.e. apostrophe-*s* (*'s*) for singular, *s*-apostrophe (*s'*) for plural: *Smith's dog* (*der Hund von Smith*), *the Smiths' dog* (*der Hund der Smiths,* bzw. *der Familie Smith*); *the American's enthusiasm for baseball* (*die Baseball-Begeisterung des Amerikaners*), *the Americans' enthusiasm for baseball* (*die Baseball-Begeisterung der Amerikaner*).

Singular names ending in *-s* are occasionally given the plural form: *Doris' headaches* (*die Kopfwehanfälle von Doris*), *Dickens' later works* (*die späteren Werke von Dickens*).

This use is becoming dated, however. The regular genitive singular is more usual nowadays (except in formal written styles): *Doris's headaches, Dickens's later works.*

009/2 Pronunciation

The pronunciation of genitive *-s* (in both singular and plural) is identical to the pronunciation of plural *-s*:

- [s] after the ***voiceless consonants*** [f], [k], [p], [t], [θ]:
  Jeff's trousers [dʒefs], *Dick's shirt* [dɪks], *the cat's tail* [kæts]
- [z] after ***vowels*** and the ***voiced consonants*** [v], [g], [b], [d], [ð]:
  Clive's wife [klaɪvz], *the dog's bone* [dɒgz], *dad's car* [dædz], *Sue's dress* [su:z]
- [ɪz] after the ***voiceless consonants*** [s], [ʃ], [tʃ], and the equivalent ***voiced consonants*** [z], [ʒ], [dʒ]:
  the boss's desk [bɒsɪz], *Rose's husband* [rəʊzɪz], *Bush's presidency* [bʊʃɪz], *the judge's remarks* [dʒʌdʒɪz].

For any word with a regular plural there is therefore no difference in pronunciation between genitive singular, genitive plural, and ordinary plural. The following phrases, for example, though distinct in written form and meaning, sound exactly the same when spoken:

(26) a. The judges notice. [dʒʌdʒɪz] Die Richter merken es.
b. The judge's notice. [dʒʌdʒɪz] Der Hinweiszettel des Richters.
c. The judges' notice. [dʒʌdʒɪz] Der Hinweiszettel der Richter.

009/3 Syntax

Syntactically, the *belonging* noun is the ***head*** of the noun phrase, and the *possessing* noun is the ***premodification***:

	Premodification	***Head***
(27)	a. Sarah's	book
	b. Jeff's	trousers

What we have here, then, is one noun phrase inside another. The first premodifies the second. As with any phrase that is part of another, the genitive noun phrase is also a self-contained noun phrase in its own right: the head is the genitive noun itself. It is important to remember this when there are other words preceding the genitive noun. These premodify the genitive noun, not the main noun. For example, in the phrase *that fat woman's dog*, the words *that* and *fat* premodify *woman*, not *dog*. It is not the dog that is fat, but the woman. Similarly, in *the little Scottish man's car* it is the man who is little and Scottish, and not the car:

(28) a.	**Main noun phrase:**	***Premodification***	***Head***
		that fat woman's	dog
		↓	
	Genitive noun phrase:	***Premodification***	***Head***
		that fat	woman's

b. **Main noun phrase:**	***Premodification***	***Head***
	the little Scottish man's	car
	↓	
Genitive noun phrase:	***Premodification***	***Head***
	the little Scottish	man's

A premodifying genitive noun phrase functions within the main noun phrase as a ***determiner*** (i.e. as an article-word). Genitives, that is, identify their heads. They answer questions formed with the interrogative determiners *which?* and *whose?*. They can also be replaced by other determiners with a pointing character, such as *this/that*, and in particular by ***possessive determiners*** (e.g. *your, his, her, their, our,* etc., see below):

(29) a. {that fat woman's} dog
↓
{which/whose} dog?
{this/her ...} dog

b. {the little Scottish man's} car
↓
{which/whose} car?
{this/his ...} car

There are various constructions in which the **belonging** noun is omitted, leaving the ***s***-genitive representing it as a kind of pronoun:

(30) a. That book is Sarah's (= Sarah's *book*).
Dieses Buch gehört Sarah.
b. Fred's garden is big, but Bob's isn't (= Bob's *garden*).
Freds Garten ist groß, aber der von Bob ist es nicht.

We call the *s*-genitive in this use the ***pronoun s-genitive***.

There are two other pronoun types closely associated with the ***s***-genitive. One, already mentioned above, is the ***possessive determiner*** (traditionally called the "possessive pronoun": *my, your, his, her, our,* etc.). This has a full pronoun form which we refer to here as the ***pronoun possessive***: *mine, yours, his, hers, ours,* etc. Possessives are dealt with in detail in chapter 3.

The of-genitive: form and syntax 010

010/1 As a postmodifying prepositional phrase

The *of*-genitive is normally regarded as forming a ***prepositional phrase*** postmodifying the **belonging** noun. As in any other prepositional phrase, the preposition is the ***head***, and the noun following it (in this case the **possessing** noun) is the ***prepositional complement***. The noun phrase *the roof of the garage* therefore has the following syntactic structure:

(31) ***Head of noun phrase*** + ***Postmodification by prepositional phrase***

	/	\
	Head of prep. phrase (preposition)	***Prepositional complement (noun phrase)***
The roof	of	the garage

The *of*-genitive is the most common type of postmodification in the noun phrase.

010/2 As part of a premodifying expression of quantity

On the other hand, in partitive and measurement expressions, and with numerals (*a cup of tea, two of the boys, some of the cake, a pound of biscuits*), the preposition is regarded as a part of the quantifying expression itself. In constructions like this, that is, what would normally be the **belonging** noun is actually the head of the whole phrase:

(32) ***Noun phrase***

/	\
Premodification	***Head***
↓	↓
Quantifying expression	***Noun***
A cup of	tea

010/3 The "double genitive"

The *of*-genitive can be combined with a ***pronoun s-genitive*** to form what is sometimes known as the "double genitive". The meaning is then "one of an undefined number":

(33) a. A book of Sarah's (= one of Sarah's (many) books)
Eins von Sarahs Büchern
b. This friend of Dave's (= this one of Dave's (many/several) friends)
Dieser Freund von Dave

c. A ball of the dog's (= this one of the dog's (many) balls)
Ein Ball vom Hund

d. A doll of my daughter's (one of my daughter's (many/several) dolls)
Eine Puppe meiner Tochter

This use is particularly common with proper nouns, but also occurs, as in c. and d., with common nouns. It is ***not*** correct in such cases to leave off the ***s***-genitive, i.e. we cannot say **a book of Sarah,* or **a bone of the dog.*
It is also ***not*** possible to postmodify a pronoun ***s***-genitive: **a bone of the dog's nextdoor.*
If postmodification is required here, an alternative construction must be used, e.g.
a bone belonging to the dog nextdoor.

Double genitives are also common with the ***pronoun possessive***:

(34) a. A book of hers (= one of her books).
Ein Buch von ihr (eines ihrer Bücher).

b. This friend of his (= this one of his friends).
Dieser Freund von ihm.

This is not surprising, as the ***pronoun possessive*** is actually the pronoun replacement for the ***pronoun s-genitive*** (see **020/2.3**).

011 The genitive in general use

011/1 Animate nouns: s-genitive
011/2 Inanimate nouns: of-genitive

011/1 Animate nouns: s-genitive

When the possessing noun refers to human beings or animals it usually takes the ***s***-genitive: *Jennifer's house, a horse's legs, the girls' hockey team, sharks' teeth.* However, there are a number of exceptions to this generalisation:

- Postmodification of the possessing noun requires the ***of***-genitive:
the umbrella of the woman at the bus-stop; the life of a person with no children; the voice of the actor who had just been speaking.
However, ***s***-genitives also occur in ***postposed*** form, i.e. not directly attached to the possessing noun, but to a postmodifying element. This often happens (especially in less formal language) with prepositional postmodifications that are parts of titles or other highly specified collocations. Most of these are themselves ***of***-genitives:
the King of Norway's son; the Leader of the Labour Party's remarks; my sister-in-law's mother.
- In spoken language the ***of***-genitive is sometimes chosen to distinguish plurals from singulars in ambiguous contexts: *my students' work* → *the work of my students.*

In many cases, however, accompanying words or larger contexts make the distinction clear and the ***of***-genitive unnecessary: *a teachers' conference, the workers' wage demands, the players' performance*.

- Genitive plurals followed by a singular head noun (as in the last example) are avoided when plural quantifiers are also involved, i.e. not * *many players' performance*, but *the performance of many players*. Similarly, *the behaviour of three visitors, the reaction of several participants, the accommodation of a few students, the situation of most politicians*, etc.
- When the possessing noun is stressed, the ***of***-genitive is always preferred. This is connected with the word-order principle of ***end-focus*** and often goes together with the contrast between a new reference and something already mentioned. Compare:
  elephants' eating habits (new reference: *eating habits*, previously mentioned: *elephants*) and *the eating habits of elephants* (new reference: *elephants*, previously mentioned: *eating habits*).
  Similarly:
  Blair's foreign policies (as opposed, for example, to his *home policies*) – *the foreign policies of Blair* (as opposed, for example, to those of *Bush*);
  Beethoven's symphonies (as opposed, for example, to his *string quartets*) – *the symphonies of Beethoven* (as opposed, for example, to those of *Mendelssohn*).
- Partly as a result of the emphasis just mentioned, the ***of***-genitive often occurs in more formal styles of writing. It is especially popular when the belonging noun refers to important characteristics, property or works of a well-known person, organization or region:
  the novels of Jane Austen, the works of Picasso, the victories of Manchester United, the policies of the president, the military empire of Genghis Khan.

For further exceptions see also under **012** below.

011/2 Inanimate nouns: of-genitive

When the possessing noun refers to something inanimate (i.e. a "thing"), it usually takes the ***of***-genitive: *the end of the street, the gate of the field, flowers of the forest, the engine of a car, the prime minister of Australia*.

But here, too, there are exceptions:

- In less formal language, organisations and geographical regions (clubs, bodies, firms, countries, etc.) are often personalised, and take the ***s***-genitive: *Australia's prime minister, a firm's profits, the club's performance, this theatre's reputation, the government's record on unemployment, NATO's next move, the town's financial position*, etc.
  This use is found particularly in speech and news reporting.
- Certain time expressions, mainly either deictic (i.e. speaker-related), or referring to the days of the week, always appear with the ***s***-genitive: *today's paper, last month's figures, tomorrow's programme, Tuesday's weather*.

Further exceptions concern the ***s***-genitive with quantifying nouns (see next section).

012 Some specific uses of the genitive

012/1 Quantifying expressions
012/2 Constitutive meaning
012/3 The pronoun *s*-genitive with localities
012/4 Genitives with verb-related nouns
012/5 Beyond the genitive: the collocational nature of "prepositional of" with verb-related nouns
012/6 The compound noun in genitive meaning

012/1 Quantifying expressions

012/1.1 Measures

These are typically followed by the ***of***-genitive. The possessing noun is the ***quantified noun***, and must be ***plural count***, or ***singular non-count***. The belonging noun is the ***measurement noun:*** *a pound of apples, two pints of milk, 50 litres of petrol, four feet of snow*

It is important to note that ***measurement nouns*** (*foot, pound, pint,* etc.) are used in the plural when they are preceded by plural numerals (i.e. *two* and above). The equivalent German constructions are quite different. No genitive is used, and the measurement noun always has the singular form, e.g. *2 Pfund Fleisch, 3 Kilo Fisch,* etc.

012/1.2 Partitives

Partitives also use the ***of***-genitive. There are two types:

a) with ***lexical quantifiers***. These are like measures, but are not exact amounts. They are simply typical ways of describing quantities of a particular substance or plural object (see **010/2** above). Here too the quantified noun must be ***singular non-count***, or ***plural count:*** *a bowl of soup, four slices of toast, a piece of cake, a bunch of flowers, that jug of milk, a crowd of people, a pinch of salt, a spoonful of sugar, a streak of oil, traces of blood, drops of water, pearls of sweat, a bar of soap,* etc.
German equivalents are similar to those under **012/1.1**, though with a tendency to put some quantifying nouns in the plural:
4 Scheiben Toast (but *2 Stück Kuchen*), *eine Schüssel Suppe,* etc.
German compound nouns are also found here, often in addition to double noun forms, though usually with slightly different meanings and stress: *ein Blumenstrauß, ein Strauß Blumen; eine Brotscheibe, eine Scheibe Brot.*

b) with ***regular quantifiers, lexical quantifiers*** and ***numerals*** (including especially ***fractions***).
This kind of partitive refers to part of "a whole". The quantified noun can be of any type: *three of the men, half of the sugar, part of a house, some of the chocolate, all of the village, two-thirds of the children, a section of the crowd, most of the book,* etc.
German uses more varied forms here: *das ganze Dorf, drei der Männer* (*von den Männern*), *die Hälfte vom Zucker/des Zuckers* etc.

012/1.3 Measures in the of-phrase

a man of 200 pounds/90 kilos (ein Mann von 90 Kilo/ein 90-Kilo-Mann), a waist of 30 inches/ 75 centimetres (eine Taille von 75 cm), a walk of five minutes (ein Spaziergang von 5 Minuten/ 5 Minuten zu Fuß/ein fünfminütiger Spaziergang), a hike of 20 miles (eine 20-Meilen-Wanderung), a flight of ten hours (ein 10-Stunden-Flug).

Unlike the case in **012/1.1**, the ***measurement noun*** here is part of the *of*-phrase. Semantically, that is, the belonging relation is reversed: it is now the belonging noun which is in the *of*-phrase, expressing the measurement as a characteristic of the possessing noun, which precedes it. There are more general examples of this in section **012/2** below.

012/1.4 Measures expressed as compound adjectives

Alternatively, the examples in **012/1.3** can be expressed like this: *a 30-inch waist, a five-minute walk, a twenty-mile hike, a ten-hour flight.*

The measurement noun loses its plural *-s*, and becomes a premodifier, with the numeral attached to it by a hyphen. We call this a ***compound adjective*** (see also chapter 4, **029/3**). It is often preferred to the *of*-phrase if there is no special end-focus. The ***compound adjective*** construction is only possible with ***count*** nouns. It is important to emphasize that the plural *-s* is always omitted.

012/1.5 Measures expressed as s-genitives

A further premodification possibility is the use of the *s*-genitive with the ***measurement*** noun. The belonging relation here is reversed semantically in the same way as in **012/1.3**: *five minutes' walk, two hours' delay, three weeks' holiday, 50 miles' drive, a day's work, a month's wages.*

This variant is used mainly with time quantities, less often with distance, but also before the noun ***worth*** in expressions of value: *Ten pounds' worth of sweets (Bonbons für zehn Pfund), fifty-thousand dollars' worth of mink (Nerz im Wert von fünfzig tausend Dollar), a hundred euros' worth of vouchers (Gutscheine im Wert von 100 Euro).*

Points to note here are:

a) The construction is only possible with ***non-count*** nouns and ***plural*** nouns.
b) Any determiner preceding the genitive noun must relate to the genitive noun, ***not*** to the main head noun (see also **008/3** above). That is, examples like *these month's wages,* or **this five minutes' walk* would be incorrect, as here the determiner obviously relates to the main head, and not to the genitive noun.
c) Nouns in the *of*-genitive following *worth* must also be ***plural*** or ***non-count***. That is, we can *say six-thousand pounds' worth of gold,* but not normally **six-thousand pounds' worth of gold watch* (except as a metaphor conveying irony).

012/2 Constitutive meaning

Here the genitive tells us what something comprises, contains, portrays, or simply "is". This is chiefly the domain of the *of*-genitive. In many cases the belonging relation is semantically reversed, i.e. it is the first noun which "possesses", and the second which "belongs". We have just met this phenomenon in **012/1.3**, and it is also the case in the categories **012/2.1**, **012/2.2**, **012/2.1–3**, and **5** following.

These categories are not totally distinct semantically. There is some overlap, for instance, between **012/2.1** and **012/2.2**, and **012/2.1** and **012/2.3**:

012/2.1 Consisting of

a family of four, a committee of experts, a panel of judges, a beam of white light, a wave of anger.

Closely related are materials that things are made of: *a dress of white cotton, tools of stone, a shirt of red flannel, curtains of thin gauze material, a necklace of pearls, eyes of pure green.*

The relation can be figurative (i.e. metaphorical): *a will of iron, a grip of steel, a complexion of smooth chocolate, a heart of stone.*

An abstract variant of this category is ***portrayal***: *the story of his rise to fame, a tale of greed and corruption, the film of the novel, a model of the new building, a plan of the city, the photo of Peter, a painting of a Greek woman, news of an earthquake, rumours of his resignation.*

012/2.2 Containing

a bag of sweets, a book of stamps, a pack of cards, a collection of porcelain, a cache of heroin, a bottle of sherry, etc.

Depending on context, some of these could be seen as partitives. Then the quantity would be emphasized. The emphasis here, however, is on the container as an object, as well as its contents.

012/2.3 Possessing/having

a teacher of great ability, a person of considerable charm, a building of character, an area of unimaginable squalor, a matter of importance, a girl of twelve (= *twelve years of age*), *a mother of four, a father of twins,* etc.

012/2.4 Caused by/resulting from

the horrors of war, the pleasure of your company, the dangers of sunbathing, the problems of unemployment, a grimace of pain, a gesture of impatience, his look of disgust, a sigh of relief, the results of the test, the fruits of his efforts, the outcome of the trial, the effects of global warming, a feat of strength, an act of will, a work of skill.

012/2.5 Equivalent to (appositives)

the island of Mykonos, the town of Bolton, the county of Sussex, a speed of 60 miles per hour, a height of ten feet, the game of chess, the age of eleven, the problem of unemployment, the topic of space-travel.

Here the first noun refers to a general entity or category, which the ***of***-noun belongs to, or specifies more closely.

This is one example of what is traditionally known in grammar as ***apposition***. It is dealt with fully in chapter 14.

012/2.6 Specification/location

Here we find the more conventional genitive meaning, with the ***of***-noun as possessing noun. In some cases it is the belonging noun which specifies a part of the possessing noun. In others, it is the possessing noun which specifies the belonging noun more closely by placing it in a particular location or category:

the centre of Edinburgh, the Moss Side area of Manchester, the West End of London, a borough of New York, the bottom of the picture, the top of a tree, the end of the line, a branch of physics, this field of philosophy, a type of screwdriver, a breed of dog, a variety of pumpkin, diseases of the brain, the history of clothes, the chemistry of the human body, Bill's style of play, etc.

A wider variation of this is the location of people and things in organizations, geographical regions, times, social contexts, and spheres of origin:

a child of famous parents, the events of 1968, a man of the working-class, a member of the club, the boss of the firm, the secretary of our department, the population of Scotland, the customs of the Sioux Indians, an author of the 18th century, the Bishop of Rochdale, the Duchess of Kent.

Social and professional ranks with ***of***-genitives can function also as official titles (as in the last two examples). They then count as ***proper nouns***. Historically, the personal names of important people also featured in ***of***-titles, usually specifying origin:
Isabella of Spain, John of Gaunt, Jesus of Nazareth.

012/2.7 Purpose

The ***s***-genitive is frequently used in standardized expressions of purpose. The genitive noun has a general meaning: *a girls' team* (*a team for girls*), *the men's toilet* (*a toilet for men*), *a children's hospital, a beginners' course, an old people's home, the steelworkers' union* (*Gewerkschaft der Stahlarbeiter*), *a boys' grammar school* (*ein Jungengymnasium*), *a nurses' home* (*ein Schwesternheim*), *a senior officers' training centre.*

Of-genitives are found here mainly in more formal institutional names and titles: *a court of law* (*ein Gerichtshof*), *the Faculty of Science, the Society of Authors, a place of worship* (*ein Ort der Andacht*), *the School of Medicine* (*die medizinische Fakultät*), *the Department of Trade, the Ministry of Labour.*

012/3 The pronoun s-genitive with localities

The ***pronoun s-genitive*** is used in a ***local*** sense to refer to particular kinds of institution, building, house or business. These are usually private homes, public institutions, shops, firms, etc. The genitive noun refers to the owner, the occupier, or person(s) that the institution is named after. Apart from personal names, this use also includes common nouns referring to relationships, occupations, trades and professions:

012/3.1 Private homes

Mainly with prepositions of place and direction:

(35) a. There is a party at Bettina's on Friday.
(= at Bettina's home, bei Bettina).

b. She's gone to a friend's for the weekend.
(= a friend's house; Sie ist übers Wochenende zu einer Freundin gefahren).
c. Bill and Sue are spending Christmas at his mother's.
(= at his mother's house, bei seiner Mutter).
d. We've been invited to the MacPhersons' this evening.
(= to their house; Wir sind heute Abend bei den MacPhersons eingeladen).

012/3.2 Firms and businesses

With or without prepositions:

(36) a. I bought this bag at Woolworth's. (= at the Woolworth store, bei Woolworth).
b. She has gone to the doctor's.
(= to the doctor's surgery; Sie ist zum Arzt gegangen).
c. Is there a Sainsbury's in the town (= a Sainsbury supermarket)?
d. I must ring the hairdresser's and make an appointment.
Ich muss den Friseur anrufen und einen Termin vereinbaren.
e. Sharon works at MacDonald's, Trisha at Barclay's.
(= at MacDonald's restaurant/at Barclay's bank)

Other familiar shops are: *the butcher's, the baker's, the greengrocer's* (*der Gemüseladen*), *the fishmonger's, the ironmonger's* (*Haushaltswarengeschäft*), *the grocer's* (*Lebensmittelladen*), *the newsagent's* (*Zeitungsgeschäft*), *the travel agent's* (*Reisebüro*), *the stationer's* (*Schreibwarengeschäft*), *the cleaner's* (*die Reinigung*), etc.

There are two connected points to note about the names of businesses and shops: firstly, they are treated as ***collective singular-plurals***, and therefore normally take a ***plural*** verb; secondly, and possibly because of this, there is often a tendency (in informal language, and sometimes even on signs) to leave the apostrophe out, and actually make them into full plurals without the genitive:

(37) a. Woolworth's have some good toys for children now.
(***collective singular-plural***).
b. Woolworths have some good toys for children now.
(conversion into full plural).

This tendency can be seen sometimes even with common nouns: *stationers* (*Schreibwarengeschäft*), *dry-cleaners* (chemische Reinigung), *fruiterers*.
However, this is a tendency only and is not officially regarded as acceptable.
This is logical, as the names themselves are singular in form: *MacDonald, Woolworth, Sainsbury, Marks and Spencer, Selfridge*, etc.

012/3.3 Other public institutions

Some traditional hotels, clubs, and entertainment establishments are also known for their apostrophes. Here is a London selection: *Claridge's* (hotel), *Ronnie Scott's* (jazz club),

Samantha's, Annabel's (disco-clubs), *Flanagan's, Khan's* (restaurants), *Madame Tussaud's* (waxwork museum), *The Duke of York's* (theatre).

The last example is named after its patron (adeliger Schutzherr), just as churches are named after their patron saints (Schutzheilige): *St. Paul's* (cathedral), *St. Martin's-in-the-Fields, St. James's, St. George's.*

It is similar with hospitals and schools: *Guy's, Queen Mary's, King George's* (London hospitals), *St. Olave's, St. Dunstan's* (London schools).

012/4 Genitives with verb-related nouns

With nouns related to verbs, an accompanying genitive may express the original ***subject*** or ***object*** of the particular verb:

(38) a. the departure of the guest (= <u>the guest</u> departed: ***subject*** of *departed*).
b. the client's needs (= <u>the client</u> needs something: ***subject*** of *needs*).
c. a love of good wines (= somebody loves <u>good wines</u>: ***object*** of *loves*).
d. Finlay's expulsion from the party (= somebody expelled <u>Finlay</u> ...: ***object*** of *expel*)

The choice of ***s***-genitive or ***of***-genitive more or less follows the principles already discussed, although ***of***-genitives with persons tend to be more frequent in this meaning than in others. This is because of information stress. Subject to this factor, the genitives in (38)a. and b. could be reversed: *the guest's departure/the needs of the client.* The ***of***-genitive, as was said above (see **011/1**), gives greater weight to the genitive noun. On their own, verbal noun phrases with genitives can sometimes be ambiguous if the original verb is transitive. For example, *the support of large families* may mean *someone/something supports large families,* or *large families support something/someone*:

(39) a. The new government measures had the support of large families.
(<u>large families</u> = ***subject*** of *support*).
b. The support of large families at home leads many poorer workers to migrate to richer areas.
(<u>large families</u> = ***object*** of *support*).

In such cases it is only the rest of the context that shows clearly which meaning is intended.

Where both subject ***and*** object are to be shown, two genitives are used. Then, it is always the ***s***-genitive which marks the ***subject*** and the ***of***-genitive the ***object***:

(40) a. Bill's love of good wines (***subject***: <u>Bill</u>; ***object***: <u>good wines</u>).
b. the company's construction of the bridge (***subject***: <u>the company</u>; ***object***: *<u>the bridge</u>*).

012/5 Beyond the genitive: the collocational nature of "prepositional of" with verb-related nouns

It should be pointed out that ***of*** is not only a grammatical device for the genitive, but also behaves as a preposition in its own right. Like other prepositions, it forms strong habitual relations (***collocations***) with some nouns, but not with others. In some cases it is therefore not grammar alone that decides usage, but also individual idiom. Certain nouns "go with" certain prepositions, just as certain verbs and adjectives "go with" certain prepositions (see chapter 6). Collocational restrictions on ***of*** affect particularly verb-related nouns. We say, for instance, *knowledge of, awareness of,* but *insight into something*. It is *an answer to* a question, and *an attack on* somebody, although we might think that as these are verb-related nouns just like any others, they ought to accept the ***of***-genitive. It is important to know, and learn consciously, which nouns combine with ***of*** and which do not.

012/6 The compound noun in genitive meaning

We have already come across the term ***compound adjective***. Compounds consist of separate words in special grammatical and semantic combinations. A common type of ***compound noun*** is one composed of two separate nouns in sequence. As a structure, this is explained more fully in the next section. Here it is the genitive meaning that interests us. The genitive meaning is often a variation on the idea of locality:

garden shed, kitchen window, garage roof, village green, car door, church spire, a London borough.

The first noun here is the possessing noun, and specifies where the second noun "belongs".

Compound nouns can also refer to material, type, purpose, origin or (in the more general sense) location (see the genitives in **012/2** above, particularly **012/2.1, 6** and **7**, in which quite a few items can actually be replaced by compounds). The original genitive meaning is weakened here. Focus is more fully on the idea of specification *("What type of?")*. Any traces of the belonging relationship still present follow the genitive patterns described above, i.e. the possessing noun here is mostly in second position:

a chocolate rabbit, a cotton dress, an iron will, a news story, resignation rumours, a brain disease, the Sioux Indians, orange juice, a bus ride, a train journey, three Liverpool women, a department store, a law court, a car park, a tennis racket, a football club.

An important point is that many of these are conventionalized, i.e. relatively fixed collocations, often thought of as comprising "one item of vocabulary".

013 Summary: s-genitive and of-genitive in contrast

013/1 The s-genitive is generally used for human beings or animals, except in the following cases

- the possessing noun is postmodified:
  the umbrella of the woman at the bus-stop;

- it is necessary to distinguish the genitive plural from the ordinary plural:
  my students' work → the work of my students;
- the belonging noun is singular and the possessing noun plural:
  the reaction of several participants;
- the possessing noun is stressed (***end-focus***):
  the eating habits of elephants (new reference: *elephants*, previously mentioned: *eating habits*); this is often the case in more formal styles of writing when the possessing noun is given more weight:
  the novels of Jane Austen, the works of Picasso.
- with partitives and quantifiers:
  a crowd of people, three of the men, most of the students;
- in constitutive senses ("consisting of", "possessing", expressing cultural or social location):
  a family of four, the photo of Peter, a father of twins, the customs of the Sioux Indians.

013/2 The of-genitive is generally used for things, except in the following cases

- In less formal language, particularly in speech and news reporting, organisations and geographical regions often take the ***s***-genitive: *Australia's prime minister, a firm's profits*
- Certain time expressions generally take the ***s***-genitive: *today's paper, last month's figures*

2.4 Noun forms

Nouns have characteristic forms which can tell us about their grammar, meaning and origin. Important elements in word-building are ***affixes***. These are syllables or syllable groups added to the beginning or end of a word to produce a new word. Affixes at the beginning are called ***prefixes***, those at the end are called ***suffixes***. The whole process of creating one word from another is called ***derivation***. The old word is known as the ***base***, and the new word as the ***derived*** word. First of all we look at typical ***suffixes*** that show "noun character". These are usually added to a base word of a different word-class to derive a noun, e.g. *good* (adjective) → *goodness* (noun). Some, however, simply derive a noun with a different meaning from another base noun, e.g. *child* (noun) → *childhood* (noun). In cases like this, the change in meaning is often from concrete to abstract.

In the examples given, the suffix is just added to the base without changing it, i.e. the base word keeps its original form in the derived word. Mostly, however, the form of the base has to be changed to fit the new suffix: *able → ability, vain → vanity.*

014 Common suffixes

014/1 Describing a state, condition or characteristic

-ance/-ence, -ancy/-ency, -cy, -ity/-ty, -ness, -dom, -hood, -ship.
The majority create nouns from adjectives, a few also from other nouns (e.g. *-hood, -ship,* and one or two instances of *-dom*): *ignorance, diligence, hesitancy, efficiency, accuracy, capability, certainty, darkness, freedom, childhood, friendship.*
Some *-ship*-nouns refer to skills, e.g. *horsemanship, seamanship.*

014/2 Describing an action or state, or the result of one

-al, -ance/-ence, -ment, -tion, -ure.
These make nouns out of verbs: *refusal, reliance, experience, statement, production, departure*

014/3 Describing a person/thing carrying out an action, or affected by one

-er/-or, -ee, -ant/-ent, -ist, -ian/an, -ess
These also create nouns from verbs: *teacher, creator, employee, defendant, student.*

In general, the suffixes *-er/-or* denote the active "doer", and *-ee* the passive role (i.e. the ***patient*** of an action, see chapter 1, **003/3.2, 3.3**), e.g. *employer* (the boss, the person who employs), *employee* (the dependent worker, the person who is employed). Similarly, a *payer* is somebody who pays and a *payee* someone who is paid.

Nouns ending in *-er* also refer to things (usually tools or other functional objects): *opener* (*Öffner*), *sticker* (*Aufkleber*), *duster* (*Staubtuch*), *runner* (*Schiene für Schubladen, Vorhänge,* etc.), *locker* (*Schließfach/Aufbewahrungsschrank*), *scraper* (*Kratzer*).

The endings *-ant/-ent* can also apply to people and things: *applicant, inhabitant, servant.* With things the reference is often to (chemical) substances or actions that have an instrumental function: *deterrent* (*Abschreckungsmittel*), *stimulant* (*Anregungsmittel*), *disinfectant* (*Desinfektionsmittel*).

The suffix *-ist,* added to nouns/adjectives, means a person practising in some field of activity (see **014/4**), such as jobs, hobbies and general fields: *journalist, machinist, economist, biologist, motorist, guitarist;* crimes: *bigamist, rapist* (*Vergewaltiger*); attitudes and beliefs: *moralist, racist, Buddhist.*

The endings *-an/-ian* are similar, but in addition can refer to nationalities: *Christian, politician, musician, republican, Indian.*

Finally, animate nouns considered to have just "male" reference are converted to "female" by the ending *-ess*: *waiter → waitress, actor → actress, lion → lioness* (*Löwin*), *tempter → temptress* (*Verführerin*).

014/4 Describing fields of study, belief, professional activity or behaviour

-ology, -onomy, -osophy, -ism, -ics.
These derive from nouns and adjectives, often of Latin/Greek origin:
theology, economy, philosophy, conservatism, economics, politics.
For the suffix *-ism,* see also under **014/5.4** below.

014/5 Suffixes with mixed reference

014/5.1 -ery/-ry

a) ***a place of activity***: *bakery, refinery, brewery, carvery* (derived mainly from verbs)
b) ***a field of activity***: *archery, slavery, chivalry, chemistry* (derived from nouns)
c) ***a collection of things or people*** (see also **008/3.1** above): *greenery, cutlery, citizenry, yeomanry* (derived mainly from nouns, ocasionally from adjectives).

014/5.2 -age

a) ***collective consequence of activity*** (see also **008/3.1** above): *wreckage, coverage, damage* (derived mainly from verbs)
b) ***functional collection of individual things*** (see also **008/3.1** above): *baggage, luggage, foliage, plumage* (derived mainly from nouns)
c) ***condition/situation:*** *bondage, dotage, suffrage* (derived mainly from verbs)
d) ***amount:*** *dosage, footage, mileage, postage* (derived mainly from nouns)
e) ***place where people live, things are kept:*** *anchorage, garage, orphanage, parsonage* (derived from nouns and verbs)

014/5.3 -ing

a) ***collective end-products of process/activity*** (see also **008/3.1** above): *clothing, painting, plumbing* (derived from verbs)
b) ***single end-products of process/activity:*** *building, crossing, landing, lining, painting, swelling* (derived from verbs)

As noted above (see **008/3.1**), *-ing*-nouns were originally gerunds, but function in the present-day language as full nouns.

014/5.4 -ism

a) ***collective activity or consequence of activity:*** *criticism, baptism* (derived from verbs)
b) ***kinds of behaviour:*** *barbarism, heroism, racism* (derived from nouns and adjectives)
c) ***kinds of language use:*** *Americanism, Germanism, archaism* (derived mainly from adjectives)
d) ***belief, idea, principle of behaviour:*** *modernism, communism, behaviourism, Buddhism* (derived from adjectives and nouns)
e) ***condition of illness or abnormal behaviour:*** *alcoholism, mannerism* (derived from nouns)

015 Prefixes

Prefixes that occur only with nouns are not so common or important in English. Unlike suffixes, they do not change word-classes. On the contrary, the same prefix usually appears in most derivations of a particular word, regardless of word-class, e.g. *possible* → *impossible* → *impossibility*. Here we will look just at prefixes which particularly affect nouns. They do this in certain general semantic ways.

015/1 Opposites

anti-, counter-, dis-, in-, non-
anti-climax, antidote (Gegenmittel), counter-revolution (Konterrevolution), discomfort (Unbehagen), inability (Unfähigkeit, cf. adjective: *unable), non-payment (das Nichtzahlen), nonsmoker (Nichtraucher).*

015/2 Describing place, order, size and rank

arch-, vice-, ex-, super-, sub-, inter-, fore-, back-, pre-, post-
archbishop (Erzbischof), vice-president (Vizepräsident), ex-prime minister (ehemaliger/abtretender Premier), supermarket, sub-category (Untergruppe), interaction (Wechselwirkung), foreground (Vordergrund), background (Hintergrund), back-payment (Nachzahlung), predecessor (Vorgänger), preview (Vorschau), post-graduate (Forschungsstudent, Doktorand).

015/3 Describing self and others

auto-, co-, pro-
autobiography, automobile (= automatic vehicle, Auto), autonomy (= freedom, independence), coauthor (Mitautor), pro-communist (= a communist sympathizer).

015/4 Referring to number and quantity

uni-, mono-, bi-, tri-, semi-
uniform, unity (Einheit), monorail (Einschienenbahn), bi-plane (Doppeldecker), tricycle (Dreirad), semi-circle (Halbkreis).

015/5 Meaning "badly/wrongly"

mal-, mis-
malfunction (Funktionsstörung), malpractice (Verstoß gegen Berufsprinzipien), misconduct (Fehlverhalten).

Compound nouns 016

016/1 Two separate nouns

The compound nouns we have met so far consist of two separate nouns:
kitchen window, cotton dress.
The first describes the second more closely, rather like an adjective. Syntactically, compound nouns are usually regarded as "double heads":

	Premodification	*Double Head*
(41)	a. Sarah's	cotton dress
	b. the	kitchen window
	c. that	car door

But in fact we could just as easily see the first noun as an adjective premodifier, and the head as a single head, as in any other noun phrase:

	Premodification	*Head*
(42)	a. Sarah's cotton	dress
	b. the kitchen	window
	c. that car	door

This analysis is simpler and more regular. It also fits the semantic facts better, since the first noun, as we have said, has the meaning of an adjective. However, compounds are often spelt with a hyphen: *car-door, bus-stop, taxi-driver, door-key.*

In this case, there is more justification for the "double head" solution, semantically as well as syntactically. This is not just a theoretical point, but also concerns the practical relation of the two nouns to each other, which is discussed in the next section.

016/2 The "hyphen" question

With many words, there are no definite rules about hyphens. The last 4 examples, for instance, often appear without hyphens: *car door, bus stop, taxi driver, door key.* Spelling is flexible, and depends on the writer's purpose. A hyphen makes it especially clear that the two nouns belong together as a unit. As we have just seen, it underlines the tendency to a "double-head" interpretation, and emphasizes that together the two words are part of one conceptual field.

Hyphens are nearly always used when either word is unique in that particular meaning: *machine-gun, cattle-trough* (*Viehtränke*), *seat-belt, dog-collar, blow-lamp,* (*Schweißbrenner*), *search-warrant* (*Durchsuchungsbefehl*), *pin-stripe* (*Nadelstreifen*), *pig-iron* (*Roheisen*), *key-ring, pot-belly* (*Hängebauch*), *nail-file, chamber-pot,* etc.

016/3 Two nouns as one

The final step to unity is when two nouns form a single word and are written together: *teapot, saucepan* (*Kochtopf*), *bulkhead* (*Schott*), *lawnmower, headroom* (*lichte Höhe*), *bedroom, bathroom, sunshade* (*Sonnenschirm*), *cowshed* (*Kuhstall*), *haystack* (*Heuschober*), *pancake, sunburn, textbook, wallpaper, beefsteak, beetroot, workman, armchair, weekend, rainbow, homework,* etc. The compound has then become conventionalized and is generally accepted in the language as being a single lexical item. Its meaning is often highly specific and amounts to more than the sum of the two parts. For example, *wrapping paper* and *toilet paper* are functional types of paper, but *wallpaper* is more, i.e. a kind of furnishing. Similarly, *homework* is not just any work done in the house, but is specifically connected with school and learning.

016/4 Singular in the first element

What does a cake shop have in common with a toothbrush and a child psychologist? Unfortunately, this is not the beginning of a funny story, but only a grammar question. If we consider that a *cake shop* sells *cakes,* a *toothbrush* cleans *teeth,* and a *child psychologist* treats *children,* then it seems logical to expect the first element of the compound to be a plural noun. In general, however, there is a tendency to avoid plurals in the first element of compounds, even when the meaning is obviously plural. Other examples are: *bookseller, bricklayer* (*Maurer*), *gun-laws, armchair, ski-rack* (*Skiständer*), *car-park, footwear* (*Schuhwerk*). This "plural → singular reduction" even affects bound plurals in some pair nouns: *trouser-zip, pyjama jacket, overall-pocket, binocular-case* (*Fernglastasche*). Other pair nouns, however, retain their plural form in compounds, e.g. *jeans pocket, glasses case* (*Brillenetui*). These are usually spelt as separate nouns, whereas the first-element singulars are hyphen- or single compounds.

016/5 Other types of compound noun

016/5.1 Proper nouns

A typical compound proper noun is a ***Christian name + surname***: *Sally Robinson, Sharon Cooke, George Mackintosh, Richard Chalfont, Bryn Williams.*

Another type is a ***title + surname***: *Mrs. Robinson, Ms. Cooke, Mr. Mackintosh, Lord Chalfont, Sergeant Williams.*

It is important to remember that title-elements are ***common*** nouns. If used without a name, they are spelt in lower case (= with a small initial letter): *At the police-station I was interviewed by a sergeant.*

If they are parts of names, as in the examples above, they are spelt with capitals.

Another important point is that the titles *Mrs.* [mɪsɪz], *Mr.* [mɪstə] and *Ms.* [məz] always appear in this abbreviated form with a full-stop after them. As common nouns Mr. and Mrs. are written in full as *mister* and *missus*.

The names of places, buildings and other institutions can also consist of a proper and a common noun. Generally, the name is first and the place (e.g. building, road or other type of location) second: *Buckingham Palace, the British Museum, the London Eye, Oxford Street, Piccadilly Circus.*

But it can be the other way round: *the River Thames, Mount McKinley, Upper Canada, West London.*

016/5.2 Adjective + noun

Adjectives sometimes form the first element in compound nouns. These are typically written as one word or with hyphens: *blackcurrant* (*Johannisbeere*), *greenhouse, longbow* (*Langbogen*), *high-street.*

But there are also many examples of separate words: *a short story* (*Kurzgeschichte*), *big game* (*Großwild*), *a front seat* (*Beifahrersitz*), *a double bed* (*Doppelbett*), *red lead* (*Bleirot*), *a yellow card* (*eine gelbe Karte*).

016/5.3 Noun/verb/adjective + prepositional phrase

Occasionally we find prepositional phrases and infinitives (always with hyphens) as the second element: *father-in-law* (*Schwiegervater,* so also *daughter-in-law, brother-in-law,* etc.), *mother-to-be* (*werdende Mutter*), *coffee-to-go* (*Kaffee zum Mitnehmen*), *a stick-in-the-mud* (colloquial, *Muffel*), *a free-for-all* (colloquial, *Rauferei*).

016/5.4 Verbs/nouns with particles

Many compound nouns have a particle element. This is a single preposition, or, more often, an adverb particle. With adverb particles, the compound is usually based on a whole ***phrasal verb*** (see chapter 8). If the particle is the first element, the compound is always a single word: *downfall* (*Sturz, Niedergang*), *downpour* (*Regenguss*), *income, outbreak* (*Ausbruch*), *underpass* (*Verkehrsunterführung*), *outfit* (*Kleidung*), *afterthought* (*nachträglicher Einfall*), *overheads* (*laufende Kosten*), *underwear* (*Unterwäsche*), *overcoat* (*Wintermantel*), *outcast* (*Ausgestoßene(r)*).

If the particle is the second element, it often has a hyphen, though single-word compounds are also common: *make-up, turn-out* (*Beteiligung*), *take-off, stop-over* (*Zwischenaufenthalt*), *press-up* (*Liegestütz*), *passer-by* (*Passant*), *set-to* (colloquial, *Rauferei*), *breakdown, touchdown, sleepover* (*Übernachtung bei Freunden*), *tearaway* (*Rabauke*), *takeover* (*wirtschaftl. Übernahme*).

There are also one or two traditional items which include an object: *forget-me-not* (*Vergissmeinnicht*), *pick-me-up* (*kräftestärkendes Tonikum*), *merry-go-round* (*Karussell*).

016/5.5 Noun-verb combinations

The majority of these are single words, but other variants occur.

Noun as first element: *earthquake* (*Erdbeben*), *milkshake, toothpick* (*Zahnstocher*), *corkscrew, haircut, car-wash, bomb scare* (*Bombenalarm*).

Noun as second element: *cookbook, repair-set* (*Reparatursatz*), *playground, dance-hall, swimsuit.*

016/5.6 Nouns with gerunds

There are two kinds of construction here; firstly, ***gerund + noun***: *walking-stick, swimming pool, ironing-board, washing machine, drinking vessel* (*Trinkgefäß*), *sailing boat, hiking boots,* etc.

Hyphens here are a matter of choice. But with or without, a gerund premodifier creates a close link. As gerunds are "verbal nouns" (see chapter 13), these combinations are traditionally regarded as compound nouns, just as if there were two ordinary nouns together. The meaning relation is purpose or function: an ironing-board is "a board for ironing clothes on", a walking stick "a stick for walking with", and so on.

The second type of construction is ***noun + gerund***: *horse-racing, sightseeing, songwriting, stamp collecting, grape-picking.*

Again, spelling habits vary. The most usual is probably with a hyphen, followed by the single-word variety. Semantically, the noun is the object of the gerund, i.e. *songwriting* = writing songs, *stamp collecting* = collecting stamps.

But with some combinations it may also be an adverbial relation: *sunbathing* (= lying in the sun), *windsurfing* (= surfing in the wind), *ice-skating,* (= skating on ice) (see also chapter 13).

016/6 Pronunciation: stress

Main stress (') can fall on either the first element or the second:

(43) a. 'bus stop
b. car 'door

In the b.-pattern, the first element is actually not entirely unstressed, but has what is known as "secondary stress". For the sake of simplicity here, though, we refer only to ***main stress***.

Spelling variations with the same words (i.e. with or without hyphens) make no difference to the pronunciation. For example, both *bus-stop* and *car-door* have the same stress pattern as in (43), where they appear without hyphens.

Apart from this factor, however, the spelling does give an indication of the stress pattern. All single compounds stress just the first element. And the same is true of most hyphen-compounds:

(44) a. 'teapot
b. 'key-ring
c. 'seat-belt

With separate nouns, there is more variation. Some follow the pattern in (43), while others put the main stress on the second element:

(45) a. 'church spire, 'clock tower, 'clutch pedal. (stress on first word)
b. kitchen 'window, garden 'shed, car 'door, village 'green. (stress on second)

These are conventions which must be learnt individually. But they are based on a general focus rule: what is stressed is where the focus lies, and the focus is on the distinguishing feature of the compound. For example, *church* is the important part of *church spire,* signifying specifically "a church and not any other type of building". With *kitchen window,* it is specifically the *window* (as opposed to any other part of the kitchen) that our attention is drawn to.

When the meaning of the two elements is *specific + general,* and the first refers to purpose or type (meaning "a type of X"), it is the first that tends to receive the main stress: *a 'news story, a 'brain disease, 'orange juice, a 'law court, a 'car park, a 'train journey, 'tennis rackets, a de'partment store, an infor'mation deficit.*

Where the first noun refers to a characteristic of form or substance (i.e. is more like an adjective), the second element gets the main stress: *a chocolate 'rabbit, a cotton 'dress, an iron 'will, the Sioux 'Indians.*

The stress pattern is exactly the same with any normal combination of adjective + noun. Compare the stress on *orange juice* in the two sentences:

(46) a. Orange 'juice ran out of the fruit. (ein orangefarbener Saft ...)
b. 'Orange juice ran all over the table. (Orangensaft ...)

In (46)a. we have an ordinary adjective, followed by a noun. The stress pattern is the same as in the last set of compound noun examples (*a chocolate 'rabbit, a cotton 'dress ...*). In (46)b. we have a compound noun, with the first element referring to type (= a type of juice for drinking).

When the first element of a compound expresses origin or place, the focus and main stress position can vary. This follows semantic principles similar to those already discussed. If the origin element specifies a more general one ("a type of X"), it is stressed: *'city people, 'Plains Indians, 'jungle animals, a Chic'ago woman, 'Arsenal players.*

The second elements here are obviously general nouns. When they are more specific, the stress pattern is the other way round: *a London 'banker, Yorkshire 'farmers, California 'students, a country 'cottage, a Shetland 'pony, a polar 'bear.*

Specificness, though, can depend on context, e.g.

(47) a. Jill and I have bought a country 'house. [normal version]
(= We've bought a house. It is in the country).
b. Jill and I have bought a 'country house.
(= The house we've bought is not in the town, but in the country).
c. Yorkshire 'farmers don't like the hot weather. [normal version]
(But other people in Yorkshire love it).
d. 'Yorkshire farmers don't like the hot weather.
(But farmers in other places love it).

Proper nouns of all types follow this principle. Main stress is usually on the second element: *Donald 'Duck, Brad 'Pitt, London 'Airport, Manchester 'United, Leicester 'Square, Hong 'Kong.*

Exceptions are where the second element is regarded as more general and the first as a specifier: *the 'Lake District, the 'Latin Quarter, the 'Circle Line, 'Fair Isle, 'Broad Street, 'Moss Brothers* (*Gebrüder Moss*).

Basically, however, these must be learnt individually. The *specific* + *general* meaning is not always obvious, and often has more to do with the origin of words than with their present-day use. We speak, for example of the *'East Side* (of New York), but of the *West 'End* (of London). Road names are stressed on the second element, except when it is *street*: *Fifth 'Avenue, Clare 'Lane, Bow 'Road,* but *'Bow Street.* With company names, the name is stressed when just the company category follows: *'Moss Brothers, 'Carver and Sons, 'Braeburn Limited.*

The second element is stressed when it expresses what the company does: *Harcourt Engin'eering, Lobos 'Travel, Framley 'Sports.*

016/7 Plural forms

Plural forms are attached to the second noun: *kitchen windows, bus stops, seat-belts, teapots, armchairs.*

The plural form is the same as for the single noun, also with irregular plurals: *workman – workmen; policewoman – policewomen; godchild* (*Patenkind*) *– godchildren.*

Care must be taken with nationality-names ending in the syllable *-man*. Not all are compound nouns.

Compounds: *Englishman – Englishmen, Frenchman – Frenchmen,* etc.

Single nouns: *Roman – Romans; Norman – Normans, German – Germans.*

In hyphen-compounds with a preposition or adverb, the plural form is attached to the noun part when there is one: *fathers-in-law, mothers-to-be, commanders-in-chief, passers-by.*

Otherwise, *-s* is added to the end of the word: *stop-overs, press-ups, set-tos, breakdowns, pick-me-ups.*

017 Compound nouns: summary and points of difficulty

017/1 Type and spelling

Compound nouns can be:

- two separate nouns: *kitchen window, coffee table;*
- two nouns joined by a hyphen: *car-door, bus-stop.*
  There are no definite rules about hyphens, but they are usual when either word (especially the first) is unique in that particular meaning: *machine-gun, seat-belt, dog-collar;*

- two nouns joined as a single word: *teapot, saucepan, textbook, wallpaper.*
  Compounds like this have become conventionalized as single lexical items with highly specific meanings.
  The first element of compounds is usually singular, even when the meaning is obviously plural, e.g. *bookseller, bricklayer, car-park, footwear.*

017/2 Pronunciation: stress

With all single compounds and hyphen-compounds (except those also spelt as separate words) main stress lies on the first element: *'teapot, 'key-ring, 'seat-belt.*

With separate words, main stress position varies: *'church spire, garden 'shed.* This is what ⚠ causes problems for German speakers, particularly when the second element is stressed (as this is unusual in German compounds).

The ***second element*** has main stress when it carries information focus, i.e.

- usually when the first element refers to a characteristic (i.e. functions more like an adjective, or actually is one): *a chocolate 'rabbit, a cotton 'dress,* the *back 'seat, big 'game,* a *short 'story;*
- when the first element expresses origin or place, and the second is specific in reference, i.e. carries new or contrasting information: *a country 'cottage* (as opposed to *a town 'flat*), *a Shetland 'pony* (as opposed to *a mountain 'lion*), *a Glasgow 'teenager* (as opposed to *a Glasgow 'policeman*).
  This can be contrasted with the first element alone as the carrier of new or contrasting information: *'city people* (as opposed to *'country people*), *'jungle animals* (as opposed to *'plains animals*), *'Arsenal players* (as opposed to *'Chelsea players*);
- usually when the whole compound is a proper noun: *Donald 'Duck, Brad 'Pitt, Leicester 'Square, Hong 'Kong, Harcourt Engin'eering.*
  Exceptions:
  certain local names, e.g. those ending in *Street, District, Quarter, Side, Line, Route* (but not *Road* or *End*): *'Bow Street* (but *Bow 'Road*), the *'East Side* (of New York, but the *West 'End* of London);
  company names when the second element refers simply to the legal or official company status: *'Moss Brothers, 'Braeburn Limited.*

Some other processes of noun formation 018

018/1 Old forms into new
018/2 Old words, new meanings
018/3 New words, new meanings

Language is constantly changing. This is partly because we need new words for new things, but also because we like to play with language. Language is flexible and ready to reflect our moods and caprices, our loves, hates and desires. It is the toy of younger generations and fashionable trends. But it also allows those who want to influence and control us to impress the world with new product names, new political concepts and complicated specialist jargon. Who can resist an insurance agent offering a *dynamically staggered, inflation-linked life and endowment policy with easy-term annulment*? We nod wisely, understand nothing, and sign the contract.

As a category, nouns are particularly open to change. Nothing succeeds like a new noun.

018/1 Old forms into new

018/1.1 Clipping

This is the reduction of a word with two or more syllables to a short form with only one, e.g. *telephone* → *phone*, *aeroplane* → *plane*, *advertisement* → *advert* (or American *ad*).

Sometimes the shortened form becomes so common that we forget where it originally came from: *pub*, for instance, is a clipping of *public house*, a *fax* is actually a *facsimile* (*eine exakte Kopie, Nachbildung*), and a *bra* (*BH*) began life as a *brassiere*; a *pop fan* with *'flu* is really a *popular music fanatic* with *influenza*. Clipped forms usually start as slang terms in spoken language. Most of them slowly gain acceptance, until some become recognized as standard lexical items. *Fax*, *fan* and *bra* have reached this status, *pub* and *pop* are on the way, while *'flu* still counts as colloquial. The apostrophe here indicates the missing first syllable. *Phone* and *plane* also originally had omission apostrophes in front of them, but since the 1950s have been always been written without them. Other examples of clipping: *exam*, *gym* (*gymnastics/gymnasium*), *maths* (American *math*, *mathematics*), *cab* (from *taxi-cab*, originally also from *cabriolet*), *lab* (*laboratory*), *bike* (*bicycle*).

In familiar language clipping is applied particularly to Christian names: *Joseph* → *Joe*, *Susan* → *Sue*, *Elizabeth* → *Liz*, *Peter* → *Pete*. In some names certain sounds change in the standard clipped forms: *Edward* → *Ted*, *William* → *Bill* (also *Will*), *Derek* → *Del*, *Richard* → *Dick* (also *Rick*), *Robert* → *Bob* (also *Rob*).

018/1.2 Diminutives

The suffix *-ie* (or *-y*) is added to a word to make it a ***diminutive*** (Verkleinerungsform). This gives the term a "smaller", more friendly and familiar sound. The effect is often childlike. Most children, for instance, first hear and learn family relation words in diminutive form: *mummy*, *daddy*, *grannie* (*grandmother*), *auntie*. Diminutives are also common with names, especially those of children and younger people. They are added straight on to one-syllable names (*Georgie*, *Hughie*). Otherwise, the name is usually clipped first and then the *-ie/-y* added: *Tommy*, *Lizzie*, *Ronnie*, *Terry* (from *Terence*).

Certain clipped forms are usual or possible only as diminutives, e.g. *Suzie* (*Suzanne*), *Wally* (*Walter*), *Betty* (*Elizabeth*), *Harry* (*Henry/Harold*), *Carrie* (*Caroline*), *Larry/Lawrie* (*Lawrence*).

In colloquial language, diminutives of common nouns are also used: *hankie* (*handkerchief*), *movie* (*moving picture*), *telly* (*television*), *barbie* (*barbecue*), *cabbie* (*cab driver*), *bookie* (*bookmaker*), *boatie* (Scottish, *boatman*), *wellies* (*wellington boots, Gummistiefel*).

In baby language also: *walkie* (*Spaziergang*), *toothie* (*Zahn, Zähnchen*), *frockie* (*Kleidchen*), *sweetie* (*Süßigkeit*), *dolly* (*Püppchen*), etc.

018/2 Old words, new meanings

018/2.1 Conversion

This is the creation of a new word simply by taking an old one and using it in a different word-class. Americans are good at creating verbs from nouns – *to can, to party, to bottle*, etc. But there are also examples the other way round. We have already discussed compound nouns with particles. These derive from phrasal verbs, as was seen above (cf. **016/5.4**). Further examples: *a printout* (*Computerausdruck*), *a takeaway* (*Essen im Straßenverkauf/vom Lieferservice*), *a let-off* (*ein glimpfliches Davonkommen*), *a lookout* (*Ausguck/Beobachter*).

A compound consisting of two verbs is *make-believe* (*Einbildung*, singular non-count). Another, derived from a verb and its direct object, is *know-all* (*ein Besserwisser*). From single verbs we have: *a guess* (*eine Schätzung, Vermutung*), *a cry/a read* (*eine Runde Weinen/Lesen*), *a go* (*ein Versuch/eine Runde im Spiel*), *a try* (*ein Versuch*), *a spy* (*Spion*), *a must* (*ein Muss*), and many more. Many of these begin their lives as colloquialisms, and some remain so (e.g. *takeaway, let-off, know-all, a go, a must*, etc.).

018/2.2 Blending

Here parts of different words are stuck together to reflect the combined meanings of the originals, e.g. *smog* (*smoke + fog*), *brunch* (*breakfast + lunch*), *workaholic* (*work + alcoholic*), *motel* (*motor + hotel*), *infotainment* (*information + entertainment*), *telex* (*teleprinter + exchange*), *Oxbridge* (*Oxford + Cambridge*).

Expressions like these are often created first as a joke or an irony. After a phase of being treated as colloquial, some become standard (e.g. currently *smog, motel* and *telex*).

018/3 New words, new meanings

018/3.1 Coinage

Coining (*Prägen*), the invention of entirely new words, occurs most frequently with nouns in the world of advertising and marketing. A new product calls for a new name, which is understood at first as a proper noun, i.e. a brand-name. It then passes into general use for that particular object, and becomes a common noun. Examples are: *aspirin, nylon, kleenex* (a paper handkerchief or cloth), *xerox* (= a photocopy), *teflon, vaseline*.

Other articles are known by the name of the firm that first made them, the inventor, or the place of origin: *hoover* (*Staubsauger*), *biro* (*Kugelschreiber*), *stetson* (= a kind of cowboy hat), *jersey* (*Pullover*), *sandwich, jeans, jeroboam* (= large wine-bottle).

018/3.2 Acronyms

Acronyms are abbreviations formed from the initials or syllable-parts of the longer expressions that they stand for. They are pronounced as words. Many public institutions, governing authorities and professional fields are referred to by acronyms:

NATO (*North Atlantic Treaty Organization*), *UNESCO* (*United Nations Educational, Scientific and Cultural Organization*), *NASA* (*National Aeronautics and Space Administration*), *TEFL* (*Teaching English as a Foreign Language*), *BAFTA* (*British Academy of Film and Television Arts*).

Common-noun acronyms tend to be technical terms or other specialized expressions:

hi-fi (*high fidelity*), *CD-ROM* (*compact disc read-only memory*), *radar* (*radio detection and ranging*), *laser* (*light amplification by stimulated emission of radiation*), PIN (*personal identification number*).

Chapter 3 Pronouns, Determiners and Quantifiers

Basically, these are quite separate categories. ***Pronouns*** are words like *you, me, anybody, who?*, etc. ***Determiners*** are 'article words' (*a, the, this, my, which?*, etc.). And ***quantifiers*** are items such as *some, each, all*, including also ***numerals*** (*one, two, ...*). But there are good reasons for dealing with them all in the same chapter. Firstly, all of them are elements of noun phrases. Secondly, the categories overlap in certain respects: quantifiers function mainly as determiners; words traditionally regarded as pronouns (e.g. *this, my, which?*) also function as determiners; and on the other hand most quantifiers and several determiners (*many, few, this/that*, etc.) can be used as pronouns too.

3.1 Pronouns

Main grammatical features 019

Pronouns are grammatical and semantic representatives of ordinary ('full') nouns. They are used in their place:

- in ***back-reference*** to a full noun phrase already mentioned, in order to avoid repeating it: *the woman ...* ← *... she; the red shoe ...* ← *... it; these flowers ...* ← *... they*, etc.;
- when person reference is ***deictic*** (speaker-related): *I, you, we, they*;
- in constructions with syntactic ***back-reference*** requiring a certain grammatical type of pronoun, e.g. with relative clauses or reflexive verbs;
- when ***back reference*** is signalled by ***head noun omission***, leaving a premodifier to represent the missing head noun, e.g. a demonstrative or pronoun ***s***-genitive (*That is John's*), a numeral (*There were three*), or some other quantifier (*Both are ill*);
- when an appropriate full noun is unknown: *somebody, anything, no-one ..., who ...?*

Strictly speaking, most pronouns replace not just nouns, but whole noun phrases: *the big sports cars in our street ...* ← *...* ***they****; the man with the black umbrella ...* ← *...* ***he***.

Syntactically in fact, pronouns are noun phrases themselves, and fill exactly the same functions:

(1) a. ***The big white dog next door*** is barking.
↕ } **subject**
It is barking.

b. The police were following ***the man with the black umbrella***.
↕ } **direct object**
The police were following ***him***.

c. The postman gave ***Jenny*** the package.
↕ } **indirect object**
The postman gave ***her*** the package.

d. Dave and Mary went to the seaside with ***the children***.
↕ } **prepositional complement**
Dave and Mary went to the seaside with ***them***.

020 Pronoun types

020/1 Personal pronouns

Personal pronouns belong to the category of ***deixis*** (= speaker-related expressions). Unlike other words in language, ***deictic*** expressions change when there is a change of speaker or listener-relationship, even if the object or person referred to stays the same.

Let us say, for instance, that I am a new teacher at a school. I am getting to know a young colleague called Jane Robinson. If ***I*** talk about ***her*** to another person, the pronoun ***I*** use is ***she***. If ***I*** talk to Jane herself, ***she*** changes into ***you***. And when ***she*** talks to ***me***, ***she*** becomes ***I*** and ***I*** become ***you***. Supposing a '***he***' now enters the staff-room. ***He*** talks to Jane. ***She*** becomes his ***you***, but ***I*** don't like this, and promptly interrupt, converting ***her*** into part of my ***we***. Jane, unfortunately, is not listening. For ***her***, this ***he*** has become all ***you***, and ***I*** am soon left alone. Too late, ***I*** discover that the ***he*** is the deputy headmaster. Perhaps it would have been better if ***I*** had let ***him*** be my ***you*** too. It is a good idea to keep on the right side of deputy headmasters. They are often powerful personalities, whether as ***he, you***, or ***I***!

Returning to language, we can see that deictic relations vary rapidly when we are talking, as each speaker communicates from his or her own perspective. Personal pronouns also vary in their levels of deictic meaning. ***You*** (= *the listener from the speaker-perspective*) and ***I*** (= *the speaker from the speaker-perspective*) are completely deictic. They do not really replace full nouns (except in a very abstract way).

This is slightly different with ***he/she/it***. Here the deictic meaning is weaker, and can be described as *not the speaker and not the speaker's listener*. More important is the objective ***back-reference*** meaning: ***he*** for male persons, ***she*** for females, ***it*** for all other entities (plants, animals, inanimate objects).

Our little story above also has a grammatical moral. Personal pronouns are the only area of English where we still find the category of ***case*** (dt. *Kasus*): there are ***subject*** forms (e.g. ***I, she***) and ***object*** forms (e.g. ***me, her***).

There are also distinctions of ***number*** (i.e. singular-plural, e.g. ***I*** ↔ ***we***).

020/1.1 Forms

Personal pronouns, then, have ***person, case,*** and ***number***:

Person/Number	Case	
	Subject	Object
First person singular	*I*	*me*
Second person singular	*you*	*you*
Third person singular	*he, she, it*	*him, her, it*
First person plural	*we*	*us*
Second person plural	*you*	*you*
Third person plural	*they*	*them*

Subject forms are used only for the ***subject*** function – except in more formal English, where they traditionally appear also as ***subject complement*** after the verb *be*: *"Who is it?" "It is* ***I****."*

Everyday English uses the ***object*** form here: *"It is* ***me****."*

In all other functions, the ***object*** form is used: *Jim saw* ***her*** *in the car* (***direct object***); *The college sent* ***me*** *a letter* (***indirect object***); *The college sent a letter to* ***me*** (***prepositional complement***).

Note that ***I*** is always spelt with a capital letter.

You is used in all forms. i.e. there is no difference between singular and plural, or subject and object. Furthermore, no distinction is made – as in German or French, for example – between a 'polite' and a 'familiar' form of the second person. German *du, Sie* and *ihr* are all ***you*** in English!

020/1.2 Points of usage

Animals, especially larger ones or pets, are often referred to as ***he***, or (if known to be female) ***she***:

(2) a. The Smiths' dog looks friendly, but he can get vicious.
b. My cat, Cindy, is sometimes moody, especially when she is hungry.

This is a personal way of referring to animals that makes them appear as part of the human world. Otherwise, in more neutral style, ***it*** is used:

(3) a. That bird looks as if it is injured – look at the way its wing is hanging down.
b. When the leading racehorse fell at the third fence, it broke a leg.

Though slightly old-fashioned, female personification is still sometimes found in references to nations and ships. The effect tends to be a little grandiose:

(4) a. The *Titanic* sank after she had hit an iceberg.
b. Scotland's independence was guaranteed after she had defeated the English at Bannockburn.

The use of ***it*** would be more normal and neutral here.

Finally, ***they*** is often used in informal language (speech, the press) to refer back to ***singular*** nouns meaning 'people of either sex':

(5) a. When a hotel-guest first arrives, they are always welcomed with a glass of champagne.
b. The person who stole my bike will regret it when they realize that the brakes don't work.

This is an economical way of preserving gender neutrality ('either a man or a woman'). The only other method is to say ***he or she***, which sounds rather formal, and is avoided in ordinary language.

020/1.3 The personal pronoun one

This is a generalized third person singular, and translates the German word *man*:

(6) a. When one first arrives, the management always welcomes one with a glass of champagne.
b. One should not let one's dog run free in this wood.

As the examples show, ***one*** remains unchanged in subject and object functions; the genitive form is ***one's***. However, ***one*** is formal and not heard much in everyday language. The preferred replacement is ***you***:

(7) a. When you first arrive, the management always welcomes you with a glass of champagne.
b. You should not let your dog run free in this wood.

A further point is that ***one*** cannot be used in the sense of German *man* when it means ⚠ a particular person, or 'people in a particular place'. The solution is either to use the ***passive voice*** (see chapter 11), or to find another noun or pronoun that fits the context. Informally ***they*** is often used for 'people in authority':

(8) a. Sie klingelte, aber man hat sie nicht gehört.
She rang the bell but nobody heard her/the people in the house didn't hear her.
b. Am Flughafen sagte man uns, die Maschine sei verspätet.
At the airport we were told that the flight was delayed/they told us that the flight was delayed.

020/2 Possessives

020/2.1 Possessive determiners

Person/number	Personal pronoun	Possessive determiner
First person singular	*I*	*my*
Second person singular	*you*	*your*
Third person singular	*he, she, it*	*his, her, its*
First person plural	*we*	*our*
Second person plural	*you*	*your*
Third person plural	*they*	*their*

Traditionally, words like *my, your, our,* etc. are known as 'possessive pronouns': firstly, because they correspond to the personal pronouns, and secondly, because in the third person they stand for full nouns in the genitive.

Syntactically, however, possessives of this kind are ***determiners***. They premodify a noun in the same way as an article (see **022/3.2** below):

(9) a. I couldn't find ***my*** glasses.
b. Mrs. Saunders drove ***her*** car into a tree.

It is important to bear in mind that the choice of possessive depends on the ***possessing*** noun, and ***not*** on the belonging noun. That is, ***John's*** *mother* = ***his*** *mother*, and ***Jenny's*** *father* = ***her*** *father*. Possessives in English do not match the noun that they premodify.

Another point is the spelling of ***its***. An apostrophe (***'s***, creating an ***s***-genitive) might seem natural here, but it is actually spelt without one. This distinguishes it from the weak form of *it is* (*it's*).

020/2.2 Possessive determiners with parts of the body

Unlike many other languages (including German), English generally uses possessive determiners and genitives with parts of the body and items of clothing:
He scratched his ear (er kratzte sich am Ohr); she injured her leg (sie verletzte sich am Bein); she broke her arm (sie brach sich den Arm); he combed his hair (er kämmte sich); she cleared her

throat (sie räusperte sich); he couldn't move his fingers (er konnte die Finger nicht bewegen); she put her hand in her pocket (sie steckte eine Hand in die Tasche); he took off his coat (er zog den Mantel aus); Diana touched Sam's arm (Diana berührte Sams Arm); the nurse massaged my temples (die Krankenschwester massierte mich an den Schläfen).

020/2.3 The pronoun s-genitive and the pronoun possessive

These two possessive types were introduced in Chapter 2 (see **009/3**). When a noun premodified by an *s*-genitive is omitted, the *s*-genitive noun 'represents' it as a kind of pronoun:

(10) a. Joan's dog is a terrier, ***Freddie's*** is a spaniel. (= Freddie's dog)
Joans Hund ist ein Terrier, der von Freddie ist ein Spaniel.
b. Tom's house is on one side of the river and his ***girlfriend's*** is on the other. (= his girlfriend's house)
Toms Haus steht auf der einen Seite des Flusses und das von seiner Freundin auf der anderen.

We call this structure the ***pronoun s-genitive***. Its main purpose is to stress a ***possessive contrast*** when the head nouns (i.e. the ***belonging*** nouns) in two or more adjacent noun phrases are identical. A ***pronoun s-genitive*** can be repeated as long as the possessor's identity has to be made clear. As soon as this *is* clear, however, pronoun ***s***-genitives are usually replaced in further back-reference by ***pronoun possessives*** (*his, hers,* etc.):

(11) a. ***Joan's*** is already 10 years old, ***Freddie's*** is only 4. ***Hers*** is called Jake, and ***his*** is called Ted. (= her dog ..., his dog).
... ihrer heißt Jake, und seiner heißt Ted.
b. ***Tom's*** is an old Victorian property, but his ***girlfriend's*** is relatively modern. ***His*** needs to be renovated, but ***hers*** is still in good condition.
(= his house ..., her house).
... seines (das Seine) muss renoviert werden, aber ihres (das Ihre) ist noch in gutem Zustand.

Pronoun s-genitives are mainly confined to the third person singular. They are unusual in the plural, and there are no first or second person equivalents. In other persons back-reference relies completely on ***pronoun possessives*** (*mine, yours, ours, theirs*):

(12) a. Joan's dog is a terrier, ***Freddie's*** is a spaniel, and ***mine*** is an Alsatian.
(= my dog: ... meiner ist ein Schäferhund).
b. Tom's house is on one side of the river, his ***girlfriend's*** is on the other, and ***yours*** is next to ***hers***. (= your house/her house: ... deines steht neben ihrem).

A full list of the ***pronoun possessives*** is given in the summary below.
Finally, a reminder of the construction known as the ***double genitive***:

(13) Tim Walcott is a friend ***of mine***/a relative ***of Sylvia's***/a neighbour of ***yours***/an employee of ***the firm's***.
... ein Freund von mir/ein Verwandter von Sylvia/ein Nachbar von dir/ein Angestellter der Firma.

Here the use of ordinary nouns and pronouns, as in German, would be incorrect. Either the ***pronoun s-genitive*** or the ***pronoun possessive*** is compulsory after *of*. ⚠

020/3 Reflexive pronouns: self and others

When the subject and object of a verb refer to the same person or thing, the ***object*** takes the form of a ***reflexive pronoun***:

(14) a. ***Sarah*** made ***herself*** ill through overwork.
b. ***We*** surprised ***ourselves*** by reaching the mountain-top in three hours.

Reflexive pronouns, that is, are *'self'*-pronouns: *myself, yourself, himself, herself, ourselves*, etc. The general form, used mainly for naming reflexive verbs in the infinitive, is *oneself*. Plural forms end in ***-selves***: *ourselves, yourselves, themselves*.

The reflexive pronouns in (14) function as the ***direct object***. The subject does something to his or her own person. Notice the contrast in meaning between the reflexive pronoun and the ordinary personal pronoun:

(15) a. The attacker was fast and ***Donald*** hurt ***himself*** when he tackled him.
Der Stürmer lief schnell, und Donald verletzte sich, als er ihn angriff.
b. ***The attacker*** was fast and Donald hurt ***him*** when he tackled him.
Der Stürmer lief schnell, und Donald verletzte ihn, als er ihn angriff.

Reflexive pronouns can also be ***indirect objects*** or ***prepositional complements***:

(16) a. ***Susan and Mary*** have bought ***themselves*** a house.
(... haben sich ein Haus gekauft.)
b. ***I*** am angry ***with myself*** for failing the exam.
(Ich bin über mich selbst verärgert, dass ich die Prüfung nicht bestanden habe.)

020/4 Reflexive pronouns: further points of usage

020/4.1 Reflexive verbs

Some verbs need a reflexive pronoun grammatically. These are ***reflexive verbs***. Many reflexive verbs are not really transitive in meaning, and the reflexive pronoun is ***not*** a direct object ***semantically***: *to enjoy oneself* (*sich gut amüsieren*), *to amuse oneself* (*sich unterhalten, die Zeit mit etwas vertreiben*), *to behave oneself* (*brav sein*), *to pride oneself on* (*stolz sein auf*), *to kid oneself* (colloquial, *sich selbst etwas vormachen*), etc.

There are not many examples like this, however. In contrast to their partners in other languages, reflexive verbs are not used much in English. Many German reflexive constructions are expressed in English by ordinary intransitive verbs: *to happen* (*sich ereignen*), *to wash* (*sich waschen*), *to dress* (*sich anziehen*), *to improve* (*sich verbessern*), *to be ashamed* (*sich schämen*), *to recover/get better* (*sich erholen*), *to get lost* (*sich verirren*), *to be mistaken* (*sich irren*), *to fall in love* (*sich verlieben*), *to adapt* (*sich anpassen*), *to remember* (*sich erinnern*), *to sit/lie down* (*sich setzen/legen*), *to withdraw/retire* (*sich zurückziehen*), *to complain* (*sich beschweren*), *to concentrate* (*sich konzentrieren*).

Others are expressed by transitive verbs in fixed collocations with noun phrases: *to catch a cold* (*sich erkälten*), *to dial the wrong number* (*sich verwählen*), *to make a slip of the tongue* (*sich versprechen*), *to have difficulties* (*sich schwer tun*), etc.

Among the intransitive verbs listed above, one or two are ***occasionally*** used reflexively:

(17) a. You should wash yourself properly.
b. Sit yourself down and have a cup of tea!
c. We have not adapted ourselves very well to the new markets in Asia.

But this is done only to emphasize the action (and/or its necessity), or to stress a command.

020/4.2 The pronoun each other

⚠ As we have seen, English reflexive pronouns always refer back to the subject. But this is not always so in German, e.g.

(18) An Weihnachten geben wir uns alle (gegenseitig) Geschenke.

Reflexive pronouns cannot be used in this ***mutual*** sense (= *gegenseitig*) in English. The pronoun needed here is ***each other***:

(19) At Christmas we all give each other presents.

Note the contrast:

(20) a. Don't do that! You might hurt ***yourselves*** (= jeder *sich selbst*).
b. Don't do that! You might hurt ***each other*** (= jeder *den anderen*).

020/4.3 Pronouns after prepositions of place

Reflexive pronouns are ***not*** used after ***prepositions of place*** in ordinary adverbial usage. Here the ordinary personal pronoun is usual: *John noticed a police-car behind him* (not **behind himself*). *They looked around them* (not **around themselves*).
Similarly: *I had no strength in me; He felt cold air above him; She saw clouds below her.*
Exceptions, however, are the two idiomatic phrases *by oneself* (*allein*), and *to oneself* (*vor sich hin*):

(21) a. I was on holiday by myself. (Ich war allein/unbegleitet im Urlaub.)
b. He was laughing quietly to himself. (Er lachte still vor sich hin.)

020/4.4 Non-reflexive use

The *'self'*-pronouns are also used non-reflexively, to ***emphasize*** the subject of an action, usually when a different subject might be expected:

(22) a. Reginald built the house himself (= no-one built it for him).
b. She fetched the parcel herself (= she didn't send anyone else to get it).

The German equivalent here is *selbst* or *selber*.

020/5 Pronoun table (summary)

Personal (subject)	Personal (object)	Possessive determiner	Pronoun possessive	Reflexive pronoun
I	*me*	*my*	*mine*	*myself*
you	*you*	*your*	*yours*	*yourself*
he, she, it	*him, her, it*	*his, her, its*	*his, hers*	*himself, herself, itself*
we	*us*	*our*	*ours*	*ourselves*
you	*you*	*your*	*yours*	*yourselves*
they	*them*	*their*	*theirs*	*themselves*

020/6 Reflexives, possessives and personal pronouns: summary of important points and common difficulties

Reference to "things": German speakers sometimes forget that all singular inanimate objects ('things') must be referred to as ***it***. In German the choice of personal pronoun is determined by the grammatical gender of the noun it refers back to. As there is ***no*** grammatical gender in English, only persons (and some animals) can be ***he*** or ***she***. Everything else requires ***it***: ⚠

(23) a. I have lost my fountain-pen. ***It*** was a present from my parents.
(*not* *He was a present …)
Ich habe meinen Füller verloren. Er war ein Geschenk …
b. Jane left her bag on the train. ***It*** was handed in to the Lost Property Office.
(*not* *She was handed in …)
Jane ließ ihre Handtasche im Zug liegen. Sie wurde zum Fundbüro gebracht.

- The personal pronoun ***one*** is not used very often, except in formal English. The more usual equivalents of German *man* are ***you***, ***they*** (informal, for authorities), or the passive voice.

- Note that the possessive determiner ***its*** is spelt without an apostrophe. The form it's means *it is*.
- Possessive determiners are used with parts of the body and other things belonging to the individual person, such as items of clothing: *The children always put their pyjamas on, before they brush their teeth.* (*Die Kinder ziehen immer den Schlafanzug an, bevor sie die Zähne putzen*).
- Back reference after s-genitives leads to simple omission of the head noun, creating a pronoun s-genitive: *Bob's car is black, but Sharon's is red.*
  If the head noun is omitted after a possessive determiner, the possessive determiner is replaced by a ***pronoun possessive***:
  Her car is red, my car is blue → *Hers is red, mine is blue.*
- ⚠ Double genitives are necessary with *of* (= *one of*): *a friend of Sarah's* (= *one of Sarah's friends*), *that book of mine* (= *one of my books*).
  The following forms are incorrect: **a friend of Sarah*, **a book of me*.
- Reflexive pronouns ('self-pronouns') in plural persons require the ending *-selves*: ***ourselves, yourselves, themselves***.
  With third person reflexive pronouns, the personal element is in the *object* form, i.e. ***him****self*, ***her****self*, ***them****selves* (the *it* in *itself* remains unchanged, of course).
  In the other person forms, the personal element is a *possessive determiner*: ***my****self*, ***your****self*, ***our****selves*.

⚠ In German, first and second person reflexive forms are identical with the ordinary object pronouns (*mich, dich, uns*). German speakers should make sure that they do not transfer these directly into English, and produce sentences like **I have hurt me* (instead of ***myself***), or **We will enjoy us* (instead of ***ourselves***).
A final point to remember is that *uns/sich gegenseitig* = ***each other***: *We visited each other when we were on holiday* (*Im Urlaub haben wir uns gegenseitig besucht*).

020/7 Other pronoun types

Several types of pronoun are connected with special syntactic structures (such as questions or relative clauses). They are introduced only briefly here, and treated more fully later in connection with their particular structures (see, for instance, chapter 14 for relative pronouns). Others are not primarily pronouns, but are really determiners (demonstratives, quantifiers and numerals) which can also have a pronoun function. These, too, are only touched upon here, and are described more fully in the determiner section.

020/7.1 Interrogative pronouns

These are words like ***who***, ***what***, ***which***, etc., which are used in questions. They refer to the identity of something unknown in the sentence which the questioner wants to find out. ***Who*** is always a pronoun (*Who gave you that?*), ***what*** mainly a pronoun but also a determiner (*What people did you see at the party?*), and ***which*** a determiner that sometimes functions as a pronoun (as, for example, in *Which of these paintings do you prefer?*). One important point of usage is the distinction between reference to a person (***who?***), and reference to a thing (***what?***). Another point is whether the question word implies choosing from a restricted selection of items (***which?***), or is quite open (***who/what?***). For more details, see under *The Interrogative* (chapter 8).

020/7.2 Relative pronouns

Relative pronouns introduce relative clauses. As we have just seen, two of them, ***who*** and ***which***, are used also as interrogative pronouns. Choice of relative pronoun also depends on whether a person (***who***), or a thing (***which***), is being referred to. A third relative pronoun is ***that***, which can be used for both people and things. For more details, see under *Relative Clauses* (chapter 14).

020/7.3 Demonstrative pronouns

The demonstratives are ***this*** (singular)/***these*** (plural), and ***that*** (singular)/***those*** (plural). As the name suggests, they have a pointing function and are ***deictic*** (speaker-related, see also **020/1** above). ***This/these*** refer to entities which the speaker feels close to, ***that/those*** to entities which the speaker feels further away from. Although traditionally regarded as pronouns, they usually function syntactically as determiners, i.e. before a noun (*this book, those people*). But they also have a pronoun function (*What's that? Who's this?*). Further information is given below, in the section on *Determiners* (see **022/6** below).

020/7.4 Quantifier and numeral pronouns

Quantifiers and ***numerals*** are used mainly as determiners: *both men, all students, some tea, few people, two girls, fifty-seven Russians*, etc. But they also feature as pronouns, especially in combination with ***of***: *All/some/few/many of the students; Twenty workers were invited to the meeting, but only eight (of them) came.*

020/7.5 Indefinite pronouns

These refer to objects and people which are not identified further: *something* (*an unidentified object*), *someone* (*an unidentified person*), *nobody* (*no person*), *everyone* (*all persons*), etc. They are 'quantifier compounds', and closely connected with quantifier meaning, see under *Quantifiers* below (**3.3**).

020/7.6 one as a prop-pronoun

One is used to replace just the ***head noun*** in a noun phrase. This must be a ***count*** noun, in the singular or plural (= ***ones***):

(24) a. "Which chemist's shop do you mean exactly?" "The one on the corner of King Street."
„Welche Apotheke meinst du denn genau?" „Die(jenige) an der Ecke der King Street."

b. I don't like the black ***shoes***, but the white ***ones*** are very nice.
Ich mag die schwarzen Schuhe nicht, aber die weißen sind sehr schön.

The ***prop-pronoun*** is used to avoid repeating a head noun already mentioned. It commonly occurs in question and answer exchanges, as in (24)a., and may equally appear in a question: *"Could you go to the chemist's in the town for me, please, Brian?" "Yes, of course. Which one shall I go to?"*

Typical is the presence of pre- and postmodifying elements to specify the alternatives, as with the prepositional phrase *on the corner* in (24)a., or the adjectives in (24)b. Instead of ***the one***, the demonstrative pronoun ***that*** is sometimes used (see **022/6.4, 6.5** below).

3.2 Determiners

021 Main grammatical and semantic features
022 Determiner types

021 Main grammatical and semantic features

Determiners are 'article-words' (definite, indefinite and zero articles, possessives, demonstratives, quantifiers, numerals and certain interrogatives). They precede nouns, though not pronouns (except prop-pronouns). The ***first*** element in a noun phrase is typically a determiner: ***a*** *large dog*, ***the*** *car*, ***my*** *brothers*, ***that*** *nice woman*, ***four*** *spoons*, ***which*** *man?*, etc.

The general semantic function of a determiner is to identify the head noun, or, with interrogatives, to ask about its identity.

022 Determiner types

022/1 The indefinite article
022/2 The definite article
022/3 The zero article
022/4 The definite article with names
022/5 The definite article in other 'borderline' uses
022/6 Demonstrative determiners

022/1 The indefinite article

022/1.1 Forms

The indefinite article has two forms, depending on the kind of sound following:
a before ***consonants***: *a dog, a cat, a bad egg.*
an before ***vowels***: *an intelligent dog, an egg, an orange bicycle.*

One point to note is that the particular sound affecting the choice is the one ***immediately following*** the article (even if this sound belongs to an adjective or some other class of word which is not a noun).

Another important point is that the ***sound***, and not necessarily its spelling, is the decisive feature. Some words, for example, have a vowel as their first letter, but a consonant as their first sound, e.g. *union* [ju:njən], *one* [wʌn]. In these cases the indefinite article is ***a***: *a union, a one-mile walk.*

On the other hand, there are words with an initial 'silent' *h* in the spelling that begin with a vowel when they are pronounced, e.g. *hour* [aʊə].

Note also that when letters or sounds are pronounced individually (i.e. in the alphabet or as initials), some begin with a vowel even though they refer to consonants, e.g. *f* [ef], *h* [eɪtʃ], *l* [el], etc. All these are cases for ***an***: *an hour, an HGV* (= *heavy goods vehicle*), *an L-plate* (= *sign meaning 'learner-driver'*), etc.

022/1.2 General usage, and the concept of indefinite reference

The ***indefinite article*** is used with ***singular count*** nouns only. It basically means the same as the numeral *one*, but in a more general sense. *One* is used for contrast to other numbers (*two, three, …*), or to single out a particular member of a group (e.g. *One boy was carrying a gun, the other a knife*). The ***indefinite article*** is more neutral and is used for unstressed singular reference, where there is no emphasis on number contrast. However, all numeral determiners, as well as the quantifiers *some* and *any*, and the ***zero article*** are similar to the ***indefinite article*** in making what is called ***indefinite reference***. What is meant by this?
Indefinite reference is reference to things or persons by ***category*** or ***type***.

(25) a. A woman on a bicycle was stopped by a policeman.
(= one representative of the category *woman*, one representative of the category *bicycle*, one representative of the category *policeman*).
b. If you see anything suspicious, tell a policeman.
(= anybody representing the category *policeman*).
c. I am a policeman (= I belong to this category).

The indefinite article, then, names categories of thing or person. It does this in three slightly different ways. (25)a. refers to a ***particular*** object and two ***particular*** people. This is an example of ***specific*** use. ***Specific*** use is typical when entities have not yet been identified individually. This is normally the case when they are introduced for the first time. After this introduction, all further reference to the same entities must be ***definite***, e.g. using definite articles and personal pronouns:

(26) A woman on ***a*** bicycle was stopped by ***a*** policeman. ***He*** told ***her*** to get off ***the*** bicycle, but ***she*** fled.

(25)b. shows the ***unspecific*** use, and means 'any representative of the category' (here of the category *policeman*). ***Back-reference*** to an ***unspecific*** use requires the pronoun ***one*** (a variant of the prop-pronoun is discussed above in **020/7**):

(27) If you see anything suspicious, tell ***a policeman***, if you can find ***one***.
After you have found ***one*** (= a policeman) tell ***him*** (= the policeman) exactly what you have seen.

Here the reference becomes specific and definite when *policeman* occurs for the third time, as the meaning is now 'the particular policeman just mentioned'.

Without a context, it may not be clear whether the indefinite article has the specific or the unspecific sense, e.g. *We're going to buy a second-hand car*:

(28) a. We're going to buy ***a second-hand car***. We'll certainly get ***one*** at MacGregor's garage. (***unspecific***)
b. We're going to buy ***a second-hand car***. We're going to collect ***it*** tomorrow from MacGregor's garage. (***specific***)

In (28)b. the car has already been chosen and reserved, i.e. it is a particular vehicle that is meant. Further back-reference is therefore definite and requires the pronoun ***it*** or the full noun with the ***definite*** article (***the*** *second-hand car*).
(28)a., on the other hand, means 'any car of that type'. Back-reference here requires the pronoun ***one*** or, alternatively, repetition of the full noun with the ***indefinite*** article (***a*** *second-hand car*).

Unspecific reference can sometimes be restricted to a particular group:

(29) a. Would you like a chocolate? (= any/one of these here in the box).
b. I'm going to buy a postcard (= one of these here on the rack).
c. Have a drink (= there are several bottles on the sideboard).

As is shown in the brackets, any reference to the group itself must be ***definite*** (... *these* ...), as the group is identified by the situation (more on this point below).

Finally, (25)c. is an example of ***generic*** use. Here the noun-phrase *a policeman* places the ***category itself*** in the forefront, rather than a single representative of it. The indefinite article is required with all categorizations of this type. The most common refer to people representing occupations, hobbies, nationality and origin, but also to those who hold beliefs, practice faiths or ideologies, or suffer from illnesses. Here German, by contrast, uses the ***zero article***:

(30) a. John is a printer, but his brother is a teacher.
John ist Drucker, aber sein Bruder ist Lehrer.
b. Sheila is an American, Roy is a Dutchman and Britta a Norwegian.
Sheila ist Amerikanerin, Roy ist Holländer, und Britta ist Norwegerin.
c. Laski was a Communist and a Catholic.
Laski war Kommunist und Katholik.
d. Her son was an epileptic.
Ihr Sohn war Epileptiker.

022/1.3 Use with numbers and quantifiers

The indefinite article is used

- as an unstressed alternative to *one* with numbers in hundreds and thousands: *a hundred, a thousand, a million;*
- with number quantifiers: *a couple* (= *two*), *a dozen* (= *twelve*), *a score* (old-fashioned for *twenty*); *dozen* and *score* also occur in stressed form with *one;*
- with indefinite quantifiers and partitive expressions: *a few, a lot, a bit, a little,* etc.; *a slice/piece/glass/cup/jug of,* etc.
- with measures: *a pint, a pound, a ton, a yard,* etc.
  Here it also functions as an unstressed alternative to *one*:

(31) I've bought a pound of tomatoes and a pint of milk.

022/2 The definite article

022/2.1 Forms

The definite article also has two pronunciation forms, depending on whether a consonant or a vowel follows. The spelling is the same in both cases, however:

[ðə] before ***consonants***:	*the dog* [ðə dɒg], *the cat* [ðə kæt], *the bad egg* [ðə bæd eg];
[ði:] before ***vowels***:	*the ugly dog* [ði: ʌgli: dɒg], *the egg* [ði: eg],
	the orange bicycle [ði: ɒrɪndʒ baɪsɪkl].

022/2.2 General usage, and the concept of definite reference

The ***definite article*** is used with nouns of all types. It always has the same grammatical form, i.e. there is no difference in form between singular and plural.

It is used for ***definite reference***. This is reference to things, people or animals with an ***established individual identity***. That is, when a speaker uses the ***definite article***, he assumes that the listener knows which particular object or person he is talking about. He can assume this for the following reasons:

a) The object, person or animal has previously been introduced in the text or dialogue, and now there is ***back-reference*** to it:

(32) ***A stray dog*** was trying to cross ***a busy road*** alone. ***A man*** went up to ***the dog*** and tried to help it, but ***the dog*** got scared and suddenly shot into ***the road*** on its own without warning. ***The man*** could do nothing.

Notice that new references are ***indefinite*** (*a stray dog, a busy road, a man*). But when the same entity is mentioned again, it becomes ***definite*** (i.e. its identity has already been established). It must therefore take the ***definite article*** (*the dog, the road, the man*). Similar points were made above in our discussion of examples (25)–(28).

b) The individual identity of the thing or person is established by a ***post-modifier*** in the noun phrase itself:

(33) *The* woman *who cleans our office on Wednesdays* lives in Willow Road.

Together with the postmodification, the definite article here means 'that particular woman'.

c) What the speaker means is indicated in the situation itself:

(34) a. I like the carpet! (= this carpet, in this room, where we are standing).
b. Could you pass the sugar, please? (= the sugar over there, on this table).

As in (33), the definite article here also means *this* or *that*, but has a stronger, more physical 'pointing' character of a ***deictic*** nature.

d) The entity is a ***known part*** of the social, cultural, local or physical context:

(35) a. The train was late this morning (= the train that I go to work on).
b. Could you go quickly to the butcher's for me, Julie? (= the butcher's where we always buy our meat).
c. The children are in the garden (= our children ..., our garden/the garden of this house).

This is reinforced in cases where the object is unique: *the Queen, the Pope, the sea, the sky, the earth, the sun,* etc.

Assumed contextual knowledge can be of a more ***general*** kind: for example, when there are certain habitual associations between elements:

(36) a. We passed a church where a wedding had taken place, but there was no sign of ***the*** bride (= the bride belonging to that wedding: where there is a wedding, there is a bride).
b. Harry bought this lamp yesterday at a store in town, but ***the*** switch doesn't work (= the switch on that lamp: lamps have switches).
c. There was an old bike leaning against our garden fence. ***The*** tyres were flat (= the tyres on that bike: bikes have tyres).

022/3 The zero article

This simply means 'no article at all'. However, this is not just a question of 'being able to leave the article out', or of the article being somehow 'unnecessary'. The ***zero article*** is a rule-governed alternative to the other articles, and has its own profile of usage, i.e. it is just as consciously chosen as any other determiner.

022/3.1 Indefinite reference with plurals and non-count nouns

One basic use of the ***zero article*** is as a substitute for the indefinite article when the indefinite article cannot be used, i.e. with ***plurals*** and ***singular non-count nouns***:

(37) a. The shop was full and customers were queuing outside.
b. Cars were parked on both sides of the street.
c. There is food on the table and beer in the fridge.

Common non-count nouns in this connection are those referring to substances and materials:

(38) a. The table was made of wood.
b. He gave her a ring of solid gold.
c. There was oil on the road where the accident had happened.
d. You have red paint on your hands and dirt on your trousers!

Equally common are ***abstract*** non-count nouns, especially those describing feelings, behaviour, illnesses, and human or social conditions:

(39) a. Charles' success caused jealousy and envy among his neighbours.
b. The atmosphere in the house was marked by excitement and joy, but also nervousness, on the day before the wedding.
c. Julia caught pneumonia.
d. Poverty and ignorance often affected Maria's life negatively in her youth.
e. Butterworth has always shown generosity and kindness towards others.
f. Communication was difficult at the meeting, and discussion virtually impossible, as everyone was full of aggression and anger.

022/3.2 Generalizations

This is a particular form of ***generic*** reference (see **022/1.2** above). When we generalize, we typically use plurals and non-count nouns with the ***zero article***:

(40) a. Milk comes from cows.
b. British universities are comparatively small.
c. I like wine, but I prefer beer.
d. Dogs eat meat.
e. Buses don't run here on Sundays.
f. Visitors must report first to the security lodge.

These are references to categories of entity, e.g. *buses* = 'this type of vehicle', *wine* = 'this type of drink'.

It is similar with abstract nouns naming beliefs, principles, and all specialized fields of human activity, such as occupations and professions, sports, pastimes, sectors of the economy, arts and sciences. All are basically references to types and categories:

(41) a. The main religions on the island are Buddhism and Christianity.
b. Communism is still the ruling ideology in China.
c. Impressionism revolutionized European painting.
d. In nineteenth century Europe, great advances took place in agriculture, industry and medicine.
e. At our school we play hockey, rugby, and cricket.
f. Crime has increased over the last few years.

The abstract nouns in (39) refer to specific instances. However, they and others like them are particularly prone to generalizations:

(42) a. Communication does not consist only of language.
b. Birth, marriage and death were the most significant events in the life of an 18th century peasant.
c. Love and hate are opposite sides of the same coin.
d. Generosity is possibly the greatest human virtue.
e. Poverty and ignorance play a central role in the misery of third world populations.

022/3.3 Generalizations: German and English in contrast

⚠ In addition to the zero article, German, unlike English, also uses the definite article for generalizations. This usually depends on style and sentence structure, but also on the kind of thing referred to. General statements about substances and materials, for instance, often attract the German definite article, especially in more formal language and when a certain emphasis is required. In English, on the other hand, the zero article is always compulsory!

(43) a. Das englische Brot schmeckt nach gar nichts!
English bread doesn't taste of anything!
b. Ein Grundelement des Universums ist der Wasserstoff.
A basic element of the universe is hydrogen.
c. Die Mosel-Weine sind vorwiegend lieblich.
Mosel wines are mainly sweet.
d. Der Strom wird in den kommenden Jahren teurer.
Electricity will get more expensive in the next few years.
e. Das Benzin wurde knapp.
Petrol became scarce.

German shows a particular preference for the definite article with abstract nouns, especially when, as in (41) and (42), they refer to social phenomena, concepts and ideas, or fields of economic and professional activity:

(44) a. Die Kommunikation ist von zentraler Bedeutung in der Ehe.
Communication is of great importance in marriage.
b. In der Medizin sind damals große Fortschritte erzielt worden.
Great advances were made in medicine at that time.
c. Die Gewalt ist eines der schlimmsten Probleme in modernen Großstädten.
Violence is one of the worst problems in modern cities.
d. Seine erste Liebe galt immer der Musik.
His first love was always music.

Here are further common English examples of generalized abstract nouns which appear in German, frequently or exclusively, with the definite article: *society* (*die Gesellschaft*), *nature* (*die Natur*), *fashion* (*die Mode*), *success/failure* (*der Erfolg/Misserfolg/das Versagen*), *labour* (*die Arbeit/Arbeiterschaft*), *capital* (*das Kapital*), *mankind* (*die Menschheit*).

References to various human qualities and characteristics: *intelligence* (*die Intelligenz*), *stupidity* (*die Dummheit*), *human nature* (*die menschliche Natur*), *common sense* (*der gesunde Menschenverstand*), *academic aptitude* (*die Eignung fürs Studium*), *physical strength* (*die körperliche Kraft*), *reading ability* (*die Lesefähigkeit*), *managerial skill* (*die Führungsfähigkeit*), *public opinion* (*die öffentliche Meinung*), etc.

General periods of human life also belong here: *childhood, adolescence, adulthood* (*die Kindheit, die Jugend, das Erwachsenenalter*), *middle-age, old age* (*das mittlere Alter, das Alter*), etc.

022/3.4 Institutions

Certain places, buildings, organizations, and various elements of activity and procedure connected with them, are sometimes regarded as ***general institutions*** rather than as individual things. The nouns referring to them, even those which are usually concrete and count, are then treated as ***abstract*** and ***non-count***, e.g. *work, home, school, college, university, parliament, bed, church, hospital, prison*. In this case they appear with the ***zero article***, often combined with prepositions. German, again, mainly uses the definite article here:

(45) a. Home is where the heart is.
Zu Hause ist man dort, wo man sich am wohlsten fühlt.
b. Bill is at college. My younger son still goes to school.
Bill ist auf dem College. Mein jüngerer Sohn geht noch zur Schule.
c. Maureen is in hospital with a broken leg.
Maureen liegt mit einem gebrochenen Bein im Krankenhaus.
d. Church was very boring this morning. I wish I had stayed in bed.
Es war heute Morgen sehr langweilig in der Kirche. Ich wünschte, ich wäre im Bett geblieben.

Other examples of 'institutionalized' terms refer to

- meals as occasions:
  breakfast, lunch, tea, dinner, supper, dessert;
- departments of firms, hospitals, and other organizations, e.g.
  surgery (*die Chirurgie*), *casualty* (*die Unfallstation*), *outpatients* (*die Ambulanz*) (hospitals); *sales* (*die Verkaufsabteilung*), *accounts* (*die Buchhaltung/Revision*), *design* (*die Designabteilung*), *security* (*die Sicherheitsabteilung*), *administration* (*die Verwaltung*) (firms, public organizations, etc.);
- education phenomena, e.g. not only teaching subjects, but also school procedures, college and university institutions: *assembly* (= *Schulandacht*), *break* (*Pause*), *homework, parents' evening, open-day* (*Tag der offenen Tür*), *term* (*Trimester*), *hall* (*Wohnheim*), *campus, refectory* (*die Mensa*); *GCSEs* (*General Certificate of Secondary Education* examinations, taken at 16 in Britain), *A-Levels* (*Advanced Level* examinations, taken at 18 in Britain, the equivalent of Abitur and Matura), *intermediates* (university – *Zwischenprüfung*), *finals* (university – *Abschlussprüfung*).
- procedures/activities in other occupational and hobby fields: *choir-practice, sport, rehearsal, surgery, registration, holiday,* etc.

(46) a. Mrs Elms had gone to lunch.
Frau Elms war zum Mittagessen gegangen.
b. Why don't you come to us for dinner on Friday evening?
Warum kommt ihr nicht am Freitagabend zum Abendessen zu uns?
c. At break tomorrow Sally and I have to prepare for the test in maths.
In der Pause morgen müssen Sally und ich uns auf den Test in Mathe vorbereiten.
d. Finals start in May. Term ends officially on 28th June. Then I'm going on holiday!
Die Abschlussprüfungen fangen im Mai an. Das Trimester endet offiziell am 28. Juni. Dann gehe ich in Urlaub.
e. Barry was at choir-practice yesterday, but did not come to rehearsal this evening.
Barry war gestern bei der Chorprobe, kam aber heute Abend nicht zur Probe.
f. Do you know where registration is?
Weißt du, wo die Kursanmeldung stattfindet?
g. Doris has to have surgery done on her knee.
Doris muss sich einem Eingriff am Knie unterziehen.

Several ***zero article*** expressions occur only or mainly with prepositions:
on site (*auf dem* (*Werk-, Bau-, Konzern-*)*Gelände*), *in/to court* (*vor/zum Gericht*), *at/to court* (*am/an den Hof*), *at/to camp* (*im/ins Zeltlager*), *in/to town* (*in der/die Stadt*), *on stage* (*auf der Bühne*).

022/3.5 The 'preposition + zero' pattern

All prepositional examples discussed above are basically part of a whole pattern of ***zero article*** collocations with prepositions: *in business* (*im Geschäft/im Geschäftsleben tätig*), *out of* *hand* (*außer Kontrolle*), *out of order* (*außer Betrieb*), *in time* (*rechtzeitig*), *on time* (*pünktlich*), *in power* (*an der Macht*), *in office* (*im Amt*), *in detail* (*im Detail*), *in theory* (*theoretisch*), *in practice* (*in der Praxis*), *under cover* (*verdeckt, geschützt*), *on demand* (*auf Verlangen*), etc. (See also chapter 6 on prepositions).

Note, again, the German tendency towards the definite article. There are some instances of this in English too, but the ***zero***-pattern is much more general. It is particularly common in expressions referring to: ⚠

- methods of transport and communication: *by bicycle, by boat, by bus, by car, on foot, on horseback, by plane, by ship, by train, by air, by rail, by road, by sea, by mail, by post, by telephone.*
  (N.B. German definite article!: *auf/mit dem Fahrrad, mit dem Auto/Flugzeug/Schiff, mit der Post, am Telefon,* etc.)
- times: *at night, at 11.30 am, at Christmas, by day, at dusk* (see below for details on time-reference.)
- physical location/condition: *at sea* (*auf See*), *on land* (*an Land*), *in space* (*im All*), *in orbit* (*auf einer Umlaufbahn*), *on course* (*auf Kurs*), *off track* (*vom Ziel abgekommen*), *in motion* (*in Bewegung*), *at rest* (*bewegungslos*), *on water, at anchor* (*vor Anker*), *in dock* (*im Dock, in der Reparatur*), etc.
- involvement in states and processes: *at war* (*im Kriegszustand*), *in battle* (*im Kampf*), *in action* (*tätig, in Bewegung*), *at play* (*im Spiel, spielend*), *in progress* (*im Gange*), *under observation* (*unter Beobachtung*), *under construction* (*im Bau*), *in print* (*im Druck erschienen*), *in stock* (*vorrätig*), *near completion* (*vor der baldigen Fertigstellung*), *on offer* (*im Angebot*), etc.
- personal condition/situation: *in form, off colour* (*kränklich*), *on edge* (*angespannt*), *to be in pain* (*Schmerzen haben*), *under strain* (*unter Druck, stark beansprucht*), *in difficulty* (*in Schwierigkeiten*), *out of work* (*arbeitslos*), *to be in employment* (*Arbeit haben*), etc.

022/3.6 Times

The majority of time references take the ***zero article***, e.g.

- all those with ***proper nouns***, i.e. the names of months, weekdays, religious festivals and public holidays. This rule applies regardless of whether prepositions are present or not, e.g. *January, Thursday, on Sunday evening, Christmas, after Easter, Whitsun.* (For time references with *at*, see further below):

(47) a. April is an unreliable month.
b. The best time to meet would be 8 o'clock.
c. We are having a party on Saturday night.

Exception: when a particular weekday, month or festival is picked out as part of a larger time period already mentioned (or understood in context):

(48) a. We spent the weekend before last at the coast. On the Saturday we went on a boat trip. We spent the Sunday hiking along the cliffs.
b. The Christmas of 1947 was one of the coldest in the century.

- most ***deictic*** expressions: *yesterday, today, tomorrow,* and those with *last* and *next*: *next week, last month,* etc. Note also the phrases *yesterday morning/afternoon/* (*gestern Vormittag/Nachmittag,* usw.) and *tomorrow morning* (*afternoon/evening*). The parts of *today,* however, are expressed by the determiner *this*: *this morning, this afternoon* (*heute Vormittag, heute Nachmittag*).
- reference to clock-times and other point-times: *ten o'clock, 3.30 pm, noon, midday, midnight,* etc.; and also to years by number, e.g. *1812, in 1928, since 2000*:

(49) a. I cannot meet you before noon.
b. Midnight is the classical time for ghosts.
c. Ten o'clock is rather a late time to eat.
d. We moved here in 1983.

- all time expressions with the prepositions ***at*** or ***by*** (in the sense of German *bei*). In addition to the festivals, clock- and point-times already mentioned (*at Christmas, at 4pm, at noon/midnight,* etc.), these include phrases relating to natural events in the 'cosmic' routine: *at/by night* (*nachts/bei Nacht*), *by day* (*tagsüber*), *at dawn* (*in der Morgendämmerung*), *at daybreak* (*bei Tagesanbruch*), *at sunrise/sunset* (*bei Sonnenaufgang/-untergang*), *at dusk* (*in der Abenddämmerung*), *at nightfall* (*bei Einbruch der Dunkelheit*), *at high-/low-tide* (*bei Flut/Ebbe*), *at full-moon,* etc.
  Exceptions are *at the weekend* (the noun *weekend* always takes the ***definite article***), and ordinary nouns referring to parts of time-spans, e.g. *at the beginning/the turn/the end of the century,* etc.
- The 'cosmic' event nouns just mentioned, like others combining with *at* and *by,* also take the ***zero article*** without prepositions:

(50) a. Sunrise would be at about 5 am.
b. Dusk was descending over the hills in the east.
c. Nightfall comes suddenly in the southern Mediterranean.

However, some of these (*dawn, dusk, sunset, sunrise*) can appear with the ***definite article.*** This is particularly favoured when it is the specific occasion or the individual process that is stressed, rather than simply the general time of day:

(51) a. The dawn was magnificent (= that particular one).
b. We went down to the beach to watch the sunset (= the process happening on that specific occasion).

- With parts of the day (*morning, afternoon, evening, night*), and seasons of the year, the definite article can always be used, but the ***zero article*** is restricted. It refers mainly to the time as a ***general phenomenon,*** i.e. to the typical features and conditions associated with it:

(52) a. We decided to wait till (the) morning (when it would be light and we could see what we were doing).
b. (The) Summer was late coming that year (= the warm weather).
c. The settlers had difficulty surviving (the) winter (= winter conditions).

The definite article is therefore more frequent here. And it is always required with parts of the day following the prepositions *in* and *during* (though not with seasons): *in the morning, during the afternoon, in the evening* (but *in winter/in the winter, in summer/in the summer*).

After the quantifier *all*, either the ***zero*** or the ***definite article*** is possible, even with parts of the day: *all (the) morning, all (the) afternoon, all (the) winter, all (the) summer*, etc.

022/3.7 Names

We have already seen that ***proper nouns*** referring to times (*Sunday, Christmas*, etc.) take the ***zero article***. In fact this applies to most other names too, whether personal, geographical, institutional, or of any other kind:

- Christian names – *Sandra, Ronald, Mike, Sheila*
- surnames – *Smith, Robinson, Jones, Wilson*
- names of countries, continents, states, towns and other regional or local areas – *Germany, Venezuela, Israel, Africa, California, East Anglia, Lancashire*
- names of town localities such as roads, squares, parks, etc. – *Lakedale Road, Tooley Street, Shaftesbury Avenue, Oxford Circus, Bedford Square, Riverside Drive, Swan Hill, Homefield Rise, Addison Terrace, Clapham Common, Richmond Park.*
- names of most topographical features such as mountains, hills, lakes (when these are singular), woods, forests, etc.: *Silbury Hill, Cardigan Bay, Sherwood Forest, Chislehurst Wood, Bewl Water.*
  Note that the titles *Mount* (for *mountain*) and *Lake* nearly always precede the name: *Mount Everest, Lake Windermere.*
- with most personal titles and all forms of address: *Lord Chalfont, Lady Bracknell, Baron(-ess) Wilde, Count(-ess) Dracula, Sir Duncan Avery, President Kennedy, Dr. Crippen, Mr. Greythorpe, Auntie Jane*, etc.
- with the names of most buildings, institutions, sports and business organisations, and market products: *Windsor Castle, Canterbury Cathedral, London University, Carnegie Hall, Moss Brothers, Glasgow Rangers*, etc.

There are a number of exceptions to these general principles, however, as the section following shows.

022/4 The definite article with names

Quite a few names take the ***definite article***. Most are combinations of proper noun + common noun (or occasionally the reverse), many with geographical meaning. Unlike those with the zero article, the common noun part here is not regarded as an integrated part of the name. Instead, it refers, as in its usual sense, to a possible range of entities.

The proper noun, functioning as an adjective, picks one of these phenomena out, i.e. identifies it uniquely, and distinguishes it from other members of the same group. For example, *the Atlantic Ocean* and *the Pacific Ocean* are expressed as 2 different members of the class 'ocean'. Referring to them together, we can call them *the Atlantic and Pacific Oceans*. But with *Oxford Street* and *Regent Street* (zero article!) the second nouns are inseparable parts of the name, and we cannot put them in the plural as **Oxford and Regent Streets*.

Definite article use with names therefore has a certain logic underlying it. Nevertheless, the kinds of phenomena it is applied to (e.g. oceans, seas, deserts, etc.) must be learnt individually. They are as follows:

022/4.1 Topographical phenomena

- ***river*** names: *the River Clyde, the River Thames, the River Seine, the River Rhine, the River Ganges.*
  With rivers on the American and Australian continents, and occasionally also elsewhere in the world, the term *River* typically follows the name: *the Ohio River, the Colorado River, the Missouri River, the Murray River, the Yangtze River.*
  With both variants, the title *River* is often omitted, and the name just used with the article: *the Thames, the Seine, the Missouri, the Yangtze.*
- plural names referring to collective landscape features, typically ***hills*** and ***mountains***: *the Rocky Mountains, the Cairngorm Mountains, the Chiltern Hills, the Berkshire Downs, the Southern Uplands, the Scottish Highlands.*
  As with *River*, the terms *Mountains* and *Hills* are often omitted. The plural ending is then attached to the naming noun: *the Rockies, the Cairngorms, the Chilterns.* In some cases this is the most usual form, or sometimes the only one: *the Cotswolds, the Pennines, the Alps, the Appalachians, the Himalayas.*
  Other examples of landscape plurals are: *the Yorkshire Moors, the Great Lakes, the Norfolk Broads, the Fens, the Great Plains, the Badlands, the Needles, the Seven Sisters;* and also groups of islands: *the Channel Islands, the Shetland Islands, the Canary Islands,* etc.
- singular names of landscape features, notably ***seas*** and ***deserts***: *the Atlantic Ocean, the Mediterranean Sea, the English Channel, the Sahara Desert.* Here also the second noun is frequently omitted: *the Sahara, the Mediterranean, the Caribbean, the Atlantic.* This only happens, though, when the proper noun is unique in that combination. For instance, *The Indian Ocean, the Dead Sea* or *the English Channel* cannot be shortened to **the Indian, *the Dead, *the English.*
  There are many other landscape singulars: *the Gower Peninsula, the Giant's Causeway, the Devil's Dyke, the Snake Pass,* etc.
  With a lot of expressions like this, the common noun element denotes a part of the larger phenomenon named, or some feature belonging to it: *the Thames Basin, the Severn Valley, the Pennine Way,* and so on.

022/4.2 Other geographical names

- *regions:*

  'Part of the whole' is also the meaning behind many terms signifying areas, regions and districts. These particularly attract the definite article when 'area-partitive' expressions (*district, quarter, side, end,* etc.) are part of the name: *the West End* (of London), *the Lower East Side* (of New York), *the West Country* (of England), *the Latin Quarter* (of Paris), *the Peak District, the Lake District* (of England), etc. The ***of***-genitive features strongly here, not just in the 'area-partitive' sense, but also with ***constitutive*** (i.e. ***appositive***) meaning (see chapter 2.2. **020/2** and **3**):

  the Vale of Evesham, the Weald of Kent, the Firth of Forth, the Bay of Biscay, the Mull of Kintyre, the Strait of Gibraltar, the Sea of Galilee, the Gulf of Suez (area-partitive/locational); *the Borough of Manhattan, the Forest of Dean, the District of Columbia* (appositive).

  A particularly common appositive is the island title *the Isle of,* as in *the Isle of Man, the Isle of Wight, the Isle of Anglesey,* etc.

- ***countries and states:***

  The definite article occurs with all ***plural names*** (mostly groups of islands, territorial unions, etc.), all combinations with *of,* plus any in which the name is followed by a term signifying the form of government or state (usually *Kingdom, Republic,* etc.): *the Bahamas, the West Indies, the Philippines, the Seychelles, the Netherlands, the United States* (*of America*), *the United Arab Emirates, the United Kingdom* (*of Great Britain and Northern Ireland*), *the Republic of Ireland, the Principality of Monaco, the Grand Duchy of Luxembourg, the Czech Republic,* etc. Here also, the ***of***-combinations are appositive.

  Apart from this there are a handful of singular names that are always or sometimes used with the definite article: *the Ukraine, the Gambia,* (*the*) *Lebanon,* (*the*) *Sudan,* (*the*) *Yemen.*

- ***buildings and other construction phenomena:***

  the Thames Barrier, the Berlin Wall, the Aswan Dam, the London Docks, the Regent's Canal.

  Bridge and tunnel names usually have no article, but some famous ones do: *the Menai Suspension Bridge, the Golden Gate Bridge, the Tamar Bridge, the Mersey Tunnel.*

  Nouns denoting institutions of art and leisure are particularly common with the definite article: *the Albert Hall, the London Palladium* (music and variety), *the Odeon, the Gaumont* (typical cinema names), *the Royal Court, the Roundhouse, the Globe* (theatres), *the Nag's Head, the Cheshire Cheese, the King's Arms* (pubs), *the Dorchester, the Plaza* (hotels), *the Tate Gallery, the Guggenheim Museum.*

  As in other cases, ***of***-constructions always have the definite article: *the Houses of Parliament, the Palace of Westminster, the Church of Our Lady, the Tower of London, the Bank of England.*

- ***roads:***

  Street names take the definite article when they consist of a single common noun, e.g. *the Beeches, the Promenade, the Close, the Avenue.* Famous London examples are *the Mall* and *the Strand.* A different case is a road named after the place it leads to. Roads can generally be identified in this way, e.g. *the London road, the Bristol road,* etc., meaning, simply, *the road leading to London/to Bristol,* etc. When expressions like this develop into actual names, the definite article is usually dropped (*London Road*). Very occasionally, however, it has been retained. London examples are *the Lee High Road*, the *Uxbridge Road, the Old Kent Road, the Mile End Road*. But these are isolated instances. Street names in foreign languages that routinely use the definite article, on the other hand, keep it in their English versions: *the Boulevard de Clichy, the Königsstraße, the Via Quattro Fontane*.

022/4.3 The personal and cultural world

- ***titles:***
  king (queen), duke, earl, count (countess), marquis, all of which take the definite article with ***of***, e.g. *the Duke of Bedford*; monarchs have an 'unseen' definite article before their number, e.g. *Henry VIII*, spoken as 'Henry the Eighth'.
- ***personal groupings:***
  Proper nouns referring to personal and social groupings: clubs, teams, bands of performers, members of social classes and sectors, political parties, government and other authorities, 'movements' in society, the arts, politics, etc., and also groups representing nations and cultures: *the London Philharmonic* (*Orchestra*), *the Beatles, the French Impressionists, the Puritans, the Conservatives* (*the Conservative Party*), *the general public, the Pittsburgh Steelers* (American football team), *the Italians, the Germans*, etc.
  With plurals, use of the definite article in this way means the group as a whole, i.e. as a social, political or national entity. In many cases, this can be very similar to zero article generalizations:

  (53) a. The Italians use mainly olive oil for cooking.
  b. Italians use mainly olive oil for cooking.

  The sentences as a whole mean roughly the same. However, the reference to *Italians* is quite different in each sentence. (53)a. identifies them as a specific (cultural or national) group and emphasizes the group concept. (53)b., on the other hand, is a generic reference to 'people of this kind'. What we have here, that is, is the usual distinction between definite and indefinite reference (see **022/1.2, 2.2** above).
  Depending on context, the ***definite article*** version (though not the ***zero*** one) could also be used in the sense of an Italian team, contingent, government, delegation, family, or any other kind of defined group.
  A common way of referring to family groups, especially informally, is by ***surname plural***: *the Smiths, the Robinsons, the McTaggarts* (*Familie Smith/Robinson/McTaggart*).
- ***certain cultural references:***
  the names of ships, newspapers and periods and events of history: *the Titanic, the Ark Royal, the Compass Rose* (ships); *the Daily Mirror, the Guardian* (newspapers); *the Jazz Age, the Renaissance, the Peninsular War, the Reformation* (historical epochs).

022/5 The definite article in other 'borderline' uses

The definite article appears in several further cases where usual rules prefer some other determiner:

022/5.1 Reference to the body

As we have already seen, the standard way of referring to parts of the body and personal clothing is with the ***possessive determiner*** (see **020/2.2** above): *She put her hand suddenly to her mouth.*

However, when the person is the direct object of the verb and the part of the body occurs in a prepositional phrase, the ***definite article*** is used:

(54) a. She kissed me on the cheek.
b. The dog bit David in the leg.
c. Mr. Hayworth scratched himself behind the ear.

The verb in such cases must be ***transitive***. Also, the verb-object meaning must be ***the same*** when the prepositional phrase is omitted (*She kissed me; The dog bit David*).

We cannot therefore say, for instance, **The wind blew him in the face*. The transitive verb *blow* in *The wind blew him*, would mean "forced him in a particular direction" (e.g. *The wind blew him against the wall*). In the starred sentence, however, *blow* has to be understood as intransitive. The construction is therefore not possible. The correct version would be *The wind blew in his face*, i.e. with the possessive.

Similar prepositional phrases occur in set expressions for complaints and diseases affecting a certain part of the body: *a pain in the leg, water on the brain, a cold in the head, hardening of the arteries, cancer of the stomach*, etc.

General reference to body organs and functions also requires the ***definite article***:

(55) a. Yoghurt is good for the digestion.
b. The most sensitive parts of the lower leg are the knees and the soles of the feet.
c. High blood pressure may affect the heart, the brain and even the kidneys.

022/5.2 Generalizations and abstractions

- ***metaphor singulars:***
  Singular count nouns with the definite article are occasionally used in generic reference, instead of the more usual zero article + plural.
  Compare:

(56) a. The present-day hotel guest has high expectations regarding food.
Der heutige Hotelgast stellt hohe Ansprüche an die Qualität des Essens.
b. Present-day hotel guests have high expectations regarding food.
Heutige Hotelgäste stellen hohe Ansprüche …

As in German, the difference is stylistic. (56)a. uses a single entity to represent the whole class. This makes the statement more elevated and abstract in tone: *The customer is always right!* (A principle often told to sales staff).

For ordinary, concrete generalizations the plural version is preferred: *Hotel guests are kindly requested not to leave their luggage unattended in the lobby; Customers may use the car-park at the rear of the building*, etc.

N.B.: plural and non-count nouns ***never*** take the definite article in generic statements.

- ***metaphor singulars and 'phenomena':***
  The same kind of reference to non-human entities (animals, plants, and inanimate objects) stresses their character as phenomena, often as species or (in the case of things) as technological or scientific items:

(57) a. The badger is a nocturnal animal.
Der Dachs ist ein nachtaktives Tier.
b. The potato was originally introduced into Europe from the American continent.
Die Kartoffel wurde ursprünglich von Amerika aus nach Europa eingeführt.
c. The most important inventions of the 20th century were undoubtedly the electric light, the motor-car, the refrigerator and the computer.
Die wichtigsten Erfindungen des 20. Jahrhunderts waren ohne Zweifel das elektrische Licht, das Automobil, der Kühlschrank und der Computer.
d. It was John Dalton who re-discovered the atom for modern science.
John Dalton war es, der das Atom für die moderne Naturwissenschaft wiederentdeckte.

- ***metaphor singulars for types and categories:***
  Other kinds of phenomena are conceptual, like the grammatical entities treated in this book (*the gerund, the article,* etc.), or forms and genres in the arts: *the ballad, the tragedy, the fairytale, the drama, the novel, the epic, the sonnet, the symphony, the madrigal, the sonata* etc.
  This kind of reference to types and categories of things is common in many other, less abstract fields also. For example, *the jive* and *the waltz* are types of dance, *the crawl* and *the backstroke* kinds of swimming technique, *the longbow* and *the sword* are weapons, *the violin* and *the piano* musical instruments, *the pillory* (*Pranger*) and *the whip* instruments of (fortunately old-fashioned) punishment. All these can function as ***metaphor singulars***, i.e. here as labels representing categories (kinds of instrument, dance, etc.):

(58) a. My daughter plays the guitar, my wife the banjo.
(= not a specific individual guitar or banjo, but those classes of instrument).
b. The saxophone is a woodwind instrument.
(= Holzblasinstrument).
c. They have been doing the jive and now they're doing the samba (i.e. those types of dance).

- ***metaphor singulars referring to 'institutions':***
  In the last section we met examples of institutional reference with the zero article (*at home, to school, in hospital,* etc.). However, certain kinds of institution (usually of a leisure or service type) are expressed as ***metaphor singulars***, and require the ***definite article***: *the theatre, the cinema, the doctor's, the library, the garage* etc. An exceptional plural form is *the shops*:

(59) a. My husband has gone to the shops and I am going to take the car to the garage.
Mein Mann ist beim Einkaufen und ich werde das Auto zur Reparatur/in die Werkstatt bringen.
b. If your headaches don't improve, you must go to the doctor's.
Wenn es mit deinen Kopfschmerzattacken nicht besser wird, musst du zum Arzt gehen.
c. John and Jean went to the cinema instead of to the theatre as they had planned.
John und Jean sind ins Kino gegangen, statt ins Theater, wie sie geplant hatten.

Here again, it is not specific and concrete individual entities (*shops, garage, doctor,* etc.) that are meant, but the general institution or implied service provided.

022/5.3 Time

There are one or two references to time that habitually take the definite article:

- the ***deictic time spheres*** (*past, present, future*):

(60) a. In the past people felt relatively secure in European cities, but now things have changed.
b. There is no time like the present if you want to put good ideas into practice!
c. We have no idea what the future will bring.

Note, however, the prepositional expressions with ***zero***: *at present* (*gegenwärtig*), and *in future* (*ab jetzt, künftig*), as opposed to *in the future* (*= at some time in the future*).

- ***dates***:
In ***written*** form, dates have the zero article: *September 23rd, May 5th, August 13th*. When ***spoken***, however, the ***definite article*** is used: *September the twenty-third, May the fifth, August the thirteenth*. (American speakers, however, use the zero article here too: *September twenty-third, May fifth,* etc.).
When the number comes first (*23rd September, 5th May*), the spoken form takes not only the definite article but also the preposition ***of*** before the month: *the twenty-third of September, the fifth of May, the thirteenth of August.*
These are spoken forms only, though. In writing the definite article and the preposition are always 'unseen'.

022/6 Demonstrative determiners

These were introduced above under their more traditional term ***demonstrative pronoun***. As pointed out, they function basically as determiners. Apart from certain quantifiers (see **3.3** below), these are the only determiners with separate grammatical forms for singular and plural (***this/these – that/those***). The term ***demonstrative*** comes from the pointing ('demonstrating') function, which we will refer to here as ***emphasized indication***. The ***deictic*** meaning of the ***demonstratives***, as mentioned above, has to do with the closeness or distance of the speaker from the object indicated. The ***deixis*** involved here, that is, is ***spatial*** in nature, and reflected also, for instance, in the adverbs *here* ('close to the speaker, in the speaker's space') and *there* ('further away from the speaker, not in the speaker's space'). We can therefore equate ***this/these*** with *here*, and ***that/those*** with *there*.

The size of the 'speaker's space', and what counts as inside it or outside it, is completely subjective, of course, and may change from sentence to sentence.

022/6.1 this/these

(61) a. I found these earrings (here in my hand) on the pavement by the car. Are they Mary's?
b. This bowl (here on the table) is from Morocco.
c. Would you show these guests (here in front of me) to their room, please, Brian?

In many cases ***this/these*** have the general communicative effect of bringing the listener into the speaker-space (if the listener is not there already), and therefore as close to the object as the speaker is. At the same time this also creates a certain communicative closeness between speaker and listener.

The closeness of the speaker to the object does not have to be physical. It may be mental:

(62) a. This friend of yours who's coming tomorrow – What was his name again?
b. Look at it this way: staying at home for the holiday means far less stress than flying to a busy resort.
c. What are all these toys on the living-room carpet, darling?

Psychological closeness is often text-related. In (62)a., for example, the speaker comes back to an earlier topic, i.e. takes up something previously talked about (*this friend*). In (62)b. we have a standard use of ***this*** to announce a following point, known as ***cataphora*** (= 'pointing forward', the opposite of ***anaphora*** – another term for 'back-reference'). In (62)c., if we assume that there is no physical closeness, the use of ***these*** is psychological. Speaker and listener could, for instance, be in another room (say the kitchen). By referring to the toys as ***these*** the speaker brings them close to him (into his 'speaker-space'), so that he is able to show them mentally to the listener.

022/6.2 that/those

(63) has the same examples as (61), except that ***this/these*** are replaced by ***that/those***. Closeness now becomes its opposite, i.e. distance:

(63) a. I found those earrings (there on the table) on the pavement by the car. Are they Mary's?
b. That bowl (over there on the sideboard) is from Morocco.
c. Would you show those guests (standing over there by their luggage) to their room, please, Brian?

The speaker now signals that the objects are not part of his speaker-space. He is pointing at them with his arm (at least figuratively speaking) outstretched.

To produce the same effect on the 'mental' examples in (62), we have to change one or two elements to fit the distance meaning:

(64) a. That friend of yours we met in town last week – What was his name again?
b. "Why don't we have the party in the old barn?" "Oh, I don't like that idea very much, I'm afraid."
c. What are all those toys on the living-room carpet, darling?

Whereas (62)a. is about present or future relevance, (64)a. looks back to something mentioned or experienced in the past. (64)b. is a typical communicative ***anaphora***, a comment on something that has just been said. This is very common when one speaker gives a judgement on another's utterance or behaviour. It is rather like stepping back from something and pointing at it. (64)c. denotes distance to the toys and would be the normal way of referring to something further away that one could not see.

022/6.3 Demonstratives as pronouns

As pronouns, the demonstratives are used in a general, indeterminate sense. They are understood to mean *this person, that object, those things*, etc., and often refer to entities not yet identified:

(65) a. "What are these?" (picking up two objects and showing them to the listener, who is a little further away).
"Oh, those are a pair of Masai spearheads I picked up in Kenya."
b. "Who's that?" (nodding or pointing in the direction of someone across the room).
"Ah, that's Iris's brother, Wayne."
c. "What was that?" (on hearing a howling noise outside on a dark night)
"It's only our cat, probably fighting with a few friends, by the sound of it."
d. "There's only one thing that bothers me about Brian's car."
"And what's that, Hermione?"
"It stinks."

With identified objects, they emphasize the speaker's reaction:

(66) a. Goodness me, Pauline, a rifle bullet! Where did you find ***this*** (***that***)?
b. Oh, lovely, a little Victorian vase. I've got just the place for ***that***!

The unstressed version uses the ordinary personal pronoun (*Where did you find it?/I've got just the place for it!*).

Demonstrative pronouns ***cannot*** be used in this sense for persons. Human references are emphasized by stressing the personal pronoun:

(67) a. Davis is an excellent coach. Where did you find ***him***?
b. What an awful band! Who on earth booked ***them***?

With person reference, in fact, demonstrative pronouns are restricted: firstly, to questions and answers concerning identity (i.e. in the sense of (65)b., and exclusively with the main verb *to be*). Furthermore, in questions they are permissible only in the singular. That is, we can say *Who's this?*, but not **Who are these?* (although *These/those are John's friends* is possible).

And because of the restriction to identity meaning, we cannot say **What is that doing?* in reference to a person. Here again the stressed personal pronoun is necessary:

(68) a. What's ***she*** doing?
b. Where are ***they*** going?

022/6.4 Demonstratives with the prop-pronouns (one/ones)

Another restriction on the pronoun use of demonstratives concerns back-reference to a specific head noun. This occurs when there are two or more noun phrases with the same head, e.g. *the black dog* and *the white dog*, and one (or more) of the head nouns is converted into a pronoun. As we saw above, this is a case for the prop-pronoun ***one/ones*** (see **020/7.6**): *the black dog and the white one*. Demonstrative determiners in such a case also require the prop-pronoun, i.e. here they cannot function as pronouns themselves: *I like this dog, but not that one* (and not **I like this dog, but not that*). This applies only to the singular, however, and not to the plural: i.e. *these* and *those* and do not normally have the prop-pronoun following. Compare:

(69) a. These apples look all right, but those are pretty rotten.
b. This apple looks all right, but that one is pretty rotten.

After an adjective, however, the ***prop-pronoun*** must be used with *these/those* as well:

(70) I'd like some apples. Those red ones look nice, or perhaps these yellow ones here.

022/6.5 Prop-pronoun alternatives: that one/the one/that

That one is often used as a more demonstrative alternative to ***the one***: *"Which chemist's do you mean?" "The one/That one in King St."* (see also example (24)a. above).

Demonstrative ***that*** points more definitively to something which the speaker thinks the listener knows well, possibly from shared experience.

A rather different case is the use of ***that*** on its own:

(71) a. The airport at Heathrow is bigger than that/the one at Stansted.
b. Under the last government, the foreign policy of Britain was very similar to that of the USA.

Here, ***that*** provides a more elegant alternative to ***the one***, and is often found in writing and more formal styles, particularly when a comparison is being made.

⚠ With concrete nouns, as in (71)a., ***the one*** would be preferred in speech as being more neutral and less formal. However, with abstract nouns, as in (71)b., there is no alternative. Here only ***that*** is possible, i.e. not **... was very similar to the one of the USA*. This overgeneralization of ***the one*** is a common error among German speakers.

It is also a mistake to use ***that one*** here, i.e. we cannot say **... similar to that one of the USA*, nor, indeed, **... bigger than that one at Stansted*, unless we really are pointing mentally to some shared experience with the listener. But the comparison of two things makes that unlikely in this example.

022/6.6 Postmodification of those

As a pronoun ***those*** can be postmodified by relative clauses and participle clauses:

(72) a. Those (tourists) who would like to climb the church tower should meet the guide at the entrance in 5 minutes.
Die(jenigen), die auf den Kirchturm steigen möchten, sollten sich mit dem Kirchenführer in 5 Minuten am Eingang treffen.
b. Mr. Miles will look after those (pupils) not coming with us on the coach.
Mr. Miles wird sich um die(jenigen) kümmern, die nicht mit uns im Bus fahren.

Here a particular sub-group is picked out of a larger one and focused upon. It can be stressed by using ***all***: *All those who would like to climb the church-tower ...* (*alle die, die ...*, cf. **024/1.7** below).

022/6.7 German-English contrasts in usage

⚠ In German the main kind of demonstrative, especially in spoken language, is the definite article (*der, die, das*), pronounced with stress. It can also freely appear as a pronoun. The English definite article, however, can never be used in this way. Compare the equivalents:

(73) a. Ich möchte ***den*** Kuchen (da). ***Der*** (dieser) hier sieht nicht so gut aus.
I'd like that cake. This one doesn't look so good.
b. Sarah? ***Die*** habe ich seit einer Ewigkeit nicht mehr gesehen!
Sarah? I haven't seen ***her*** for ages.
c. Wie wäre es denn mit den braunen Schuhen? Die flachen meine ich (die du letzten Winter gekauft hast).
What about the brown shoes? I mean those flat ones (that you bought last winter).

Of course, if the German article in (73)c. is understood as being without the demonstrative ('pointing') emphasis, then the English definite article could be used as well: *Ich meine die flachen, die du letzten Winter gekauft hast – I mean the flat ones that you bought last Christmas.*

022/6.8 German-English plurals

As a general demonstrative, German *das* can be followed by a plural verb (usually only *sind/waren*). But it is not possible in English to say **that are*. In English singular subject pronouns always require a singular verb form; a plural verb form needs a plural subject pronoun (here ***these/those/they***):

(74) a. Das sind meine Freunde!
Those/they are my friends.
b. Das hier sind die Bilder, die ich dir zeigen wollte.
These are the pictures I wanted to show you.

Even with a singular verb, standard English tends to avoid using a singular subject with a plural subject complement, unless the plural stands for an entity that can be seen as a unit, i.e. *That's John's parents, That's the Smiths*, but not **That's our two cats*, or **That's the photos we took*. The correct versions of these last two are: *Those/these are our two cats* and *those/these are the photos we took*.

022/6.9 Particular uses of this/these

- ***first-time introductions:***
  "Oh, Tim, this is Maya, my wife. Maya, this is Tim, our new colleague."
  The phrase *this is* is used also with more than one person: *Jane, this is Roland and his wife Maya.*
  But for actual plurals *these are* is preferred: *Jane, these are my two colleagues, Bill Walmsely and Ciaron O'Shea.*
  Mr. Walmsely, these are our twin daughters, Gale and Lavinia.
- ***telephone identification:***
  "Hello, Mrs. Singh, this is Jenny. Can I speak to Yasmina, please?"
- ***in the sense of 'here':***
  In this firm overtime is compulsory (*Hier in dieser Firma sind Überstunden Pflicht*).
  In this family we do things differently! (*In dieser Familie machen wir die Dinge anders!*).
  In this valley there were many farms, whereas in the others there were none (*In diesem Tal gab es viele Bauernhöfe, während es im anderen keine gab*).
- ***in the sense of 'now':***
  this morning, this afternoon, this evening (*heute Morgen/Nachmittag/Abend*). These contrast, for instance, with *yesterday morning* (*gestern Morgen*), *tomorrow afternoon* (*morgen Nachmittag*), etc. Also: *this week, this month, this year* (*diese Woche, diesen Monat, dieses Jahr*), all of which contrast with *last week/month/year*, and *next week/month/year; these days* (= *nowadays*).
  A variation of this use is with *this time* to indicate an occasion in the immediate future: *This time you'll pass the exam, don't worry!* (*Diesmal wirst du die Prüfung bestehen. Mach dir keine Sorgen!*).
- **this *with adjectives in the sense of 'so':***
  I haven't brought a sweater. I didn't realize it would be this cool in the evening. (*... Mir war nicht bewusst, dass es abends so kühl sein würde*).

An alternative expression here is *as cool as this*. The use of *this* indicates that the speaker is experiencing the condition mentioned (= *as cool as I'm experiencing now*). See also under ***that*** below for a similar meaning.

- ***colloquial* this *in introductions as an emphasized indefinite article:***
  In informal language, ***this*** is sometimes used to introduce things into dialogue for the first time, particularly when emphasis is required: *We were in the High St. yesterday shopping, when we saw this peculiar-looking man outside Smith's.*
  This functions here as an emphatic form of the indefinite article, signalling to the listener that 'the man' is going to be talked about. It often draws attention to something special or extraordinary: *I looked out of the window one day a couple of weeks ago, and there was this big dog in the front garden eating our flowers.*
  It is a common opener for jokes and anecdotes: *This attractive blonde was sunbathing on the beach in Brighton …*

022/6.10 Particular uses of that/those

- ***together with* this *for contrastive pointing/showing:***
  Speaker A: *"That's the key for the front-door"* (handing it to B).
  "That's the key for the side-door" (handing B a second key).
  "And this is the key for the front-door" (emphasizing the third key before handing it to B).
- ***comments, reactions:***
  "That's a nice hairstyle. It makes you look younger!"
  „Das ist eine schöne Frisur. Sie macht dich jünger!"
  "Where did you get that blouse? It's very nice."
  „Wo hast Du die Bluse (die, die du gerade an hast) gekauft? Sie ist nämlich sehr schön."
  "That was rather a nasty remark. I think you ought to apologize!"
  „Das war eine etwas böse Bemerkung. Ich finde, du solltest dich entschuldigen."
- ***distance identification:***
  Isn't that Bob and his wife at the table over there on the right?" (*„Sind das nicht Bob und seine Frau am Tisch da drüben rechts?"*)
- ***in the sense of 'then':***
  (on) that morning/afternoon/evening (*an dem damaligen Vormittag/Nachmittag/Abend*); *at that time* (*damals*), *on that day* (*an jenem Tag*), *in those days* (*in der damaligen Zeit*).
- ***in reference to shared past experience:***
  D'you remember that film we saw in Manchester? What was it called?
  By the way, where does that cousin of yours in Scotland live exactly?
  (see also (64)a. above)
- ***with* wh-*adverbs as an explanation or emphasis of something just mentioned or already known:***
  Phil's shoes are too tight. That's why he can't walk properly.
  (*… Deswegen kann er nicht …*)
  Then the man asked us for money. That's when we started to get suspicious. (*… Spätestens dann fingen wir an, Verdacht zu schöpfen*).
  A neighbour of mine saw Tanya in a café. That's how I knew she hadn't been to work that day. (*Daher wusste ich, dass sie …*).

- ***explanatory* that is*:***
  Marston is going to be away all week. That is, he will miss the meeting on Thursday. (... *Das heißt, er wird die Sitzung am Donnerstag verpassen*).
  The abbreviation for ***that is*** is ***i.e.*** (for Latin *id est,* German *d.h.*), which by now you should be familiar with from this book!
- **that *with adjectives in the sense of* so*:***
  Is the firm's economic position really ***that*** *serious? (= as serious as you've just told me: ... so schlimm).* An alternative expression here is *as serious as that.*
  That can only be used in the sense of *so* if the particular condition is visible or has already been mentioned. It is not possible, for example, to say **I was that tired* (meaning *so tired*), unless a degree of tiredness had already been expressed or implied in some way. As seen above, there is a similar use of ***this***, which suggests more closeness to the condition and more involvement in it than ***that*** does. For example, *I didn't think the play would be* ***that*** *good* (said after the performance, or when someone else has told me about it); *I didn't think the play would be this good* (said by me as I am experiencing the performance).

3.3 Quantifiers

023 Main grammatical and semantic features

Quantifiers are basically determiners. They express amount, number and extent (or range). There are three semantic types: those referring to the whole of particular groups and categories, or to specified parts of them, such as *all, both, no, each,* etc. (***distributives***); those referring to indefinite quantities, like *some, any, few, much, more, several,* etc. (***indefinite quantifiers***); and numbers themselves (***numerals***).

Apart from their grammatical role as determiners, most quantifiers also appear as pronouns, some as adjectives and adverbs, and a few in a special category applying only to quantifiers, called ***pre-determiners***. A quantifier functions as a ***pre-determiner*** when it can be placed before other determiners, such as articles, possessives, etc., as in, for example, *all the people.* There is a variant with ***of*** which we will call here the ***partitive pre-determiner***: *all of the people.*

Further examples of these varying roles are:

- ***determiner***: *both animals*
- ***pre-determiner***: *both the animals*
- ***partitive pre-determiner***: *both of the animals*
- ***pronoun***: *both,* as in *Both were hungry.*
- ***adverb***: *They were both hungry.*

The ***adjective*** role does not occur with distributives, but is found with certain indefinite quantifiers, and also with numerals: *The few/many/three animals in my private zoo.*

Only the distributives *all* and *both* and the numeral *half* can take the role of a direct ***pre-determiner***. The ***partitive pre-determiner*** function is much more common, however, and occurs with most quantifiers, e.g. *a few of the people, some of the beer, three of the men,* etc. Where both ***pre-determiner*** types are possible (i.e. with *all, both, half*) they mean the same, e.g. *half the money = half of the money*.

There are quite a few similarities between German and English quantifiers, but also significant differences, as the discussion following shows.

Distributives 024

Distributives refer to definite quantities, chiefly in the sense of 'all or nothing'. That is, ***they*** relate to range and extent within groups and categories.

024/1 all

All refers to a whole group or quantity. It is used mainly with ***plurals*** and ***singular non-count*** nouns, but can appear also with certain types of singular count noun. With plurals, ***all*** means three or more. It cannot be applied, that is, to groups consisting of only two elements.

Its principal syntactic functions are as a ***determiner*** (*all cats*), ***pre-determiner*** (*all the cats*), and ***partitive pre-determiner*** (*all of the cats*). It also has restricted uses as a pronoun and adverb.

024/1.1 As a determiner

(75) a. All cats like milk.
Alle Katzen trinken gern Milch.
b. The town centre is now closed to all traffic.
Die Stadtmitte ist jetzt für den Verkehr gesperrt.

The meaning here is ***generic***, i.e. what is being referred to is the 'general category of thing named' (*all cats* in general, *all traffic* in general). This is therefore similar to using the ***zero article*** alone, for this also refers to category or type (see **022/3** above): (75)a. essentially means the same as *Cats like milk*. Adding ***all*** simply emphasizes the *whole* category and intensifies the reference.

Generic use may be restricted to a defined, specific location:

(76) a. The message was received by all pilots in the region.
b. All holidaymakers on the island were evacuated.
c. All pupils at the school were sent home.
d. All work at the plant stopped.

The meaning here is 'that category of persons in that place', e.g. *all pupils* (but not, for instance, the staff), *all holidaymakers* (as well as the inhabitants), *all pilots* (that professional group); and with non-count nouns 'that type of phenomenon/activity completely': *All work stopped and demonstrations and picketing started.* (See also under **024/1.3**).

024/1.2 As a pre-determiner and partitive pre-determiner

(77) a. All (of) the cats have been fed.
b. Merrick has lost all (of) his money.
c. All (of) those people are staying in our hotel.

Reference in this case is always to a ***specific*** individual group. This is obvious with possessives and demonstratives, but the definite article sometimes causes misunderstandings. A phrase like *all the people* means 'all the people in the group I am talking about'. It can ***never*** be used to mean 'people in general'. There is no semantic difference between the ordinary and partitive forms; the ***of***-form, however, lends more emphasis to the quantifier.

024/1.3 Distinctions in determiner and pre-determiner use

We will return for a moment to the contrast between ***generic*** and ***specific*** meanings. We have seen that in ***generalizations*** we must use ***all*** without a definite article following:

all cats (= the whole species), *all milk* (= this type of liquid), *all people* (= everyone everywhere). With the article, reference is to a ***specific*** and ***identified*** individual group: *all the cats* (= the entire group that I am talking about, e.g. *all the cats in this town*); *all the milk* (= here, in this kitchen); *all the people* (= all the people in the group referred to, e.g. *all the people on this ship*).

The two types of meaning may not be quite so easy to distinguish when generic reference is also restricted in location, as in (76) above. Compare (78)a. and b., and (78)c. and d., respectively:

(78) a. All holidaymakers on the island were evacuated.
b. All the holidaymakers on the island were evacuated.
c. All pupils at the school were sent home.
d. All the pupils at the school were sent home.

In most contexts either version would fit. So on the surface, there does not appear to be much difference. Nevertheless, the two types of reference are quite distinct. The ***determiner*** versions (without the definite article, as in a. and c.) are normal only when the category ***as such*** is meant (i.e. in possible contrast to some other group or category). The

pre-determiner versions (with the article, as in b. and d.) tend to focus more on the specific group and its individual members:

(79) a. All holidaymakers on the island (but no inhabitants) were evacuated.
b. All the holidaymakers on the island were evacuated (and not just some of them, *or*: ... as opposed to those on the mainland, who were allowed to stay).
c. All pupils at the school were sent home (but the staff stayed).
d. All the pupils at the school were sent home (and not just some of them, *or*: ... the pupils in this school were sent home, as opposed to those at another school, who were not).

The German translation in every case here is *alle* (*alle Urlauber, alle Schüler*). So this will not help in distinguishing between the two English versions.

A simplified rule is to use the ***determiner*** version (***no article***!) only for ***generalizations***, and the ***pre-determiner*** version (***with article***!) for all other cases.

024/1.4 With concrete singular count nouns

(80) a. I haven't yet read all of the book.
b. You haven't eaten all of your meal (= You've left some of it untouched).
c. All the playground is under water.
Der ganze Kinderspielplatz steht unter Wasser.
d. Chessington Zoo: a treat for all the family!
Der Chessington-Tiergarten: ein Vergnügen für die ganze Familie!

References of this kind, obviously, are to entities that can be divided mentally into 'portions' or parts, at least in the relevant context. The nouns are usually concrete: that is, ***all*** tends to be avoided with abstract count nouns (though there are certain exceptions, e.g. 'time-nouns', see below). A third point is that the ***non-partitive*** version (without ***of***), as in (80)c. and d., is generally regarded as informal. In more neutral to elevated style the ***partitive*** version (+ ***of***) is preferred. It is generally obligatory in all cases with personal pronouns and the indefinite article:

(81) a. I haven't yet read all of it.
b. Timmy drinks all of a bottle of milk every morning.
c. All of it is under water.

A lexical alternative to ***all*** is the adjective/pronoun ***whole*** (with singulars only): *I haven't read the whole (of the) book yet; The whole (of the) playground is under water.*

With abstract count nouns it is the preferred alternative: *the whole idea, the whole period, the whole joke.*

(82) a. I haven't yet read the whole of it.
b. Timmy drinks a whole bottle of milk every morning.
c. The whole of it is under water.

024/1.5 With proper nouns referring to geographical areas

(83) a. All Manchester celebrated the team's victory.
b. All the West of England has had rain today.

This is a similar case to that in **024/1.4**, i.e. with a singular noun that can be thought of as 'whole' or 'in parts'. It occurs mainly when the noun is subject, but occasionally also after prepositions: *He has travelled in all India*.

Except in cases like (83)a., where the meaning is essentially 'the people in the area', the partitives *all of* or *the whole of* are preferred for area references of this kind: *All of the West of England ...; ... in the whole of India*.

024/1.6 As an adverb

As a less emphatic alternative to the other uses, ***all*** can appear as an ***adverb***:

(84) a. The children were all playing in the garden (= all of the children).
b. Filmstars all love to be adored (= all filmstars).
c. The men all had knives with them (= all of the men).

With full nouns, this is only possible when they are the ***subject***. But there is no restriction with pronouns:

(85) a. They were all playing in the garden.
b. Filmstars in those days were like gods, and the public adored them all.
c. Best wishes to you all.

The position of all as an adverb with subject nouns and pronouns is either verb-***phrase-internal*** (i.e. following the first auxiliary verb), or between the subject and the main verb (cf. chapter 5). With pronouns in other positions, ***all*** follows them directly, as in (85)b. and c.

There is another, quite different adverb use before ***adjectives***:

(86) a. The boy had been playing football and was all muddy.
... war ganz verdreckt.
b. I'm all wet!
Ich bin ganz nass!
c. Your eyes are all red.
Deine Augen sind ganz rot.

This is only possible with adjectives used ***predicatively***, i.e. in the ***subject complement*** function. Secondly, the adjective normally describes a negative or at least an unusual condition. Thirdly, the condition is usually concrete, though in colloquial usage it may sometimes be an internal or behavioural state: *He got all upset* (*Er wurde ganz sauer.*); *She went all sentimental* (*Sie wurde ganz sentimental.*); *I'm all confused* (*Ich bin ganz durcheinander.*).

Finally, ***all*** confers a similar meaning on many ***prepositional phrases***:

(87) a. We drove all through the night.
... die ganze Nacht hindurch.
b. She had spilt the wine all down her dress.
... über ihr ganzes Kleid.
c. He came to the party dressed all in black.
... ganz in schwarz gekleidet.

024/1.7 Further points of note

- ***with times:***
determiner (no definite article): *all day, all night*
determiner or pre-determiner (definite article optional): *all (the) morning/afternoon/evening, all (the) week/month/year.*
The article is also optional with seasons and festivals: *all (the) winter/spring/summer/autumn/Christmas,* etc.
Note also: *all my life (your/his/her,* etc.) – *mein ganzes Leben; all the time – die ganze Zeit.*
- ***with numerals:***
Before numerals ***all*** can emphasize the group as a whole: *All four men were wearing masks; All 40 passengers escaped serious injury,* etc.
- ***with demonstratives:***
All + demonstrative determiner can mean 'so much': *We've been waiting all this time!* (= so long up to now). *And you spent all that money!* (= so much money). *So you like Christmas, eh, Timmy? – all those presents!* (= so many presents). *All these difficulties (which we're now having)! Will they ever stop?* (= so many difficulties)
All that + adjective with negative verbs is used (mainly in spoken English) to mean 'not very': *The situation doesn't look all that good (... sieht nicht sehr gut aus.); It's not all that bad! (So schlimm ist es nicht!); I'm not all that well (Ich fühle mich nicht so gut.).*
- ***with postmodified* those*:***
All gives more emphasis to postmodifications with ***those:*** *All those who invested in that company have lost their money. All those needing transport home can come with me in the mini-bus.* (See also **024/6.6**).
- ***as a pronoun:***
All is not generally used as an indefinite pronoun. The usual English equivalents of German *alles/alle* are *everything/everyone* (see **024/3.1** below). An exception is when the pronoun is ***postmodified by a relative clause***. Here ***all*** is permissible, and often preferred when the message has to be brief and to the point: *Have our guests got all/everything (that) they need? (Haben unsere Gäste alles, was sie brauchen?); I don't remember all/everything (that) she said (Ich erinnere mich nicht an alles, was sie gesagt hat); After all/everything Bill has done for them, their behaviour seems ungrateful, to say the least (Nach allem, was Bill für sie getan hat, scheint ihr Verhalten, milde ausgedrückt, etwas undankbar zu sein).*
As indicated, the relative pronoun can be omitted in appropriate cases (see also chapter 14).

There is a further instance where ***all*** is not only permissible, but in fact ***obligatory***: this is when the meaning is 'not more' or 'the only thing(s)': *All* (*that*) *he said was that he was not coming to the meeting, but he gave no reason* (*Alles, was er sagte, war, dass er nicht ...*); *All (that) I did was turn off the heating (Ich habe doch nur die Heizung abgedreht, sonst nichts); All (that) she possesses is a few clothes and two stray cats (Alles, was sie besitzt, sind ...); All I mean is that we need to save a little money* (*Ich meine doch nur, dass wir ...*).

To the last three examples we could also add the phrase *that's all* (*das ist alles/mehr nicht*).

Everything, then, although generally the more usual equivalent of German *alles,* cannot be used in these examples.

⚠ Finally, a reminder: German *alles, was ...* can ***never*** be rendered in English as **all what ...*! In standard English *what* cannot be used as an ordinary relative pronoun (see chapter 14).

Apart from the systematic exceptions just discussed, ***all*** is additionally found as a pronoun (with the meaning of both *alle* and *alles*) in a few set phrases: *All's well again* (*Es ist alles wieder gut*); *All is lost, I'm afraid* (*Es ist leider alles verloren*); *Now it's all or nothing* (*Jetzt geht's um alles oder nichts!*); *It was embarrassing for all concerned* (*Es war peinlich für alle Beteiligten*); *A good time was had by all* (*Es hatten alle ihren Spaß*).

- ***some other common idiomatic expressions:***

  At all (= *completely, in any way,* with negatives and questions): *I didn't see him at all (Ich habe ihn gar nicht/überhaupt nicht gesehen);The cat's not at all well* (*Der Katze geht es gar nicht gut*); *Did you find out anything at all?* (*Haben Sie überhaupt etwas darüber herausgefunden?*)

  In all *(= altogether, a total of)*: *There were four of us in all* (*Wir waren insgesamt zu viert*); *In all that will cost you about £500* (*Insgesamt wird Sie das etwa 500 Pfund kosten*).

  X of all Ys (= *X is particularly surprising, annoying, paradoxical,* etc.): *And now this of all things!* (*Und jetzt ausgerechnet das!*); *Sandra of all people* (*Ausgerechnet Sandra!*); *Today of all days!* (*Ausgerechnet heute!*)

  For all (= *despite*): *For all his wealth, he's the meanest person I know* (*Trotz seines Reichtums ist er der geizigste Mensch, den ich kenne*).

  For all X knows/cares (= *X doesn't know and/or doesn't care that ...*):
  For all I care you can dye your hair blue! (Und wenn du dir die Haare blau färben lassen würdest, wär's mir doch wurscht!); For all I know, he's still in America (Er ist wohl noch in Amerika, was weiß ich, ist mir doch egal).

024/2 both

Both refers to a group of two, usually already identified. It is what might be called the 'dual' equivalent of ***all***, in the sense that it stresses the 'whole group' (as opposed to just one of the two members). It is used exclusively with ***plurals***. Like ***all***, it functions syntactically as a ***determiner*** (*both cats*), ***pre-determiner*** (*both the cats*), and ***partitive pre-determiner*** (*both of the cats*). It can also be used as a pronoun and adverb.

024/2.1 As determiner, pre-determiner, partitive pre-determiner

(88) a. Two young women got into the car. Both women were wearing evening-dress. [***determiner***]
... Beide Frauen trugen Abendkleider.
b. ... Both the women were wearing evening-dress. [***pre-determiner***]
c. ... Both of the women were wearing evening-dress. [***partitive pre-determiner***]

There are no differences in meaning here at all, and the German equivalent is the same in each case.

024/2.2 As a pronoun/adverb

(89) a. Two young women got into the car. Both were wearing evening-dress.
... Beide trugen Abendkleider [***pronoun***]
b. They were both wearing evening-dress. [***adverb***]

This kind of adverb usage is the same as with ***all*** (see **024/1.6**).

There is a further type, specific to ***both***, which we will call ***co-ordinate pair reference***. The effect here is to emphasize the association of two elements joined together by ***and***:

(90) a. Both Marianne and Gudrun are coming to the party.
Sowohl Marianne als auch Gudrun kommen zum Fest.
b. They were both tired and hungry.
Sie waren sowohl müde als auch hungrig.

Note that there is ***no comma*** following ***both***!

024/2.3 both and German beide

Both and *beide* are not entirely the same in meaning and use. *Beide* is frequently used as an adjective following the definite article or some other determiner, e.g. *Am Tag darauf gingen die beiden Mädchen im Park spazieren*, or *Gerade diese beiden traf ich einige Wochen später auf einer griechischen Insel.*

Both can ***never*** follow a determiner in this way. ***Both*** must either be a determiner itself, or it must precede a determiner. Secondly, ***both*** cannot be used in the English version of these sentences. The correct English rendering here is ***the/these two***: *The next day the two girls went for a stroll in the park; I met precisely these two on a Greek island a few weeks later.*

In short: *beide* = ***both***, *die/diese beiden* = ***the two***. Here for clarification is a further example:

(91) a. Beide Brüder wurden des versuchten Mordes für schuldig befunden.
Both brothers were convicted of attempted murder.
b. Die beiden Brüder wurden des versuchten Mordes für schuldig befunden.
The two brothers were convicted of attempted murder.

The difference in meaning, to make the point absolutely clear, is that (91)b. is simply a way of referring to two associated people, whereas (91)a. says that (perhaps contrary to expectation) not just one brother was convicted, but 'the whole pair' (= *alle beide*).

024/3 every

Every means the same as ***all***, i.e. the total number of things or people in a group. But it refers to them individually and in the singular. Like ***all***, it can be used in a general sense to mean 'the whole category', or limited to a particular group:

(92) a. Every cat likes milk. [***generic***]
Jede Katze ...
b. The teacher gave every child in the class a sweet. [***specific***]
Die Lehrerin gab jedem Kind in der Klasse ein Bonbon.

Like ***all***, ***every*** must refer to a group of at least three entities. Unlike ***all***, it combines only with ***singular count*** nouns. Another difference is that it can only be used as a determiner – never as a pre-determiner, adverb or pronoun. Repetition of a head noun with ***every*** is avoided by using the ***prop-pronoun***: *The glasses had all been washed. Every one was sparkling clean.*

024/3.1 Compounds of every as indefinite pronouns

Indefinite pronouns (see **020/7** above) with ***every*** are: *everyone/everybody* (= *all people*) and *everything* (= *all things*); *everywhere* (= *in all places*) is the corresponding ***indefinite adverb***.

As to be expected, the primary stress in pronunciation is on the first element. This is different when ***every*** is a separate word. Here primary stress is on the noun or pronoun following. Compare:

(93) a. everyone ['evrɪwʌn] (*jede/r, jedermann*)
b. every one [evrɪ'wʌn] (*jede/r/s Einzelne*)

024/3.2 Expressions of frequency

- ***plurals:***
In expressions of frequency ***every*** appears (exceptionally) with plural nouns. These refer to measures (usually time or distance). ***Every*** is followed by a numeral or indefinite quantifier: *every 5 days* (*alle 5 Tage*), *every 6 months* (*alle 6 Monate*), *every few metres* (*alle paar Meter*).
The likely explanation for the use of ***every*** in such cases is that it stands for an ellipted singular noun: *every 5 days = after every period of 5 days.*
- ***singulars:***
Note also singular expressions of frequency: *every minute/hour/morning/afternoon/evening*, etc.; *every day/week/month/year*, etc.
A point to remember is that *every day* (*jeder/n Tag*) is usually written as two words (with stress on the second: *every 'day*), even in adverbial function, e.g. *He comes here*

every day. It is only considered to be one word when used as a premodifying adjective (= German *alltäglich*); stress is then on the first element (*'everyday*): *Our everyday life is rather boring, I'm afraid.*

- ***with ordinal numerals:***
  Frequency within a sequence (i.e. a series of events, times or other entities) is often expressed by ordinal numeral: *every fourth year, every second day*. It is common in statistical reference: *every third child* (*jedes dritte Kind*), *every tenth worker* (*jeder zehnte Arbeiter*), *every fourth car produced*, etc.
  The expression *every other* is sometimes used as an alternative for *every second*, e.g. *every other day* (= *every second day, jeden zweiten Tag*), *every other household* (*jeder zweite Haushalt*). There may be some ambiguity here, as *every other* more regularly means *all other* (= *jedes andere/alle anderen*). The context must decide, of course: *Every other car in the wedding parade was a cadillac* (*Jedes zweite Auto in der Hochzeitsparade/alle anderen Autos* ...).
- ***some other common expressions:***
  in every way/respect (*in jeder Hinsicht*), *every minute* (*jede Minute*), *every time* (colloquial for *whenever*), *every single* ... (*jede/r/s einzelne* ...), *every bit as* (informal for German *genauso*), *every* + abstract noun, e.g. *hope/chance/reason/opportunity/success*, etc. (= *all possible* ...), *every now and then/every so often* (*occasionally, but not often*):

(94) a. It was a great show in every way and we enjoyed every minute of it. Every single performer was brilliant!
b. Every time McClintock gets the ball, he's dangerous. He's every bit as good as Cormick, if not better.
c. You will have every opportunity to improve your career prospects in London, and we wish you every success.
d. We see Sally every so often in town, but never Arrol.
Wir treffen Sally dann und wann in der Stadt, aber Arrol nie.

024/4 each

Each refers to two or more entities in an identified group. It cannot be used generically, but is otherwise similar in meaning to ***every***, and in many contexts interchangeable with it. However, whereas ***every*** looks at the whole group together (i.e. as a collection), ***each*** focuses on the individual members separately. For comparison:

(95) a. The teacher gave ***every*** child in the class a sweet (= the whole group got one sweet per child and no child was left out).
Die Lehrerin gab jedem Kind in der Klasse ein Bonbon.
b. The teacher gave each child in the class a sweet (= the individuals, one by one, got a sweet of their own).
Jedes Kind in der Klasse bekam von der Lehrerin ein (eigenes) Bonbon.
c. The girl had a ring on every finger of her left hand.
Das Mädchen hatte an jedem Finger ihrer linken Hand einen Ring.
d. The girl had a ring on each finger of her left hand.
Jeder Finger an der linken Hand des Mädchens hatte seinen (eigenen) Ring.

(95)c. remarks on the fact that the girl had a lot of rings on her fingers. (95)d., on the other hand, invites us to look at the individual rings separately, possibly with the suggestion that they are all different, or that the character of the individual fingers is affected in some way.

The problem for German speakers here is one that all language learners come across regularly, regardless of the language they are learning or the one they speak already: a single term in the native language (*jede/r/s*) corresponds to two (*every/each*) in the target language. The best advice in cases of doubt is to use ***every*** – assuming, of course, that ***every*** is grammatically possible. For ***each*** has a wider grammatical range and can function as a ***determiner***, ***partitive pre-determiner***, ***pronoun*** and ***adverb***:

(96) a. The teacher gave ***each*** child in the class a sweet. [***determiner***]
b. The teacher gave ***each*** of the children in the class a sweet. [***partitive pre-determiner***]
c. The children ***each*** got one sweet. [***adverb***]
Jedes der Kinder bekam ein Bonbon.
d. The children got one sweet ***each***. [***adverb***]
Die Kinder bekamen je ein Bonbon.
e. The three men came closer. ***Each*** was wearing a blue raincoat. [***pronoun***]

The use of ***each*** as a pronoun, as in (96)e., is elevated and literary. In normal use the ***prop-pronoun*** is preferred: *Each one was wearing …*

As can be seen from (96)c. and d., ***each*** has 2 possible adverb positions. The first, in c., is the same as with ***all*** and ***both***, i.e. between subject and verb, and signifies the same kind of less emphatic alternative to the uses in (96)a. and b. It is only possible when the related noun is ***subject*** (cf. the equivalent point above with ***all*** and ***both***).

The second position, in (96)d., is unique to ***each***, and has a different meaning, i.e. *per person*. Other examples: *These apples cost 75p each* (= *per apple*); *We bought two apples each* (= *two apples per person*, i.e. one person bought two apples).

A point of note is that ***'adverb each'***, as in c. and d., relates to ***plural*** nouns. Otherwise ***each*** is ***singular***, and if it is part of the subject takes a ***singular*** verb form: *Each child was given a present.*

024/4.1 Some further points on each and every

Like ***all***, ***every*** can be premodified by certain adverbs of degree (*almost every guest, absolutely every politician, virtually every teacher*, etc.), but ***each*** cannot (**almost each guest*). Similarly, ***every*** and ***all*** can be negated (*not all guests, not every politician*), but ***each*** cannot (**not each guest*). See also **024/6** below for negatives. And finally, ***every*** is sometimes given emphasis by the adjective *single* following it: *every single guest* (= *absolutely every one*). This is not possible with ***each***: **each single guest.*

Generally speaking, ***each*** cannot replace ***every*** in the types of collocation listed in **3.2**. Among the frequency expressions, however, there are certain exceptions:

(97) a. Each/every time I see them in the street they ignore me.
b. A nurse visits him each/every day at home.
c. We spend our holidays each/every year in the west of France.

The ordinary difference in emphasis between ***each*** and ***every*** is felt here too. ***Each*** stresses the single occasion more, isolating it for separate inspection. Attention is therefore drawn more to the individual event and the way it happens, or what it consists of.

024/4.2 each and both

We have already said that ***each*** (unlike ***every***) can refer to two things only. What, then, is the semantic difference between ***each*** and ***both***?

(98) a. Both girls were wearing make-up.
Beide Mädchen waren geschminkt.
b. Each girl was wearing make-up.
Jedes der beiden Mädchen war geschminkt.

If we take ***both*** as being the 'dual' equivalent of ***all/every***, then we can see that (98)a. means 'not just one of them, but the two together'. (98)b., as always with ***each***, invites single inspection of the girls separately. In German this could indicate, for instance, *Jedes Mädchen war unterschiedlich/auf ihre eigene Art geschminkt*, or *Jedes Mädchen war geschminkt, aber beim einen ist es kaum aufgefallen*. These, of course, are just two of any number of implications – and they *are* just implications. But whatever the actual case, with (96)b. our view focuses first on one girl and then on the other; with (98)a. it is on the two girls together, as a 'unit'.

024/5 either

This has two distinct pronunciations in Britain and America: British: [aɪðə]; American: [i:ðə].

Either is also a little complex semantically. It has several slightly different meanings, and as a result there is no single German equivalent. A further problem is that the general German translations of ***either*** are *jede/r/s* and *beide/s*.

The most common English equivalents of these, however, are ***every*** and ***both*** – which in a sense are actually opposites of ***either***!

024/5.1 One out of a choice of two

The meaning here is 'one or the other':

(99) a. There are two clean glasses on the kitchen table. Take either glass/Take either of them/Take either. [***determiner, partitive pre-determiner, pronoun***]
... Nimm eines davon/Nimm egal welches.
b. "Shall we meet on Thursday or Friday?"
"Either day suits me."
Mir passt beides.

c. Can either of you (two) help me?
Kann mir einer von euch (beiden) helfen?

d. That oven-glove is for either hand. The back and front are the same.
Der Ofenhandschuh passt an beiden Händen ...

Another way of describing the meaning here is: 'only one of the two, but it doesn't matter which one'.

Instead of ***'pronoun either'***, as in (99)a., the ***prop-pronoun*** can be used (i.e. added to *either*, thus making it a determiner): *Take either one.*

024/5.2 either ... or

Either is used together with ***or*** as a ***double conjunction***, stressing a pair of alternatives. It is a further example of ***co-ordinate pair reference*** (like ***both ... and***, see **2.2** above):

(100) a. I'm going to have either chicken or fish, I think.
Ich glaube, ich nehme entweder Huhn oder Fisch.

b. The trade fair is either in Frankfurt or Stuttgart. I'm not sure which.
Die Messe findet entweder in Frankfurt oder in Stuttgart statt ...

c. Either she left her umbrella on the train, or somebody took it while she was in the tearoom.
Entweder sie hat den Regenschirm im Zug liegen lassen, oder jemand hat ihn mitgenommen, während sie im Café war.

d. Either Jarvis or Mabeline will be on duty tomorrow in Ward 10.
Entweder Jarvis oder Mabeline wird morgen auf der Station 10 Dienst haben.

024/5.3 In the sense of each (of two things)

This use is found typically in prepositional phrases referring to position and location (e.g. with words like *side, end,* etc.):

(101) a. There are lifts at either end of the hall (= at each end/both ends).
Es gibt Fahrstühle an beiden Enden vom Flur.

b. I walked carefully along the narrow mountain path: on either side of me was a 300-foot drop (= on each side/both sides).
... auf beiden Seiten von mir war jeweils ein 300 Fuß tiefer Abgrund.

This seems to be the opposite of the meaning in **024/5.1**, but in fact it is logically connected, since the implication here is also 'no matter which', i.e. *Whichever end of the hall you go to, you will find a lift; No matter which side of the path I looked at – the view was terrifyingly the same!*

Here, too, in other words, ***either*** implies an alternative. If there is no such implication, we have to use ***each*** or ***both***:

(102) a. There are exits at either end of the main stand (said, for example, by an official to a spectator, and meaning *It doesn't matter which one you choose*).
Ausgänge gibt es an beiden Enden der Haupttribüne.
b. There are exits at both ends of the main stand (normal manner of reference, and meaning *Each end of the stand is equipped with an exit*).
Beide Enden der Haupttribüne haben einen Ausgang.

024/6 Negative distributives: not + either/neither/nor

Negative distributives negate whole categories or parts of them. We describe this in the following as ***whole-group negation*** and ***part-group negation***:

024/6.1 not + either as negative both

Not + either means 'both things not', i.e. zero. It is therefore the ***whole-group negation*** of ***both***. It can relate not only to nouns, but also to adjectives and complete verbal expressions. The negative is always attached to the verb, and ***either*** follows (as ***pronoun***, ***determiner*** or ***partitive pre-determiner***):

(103) a. At Dawson's they only had two sweaters left in my size, and I didn't like either (of them).
Bei Dawson hatten sie nur noch 2 Pullover in meiner Größe übrig, und keiner der beiden hat mir gefallen.
b. Bruce looked for his friends in the two High Street pubs, but they weren't in either (one).
... aber sie waren in keinem der beiden (Lokale).
c. His doctors told him to take more exercise and eat less, but he didn't do either (thing).
... aber er hat keines von beidem getan/weder das eine noch das andere getan.
d. I had hoped for a husband who was kind and generous, but mine, as it turned out, wasn't either (of these things).
... war keines von beidem.

Either cannot be directly premodified by ***not***. In ***subject*** position at the beginning of clauses it therefore requires a special negative equivalent. This is ***neither*** (Am. [ni:ðə], Brit. [naɪðə]), usually singular, but regarded in less formal language also as plural. It takes a ***positive*** verb (not a negative one):

(104) a. I tried on two sweaters, but neither sweater was/neither(of them) was/were big enough.
... aber keiner (von beiden) war groß genug.
b. Brian and Trisha both came to the party, but neither (of them) looked very happy.
... aber keiner der beiden (bzw. weder der eine noch der andere) sah sehr glücklich aus.

Neither occurs also as ***subject complement***, and, less often, as ***object***:

(105) a. I had hoped for a husband who was kind and generous, but mine, as it turned out, was neither (of these things). [cf. (103)d.]
... aber meiner, wie sich herausstellte, war weder das eine, noch das andere.
b. His doctors told him to take more exercise and eat less, but he did neither (thing).

In these positions, ***neither*** is a rather more forceful and emphatic alternative to ***not either***.

Finally, a note on German *kein/keiner/keines/keine*: when these mean *kein(e/r/s)* ***von beiden*** the English counterparts are always ***not + either/neither***.

024/6.2 not + either as negative equivalent of also

The adverb ***also*** does not combine with negatives (apart from one or two exceptions). The equivalent of ***also*** in negative sentences is ***either*** (in this case an ***adverb***, and placed in final position):

(106) a. Bill isn't coming to the wedding, and Jane isn't (coming) either.
Bill kommt nicht zur Hochzeit, und Jane auch nicht.
b. "I don't speak French." "I don't either."
"Ich spreche kein Französisch." "Ich auch nicht".

The main verb is usually omitted in the second clause, or, as in (106)b., in the reply (cf. also chapter 8 on response tags).

Like ***not*** alone, ***not + either*** can focus on specific parts of the sentence. These can be implied contextually, or indicated by the syntax. The examples in (106) would normally be understood as ***subject***-focused, depending on context and intonation. Here are examples of focus on other functions. Note that the verb is left out in these cases:

(107) a. They didn't invite Brenda, and not me either. [***direct object***]
... und mich auch nicht.
b. We aren't giving Bob a Christmas present this year, and not Moira either. [***indirect object***]
... und (der) Moira auch nicht.
c. We didn't go to Scotland, and not to Wales either.
... und auch nicht nach Wales. [***prepositional phrase as adverbial***]

Focus may also be on the verb and the action. This is most often the case when the second clause contains a different main verb and refers to a different action. Here, the first clause need not be in the negative. The first verb, that is, can be positive or negative, depending on the sense:

(108) a. It was a lovely meal, and it didn't cost much either.
... und hat auch nicht viel gekostet.
b. They left early, and (they) didn't say goodbye either.
Sie sind früh gegangen und haben sich auch nicht verabschiedet.
c. We didn't visit Scotland and didn't manage Wales either.
... und schafften es auch nicht nach Wales.

For ***either*** to make sense in cases like this, the second clause must fill the same communicative intention as the first clause, and reinforce it pragmatically. In (108)a., for example, the approval expressed in the first clause is underlined by a further point of appreciation in the second. In (108)b. the 'leaving early' is a critical point, and is compounded by a second criticism in the second clause. In (108)c. the two actions are obviously both examples of 'things we didn't have time for during our British holiday'. There must, in other words, be some kind of logical communicative link between the two points.

024/6.3 neither/nor as negative also

Another way of rendering German ***auch nicht*** is with the ***negative adverbs neither*** or ***nor***. These must start the clause or sentence. The verb is then positive, but must be ***inverted*** (i.e. subject and verb are reversed, as for a question). Again, the main verb is usually omitted:

(109) a. Bill isn't coming to the wedding, and neither/nor is Jane.
Bill kommt nicht zur Hochzeit, und Jane auch nicht.
b. "I don't speak French." "Nor/Neither do I."
„Ich spreche kein Französisch." „Ich auch nicht".

Note that the positive equivalent has the same syntactic pattern with ***so***:

(110) a. Bill is coming to the wedding and so is Jane.
Bill kommt ..., und Jane auch.
b. "I speak French." "So do I."
„Ich spreche Französisch." „Ich auch."

As with ***either*** in (108), the second clause may have a different main verb from the first. Unlike ***either***, however, ***neither/nor*** definitely require a negated verb in the first clause:

(111) a. The food isn't bad at all, and neither/nor does it cost much.
Das Essen ist weder schlecht, noch kostet es viel/Das Essen ist nicht schlecht und kostet auch nicht viel.
b. They don't like fish and neither/nor do they eat much meat.
Sie mögen keinen Fisch und essen auch nicht viel Fleisch.
c. We didn't visit Scotland and neither/nor did we manage Wales.
Wir haben Schottland nicht besucht und schafften es auch nicht nach Wales.

024/6.4 Nor as a phrasal conjunction

Nor can be used to add something to a negated main clause:

(112) a. They didn't invite Brenda, nor me.
... und mich auch nicht.
b. I didn't have to pay for the meal, nor for the drinks.
... noch für die Getränke.
c. Fred hasn't cleaned the kitchen yet, nor the hall.
Fred hat die Küche noch nicht sauber gemacht, und den Flur auch noch nicht.

Nor functions itself as a ***conjunction*** here, as it stands also for ***and*** (which must be left out). These examples are equivalent to those with ***not + either*** in (107). ***Nor*** provides a neater alternative (though a less emphatic one). Even less emphatic would simply be ***or***, which also functions as the equivalent of ***and*** (in its 'additive' sense) when the verb is negated (see also chapter 7 on conjunctions):

They didn't invite Brenda, or me; I didn't have to pay for the meal or the drinks; Fred hasn't cleaned the kitchen yet, or the hall.

A point to note here is, firstly, that this use of ***nor*** does not apply to ***neither***. Secondly, ***nor*** cannot be used as a conjunction introducing a clause. This requires ***and + nor/neither*** as adverbs, as in (109)a. and (111), e.g. *They didn't invite Brenda, and nor did they invite me.*

024/6.5 double conjunctions: neither ... nor, not + either ... or

These are further variants for expressing combined negatives, but as a ***co-ordinate pair reference*** (see **024/2.2** and **5.2**).

Double conjunctions, that is, unify the two elements, stressing the fact that they belong together, rather than simply adding one to the other. These two double conjunctions are the negative equivalents of ***both ... and ...***

They have a slightly elegant ring to them, and are found more in writing than in speech:

(113) a. Neither Bill nor Jane is coming to the wedding.
Weder Bill noch Jane kommt zur Hochzeit.
b. I am neither mad, nor drunk.
Ich bin weder verrückt noch betrunken.
c. Fred has cleaned neither the kitchen yet, nor the hall.
Fred hat weder die Küche, noch den Flur schon sauber gemacht.
d. I went neither to the butcher's nor (to) the baker's.
Ich ging weder zum Metzger noch zum Bäcker.

Not + either ... or could be substituted before ***objects*** and ***prepositional phrases***, as in (113)c. and d. respectively. In less formal language, in fact, this would be the preferred form:

(114) a. Fred hasn't cleaned either the kitchen or the hall yet.
b. I didn't go either to the butcher's or the baker's.

In (113)a. and b., however, this is not possible: ***not*** + ***either*** cannot be used for subjects (see **024/6.1**), and in the double conjunction variant is usually also avoided with subject complements.

024/7 Other negative distributives

024/7.1 not + all/every/both

All and ***every*** are directly negated (i.e. premodified by ***not***) in ***subject*** position. Otherwise, negation is usually verb-attached:

(115) a. Not all the students are from America.
b. The students aren't all (are not all) from America.
c. I did not interview all the students.

What is negated here semantically is not the group as a whole, but the wholeness of the group, so to speak, i.e. its totality (= German *nicht alle*). The term ***part-group negation*** was introduced above to account for cases like this (see **024/6**). With generic and non-specific meaning there is, of course, no determiner: *Not all sharks are dangerous* (*Nicht alle Haie sind gefährlich*).

The implication in a. and b. is that at least ***some*** (and possibly ***most***) of the students were from America, but that others in the group were not. Similarly, in c. at least a certain number of students were interviewed, but not the whole group. The same applies to ***not every*** (German *nicht jeder*):

(116) a. Not every student is from America.
b. I did not interview every student.

With ***both*** this kind of negation (i.e. ***not both***) means 'only one':

(117) I did not interview both students (but just one of them).

Both, however, is not directly negated in subject position. In reference to a subject, it is negated adverbially, like ***all*** in (115)b.:

(118) Maureen and Denise aren't both/are not both from America (only one is).

Remember that 'both not' is expressed by ***not*** + ***either*** and ***neither*** (see **6.1** above): *I did not interview either student* (= *keinen der beiden*).

024/7.2 not + any

This is the most common ***whole-group negative*** of ***all***. With ***plurals*** it must refer, like ***all***, to 'more than two':

(119) a. At Dawson's they only had three sweaters left in my size, and I didn't like any of them.
Bei Dawson hatten sie nur noch 3 Pullover in meiner Größe übrig, und keiner der drei hat mir gefallen.
b. Bruce looked for his friends in the five High Street pubs, but they weren't in any of them.
... aber sie waren in keinem der fünf Lokale.
c. I had hoped for a husband who was kind, generous and wealthy, but mine, as it turned out, wasn't any of these things.
... war nichts von alledem.

As the examples show, the relationship of ***not + any*** to ***all*** is the same as that of ***not + either*** to ***both***. Note that German uses *keine/r/s* regardless of how many entities are involved. In other words, although German differentiates between *beide* and *alle* in their positive forms, it does not differentiate in the negative. English does, however, as we have seen. Care must therefore be taken when translating *keine/r/s* into English: 'two not' = ***not + either***, but 'more than two not' = ***not + any***.

The partitive form (i.e. with ***of***) is usual in reference to a specific and defined group, as in (119). The full pronoun use of ***any*** (without ***of***) is generally avoided in cases like these.

Like ***all***, ***not + any*** also appears with ***singular non-count*** nouns. Here, the pronoun use of ***any*** is common:

(120) a. I had put a bowl of fruit on the table, but the guests didn't eat any (of it).
b. The children didn't drink any of the milk I had given them.

The German equivalent here is *nichts (davon)*.

Not + any does **not** occur:

- with singular count nouns (**I haven't got any car)*.
  Correction: *I haven't got a car* (*Ich habe kein Auto*).
  See under **7.5** below.
- at the beginning of sentences or clauses (**Not any milk was drunk*).
  Correction: *None of the milk was drunk* (*Es wurde nichts von der Milch getrunken*).
  See immediately below.
- as the negation of the zero article in 'identifying generalizations' (**This is not any tea, but coffee)*.
  Correction: *This is not tea, but coffee* (*Das ist kein Tee, sondern Kaffee*).

024/7.3 none

A further whole-group negative of ***all*** is ***none***. This is the 'two-plus' equivalent of ***neither***, but functions only as a ***partitive pre-determiner*** and ***pronoun*** (and never as a determiner). It serves as a replacement in clause-initial position for ***not + any***, and is particularly common in group-specific reference. The accompanying verb-form is ***positive*** and normally ***plural*** when referring to plural nouns:

(121) a. None of the students are from America.
b. I tried on three sweaters, but none of them were big enough.
... aber keiner war groß genug.
c. Brian, Trisha and Jane all came to the party, but none of them looked very happy.

In reference to a specific and defined group, as in (121), the ***partitive*** form is usual, except after *there are*:

(122) There are students from Africa (in the group), but none from America.

Like ***any***, ***none*** may also refer to ***singular non-count*** nouns. Here full pronoun use is possible:

(123) a. I had put a bowl of fruit on the table, but none (of it) had been eaten.
b. None of the milk I had given the children had been drunk.

The German equivalent, again, is *nichts (davon)*.

Like ***neither***, ***none*** is used in other sentence functions (i.e. as ***complement*** or ***object***) for emphasis. It then sounds slightly more formal:

(124) a. I had hoped for a husband who was kind, generous and wealthy, but mine, as it turned out, was none of these things. [cf. (119)c.]
... war nichts von alledem.
b. I had put a bowl of fruit on the table, but the guests had eaten none of it).

With ***generic*** meaning, ***none*** is used only as a pronoun (i.e. never as a partitive):

(125) All cats like milk, but none like dogs.
... aber keine mögen Hunde.

024/7.4 not + zero article

Like ***not + any***, this is used with ***plurals*** and ***non-count nouns***, but mainly in ***generic*** statements. It is the most usual form in ***generalizations***:

(126) a. I don't drink wine.
b. The guests did not eat meat (= they were vegetarians).

Although ***not + any*** is occasionally also found here, the preferred form is ***not + zero***. It is absolutely obligatory in references to type or category that concern ***identification***:

(127) a. The guests were not eating meat (= it wasn't meat that they were eating, but something else).
b. She didn't have make-up on her face (= it was something else, e.g. a form of body paint).

Here, ***not + any*** cannot be used at all. The rule is particularly clear-cut with the verb *to be*:

(128) a. Those animals are not goats (but sheep).
*... are not any goats ...
Diese Tiere sind keine Ziegen (sondern Schafe).
b. We are not Catholics (but Protestants).
*... are not any Catholics ...
Wir sind keine Katholiken (sondern Protestanten).
c. This is not tea, but coffee.
*... not any tea ...
Das ist kein Tee, sondern Kaffee.
(See also under **024/7.2**)

On the other hand, ***not + zero*** tends to be avoided in specific usage, where the positive zero article is usually negated by ***not + any***:

(129) a. I saw children in the street. [positive]
I didn't see any children in the street. [negative]
b. She had make-up on her face. [positive]
She didn't have any make-up on her face. [negative]

Note the difference between the negative in (129)b. and the sentence in (127)b.:

(130) a. She didn't have any make-up on her face.
Sie trug keine Schminke im Gesicht (ihr Gesicht war ungeschminkt).
b. She didn't have make-up on her face.
Schminke war's nicht, was sie im Gesicht hatte.

A further negative alternative in (129) – though certainly not in (128) – is provided by ***no*** (see **024/7.6**).

Not + zero does **not** occur in initial position or after *there is/are* (**Not children were in the street; *There weren't children in the street*).

024/7.5 not + indefinite article

The negative of ***a/an*** is ***not + a/an***. It is the most common ***singular count*** equivalent of ***not + any*** (included for comparison in the following examples):

(131) a. We didn't have an umbrella with us.
Wir hatten keinen Regenschirm dabei.
b. We didn't have any umbrellas with us.
Wir hatten keine Regenschirme dabei.
c. The committee didn't make a statement.
... gab keinen Kommentar.
d. The committee didn't make any statements.
... gab keine Kommentare.

It is also used for ***generalizations*** and other forms of ***generic*** utterance, and is then the ***singular count*** equivalent of ***not + zero***:

(132) a. I don't read a daily newspaper.
Ich lese keine Tageszeitung.
b. My son doesn't wear a helmet for cycling.
Mein Sohn setzt zum Radfahren keinen Helm auf.

It is the only possible form in references to type or category that concern ***identification***:

(133) a. Martha doesn't work in an office (= it is a different type of environment that she works in).
Martha arbeitet nicht in einem Büro.
b. The robbers did not escape in a car (but on foot).
Die Räuber flohen nicht in einem Auto, sondern zu Fuß.

This is particularly the case with the verb *to be*:

(134) a. Mr. Mercury is not a good teacher.
... ist kein guter Lehrer.
b. That is not a dog, but a cat.
Das ist kein Hund, sondern eine Katze.
c. I was a government official, but not a politician.
Ich war Regierungsbeamter, aber kein Politiker.

Like its 'partners', ***not + a/an*** is generally avoided in subject position. A notable exception is when there is special emphasis, often heightened by adjectives like *single, solitary*, etc.:

(135) a. Not a (single) word was said.
b. Not a single pupil had done the homework.

An alternative here is ***not + one*** (often with partitive ***of*** in reference to a specific group):

(136) a. Not one word was said.
b. Not one pupil (not one of the pupils) had done the homework.

Another alternative in unspecific references is ***no***: *No word was said* (see next section).

024/7.6 no

No can occur with all noun types. It is a further ***whole-group negative*** of ***all***, meaning ***not + any***. But it can also negate ***singular count*** nouns, and is then equivalent to ***not + a/an***. The German translation, again, is *keine/r/s*.

No functions exclusively as a ***determiner***. The accompanying verb-form is ***positive***. The negation is therefore focused on one word, which gives the negative meaning more prominence and emphasis (as with ***none***). In initial position, it is used mainly for generalized (i.e. unspecific) meaning:

(137) a. No cats like dogs.
b. No sympathy was given.
c. No friend would say a thing like that.

This position stresses the negative with particular force. It is often found in formal or official language, especially for announcements and warnings on public notices. Gerunds and participles are also common here when the message is a prohibition:

(138) a. No children under 12 allowed in the hotel bar.
b. No dogs are permitted on the beach.
c. No trains will run tomorrow between Cannon Street and London Bridge.
d. No smoking/no fishing/no trespassing/no parking/no entry, etc.

Introductory ***there is/are*** creates a less emphatic, more neutral tone, and is often preferred in normal language. The negated noun then follows, with the main body of the message placed in a postmodification:

(139) a. There will be no trains running tomorrow between Cannon Street and London Bridge.
b. There are no shops in this area that sell furniture.
c. There were no children playing in the street at that time.

This is the usual form for group-specific reference (where the initial position is generally avoided):

(140) There are no students from America in the group.

In other sentence positions ***no*** has a less forceful effect, and is more common. But it still has greater emphasis (and slightly more formality) than ***not any***:

(141) a. We were hungry, but we didn't have any food with us. [neutral]
We were hungry, but we had no food with us. [more emphatic]
b. She didn't give us any personal information. [neutral]
She gave us no personal information. [more emphatic]

Everything said so far applies equally to ***singular count nouns***: i.e. the initial position is possible for emphasis, but preference in ordinary usage is for ***there is***:

(142) a. There was no word said.
b. There is no table in the kitchen.
c. There will be no doctor on duty here this evening.
Heute Abend wird hier kein Arzt Dienst haben.

As with non-count and plural nouns, ***no*** occurs more often in the object function than the subject function. Here, too, though, it is more emphatic and formal than the ***not***-equivalent:

(143) a. We had no umbrella with us. [emphatic]
b. We didn't have an umbrella with us. [neutral]
c. The committee made no statement. [emphatic]
d. The committee didn't make a statement. [neutral]

As a reminder: the German equivalent of both versions is *keine/r/s*.

024/7.7 no: errors and restrictions on use

There is a tendency for German speakers to use ***no*** as a general equivalent of *keine/r/s*. ⚠ This leads to errors, firstly, in style: ***no*** should ***not*** be used unless there is a special need for emphasis, and/or formality.

Secondly, as we have seen, it ***cannot*** be used in ***identifying*** references. German *keine/r/s* must be rendered in this case by ***not + zero*** or ***not + a/an***:

(144) a. Those are not goats; they are sheep.
Das sind keine Ziegen, sondern Schafe.
b. They were not drinking beer, but wine.
Sie tranken kein Bier, sondern Wein.
c. I am not in a bad mood!
Ich habe keine schlechte Laune!
d. Einstein was a scientist, not a politician.
Einstein war Naturwissenschaftler und kein Politiker.

Indefinite quantifiers 025

025/1 some
025/2 any
025/3 much/many/a lot of
025/4 little/few/a little/a few/several
025/5 more/most, less/least, fewer/fewest

Indefinite quantifiers are a further form of ***indefinite reference***, as the name suggests. In a similar way to the zero article, they function as a 'version' of the indefinite article with ***plurals*** and ***non-count singulars***. In addition, however, they specify certain 'levels' of quantity, mainly in the general sense of 'a big amount' or 'a small amount'.

025/1 some

Of all the words in this group, ***some*** is closest in use to that of the indefinite article. It means 'an unspecified, but small quantity of', and occurs with both ***plurals*** and ***non-count singulars***. The plural meaning is 'three or more':

025/1.1 As a determiner

(145) a. A car stopped and some people got out.
… und Leute stiegen aus.
b. I'm going to buy some fish for supper.
Ich kaufe Fisch zum Abendessen.

As seen from the translations, the normal, neutral German equivalent is the zero article. This is also possible in English, of course, but would usually shift the focus to the ***generic*** meaning, i.e. to the ***phenomenon*** itself:

(146) a. I'm going to buy fish for supper (i.e. not meat or anything else).
b. We're police officers (that's our job/function).

(For ***generic*** meaning, see also **022/1.2** above). Compare, again:

(147) a. Mave keeps goats in her back-garden (that's her hobby/that's why the grass is short).
b. Mave keeps some goats in her back-garden (so don't be surprised when you see them!).

025/1.2 As a partitive pre-determiner

This means part of an identified larger quantity:

(148) a. Some of her books are still in the cellar.
Manche/einige ihrer Bücher …
b. I think I'd like some of that coffee!
Ich glaube, ich hätte gern etwas von dem Kaffee da!

Partitive use occurs frequently when there is a contrast with the rest of a particular group: *Some of Mary's books are still in the cellar, but most are now in her study* (see also under **025/1.4**).

025/1.3 As a pronoun

(149) a. All the guests wore carnival costumes. Some were fantastic!
Einige/manche waren ...
b. We've just made some soup. Would you like some?
... Hättest du gern davon?

025/1.4 some in contrast to others, many, all, etc.

As a determiner, ***some*** in this meaning is usually generic:

(150) a. Some people don't like dogs, but others love them.
b. Some cars nowadays run on biological fuel.

Otherwise, with particularized groups, the ***partitive*** use is preferred:

(151) a. The fire damaged some of the paintings, but most were unharmed.
b. Some of the films we saw last year were interesting, but many were boring.

In this meaning ***some*** is usually stressed: *'some people ..., 'some cars ..., 'some of the paintings ...*, etc., and also as a pronoun: *'Some were fantastic.*

025/1.5 Special meanings of some

Some is commonly used (particularly informally) in the sense of 'rather a lot'. In this case it is also stressed: *I've had this job for 'some years now* (i.e. *quite a lot*); *It's 'some distance from London to Brighton* (i.e. *quite a long way*). Another use is with ***singular count nouns*** referring to persons or things that are not exactly known: *For some reason she left the party early; He works at some bank (or other) in London; Barbara married some cowboy from the Midwest.*

025/1.6 Compounds of some as indefinite pronouns

These are ***someone/somebody*** and ***something***. ***Somewhere*** is the corresponding ***indefinite adverb***. Their meaning actually derives from the *unknown/unspecified* sense of ***some*** just mentioned in **1.5**:

(152) a. Someone has broken our garden gate (= an assumed person of unknown identity – dt. *irgendwer*).
b. Look, there's something lying over there in the grass (= a particular object, but not yet identified – dt. *irgendwas*).
c. Dick lives somewhere in Liverpool (= at an unknown place – dt. *irgendwo*).

025/2 any

Any is used as a ***determiner***, ***partitive pre-determiner***, ***pronoun*** and ***adverb***. We have already encountered it in the negative collocation ***not any*** (= ***none***), and will now look at other, similar uses. All of these stem from the same basic meaning, which is a little abstract. On the one hand, ***any*** has a certain similarity to ***all/every***, i.e. it refers to the whole of a category or group. It does so, however, in a way that makes it different not only from these two, but also from all the other distributives: on its own, ***any*** does not give an exact quantity, but rather ***a range of possibility***. It therefore tends to have a certain speculative character.

025/2.1 As equivalent to the zero article (determiner)

With ***plurals*** and ***non-count*** nouns, ***any*** means 'at least one' or 'the smallest amount' of the entity named: *any children = at least one child; any blood = at least a very small (the smallest) amount or quantity.*

The emphasis here is on a manifestation of the phenomenon itself, i.e. on a sign of its existence. In this meaning, ***any*** is used only ***after negatives*** (i.e. as ***not any***, see above), and in ***questions***. It does not occur in positive statements, nor, in this case, with singular count nouns.

(153) a. Were there any children at the wedding? (= Was the phenomenon/category 'child' represented at the wedding?)
Waren Kinder auf der Hochzeit?
b. Did you see any blood on the carpet?
Haben Sie (irgendwelche) Blutspuren auf dem Teppich gesehen?

Any therefore means the same here as the ***zero article*** (see also **022/3** above). The ***zero article*** is also possible (*Were there children at the wedding?; Did you see blood on the carpet?*), but ***any*** is usually preferred, as it is more emphatic.

An exception is with references to ***identification***. Here the ***zero article*** is obligatory:

(154) a. Were the guests eating meat? (= Was it meat they were eating, or something else?)
Aßen die Gäste Fleisch?
b. Are they Catholics?
Sind sie Katholiken?

025/2.2 In 'hidden' or implied negatives and questions

Any occurs in several kinds of positive statements that imply questions or negatives:

- ***indirect questions:*** *She asked if there were any flights to Scotland in the afternoon.*
- **if*-clauses implying doubt or uncertainty:*** *If we have any money left after the holiday, we'll buy a new carpet.*
- ***with negative adverbs, prepositions, conjunctions:*** *I rarely (seldom, never, etc.) do any sport these days; Try and write the letter without making any spelling mistakes, Peter; Let's interrupt the meeting here for a short coffee break – unless there are any objections.*
- ***consecutive clauses after*** **too:** *I was too surprised to make any protest.*

025/2.3 In group-specific reference (determiner, partitive pre-determiner)

(155) a. Were any (of the) guests at the party eating meat?
Aßen irgendwelche (der) Gäste Fleisch?
b. Has Roger seen any of his close friends lately?
Hat Roger in letzter Zeit (irgendwelche) enge(n) Freunde getroffen?

025/2.4 As an adverb

Any features sometimes as an ***adverb*** before ***comparatives***. The normal conditions for ***any*** must apply, i.e. only in questions, negatives, or ***if***-clauses of the kind just shown under **2.1** and **2.2**:

(156) a. Jill doesn't seem to have got any older.
Jill scheint kein bisschen älter geworden zu sein.
b. If I eat any more cake, I'll burst!
Wenn ich noch ein Stück Kuchen esse, platze ich!
c. Any more wine, Sir?
Noch Wein, mein Herr?
d. Can't you drive any faster, Cecil? We're late enough, as it is!
Kannst du nicht etwas schneller fahren ...?

One or two adjectives combine idiomatically with ***any*** in their ordinary forms. This also applies to the noun *use*:

(157) a. Nice to see you again, Fred! You don't look any different!
... Du hast dich kein bisschen verändert.
b. This bread-knife isn't any good/any use. It's blunt.
Dieses Brotmesser taugt nichts. Es ist stumpf.

025/2.5 In the meaning 'of whatever kind' (determiner)

A slightly different (though related) sense of ***any*** is 'of whatever kind' or 'it does not matter which':

(158) a. You can buy any beer you like (= You can choose the type/brand/quantity yourself).
Du kannst jedes Bier kaufen, das du willst.
b. Any flowers will do, just as long as they are red or yellow (= it doesn't matter what kind they are, but they should be red or yellow).

In this case, ***any*** is usually stressed when spoken. It can also be used in this sense with ***singular count*** nouns, and means 'a member of the named group, but no particular one':

(159) a. Ask any doctor and he'll tell you the same thing.
Frage irgendeinen Arzt und er wird dir das Gleiche sagen.
b. If you have any problem, let me know.
Wenn du irgendein Problem hast, sag Bescheid.

This can be regarded as a stressed form of the ***indefinite article*** in its unspecific use. Less emphatically, that is, we could render (159) as: *Ask a doctor, and he'll tell you …; If you have a problem …*

025/2.6 Differences between any and every

Sometimes there appears to be no difference between ***any*** and ***every***. Certain contexts will allow either without changing the overall meaning.

(160) a. Any decision taken on this question must involve the workers themselves.
b. Every decision taken on this question must involve the workers themselves.

Both versions can be rendered in German by *jede Entscheidung*. Nevertheless, the basic semantic distinction between ***any*** and ***every*** remains even here, and affects the interpretation of each sentence in a different way.

(160)b. assumes in advance that there will be a number of decisions (i.e. at least three). (160)a., on the other hand, leaves not only the number open, but also the possibility that there may not even be one. It has the force of a conditional clause: *Falls Entscheidungen gefällt werden, dann müssen die Arbeiter daran beteiligt sein.*

Even in reference to known events (e.g. in the past), ***any*** is used when the speaker does not mean a definite number, or is stating a general truth or principle. ***Every*** is reserved for specific cases:

(161) a. Any player who broke the rules was expelled from the club.
(= If a player broke the rules, then …).
b. Every player who broke the rules was expelled from the club.
(= There were a number who broke the rules, and all of them were expelled).

Because of its more speculative or conditional meaning in positive statements, ***any*** does not make sense in situations where something is assumed to occur definitely and without exception:

(162) a. Every golfer must report to the clubhouse before beginning a round.
Jeder Golfspieler muss sich im Vereinsbüro melden, bevor er mit einer Runde beginnt.
b. *Any golfer must report to the clubhouse before beginning a round.

Here, of course, it must be supposed that all those who come to the golf club are golfers, and will at some point begin a round. As there are no exceptions, ***any*** cannot be used. Compare this with *Any guest player must be accompanied by a member.* Here we have the conditional-type meaning once more (*Eventuelle Gastspieler müssen in Begleitung eines Clubmitglieds sein*), and ***any*** is permissible.

025/2.7 Compounds of any as indefinite pronouns

These are similar to those of other quantifiers, i.e. ***anyone/anybody*** and ***anything***, with ***anywhere*** as the main ***indefinite adverb***.

(163) a. Has anybody seen my dog? (= a person of whatever identity – dt. *irgendeiner/ irgend jemand/wer auch immer*)
b. Look, there isn't anything lying over there in the grass (= no object whatever, nothing – dt. *Da drüben liegt nichts …*).
c. Dick doesn't live anywhere in Liverpool (= at no place in Liverpool – dt. … *wohnt überhaupt nicht in … / … wohnt nirgendwo in …*).

Two further ***any***-related adverbs are *anyhow* and *anyway*. However, these are not indefinite adverbs in the semantic sense, and therefore play no part here.

025/2.8 Differences between any and some

Questions are the main source of confusion here. Although ***any*** is typically associated with questions, there are certain kinds that require ***some***. Compare:

(164) a. Aren't you going to buy any brushes?
b. Aren't you going to buy some brushes?
c. Did you leave any money in the car?
d. Did you leave some money in the car?
e. Would you like any wine?
f. Would you like some wine?
g. Does Dick live anywhere in Yorkshire?
h. Does Dick live somewhere in Yorkshire?

In general, ***some*** is used to refer to ***specific*** things: these are present, for example, in the situation or in the speaker's mind (perhaps because they have already been mentioned). (164)b., for instance, might refer to a plan which the listener has forgotten (dt. *Du willst/ wolltest doch Pinsel kaufen, oder?*). (164)d. implies that a certain sum of money has been found or seen in the car and the questioner wants to find out who it belongs to. (164)f. refers to wine that is present and accessible for the listener, e.g. on the table in front of him. Similarly, (164)h. would be used if the questioner had a reason for thinking that Dick lives in Yorkshire, e.g. because of his accent or the fact that he has mentioned the county several times before.

The ***any***-variants are more theoretical and less concrete or specific in reference. (164)a., for example, would not refer to particular brushes or to a previous plan. It could just be a reaction, reminding somebody who has bought paint that brushes are also generally necessary for painting. (164)c. could be prompted by the wish not to have valuables or money left in the car because of possible thieves. If it is the waiter who is offering wine, he will use (164)e., to avoid appearing too definite or pushy. The difference here is between a strong invitation by a private host (***some** of **this** wine – Do have some*!) and a more discreet and neutral offer by a person who is selling a range of services (***any***). Whereas (164)h. could be a guess about Dick based on specific evidence, the ***anywhere***-variant is simply a neutral call for information: ... *because if he does live there, he may be a victim of the terrible weather conditions in Yorkshire at the moment.*

025/3 much/many/a lot of

These refer to high quantities, and all express German *viel*. ***Much*** goes with ***singular non-count*** nouns (*much tea, much paper*); ***many*** is used with ***plural count nouns*** (*many books, many places*); ***a lot of*** occurs with both (*a lot of paper, a lot of books*).

⚠ As German *viel* is used for singular and plural, there is a tendency among German speakers to forget the singular-plural distinction of ***much*** and ***many***. The most common error is to use ***much*** for plurals (**much books*).

025/3.1 Usage

In ordinary everyday language ***much*** and ***many*** occur only in ***questions*** and ***negatives***:

(165) a. Have you got many students in your classes?
b. Has Brian done much work for his exams?
c. We don't have many visitors these days.
d. Sharon didn't earn much money as a waitress.

Positive statements use mainly ***a lot of***:

(166) a. I have a lot of students in my classes.
b. Brian has done a lot of work for his exams.

We cannot say here **Brian has done much work ...*, unless using a marked poetic style. ***Many***, however, ***is*** found in positive statements in more normal, though slightly more formal style: *I have many students in my classes.*

A lot of is used everywhere, i.e. not only in positive statements, but also in negatives and questions.

025/3.2 Syntax

All three expressions occur as ***determiners***, ***partitive pre-determiners***, and ***pronouns*** (***a lot*** then without the preposition). ***A lot*** and ***much*** can also be ***adverbs***:

(167) a. Are many of/a lot of the students at your college English majors? [***partitive pre-determiners***]
b. Yes, many/a lot are. [***pronouns***]

c. I didn't sleep much/a lot last night. [***adverbs***]
d. We don't have many/a lot of visitors these days. [***determiners***]

As adverbs, ***a lot*** and ***much*** can premodify adjectives and adverbs in ***comparative forms*** (see chapter 4); ***much*** can also intensify ***too*** in ***consecutive constructions*** (see chapter 14): *a lot more successful; much faster; much too expensive.*

025/4 little/few/a little/a few/several

025/4.1 little/few

Little is the opposite of ***much***, and is similarly used with ***singular non-count*** nouns: *little sleep, little wood, little love.*

Few is the plural equivalent and is the opposite of ***many***: *few books, few places.*

The German rendering of both is *wenig.*

In contrast to ***much*** and ***many***, ***little*** and ***few*** are not restricted to questions or negatives. Quite the contrary: because of their meanings, ***little*** and ***few*** tend to occur mainly in positive statements: *I had little sleep last night; Few people attend our meetings nowadays.* The style is slightly formal. Everyday language prefers ***not much*** and ***not many***: *I didn't have much sleep last night; Not many people attend out meetings nowadays.*

Syntactically, ***little*** and ***few*** behave in the same way as ***much*** and ***many***:

(168) a. She ate little of the food/few of the sandwiches that she had brought. [***partitive pre-determiners***]
b. Many (people/cinema-goers) like action films and romances, but few are interested in political dramas, and cinemas do little to encourage this. [***pronouns***]
c. During our journey we slept and ate little. [***adverb***]
d. We have few visitors and little excitement these days. [***determiners***]

025/4.2 a little/a few

These behave grammatically in the same way as ***little*** and ***few***, and also mean 'a small amount/number of', but in a slightly different sense, just like their German equivalents *ein wenig/etwas/einige/ein paar*:

(169) a. She ate a little of the food/a few of the sandwiches that she had brought. [***partitive pre-determiners***]
b. All her love affairs have been romantic, and a few even dramatic. [***pronoun***]
c. "Would you like a little wine, Daphne?" "A little, Tom. Thank you." [***determiner, pronoun***]
d. "And how about a few nuts?" "Well, yes, just a few. Thank you." [***determiner, pronoun***]
e. "I think I'll try and sleep a little." "Alright, Mother. I'll wake you when we arrive." [***adverb***]

Whereas ***little/few*** stress that the quantity is small rather than large, ***a little/a few*** stress 'some', rather than 'none at all', or pick out a small quantity from a larger one, as in (169)a., b., c., and d.

As an adverb, ***a little*** can premodify adjectives and adverbs: *After three glasses of wine, Daphne's face had turned a little red; You're driving a little fast, Henry!*

It can also precede ***comparative forms*** and ***consecutive constructions*** (see also ***much*** and ***a lot*** above): *a little more successful; a little faster; a little too expensive.*

A colloquial version of ***a little*** is ***a bit*** (dt. *ein bisschen*), used in particular as an adverb: *I think I'll try and sleep a bit; a bit red; a bit more successful; a bit faster; a bit too expensive.*

025/4.3 several

Several combines only with ***plural count*** nouns. It functions as a ***determiner, partitive pre-determiner***, and ***pronoun***, and means 'a small number, but more than three'. The German equivalent is *mehrere*: *I called them several times, but they were out; Several neighbours were standing around Briony's car, pointing at the wheels; Several of my students are going to America this year; There are also several in Canada at the moment.*

Several means roughly the same as ***a few***, but tends to indicate an individual number and stress that it is 'larger than just one, two or three'.

025/5 more/most, less/least, fewer/fewest

These are ***comparative*** and ***superlative*** forms of all quantifiers, including numerals. That is, they mean 'a larger or smaller quantity than the quantity mentioned'. They too are used as ***determiners, partitive pre-determiners*** and ***pronouns***, and in addition (except ***fewer/fewest***) also as ***adverbs***. It is important to note that ***less*** refers to ***singular non-count nouns*** and ***fewer*** to ***plural count nouns***. ***More*** and ***most*** are not restricted. ***Most*** can mean 'almost all', or 'the larger proportion of':

(170) a. We eat more/less meat now than in the past. [***determiner***]
Wir essen jetzt mehr/weniger Fleisch als früher.
b. Sue plays a lot of tennis, but Charles plays even more. [***pronoun***]
c. There were fewer than ten people at the ceremony. [***pronoun***]
... weniger als zehn Leute ...
d. I've cleared most of the empty bottles out of the cellar.
... die meisten Flaschen ... [***partitive pre-determiner***]
e. I sleep least when I'm working on a book, and most when I'm on holiday. [***adverbs***]

⚠ Danger signals for German speakers are the superlatives ***most*** and ***least***. Unlike the German equivalents, these are not normally preceded by the definite article before nouns (unless, that is, they form a superlative adjective), i.e. *most people* and not **the most people, most of the empty bottles*, and not **the most empty bottles*. There are one or two exceptions to this rule, but these are dealt with in the next chapter, where we look at comparative and superlative forms in detail.

Chapter 4 Adjectives

Basic features 026

A further class of word typically associated with nouns and noun phrases is the ***adjective***. This is a descriptive element which refers to the ***characteristics*** of nouns: *the **yellow** rose, a **clean** kitchen, the **large** garden, **big** trees, two **small** boys.*

Together with other members of the noun phrase, adjectives are ***morphologically invariant***: as there is no grammatical gender or case in English, adjectives do not have grammatical endings depending on the noun they relate to. This applies also to the plural. Adjectives have the same form in singular and plural. Another point is that like the members of other word-classes, adjectives have no definite or obligatory form. As individual words, many cannot be distinguished from nouns or verbs. However, there are certain ***suffixes*** (i.e. endings) which are only found with adjectives and which do occur with quite a large number, e.g. *-ful* (*wonderful*), *-able* (*capable*), *-ive* (*aggressive*).

Another grammatical phenomenon typical of adjectives is the category called ***comparison***: *dangerous* (***base form***), *more dangerous* (***comparative***), *most dangerous* (***superlative***). This reflects the fact that many characteristics referred to by adjectives can be thought of as being more, or less, intense. A similar aspect is that many (though certainly not all) adjectives occur with ***adverbs of degree***: *very good, quite right, rather awkward.* Adjectives like this are said to be ***gradable***.

A general semantic feature of many individual adjectives is that they can combine with some noun-types but not others, although the meaning is similar. For example one speaks of *heavy rain* but *strong winds,* of *weak tea,* but *thin soup.* A meal containing spices like fire is said to be *hot*; without them, it would be *mild*; wine can be *sweet* or *dry*. Milk that is no longer fresh might be *sour*; butter in the same state would be *rancid,* and lemons are described as *sharp*. Combinations like these are known as ***collocations***. They are one element (among others) in the idiomatic quality of language.

Finally, there is a strong association between ***adjectives*** and ***adverbs***. In some senses they are two grammatical sides of the same coin: both have a descriptive function semantically, but ***adjectives*** relate to ***nouns***, whereas ***adverbs*** relate typically to ***verbs*** and ***adjectives***.

027 The syntax of adjectives

027/1 Position and function

Adjectives occur in two major syntactic positions: firstly, ***attributive***, i.e. inside noun phrases, as part of the ***premodification***; and secondly ***predicative***, i.e. in the sentence functions of ***subject complement*** (**Cs**), or ***object complement*** (**Co**):

(1) a. two ***small*** boys [***attributive***, part of the ***premodification***]
b. The boys were ***small***. [***predicative***, as **Cs**]
c. The food made the guests ***ill***. [***predicative***, as **Co**]

Most adjectives appear in both positions, but some are confined to one or the other. For example, *well* is ***predicative-restricted***, i.e. we can say *He is well*, but not **a well person*. The adjective *entire* is ***attributive-restricted***, i.e. we can say *the entire world*, but not **The world is entire*. Certain other adjectives are confined to a particular position in one of their meanings only. For example, *old* is ***attributive-restricted*** in the meaning 'former, belonging to the past', as in *my old firm* (= *the one I used to work at*). In the ordinary meaning (= *not young, advanced in age*) it can appear in either position.

When used ***attributively***, i.e. inside noun phrases, adjectives generally ***premodify*** their noun. But there are some cases where the adjective ***postmodifies*** it, e.g. *the tickets available* (*die verfügbaren Karten*), *the managers responsible* (*die verantwortlichen Manager*). As we will see later, many adjectives which are otherwise ***predicative-restricted*** can be used ***attributively*** when they occur in ***postmodifying*** position.

Regarding sentence function, an adjective typically takes the role of ***subject complement*** or ***object complement***, as shown above in (1); also possible, though less frequent, is the role of ***adverbial***:

Adverbial (A)

(2) Last night Sandra came home ***angry***.

Details on all of these points are given further below.

027/2 The adjective phrase

Like nouns, adjectives themselves can combine with certain other elements to form a grammatical unit or ***phrase***, in this case an ***adjective phrase***. Typical members of adjective phrases are adverbs of degree (*very ill, too fat*) and prepositional expressions (*blue with cold, good at maths*). Here it is the ***adjective***, of course, that is the ***head***; elements preceding the head are called the ***premodification*** (as in a noun phrase); those following the head form the ***adjectival complement***:

	Premodification	*Head*	*Adjectival Complement*
(3)	very	good	at maths
	quite	content	with the results
	rather	envious	of his friend's luck

As with noun phrases (and any others), it is the ***phrase as a whole*** that fills any given syntactic function:

		Subject Complement (Cs)	
(4)	a. Roger became	*rather envious of his friend's luck.*	
		Direct Object (Od)	***Object Complement (Co)***
	b. The lottery win made	Roger	*rather envious of his friend's luck.*
		Adverbial (A)	
	c. Joan started her new job	*full of enthusiasm.*	

Adjective meaning and adjective grammar 028

028/1 Common semantic categories

Most adjectives can be categorised in the following areas of meaning: dimension and volume (e.g. *thick, fat, short, round, weak, wealthy*); colour and light (*pink, blue, bright*); material and texture (*woollen, sandy, wet, smooth*); other sensory qualities (*sweet, smelly, hot*); time, age and condition (*recent, old, new, fresh*); movement and process (*fast, direct, brisk, sluggish*); origin and type (*French, Asian, Expressionist*); behaviour (*cruel, quiet, awkward*); feelings and disposition (*well, ill, faint, relaxed, afraid, brave*); general evaluation (*good, nice, nasty, inconvenient*).

These semantic groupings are not defined exactly and may sometimes partly overlap or shade into one another. *Cruel, smelly, intelligent* and *weak*, for example, in addition to their basic semantic types, also carry evaluative meanings. Other adjectives have more than one meaning, and because of that belong to different semantic categories at the same time.

Although rather vague and general, such semantic categorization makes sense, as it is relevant grammatically in several ways. For example, two or more adjectives premodifying a noun tend to occur in a certain ***sequence of meaning***. Secondly, semantics affect the

gradability of an adjective, explained below in section **028/8**. Thirdly, meaning can influence the ***position*** of an adjective in a sentence. Fourthly, semantics determine certain relations to other word-classes. For example, some adjective types are closely related in meaning to adverbs; others function like nouns, while nouns, on the other hand, can be used under certain meaning conditions like adjectives; so, too, can participles, numerals and quantifiers. Finally, many adjectives denoting origin and type function as ***proper adjectives*** (with grammatical consequences for spelling).

Within these general categories there are important variations.

028/2 Some special sub-types

We will turn now in more detail to certain sub-types. Most of the following belong to the general ***dimension*** category. But they have a common feature distinguishing them from others in the same group: they do not refer to intrinsic qualities but to ***relational*** ones. That is, they characterize the entity externally, in its connection to other entities, or to roles in particular contexts:

028/2.1 Quantity

the whole cake, my one friend, the three ducks

Numerals and other quantifiers (e.g. *many, few,* etc.) can function as adjectives, as well as determiners.

028/2.2 Sequence

first, second, third

Ordinal numerals function mainly as adjectives and adverbs, together with other expressions of sequence, such as *last, next,* etc.

028/2.3 With action-related nouns

a great believer, a strong swimmer, a hard worker, a heavy smoker, a big liar

The adjectives here refer to actions, and are therefore equivalent to adverbs and adverbial expressions: *a hard worker = someone who works hard; a big liar = someone who lies a lot; a heavy smoker = someone who smokes heavily,* etc.

028/2.4 Intensifiers

the very thought, complete nonsense, utter rubbish, an absolute lie, a total stranger, sheer laziness, mere chance

These emphasize qualities expressed in the noun and mean 'extremely' or 'nothing but', which gives them a certain adverbial sense: *a total stranger = someone who is totally strange/unknown; the very thought* = dt. *schon der Gedanke; mere chance = only/nothing but chance.*

In many contexts intensifiers tend to express speaker-attitudes and therefore have a certain modal coloration. Besides dimension, that is, they can express ***evaluation***.

028/2.5 Adjectives of degree

a close relative, his best friend, a reasonable effort, a hopeless case, a distant acquaintance

028/2.6 Focus adjectives

a particular case, the sole reason, the same child, the main factor, the only guests

These profile individual entities and also clarify and identify: *his exact address, the real problem, the actual difficulty, the very thing* (*very* in this case meaning 'exactly that one').

028/2.7 Time adjectives

an old friend, my old boss, her present job, Sally's former husband, our past life, a late film

028/2.8 Modal adjectives

poor John, dear Anne, little Dorrit

These are variants within the category of ***general evaluation***. They show positive or negative speaker attitudes, but without actually referring to them explicitly. *Poor*, for example, conveys sympathy, *dear* affection and *little* both affection and protectiveness. Adjectives of this type often occur with names, but also with common nouns, especially in colloquial language: *old Tom* (*der gute Tom*), *the bloody lawnmower* (*der Scheißrasenmäher*), *my stupid car* (*mein blödes Auto*).

028/3 Adjective position: attributive only

Generally speaking, ***attributive-restricted*** adjectives are the types listed in 028/2, those that is, with ***relational*** rather than ***intrinsic*** meanings. This does not apply to all cases, certainly, but it does to most.

028/3.1 Quantity

the three ducks → **The ducks are three.*

Similar ***attributive-restricted*** example: *entire* in the sense of *whole*.

Exceptions: *whole* in the sense of *intact/not damaged* (dt. *heil*): *None of the cups were whole* (= all were damaged in some way); *Few* and *many* in rather poetic and old-fashioned use sometimes occur predicatively: *His talents were few and his faults many*.

Ordinal numerals and other expressions of sequence all occur predicatively: *Britta was next and I was last*.

028/3.2 All 'adverbial', action-referring adjectives

the heavy smoker ≠ The smoker is heavy; the strong swimmer ≠ The swimmer is strong.

The adjectives *heavy* and *strong* (and several others here), have other meanings of an intrinsic kind, of course, which naturally allow either position, e.g. *The swimmer is strong* (= has a lot of strength); *The smoker is heavy* (= weighs a lot).

028/3.3 Intensifiers

complete nonsense → **The nonsense is complete*. Other meanings, of course, can be intrinsic, and allow both positions: *the complete set of paintings* → *The set of paintings is complete.*

028/3.4 Adjectives of degree

his best friend ≠ *His friend is best*. Exceptions: *reasonable, hopeless*

028/3.5 Focus adjectives

a particular case → **The case is particular; the real problem* ≠ *The problem is real.*

028/3.6 Time adjectives

an old friend/my old boss ≠ *The friend/My boss is old.*

028/3.7 Modal adjectives

poor John ≠ *John is poor.*

028/4 Adjective position: predicative only

The following are ***predicative-restricted***:

028/4.1 All adjectives with complements (e.g. prepositional expressions)

He was keen on fishing → **A keen on fishing person*

028/4.2 Adjectives with the prefix a-

afraid, alight (*brennend*), *alike* (*gleich, ähnlich*), *alive* (*lebendig*), *alone, asleep, awake*, etc.

028/4.3 A few adjectives referring to health

ill, poorly, well, unwell, fine

For attributive use these have to be replaced by equivalents: *The people are ill* → *the sick people; My health is fine* → *I'm in good health.*

028/4.4 Some adjectives referring to feelings and other mental states

content, glad, upset, sorry, certain, sure.

Again, attributive use requires equivalents: *The passengers were glad* → *the happy passengers.*

Some of these have attributive uses in particular senses, especially with things rather than people (e.g. *a certain cure for an upset stomach*).

028/4.5 Several adjectives referring to size and distance

near, far, close. The station is near/far/close → *the nearby/distant station*

028/4.6 A few focus adjectives – exceptionally – belong here too

responsible, present, involved, concerned, etc.

An important point to note is that some ***predicative-restricted*** adjectives can be used ***attributively*** in ***postmodifying*** position (see **027/1** above). Adjectives with complements, for instance (e.g. **A keen on fishing person,* see above), are permissible in ***attributive*** function when they ***follow*** the noun, e.g. *a person keen on fishing*. This is because ***postmodifying*** adjectives (although ***attributive***) are derived from ***predicative*** use. They are the result of a phenomenon we call ***clause reduction***, explained in the next two sections.

028/5 Clause reduction

Clause reduction is a general feature affecting subordinate clauses. Certain types of clause are reduced to phrases by the ellipsis (i.e. omission) of subject and predicator. ***Adjectives***, especially, are involved in ***clause-reduction***:

(5) a. ***If possible***, could you tell me tomorrow?
(= if ***it is*** possible ...)
b. ***Although very nervous***, Claire spoke loudly and clearly.
(= although ***she was*** nervous ...)
c. Fish should be eaten only ***when completely fresh***.
(= only when ***it is*** completely fresh)

Apart from the conjunction, then, the subordinate clause is reduced here to the adjective phrase. In the full clause, this functioned as ***subject complement***. Now it represents a whole clause. Syntactically the clause remains, and is known in this case as a ***verbless clause*** (in the function of ***adverbial***). Other examples are:

(6) a. ***Certain of the facts***, I spoke confidently to the police.
b. We went to bed ***hungry***. (see also (2) above)

These, then, are examples of ***adjective phrases*** functioning (with or without conjunctions) as ***clauses***. What is relevant here is the connection between ***clause reduction*** and ***adjective position***. This has to do with the fact that ***clause reduction*** also affects ***relative clauses*** (see also chapter 14):

(7) a. The village was a place ***full of old-world charm***.
(= ... a place ***which was*** full ...)
b. I know a man ***famous for breeding monkeys***.
(= ... a man ***who is*** famous ...)
c. We need a lady ***willing to clean for us on just one day a week***.
(= ... a lady ***who is*** willing ...)

With ***relative clause reduction***, adjectives used ***predicatively*** in the full relative clause (i.e. as subject complement) now become ***attributive*** – but in ***postmodifying*** position. This offers an attributive solution particularly for adjectives with complements, which cannot appear in premodifying position, as we have already seen. The majority of postmodifying attributives are, in fact, adjectives with complements, as in (7). Otherwise, the usual attributive position for all adjectives is the premodifying one, i.e. before the noun. There are one or two exceptions, however, and these are shown in the next section.

028/6 Attributive postmodification

Attributive postmodification affects the following cases:

028/6.1 Predicative-restricted adjectives with complements

Adjectives that are otherwise ***predicative-restricted*** can become ***attributive***, as we have just seen, by ***relative clause reduction***, which converts them into ***attributive postmodifiers***. This is most common with complemented adjectives, i.e. the type we have just been discussing, mentioned also under **028/4.1**:

(8) a. This is a road notorious for its traffic congestion.
b. He was a man capable of anything.

028/6.2 Predicative-restricted adjectives with an a-prefix

This type is listed under **028/4.2**:

(9) a. A traveller alone travels farthest.
b. Children asleep are like angels.

028/6.3 General, non-restricted adjectives

A few non-restricted adjectives, mainly ending in *-ed* and *-able/-ible* can be used in both ***premodifying*** and ***postmodifying*** positions:

(10) a. Please inform us of any ***available*** tickets.
b. Please inform us of any tickets ***available***.
(Bitte informieren Sie uns über verfügbare Karten)

There is no real difference in meaning between the two sentences. However, the postmodifying version in (10)b. gives more stress to the adjective: *Please inform us of any tickets 'available* (compared with *Please inform us of any available 'tickets*).

If the speaker wants to know if it is still possible to buy a ticket (or whether they have all been sold), the choice would normally fall on the postmodifying variant, since the enquiry is focused on the question of availability.

028/6.4 Predicative-restricted adjectives of the focus type

These were listed under **028/4.6**. Principle examples are *responsible, present, involved, concerned*. These occur also in ***both*** attributive positions, but with a difference in meaning. In the ***focus*** meaning they ***postmodify***. In other meanings, they ***premodify***:

(11) a. I would like to speak to the manager ***responsible***.
(**postmod.** = *zuständig, verantwortlich*)
We need a ***responsible*** manager in charge of our sales department.
(**premod.** = *verantwortungsbewusst*)
b. Among the guests ***present*** were several famous film stars.
(**postmod.** = *anwesend*)
The ***present*** guests are very satisfied with their rooms.
(**premod.** = *jetzig, gegenwärtig*)
c. The pupils ***involved*** were questioned by the police.
(**postmod.** = *beteiligt*)
This is a rather ***involved*** problem.
(**premod.** = *schwierig, komplex*)
d. The holidaymakers ***concerned*** contacted their travel agent.
(**postmod.** = *betroffen*)
The ***concerned*** holidaymakers contacted their travel agent.
(**premod.** = *besorgt*)

028/6.5 Indefinite pronouns

Adjectives attached attributively to ***indefinite pronouns*** always ***postmodify*** the pronoun: *something nice, nobody special, nothing wrong, anyone sensitive*.

028/6.6 Formal expressions

There are a small number of adjectives in a few stereotyped phrases, formal titles, and names for ranks and institutions, which always follow the noun: *Director General* (*Vorstandsvorsitzender*), *Attorney General* (*Justizminister*), *Poet Laureate* (*Nationaldichter*), (*from*) *time immemorial* ((*seit*) *jeher*), *body politic* (*das Staatswesen*), *court martial* (*Militärgericht*), *sergeant major* (*Hauptfeldwebel*).

This type derives from older stages of the language that were influenced by French and Latin. The adjective positions that are usual in those languages were either simply copied, or came into English through the direct borrowing of a word.

028/7 Attributive premodification

We return now to the usual attributive position for adjectives, i.e. the premodifying one.

028/7.1 Order of premodifying adjectives

Although there are no definite rules, adjectives in sequence usually come in a more or less fixed order. This is determined by certain semantic categories, and their contribution to the identity of the particular noun. Those referring to more intrinsic, or essential, characteristics come closest to the noun. The further they are from the noun (i.e. to the left), the less intrinsic the named features become. The following table is for illustration only. Adjective sequences are rarely as long as shown here, of course.

	General Quality/ Assess-ment	***More specific Quality/ Assess-ment***	***Size***	***Age***	***Shape***	***Colour***	***Origin***	***Material***	***Purpose and type***	***Noun***
a	*lovely*		*thick*	*old*	*shapeless*	*green*	*English*	*woollen*	*gardening*	*pullover*
a	*nice*	*good-looking*	*slim*	*young*		*fair-haired*	*Welsh*		*piano*	*teacher*
	horrible	*foul-smelling*		*ancient*		*black*		*flake*	*pipe*	*tobacco*
a	*fine*			*new*	*round*	*blue*	*Italian*	*metal*	*jewellery*	*box*
a			*large*	*fresh*	*plump*		*Norfolk*		*roasting*	*chicken*
the			*cramped*	*18th century*			*East-coast*	*wooden*	*sailing*	*ships*
	beautiful		*big*	*antique*			*Spanish*	*crystal*	*wine*	*goblets*

028/7.2 Commas

Commas are sometimes used to separate adjectives. But there are no strict rules on this point. As commas mark pauses (see also chapter 7), they are avoided when there are no pauses necessary in the spoken form, i.e. when several adjectives would be spoken in one breath-group. Most adjectives are 'run together' like this when they are short, common, and there are only two or three: *a large red glowing sun.*

On the other hand, commas and pauses can be used to stress adjectives for reasons of style: *a large, red, glowing sun.*

But there is no obligation to use them, even in longer sequences. They would rarely occur, for example, between adjectives of the five most intrinsic categories: *a round blue Italian metal jewellery box.*

This is because the adjectives here are quite distinct in meaning. When the similarities are greater, the need is felt more to separate them. This happens particularly with the less intrinsic, more general and evaluative categories: *horrible, foul-smelling, ancient black flake pipe tobacco.*

Essentially, then, the use of commas here, as in most other fields in English, is a semantic rather than a grammatical problem.

028/7.3 Colour combinations

Two colour adjectives are connected by *and* when they refer to an object with different colours: *a red and white flag* (= partly red and partly white, *eine rotweiße Flagge*); *a green and yellow football shirt* (= part of it green, part yellow, *ein grüngelbes Fußballtrikot*). Sometimes hyphens are used: *a red-and-white flag*. With three colour words a comma separates the first two: *a red, white and blue flag, a black, yellow and red scarf.*

Colour ***mixtures*** (as opposed to combinations) are expressed using hyphens: *blue-black ink* (*blauschwarze Tinte*); *grey-green eyes* (*graugrüne Augen*).

028/8 Gradable and non-gradable adjectives

This distinction has to do with whether an adjective can appear with ***adverbs of degree*** (such as *very, rather, quite, completely,* etc.). We can say, for instance, *rather slow* or *too quiet,* but not *very dead* (except as a metaphor or a joke). This is because *dead* refers to an ***absolute*** condition, one that exists either totally or not at all. Most conditions and qualities can be thought of as being ***relative***: this means that they can exist in varying 'amounts' or ***to a varying degree***. The adjectives referring to them are ***gradable***, i.e. can occur with adverbs relating to different levels of intensity (= ***adverbs of degree***): *slightly cold, very pale, quite healthy.* Adjectives referring to ***absolute*** conditions are ***non-gradable***: *dead, present, absent, married, excellent,* etc.

Other adjectives are ***partly gradable***. They refer to conditions that have a limited range of intensities, usually because they are located at the top or bottom end of a scale of qualities. *Beautiful,* for instance, means *at the top end of an 'attractiveness' scale.* It can be further intensified by *very,* but will not combine with adverbs relating to attractiveness-levels that are below the '*beautiful*-range'. We therefore cannot say **slightly beautiful* or, to take another example, **fairly fine,* since these adverbs of degree lie outside the range on the quality scale that the particular adjective refers to.

Gradability also affects the grammatical category of ***comparison*** (see below).

028/9 Proper adjectives

Proper adjectives derive from ***proper nouns***, i.e. names. They are always spelt with an initial capital letter. They typically refer to categories of ***identity*** like the following:

a) nationality: *Russian tea, Swiss chocolate, Irish beer, Thai spices;*
b) other kinds of local and geographical origin: *Bavarian cows, Nordic walking, Arctic sea-birds, Alpine landscapes;*
c) historical periods, cultural, political and scientific movements, styles, theories, etc.: *Victorian furniture, Freudian psychoanalysis, Impressionist painters, Celtic languages.*

A point to note is that German (and other European languages) generally do not use initial capital letters here (*russischer Tee, viktorianische Möbel, keltische Sprachen*). Capital letters ***must*** be used in English, however! ⚠

Adjective forms 029

029/1 Affixes

Like the members of other word-classes, English adjectives have no obligatory form. Many cannot be distinguished – as individual words – from nouns or verbs, for instance. Nevertheless, there are certain ***affixes*** (= attached syllables) which are specific to adjectives, or at least very common with them. Among these, the ***suffixes*** are ***derivational*** in nature. That is, they convert representatives of other word classes into adjectives.

029/1.1 Suffixes added to nouns

a) *-ful* generally means 'having' or 'full of': *careful, beautiful, colourful, dutiful, hurtful.*

b) *-ous/-ious/-eous* are similar: *conscious, virtuous, envious, mountainous.*

c) *-less* is the negative of *-ful* and means 'without, lacking': *careless, colourless, cheerless.*

d) *-ic/-al/-ial* mean 'of' or 'belonging to': *tragic, romantic, public, poetic, economic, postal, central, universal, legal, dictatorial.* They can also function as noun endings (*music, mechanic, public, criminal*). The adjective may then have the same form (*public, criminal*), or in the case of *-ic* may have *-al* added (*tropical, comical, mechanical*). Some adjectives have an *-ic* and an *-al* form. Here the meaning may be more or less the same (*comic, comical*) or quite distinct (*economic* = relevant to the economy, *economical* = cheap).

e) *-y* means 'full of': *dirty, hairy, icy, messy, rainy*; and also 'like': *wavy* (= like a wave), *silky* (= like silk).

f) *-ly* also has the sense of 'like', or 'with the character of': *friendly, fatherly, leisurely.* Some adjectives of this kind have developed more specific meanings a little away from their direct roots, e.g. *lovely* (= nice, beautiful), *lively* (= high-spirited, energetic, vigorous), or those referring to periods of time such as *daily, weekly, monthly* (= once every day/week/month). One or two derive from other adjectives, e.g. *kindly, lonely.*

   A problem with *-ly* is that it is also a typical ***adverb*** suffix. Consequently, there may be some confusion with adverbs. The problem is increased by the fact that some *-ly-* adjectives can actually be used as adverbs too (i.e. those of the type *daily/weekly/monthly,* and also *kindly*). Most, however, cannot. We cannot say **He talked to me fatherly* or **She treated me friendly,* but have to find adverbial paraphrases (e.g. *in a fatherly way, in a friendly manner*).

g) *-ish* is often found with ***proper adjectives*** referring to nationality, race, and other types or origin: *Jewish, Polish, British.* It is also used for equivalent proper nouns.

   With common adjectives it means 'like', or 'with the character of', though mainly in a negative sense: *foolish, selfish, snobbish, childish.*

   A third meaning is 'tending to be' or 'about'. This is added mainly to existing adjectives (and one or two nouns) and relates especially to colours, dimensions and ages: *a whitish/reddish/greenish* substance (*ein weißlicher/rötlicher/grünlicher Stoff*); *a fattish person* (*dicklich*); *He's thirtyish* (*um die Dreißig*).

h) *-ian/-ean/-an* are also typical ***proper adjective*** endings referring to nationality, local origin, and in addition beliefs and cultural identities or traditions: *Persian, Korean, Virginian, Christian, Shakespearean, Elizabethan, Unitarian.* A few common adjectives belong to the same type, but with the suffix usually expanded into *-arian*: *totalitarian, agrarian, sectarian.* The sense, again, is 'of a particular group, belief or interest'.

All the adjectives in this group can be nouns as well (see under **30/1** below).

i) *-ese* is similar to *-ish* and *-ian/-ean/-an*. It is found with ***proper adjectives*** of nationality and language: *Chinese, Portuguese, Maltese* (= from Malta).

029/1.2 Suffixes added mainly to verbs

-able/-ible derive adjectives mainly from transitive verbs. The adjective refers to the potential ***direct object*** of the verb and means 'can/should have this action done to it': *admirable* (= can/should be admired), *avoidable,* (= can/should be avoided), *enjoyable* (= can be enjoyed), *edible* (= can be eaten), *notable* (= should be noted), *predictable* (= can be predicted).

-able/-ible occur also with noun bases, however, and then mean 'possessing/providing that thing or quality': *comfortable* (= providing comfort), *fashionable* (= possessing fashion), *knowledgeable* (= possessing knowledge).

-ive relates to the potential ***subject*** of verbs and means 'doing or able to do': *attractive* (= able to attract/attracting), *explosive* (= exploding/likely or able to explode), *sensitive* (= able to sense).

-ant/-ent have the sense of 'doing/resulting from doing': *consistent* (= maintaining the same standard), *different* (= differing), *pleasant* (= pleasing), *significant* (= signifying something important), *triumphant* (= state resulting from triumphing), *vacant* (= being empty), *violent* (= applying violence). Further examples are *arrogant, buoyant, elegant, jubilant, rampant, sufficient.* Most of these derivations have their verbal bases in Latin or French.

-ate (pronounced [ət]) means 'having this quality/behaving in this way'. Apart from being added to a verbal base, it may also just replace the verb suffix *-ate,* which is identical in spelling, but pronounced [eɪt]: *animate* (= living, alive), *appropriate* (= belonging or suitable to), *considerate* (= kind to others), *delicate* (= possessing fineness, lacking robustness), *degenerate* (= having fallen in moral or other qualities). It is also added to nouns: *affectionate, passionate.*

-y added to verbs means 'having a tendency/ability to do': *bendy* (= able/tending to bend), *floppy* (= tending to flop). So also *dreamy, runny, sleepy, sticky.*

029/1.3 Prefixes with adjectives

Prefixes do not signal specific word-classes, and the following are not confined to adjectives. Nevertheless, they are very common with adjectives, especially those in (a)–(e), which create ***negative opposites***:

a) *un-*: *unnecessary, unable, uncertain;*
b) *in-*: *inactive, incapable, inconsiderate, insecure;*
c) *im-*: *impolite, impossible, immobile;*
d) *ir-*: *irresistible, irresponsible, irresolute;*
e) *dis-*: *disloyal, disreputable, disorderly.*

Prefixes with other meanings:

f) *pre-* (= *before*): *preliminary* (*Vor-*), *premature* (*verfrüht*), *preoccupied* (*in Gedanken*), *precocious* (*frühreif*);
g) *a-* (= *in a particular state or condition*): *afraid, alight* (*brennend*), *alike* (*gleich, ähnlich*), *alive* (*lebendig*), *alone, asleep, awake.*
   These are used only ***predicatively*** (see below).
h) *ob- (also oc-, of-, op- before c, f, p): obese (= very fat), obsolete (= old-fashioned), obstinate* (= *stubborn*), *obvious* (*offensichtlich*), *opportune* (*günstig, passend*).

The prefix under h) derives from Latin. It has no concrete uniform meaning in modern English, but carries the abstract sense of the prepositions *to* or *against* (i.e. preventing or blocking something, or presenting itself to the senses).

029/2 Other words in adjective functions

029/2.1 Nouns

As we saw in chapter 2, nouns often premodify other nouns: *kitchen window, garage roof, car door, truck driver, violin case.*

Premodifying nouns are similar to adjectives in function. They specify or characterize the head noun particularly closely when they refer to place or purpose, as in the examples just given, or to the material that something consists of: *an iron door, a brick wall, a grass slope, a stone path.*

On the other hand, they are still generally considered, as a word-class, to be nouns. This is because they have no other features typical of adjectives: they cannot, for example, be premodified by adverbs, nor can adverbs be formed from them (see following chapter); there are no comparative forms, and usually there is no predicative use.

Exceptions on this last point are some nouns denoting materials; *concrete, plastic, iron, brick,* and sometimes *stone* are used predicatively (at least with the verb *to be*): *That wall is brick; The door is iron; The handles were plastic.*

The same applies, particularly in informal language, to certain food nouns, especially ones referring to content and flavour: *The ice-cream is chocolate and the milkshake is strawberry.*

These nouns are therefore more adjective-like. With predicative usage, in fact, some dictionaries list them as both adjectives and nouns.

029/2.2 Present participles

Present participles can also premodify nouns: *a shooting star, falling leaves, a passing car, a flying object.* They can be paraphrased by relative clauses: *falling leaves* = leaves that are falling; *a passing car* = a car that is passing.

The participle refers, that is, to an act which the head noun performs. Here too, then, we have a word in the adjective position that to a certain extent keeps its original word-class identity: this time as a verb. But the participle also loses some of its verbal character. Premodifying present participles never just refer to individual actions. We cannot, for instance, call a woman who is reading **a reading woman*, or a boy who is playing **a playing boy*. In cases like these the participle must follow the noun as a postmodifier: *a woman reading, a boy playing*. Premodifying participles signify a characteristic form of behaviour, and place the head in a particular category: a *shooting star* is a type of star, a *passing car* a category of vehicle (i.e. one that is moving). Such constructions cannot be formed spontaneously. They are collocations that must be learnt.

All this shows that the present participle has at least a semi-adjectival function. It cannot be used predicatively, however. Although we can say *The object seemed large*, we cannot say **The object seemed flying*. The participle can follow the verb *be*, of course: *The object was flying*. But it then simply becomes part of the progressive form, and is no longer adjectival in nature.

There are a number of participles that have lost their verbal identity entirely and have become full lexical and grammatical adjectives: *boring, interesting, annoying, surprising, exciting, fascinating, tiring*. Unlike ordinary participle premodifiers, they have comparative and superlative forms (*more interesting, most exciting*) and can also be used predicatively: *The book looked interesting*.

029/2.3 Past participles

Whereas present participles have an active meaning, ***past participles*** refer to ***states*** as ***consequences*** of actions. Usually, these are states which have been imposed on the noun and place it in a ***passive*** role: *a parked car* (= a car that has been parked), *a closed door* (= a door that has been closed), *a wrapped gift* (= a gift that has been wrapped). In general, past participles of this kind are closer to real adjectives than ordinary present participles. They are used more freely (not just in fairly restricted collocations), and can also appear predicatively: *The car was parked; The door seemed closed*.

There are quite a lot of exceptions to the passive meaning, however. These occur with past participles deriving from ***intransitive*** verbs, which place the head noun in an active role. In this respect they are more like present participles: with the difference, however, that here the act is over ('something that the noun has done'), and we see its ***consequence***:

a fallen tree (= a tree that has/had fallen); *an escaped prisoner* (= a prisoner that has/had escaped); *faded colours* (= colours that have/had faded).

Others like this are: *disembarked passengers, a retired teacher, departed guests, an increased danger, his improved health*.

With regard to position, there is a lot of individual variation:

- ***attributive-restricted***: *fallen, escaped, disembarked, departed*, etc.;
- ***predicative-restricted***: *gone* (*weg, verschwunden*), *recovered* (*genesen*), *set* (*fest, erhärtet*), *drunk* (German *betrunken*; attributive usually *drunken*), etc.;
- ***non-restricted***: *faded, retired, engaged, married, divorced*, etc.

029/2.4 'False' participles

There are a few adjectives with a past participle form not actually derived from a real verb. They have usually been formed by analogy (i.e. 'copying'):

- genuine participles negated: *unexpected, unmarried, disinterested.*
  The positive equivalents are genuinely verb-derived, but the negatives are not. There are no verbs like **to unexpect* or **to unmarry.*
  These contrast with negative participles derived from genuine negative verbs, e.g. *inconvenienced* (from *to inconvenience*), *incapacitated* (from *to incapacitate*).
- derived from nouns: *talented, gifted, ribbed, cross-eyed, red-haired, fair-skinned, jet-lagged*
- adjectives in [ɪd]: *crooked, wretched, wicked, naked, jagged,* etc.
  Care must be taken to pronounce the vowel and voice the consonant: [krʊkɪd], [wɪkɪd], [neɪkɪd], etc.

029/2.5 Gerunds

Like premodifying nouns, premodifying gerunds are also regarded sometimes as parts of compound nouns (see also chapter 2). The close link to the head noun is underlined by the (usually optional) use of hyphens: *dining-room, gardening gloves, swimming-trunks, diving-board, fishing rod, breathing apparatus, singing lessons.*

The relation to the head is similar to that of a premodifying noun, i.e. in a grammatical sense the gerund is less 'adjectival' and more nominal than participle premodifiers. Nevertheless, just as premodifying nouns have a certain adjective function semantically, so also do gerunds. They specify the head noun in terms of ***type*** and ***purpose***: *dining-room* = a room for dining in; *gardening gloves* = gloves for gardening, *a fishing rod* = a rod for fishing with; and so on.

This is the important semantic distinction between a gerund and a present participle before nouns. The gerund tells us the type of noun and what it is for. The participle tells us what the noun is doing. The difference is heard also in the pronunciation. Gerunds are stressed (*'dining-room*). Participles are not: here the head noun is stressed (*passing 'car*).

Like premodifying nouns, gerunds are ***attributive-restricted.***

The syntax and semantics of participles and gerunds are discussed fully in chapter 13).

029/2.6 Adverbs

Adverbs and adverb particles regularly occur as premodifying adjectives, though often in fairly fixed collocations. Most refer to place and direction: *the back entrance, the front garden, an away game, a forward pass, a sideways glance, backward areas, outside interests, further details, the above address, an off-day, the in-box, the out-tray, a down train, a through-road.*

Compound adverbs, principally in noun combinations, are also common. Many of them, again, are restricted to certain collocations: *our downstairs toilet, the nextdoor neighbour, an uphill struggle, offshore islands, off-peak travel, online banking.*

As adjectives these are ***attributive-restricted***. This is in keeping with the fact that almost all are ***relational*** rather than intrinsic. Some can appear predicatively, but then have ***adverb*** status and function ***adverbially***, e.g.

		Adverbial
(12)	a. The address is	above.
		Adverbial
	b. Our toilet is	downstairs.

Here the focus shifts from a relational characteristic to pure location. In (12), that is, I am saying where the subject is, and not what it is. This may not affect the meaning radically, but there are at least nuances of difference:

Our toilet is downstairs says that there is one toilet in that location.

Our downstairs toilet, on the other hand, implies that there is more than one, and that it is the downstairs one that I am referring to.

029/2.7 Quantifiers and numerals

Numerals are usually determiners (see chapter 3). If they are preceded by other determiners, however, they become adjectives: *the three bears, these five men, all six boats.*

Only certain quantifiers can be used in this way, i.e. *few, little,* and *many*: *the many holidaymakers on the beach; the little money in his pocket.*

In ordinary language these are attributive-restricted, but they can appear predicatively in more poetic styles: *His problems were many and his pleasures few.*

029/3 Compound adjectives

Compound adjectives are combinations of (usually) two words. At least one of these is normally (though not necessarily) an adjective. The two parts are typically joined by hyphens, but they may also form a single word. The semantic relation between them varies. Stress patterns depend on which part carries the main semantic weight (or individual meaning), and which part is more 'functional'.

029/3.1 Noun + adjective

waterproof, heat-resistant, homesick, airtight, carefree, jet-black, sky-blue

The adjective here typically stands in a prepositional relation to the noun: 'resistant to/against heat/air/water', 'sick for home', 'without care'. Main stress here is on the noun: *'carefree*. The colour words mean 'a type/shade of' (blue, black, etc.). In this case, the second element is given main stress: *sky-'blue*.

029/3.2 Adjective + noun

free-range, red-brick, large-scale, high-level, low-grade

Here the adjective describes the noun. The expected stress pattern would accentuate the head, as with normal noun phrases. In our examples, though, this is only the case with *red-'brick*. With the others the noun is a term of measurement and therefore functional. Semantic weight – and therefore stress – thus lies on the first element: *'large-scale, 'high-level.*

029/3.3 Adjective + adjective

bright-red, dark-brown, grey-green, blue-black, black-and-white

This kind of combination is found typically with colour references. The first adjective premodifies the second. It is therefore the second (as head) which receives main stress: *blue-'black*. Terms like the first two denote shades of one colour (*hellrot, dunkelbraun*), whereas the type *grey-green* refers to 'green mixed with grey' (German *graugrün*). Combinations like *black-and-white* mean the separate colours together on one object: *a black-and-white scarf* (*ein schwarz-weißer Schal*).

029/3.4 Noun + participle

smoke-filled, diesel-driven, breast-fed, pipe-smoking, thought-provoking, meat-eating, home-brewed, leather-bound, snow-capped

The past participle is passive and the noun is part of a prepositional phrase denoting an adverbial relation, usually referring to an agent, a material feature, or a place of occurrence: *a smoke-filled room* = a room filled by/with smoke; *homebrewed beer* = beer brewed at home. The present participle is active and the preceding noun the potential direct object: *a thought-provoking remark* = a remark which provokes thought; *a pipe-smoking professor* = a professor who smokes a pipe. In all cases the first element is stressed: *'meat-eating, 'breast fed.*

029/3.5 Adjective + participle

hard-working, deep-frozen, quick-witted, simple-minded, widespread, easy-going, smooth-talking, high-ranking, bad-tempered, good-looking

The adjective here typically stands for an adverbial element: *hard-working* = working hard; *quick-witted* = reacts quickly; *widespread* = widely spread.

But it may also represent a hidden subject complement: *Simon is bad-tempered* = Simon's temper is bad; *John is good-looking* = John looks good. Main stress here lies on the participle: *smooth-'talking, high-'ranking.*

029/3.6 Adverb + participle

finely-tuned, highly-paid, badly-behaved, well-built, smartly-dressed, forward-looking, back-dated

Adverbs premodifying participles usually follow the same pattern as the adjectives in **029/3.5**, i.e. they are regarded as part of a compound and joined to the participle by a hyphen. However, this is only the case in ***attributive*** position.

In ***predicative*** use hyphen and compound disappear, leaving the adverb as a separate premodifier: *a finely-tuned engine → The engine was finely tuned.*

Stress is generally on the participle with adverbs of manner: *highly-'paid, badly-'behaved*. With other types, the adverb is often stressed, though context also plays a part:

'forward-looking politicians, 'scientifically-minded pupils, 'nautically-inclined guests; a musically-'interested (though not musically-'gifted) woman.

029/3.7 Numeral + noun

ten-storey, three-volume, five-year, twenty-minute, six-mile (***attributive only***); *third-rate, second-hand, first-degree.*

We saw in the chapter 2 (**012/1**) that measurement expressions of this kind are formed with ***singular*** nouns: *a ten-storey building* = a building with ten storeys; *a six-mile walk* = a walk of six miles. Those with cardinal numbers (*two, three,* etc.) can only be used ***attributively***. Stress is on the numeral: *a 'three-volume novel, a 'twenty-minute journey.* Compounds with ordinal numbers (which can also be used ***predicatively***) stress the numeral too: *a 'first-degree murder, a 'third-rate film.*

029/3.8 Numeral + noun + adjective

seven-year-old, four-hour-long, three-inch-wide (***attributive only***)

Here an adjective referring to the kind of dimension (*How long? How old? How wide?*) has been added to compounds of the type in **029/3.7**: *a seven-year-old child, a four-hour-long exam.*

In ***predicative*** use the compound disappears, leaving an ordinary adjective premodified by an ordinary plural noun: *The child was seven years old; The exam was four hours long.*

029/3.9 Verb + adverb particle or preposition

a drive-in cinema, a takeaway meal, a see-through blouse, a stand-up comedian, a roll-on deodorant

These are restricted collocations, often invented by media and advertising for very specific objects. But the form itself is frequent.

Aspects of usage 030

030/1 Adjectives as nouns

In German, French, and many other languages, adjectives can be used freely as nouns, ⚠ e.g. *der Alte, die Kleine, das Unangenehme,* etc. This ***nominalization*** of adjectives is ***not*** generally possible in English. English equivalents here require the addition of full nouns: *the old man, the little girl* (*woman,* etc.), *the unpleasant thing.*

Certain restricted types of adjective, however, do allow ***nominalization***, among them ***proper adjectives*** denoting people in terms of origin, race, and nationality. In most cases the same adjective is also used for the particular language spoken. Proper adjectives can also refer to other forms of affiliation, for example to religious, political or cultural groups (*Catholics, Liberals, Impressionists*). A further type comprises ordinary adjectives which identify people according to social types or categories, e.g. *the poor and the needy* (*die Armen und Bedürftigen*).

030/1.1 Nationalities

As already pointed out, nationality names are ***proper adjectives*** and begin with a ***capital letter*** (*an American film-star*). Those ending in *-an* or *-on* are ordinary count nouns and take *-s* in the plural: *an American, two Americans*. So also *Nigerians, Britons*, etc.

Those ending in *-ese* are also count nouns, but have the same form in singular and plural: *a Chinese, two Chinese*.

Those ending in *-sh*/*-ch* are ***adjectival collectives*** (see chapter 2, **016/3**), i.e. they are used only in the collective sense, and as singular-plural nouns: *the Irish, the French* (= all of them, the whole nation), etc. They have other noun forms for individualized meaning (most frequently ending in *-man*/*-woman*): *an Irishman, a Frenchwoman* (*Irishmen, Frenchwomen*, etc.).

030/1.2 Articles with nationality nouns, and other nominalized proper adjectives

Adjectival collectives always take the definite article: *The French have good wine; the Irish have good whiskey.*

⚠ Individualized nouns after the verb *to be* take the ***indefinite article*** (in contrast to the case in German): *I am an American* (*Ich bin Amerikaner*). It is the same with other nominalized proper adjectives: *He is a Catholic/a Moslem/a Buddhist/a Conservative/a Liberal.*

Individualized nouns of this type are ordinary count nouns, of course, and can be used in the plural, with all types of determiner: *the Liberals* (= *the Liberal Party*), *four Americans, those Conservatives who voted against their party*, etc.

Note with ***languages*** that the ***zero article*** is used: *What's this word in German?; The four singers were speaking Chinese.*

When the word *language* is added, however, the ***definite article*** is required: *He writes his novels in the English language, but generally speaks Italian.* (And not: **He writes his novels in English language …*)

030/1.3 Geographical names

The head noun is often omitted after proper adjectives referring to many geographical phenomena like oceans, mountains and groups of islands. The definite article is necessary here, too, of course (see also chapter 1): *the Atlantic* (*Ocean*), *the Baltic* (*Sea*), *the Cotswolds* (*the Cotswold Hills*), *the Appalachians* (*the Appalachian Mountains*), *the Canaries* (*the Canary Islands*).

030/1.4 Generalized social groups

Adjectival collectives can also refer to social categories or groupings: *the rich, the poor, the young, the old, the sick, the handicapped, the deprived.*

As with all adjectival collectives, these are treated as non-count plurals. They appear almost always with the definite article, as it is a defined general group that is meant. Exceptions are certain collocations with *and*, stressing 'totality' ('everyone, no matter who, or of what kind'): *The whole town was at the fair, young and old, rich and poor.*

030/1.5 Nominalizations as fixed expressions

Nominalized adjectives are occasionally used (especially in more elaborate style) to refer to abstract concepts or entities representing them: *London is a good place to see the old and the new, the ancient and the modern, the beautiful and the ugly*. Expressions like these are fairly fixed, although new ones can certainly be coined. As mass nouns, they are non-count singulars; the definite article is usual.

More specific fixed nominalizations occur in the specialized language of certain subject fields, e.g. law and administration (mainly as participle adjectives): *the accused* (*der/die Angeklagte*), *the deceased* (*der/die Verstorbene*), *the undersigned* (*der/die Unterzeichnete*).

These are most common with the definite article, although other determiners are possible. As individual nouns they can be plural, but then keep the same form: *The three accused were brought into the court.*

Grammatical terminology also has many nominalizations: *the present* (*tense*), *the passive* (*voice*), *the dative* (*case*). These are individual nouns, and take normal plurals, most often in the sense of particular examples or representatives: *That is a dative* (= a word in the dative case); *Those are passives* (= verbs in the passive voice).

Further examples of fixed expressions are: *a classic* (*ein Klassiker*), *a native* (*speaker/person/inhabitant*), *a superior* (*ein Überlegener/Vorgesetzter*), *an inferior* (*ein Untergebener/Untertan*), *an equal* (*ein Gleichgestellter*), *a noble* (*ein Adliger*), *a relative* (*ein Verwandter*), *particulars* (*Einzelheiten*), etc.

030/1.6 Back-reference with the prop-pronoun

In German, nominalized adjectives are used to avoid repeating nouns that have just been mentioned. In English, ***back reference*** of this kind to ***count nouns*** requires the ***prop-pronoun***, that is, the addition of ***one/ones*** (see also chapter 3, **028/7**): ⚠

(13) a. Welches Stück möchtest du? ***Das große*** oder ***das kleine***?
Which piece would you like? The ***big one*** or the ***small one***?
b. Ich möchte bitte 4 Rosen: ***eine rote*** und ***drei weiße***.
I'd like 4 roses, please: ***a red one*** and ***three white ones***.

Note again that the prop-pronoun replaces just the ***head*** of the noun phrase. The rest of the phrase remains as it is.

An important point is that the ***prop-pronoun*** is used ***only*** for back-reference: that is, it must relate to a noun mentioned just previously. German nominalized adjectives can ⚠

refer to individual nouns when there is no back reference. In English, the prop-pronoun is ***not*** possible in this case. Appropriate full nouns are necessary (see also the beginning of this section):

(14) a. Drei Verletzte wurden im Krankenhaus behandelt.
Three injured people (passengers, passers-by, etc.), were treated in hospital (*not* *three injured ones).
b. Die Firma stellte zwanzig Arbeitslose ein.
The firm hired twenty unemployed workers (*not* *twenty unemployed ones).
c. Dieses Fahrzeug ist speziell für Behinderte.
This vehicle is specially for handicapped people.

It is a similar case with German evaluative nominalizations:

(15) a. Das Seltsame/Lustige/Gute daran, war …
The strange thing/funny thing/good point about it was …
b. Das Blöde ist, dass er am nächsten Tag eine Prüfung hat.
The awkward thing is that he's got an exam the next day.

030/1.7 Back-reference without the prop-pronoun

The prop-pronoun is ***not*** used for back-reference to ***singular non-count nouns***. Here the adjective is just nominalized, as in German:

(16) a. Would you like red wine or white?
b. As they had no Indian tea, I bought Chinese.
c. I think we'll use the white paint here rather than the blue.
d. You can buy fresh fish or frozen. It doesn't matter.

With one or two exceptions in informal language, ***plural non-count nouns*** also take no prop-pronoun. As nominalization is not possible here either, alternative expressions must be found:

(17) a. The surroundings were shabby, and after a while I started to long for a brighter environment (*not* *brighter ones).
b. We had hoped for higher wages, but they threatened us with wage-cuts (*not* *lower ones).

Exceptions are found occasionally in colloquial language, mainly regarding items of clothing, in particular pair nouns: *Her jeans were old and worn, and she decided to buy new ones.*
In 'better' style, though, this would be avoided: … *decided to buy a new pair.*

Finally, prop-pronouns are usually avoided in neutral reference to people:

(18) a. I mean the small man, not the big guy next to him (*rather than* ?* the big one next to him).
b. The Japanese student was better in her studies than the American student (*not* *... than the American one).

When prop-pronouns are used, they tend to confer a certain collective, 'labelling' quality. This can sound a little derogatory, or at least familiar, and may suggest that the speaker has a higher status (as, for instance, when referring to children):

(19) a. In my class the good pupils are interested in everything, but the bad ones get bored easily.
b. Some guests were restrained at the buffet, but the hungry ones piled their plates high with food.

030/1.8 Nominalization with comparatives and superlatives

Comparatives follow the normal adjective rule and take the prop-pronoun. Superlatives can do the same, or, alternatively, stand alone:

(20) a. I bought these roller-blades for John, but he needs larger ones.
b. This castle is the oldest (one) in Wales.

030/1.9 Head noun ellipsis

The omission (***ellipsis***) of head nouns is common in certain stereotyped contexts:

(21) a. Two returns to Carlisle, please (= two return tickets, e.g. for a train).
b. I'd like one small and one family-sized, please (= portions, e.g. of food from a fast-food restaurant).
c. Three large and one medium (e.g. cups of coffee).

030/2 Some special cases

030/2.1 The adjective own

The adjective ***own*** must be preceded by a genitive or possessive. In contrast to its German equivalent, it cannot appear with other kinds of article words: ⚠

(22) a. I have founded my own company (*not* * an own company).
Ich habe eine eigene Firma gegründet.
b. It's nice to be in one's own garden (*not* *the own garden).
Es ist schön, im eigenen Garten zu sein.

On the other hand, ***own*** is used in nominalized form (i.e. without the prop-pronoun):

(23) a. This company is my own (= it belongs to me).
b. Celia won't need her mother's car now that she has one of her own.

030/2.2 Adjectives of dimension and measure

Adjectives referring to a dimension or standard of measurement are premodified, when necessary, by quantified plural nouns: *three years old, eight feet high, four inches thick, six feet wide.*

As already pointed out (see under **029/3.7** and **8** above), such expressions only occur ***predicatively***. In ***attributive*** position, the corresponding compound adjectives must be used. The nouns involved are then ***singular***: *a three-year-old child, a four-inch-thick wall, a six-foot-wide path.*

When the dimension or standard is clear (e.g. from common usage) the general adjective (*tall, long,* etc.) is omitted: *a three-year prison sentence, a six-foot policeman, a 15-stone rugby player, a five-hour wait.*

030/2.3 Consecutive modifiers

Gradable adjectives can be modified by the adverbs ***too*** and ***enough***. These are known as ***consecutive modifiers***. They relate the quantity of a certain characteristic to its consequences. The adverb ***so*** can also have consecutive meaning:

(24) a. I didn't go to the party as I was too tired.
b. If you're not warm enough, I'll lend you a sweater.
c. Jessica was so surprised: she could hardly say anything.

Note that ***too*** and ***so*** precede the adjective, but ***enough*** follows it. The consequence is often expressed by a phrase or clause functioning as an adjectival complement (i.e. integrated into the adjective phrase, see below):

(25) a. I was too tired to go to the party.
b. The weather is not good enough for an outing to the coast.
c. Jessica was so surprised that she could hardly say anything.

030/3 Adjectival complements

As we have already seen, an adjectival complement is the part of an adjective phrase following the head. It is the 'postmodification', so to speak, of the adjective.

⚠ One important point to note is that adjectives with complements can ***never*** premodify nouns in English. We can say in German, for example, *ein von Kummer gezeichnetes Gesicht.* The English equivalent, however, requires a postmodification or predicative position: *a face (that is) lined with worry.*

Adjectival complements have typical structures:

030/3.1 Prepositional phrases

Adjectives have an attraction for prepositions. Prepositions relate an adjective to a specific entity, usually in the general meanings of 'regarding/concerning', or 'caused by': *short of money, weak in the head, blue with cold, anxious about Jim.*

Individual prepositional meaning here is mainly idiomatic, i.e. confined to the association with the particular adjective (or adjective type), and different from the normal independent meaning. More details on this will be found in the chapter on prepositions.

With adjectives that comment on an action, focus on the subject of the action can be introduced with *of*: *It was clever of you to think of a solution; It was kind of Sheila to help the old lady across the road.*

For the use of the infinitive here, see chapter 13.

Finally, prepositions complementing adjectives can also attract gerunds (see under **030/3.3**).

030/3.2 Finite clauses

That-clauses are typical complements of adjectives describing feelings or states of mind: *happy/sorry/afraid/sure that ...*

The adjective shows a certain (emotional or mental) attitude towards the fact referred to in the *that*-clause, e.g. *I was disgusted that Bill treats his family so badly.*

Adjectives relating to knowledge of facts (*sure, certain, clear,* etc.) also occur with ***wh***-clauses (= ***indirect questions***, see chapter 11), particularly in the negative, e.g. *She is not certain why she is here; Jason was doubtful whether he would get the job.*

Clauses of this kind can also follow prepositions: *I wasn't quite clear on where I had to go; She was uncertain about when she should come.*

In this connection the complex preposition *as to* (meaning 'regarding/concerning') is heard also in slightly higher style: *She was uncertain as to when she should come.*

030/3.3 Non-finite clauses

Gerunds frequently follow prepositions when adjectives refer to activities (usually in terms of attitude or ability): *keen on learning French, tired of telling jokes, interested in collecting fossils, bored with watching television, good at repairing cars.*

Infinitives occur with volitional (i.e. 'wanting') adjectives (*ready/willing/reluctant to go*), adjectives expressing emotional reactions (*sorry/happy/angry to hear that ...*), and in consecutive constructions of the type shown in (25) above (*too tired to go to the party*).

The adjective *busy* (and others of similar meaning, such as *occupied* and *active*) take present participles: *Mother was busy talking to Uncle Roy.*

It should be noted, however, that not all clauses following adjectives are necessarily adjectival complements. For example, infinitive constructions like those in *It is impossible to see him,* or *Bill is hard to convince* are not syntactically part of the adjective phrase, but what we call extrapositions (see also chapter 7).

All points mentioned in this section are discussed more fully in chapter 13 on non-finite verbs.

031 Comparison

The category of ***comparison*** is applied only to ***gradable*** adjectives. In general, we use it in order to say how much of a particular characteristic one entity has in relation to another, i.e. ***more***, ***less***, or the ***same amount***.

031/1 Types of comparison

As an illustration of what has just been said, we will take the four novelists Sue, Dennis, Jane and Henry, and compare their success as writers:

(26) a. Sue is ***more successful than*** Dennis.
b. Henry is ***less successful than*** Dennis.
c. Jane is ***as successful as*** Dennis.

If we list them in the order of their success, Sue comes first, Dennis and Jane both second, and Henry last. So in reference to Sue and Henry, we can say

(27) a. Sue is the ***most successful*** of the four (people).
b. Henry is the ***least successful*** of the four (people).

Semantically, (26)a. and (27)a. show a relation of ***more***, or as we will call it here, ***surplus comparison***. (26)b. and (27)b. show a relation of ***less***, or in our terms ***deficit comparison***. And (26)c. demonstrates the ***same amount***, or ***equative comparison***.

Grammatically, the categories are arranged in a slightly different way: *more successful* and *less successful* are ***comparative forms*** of the adjective *successful*; *most successful* and *least successful* are ***superlative forms*** of the adjective *successful*; and the phrase *as successful as* is an ***equative construction***.

The semantic and the grammatical categories do not correspond to one another in a neat way. This is because the ***surplus*** and ***deficit*** categories each have their own distinct ***comparative*** and ***superlative*** forms.

But an overview can simplify things a little:

(28)

surplus		*deficit*		*equative*
/	\	/	\	|
comparative	*superlative*	*comparative*	*superlative*	|
|	|	|	|	***equative construction***
more	*most*	*less*	*least*	|
				as + adj. + *as*

Finally, *than*/*as Dennis*, in (26), are ***comparative phrases***, *than* and *as … as* function as ***comparative particles***, and the noun following them (*Dennis*) is the ***comparative complement***. All these terms are important in the discussion following.

031/2 Forming the comparative and superlative

There are actually two ways of forming comparatives and superlatives. One we have already met. Here the adverbs *more* (*less*) and *most* (*least*) are simply added to the ***base form*** of the adjective as separate premodifiers:

successful → more/*less successful → most*/*least successful*

These are called ***periphrastic*** forms.

The other method is to add the ***inflections*** *-er* and *-est* to the ***base form*** of the adjective:

cheap → cheaper → cheapest

These are ***inflectional*** forms.

There are no inflectional forms for ***deficit comparison***. Deficit comparison is only ***periphrastic***.

With a number of adjectives both the ***periphrastic*** and ***inflectional*** forms of comparison are possible. Many, however, take only one form or the other. In general, this depends on whether the adjective is long or short (i.e. on the number of syllables). A few adjectives also have irregular comparative and superlative forms.

031/2.1 Adjectives of one syllable

Most of these take the ***inflections*** *-er* and *-est*. After short vowels a single final consonant in the spelling is doubled. Adjectives already ending in *-e* just add *-r* and *-st*:

base form	**comparative**	**superlative**
small →	*smaller →*	*smallest*
dark →	*darker →*	*darkest*
hot →	*hotter →*	*hottest*
mean →	*meaner →*	*meanest*
large →	*larger →*	*largest*
sad →	*sadder →*	*saddest*

With adjectives ending in *-ng* the *-g* is pronounced in comparative and superlative forms:

base form	***comparative***	***superlative***
long [lɒŋ]	*longer* [lɒŋgə]	*longest* [lɒŋgɪst]
young [jʌŋ]	*younger* [jʌŋgə]	*youngest* [jʌŋgɪst]

Exceptions:

a) The adjectives *real, right* and *wrong,* plus all participles, take the ***periphrastic*** form: *more real, more bored.*
b) Either the ***inflectional*** or the ***periphrastic*** form is taken by a few one-syllable adjectives with abstract meanings, e.g. *brave, clear, keen, free, safe, sure, true, wise* (*keener/more keen, truer/more true*), etc.
c) The adjectives *good* and *bad,* plus one or two others, have irregular comparative and superlative forms (see below).

031/2.2 Adjectives with two or more syllables

Most adjectives of two syllables, and almost all those with more than two, take the ***periphrastic*** form:

base form	***comparative***	***superlative***
certain →	*more certain →*	*most certain*
violent →	*more violent →*	*most violent*
attractive →	*more attractive →*	*most attractive*
considerate →	*more considerate →*	*most considerate*
knowledgeable →	*more knowledgeable →*	*most knowledgeable*

Exceptions:

a) Two-syllable adjectives ending in *-er, -y, -ow, -le* can take either form. If inflections are added, final *-y* changes to *-i.*
b) Negatives of these with prefixes (*unlucky, unhappy*) behave in the same way, although they have three syllables.
c) Belonging to this group are also the adjectives *quiet, pleasant* and *common.*
d) Two-syllable adjectives with stress on the second syllable can also take either form.

Here an overview of the two-syllable exceptions:

base form	***comparative***	***superlative***
lucky →	*luckier* → *more lucky* →	*luckiest* *most lucky*
happy →	*happier* → *more happy* →	*happiest* *most happy*
bitter →	*bitterer* → *more bitter* →	*bitterest* *most bitter*
shallow →	*shallower* → *more shallow* →	*shallowest* *most shallow*
simple →	*simpler* → *more simple* →	*simplest* *most simple*
common →	*commoner* → *more common* →	*commonest* *most common*
quiet →	*quieter* → *more quiet* →	*quietest* *most quiet*
unlucky →	*unluckier* → *more unlucky* →	*unluckiest* *most unlucky*
compact → [kəm'pækt]	*compacter* → *more compact* →	*compactest* *most compact*
polite → [pəl'aɪt]	*politer* → *more polite* →	*politest* *most polite*

031/2.3 One-syllable adjectives with irregular forms

A handful of forms are completely irregular:

base form	***comparative***	***superlative***
good →	*better* →	*best*
bad →	*worse* →	*worst*

The adjectives *old* and *far* each have two sets of forms with two separate meanings:

base form	***comparative***	***superlative***	
far →	*farther* →	*farthest*	(distance meaning only)
	further →	*furthest*	(all meanings)

base form	***comparative***	***superlative***	
old →	*older* →	*oldest*	(***regular:*** all meanings)
	elder →	*eldest*	(***attributive-restricted***, meaning senior and applied to family members)

To these we must add the ***comparative quantifiers*** *more* and *less*, and their ***superlatives*** *most* and *least*. Formally these are related to the base forms *little* and *much/many*. All of these can be used as adverbs, and also (except for *much*) as adjectives.

base form	***comparative***	***superlative***
little →	*less →*	*least*
many →	*more →*	*most*

The quantifier *few*, like *many* and *little*, also occurs as an adjective, but it is ***regular***:

base form	***comparative***	***superlative***
few →	*fewer →*	*fewest*

031/3 Use of comparative and superlative

Comparative forms are used when we compare ***two*** elements:

(29) a. Wendy is ***braver than*** Tom.
b. Sausages are ***cheaper than*** steak.

The two elements do not have to be equal in size, however. With a group of more than two members, we can pick out one of them, and compare that member with the rest ***collectively***, e.g.

(30) a. Wendy is ***braver than*** Tom and Jerry.
b. Sausages are ***cheaper than*** steak or chops.

Here we simply reduce each group to two unequal parts, so that it is possible to compare on the basis of ***two*** (i.e. 'one versus the rest'), even though there are three members involved altogether.

It is necessary to emphasize this point, because with groups of more than two members we have an alternative method of comparison, as in (31): the ***superlative***:

(31) a. Wendy is the ***bravest*** of the three (people).
b. Sausages are the ***cheapest*** of the three (kinds of meat).

The ***profiled*** member (*Wendy, sausages*) is now included in the group as a whole. That is, we relate the profiled member to the ***whole*** group and not just to the 'other part' of it. For this we use the ***superlative forms*** of the adjectives *brave* and *cheap*, i.e. *bravest* and *cheapest*. In this case there is ***no*** comparative particle (*than*). The ***partitive of-genitive*** is used instead. Superlatives usually have the definite article before them, although this can be left out under certain circumstances (see under **031/7.3** below).

So far we have illustrated comparative and superlative usage with examples from ***surplus*** comparison. The same principles apply to ***deficit*** comparison – with the difference, as already stated, that only ***periphrastic forms*** are used:

(32) a. John is ***less lucky than*** Sharon and Bob.
b. John is the ***least lucky of*** the three (people).

031/4 Equative comparison

Here we do have a one-to-one correspondence between structure and meaning, as there is a special ***equative construction***, *as* + adjective + *as*:

(33) a. Mike is ***as successful as*** Brian.
b. Jane is ***as happy as*** Sarah.

Here, too, there is only the periphrastic construction, and no inflectional alternative.

Equative constructions in the ***negative*** are frequently used for ***deficit comparative*** meaning, i.e. in place of *less*:

(34) a. John is ***not as lucky as*** Sharon and Bob.
(= John is less lucky than Sharon and Bob, see (32)a.)
b. Tom is ***not as successful as*** Wendy.
(= Tom is less successful than Wendy.)

The ***negative equative*** version is often preferred in informal language and speech, as it is more emphatic. *Less* is more restrained and more formal.

Equative meaning itself, on the other hand, can also be given greater emphasis by using ***surplus*** or ***deficit comparatives*** in the ***negative***:

(35) a. Mike is ***no(t) less successful*** than Brian. (see (33)a.)
b. Brian is ***no(t) more successful*** than Mike.

It is usual here to replace the less emphatic *not* by *no*.

031/5 Deficit and surplus comparatives compared

Examples like (35) show that ***deficit*** and ***surplus*** comparatives can be used to convey the same message when certain changes are made. In (35), of course, the subject and complement nouns *Mike* and *Brian* must exchange positions.

Deficit and surplus comparisons can also function as rough semantic equivalents with ***lexical opposites*** (or ***antonyms***). For instance, instead of saying *happier*, we can say *less unhappy*, and the other way round, i.e. *unhappier* for *less happy*.

(36) a. Mary is happier than Maurice.
b. Maurice is less happy than (not as happy as) Mary.
c. Mary is less unhappy than (not as unhappy as) Maurice.
d. Maurice is unhappier than Mary.

However, there are differences in semantic emphasis. Firstly, the opposing adjectives (= ***antonyms***) express different ***standards of comparison***. (36)a. and b. measure the relative amount of happiness, and c. and d. the relative level of unhappiness. That is, they refer to the same coin, but focus on different sides of it.

Secondly, ***surplus comparatives*** tend to relate the ***base form adjective*** more emphatically to the ***subject***, whereas ***deficit comparatives*** tend to relate it more emphatically to the ***comparative complement***. (36)a. and b. therefore both imply *Mary is happy*, and (36) c. and d. both imply *Maurice is unhappy*, though the 2 sentences of each pair have different subjects (Mary in a., Maurice in b; Mary in c., Maurice in d). Further examples of this are:

(37) a. Wendy is stricter than Tom. (= Wendy is strict)
b. Tom is less strict than (not as strict as) Wendy. (= Wendy is strict)
c. Wendy is less lenient than (not as lenient as) Tom. (= Tom is lenient)
d. Tom is more lenient than Wendy. (= Tom is lenient)

Here, too, then, there are shifts of emphasis between the sentences. (37)a. and c. both focus on Wendy but c. emphasizes Tom's lenience rather than her own strictness. The same applies in reverse to b. and d., both of which focus on Tom, but with b. stressing Wendy's strictness rather than his lenience.

What often adds to this effect is that some adjectives lose their base form meanings – or one of their principle base form meanings – in their comparative and superlative forms. For example, *tall* in *Charlene is tall* means 'having more than average height'.

(38) a. Charlene is taller than Mike.
b. Mike is less tall than Charlene.
c. Mike is shorter than Charlene.
d. Charlene is less short than Mike.

In (38)a., however, *taller* does not mean this. Here it means 'having more height than someone else'. So, for instance, (38)a. can be true even if Charlene is in fact short. In (38)b., on the other hand, *tall* has its base meaning of 'having more than average height'. Therefore a. and b. are not equivalent semantically.

Similarly, (38)d. means that Mike is short, but not (38)c., which simply says that he has less height than Charlene, though in general terms he may in fact be tall.

We are used to thinking that *comparative-x* means 'more of x' than the base. And so it does in many cases. For example, *My clothes are dirtier (than yours)*, implies that my clothes are dirty. But where base and comparative meanings diverge, as in (38), the surplus meaning may not apply in the sense of the base. As another example, *My clothes are newer (than yours)*, does not necessarily imply that the speaker's clothes are new; here *newer* is not an intensification of *new*, but simply conveys an age comparison.

This leads to what is sometimes rather jokingly called the 'comparative paradox'. As *newer* may not mean '*new*-plus', so *older* may not mean 'more old'. A sentence like e.g. *Sally is older now* implies, in fact, that the subject is 'no longer young', but nevertheless 'not yet old'.

These are chiefly semantic problems, of course. But as we have seen, they affect the grammar of comparison, or interact with it, in various ways.

031/6 Comparative constructions and their syntax

So far we have concentrated on just the adjective. Now we will take a look at the other elements in comparative constructions.

031/6.1 The comparative particles

As we have already seen, these are ***than*** (for ***surplus*** and ***deficit*** comparison), and ***as*** + adjective + ***as*** (for ***equative*** comparison):

(39) a. The lounge is warmer than the bedroom.
Das Wohnzimmer ist wärmer als das Schlafzimmer.
b. The bedroom is less warm than the lounge.
Das Schlafzimmer ist weniger warm als das Wohnzimmer.
c. Olivia is as tall as Matthew.
Olivia ist so groß wie Matthew.

Learners should distinguish carefully between ***than*** and ***as ... as***. A common mistake ⚠ among German speakers is the use of ***than*** for ***as*** in the equative construction, i.e. **Olivia is as tall than Matthew*.

Comparative particles in this constructions are ***prepositions***. Pronouns following them are placed (where necessary) in the ***object*** form, e.g. *Olivia is as tall as me/him/her; We are richer than them*.

Older forms of English used the subject forms. Occasionally this is still found with the first person pronoun (... *as tall as I*), but it is regarded as very formal. The comparative particle is in this case not a preposition but a conjunction (see **031/6.4**).

031/6.2 The comparative phrase

As already said, the noun following the comparative particle is called the ***comparative complement*** (e.g. *bedroom*). Particle and complement together form the ***comparative phrase*** (e.g. *than the bedroom*).

Comparative phrases are not always necessary. The intended comparative complement may be clear from the context:

(40) We prefer the lounge to the kitchen, but the kitchen is warmer.

In the examples so far, the ***comparative phrase*** (e.g. *than the bedroom*) functions as an ***adjectival complement*** within an ***adjective phrase***:

		Head	Adjectival Complement
(41) a.		warmer	than the bedroom.
	Premodification	*Head*	*Adjectival Complement*
b.	less	warm	than the lounge.
	Premodification	*Head*	*Adjectival Complement*
c.	as	tall	as Matthew.

031/6.3 Comparatives within noun phrases

Instead of being the head of an adjective phrase, as in **031/6.2**, the compared adjective may premodify a noun, e.g. *The lounge is a warmer place than the bedroom*. In this case the adjective is part of a ***noun phrase***, with the comparative phrase now functioning as the ***postmodification*** of the noun:

	Premodification	Head	Postmodification
(42) a.	a warmer	place	than the bedroom.
	Premodification	*Head*	*Postmodification*
b.	a less warm	place	than the lounge.
	Premodification	*Head*	*Postmodification*
c.	as tall a	person	as Matthew.

In equative constructions of this type, as in (42)c., the indefinite article follows the adjective. Other examples: *as great a success as this, as big a car as yours*, etc. This has a slightly formal ring to it, though. A more neutral alternative (obligatory with plurals) is to place the whole of the comparative construction in the postmodification:

	Head	Postmodification
(43) a.	a person	as tall as Matthew.
b.	a car	as big as yours.
c.	successes	as great as these.

A further alternative for both singular and plural is with *such*:

	Premodification	Head	Postmodification
(44) a.	such a tall	person	as Matthew.
b.	such great	successes	as these.

031/6.4 Verbs after comparative particles

A verb can be added to the comparative phrase. This makes it into a ***clause***. The ***comparative particle*** becomes a ***conjunction***. What was the comparative complement (e.g. the bedroom, *the lounge*) now becomes the ***subject*** of the comparative clause:

(45) a. The lounge is warmer than the bedroom is.
b. The bedroom is less warm than the lounge is.
c. Olivia was as tall as Matthew was.

Like *have* and *be*, other main verbs in the ***comparative clause*** can also be repeated. However, they are usually replaced by their ***auxiliary pro-forms*** (see chapter 8):

(46) a. The lounge feels warmer than the bedroom does (than the bedroom feels).
b. Jim looked more successful than Bob did (than Bob looked).

031/6.5 Various comparative relations

Semantically, the examples so far have all shown the same relation of comparison: with phrases, between the ***subject*** of the sentence and the ***comparative complement*** (e.g. ***The lounge*** *is warmer than* ***the bedroom***); with clauses, between the ***subject*** of the main clause and the ***subject*** of the ***comparative clause*** (e.g. ***The lounge*** *is warmer than* ***the bedroom*** *is*). However, there are several other possibilities. The whole range is as follows:

(47) a. ***My wife*** is a better driver than ***me***/than ***I*** am.
(main clause subject ↔ comparative complement/comparative clause subject)
b. ***My wife*** drives a bigger car than ***me***/than ***I*** do.
(main clause subject ↔ comparative complement/comparative clause subject)
c. My wife drives ***a bigger car*** than ***mine***.
(object head noun ↔ comparative complement)
d. The new cosmetics line has been ***more successful*** than ***we expected***.
... has had ***greater success*** ...
(main clause subject complement/direct object ↔ whole comparative clause)
e. The lounge ***is*** warmer than it ***was***.
(main clause predicator ↔ comparative clause predicator)
f. We're making ***larger profits*** than ***in 2006***.
(direct object ↔ adverbial)

(47)a. shows the pattern of previous examples. A slight difference with this sentence is that the comparative complement is a personal pronoun. The object form is usual after *than*, though in more elevated speech the subject form is also possible (*than I*). In other persons the object form, where it exists, is compulsory (*than her/him/us/them*). In the clause version, of course, the subject form is compulsory.

A further point is that all examples up to here have been ***intransitive***. In (47)b., with the same pattern of comparison, we encounter a ***transitive*** verb for the first time. Here, that is, we have a direct object (*a bigger car than me*). This is also true of (47)c. Despite the same sentence pattern, however, the comparative complement in (47)c. is related to *car*, not to *my wife*. In other words, the comparative relation here is between the ***comparative complement*** and the ***direct object head noun*** (and ***not***, as in a. and b., between the ***comparative complement*** and the ***subject***). With some sentences it may be unclear, out of context, whether the intended meaning is that of (47)b. or that of (47)c. In the following, for instance, (48)a. is ambiguous, and can mean either (48)b. or (48)c.:

(48) a. I have nicer friends than Madeleine.
b. I have friends who are nicer than Madeleine.
(relation = direct object ↔ comparative complement, as in (47)c.)
c. Madeleine's friends are not as nice as mine.
(relation = subject ↔ comparative complement, as in (47)b.)

The ambiguity would be resolved in the clause versions:

(49) a. I have nicer friends than Madeleine ***is***. (= (48)b. meaning)
b. I have nicer friends than Madeleine ***has***. (= (48)c. meaning)

We deal with (47)d., e., and f. in the next section.

031/6.6 Comparative clauses, ellipsis, and postponement

The use of clauses makes a greater range of comparison possible, as it includes the verb as a possible 'comparison partner'. A quite different comparative verb, as in (47)d. (*The new cosmetics line has been more successful/had greater success than we expected*), is often used to contrast facts with opinions, attitudes and predictions. A further example would be: *The team has done far worse than we ever imagined.* Here the comparison partners are the main clause predicator and the whole comparative clause.

With (47)e. (*The lounge is warmer than it was*) the partners are just the different predicator forms, i.e. the two distinct tense forms of the same verb. Semantically, this creates a purely time-level contrast.

Comparative clauses are necessary when the comparison rests on distinctions between verbs or their forms, as in (47)d. and e. Clauses are also used for emphasis or clarification when the phrase comparison is felt to be less clear.

Otherwise, the phrase is usually preferred in everyday language, as it is more 'economical'. A good example of this is when the comparative complement has an adverbial character (usually a noun phrase or a prepositional phrase), as in (47)f., *We're making larger profits than in 2006*. Further examples: *This is better weather than at home; We had a nicer time than last year.*

Sentences like this are a consequence of ***ellipsis***, i.e. omitting certain elements in more complex structures to produce a 'totally shortened' phrase. This can be illustrated in the following steps:

(50) a. We're making larger profits than the profits which we made in 2006.
↓
b. We're making larger profits than we made in 2006.
↓
c. We're making larger profits than in 2006.

Strictly speaking, then, the prepositional phrase in (50)c. is not the 'real' comparative complement semantically. It is simply part of the underlying comparative clause in (50)b., where the comparative elements seem to be the different tense forms of the same verb. However, even these can be regarded as products of ***ellipsis***, if we go back further to (50)a. This shows us that the 'original' comparative partners are direct object and comparative complement; the comparative complement is a noun phrase postmodified by a relative clause. Ellipsis of the head noun turns the relative clause into the comparative clause in (50)b., and further ellipsis of the subject and predicator leaves just the prepositional phrase.

Most of the comparative variations shown in (47) are products of ellipsis. This applies especially to the comparative phrases, but also to the clauses. For example, (47)d. (*The new cosmetics line has been more successful than we expected*) can be expressed more fully as ... *more successful than we expected it to be*.

A final point is that the comparative phrase or clause may not directly follow the adjective or noun that it is related to syntactically. Other clause elements may come in between:

(51) a. My working hours were longer yesterday than yours.
b. We made bigger profits last year than this year.
c. A larger number of people read newspapers than novels.
d. Judy is better at maths than I am.

This is what we call the ***postponement*** of the phrase or clause. It is an interruption of a particular sequence of words that belong together syntactically, and is a general phenomenon that affects other clause types as well (see also chapter 14). The 'interruption' can be removed if the expressions in between are not directly related to the words they follow, as (51)a. or b., where *yesterday* and *last year* can easily be placed somewhere else, e.g. *Yesterday my working hours were longer than yours*. In (51)d. the interrupting expression *at maths* is itself strongly attached to its position, as it is also an adjectival complement of *better*. It is possible, however, to postpone this, instead of the comparative clause: ... *better than I am at maths*.

There is no alternative, though, when the comparative adjective is part of the subject of a sentence, as in (51)c.

031/6.7 Nominalization of comparatives

Comparative adjectives can also feature in a construction similar to that of superlatives, with the definite article preceding and a ***partitive* of*-genitive*** following (instead of a comparative phrase).The starting-point is the presence of a head noun, as in **031/6.2** However, it may be left out, making the adjective itself into a noun. A context is required. Thus, if I am already talking about Mary and John, and want to express that *Mary is a nicer person than John*, I could use the forms in (52)a. or b.:

(52) a. Mary is the nicer person of the two.
b. Mary is the nicer of the two.

The nominalized adjective, as in b., is essentially a pronoun, i.e. it stands for the missing head noun (or one of the same type), which in a. is present.

The construction is a little formal with comparatives, but is standard with superlatives (see under **031/3** above and **031/7** below). Note the use of the ***definite article*** here.

031/6.8 Premodifiers with comparatives

Whereas base forms of adjectives are intensified by *very*, comparatives are intensified by *much*, i.e. *very warm*, but *much warmer*. It should be noted that *much* is being used here as an ***adverb*** (like *very*), not as a quantifier. This means that it stays the same, regardless of what kind of noun follows, e.g. *a much warmer room for much nicer people*.

With periphrastic forms, of course, *much* precedes *more* and *less*, as, for example, in *much more interesting, much less warm*.

Much can itself be further intensified. Here we use *very* again. So although **very warmer* is not possible, we can say *very much warmer*. So, also *very much more interesting*. Certain other premodifiers are possible too, e.g.:

- *no, not much, hardly any:*
  My car is no bigger/not much bigger/hardly any bigger than yours.
  (*... kein bisschen größer/nicht viel größer/kaum größer als ...*)
- *a little/a bit/a little bit:*
  My car is a little/a bit/a little bit bigger than yours.
  (*... etwas größer/ein bisschen größer/ein kleines bisschen größer als ...*)
- *far/even:*
  My car is far/even bigger than yours.
  (*... viel/weitaus größer/(sogar) noch größer als ...*)

031/6.9 Double comparatives

Double comparatives express a continuous process of increase. Inflectional forms are repeated and joined by *and*. Periphrastic forms just repeat the *more*:

(53) a. Stanley is getting fatter and fatter.
Stanley wird immer dicker.
b. His wife is getting more and more anxious.
Seine Frau wird immer besorgter.

The following construction shows a slightly different kind of double comparative, where the two adjectives (and often the verbs) are different. This type relates two processes of increase to one another:

(54) a. The fatter Stanley gets, the more anxious his wife becomes.
Je dicker Stanley wird, desto besorgter wird seine Frau.
b. The richer she gets, the more problematic her life becomes.
Je reicher sie wird, desto problematischer wird ihr Leben.

c. The hotter it gets, the less active we are.
Je wärmer es wird, desto weniger aktiv sind wir.

031/7 Superlatives

We now return to superlatives, which are syntactically less complex than comparatives. As already explained, superlatives pick out one element from a particular group of three or more members. The group is often implied by context, but can be referred to explicitly in an ***of***-phrase or other prepositional expression. We refer to this as the ***specifying element***:

(55) a. (In our family) Julie is the tallest of us all.
b. Sally and Alan are very intelligent, but Maria is the most interesting (of the three).
c. We have many good paintings, but this is the best in our collection.
d. Wendy is the bravest of the three.

031/7.1 Superlatives: nouns or adjectives?

Superlative forms, as typified in (55), are ***nominalized adjectives***, i.e. essentially pronouns standing for a missing head noun. The head noun could also be added, or expressed in a prop-pronoun, e.g. *the most interesting person, the best painting, the bravest one,* etc. Where the head noun cannot be inferred from the context, it must be included:

(56) a. Molly is the cleverest pupil at the school.
b. The least expensive beer (in the shop) is Browns Lager.
c. He makes the most stupid remarks that I have ever heard.

In these cases, the superlative is a ***premodifying adjective***. Note that the identifying reference is a definite one, and therefore requires the definite article.

031/7.2 Specifying elements: type and position

In addition to prepositional phrases, ***specifying elements*** can also be relative clauses, as in c. Specifying elements generally follow the noun, and function as postmodifiers. Prepositional phrases may sometimes be split off, however, and placed elsewhere (usually at the beginning of the sentence). They then function as separate adverbials, e.g. *At the school, Molly is the cleverest pupil; Of the three, Wendy is the bravest*. This gives them particular profile. The normal position is the postmodifying one. Relative clauses, of course, must always postmodify.

031/7.3 No article

The article is omitted in cases like the following:

(57) a. Steaks are juiciest in Texas.
b. Bananas used to be cheapest at the market.
c. For me, jogging is most effective in the evenings.
d. Fred was most charming when he was drunk.

This is a rather different sense of the superlative from the one discussed so far. Here it is not the noun itself that is profiled (i.e. in the 'one of a group' meaning), but its state or behaviour under particular circumstances. Although the superlative is used as a ***predicative adjective***, it has a kind of adverbial meaning, e.g. *Bananas could be bought most cheaply …; … jogging is done most effectively …; Fred behaved most charmingly*. An alternative which reflects this meaning closely is one with a prepositional phrase (i.e. also an adverbial expression). Note the similar German equivalent:

(58) a. Steaks are ***at their juiciest*** in Texas (= *am saftigsten*).
b. Bananas used to be ***at their cheapest*** at the market (= *am billigsten*).
c. For me, jogging is ***at its most effective*** in the evenings (= *am effektivsten*).
d. Fred was ***at his most charming*** when he was drunk (= *am charmantesten*).

031/8 Non-adjective comparison

The category of ***comparison*** is fundamental to adjectives and adverbs (see next chapter for adverbs). But it also affects ***quantifiers***. In this section we will deal with ***quantifier comparison***. The quantifier use of *more* and *most* is very similar to that of adjective comparison. But there are one or two additional points to note.

031/8.1 more (= a larger number/amount than)

More is used with plurals and singular non-count nouns. Structurally, it is the comparative form of *much/many*, as we saw above. Semantically, however, ***more*** is the comparative of all indefinite determiners that refer to plurals and singular non-count nouns (like *some*, the zero article, the numerals, etc.):

(59) a. Many people like rugby, but more (people) like soccer.
b. A few guests were still on the terrace, but more (guests) were in the dining-room.
c. Mike eats some rice, but he eats more potatoes.

Like other determiners, *more* can be used as a pronoun, as in (59)a. and b., where the nouns in brackets can be left out. Overt comparisons with *than* (as in the case of adjectives) are most common in the phrase form. Verbs can be added, of course, as in the brackets below. The verb type used varies slightly, depending on the sentence function of the noun phrase concerned:

(60) a. More people like soccer than (like) rugby.
b. Mike earns more money than Jenny (earns/does).
c. Mike eats more potatoes than (he eats/does) rice.

Replacement by auxiliary pro-form is possible and usual in all functions of the noun phrase except subject. In this case, as in (60)a., the main verb has to be repeated.

031/8.2 more in general and specific meanings

Most examples in (59) and (60) have ***general*** reference. An exception is (59)b., where ***specific*** reference is implied, i.e. 'guests at that hotel'. Specific reference can be made explicit, as here by postmodification, *... at that hotel.* Similarly, we could say *More people in this town like soccer ...*, or *Mike ate more potatoes from the buffet than anyone else.*

Another possibility to specify is to use ***more of***:

(61) a. More of the people in this town like soccer than rugby.
b. Mike ate more of the potatoes from the buffet than anyone else.

As with other quantifiers used ***partitively*** (*some of, few of, any of*, etc.), ***more of*** must refer to a ***specific*** entity, and must be followed by ***a determiner***, usually the definite article, or some other definite determiner (demonstrative, possessive, etc.). It can ***never*** be used in a general sense. Thus if I say *more of the people*, I do not simply mean *mehr Menschen (überhaupt)*, but *mehr von den Menschen, von denen jetzt die Rede ist.* On the other hand, ***more*** alone (i.e. used itself as a determiner), can be specific, as well as general in meaning.

031/8.3 more in the sense of 'an additional quantity'

More is used in the meaning of 'a further, additional quantity', i.e. it is the plural and non-count equivalent of *another*. It is often preceded by other (modifying) quantifiers:

(62) a. I'd like some more information, please.
... noch ein paar Informationen ...
b. Would you like a little more tea, Mrs. Brown?
... noch etwas Tee ...?
c. She did not want any more cake.
Sie wollte keinen Kuchen mehr (nichts mehr von dem Kuchen).
d. We need more tickets.
Wir brauchen noch Karten.

Note that although *more* itself can refer to singular or plural, preceding quantifiers and other modifiers must take account of the difference where necessary, i.e. *a little more tea*, but *a few more cakes*; similarly, *much more trouble*, but *many more difficulties.*

Numerals are also common: *three more tickets* (*noch drei Karten*), *four more hours* (*noch vier Stunden*). Perhaps rather strangely, an alternative to *more* with numerals is *another* + numeral: *another three tickets, another four hours.*

In this meaning, *more* also postmodifies ***indefinite pronouns***: *nothing more, something more, anything more*, etc., e.g. *I have nothing more to say on the matter* (*Ich habe nichts mehr dazu zu sagen*).

031/8.4 more as a general or 'indefinite' pronoun and adverb

More not only modifies indefinite pronouns. It also has a general pronoun use of similar meaning:

(63) a. Dudley would like to do more for the community, but unfortunately his job takes up all his time.
b. I could say more on that issue, but I won't do that now.
c. More has been written about Hitler than about any other contemporary historical figure.

And likewise as an adverb:

(64) a. Dudley would like to help us more, but unfortunately he has no time.
b. You ought to think more of your health.
c. I had hoped to walk more while on holiday, but the weather was too bad.

A different kind of adverb use is in the sense of *rather*:

(65) a. Your hat looks more like a wig.
... sieht eher aus wie eine Perücke.
b. Her occupation is more a hobby than a real job.
... ist eher Hobby als echter Job.

031/8.5 most (= 'the majority/major portion of')

This is the superlative form of *more* and is likewise used with plurals and singular non-count nouns. It also occurs as a simple ***determiner*** (i.e. ***without*** partitive *of*) for both ***general*** and ***specific*** reference:

(66) a. Most people (in general) like soccer.
Die meisten Leute (überhaupt), mögen Fußball.
b. Most lamb eaten in Britain comes from New Zealand.
Das Lamm, das in Großbritannien gegessen wird, stammt zum Großteil aus Neuseeland.
c. I spoke to most people (who were) at the party.
Ich sprach mit den meisten Gästen, die auf dem Fest waren.
d. Fred drinks most whisky (but he doesn't like Canadian).
Fred trinkt die meisten Whiskysorten (mag aber den kanadischen Whisky nicht).

Most here means *the largest part or number of*. Taken literally, this can be any quantity above 50%. In practice, however, ***most*** is usually reserved for 'large majorities' and frequently has the sense of *almost all*.

⚠ Important for German speakers: the definite article is ***never*** used here in English!

031/8.6 most and most of

We have just seen that ***most*** can be used for specific reference, as in (66)b. and c. An alternative which makes the specific reference quite clear is ***most of***.

(67) a. Most of the lamb eaten in Great Britain comes from New Zealand.
b. I spoke to most of the people at the party.

Like *more of*, ***most of*** needs a ***determiner*** following it – usually the definite article, demonstrative, or possessive. Also similar to *more of* is the fact that ***most of*** can only appear in ***specific*** references, ***never*** in general ones.

031/8.7 most and the most (= 'a larger number/quantity than others')

As a quantifier, ***most*** also has another, rather different specific meaning (though one similar to that of superlative adjectives), i.e. *more of something than any other members of a particular group*. In this use a preceding definite article is permissible and also usual, especially with subject nouns:

(68) a. The most points went to the song from Finland.
(= Finland got more points than any other country).
b. I spoke to (the) most people at the party.
(= to more people than anyone else spoke to).
c. Roger ate (the) most sandwiches.
(= more than anyone else ate).

The German translation here too is with the article (e.g. *die meisten Punkte/mit den meisten Leuten*). German, that is, does not distinguish this meaning (*more than anyone else*) from the meaning discussed in **031/8.5** (*the largest portion*).

In this sense ***most/the most*** are also used as pronouns and adverbs.

(69) a. We all ate some sandwiches, but Roger ate (the) most.
(= die meisten).
b. My wife likes these chocolates (the) most.
(= … mag diese Pralinen am liebsten).
c. I sweat (the) most when I'm nervous.
(Ich schwitze am meisten, wenn ich nervös bin).

Note also the use of the adverbial set phrase ***at the most*** (= *höchstens*): *How long are you staying? Three days at the most.*

031/8.8 less and fewer

The quantifiers ***less*** and ***fewer*** are the ***deficit comparative*** equivalents of ***more***. Structurally, their respective base forms are *little* and *few*, but like *more*, they function as the comparative of all indefinite determiners with plural and singular non-count reference.

Whereas *more* is used for both plurals and singular non-count nouns, the deficit comparatives make a distinction, viz., ***fewer*** for ***plurals*** and ***less*** for ***singular non-count***. Otherwise, they behave grammatically in the same way as *more*:

(70) a. Many people like soccer, but fewer (people) like rugby.
b. Fewer people like rugby than soccer.
c. Mike eats less rice than potatoes.
d. Jenny earns less money than Mike (earns/does).

Mixed reference of singular and plural, as in (70)c., is rather colloquial. More formally, ***less*** would be avoided as a quantifier with a plural following as comparative complement. The solution is to place *less* after *rice* as an adverb: *Mike eats rice less than (he eats/does) potatoes.*

In neutral and less formal language, the negative equative ***not as many/much*** is often preferred to *fewer* and *less*, especially when no comparative phrase or clause follows:

(71) a. A lot of people like soccer, but not as many (people) like rugby.
b. Jenny doesn't earn as much money as Mike.

The negative equative versions generally give more emphasis.

Fewer of and *less of* function in the same way as *more of* (but again, only with ***specific*** meaning!):

(72) a. Fewer of the people in this town like rugby than soccer.
b. Jenny has to pay less of her salary in tax than Mike.

Preceding adverbial modifiers are *much* (with *less*), *a lot* (usually with *less*, occasionally also with *fewer*), and *far* (with both *less* and *fewer*).

Numerals generally precede ***fewer***, although numbered quantities of ***weight, distance, cost, time***, etc. usually combine with ***less***:

(73) a. Far fewer people in this town like rugby.
b. They spent far/much/a lot less money on their house than we did.
c. Tomatoes cost 50 cents less here than at the other shop.
d. I weigh 6 pounds less than last year.
e. There were only ten members at the committee meeting: 9 fewer than at the last one.

Finally, *less* can be used in the same way as *more* as a general or 'indefinite' pronoun and adverb:

(74) a. Dudley does less for the community than his wife does.
b. Less has been written about Churchill than Hitler.
c. Diana helps us much less in the garden than our other daughter does.

d. Your hat looks less like a hat than a wig.
e. Joe was less tired than depressed.

031/8.9 least and fewest

These are the superlative partners to *less* and *fewer,* and are also the ***deficit superlative*** equivalents of *most.* Unlike *most,* however, they are used in general meaning with the definite article (i.e. not as determiners, but as quantifying adjectives). More widespread in informal language are the phrases *the least amount of/the least number of,* where ***least*** means 'lowest' or 'smallest':

(75) a. The least number of girls (the fewest girls) like soccer.
Die wenigsten Mädchen mögen Fußball.
b. The least (amount of) beef eaten in Britain is now of British origin.
Das Rindfleisch, das in Großbritannien gegessen wird, stammt heutzutage zum geringsten Teil aus Großbritannien.

A stylistically more elaborate version of (75) is with *the fewest of, the least of: The fewest of girls like soccer; The least of the beef eaten in Britain ...*

Generally speaking, ***least*** and ***fewest*** are not heard as much in everyday language as *more* and *most.* The usual preference is just to refer to small quantities, using *very little, very few, not very many/much,* etc.: *Very few girls ...; Very little beef ...,* etc.

Least and ***fewest*** are more common in the specific meaning *less/fewer of something than any other members of a particular group* (the equivalent of *most* under 031/8.7). Here a preceding definite article is usual, but may also be left out:

(76) a. (The) Fewest points went to the song from Finland.
(= Finland got fewer points than any other country).
b. Roger drank (the) least alcohol (of anyone) at the party.
(= Roger drank less than anyone else).

Like ***most/the most*** they also occur as pronouns and adverbs.

(77) a. We all ate some sandwiches, but Roger ate (the) fewest.
(= die wenigsten).
b. My wife likes these chocolates (the) least.
(= ... mag diese Pralinen am wenigsten).
c. I sweat (the) least when I'm relaxed.
(Ich schwitze am wenigsten, wenn ich entspannt bin).

Note also the use of the adverbial set phrase ***at least*** (= *wenigstens, mindestens*):

(78) a. At least sit down for 5 minutes, even if you can't stay long.
Setze dich wenigstens 5 Minuten lang, auch wenn ...

b. I didn't count the guests at the party, but I would say there were at least a hundred.
(... mindestens hundert).

031/9 Summary of different comparative types and structures

031/9.1 Overview

Comparison has to do with a relation of ***more*** (= ***surplus comparison***), ***less*** (= ***deficit comparison***), or the ***same amount*** (= ***equative comparison***). ***Surplus*** and ***deficit*** comparison each have two levels: ***comparative*** (***more/less***), and ***superlative*** (***most/least***).

Surplus comparatives and superlatives occur in two possible forms, ***periphrastic*** (*more/less clear, most/least clear*), and ***inflectional*** (*clearer, clearest*). ***Deficit*** comparatives and superlatives occur only in ***periphrastic*** forms.

031/9.2 Comparative/superlative forms, general rule

Inflectional forms: adjectives of ***one syllable*** add ***-er*** and ***-est*** to the base form (*cheap → cheaper → cheapest*).
Periphrastic forms: adjectives of ***more than one syllable*** are preceded by ***more/less, most/least*** (*successful → more/less successful → most/least successful*).
Deficit comparison is only ***periphrastic***.

031/9.3 Comparative/superlative forms; exceptions with one-syllable adjectives

a) *real, right* and *wrong,* plus all participles, take the ***periphrastic*** form (*more real, more bored*).
b) The following (abstract meanings) can take either the ***inflectional*** or the ***periphrastic*** form: *brave, clear, keen, free, safe, sure, true, wise* (*keener/more keen, truer/more true*), etc.
c) The one-syllable adjectives *good* and *bad* have ***irregular*** comparative and superlative forms: *good → better → best; bad → worse → worst*
d) For *old* and *far* there are ***two*** sets of ***inflectional*** forms with two separate meaning fields:
far → farther → farthest (distance meaning only)
further → furthest (all meanings)
old → older → oldest (***regular***: all meanings)
elder → eldest (***attributive-restricted,*** meaning *senior* and applied to family members)
e) ***Quantifiers:*** *little → less → least; many → more → most; few → fewer → fewest* (***regular***)

031/9.4 Comparative/superlative forms; exceptions with adjectives of two syllables

Either form:
Adjectives ending in *-er, -y, -ow, -le* can take either form (with inflections final *-y → -i*). Applies also to prefix-negatives:

(un)lucky	→	*(un)luckier*	→	*(un)luckiest*
	→	*more (un)lucky*	→	*most (un)lucky*

Also *quiet, pleasant, common,* and those with stressed second syllable (e.g. *compact, polite*):

compact	→	*compacter*	→	*compactest*
[kəm'pækt]	→	*more compact*	→	*most compact*

031/9.5 Use and syntax

a) ***comparative*** (used to compare ***two*** elements):
Wendy is ***braver than*** Tom. (***surplus*** comparison)
Tom is ***less*** brave ***than*** Wendy. (***deficit*** comparison)

b) ***equative*** (used to compare ***two*** elements):
Jane is ***as happy as*** Sarah.
Tom is ***not as*** brave ***as*** Wendy.
(***Negative equative*** comparison often preferred, especially informally, to ***deficit*** comparison).

c) ***The comparative particles and the comparative phrase/clause:***
Learners should distinguish carefully between ***than*** (in ***surplus/deficit*** comparison) and ***as … as*** (in ***equative*** comparison). German speakers tend to confuse ***than*** and ***as***, e.g. **Wendy is braver as Tom,* or **Tom is not as brave than Wendy.* ⚠
In *Wendy is braver than Tom* and *Tom is not as brave as Wendy*, the phrases *than Tom* and *as Wendy* are the ***comparative phrases***, with the ***comparative particles*** *than* and *as* functioning as ***prepositions***. Any personal pronouns following are usually in the ***object form*** in modern English: *… as me/… than him*, etc.
If a verb is added, the phrase becomes a ***comparative clause***, with the ***comparative particles*** functioning as ***conjunctions***: *Wendy is braver than Tom is.* Note that *Tom* is now the subject of the comparative clause. As a pronoun it must therefore be in the ***subject form***: *Wendy is braver than he is.*
Although main verbs in the comparative clause can be repeated, they are usually replaced by their ***auxiliary pro-forms***, e.g. *The lounge feels warmer than the bedroom does* (*than the bedroom feels*).

d) ***superlative:***
This picks out one element from a particular group of ***three*** or more members. The group may be implied, or expressed explicitly (***of***-phrase or other prepositional expression):
(In our family) Julie is ***the tallest*** (of us all).
Wendy is braver than Tom and Jerry = Wendy is the ***bravest*** of the three.
John is ***less lucky than*** Sharon and Bob = John is (the) ***least lucky of*** the three (people).

Chapter 5 Adverbs

032 Basic features

As already pointed out, ***adverbs*** are closely related to adjectives. Many have a similar descriptive meaning, and a large number are derived from adjectives: the ending ***-ly*** is added to an adjective to form an appropriate adverb:

quick → ***quickly***; *slow* → ***slowly***; *public* → ***publicly***; *serious* → ***seriously***; *nice* → ***nicely***.

This indicates on the one hand a similarity in meaning, but on the other a difference in grammatical function. Whereas adjectives are associated with nouns, ***adverbs*** are typically connected with ***verbs***, as the term itself suggests (*ad-verb*):

(1) a. She showed a quick reaction/She reacted quickly.
b. John is a nice dancer/John dances nicely.

The ***-ly*** ending often causes problems for German learners, as adverbs in German do not have a special suffix to mark them. The adjective itself is simply used as an adverb, e.g. ⚠ *Sie reagierte schnell.* A typical German-influenced error in English would be to translate this as **She reacted quick*. True, this would not be a mistake in certain colloquial forms of English where some adjectives are used as adverbs in a similar way. In standard English, however, this is not acceptable. More precisely, it is not acceptable when the adverb must be marked. And this is the next problem: a great many adverbs have no special ending at all, in particular those that are not related to adjectives.

So although the majority are marked by the suffix, a very large minority are not. This makes it additionally difficult to develop the habit of 'not forgetting' the ***-ly*** ending when it is necessary.

Adverbs typically describe actions and states, when these are expressed by verbs, as in (1). They tell us ***how***, ***when***, ***where***, ***how often***, or ***to what extent*** ('how much') something happens. In this case, they are said to ***modify*** the verb grammatically. This is a central function, but not the only one. In fact, adverbs as a class fill a whole range of varied semantic and grammatical roles. Some, for instance, may modify adjectives or other adverbs (*very big/quite seriously*), or in certain cases even nouns (*only a cat*). They can also relate to whole sentences, connecting one statement to another (*however, so, therefore*), or referring to speaker attitudes and intentions (*frankly, perhaps, unfortunately*). Specific adverbs are also used to form questions (*When?; How?; Where?*). Even when referring to an action, an adverb may modify not just the verb, but the verb plus its complementation, e.g. *Sharon got to the station quickly*.

A particular issue with adverbs is their position. Where should an adverb be placed in a sentence? The answer depends on its type of meaning, on the part of the sentence it refers to, and occasionally also on emphasis. There is often a certain choice of position, and this can make it difficult to give clear rules, especially when considerations of style are involved. On the other hand, there are definite 'taboos', and these may contradict the position principles of other languages. German, for instance, often places adverbs between the verb and its objects (or other compulsory elements of complementation): *Sie überquerte schnell die Straße; Wir benutzen häufig öffentliche Verkehrsmittel.* This cannot be ⚠ copied in English (**She crossed quickly the street; *We use often public transport*). In the first case the most common English version would be *She crossed the street quickly* (following the object), and in the second *We often use public transport* (i.e. between subject and verb, which is, of course, strange for German-conditioned ears and eyes).

Like adjectives, ***adverbs*** can be ***gradable***, i.e. appear in the ***comparative*** and ***superlative*** (*quickly → more/less quickly → most/least quickly*), and occur with ***adverbs of degree*** (*very/quite quickly*).

Finally, a note on the terms ***adverb*** and ***adverbial***. These are often wrongly used in the same meaning. It is important to differentiate between them. An ***adverb*** is a representative of a particular ***word-class*** (in the same way that terms like *noun, adjective, preposition, conjunction*, etc., also refer to word-classes). The expression ***adverbial***, on the other hand, refers (like *subject, object, subject complement*, etc.) to a ***syntactic function***. Not only adverbs can function as adverbials, but also, for example, prepositional phrases (*on the table*), and noun phrases (*last week*). Sometimes these are also called 'adverbs'. However, this confuses two separate levels of analysis that should be carefully kept apart. It is important to remember this point, even when dealing with adverbs themselves, for as we will see later, adverbs do not always function as adverbials.

The adverb-adverbial confusion is encouraged by the fact that both have the same categories of meaning (e.g. *time, manner, place*, etc.), and often occupy similar sentence positions.

Nevertheless, it is necessary, as we have said, to make a clear distinction between the ***adverb*** as a ***word-class***, and the ***adverbial*** as a ***function***.

Adverb meaning 033

033/1 Semantic types
033/2 The adverb phrase and its functions
033/3 Adverb position: general
033/4 Adverb position according to meaning
033/5 Position of other adverbials
033/6 Usage: some special cases

As the meaning of an adverb strongly influences its function and position in the sentence, we will take semantics as the starting point.

033/1 Semantic types

033/1.1 Adverbs of manner

This is the largest and most open category. Adverbs of manner express ***how*** (i.e. in what way) something is done:

(2) a. He drove the car ***dangerously***.
b. The teacher answered our questions ***patiently***.

033/1.2 Adverbs of time

It seems obvious that adverbs of time should tell us ***when*** something happens. However, most of them do not do this in any ***definite*** sense. ***Definite*** time is referred to mainly by prepositional and noun phrases in the adverbial function (*at 8 o'clock, on Monday, last January,* etc.). The few actual adverbs that do refer to ***definite*** times are ***deictic*** (i.e. speaker-relative): *today, tomorrow, now*. The rest are ***indefinite*** and mostly what we will call ***context-relative***, i.e. they refer to contexts already mentioned or being spoken about: *then, again, finally, early/late, immediately, afterwards, beforehand, first, second, next,* etc. Some of these are understood as deictic if there is no further context: *still, yet, already, just, recently, soon, formerly,* etc.

Many of these have little direct relation to ***when?*** They concern time in a broad range of senses, e.g. ***how long?*** (*soon, finally, just, immediately*), ***how punctual?*** (*early/late*), ***in what order?*** (*first, second*). *Still, yet* and *already* have a modal meaning connected with speaker expectation, and in some ways so do *just* and *again*. Individual adverbs are discussed more fully below.

033/1.3 Adverbs of frequency

These also concern time, but in the sense of ***how often***?

Definite frequency is expressed by the numeral adverbs *once* and *twice*, and interval adverbs such as *hourly, daily, weekly, monthly,* etc. Apart from these, it is prepositional and noun phrases here, too, that are chiefly responsible for ***definite*** reference: *every morning/night/week/month/year,* etc., *three times a day, on Saturdays.*

Ordinary time adverbials, such as *in the summer, at Christmas, during the spring holiday,* can in context take on the role of frequency adverbials, e.g. *We (usually) go to California during the spring holiday.* Most of the adverbs in this category express ***indefinite*** frequency: *always, often, sometimes, occasionally, seldom,* etc. ***Never*** also belongs here, but is in a sense definite.

033/1.4 Adverbs of place and direction

These tell us ***where*** an event happens and in ***what direction*** something moves.

Most adverbs of place can equally express direction: *here/there, away/back, abroad, ahead, left/right,* etc., and the ***indefinite adverbs*** *somewhere/anywhere/nowhere/everywhere.*

A few, such as *backwards, forwards, sideways,* etc. express direction alone.

A particular feature of English are ***adverb particles***. These are prepositions used as adverbs, e.g. *above, below, behind, outside/inside.*

(3) a. We waved to our guests from the garden, and then went ***inside*** (= inside the house).
b. John drove the car in front and Bettina the one ***behind*** (= the one that was behind the one in front).

The particles listed above are treated as independent adverbs (i.e. functioning as adverbials, see also below). Others, such as *up, down, over, across, in, out,* etc., are regarded as independent only when they relate to place and follow verbs like *to be, to stay,* etc. With verbs of motion, when they refer to direction, they are considered part of the verb (i.e. as belonging to the ***predicator***):

Predicator (P)
(4) a. Cathy is ***coming over*** on Sunday (= she is visiting us).
Predicator (P)
b. Nobody answered the door. Clearly, the family ***had gone out***.
Adverbial (A)
c. Nobody answered the door. Clearly, the family was ***out***.

Combinations of verb + adverb particle, as in (70)a. and b., are ***phrasal verbs*** (see chapter 8 under *Particle verbs*).

033/1.5 Adverbs of degree

Typical adverbs of degree are *very, rather, quite, too, enough, partly, totally, completely,* etc.
They express ***to what extent*** something happens, or a particular condition exists. They modify not only verbs, but also adjectives and other adverbs:

(5) a. We ***completely*** forgot to buy bread.
b. That book is ***very*** good.
c. Sheila did ***rather*** badly in the exam.

Degree adverbs tend to form particular ***collocations***, especially with adjectives and other adverbs. For instance, we say *much better*, but *very ill; seriously* also collocates with *ill,* but not with *sick. Badly* (like *seriously*) can modify other adjectives expressing damage or harm (*injured, hurt, damaged, harmed,* etc.), and yet we cannot say **badly ill.* The various fields of meaning have their special 'adverb intensifiers'. One can be *highly praised* or *strongly criticized;* some things are *extremely dangerous,* others *completely safe;* people can be *totally wrong* or *absolutely right, thoroughly lazy* or *very hard-working,* and so on.
A connected point is that not all degree adverbs can modify all three classes of word. *Too, very* and *fairly* (= *quite/rather*) are confined to adjectives and adverbs, for example. *Rather* and *quite,* on the other hand, can also modify certain verbs:

(6) a. I ***rather/quite*** enjoyed the concert.
b. We ***quite*** forgot your birthday. Sorry!

For details on the meanings of *quite, rather* and other common degree adverbs, see section **033/6** below.

033/1.6 Adverbs of focus

These give sentences, or individual elements in them, a certain meaning ***perspective*** from which they are to be understood. Sub-categories are ***emphasis*** (*particularly*), ***restriction*** (*only*), ***addition*** (*also*), and general ***viewpoint*** (e.g. *socially, psychologically, professionally,* etc.):

(7) a. ***Politically*** and ***socially***, Germany reached a turning-point in 1989.
b. Our firm exports ***mainly*** to Asia, but ***also*** to America.
c. ***Basically***, we deal ***just*** in antique furniture, but recently we have started selling a few modern items ***too***.

033/1.7 Connective adverbs

Connectives relate one statement to another. They are also known as ***relational adverbs*** or ***conjuncts***. Main sub-types are ***conclusion/consequence*** (*so, therefore*), ***contradiction/concession*** (*however, nevertheless*), ***sequence*** (*firstly, secondly, next*), ***addition/reinforcement*** (*furthermore, moreover*), ***transition*** (*incidentally, meanwhile*), ***comparison*** (*similarly, likewise*), ***contrast*** (*instead*), ***apposition*** (*namely*), ***re-phrasing*** (*rather*), ***replacement*** (*alternatively*).

Connectives modify whole clauses and sentences, and are placed typically at the beginning or end. They are often separated from the rest of the sentence by a comma. This suggests a pause, and shows that connectives are not actually part of the content of the sentence itself. Instead, they signal to the reader or listener how one sentence or clause is linked to another in meaning. They help to give shape to groups of sentences or statements, and can play an important part in shaping whole texts logically. This is particularly important when explanations are given, processes described, or arguments presented. But ***connectives*** are also crucial in dialogues to show the reaction of one speaker to what another says. Good use of connectives is essential in many speech intention fields, such as agreeing and disagreeing, expressing likes/dislikes, showing understanding and non-understanding, or verbalizing sympathy and decision processes. They are important aspects of differentiated expression and appropriate reaction behaviour.

(8) A: ***So*** you don't want to come with me, ***then***?
B: ***Well***, I would prefer to stay at home, or ***rather***, work in the garden.
Firstly, I have a lot to do, and ***secondly***, I don't like Brenda's friends.
A: ***Still***, it is a fortieth birthday.
B: ***Maybe***. But ***even so***, it's a bad time for me. And ***anyway***, we'd have to stay the night there. And that would be very awkward with Rachel coming back tomorrow.

033/1.8 Adverbs of comment

These are similar to connectives in several ways: they are not part of the sentence content, they are often placed at the beginning of sentences and clauses, and are usually then separated from the rest by commas. But in contrast to connectives, ***adverbs of comment*** signal the speaker's attitude to what is expressed, its relationship to reality, or how it should be generally understood.

Sub-types are ***speaker style*** (*frankly, honestly, personally*), ***content evaluation*** (*fortunately, hopefully, sadly*), and ***content truth/certainty*** (*obviously, perhaps, possibly*).

(9) a. ***Secretly***, I'm rather glad Bob didn't marry Sylvia.
b. ***Hopefully***, we'll be more successful next time.
c. ***Clearly***, the team needs new players.

033/2 The adverb phrase and its functions

The grammatical unit centred around an adverb is an ***adverb phrase***. As with other phrases, the main word is called the ***head***. In an adverb phrase the head must, of course, be an adverb. The phrase may consist just of the head alone (i.e. a single adverb) or include other elements. Typically, these are also adverbs (usually of degree, e.g. *very, rather, quite,* etc.), which ***premodify*** the head. Patterns are similar to those of the adjective phrase:

(10)

Premodification	***Head***
very	quickly
quite	proudly
rather	soon

As with adjectives, elements following the head form the ***complement***, here the ***adverb complement***. Adverb complements are less common than adjective complements. In fact, the adverb phrase is generally less complex in structure than adjective or noun phrases. Adverb complements occur most frequently with ***consecutive*** or ***comparative*** constructions (see chapter 4, **031** and chapter 14):

(11) a. The language teacher speaks ***too fast for beginners***.
b. Uncle Norman drives ***more slowly than father***.

The structure of these phrases is:

(12)

Premodification	***Head***	***Adverb Complement***
too	fast	for beginners
more	slowly	than father

As with other phrases, it is always the ***phrase as a whole*** that fills any given syntactic function:

Adverbial (A)

(13) Joan started her new job ***quite enthusiastically***.

From now on, we will refer for simplicity just to 'adverbs' rather than to 'adverb phrases', bearing in mind that the term *adverb* always means 'the adverb phrase as a whole'.

Adverbs are found in two basic types of general function. When they modify verbs or whole sentences or clauses, they have an ***independent sentence function***, as in (14)a. When they modify other word classes (typically adjectives and other adverbs), they have a ***phrase modifier function***, as in (14)b.:

(14) a. *She* ***certainly*** *dances* ***beautifully***, ***though***.
b. *She spoke* ***quite*** *impressively at a* ***very*** *important political conference yesterday.*

In (14)a. all three adverbs are independent, and function as ***adverbials***. In (14)b. the adverbs *quite* and *very* are ***premodifiers*** inside an adverb and an adjective phrase, respectively.

We will now look more closely at these factors.

033/2.1 Adverbial (A)

The only independent sentence function filled by adverbs is that of ***adverbial*** (***A***). Adverbs can never be subjects, objects or complements:

(15) a. You must buy the ticket ***here*** (*A*) ***quickly*** (*A*) ***tomorrow*** (*A*).
b. ***Actually*** (*A*), Phil ***always*** (*A*) arrives ***late*** (*A*).

The adverbs here show a range of meanings and relate to the sentence and its parts in varied ways. In a. adverbs of ***place*** (*here*), ***manner*** (*quickly*) and ***time*** (*tomorrow*) modify the verb and its complementation (here a direct object). In b. the adverb of ***time*** (*late*) modifies the verb alone; the adverb of ***frequency*** (*always*), modifies the verb and its complementation (here the adverb *late*); the ***relational adverb*** *actually* connects the meaning of the whole sentence to a previous one.

Note, however, that despite this variety in reference, all these adverbs are ***independent***, i.e. they are not parts of other phrases, and therefore have their own individual function in the sentence as a whole: that of an ***adverbial***.

033/2.2 Adjective modifier

These are usually adverbs of ***degree*** (*very, quite, rather,* etc.) and premodify the adjective (*quite good*). Sometimes they can be ***viewpoint*** adverbs (i.e. ***focus***): *socially irresponsible, politically correct.* These can postmodify the adjective too: *Bill is critical intellectually but naïve emotionally.*

There is one adverb of ***degree*** that always postmodifies: *enough*, e.g. *Is he good enough?*

A particular point concerns *such, quite* and *rather* with adjectives premodifying nouns: if the noun has an ***indefinite*** article, the modifiers usually ***precede*** it: *such a good player, quite a nice party, rather a shabby house*. At first sight, this position makes it look as if the whole noun phrase is being modified. But this is not so. The adverb refers only to the adjective.

The position is obligatory for *such*, usual with *quite* and frequent in the case of *rather*. With nouns in subject position, *rather* is generally preferred ***after*** the article: *A rather expensive wine was served with the meal.*

Another member of this group is *what*, used in exclamations as an adverb: *What a surprise! What terrible weather!* (dt. *Was für eine Überraschung! Welch scheußliches Wetter!*).

(For *such, quite, rather* and *what* as noun modifiers, see **033/2.6** below).

033/2.3 Adverb modifier

These, too, are adverbs of ***degree***: *rather suddenly, so violently, terribly fast*. Again, *enough* postmodifies: *slowly enough*.

Special ***degree*** adverbs can premodify adverbs of ***place*** and ***direction*** (including many adverb particles), with which they form strong and often restricted collocations: *straight on, sharp left, right behind, well ahead, close by, far away*. And also adverbs of time: *just then, right after, just now, right now*.

Particles of ***place*** and ***direction*** themselves often modify *here* and *there*: *down here, up there, over there, out here*.

In many similar types of expression (also for time) the first word is a ***preposition*** (and ***not*** an adverb particle): *through here, along there, from here, until later, by now, since then*. Although they belong to the same field of meaning, these are not cases of modification grammatically. Only the second element is an adverb here. The preposition combines with it to form a prepositional phrase, in which the adverb has the role of prepositional complement. We will not pursue this technical point here. It is fully explained in the chapter on prepositions (see chapter 6).

033/2.4 Prepositional phrase modifier

This is similar to adverb premodification: *right outside the door, entirely against the plan, quite within his rights, completely in agreement, just at that moment, all along the watchtower*.

Here, too, the premodifier can be an adverb particle (of ***place*** or ***direction***): *down in Louisiana, over in the pub, up through the chimney, out into the woods*.

033/2.5 Quantifier modifier

Certain adverbs of ***degree*** can premodify definite quantifying expressions (such as numbers, *all/none*, etc.): *about forty people, over 18 years of age, almost all my money, practically every house in the street*. This applies also to indefinite pronouns with a 'quantity' meaning: *nearly everybody, virtually nothing, just about anybody*.

033/2.6 Noun phrase modifier

Adverbs do not typically refer to nouns, but there are some that do. These are mainly ***focus*** adverbs, and occasionally adverbs of ***degree***: *even Brian, only dogs, mainly children.* Here again *such, quite, rather* and *what* (in exclamations) can occur. They emphasize an evaluation or quality expressed by the noun, and must precede an indefinite article: *He's such a liar* (dt. ... *ein solcher Lügner*); *She's quite a heroine* (dt. ... *ganz die Heldin*); *He's rather a bore* (dt. ... *ein ziemlicher Langweiler*).

Such and *what* (but not *quite* or *rather*) can precede plurals and non-count nouns too (*such idiots, What incompetence!*).

033/3 Adverb position: general

The first factor affecting adverb position is the function. In the ***phrase modifier function***, as shown in 033/2.2–6, the adverb generally comes immediately ***before*** the item that it modifies, e.g.: *quite good, socially irresponsible, rather suddenly, just then, over there, completely in agreement, down in Louisiana, about forty people, even Brian.*

Minor exceptions are: the adjective modifiers *quite, rather, such* and *what* preceding the indefinite article (*quite a nice house*); the postmodifying positions of *enough,* and sometimes certain focus adverbs (*good enough, irresponsible socially*).

In ***independent sentence function***, there are three basic sentence positions: ***initial*** (***I***), ***medial*** (***M***) and ***final*** (***F***).

(16) a. ***Politically***, the rabbi is left-wing. (***I***)
b. Simon ***usually*** cooks for the family. (***M***)
c. Jenny bought a new car ***yesterday***. (***F***)

Initial (***I***) means at the beginning of the sentence or clause; ***final*** (***F***) means at the end, after any objects or other necessary complementation:

Generally, the favoured position for most adverbs is (***F***). If there are two or more at (***F***), they normally occur in a certain order according to type of meaning (see below).

(17) a. We lived in Cornwall ***then***.
b. She put the letter on the table ***quickly***.
c. Donna feels very happy ***here***.

- The ***medial*** position (***M***) is verb-centred, and varies slightly according to the kind of verb phrase:
- If there are no auxiliary verbs (i.e. just a main verb), the adverb comes between subject and verb $(\boldsymbol{M})_1$.
- If there is an auxiliary the adverb is placed after it (or after the first auxiliary if there are two or more) $(\boldsymbol{M})_2$.
- Finally, there are two exceptional positions: $(\boldsymbol{M})_3$ is optional and follows the modal perfects *will have, would have* and *must have*; even here, though, $(\boldsymbol{M})_2$ is the more normal alternative. $(\boldsymbol{M})_4$ affects only the verb *to be* as a main verb, and is the position immediately following it.

(18) a. Maria ***often*** plays tennis. $(\boldsymbol{M})_1$
b. Maria has ***often*** played tennis. $(\boldsymbol{M})_2$
c. Maria has ***probably*** been playing tennis. $(\boldsymbol{M})_2$
d. Maria would have ***normally*** been playing tennis. $(\boldsymbol{M})_3$
e. Maria is ***probably*** at the tennis club. $(\boldsymbol{M})_4$

The adverbs in (18)b. and c. have the same position $(\boldsymbol{M})_2$. The difference is that b. has only one auxiliary (*has*), whereas c. has two (*has* and *been*), with the adverb *probably* between them.

As we have already said, the $(\boldsymbol{M})_3$ position, following the two auxiliaries *will/would* + *have*, is an exception. It sometimes occurs, especially in speech, when a third auxiliary (here *been*) is present. The position is optional, however, and the adverb could also occupy the $(\boldsymbol{M})_2$ slot: *Maria would* ***normally*** *have been playing tennis.* This in fact sounds slightly better stylistically.

Finally, one or two general points on the (***I***) position. Adverbs here tend to modify the sentence as a whole. They are separate from the main body of the message (an effect usually underlined by a comma following), and often express a comment, an introduction or a certain perspective from which the sentence is to be understood. This introductory function also emphasizes the adverb. (16)a. above shows the perspective function: ***Politically***, *the rabbi is left-wing.*

(***I***), (***M***) and (***F***) show the whole range of possible adverb positions. But this does not mean that all adverb types can occur in any or every position. Some are restricted, while others have preferred slots in certain contexts. The choice in a particular case may also have to do with emphasis and how many other adverbs there are in the sentence.

033/4 Adverb position according to meaning

033/4.1 Adverbs of manner

(***F***) is the most common. But (***I***) and (***M***) are also possible:

(19) a. The teacher answered our questions ***patiently***. ***(F)***
b. ***Patiently***, the teacher answered our questions. ***(I)***
c. The teacher ***patiently*** answered our questions. ***(M)***

The (***F***) position in (19)a. places a certain focus on the adverb. Nevertheless, this is the most neutral version. The other positions are ***marked***, i.e. they convey special shades of meaning or style. Neither are used much in speech or everyday language. They are found mainly in narrative style.

Manner adverbs at (***I***), usually with a comma following, emphasize the ***behaviour*** of the subject, rather than just characterizing the action. (19)b. means, roughly, *The teacher was patient when she answered our questions.* (***I***) manner adverbs are also a little detached from the main message, creating the effect of a separate clause. This produces a slight pause, often used as a stylistic effect: for instance to profile the action following, and perhaps also raise drama or suspense.

At (***M***) the adverb is also more subject-related than action-related, but less prominent. For adverbs of manner (***M***) is the 'weaker' version of (***I***).

(***I***) and (***M***) are usually restricted to manner adverbs which can express subject behaviour in this more general way. For example, we would probably not say **Dangerously, he drove the car*; or **He dangerously drove the car*, because *dangerously* does not in this case refer to subject behaviour. An indication, where there is a corresponding noun, is whether the adverb can be replaced by *with* + noun, e.g. *The teacher answered our questions with patience*. We cannot say **He drove the car with danger*. (***M***) is also marked stylistically as being slightly more elevated and 'literary'.

033/4.2 Adverbs of manner: position change and meaning change

Some adverbs of manner change their meanings in particular positions. A few, for instance, become adverbs of ***comment*** when they occur at (***I***) and (***M***):

(20) a. She gave money ***generously***.
  (***F***) = ***manner***: in a generous way.
 b. She ***generously*** gave money.
  (***M***) = ***comment***: It was generous of her to give money.
 c. Mrs. Farrars taught the children ***kindly***.
  (***F***) = ***manner***: in a kind way.
 d. Mrs. Farrars ***kindly*** taught the children.
  (***M***) = ***comment***: It was kind of Mrs. Farrars to teach the children.
 e. They chose a house ***wisely***.
  (***F***) = ***manner***: in a wise way.
 f. They ***wisely*** chose a house.
  (***M***) = ***comment***: It was wise of them to choose a house.

Summarizing the difference, we can say that: at (***F***) the adverb modifies the verb in the normal way, i.e. describes how the action is done; at (***M***) the adverb gives a comment or judgement on the fact that something happens and on the person who does it.

Except *kindly*, most adverbs in this group can also appear at (***I***), and then have the same meaning as at (***M***), e.g. *Wisely, they chose a house*.

Other adjectives of manner that behave in the same way are: *bravely, clearly, courageously, cunningly, erratically, foolishly, stubbornly*, etc.

Simply belongs here too, but changes into a ***focus*** adverb:

(21) a. He spoke to the crowd ***simply***.
  (***F***) = ***manner***: in a simple way.
 b. He ***simply*** spoke to the crowd.
  (***M***) = ***focus***: He just spoke to the crowd (and nothing more).

033/4.3 Adverbs of time

Here, too, (***F***) is the standard position for all definite and many indefinite time adverbs. (***I***) is possible, but introduces a special focus:

(22) a. We're going to Brighton ***tomorrow***.
b. ***Tomorrow***, we're going to Brighton.

(22)b. would be used to stress the adverb, possibly in answer to the question *What are you doing tomorrow?* That is, whereas (22)a. tells us about the visit, (22)b. tells about *tomorrow* and 'what tomorrow will contain'.

In adverb sequences at (***F***), adverbs of ***time*** tend to come ***after*** adverbs of ***manner***. ***Definite*** adverbs of time (*today, tomorrow,* etc.) tend to follow ***indefinite*** ones (*early/late,* etc.):

(23) a. We're going to Brighton ***quickly tomorrow***. (***manner*** + ***time***)
b. We're going to Brighton ***early tomorrow***. (***indefinite time*** + ***definite time***)

Certain ***indefinite*** time adverbs occur at (***M***). With ***still*** and ***just*** this is obligatory. With ***yet*** and ***already*** it is common when they are not stressed. Otherwise they appear at (***F***):

(24) a. Sarah has ***just*** finished her homework.
b. The stranger was ***still*** watching the house from the other side of the street.
c. Sarah has (***already***) finished her homework (***already***).
d. Sarah has not (***yet***) finished her homework (***yet***).
e. Has Sarah finished her homework ***yet***?

In questions with ***yet***, as in (24)e., (***F***) is obligatory. A number of further indefinite time adverbs can optionally appear at (***M***): *eventually, immediately, now, then, recently, suddenly,* etc. With most of them (***I***) is also possible for special focus:

(25) a. (***Eventually***) we (***eventually***) sold the house (***eventually***).
b. (***Immediately***) the man (***immediately***) pulled out a knife (***immediately***).
c. (***Now***) I am (***now***) working somewhere else (***now***).

There is most emphasis at (***I***), as with adverbs of manner, and least at (***M***).

033/4.4 Adverbs of frequency

(***F***) is the standard position for adverbs of ***definite*** frequency, such as ordinal numbers (*once, twice,* etc.), and time interval adverbs (*weekly, monthly,* etc.).

(***M***) is the standard position for adverbs of ***indefinite*** frequency, such as *often, sometimes, always, never, usually,* etc.:

(26) a. We ***always*** pay the milkman ***weekly***.
b. They have ***never*** been to America.
c. If I ask him to help me, he ***usually/often/sometimes*** does.

Note that with ***tags*** (i.e. ***auxiliary pro-forms***, see chapter 8), as in (26)c., adverbs of ***indefinite*** frequency take the (***M***)$_1$ slot, even though in this case the adverb is before an auxiliary.

In sequences at (***F***), ***frequency*** adverbs tend to come ***before*** adverbs of ***time***, and ***after*** adverbs of ***manner***:

(27) She spoke to him ***sharply twice yesterday***. (***manner*** + ***frequency*** + ***time***)

033/4.5 Adverbs of place and direction

Here, too, (***F***) is the standard position. (***M***) never occurs, and (***I***) generally when there is particular emphasis or contrast:

(28) a. As the weather was good, we held the party ***outside***.
b. ***Downstairs*** everything was dark, but ***upstairs*** a candle was burning in one of the windows.

In sequences at (***F***), ***place*** adverbs come ***before*** time adverbs, but tend to occur ***after*** adverbs of ***manner***:

(29) a. People were dancing ***wildly everywhere tonight***. (***manner*** + ***place*** + ***time***)
b. Donoghue rode ***brilliantly there yesterday***. (***manner*** + ***place*** + ***time***)

It is important in this connection to distinguish between place adverbs at (***F***) and place/direction adverbs which are part of the ***obligatory verb complementation***:

(30) a. Please get ***here*** quickly tomorrow. (***obligatory verb complementation***)
b. She drove ***there*** fast yesterday. (***obligatory verb complementation***)
c. She drove fast ***there*** yesterday. (***part of (F)-sequence)***

In (30)a. and b. the direction adverbs *here* and *there* (dt. *hierher/dorthin*) are grammatically necessary to complement the verbs of motion, *get* and *drove*. They must therefore follow the verb immediately. They are not part of the (***F***)-sequence itself. In a. the (***F***)-sequence consists just of *quickly tomorrow* and in b. of *fast yesterday*.

In (30)c., on the other hand, the place adverb *there* (dt. *dort*) does ***not*** complement *drove*. Like *rode* in (29)b., *drove* here refers to an activity (e.g. *drove in a race*), and does not mean 'motion towards a particular place'. The adverb *there* is therefore part of the (***F***)-sequence and follows the adverb of manner *fast*.

033/4.6 Adverbs of degree

The standard position here is (***M***). Exceptions are the adverb quantifiers, which come at (***F***):

(31) a. I ***completely*** forgot the flowers.
b. She was ***totally*** bored with her new job.
c. We were ***almost*** knocked over by the speeding taxi.
d. Jonathan ***rather*** likes Denise.
e. I don't mind coffee, but I like tea ***more***.
f. We don't go to London ***much*** now.

033/4.7 Adverbs of focus: emphasis, restriction, addition

Here, too, the usual position is (***M***):

(32) a. Matthews has ***only*** been at the firm for three weeks.
b. After the argument with the waiter, we ***simply*** got up and left the restaurant.
c. What a coincidence! We were ***also*** in Berlin at that time.
d. We ***particularly*** liked the trip to Wannsee.

An exception is *too*, which generally occurs at (***F***). Also occasionally found at (***F***), for reasons of stress, are *also* (sounding then rather formal), and ***emphasis*** adverbs like *particularly, especially,* etc.:

(33) a. We were in Berlin at that time ***too***.
b. We were in Berlin at that time ***also***.
c. We liked the trip to Wannsee ***particularly***.

In this connection it is necessary to look briefly at *too* and *also* in their ***phrase modifying function***. A point to note is that as ***phrase modifiers*** *too* and (usually) *also* follow the word they modify:

(34) a. We ***too/also*** were in Berlin at that time.
b. Frank ***also*** had been in the restaurant on the night of the murder.

At first sight this may look like the (***M***) position, but the adverbs here are ***not*** sentence modifiers. They modify the subjects *we* and *Frank* as ***phrase modifiers***. As sentence modifiers they would be in the wrong positions: i.e. *too* would have to be at (***F***), and *also* after *were* and *had*, respectively:

(35) a. We were (***also***) in Berlin at that time (***too***). (see also (32)c. and (33)a.)
b. Frank had ***also*** been in the restaurant on the night of the murder.

Interestingly enough, though, (35) can mean the same as (34). In fact, as (34) is rather formal, (35) is the more usual and neutral way of expressing the same thing. The only difference is that (34) refers unambiguously to the individual words *we* and *Frank*, whereas (35) may have other meanings as well. For comparison, here are the b.-sentences in (34) and (35) again:

(36) a. Frank ***also*** had been in the restaurant on the night of the murder.
b. Frank had ***also*** been in the restaurant on the night of the murder.

(36)a. means only: *Among other people, Frank had been in the restaurant too.* (36)b. could mean the same, but it could also mean *Frank had been in the restaurant, as well as in other places on the night of the murder,* or *Frank had been in the restaurant on other nights as well as on the night of the murder.*

The message here is that in ***sentence-modifying function*** focus adverbs may be ambiguous in their reference. Another example is *only*. For instance, (32)a., *Matthews has only been at the firm for three weeks*, can be variously interpreted as (37)a. or b. In speech, the meaning distinctions would be conveyed by differences in stress, as shown:

(37) a. Matthews has only been at the firm for three 'weeks.
(… for ***only*** three weeks, i.e. he is a new employee).
b. Matthews has only been at the 'firm for three weeks.
(… ***only*** at the firm, i.e. nowhere else but at the firm).

Alternative word order for the b. meaning is *For three weeks Matthews has only been at the firm*, but not, of course, for the a. meaning.

033/4.8 Adverbs of focus: viewpoint

The standard positions here are (***I***), and, less profiled, (***F***):

(38) a. ***Psychologically***, this presents a very thorny problem.
b. ***Basically***, I deal with all sales enquiries.
c. The film is often inaccurate ***historically***.
d. The sixteenth century had a great impact on London ***culturally***.

(***I***) gives a stylistically weightier effect, as it has the character of an 'announcement'. (***F***) is sometimes chosen to give the more associative impression of an afterthought. But this is not necessarily always the case. (***M***) is possible after the verb *to be*. It is the least profiled position: *The company is financially in considerable difficulty*.

033/4.9 Connective adverbs

These can vary a little in position, depending on the individual adverb. (***I***) is the standard for many, in particular ***additives*** and ***reinforcers*** like *moreover* and *furthermore*:

(39) a. He doesn't sing well at all. ***Furthermore***, he's never on time for choir practice.
b. Teri should be treasurer, with her financial experience. ***Also***, she's the longest-serving committee member.

Note that ***also*** is being used in a ***connective*** meaning here. It could occupy the ordinary (***M***) position here too, but would then be less profiled. (***I***) is also most common for ***sequence*** adverbs (i.e. *firstly, secondly, finally, next*, etc.), and those of ***contradiction/concession***, such as *however, nevertheless, yet* and *still*. Certain of these, like *however* and *anyway*, can occur at (***F***) and are then less profiled. In more elevated style, *however* and *nevertheless* are sometimes 'tucked away' at (***M***) (*however* then usually inside commas).

A general exception here is ***though***, which never appears at (***I***), and most ommonly takes (***F***):

(40) a. ***Secondly***, I would like to mention Max.
b. Teri would be the best treasurer. ***However***, she does not want the job.
c. She does not, ***however***, want the job.
d. She does not want the job, ***though***.
e. ***Even so***, I think we should ask Teri again ***anyway***.

It is important to remember that connectives cannot be used as conjunctions, i.e. to join clauses together. In German this is sometimes possible: *Teri wäre die beste Kassenwartin, doch sie will die Aufgabe nicht übernehmen*. The English version must remain as it is in (40)b. We cannot say **Teri would be the best treasurer, however she does not want the job*. This is a grammatical mistake.

Among the ***conclusion/consequence*** adverbs, *so* occurs at (***I***). The same applies to *thus* (elevated, formal) and *therefore*, although (***M***) is often favoured as a 'neater' and more elegant position if less weight is intended.

Then in the sense of *so* sometimes takes (***I***), but sounds softer at (***F***):

(41) a. Jean's daughter has just had a baby. ***So*** Jean wants to stay in this area now, and not move.
b. … ***Therefore*** Jean wants to stay in this area now… (weighty, and rather formal).
c. … Jean ***therefore*** wants to stay in this area now …
d. 'I want to get the ten-thirty train.' '(***Then***) you should leave now (***then***).'

Other connective types, such as ***concluding*** (*altogether*), ***transitional*** (*incidentally, now, meanwhile*), ***comparative*** (*similarly, likewise*), ***contrastive*** (*instead*) and those of ***replacement*** (*alternatively*) usually take (***I***), some of them also with the option of (***F***) for less profile:

(42) a. (***Altogether***,) it's been a successful week (***altogether***).
b. ***Now***, what shall we have for supper? (no alternative possible)
c. He was supposed to deliver the newspapers, but (***instead***) he dumped them all in the river (***instead***).

033/4.10 Adverbs of comment

Usual positions here are either (***I***) or (***M***). ***Speaker style*** adverbs are preferred at (***I***). ***Content evaluation*** adverbs occur at (***I***) if profiled, or long (e.g. more than three syllables), otherwise at (***M***). ***Content truth/certainty*** adverbs also occur at either: *perhaps* is usually preferred at (***I***); others, unless stressed, are generally placed at (***M***):

(43) a. ***Frankly***, I don't like her.
b. ***Unfortunately***, we can't come to the party on Saturday.
c. She ***bravely*** blocked the robbers' path.
d. ***Perhaps*** you need a change of air and scenery.
e. You ***probably*** need a change of air and scenery.

The simple rule, therefore, is: adverbs of comment at (***M***), except long ones and ***speaker style*** adverbs.

033/4.11 Negation and adverbs at (M)

The $(\boldsymbol{M})_2$ rule in the case of auxiliaries does not apply to many negatives. In the following example, the positive version in a. follows the $(\boldsymbol{M})_2$ rule, as we would expect. The negative version in b., however, does not:

(44) a. He will ***probably*** come on Monday.
b. He ***probably*** won't come on Monday.

The reason is that the negative particle ***not*** generally precedes what it negates (but see also chapter 8). When attached to an auxiliary, ***not*** therefore negates any adverb following at $(\boldsymbol{M})_2$. So if an adverb is to keep its positive meaning, it must be placed at $(\boldsymbol{M})_1$. This explains the position of ***probably*** in (44)b. If, on the other hand, the adverb is to be negated as well, it stays at $(\boldsymbol{M})_2$, e.g. *He won't* ***necessarily*** *come on Monday.*

In certain cases this leads to two negative versions of the same sentence, each with a different meaning: one has the adverb at $(\boldsymbol{M})_1$, and the other at $(\boldsymbol{M})_2$. The adverb categories involved are generally ***comment***, ***degree*** and ***focus***, but also occasionally ***time*** and ***frequency***:

(45) a. He ***definitely*** isn't coming on Monday. (= It is definite that he *isn't* ...)
(dt. Er kommt sicher nicht am Montag.)
b. He isn't ***definitely*** coming on Monday. (= It *isn't* definite that he is ...)
(dt. Er kommt nicht unbedingt am Montag.)
c. He ***still*** isn't working. (= He hasn't yet started to work.)
(dt. Er arbeitet immer noch nicht (wieder).)
d. He isn't ***still*** working. (= He has stopped working.)
(dt. Er arbeitet nicht mehr.)
e. She ***often*** doesn't do her homework. (= She frequently neglects it.)
(dt. Sie macht oft ihre Hausaufgaben nicht.)
f. She doesn't ***often*** do her homework. (= She mostly neglects it.)
(dt. Sie macht nicht oft ihre Hausaufgaben.)
g. We ***particularly*** didn't like the food. (= Most of all, we didn't like ...)
(dt. Wir mochten insbesondere das Essen nicht.)
h. We didn't ***particularly*** like the food (= We didn't like the food that much.)
(dt. Wir mochten das Essen nicht besonders.)
i. He ***simply*** doesn't like maths. (= Quite simply, he doesn't like maths.)
(dt. Er mag Mathe ganz einfach nicht.)
j. He doesn't ***simply*** like maths. (= ... but also physics and chemistry)
(dt. Er mag nicht nur Mathe, sondern ...)

Another interpretation of (45)j. is that *simply* modifies *like* (rather than *maths*): *He doesn't simply 'like maths: he 'loves it!*

Occasionally, positional change alters the adverb meaning slightly, too:

(46) a. He ***possibly*** can't come on Monday. (= It is possible that he can't ...)
(dt. Möglicherweise kann er am Montag nicht kommen).
b. He can't ***possibly*** come on Monday. (= It is impossible that he can ...)
(dt. Er kann unmöglich am Montag kommen).

033/5 Position of other adverbials

By 'other adverbials' we mean ***prepositional phrases*** and ***noun phrases*** that function as ***adverbials*** (***A***). Basically, these follow the same position rules as adverbs. But in general they are less flexible and tend more to (***F***) because of their length. With mixed (***F***)-sequences consisting of phrases and adverbs, there is a general 'length principle': adverbs come first and phrases follow. It may be overruled, however, by other factors, in particular the need for ***end-focus***, i.e. the tendency to place stressed elements in a sequence last.

033/5.1 Adverbials of manner

(***F***) is standard, (***M***) very rare, and (***I***) strongly profiled, as with single adverbs:

(47) a. Sandra started her new job ***with great enthusiasm***.
b. She had left her old firm ***in a hurry***.
c. ***In a panic***, the crowd fled from the stadium.

(***I***) focuses on the subject, and its behaviour or feelings in that situation, e.g. in (47)c. the crowd's fear is emphasized. Similarly, if we turn (47)a. around, attention is directed strongly to *Sandra* and her feelings: ***With great enthusiasm****, Sandra started her new job*. (***I***) is not often found outside written texts.

In (***F***)-sequences of manner alone, single adverbs precede phrases ('length rule') and are usually joined to them by a co-ordinating conjunction (*and/but*): *She had left her old firm* ***sadly*** *and* ***in a hurry***.

033/5.2 Adverbials of time

Again, the usual position is (***F***), and the particular profile option at (***I***). With (***F***)-sequences consisting only of time adverbials, the main principles (apart from the length rule) are: ***indefinite + definite time*** (*at some time next Saturday*); and ***shorter time + longer time*** (*at 3.30 this afternoon*). However, in particular cases, either one may override the other (or the length rule), depending on importance and emphasis:

(48) a. Sandra is flying to New Zealand ***on Wednesday next week***.
b. We got back ***late last night***.
c. Building starts ***in January next year***.
d. We are setting out ***at dawn tomorrow***.

Manner adverbials tend to precede ***time*** adverbials, and also ***time adverbs*** (thus overriding the length rule):

(49) a. Sandra is flying to New Zealand ***with Austrian Airlines on Wednesday next week.***
(***manner + shorter time + longer time***)
b. She went to work ***with a headache yesterday***.
(***manner + time adverb***)

(And as a reminder: the direction adverbial *to New Zealand* in (49)a. is ***compulsory complementation***, and not part of the (***F***)-sequence!)

If there is no special stress and all elements are equally prominent, the sequence in (49) would be the normal one. If one element is to be profiled, however, it will normally be placed at the end (according to the ***end-focus*** principle). This does not mean that final elements are always stressed, but that if stress is required, it will naturally be given to the last member of the sequence: *She went to work yesterday* ***with a headache***. This order would give 'her headache' slightly more prominence than in (49)b. Similarly, if the name of the airline is to be profiled in (49)a., this would probably come last (with one of the time adverbials left out): *Sandra is flying to New Zealand on Wednesday* ***with Austrian Airlines*** (*and not with Air France, as she did last time*).

033/5.3 Adverbials of frequency

(***F***), again, is the standard position. The (***I***) slot is used for prominence, but with frequency adverbials (especially ***indefinite***) also as an alternative to a phrase cluster in final position. This spreads the 'adverbial load' over the whole sentence, which is sometimes stylistically preferable to having all the adverbials at the end.

When they occur, (***F***)-sequences are similar to those for adverbs, i.e. usually in the order ***manner + frequency + time***. Note that the (***M***) slot is good for single adverbs, but ***not*** for whole phrases:

(50) a. We are ***always*** in St. Ives ***every year***.
b. (***Now and again***) they went to London ***by train*** (***now and again***) ***during their holiday***.
c. (***On Sundays***) Bill and Irene ***often*** took their children swimming (***on Sundays***).
d. Farrars drove to the village ***in the van twice yesterday***.

Here, too, ***end-focus*** can lead to a different order:

Farrars drove to the village twice yesterday ***in the van*** (*and did not go by bike as usual*); or: *Farrars drove to the village in the van yesterday* ***twice*** (*and not just once as usual*).

033/5.4 Adverbials of place and direction

(***F***) is also the preferred position for place and direction adverbials, but their position in (***F***)-sequences varies. Generally speaking, as with adverbs, the order is ***manner + place + time***:

(51) a. She saw him ***clearly in the shop at that moment***.
b. I tried to call you ***from my mobile in the supermarket just now***.

In some contexts, however, the speaker may feel that the place element is closer in meaning to the verb than the other elements are. In this case ***place*** will come first: *I tried to call you* ***in the supermarket*** *just now from my mobile*. The ***manner*** element could now, optionally, be given ***end-focus*** stress (though this need not be the case).

A further reason for putting (particularly) place and direction adverbials first in the (***F***)-sequence is that they are ***known information***. There is a general tendency in English to place anything that is known, or has already been mentioned, ***before*** new references, or new information. If the subject of the sentence is known to have been 'in the supermarket', this would also justify putting the place adverbial first.

Finally, there is an important factor which we will call ***referent adjacency***. In cases of doubt, it is generally assumed that adverbials modify particularly those elements that they are ***closest*** to. Consider:

(52) a. Ronald watched Sonia and Dan ***in the garden***.
b. Ronald watched Sonia and Dan ***in the garden on the roof***.
c. ***On the roof***, Ronald watched Sonia and Dan ***in the garden***.
d. Ronald watched Sonia and Dan ***in the garden*** with bitterness in his heart.

In (52)a. Sonia and Dan are definitely ***in the garden***, and Ronald might or might not be (i.e. Ronald's position is left open). In (52)b. it is ***the garden*** that is ***on the roof*** (and, logically, Dan and Sonia too, as they are in the garden). Ronald's position, again, is left open. In (52)c. Ronald is definitely ***on the roof***, while the garden now is definitely not. Sonia and Dan, though, are still definitely ***in the garden***, though no longer on the roof.

The principle of ***referent adjacency*** illustrated here can affect adverbial position in an (***F***)-sequence. This is shown in (52)d., where the ***place*** adverbial ***must*** precede the ***manner*** adverbial.

The principle of reference adjacency also affects adverbials at (***I***), as shown in (52)c. Generally speaking, adverbials at (***I***) refer to the ***subject*** of the sentence. This is shown, for example, if we put (52)c. in the passive: *On the roof, Sonia and Dan were watched by Ronald in the garden*. Now it is Sonia and Dan who are ***on the roof***. Ronald has also been affected by reference adjacency. Having changed position in the sentence, he is now not on the roof but ***in the garden***.

In principle, reference adjacency applies to any type of adverbial. However, it is place and direction adverbials that are most noticeably affected, because of their large range of possible referents and greater potential for ambiguity.

033/5.5 Adverbials of degree, focus, comment and connection

With one or two exceptions, these all have a general preference for (***I***):

(53) a. ***To some extent/on the whole/in general***, I can sympathize with Tom's views. (***degree***)
b. ***In my opinion/from my point of view***, he's right. (***focus***)
c. ***Of course***, that is only part of the problem. (***comment***)
d. ***On top of that*** we're having difficulties with the heating. (***connection***)

Among the ***degree*** adverbials, ***quantifiers*** such as *a little, a lot, a great deal,* etc., and ***negation intensifiers*** like *at all, in the least,* or *in the slightest* occur only at (***F***): We go swimming ***a lot***; I don't know anybody here ***at all***.

In addition, (***M***) will occasionally accommodate some of the more frequent degree adverbials (*I can on the whole sympathize with Tom's views*), and one or two from the comment field (*The flight may of course be delayed*), though this tends to be done mainly in parenthesis, i.e. as a more elevated stylistic interruption, often with pauses (and commas in writing): *I can, on the whole, sympathize …* Otherwise, in more neutral and informal language (***F***) is often chosen for degree, focus, comment, and for certain connectives:

(54) a. I can sympathize with Tom's views ***to some extent***.
b. He's right ***in my opinion***.
c. That's only part of the problem, ***of course***.
d. We're having difficulties with the heating, ***for one thing***.

Adverbials in this group lose a lot of their emphasis at (***F***) and have more of an 'afterthought' character.

033/5.6 Some other adverbial categories and their positions

We have presented the main categories of adverbial, but there are one or two others that still have to be mentioned. They have not been discussed up to now as they have no (or few) equivalent single adverbs.

- ***Reason:***
  Owing to his illness *Mackenzie has resigned from the committee.*
  (***I***), occasionally (***F***).
- ***Purpose:***
  With this aim in mind, he set out for Edinburgh.
  (***I***) or (***F***); *on purpose* usually (***F***).
- ***Circumstance:***
  She limped off the field ***in great pain***.
  Usually (***F***); (***I***) for profile.
- ***Condition:***
  They accepted the decision ***on our terms***.
  (***F***) only in this case; (***F***) or (***I***), depending on phrase.

033/5.7 Inversion

Inversion is the reversal of subject and verb, as necessary, for instance, in forming questions, e.g. ***Have you*** *paid the electricity bill yet?*

Inversion is actually not limited to questions, though. It is sometimes required in statements. In German, in fact, ***inversion*** is necessary whenever a sentence does not begin with the subject: ***Martin kaufte*** *letzte Woche ein Haus* → *Ein Haus* ***kaufte Martin*** *letzte Woche* → *Letzte Woche* ***kaufte Martin*** *ein Haus.*

The most typical examples are sentences like the last one, beginning with an adverbial. English word-order is in general much more stable than this. But English also requires inversion with a small number of special adverbials. These are adverbials with a ***negative*** or ***restrictive*** meaning: *never, hardly, scarcely, barely, under no circumstances, neither, nor, only + adverbial* (*only then, only when, only like this,* etc.), *not only, nowhere,* etc.:

(55) a. ***Hardly had I*** sat down to lunch when the phone rang again.
b. ***Under no circumstances must you*** leave your luggage unattended.
c. I don't eat fish and chips, and ***neither does my wife***.
d. ***Not only do they*** disturb us with their noise: they also throw garbage in our garden.

One adverb requiring inversion is outside this negative/restrictive group: ***so***, in the meaning of 'also' (*'I'm tired.' 'So am I.'* See below under 6.).

A point to note is that inversion is only possible in English with an auxiliary verb. If there is no auxiliary present, *do* has to be introduced (see ***do-support***, chapter 8).

033/6 Usage: some special cases

A few common everyday adverbs require some explanation as far as meaning and use are concerned. Most are adverbs of degree (033/6.8).

033/6.1 quite

Like German *ganz*, ***quite*** has two opposite meanings: firstly, *moderately* (i.e. *more than a little, but not very*); and secondly, *totally*.

- The first is more common in everyday speech. In this meaning, ***quite*** appears only with gradable expressions, and on a 'scale of degree' would be between *a little* and *very*, e.g. *a little tired* → ***quite*** *tired* → *very tired*.
  In this sense, it often serves as an ***understatement*** for *very* or a *great deal; We used to go to concerts* ***quite*** *a lot* (= *very often*); *You need some after-sun lotion – your back is* ***quite*** *red* (i.e. 'looks bad').
  With nouns it is used in the similarly ***understated*** sense of *considerable* or *notable*: *It's* ***quite*** *a distance to the station from here; My son is* ***quite*** *an expert on computers.*
  Its use with verbs is restricted mainly to *like* and *enjoy*: *I'm* ***quite*** *enjoying this soup* (dt. *Die Suppe schmeckt mir ganz gut*).
  Quite cannot be used with comparative forms of adjectives and adverbs (**quite more expensive*). Here we need *rather*, or other equivalents like *a bit*, and *a little* (see below).
- The second meaning of ***quite*** (*totally, completely*) is found with expressions that are either non-gradable, or at the extreme end of a gradable scale: *The box, when we opened it, was* ***quite*** *empty* (= *completely empty*); *Outside, the streets were* ***quite*** *deserted* (= *totally/absolutely deserted*); *I'm sure you'll find the martini* ***quite*** *perfect, Mr. Bond* (= *shaken, but not stirred!*).

This is also the sense of ***not quite***: *What you said just now is **not quite** correct* (*= not totally correct*).
In rather formal style, ***quite*** is occasionally found with a small number of verbs: *I have quite* (= *completely*) *finished; I had quite forgotten that guests had been invited.*
The negative is more neutral and more widespread: *She has **not quite** recovered from her illness yet; They did **not quite** make it to the summit* (dt. *Sie haben es nicht ganz bis auf den Gipfel geschafft*).
A final note on spelling: learners sometimes confuse ***quite*** with *quiet* (dt. ruhig), which is completely different not only in spelling and meaning, but also in pronunciation.

033/6.2 rather

This has several meanings:

a) like *quite*, but a little stronger, and often in the sense of 'tending to be'. It is used mainly with expressions that have a ***negative*** meaning, e.g. *rather boring, rather lazy, rather fat*; or it gives a negative meaning to neutral expressions, e.g. *rather young* (= *not old enough*), *rather surprising* (dt. *etwas befremdlich*), *rather long* (= *too long*).
It can also premodify comparative forms: *That's **rather** more expensive than I imagined.*
b) like *quite*, with ***positive*** expressions, but usually in the sense of 'contrary to expectation': *The film was **rather** good, actually (although we were expecting it to be bad); She did **rather** well in her exams (although she had done almost no work for them).*
In this sense it is often used with verbs of liking (*like, enjoy*) and occasionally disliking (*resent, object, dislike*): *A lot of people object to his accent, but I **rather** like it; I **rather** resent his constant good humour, I must say.*
c) with *would* in the sense of *prefer*: *I **would rather** go to a concert than see a film.* Note in this case that an infinitive (without *to*), and ***not*** a gerund follows *than*. The *would* is often shortened in speech to *'d* (*I'd rather go ...*).
If the preference refers to another person's action (i.e. with a different subject) a finite sub-clause is used. The verb must then be in the (unreal) past tense or past perfect: ***I'd rather*** *you got here tomorrow before 8 o'clock* (= *I would prefer you to get here before 8 o'clock*); ***I'd rather*** *you hadn't arranged the meeting for a Sunday* (= *I would have preferred it if you hadn't arranged ...*).
Rather than is also used without *would* in the meaning *in preference to*: *I think I'll have a coffee **rather** than another beer; She decided to go for a walk in the park **rather** than stay at home on her own.*
d) with *or*, to correct something that has been said, or to make it more precise: *We walked, **or rather** ran, to the station this morning* (dt. *... oder besser* (*gesagt*) *rannten ...*); *My parents used to run a hairdresser's, **or rather** my mother did.*

033/6.3 fairly, pretty

These are variations of *quite*, and *rather* in senses (a) and (b). ***Fairly*** modifies positive adjectives. It has roughly the same meaning as *quite*, but is often a little less positive on the degree scale, i.e. ***fairly** good* could be taken as being 'less good' than *quite good*. It cannot modify comparatives or verbs.

Pretty is similar, but can also modify negative adjectives (*pretty good, pretty bad*). It is informal/colloquial, and is used as an equivalent of *rather* (meaning (a)) more in American than in British English. It cannot modify comparatives or verbs, except in the idiom *pretty much* (Am. *pretty near*) = *almost/more or less*: *He has pretty much retired* (dt. *Er ist mehr oder weniger im Ruhestand*).

033/6.4 a little/a bit, somewhat

The noun phrases ***a little/a bit*** are quantifier nominalizations and not adverbs. But they are very common as degree adverbials and should certainly be mentioned here, especially as they also premodify adjectives in the way that ordinary adverbs do.

A little is stylistically neutral to elevated, while ***a bit*** is colloquial and informal. They both mean *to a small extent* and are therefore at the lowest end of the 'degree scale'. One of their most common uses is to 'soften' adjectives and other expressions that are felt to be rather direct: *I am feeling a little worried* (dt. *Ich bin etwas besorgt*); *Old Davis was a bit upset after the quarrel* (dt. ... *war nach dem Streit ein bisschen pikiert*).

They could also be seen here (from the opposite perspective) as ***understatement*** forms for *quite* and *rather*.

They can also modify verbs: *Sit down a bit and have a rest!*

Combined with *only* they mean *not very much*: *John only played a bit last season.*

Somewhat (dt. *etwas*) has the same meaning, but is rather formal and usually avoided in ordinary language, especially with verbs: *The sky was somewhat overcast* (literary: dt. ... *leicht bedeckt*).

033/6.5 much, little

As in its quantifier uses, ***much*** features mainly in questions and negatives. It chiefly modifies verbs, in the sense of *often*: *The old couple didn't go out* ***much***; *Do you play* ***much*** *at the tennis club these days?*

Much generally premodifies adjectives and adverbs only when they are in ***comparative*** forms (*much smaller, much more, much more quickly*), although then even in positive statements (*I play much more these days*). But it cannot occur with base forms (**much big, *much quickly*), except in one or two standard idioms and collocations (e.g. *much needed, much loved*). As a verb modifier in positive statements it occurs only when it is premodified itself by the degree adverbs *so* and *too* (*so much, too much*). With *very* it also features mainly in questions and negatives (*They didn't go out* ***very much***), but in a restricted number of collocations (usually with verbs of liking) also in positive statements: *We enjoyed our holiday* ***very much***; *I am* ***very much*** *in favour of better childcare.*

Too much and ***so much*** occur quite freely in positive statements and are the usual equivalents of German *zuviel* and *soviel*: *There is so much/too much traffic on the road nowadays.*

Little, the polar opposite of *much*, is not used a great deal as an adverb, except when premodified by *very*: *She spoke* ***very little*** *during the party*. Even this is slightly elevated in style, but without *very*, it would sound formal and literary. In ordinary neutral language, ***not much*** is preferred instead: She *didn't speak* ***much*** *during the party.*

Apart from this, ***little*** is found in just a few standard phrases and collocations, and occasionally with comparatives (e.g. *little better*). ***Little*** should not be confused, incidentally, with ***a little*** (see also chapter 3). ***Little*** means *almost nil*, i.e. it stresses how small the quantity is in contrast to an expected larger one. ***A little***, on the other hand, simply means 'a small amount of ' in contrast to nothing at all.

033/6.6 a lot, very

Like *a bit/a little*, the phrase ***a lot*** is a quantifier nominalization, i.e. grammatically a noun phrase. It functions here as an adverbial and, to some extent, an adjective premodifier. It is the usual equivalent of German *viel* in positive sentences: *I play tennis* ***a lot***.

Like *much*, it can modify adjectives and adverbs only in the comparative form: *The journey is* ***a lot quicker*** *by car*.

It can be premodified itself by *quite* and *rather*: *Jonathan talks* ***rather a lot***.

And it can also appear in the negative (i.e. as an equivalent of *not much*): *I* ***don't*** *play tennis* ***a lot*** *these days*.

Very is the most common intensifying degree adverb. It premodifies adjectives and other adverbs in the base form, but not the comparative: ***very good/very well*** (not **very better*). Unlike German *sehr*, ***very*** cannot modify verbs. The English translation of *Er liebt sie sehr* is *He loves her a lot/very much*.

033/6.7 almost, nearly

These both mean the same and translate German *fast*. However, ***nearly*** is more restricted in use. It refers to states or conditions with clear borders or dividing lines marking them off from what they are not. That is, ***nearly x*** means 'close to x, but not x': ***nearly*** *finished*, ***nearly*** *asleep*, ***nearly*** *ready*, ***nearly*** *dry*.

Almost can have the same meaning, and could replace ***nearly*** in these examples. But ***almost*** additionally means 'as good as', 'partly', or 'all but', i.e. 'in effect, if not in fact'. That is, it is used also for states without clear divisions, often abstract, and with an area of transition or mixture in their 'border regions': *We are* ***almost obliged*** *to go* (dt. ... *beinahe verpflichtet hinzugehen*); *She was* ***almost afraid*** *now*; *The cat is here so often it is* ***almost*** *our own*; *We're so near the coast you can* ***almost*** *smell the sea*.

In these examples, ***nearly*** cannot replace ***almost***. In (56)a. and c. it can. But if we assume the second meaning of ***almost*** ('as good as') for (56)b. and d., then there are contrasts between a. and b., and c. and d.:

(56) a. She ***nearly/almost*** apologized (but then kept her mouth shut).
b. She ***almost*** apologized (= as her words expressed so much regret).
c. I ***nearly/almost*** forgot the beer (but then I remembered to bring it at the last minute).
d. I ***almost*** forgot how beautiful the country is (but these pictures are reviving my memory).

033/6.8 too, also, either, so, neither/nor

Also and ***too*** cannot be used with negatives. Their negative equivalent is ***either***: *Bella has retired and her husband does**n't** work any more **either**.*

Returning to the positive version with ***too/also***, we should note that when the same main verb refers to both clauses, it can be omitted in the second: *Bella has retired and her husband **has too**.*

The auxiliary is left standing as an auxiliary ***pro-form*** (see also chapter 8). If there is no auxiliary present, *do* must be introduced: *Bella worked for Siemens, and her husband **did too**.*

So offers a more common alternative way of expressing this: *Bella worked for Siemens, and **so did** her husband.*

There are three points to note here. First, of course, the meaning of ***so*** here is different from the meaning already discussed in **033/1.7**. above. ***So*** here has the sense of ***too/also***. Second, its position is (***I***). Third, subject-verb ***inversion*** must follow (see **033/5.7**).

Now we come to the ***negative*** equivalent of ***so***. This is ***neither/nor***, again at (***I***), and again with ***inversion***: *Bella doesn't work anymore, and **neither does** her husband* (***nor** does her husband*).

The alternative equivalent here is the version with ***either***, which brings us back to our starting-point above: *Bella doesn't work anymore, and her husband does**n't either**.*

(57) gives a summary overview of the sentence examples just discussed:

(57) a. Bella has retired and her husband does**n't** work any more **either**.
b. Bella has retired and her husband **has too**.
c. Bella worked for Siemens, and her husband **did too**.
d. Bella worked for Siemens, and **so did** her husband.
e. Bella doesn't work anymore, and **neither does** her husband (**nor** does her husband).
f. Bella doesn't work anymore, and her husband does**n't either**.

033/6.9 hardly, barely, scarcely

These all have the same meaning, and translate German *kaum*. They modify mainly verbs and expressions of quantity. As they are negative in meaning themselves, they must combine with positive verbs and quantifiers. ***Hardly*** is the most frequently used: *I have **hardly any** money left (= almost none); Tom and Sarah **hardly** knew each other before they married; They **hardly ever** go on holiday (= almost never).*

A common construction is ***hardly/scarcely ... when*** (= *immediately x happened, y happened*): *He had **scarcely** sat down, when the phone rang* (*Kaum hatte er sich hingesetzt, als ...*).

In this construction they can be placed at (***I***) for more emphasis, and then require ***inversion*** (see **033/5.7** above): ***Scarcely had he** sat down, when the phone rang.*

An alternative construction with the same meaning is ***no sooner ... than***: *No sooner had he sat down, than the telephone rang.*

034 Adverb forms

034/1 Derived adverbs

034/1.1 Adverbs ending in -ly

The majority of adverbs are derived from adjectives. As we saw above, the suffix *-ly* is added to the adjective: *strong* → ***strongly***; *rapid* → ***rapidly***; *beautiful* → ***beautifully***.

There are a few special points to note:

- with adjectives ending in *-y* the *-y* is dropped and replaced by *-ily*: *happy* → ***happily***; *funny* → ***funnily***; *easy* → ***easily***.
- certain one-syllable adjectives ending in *-y* keep the *-y*: *sly* → ***slyly***; *shy* → ***shyly***; *dry* → ***dryly*** (but also ***drily***).
- with adjectives ending in *-le* the *-e* is dropped and replaced by *-y*: *gentle* → ***gently***; *possible* → ***possibly***; *simple* → ***simply***.
- the adjectives *whole, true* and *due* also drop the *-e*, but add *-ly*: *whole* → ***wholly***; *true* → ***truly***; *due* → ***duly***.
- Otherwise, adjectives ending in *-e* keep the *-e*, and just add *-ly* in the normal way: *safe* → ***safely***; *extreme* → ***extremely***; *blithe* → ***blithely***.
- adjectives ending in *-ic* add *-ally* in the written form, although the *-a* is not pronounced: *basic* → ***basically*** [beɪsɪklɪ]; *fantastic* → ***fantastically*** [fæntæstɪklɪ] ; *systematic* → ***systematically*** [sɪstəmætɪklɪ].
  A spelling exception is the adjective *public*, which adds *-ly* directly:*public* → *publicly*.
- participle adjectives also form regular *-ly* adverbs: *boring* → ***boringly***; *deserving* → ***deservingly***; *hurried* → ***hurriedly***.

034/1.2 Adverbs with other suffixes or compound elements

There are one or two other adverb suffixes, but they are confined to a small group of specific adverb types:

- ***-wards*** (American also ***-ward***) signals direction. It is added mainly to other adverbs or nouns: *backwards, forwards, upwards, downwards, westwards, eastwards*, etc. The equivalent adjective omits the *-s*: *in a forward/upward/westward direction*, etc.
- ***-ways*** and ***-wise***, added to nouns, also mean direction: *clockwise, crossways/crosswise, lengthways/lengthwise, sideways*, etc.;
  -wise is also used in the sense of 'regarding/concerning', or 'from the viewpoint of': *timewise, taxwise, workwise*, etc.
  Direction adverbs ending in ***-ways*** and ***-wise*** are used as adjectives, too: *a sideways glance, in a clockwise direction*, etc. This does not apply, though, to ***-wise***-adverbs with a viewpoint meaning, which have no direct adjective equivalent.

- ***-where***, added to the quantifiers *some, any, every,* and *no* form what are known as ***indefinite adverbs*** referring to place: *anywhere, everywhere, nowhere, somewhere.*
  These are actually ***compounds*** (i.e. combinations of two or more words), and are the adverb equivalents of indefinite pronouns (*anybody, someone, no-one,* etc.). Other compound elements of indefinite adverbs are ***-time(s)***, referring to time or frequency (*sometimes, anytime,* etc.), and ***-how***, indicating manner (*somehow, anyhow*).

034/2 Non-derived adverbs and other special groups

Many adverbs, including a lot of common ones, have no suffix of any kind: *very, enough, too, here/there, then, often, perhaps, however, so, now,* etc. Most are not related to adjectives. Some are, but have the same form as the corresponding adjective: *hard, fast, near/far, high/low,* etc. (see below). Others are identical with nouns: *today, tomorrow* and *yesterday,* for example, occur as both adverbs and nouns. A particular group to mention here are the ***adverb particles***. These are prepositions used as adverbs (*in, over, under, across, up, down,* etc.) usually in strong connection with verbs (see below).

Finally, there is one ***irregular*** adverb formation: *good* → ***well.***

This is a particular candidate for mistakes among German-speaking learners. Note, for example, that the English translation of *Meine Tochter kann gut lesen* is *My daughter reads* ***well***, and ***not*** **My daughter reads good.* In colloquial varieties of English (especially in America) *good,* like certain other adjectives, is used as an adverb. But this is ***not*** standard! ⚠

034/2.1 Adverbs and adjectives with the same form and meaning

A few examples of this phenomenon have just been mentioned. The following is an overview:

- *big, close, fast, free, hard, straight* (manner)
- *early, late, long* (time/frequency)
- *deep, far/near, high/low, home, outside/inside, first/second, next/last,* etc. (place/sequence)
- *better/best, worse/worst* (comparative/superlative forms)

Selected examples: *to talk big/a big talker; to get close/a close race; to get something free/a free ticket; to walk straight/a straight line; to stay long/a long stay; to dig deep/a deep hole; a near miss/to come near; home cooking/to come home; her first win/to come first; an outside toilet/to go outside.*

The group includes a small number of ***-ly*** adverbs. In these cases, the equivalent adjectives also end in ***-ly***: *hourly, daily, weekly, monthly, yearly* (frequency), and *kindly* (manner): *to pay weekly/a weekly paper; to act kindly/a kindly person.*

034/2.2 Adjectives ending in -ly with no equivalent adverb

Most other ***-ly*** adjectives cannot be used as adverbs: *cowardly, elderly, friendly/unfriendly, lively, lovely, lonely, likely/unlikely, manly/womanly, motherly/fatherly/brotherly/sisterly, silly, ugly.*

They have no other equivalent adverbs either. For adverbial use, appropriate prepositional phrases are required, e.g. *She kissed him in a sisterly way and he smiled in an ugly manner.*

034/2.3 Adverbs and adjectives with the same form but different meanings

Here, adverb and adjective are the same word, but unlike the examples under **034/2.1** have different meanings (in some cases related, in others quite unrelated):

- ***well*** (adverb) = dt. *gut*: *Maggie sings well.*
  well (adjective) = dt. *fit, gesund*: *Maggie feels very well.*
  Note that ***adverb*** *well* is the irregular adverb form of the adjective *good* (see also **034/2** above).
  Adjective *well* is only predicative in use, and does not appear attributively.
- ***only*** (adverb) = dt. *nur*: *Only Cindy was invited to dine with the Donaldsons.*
  only (adjective) = dt. *einzig*: *Cindy was the only guest. There were no others.*
  Note that ***adjective*** *only* is purely attributive, and does not appear predicatively.
- ***still*** (adverb) = dt. *noch, immer noch*: *The cinema in the high street was knocked down years ago, but the café next door is still there.*
  still (adjective) = dt. *ruhig, still*: *There was no breeze at all. The air was quite still.*
  Note that ***adverb*** *still* has other meanings too, e.g.: *nevertheless* (dt. *trotzdem*); *even* (dt. *noch*): *Sally is tall, but Jonathon is taller still.*
- ***very*** (adverb) = dt. *sehr*: *Jonathon is very tall.*
  very (adjective) = dt. *allein, gerade, bloß*: *The very thought makes me shudder* (*Allein der Gedanke daran schüttelt mich*); *At that very moment a bus appeared on the hill* (*Gerade in jenem Augenblick* ...).
  Note that ***adjective*** *very* is attributive only.
- ***poorly*** (adverb) = dt. *schlecht*: *She did poorly in her exams.*
  poorly (adjective) = dt. *krank*: *She was poorly at the time.*
  Note that ***adjective*** *poorly* is predicative only. ***Adverb*** *poorly* is directly derived from the adjective *poor* and related to it in meaning.
- ***pretty*** (adverb) = dt. *ziemlich*: *She did pretty poorly in her exams.*
  pretty (adjective) = dt. *hübsch*: *That's a pretty little cottage!*
  Adverb *pretty* is colloquial for the stylistically more neutral *rather* and *quite*. It is an adverb of degree and only premodifies adjectives and other adverbs.
  There is also a regular adverb *prettily* (see next section **034/2.4**).
- ***just*** (adverb) = dt. *eben/soeben/gerade*: *We have just sold our house.*
  just (adjective) = dt. *gerecht*: *It was a just decision.*
  There is also a regular adverb *justly* (see next section **034/2.4**).

034/2.4 Adverbs with two forms

Many adverbs without ***-ly*** have an ***-ly*** form as well, but with a different meaning. In some cases, the ***-ly*** form has a restricted or specialized sense. With others (such as *pretty* and *just*) it is the ***-ly*** version that is the regular one (conforming to the sense of the equivalent adjective), and the non-suffix adverb that tends to have the special or unrelated meaning.

Here are the most common examples:

- ***close*** = *near* in a concrete sense: *I couldn't see the stage properly as I could not get close enough* (dt. *nahe/nahe dran*).
  closely = more abstract or metaphorical: *Watch this closely/The two aspects are closely connected* (dt. *genau/eng*).
- ***deep*** = *a long way below/behind the surface* in a concrete sense: *They had to dig deep to find the treasure.*
  deeply = more abstract, and generally reserved for emotional senses: *She cares deeply about him* (dt. *Sie liebt ihn sehr*).
- ***free*** = *without cost*: *Pensioners travel free on the buses here* (dt. *umsonst*).
  freely = *without restriction or reservation*: *Can I speak freely?* (dt. *ohne Einschränkung, ohne Hemmung*). *He freely admitted his mistakes* (dt. *vorbehaltlos, ohne Einschränkung*).
- ***hard*** = *with energy or force.*
  hardly = *scarcely*: *I have hardly any money left* (dt. *kaum*).
- ***high*** = *a big distance above the ground or upwards.*
  highly = *very much*: *highly praised* (dt. *hoch gelobt*).
- ***late*** = *after the time expected.*
  lately = *recently*: *Have you been to the cinema lately?* (dt. *in letzter Zeit*).
- ***last*** = *after everything else, in final position, on the last occasion*: *We will discuss that topic last* (dt. *als letztes*); *When did you last see her?* (dt. *zum letzten Mal*).
  lastly = *finally* (introducing the last item in a list, dt. *schließlich*).
- ***near*** = *close, not far away* (dt. *nahe*).
  nearly = *almost* (dt. *fast*).
- ***pretty*** = colloquial for *rather* (see above under **034/2.3**).
  prettily = *in a pretty way*, dt. *hübsch*: *He had arranged the flowers prettily on the table.*
  Here it is actually the ***-ly*** form that is semantically regular and identical in meaning with the adjective.
- ***just*** = dt. *eben/soeben/gerade* (see above under **034/2.3**).
  justly = *fairly*, dt. *gerade.*
  In this case too the ***-ly*** form is the regular one.

Other 'double forms' have little or no meaning difference between them. For instance, ordinal numbers (*first, second, third*, etc.) can be used as listing adverbs with or without the ***-ly***:

First/Firstly, let me say how happy I am to be here with you tonight.

Other examples are *loud/loudly, slow/slowly*, and *dear/dearly* in certain collocations and contexts.

034/2.5 Further -ly adverbs different in meaning from corresponding adjectives

Apart from the cases with double forms just discussed, there are also single ***-ly*** adverbs with meanings more or less different from those of their equivalent adjectives:

- ***coldly, coolly, hotly, warmly*** are generally used in an emotional sense, e.g. *My hosts welcomed me warmly. They told her coldly to leave* (= *in an unfriendly way*).
- ***barely*** and ***scarcely*** (= *hardly*, dt. *kaum*)
- ***largely*** (= *mainly*, dt. *hauptsächlich*)
- ***shortly*** and ***presently*** (= *soon*, dt. *bald*)
- ***expressly*** (= *deliberately*, dt. *absichtlich*)
- ***fairly*** (= *quite/rather*, dt. *recht/ziemlich*)

Shortly and ***fairly*** have other meanings closer to those of their adjectives: *"I've told you that already," she said shortly* (= *impatiently*, dt. *kurz angebunden*); *The boss treats us very fairly* (= *with fairness*, dt. *gerecht*).

034/3 Comparison of adverbs

The basic features of comparison were described in chapter 4. Adverb comparison is more or less the same, but simpler. Here a summary of comparison 'basics', applied to adverbs:

- ***comparison*** is applied only to ***gradable*** elements (here ***gradable adverbs***).
- Gradable adverbs can be modified by adverbs of degree, e.g. *very, rather,* etc.: *very quickly, rather slowly.*
- ***grades*** of comparison: ***base*** form (*slowly*) → ***comparative*** form (*more slowly*) → ***superlative*** form (most slowly).
- ***comparative*** forms compare ***two*** elements with one another: *John drives more carefully than Mary/Mary drives less carefully than John.*
- ***superlative*** *forms* pick out and profile one member from a group of three or more: *Of all the teams in Scotland, Rangers are playing most aggressively at the moment.*
- ***surplus comparative*** = ***more***, as in ***more*** *slowly.*
- ***surplus superlative*** = ***most***, as in ***most*** *slowly.*
- ***deficit comparative*** = ***less***, as in ***less*** *slowly.*
- ***deficit superlative*** = ***least***, as in ***least*** *slowly.*
- ***equative comparison*** = ***the same as***, as in ***as*** *slowly* ***as***.
- ***comparative particles***: ***than*** (*surplus* and *deficit comparatives*), ***as … as*** (*equative*).
- ***comparative*** *and* ***superlative forms: inflected*** (faster, fastest), ***periphrastic*** (*more slowly, most slowly*).

034/3.1 Forming the comparative and superlative

Adverbs of one syllable have ***inflectional*** forms, i.e. add *-er* and *-est* to the ***base*** form of the adverb:

base form	***comparative***	***superlative***
high →	*higher* →	*highest*
soon →	*sooner* →	*soonest*

Most others have ***periphrastic*** forms:

base form	***comparative***	***superlative***
patiently →	*more patiently* →	*most patiently*
wisely →	*more wisely* →	*most wisely*

Exceptions: the following are ***irregular***:

base form	***comparative***	***superlative***
well →	*better* →	*best*
badly →	*worse* →	*worst*
late →	*later* →	*latest/last/lastly*
early →	*earlier* →	*earliest*
little →	*less* →	*least*
much →	*more* →	*most*
far →	*farther/further* →	*farthest/furthest*

034/3.2 Use of comparative and superlative

Individual cases:

- *further/furthest*: used in all senses concrete and abstract.
- *farther/farthest*: used only in the concrete sense of distance.
- *latest*: used in the ordinary ***time*** sense (*Of all days this week I'll probably arrive home latest on Thursday*).
- *last*: used in the sense of ***time sequence*** (*Do the least important things last*).
- *lastly*: a connective used for ***enumeration***. (*Firstly,... secondly ..., and lastly, I would like to thank the club chairman for his great help*).

Here some examples from general usage, and a few comments:

(58) a. Jane generally drives ***faster than me*** (***than I do***).
[***surplus comparative***]
b. The builders worked ***less efficiently than*** we expected.
[***deficit comparative***]
c. I got home ***earlier*** today ***than*** I have done all week.
[***surplus comparative***]
d. Of all the people in the office, Frank works (***the***) ***hardest***.
[***superlative***]
e. Olivia sings ***most beautifully*** when she sings alone.
[***superlative***]
f. The builders did not work ***as efficiently as*** we expected.
[***equative***]
g. Can we check in at the hotel ***as late as*** 10 pm?
[***equative***]

Note, firstly, that the comparative particle ***than*** can be followed by a noun or pronoun, as in (58)a. (*than me*), and is then a ***preposition***; or it introduces a comparative clause, and is then a ***conjunction***, as in (58)a. (brackets), or (58)b. The same applies to the equative particle (***as…as***). In (58)f., it is a conjunction introducing a clause, and in (58)e., a preposition before a noun phrase.

Secondly, deficit comparatives, as in (58)b., are less common in speech and informal language than equivalent negative equative constructions, as in (58)f. Thirdly, note that the entities of comparison vary. In a. (*Jane* and *I*) and d. (*Frank* and *the people in the office*) it is the subjects of the sentence that are compared. But this is not always the case. In b. and f. it is two predicators (the actual and the expected performance of the builders). In c. and e. time adverbials (referring to different occasions of the same event) are compared, and in g. also, where an implied check-in time and *10 pm* are compared on a scale of 'lateness'.

Fourthly, when a superlative focuses on a subject, as in d., the definite article can optionally precede it.

Chapter 6 Prepositions

Basic features 035

Prepositions and prepositional phrases have been mentioned quite a lot so far during our discussions of other phenomena. But we will now look at prepositions in their own right, bottom up, starting with the basic characteristics.

Prepositions are associated with nouns. They express certain types of syntactic and semantic connection to a noun, e.g. ***on*** *the table*, ***at*** *that time*, ***during*** *the match*, ***after*** *her lecture*.

For a large number of prepositions, meaning categories are similar to those of many adverbs and adverbials: *place*, *direction*, *time*, etc.

Like other word-classes, prepositions form grammatical units with other elements. These units are ***prepositional phrases***. They consist of a preposition as ***head***, and a ***prepositional complement***, which is usually a noun phrase:

	Head	*Prepositional Complement*
(1)	on	the table
	at	that time
	during	the match

As seen in the last chapter, prepositional phrases in independent sentence function have the role of ***adverbials*** (***A***). And in fact this is their only independent function. They can never be subjects, objects or complements:

(2) a. The book was ***on the table***. [*A*]

b. Five players were injured ***during the match***. [*A*]

As parts of other phrases, prepositional phrases can be:

(3) a. ***adjectival complements***: good at maths.
b. ***postmodifiers in noun phrases***: the pub on the corner.

Prepositions do not just appear in prepositional phrases, however. They also combine with verbs to form ***prepositional verbs***, e.g. *to wait for*, *to deal with*, *to laugh at*, etc. The preposition here is part of the verb, i.e. part of the ***predicator*** function (***P***). Prepositional verbs are always followed by ***direct objects*** (***Od***):

P Od

(4) a. Three other people *were waiting* ***for*** the train.

P Od

b. Sally *had been dealing* ***with*** a difficult customer.

Prepositional verbs are sometimes confused with a rather similar phenomenon, ***phrasal verbs***, e.g. *to sit down, to put up, to break off,* etc. In this case, the word following the verb is not a preposition but an ***adverb particle***. Most particles are identical with prepositions, but behave quite differently syntactically. It is therefore important to distinguish carefully between adverb particles and prepositions, and between prepositional verbs and phrasal verbs (for details see chapter 8, **042/2**).

Finally, there are some prepositions which consist of more than one word, e.g. *out of, due to, because of,* etc. We will refer to these as ***composite*** (or ***complex***) ***prepositions***.

036 Individual prepositions and their meanings

036/1 Prepositions of place and direction

036/1.1 to/towards

Movement in a particular direction is expressed by ***to***.

(5) a. We are flying ***to*** London for the weekend (dt. *nach*).
b. When she heard the knock, she ran ***to*** the door (dt. *an*).
c. I must go ***to*** the butcher's quickly (dt. *zu*).

In many contexts ***to*** implies that the objective is reached. For instance, *Cook sailed to Australia,* means not just in the direction of Australia, but also that Cook actually got there. If it is necessary to differentiate, ***towards*** can be used, meaning simply *in the direction of* and nothing more: *Cook sailed towards Australia.*

In general reference to certain institutions, the article is left out: *to work, to school, to university, to church, to hospital.*

There need not be any real movement or change of position involved; ***to*** can mean generally 'in the direction of', i.e. refer to the aim or orientation of the action in a broader sense. Typical examples are gestures and acts of communication: *to wave to s.o., to nod to s.o., to point to sth., to say/give/send/show/explain sth. to s.o.,* etc.

In a large number of expressions like this, ***to*** refers to the ***recipient*** of an action, which in many cases (though not all!) can also be expressed by an ***indirect object***:

Oi
(6) a. I sent ***them*** a letter.
A
b. I sent a letter ***to them***.

However, care should be taken on this point. German datives do ***not*** automatically correlate with indirect objects in English. Only some ***to***-phrases in English can convert into indirect objects. A greater number in fact cannot. So although there is a high correspondence between the German dative and ***to***-phrases, this does not mean that any German dative noun automatically translates into English as an indirect object. This is a continual source of error among German-speaking English learners. Verbs that can take indirect objects in English must be learnt on an individual basis. ⚠

Further examples of the figurative 'direction' sense of ***to*** in communicative meaning (especially with verbs, and derived nouns) are: *to apply to, to agree to sth., to appeal to, to listen to, to complain to s.o., to object to, to refer to, to reply to, to speak to s.o., to turn to, a reply/answer/remark/appeal/address/speech/letter/e-mail/telegram to,* etc.

Also strongly represented here are 'double complement' verbs (i.e. with an object between the verb and the preposition, see below): *to say sth. to s.o., to introduce s.o. to s.o., to suggest/propose sth. to s.o., to explain sth. to s.o., to demonstrate sth. to s.o., to describe sth. to s.o.,* etc.

Note that none of these typical German 'dative' relations correspond to indirect objects in English (**He explained me the route;* correct: *He explained the route to me*).

A specific sub-meaning of direction in both figurative and concrete senses is 'as far as': *right to the limit, up to a point, to a certain extent, to a considerable degree,* etc. e.g.: *We were up to our knees in water; We didn't make it to the summit* (dt. *Wir haben's nicht bis zum/bis auf den Gipfel geschafft*).

Feelings and attitudes also express their 'direction' through ***to***: *to be kind/nice/good/friendly/polite/considerate/grateful,* etc., ***to*** *someone* (also ***towards***, dt. *gegen, zu*).

Nouns expressing emotional reactions often combine with ***to*** as prepositional complements, in the sense of ***cause*** (dt. *zu/auslösend*): *to my surprise* (*zu meiner Überraschung*), *to my regret* (*zu meinem Bedauern*), and similarly, *to my liking/disgust/joy/astonishment,* etc.

Another typical semantic field is that of belonging and joining: *to join/add/fasten/attach/ascribe/attribute/limit/confine x to y.; to stick (x) to (y), to correspond to, to belong to,* etc.

Further adjective groups with an attraction for ***to*** are those expressing relationships:

- belonging relations: *relevant, pertinent, native, intrinsic, inherent, peculiar, specific, essential, favourable, applicable, related, restricted, useful, used,* etc., **to**, e.g. *Cumin and coriander are essential to the flavour of many Asian dishes.*
- logical or ranking relations between entities: *equal, similar, inferior, superior, equivalent,* etc. ***to***, e.g. *Bill and Brian are very similar to each other;* also after nouns with other prepositions, meaning *concerning/regarding* (dt. *betreffend/bezogen auf*): *in/with regard to, in/with reference to, with respect to, in answer to,* etc., e.g. *I have a question with respect to savings accounts at your bank.*

Nouns related to these groups also take ***to***: *equivalence to, inferiority to, restriction to,* etc.

036/1.2 from

The opposite of *to/towards* is ***from***, which refers to a ***starting-point***:

(7) a. We are flying to Spain ***from*** Stansted Airport (dt. *von*).
b. Flight LU 235 ***from*** Barcelona will be delayed by half-an-hour (dt. *aus*).

As with *to* in general institutional reference, so also with ***from*** the article is left out: *from work, from school, from hospital*, etc.: *I was coming home from work one day, when …; Jamie is not home from school yet.*

From … to refers to a stretch of distance, an amount of space, e.g. *It was 3 metres* ***from*** *one wall* ***to*** *the other*. N.B. also the phrases: *from start to finish, from beginning to end, from A to B (= from one place to another)*.

From … to can also refer to a stretch of time (see below), or quantity, including number and age: *from 70 to 80 kilos, from (the age of) 18 (onwards); Think of a number from 1 to 20!* ***From*** expresses 'starting-point' here in the sense of the 'lower limit'.

As with ***to***, there need not be any actual movement involved. ***From*** can simply signal the standpoint taken for observing or considering something else, e.g. *Look! You can see the sea from here*: and also figuratively: *From the economic angle, things look different; From our point of view there are no objections to the plan.*

On the other hand, it may signal the starting-point for ***movement towards*** the speaker or observer: *Black smoke was pouring over our fence* ***from the garden next door.***

This is the basis for reference to ***origin***:

(8) a. Mette is from Norway (dt. *aus*).
b. … And this present is from me (dt. *von*).
c. Sandra was feeling faint from the heat (dt. … *matt von der Hitze*).
d. Yoghurt is made from milk (dt. *aus Milch hergestellt*).

Note that when the ***originator*** is referred to, the preposition is not *from*, but *by* (e.g. *a poem by Keats*). This applies particularly to passives, e.g. *Her faintness was caused by the heat* (see below).

(8)d. refers to a basic material from which a ***new*** material is produced, i.e. there is a change of substance. But when we talk about the material of a particular object, the preposition is *of*. Compare *Glass is made* ***from*** *silicon* and *A bottle is made* ***of*** *glass* (see also below).

From can precede other prepositional phrases that refer to places as standpoints or starting-points: ***From above the clouds*** *it sometimes looks as if you're flying over snow; Strange noises were coming* ***from behind the shed****; A small animal suddenly ran out* ***from under the sofa****.*

Note also: *from here/from there* (dt. *von hier/dort aus*).

Finally, another variant of the base meaning is that of ***separation***. This is underlined in certain adverb combinations: *Keep* ***away from*** *the edge of the platform, children!; Who else is missing,* ***apart from*** *Sharon?* (dt. … *abgesehen von Sharon*).

And also with adjectives and verbs: *different, safe, separate/separated, cut off/isolated* ***from****; to steal/take something* ***from*** *someone, to tell/distinguish X* ***from*** *Y, to stop/prevent/keep somebody/something* ***from doing*** *something, to protect someone/something* ***from***, etc.

036/1.3 at

This refers to a ***location***, i.e. tells us where something is or where it happens. It is usually applied to ***social environments*** like ***shops*** (*at the baker's, at Sainsbury's*), ***houses*** (*at Bertha's, at my grandmother's, at 44 Arnfield Avenue*), ***work, leisure*** and other ***social institutions*** (*at the office, at the swimming-pool, at the dentist's, at a club, at a stadium*, etc.), and also to ***events*** (*at a party/concert/race/lecture/wedding*, etc.).

With a few generalized institutions, the article is left out: *at work, at school, at home, at college, at university, at church*; also with meals (as 'events'): *at lunch/dinner/tea/breakfast.*

At is also used for ***localized points and places***: *at the top/bottom of the ladder, at the side of the house, at the door/window*; also for places within wider localities or areas: *at the crossroads between Bourne Grove and Fulton Way, at the bus-stop/traffic-lights/pedestrian crossing*, etc.

We also say *to go* ***at*** *a certain speed* (e.g. *to drive at 50 miles per hour, to sail at 20 knots*, etc.). The German equivalent with speeds, of course, is *mit.*

But the usual German renderings of ***at*** are *an, in,* or *bei*, and (with events) *auf*: *beim Arzt* (*at the doctor's*); *am Bahnhof* (*at the station*); *auf einer Tagung* (*at a conference*), *in der Walcott Street Nr. 13* (*at number 13 Walcott Street*).

Note the use of the ***genitive*** with the names of businesses, and the homes of persons: *at Woolworth's* (*bei Woolworth*), *at Susan's* (*= at Susan's house, bei Susan*), *at Siemens'* (*bei Siemens*).

Difficulties can arise with German *in*, which is translated sometimes as ***at*** and sometimes as *in* (see also below). Generally speaking, ***at*** = German *in*, in the sense of German *an* or *bei*: *im Kino* (*= dabei, einen Film anzuschauen*) *=* ***at*** *the cinema; in der Kirche (beim Gottesdienst)* = ***at*** *church; an der Kunstakademie* (*beim Studieren*) = ***at*** (*the*) *art college.* ⚠

There is a 'partner' relation between ***at*** and ***to***: one goes ***to*** *a place*, and is then ***at*** *that place.*

As with ***to***, reference to certain institutions has no article: *to be* ***at*** *school/****at*** *church,* ***at*** *home*, etc.

Note that we say, exceptionally, *in hospital* (see also below).

At is used in the figurative sense of 'location' following many adjectives and some nouns*: good/bad/clever/skilled* ***at***, etc.; also with those denoting emotions, in the meaning of *about: angry/surprised/shocked/amused* ***at***, etc.

Rather surprisingly, ***at*** can also express direction, though only in fairly idiomatic combinations, and in the mainly figurative sense of 'aim': *to throw at, to aim at, to shoot at*; and, more commonly: *to look at, to glance at, to stare at, to point at, to smile at*, etc. *To smile at* can also mean 'to be amused about' (mainly with things); *to laugh at* is similar.

Other phrases: *at last* (*endlich*), *at least* (*wenigstens*), *at* (*the*) *most, at best* (bestenfalls).

036/1.4 in/into

In refers to a space or substance as a kind of 'container' which encloses something: *in the garage, in water, in my pocket* (= *enclosed by*, respectively, *the garage, water, my pocket*). These are three-dimensional spaces, but the enclosing space can also be flat: *in the street, in the park, in the field.*

In is used also for geographical areas, such as towns, villages, countries, regions, etc.: *in Berlin, in Africa, in Canada, in Yorkshire*. The usual German equivalent is also *in*, although with flat spaces sometimes *auf*: *auf der Wiese* (***in*** *the field/meadow*), *auf dem Trafalgar Square* (***in*** *Trafalgar Square*), *auf dem Bild* (***in*** *the picture*), *auf dem Land* (*in the country*).

Like *to* and *at*, ***in*** can refer to certain states, places and institutions without an article: *to be in hospital, in prison, in bed*, etc.

In refers basically to ***place***, but with certain verbs (mainly general verbs of motion like *come* and *go*) to ***direction*** as well, especially in informal and colloquial language: *The children went in the park; Come in the house, out of the rain!; Don't fall in the water*!

It is nearly always used for movement with verbs of 'placing': *He put his pen in his pocket; Jane placed her hand in Tom's; The child stuck its thumb in its mouth*. Usually also with directions: *She looked in the window/in the mirror; Trains run from here in every direction*; and with expressions describing bodily contact: *The ball hit Brian in the stomach; The wind blew in our faces*, etc.

Otherwise, entering a particular space or place is generally expressed by ***into***: *We went into the church; She poured a little wine into her glass; The child ran into the road.*

Into also expresses collision (*Zusammenstoß*): *The car ran into the back of the truck; The man walked into a lamp-post; The two clowns bumped straight into the elephant.*

⚠ It is important to distinguish between ***into*** and ***to***, as German uses *in* for both: *She went to the cinema* (*Sie ist ins Kino gegangen*); *She went into the cinema* (*Sie ist ins Kino(-Gebäude) gegangen*). ***Into*** denotes very ***local*** movement and means here, e.g.: *She was outside/in front of the cinema and then she went into it.*

Similarly, we must differentiate carefully between ***in*** and ***at***, as, again, German uses *in* for both: *She was at the cinema* (*im Kino, und nicht z.B. in der Schule*); *She was in the cinema* (*Sie war im Kino (drinnen), und stand z.B. nicht mehr davor*). The difference is between general location (***at***) and specific position (***in***). A further example is: ***in*** *the swimming-pool* (= *in the water*), and ***at*** *the swimming-pool* (= e.g. *there, and not at home or at work*).

036/1.5 Idiomatic expressions with in/into

The following is a selection of various idioms and figurative expressions with ***in/into***. All are derived from the basic meanings of space and direction:

Typical adverbial uses:

- ***manner***, ***relation***, ***comment***: *in addition, in any case, in fact, in general, in particular, in detail, in my opinion, in English/German/French*, etc., *in good faith, in all honesty.*
- ***manner***, describing physical and emotional states, often accompanying actions: *in shame/horror/disbelief/despair, in poverty/comfort, in a bad/good mood, in high/low spirits, in good/bad health, in pain, in tears, in a low/high/loud/soft voice, in fear/panic*, etc.
  Other emotions or conditions: *in love, in danger, in trouble/difficulty*, etc.

- ***manner***, describing material media in creative activities: *in ink, in watercolour, in oil, in stone, in plastic,* e.g. *to write in ink, to paint in watercolour/in oil, to model in clay, to cast in bronze,* etc.
- ***manner***, describing shapes, arrangements, quantities: *in groups of three, in a straight line, in a queue, in a bunch, in a crowd, in alphabetical order, in four pages/ten lines/three acts/ seven verses,* etc.
- ***place***, referring to subject areas/fields of activity: *in sport, in history, in business, in politics, in films, in music,* etc.

Other uses:

- Composite prepositions: *in favour of, in front of, in spite of, in view of, in terms of.*
- ***in*** with verbs: *to believe in s.o./sth., to deal in sth., to succeed/fail in sth., to trust/confide in s.o., to dress in* (certain colours or types of clothes), *to take part in, to participate in.*
- ***in*** with nouns relating to activity or process: *interest/involvement/share/participation/ complicity/partnership in.*
- ***in*** with nouns relating to 'more or less of' sth.: *increase/rise/decrease/fall/decline in.*
- ***into*** with verbs: *to look into/to enquire into (a question/problem), to get into (trouble),* see also below; *to change into* (e.g. *more comfortable clothing* – dt. *sich umziehen*), *to change/ turn into* (e.g. *a pillar of salt* – dt. *sich verwandeln*), *to divide sth. into (parts/pieces), to translate sth. into, to integrate s.o./o.s. into sth.*
- ***in*** as an ***adverb particle***: *I rang the bell several times, but they were not* ***in*** (= *at home*); *Come in*! (dt. *Herein*!). See also under ***Phrasal Verbs*** in chapter 8.
  Note the expressions *in here/there* (dt. *hier/dort drinnen*).

036/1.6 out of

Out of is a ***composite*** (or ***complex***) preposition, i.e. one that consists of more than one word. It is used mainly as a preposition of direction, and means the opposite of *into*: *When the fire broke out, the people ran* ***out of*** *the building in panic* (dt. … *aus dem Gebäude heraus*).

In certain collocations it refers to place rather than direction and is then the opposite of *in*: *out of prison/hospital/danger* (*no longer in prison/hospital/danger*); *out of work* (= *without a job*); *out of luck/money/petrol,* etc. (= *having no luck/money/petrol,* etc.); *out of sight/reach/ touch/earshot* (*not able to be seen/grasped/contacted/heard*); *out of the way* (= *in an isolated place*; or *not 'in the way'*, i.e. *not blocking anyone's path*).

And with abstract nouns: *out of interest/generosity/kindness,* etc. (= *because of*): *I gave her the money* ***out of*** *kindness: I had no other motives.*

In colloquial language and dialect, ***out*** is sometimes used alone as a preposition, i.e. without *of* (*He just threw it out the window*). However, this is not standard English. The standard use of *out* on its own is as an ***adverb particle***: *I don't really want to go* ***out*** *tonight, so I'll just stay at home.*

036/1.7 inside/outside

Outside and ***inside*** have the same meanings as *out of* and *in*(*to*), and are used to emphasize them: *She put the frozen chicken **inside** a large plastic bag* (i.e. *so that it was completely covered*); *Don't let the children go **outside** the garden* (i.e. *don't let them leave the garden*).

The emphasis may underline an *inside-outside* contrast, or signal a change of perspective from one to the other: *The light switch is just **inside** the front door on the right* (i.e. *when you approach the house from the street **outside** it*); ***Inside** the car it was warm* (*as opposed to **outside** it*); *Even after the film had begun, there were a lot of people still waiting **outside** the cinema* (i.e. *waiting to get **inside** the cinema*). As in this last example, ***outside*** often translates German *vor*: *I'll meet you tomorrow **outside** Oxford Circus tube station.*

Inside/outside can also be:

- adverbs (*Please go outside if you wish to smoke*);
- nouns (*On the outside the house looked old and dirty, but the inside was modern and luxurious*);
- adjectives (*an outside toilet*);

Some idiomatic collocations and derived meanings: *inside out* (e.g. of clothing, dt. *links herum*), *insider* (a member of an organization who has special knowledge or experience), *inside information* (= known only to insiders), *to be inside* (= in prison), *outsider* (somebody outside a particular group, or somebody excluded from something socially); *inside lane* (dt. *Innenspur*), *outside lane* (dt. *Überholspur*).

036/1.8 on/onto

On means 'touching, or part of, a particular surface': *on the ceiling* (dt. *an der Decke*), *on the wall* (dt. *an der Wand*), *on the floor* (dt. *auf dem Fußboden*). The general German equivalents are *auf* and *an*, depending on the direction of contact (*auf* = 'with the surface below', *an* = 'with the surface above', or 'touching from the side').

On is also used for certain parts of the body (hands, feet, wrists, fingers, toes) in the sense of *around*, and also for the skin in the sense of 'attached to, or part of, the surface'. Here, again, German uses *an*:

(9) a. She wore rings ***on*** most fingers and ***on*** three of her toes (dt. *an*).
b. There was a bruise ***on*** Sam's arm (= on the skin of Sam's arm) where the stone had hit him (dt. *an*).
c. Davies owned an expensive watch, but it was never ***on*** his wrist (dt. *an*).
d. There was a scar ***on*** his forehead and a wart ***on*** his nose (dt. *an der Stirn, an/auf der Nase*).

⚠ A particular contrast to German are the following: ***in*** *the picture* (not **on the picture*, dt. *auf dem Bild*), e.g. *What can you see **in** this picture, children?*; and ***on*** *the blackboard* (not **at the blackboard*, dt. *an der Tafel*). It is also ***on*** *the screen* (dt. *am/auf dem Bildschirm*), ***on*** *the notice-board* (dt. *am schwarzen Brett*), ***on*** *the sign* (dt. *auf dem Schild*).

Note other cases of ***on*** as 'attached to' (where German, again, mainly uses *an*): *a balloon on a piece of string, a dog on a lead, a shelf on the wall, a notice on the door,* etc.

On is used, like German ***auf***, for geographical surface areas: *on the continent, on an island, on the mainland;* also: *on a planet,* i.e. *on the moon, on Mars,* etc. Note that although we say *on the Earth,* it is nevertheless *in the world* (contrast German *auf der Welt*). For ***direction*** in these cases (i.e. movement in flight), we use ***to*** (as opposed to German *auf*): *to fly to the moon, to return to the Earth,* etc. And similarly with islands: *to fly to Crete/Majorca/Madeira/the Channel Islands,* etc. One lives/stays, etc., ***on*** *an island,* and ***on*** smaller islands referred to by name: *on the Isle of Wight, on Skye,* etc. With the names of larger islands ***in*** is preferred: *in Crete/Majorca, Madeira/Jersey,* etc.

On is used for local surface areas (again, in the sense of German ***auf***): *on the beach, on the village green, on the golf course.*

Like *in,* ***on*** may sometimes compete here with ***at***. Again, the difference here is between general location (***at***) and specific position (***on***), e.g. ***at*** *the golf course* (= e.g. *not at home or at the cinema*); ***on*** *the golf-course* (= e.g. *playing golf and not in the clubhouse having a drink*). Similarly, ***at/on*** *the beach,* ***at/on*** *the tennis-court,* ***at/on*** *the race-track,* etc.

On also competes with ***in***. Normally, the distinction is clear: *on the grass* (= *touching the surface*), *in the grass* (= *surrounded or enclosed by blades of long grass*); *on the sand* (= *on top of it*), *in the sand* (= *enclosed or covered by it*). With larger local areas, however, the difference is not so easy to recognize: *in a field* means 'enclosed by a fence or some other boundary'. Similarly, we say *in a street/road/square* (= *enclosed by buildings*). American English here often uses *on* (*on Sunset Boulevard, on Riverside Drive*). A point of confusion in British English (and an exception) is that the position ***on*** the driving surface of a road (i.e. the part that vehicles use) is seen as ***in*** *the road.* British parents tell their children not to go ***in*** *the road,* but to stay ***on*** *the pavement* (dt. *auf dem Gehsteig*). Both British and American English say ***in*** *a lane* (dt. *auf einer Fahrspur*).

Apart from these individual differences, Britons and Americans agree that the general place relation to a road or path in the sense of German *auf* is ***on***: ***on*** *the way/path/road/route to the west.* Similarly also: *on the rails/track/trail,* etc. With rivers ***on*** expresses both German *auf* and German *an*: ***on*** *the Thames* (dt. *auf dem Wasser der Themse,* bzw. *an der Themse*): *the boats on the Rhine; Cologne stands on the Rhine.*

Onto can be written as one word or two (***on to***). In more conservative spelling, the two-word version is preferred. Like *into,* ***onto*** expresses direction or movement. With ***onto***, the movement is from a particular place to a surface: *A large apple fell from the tree onto the garden table; The cat jumped from the flower-bed on to the garden wall.* The starting position does not have to be mentioned. It can simply be implied by context: *The dog trotted into the room and climbed onto Mary's lap* (i.e. *from the floor of the living-room*). As with *into,* ***onto*** is rarely used with 'placing' verbs like *put, place, lay, stand,* etc. Here ***on*** is preferred, even for ***direction***: *He put the book on the table; She placed her hands on her hips,* etc. ***Onto*** is usually reserved for movement across space or distance, or implying effort, particularly when the direction is up or down. It tends to occur most often with verbs such as *to get, to climb, to jump, to leap, to hop,* etc. Note, however, that we nevertheless use ***on*** (and ***not*** *onto*) with the verb *to land*: *They landed* ***on*** *the moon; The pilot landed* ***on*** *an airstrip in the jungle; They landed* ***on*** *a deserted beach,* etc.

036/1.9 Idiomatic expressions with on/onto

The following is a selection of various idioms and figurative expressions with ***on/onto***. Typical adverbial uses are:

- ***place***, in local and socially figurative senses: *on the phone, on (the) television/radio, on video/DVD/hard-disc/diskette/computer/podcast,* etc.; *on a committee/panel/board/council/staff,* etc. (American usage also: *on a team*); *on a list/roster/rota/schedule,* etc.
  In a more concrete sense, ***on*** can precede various terms referring to farms and land: *on a farm/ranch/estate,* etc.
  And for ***place deixis***: *on the right/on the left.* Also for types of land or water surface: *on land, on sea, on water, on snow, on sand.*
- ***manner/state***: *on (one's) guard, on the attack, on the defensive, on sale, on fire, on one's own (= alone), on the increase, on a trip/journey, on holiday, on duty, on call, on leave, on business, on purpose, on principle, on time,* etc.
- ***relation, comment***: *on no account, on average, on the contrary, on condition, on the whole,* etc.

Other uses:

- composite prepositions: *on account of, on behalf of, on the part of.*
- with verbs: *to count/depend/rely on s.o./sth., to decide on, to insist on, to congratulate s.o. on sth., to call on s.o., to decide on, to live/feed/exist on, to encroach/impinge on sth.*; also in the sense of ***about***: *to comment on sth., to lecture/talk/speak on certain subjects* (usually in monologue form and for an audience).
- with nouns related to the verb types just listed: *dependency/reliance/insistence/congrulations on,* etc.
  Note also: *(to have) an effect on s.o./sth.*
  And similarly after reference to communication processes *about* certain topics: *a lecture/talk/article/book/programme, advice,* etc. ***on*** *a subject/theme/topic/field/area,* etc.
- before nouns referring to vehicles and methods of travel: *on a bus/boat/train/plane/bicycle/motor-cycle,* etc. Also: *on skates/skis/stilts/a skateboard/a surfboard,* etc.; and similarly with animals: *on a horse/donkey/elephant,* etc. But: ***in*** *a car/**in** a taxi.*
  Note also the verbal expressions *to **get on/get off** a bus/plane/bicycle/train/elephant,* etc. But: to ***get into/out of*** cars/taxis/lorries.
  In reference to ***methods*** of travel (in the abstract), ***on*** is used only in the phrases *on foot, on horseback.* There is no article. With vehicles and animals (except horses), the usual preposition here is ***by*** (see also below): *by bus/boat/train/plane/car/taxi/camel,* etc.
- before nouns referring to instruments of media and communication: *on (the) television/ radio, on the air* (dt. *auf Sendung*), *on the phone.*
- ***on*** as an ***adverb particle***: Like *in,* ***on*** can be used as an adverb particle (see also in chapter 8 under ***Phrasal Verbs***):
  a) in the sense of the preposition: *Milk has spilt out of the bottle because the top wasn't **on** (= on the bottle).*
  b) in derived senses: *She had a blue blouse **on** (= she was wearing one); The television/oven,* etc. *is **on** (= running).*

c) in the meaning of progress/continuation: *to carry on* (dt. *weitermachen*), *straight on* (dt. *geradeaus*), *further on* (dt. *weiter auf dem Weg*).

036/1.10 off

This is the opposite of *on/onto*, and means movement away from a surface: *The picture fell **off** the wall; The wind blew the cap **off** my head.* Direction of movement is usually up or down, but can be on the same level, e.g. *The singer just turned and walked off the stage; The spectators booed as the players came off the field.*

Extensions of this meaning are: the idea of 'removal or disappearance' from a surface (*I rubbed the writing off the board; She wiped the chocolate off her son's face*); and detachment from something (*We cut the dead branches off our fruit-trees; She took the watch off her wrist*).

The most common German equivalents here are *von/von … herunter/von … ab*, or sometimes simply dative + *ab*: *Security officials took four knives off passengers booked on the Istanbul flight; I bought the car off a man in Bristol.*

In certain collocations ***off*** can also convey the idea of ***place***: *The village is in North Kent, just off the Dover road* (= dt. *direkt neben*); *The island is about two miles off the coast* (= dt. *vor der Küste, von der Küste entfernt*).

It is occasionally also found in the sense of *above*: *The lowest branch of the tree was 3 metres off the ground* (dt. *drei Meter über dem Boden*).

Certain phrases with ***off*** imply place in a figurative sense. Several of these have ***on***-equivalents: *off duty* (dt. *nicht im Dienst*, cf. *on duty*); *off one's guard* (dt. *auf einen Angriff nicht vorbereitet*, cf. *on one's guard*). A further pair are *off shore* (more frequently *offshore*, dt. *vor der Küste/ablandig*) and *on shore* (sometimes *on-shore*, dt. *an Land/anlandig*).

Other phrases: *off balance* (*aus der Balance*), *off course* (cf. *on course*), *off-line* (cf. *on-line*), *off limits, off one's hands* (*einen nicht mehr belastend*, cf. *on one's hands*), *off work* (dt. *krank gemeldet*). In some cases these can be used also for ***direction***: *to go on/off duty; to go off course/off limits*, etc.

Off occurs as an ***adverb particle***, usually in the German meaning of *ab/weg*: *to drive off/walk off/go off.* Also: *to fall off* (figurative, dt. *nachlassen*), *to leave off* (dt. *nachlassen, weglassen*), *to take off* (dt. *starten*), *to see s.o. off* (dt. *jemanden verabschieden*), etc.

036/1.11 by

This means *next to/beside*, or *very near*: *the table by the window* (dt. *am Fenster*); *the lamp standard by the couch* (dt. *neben der Couch*); *the tree by the gate* (dt. *neben dem Tor*).

By also has a direction meaning in the sense of *past*: *She walked by me without seeing me* (= dt. *an mir vorbei*).

An important figurative sense of 'direction' is expressed when ***by*** refers to the source or origin of an action or state (dt. *von/durch*):

- *She was frightened **by** a sudden noise under the bed* (= ***agent*** in a ***passive*** sentence).
- *That painting is **by** my sister; This is a book **by** Tolkien* (= ***agent*** as creator of a 'product'). N.B. A widespread error here is using *of*, instead of ***by***: **a book of Tolkien.* ⚠
- *We met them **by chance**; She's French **by birth**, and a lawyer **by profession*** (dt. *von Geburt, von Beruf*); *I took your book **by mistake/by accident*** (dt. *aus Versehen*).

Closely related to this is ***instrument*** or ***method***, i.e. showing a way of doing something, or the circumstances under which it is done:

- *We went* ***by*** *car/bus/train; I came in* ***by*** *the back entrance; John drove to Brighton* ***by*** *the scenic route; The burglars got into the house* ***by*** *climbing through a window.*
- *I learn all vocabulary* ***by heart*** (dt. *auswendig*); *You can contact me* ***by*** *phone/****by*** *e-mail at any time* (dt. *telefonisch/per E-Mail*); *The letter was delivered* ***by hand****; I know Jenny* ***by sight*** (dt. *vom Sehen her*); *She came to the party* ***by herself*** (= *alone*).
- *He grabbed her* ***by*** *the wrist (*dt. *am Handgelenk); Hold the knife* ***by*** *the handle!* (dt. *am Griff*); *He does not play* ***by*** *the rules* (= *according to,* dt. *nach*); *What do you mean* ***by that****?* (= *by saying that,* dt. *mit/damit*).

Another close relation is ***quantity*** or ***dimension***:

- *Bryant won the election* ***by*** *five votes* (dt. *um/mit einem Abstand von*).
- *If you multiply 4* ***by*** *2, you get 8, and if you divide 4* ***by*** *2, you get 2* (dt. *mit/durch*); *My bedroom at home measures 9 feet* ***by*** *6* (dt. *auf*).
- *We're losing our fortune bit* ***by*** *bit* (= *gradually,* dt. *Stück für Stück*).

As an ***adverb particle, by*** means *past* (dt. *vorbei*): *We waved as the train went* ***by*** (= *past us*). Note also to *drop/call/come* ***by*** (= *to visit informally,* dt. *vorbeikommen*).

036/1.12 up, down

These mean 'in a higher or lower place/direction'. They are the most common prepositions describing relations between different levels (or ***planes***). Both also occur as adverb particles.

Up (= *towards/in a higher place*) and ***down*** (= *towards/in a lower place*) are opposites of one another. They are most frequently used for direction: ***up/down*** *the hill.* Note that in English these are straightforward prepositions like any others. German is more complex here, and can only express this in the form of 'postpositions' which are a mixture of prepositions and adverbs: *den Berg hinauf/hinunter.*

Down is also used to mean *along,* usually in the sense of 'away from the speaker': *The bathroom is down the corridor to the right; The mysterious black car drove slowly down the street.* This use is particularly common in spoken and informal English. With verbs indicating a change of direction, ***down*** can also mean *into and along*: *The car turned down a sidestreet.*

As adverb particles, ***up/down*** are also mainly used in the sense of direction. As with other particles in concrete use, it is the context which makes the meaning clear: *Come* ***down*** (e.g. *from that ladder you're rather dangerously balanced on*)!; *I'll just go* ***up*** *and see to the children* (*who are upstairs in bed*).

Up/down often combine with *to* when movement towards something also involves a vertical change of place: *We went* ***down to*** *John's for the weekend.* This suggests that we live on higher ground than John. For the reverse visit we would then say *John's coming* ***up to*** *us for the weekend.* Another meaning could be *north* vs. *south,* indicating that we live north of where John lives. Regions far apart are stressed in this way, e.g. in Britain a southerner could go *up to Scotland* and a northerner *down to London.* But often the difference is cultural or psychological. The phrase *up to London*, for instance, is often heard at standpoints in the southern suburbs or on the south coast. Similarly, New Yorkers speak of 'uptown' (= north of the main city centre) and 'downtown' (= the city centre from an uptown, i.e. northerly, standpoint).

Note also that the phrase ***up to*** expresses German *auf ... zu*: *A woman came up to me as I was waiting for the bus* (dt. *...kam auf mich zu*).

Up to/down to also refer to levels and amounts: *The water in the flooded cellar came up to our knees; This car can carry up to five passengers; Unemployment is now down to the level of ten years ago.*

Note ***up*** in the sense of *not in bed*: *Sally is never up before noon on Saturdays.*

Up/down combine also with other place prepositions: *up at Craggs' farm, down in Alabama, down on the beach*, etc. Also with *here/there* for emphasis: *down here/there* (*hier/dort unten*), etc.

The adverbs ***upwards/downwards*** are used to emphasize movement in the direction of up or down. They also appear (without *-s*) as adjectives: *in an upward/downward direction.*

Typical phrasal verbs showing the concrete meanings of ***up/down*** are: *to pick up* (dt. *aufheben/in die Hand nehmen*), *to put down* (dt. *hinlegen/hinstellen*); *to get up* (dt. *aufstehen*), *to lie down* (dt. *sich hinlegen*), etc. Others are listed in chapter 8, **042/2**.

036/1.13 over, under, above, below

This is a further set of prepositions referring to higher and lower planes.

Over refers to a position which is 'higher' in a ***vertical*** (ninety-degree) direction. One meaning is 'not touching, but quite close', often implying that the lower object is covered in some way: *the roof over our heads; The grill hangs on a chain over the fire; We placed the armchair over the stain on the carpet.* The German equivalent is *über*, in the sense of *direkt darüber.*

Another, closely related meaning is 'touching and covering from the top or the side': *She pulled the blankets over her head and fell asleep again; The man had a patch over (= covering) one eye; there was a metal cover over the hole in the ground.*

A third meaning is 'up, across and down', i.e. from one side to the other: *The dog jumped over the gate; She threw the rubbish over her neighbour's fence.*

For movement and direction, ***over*** is preferred in this sense to *across.*

Finally, as a figurative extension of place reference, ***over*** is used to mean *more than*, especially in the sense of 'past a particular limit'. This is a figurative extension of the place meaning: *over 21 years of age; He weighs over a 100 kilos; We're over ten miles from the village.*

Under is the 'lower' equivalent: *The cat lay under the sofa; There was a small terrace under the upstairs balcony; He was wearing just a T-shirt under his anorak* (dt. *unter* (*... darunter*)); *Sam slid the envelope under the professor's door; Are you under 18?*

Above is sometimes used like ***over*** in the sense 'not touching, but quite close': *a mirror above/over the fireplace* (dt. *über dem Kamin*); *a small window above/over the door.* Unlike ***over***, however, ***above*** is used in the more general sense of 'at a higher level than', even when the direction is ***not*** vertical: *On our left the track wound up the mountainside above us*

(= *to a much higher level than where we were standing*); *This town is a thousand feet above sea-level* (dt. ... *über dem Meeresspiegel*).

It is also preferred, as a rule, when the distance is stated: *There was a scar about a centimetre above his right eye; The helicopter circled 1500 feet above us.* Similarly also for 'vertical' measuring scales: *The temperature now is only two degrees above zero* (dt. ... *über Null*).

On the other hand, ***above*** cannot mean ***over*** in the sense of *across*, i.e. *The dog jumped* ***above*** *the fence* means 'higher than the top of the fence', but ***not*** 'from one side to the other'.

With expressions of movement, then, ***above*** = upward direction alone, and ***over*** = *across*.

Compare: *The plane flew quickly above the mountains* (= *to a higher level in the sky*), and *The plane flew quickly over the mountains* (= *crossed them*).

Below is the 'lower' equivalent of ***above***: *On our left the track wound down the mountainside below us* (= *to a much lower level than where we were standing*); *This town lies a hundred feet below sea-level; The temperature is 5 degrees below zero.*

Below and ***under*** contrast in the same ways as *above* and *over*. ***Below*** is preferred when distances are quantified or otherwise emphasized. When movement is expressed, ***below*** = downward direction alone, ***under*** = 'from one side to the other', or 'into a position under ...': *The dog crawled under the fence; Come under my umbrella in this heavy rain.*

'In(to) a position under ...' can be emphasized by the preposition ***underneath*** (= dt. *unterhalb*): *When the dog appeared, the cat shot underneath the sofa.*

Over, under, above, below are all used as adverb particles for both place and direction, e.g. *to go over/above/below* (dt. *hinüber-/hinauf-/hinuntergehen*); *Mary is over* (= *has come over to us*) *for the weekend; There was a cry from above/below.* The precise meaning, of course, is context-dependent. On its own, ***under*** has a restricted adverb use meaning *under water* (*The ship went under*, i.e. *sank*). ***Under*** and ***over*** frequently combine with *here* and *there* to emphasize them: *over here/there* (dt. *hier/da drüben*), *under here/there* (dt. *hier/dort unten*).

Above and ***below*** are themselves sometimes emphasized by *up/down*, respectively: *up above, down below.*

For details on phrasal verbs, see chapter 8, **042/2**.

036/1.14 Other place/direction prepositions

- ***across***: ***Across*** means the same as *over* in the sense of 'from one side of a surface to the other': *We walked across (over) the field; They rowed across (over) the river* (dt. *über ... hinüber/herüber*).
  It is also used for place, meaning 'at the other side': *There was a pub across (over) the road* (dt. ... *auf der anderen Straßenseite*).
  But it is only used for places and directions ***on the same level***, and ***cannot*** replace *over* in the sense of 'up and down': *The boys climbed over the fence* (not **across the fence*); *The coach came over the hill* (not **across the hill*).
- ***against:*** This translates German *gegen/an* in the sense of 'touching/hitting an upright surface': *A man was leaning against the wall of the pub; The rowing boats in the harbour started to knock against each other as the wind increased.*

In certain collocations it can mean 'in the opposite direction to' in the sense of resisting or fighting: *Don't try to swim against the current; It was a hard job sailing against the wind*. More frequently it is used in this sense figuratively (i.e. meaning 'in opposition to'): *Our partners have decided against the plan; What you did was against the law; Then the other team scored against the run of play.*

It cannot be used in the sense of German *zu/entgegen*. The English equivalent here is *towards*: *There was a car coming towards us; He has a negative attitude towards/to his job.* ⚠

Against is not used as an adverb particle.

- ***along: Along*** = 'following the length of something', 'from one end towards the other' (dt. *entlang*). It is only used in a horizontal sense. It contrasts with *across* (= 'from one side to the other'): *along the road* (dt. *die Straße entlang*), *across the road* (dt. *quer über die/der Straße*), *along the beach* (= *following the line of the sea*), *across the beach* (= *from sea to land or from land to sea*). It is used for both place and movement: *There were trees along one side of the road; He walked along the road.* A common alternative, especially in informal use, is *down*: *He walked down the road* (see also under ***Down*** above). As an adverb particle it conveys the idea of 'accompanying': *You can come along too* (*Du kannst auch mit uns mitgehen*).
- ***Around*** something = 'in the shape of a circle with the object in the middle' (dt. *um ... herum*): *The children joined hands and danced around the tree.*

  Similar meanings are 'surrounding' (*The entire family sat around the table; There was a fence around the field*), and 'following a curved line' (*The mountains came into view around a bend in the road*). In this sense it is used as the opposite of *through* or *over*, often with the idea of 'avoiding': *People were walking around the man lying on the pavement; We will be going around London on the south side.*

  On the other hand, ***around*** can mean 'throughout' or 'at/to many places inside': *Brian spent the morning working around the house; Guests from abroad were being shown around the company.*

  Around is often converted simply to ***round***, especially in informal language: *The park has no fence or hedge round it; We went on a tour round Tokyo on our third day.*

  As an adverb particle ***around*** has several similar meanings. Most, though not all, are related to the prepositional ones:
  - *The big wheel started to go a/round* (= 'move in a circular direction', dt. *sich drehen*);
  - *There were a lot of people standing a/round outside the pub* (= 'here and there in a particular area', dt. *herumstehen*);
  - *Children were running around in the garden* (= 'here and there/in all directions', dt. *herumrennen*);
  - *We spent the first week in Israel travelling around* (= 'in various directions', dt. *herumreisen*);
  - *At the club there was no-one around* (= 'there/available to talk to', dt. *da/dort*); *That singer is fairly old: He's been around for years* (informal, 'in existence', dt. *Den gibt's seit Jahren*);
  - *Is there any food around ?*(= 'here/available', dt. *Gibt es hier zu essen?*);
  - *There are no good restaurants a/round here* (= informal, 'in this area', dt. *in dieser Gegend*);

- *She heard a noise behind her and turned a/round suddenly* (= 'in a half-circle/facing the opposite direction', dt. *sich herumdrehen*).

- ***behind, in front of:*** These are opposites and translate German *hinter/vor*, respectively. They refer to relative positions in a sequence or order, seen from a front-to-back or back-to-front perspective.
  Concrete individual senses of ***behind*** are 'at the back of' (*There was a shed behind the house*), 'following' (*In my driving mirror I could still see the big black car behind me*) and also 'covered/hidden by' (*The sun went behind the clouds; There was a safe on the wall behind a large painting*). In this last sense, ***behind*** is the horizontal equivalent of *under*.
  With sequences, queues, competitions and other types of comparison, ***behind*** means 'further back than'/'not as far forward as': *Saunders was well behind Matthews at that stage of the race; In the football league table, Liverpool are just behind Arsenal at the moment.*
  In front of is the opposite, and means, concretely, 'placed before' (*A caravan was parked in front of the house; At the traffic lights there were four cars in front of me*), or 'further forward than' (*Matthews was well in front of Saunders at that stage of the race*). An alternative is ***ahead of***, used especially when there is some distance between entities: *About 100 yards ahead of our boat there was a group of rocks.*
  All can be used as adverb particles (again depending for the exact meaning on context): *Matthews was well in front; Saunders was a long way behind; There was a group of rocks about 100 yards ahead.*

- ***before, after:*** Although generally preferred for time relations (see below), these are sometimes used for *in front of* and *behind*, especially for queues, and for other kinds of sequence that have a certain time association: *There were two women before me at the supermarket check-out; S comes before V in the alphabet* (*= earlier than*), *but after P* (*= later than*).
  Before and ***after*** are preferred also in 'sideways' ('shoulder-to-shoulder') sequences: *The hairdresser's is after the baker's just before Woolworth's on the right-hand side.*
  Before (though not ***after***) is used for general space relations in more formal style: *The great Rocky Mountains rose before us across the plain; I stand before you today not as your teacher, but as a private person.*

- ***past, through:*** As a movement preposition, ***past*** generally means 'passing on one side/going by' (dt. *an … vorbei*): *The train sped past fields, forests and lakes; We walked past McDonald's and the pet shop to the bank on the corner.*
  As a preposition of place, it means 'after/beyond' (dt. *jenseits*): *The hairdresser's is past the baker's on the right-hand side*. This meaning also occurs with certain verbs of motion: *Let's get past London, and then we'll have a break* (dt. *Lassen wir London erst hinter uns …*).
  Note that with geographical locations German *hinter* is generally rendered by ***past*** or ***after***: *The village of Masefield is past Stow in the direction of Cirencester.*
  Through (dt. *durch … hindurch*) means 'into and out of a space', or movement inside an enclosed area from one side/end to the other: *The dog got into the garden through a door/gate/gap in the hedge; We walked through the wood; The train went through a tunnel; You could not see through the window, as it was so dirty.*
  It is also used in a quite different and more abstract sense of cause (= *because of*): *Through your carelessness we've lost our tickets; Through the breakdown on the motorway, our journey was delayed by about three hours.*

Both can be used, contextually, as adverb particles: *Parker ducked behind a bush as the riders went past* (also ... *went by*, German *vorbei*); *At the factory gate they just waved us through without asking for any identity.*

- ***between, among: Between*** (dt. zwischen) usually refers to the space separating two things or people: *There is no bus stop between here and the next village; The railway line ran between rows of small houses; In the cinema I sat between Suzanne and Ali.*
  But it can also mean simply 'dividing': There was a thick hedge between the two fields; The wall between this room and the kitchen is made of wood. Or, indeed, 'connecting', also in an abstract sense: *The ferry between the two islands was not operating due to bad weather; The professional relationship between Steadman and me was good; A quarrel between the two men had also led to silence between their wives.* Reference to 'space' may also be abstract, e.g. separating numbers or quantities: *This granite block weighs between 6 and 7 tons; Sirtaz earns between forty and fifty thousand pounds a year.*
  Among (dt. *unter*) is the equivalent of *between* when more than two entities are involved: *Divide the sandwiches equally among the three of you*!; *The five students should first discuss the matter among themselves; I could see several deer among the trees in the distance.*
  It can also convey the idea of 'within a group': *There is no one among us in the office who can speak good Spanish; Dissatisfaction among the workers in the company has been steadily increasing over the past months; I searched among my papers, but could not find the document.* Or 'in the middle of': *You are among friends here.*
- ***opposite, near: Opposite*** (dt. *gegenüber*) means 'on the other side of something but facing': *The house opposite ours is for sale; The chemist's is on the left of the High Street opposite a betting shop.* Contextually it is used as an adverb, e.g. *the house opposite* (i.e. *facing ours*).
  Near = 'a short distance away/close to/not far from' (dt. *nahe/in der Nähe von*): *There is a sports centre near the station; Don't go near the fire, children!*
  Near is also used as an adjective and adverb with *to*, in the same sense as the preposition: *There is a sports centre quite near to the station.* In informal language, the distinction preposition-adverb/adjective is often blurred, so that even the preposition takes on certain adjective/adverb forms, e.g. gradability (*very near the station*) and comparative and superlative: *The post office nearest here is in the town; My daughter and her children are moving nearer me next year.*

036/2 Prepositions of time

Several prepositions with place meaning are also used for time. The major ones are ***in***, ***on***, and ***at***, followed by ***after*** and ***before***. Less prominent are ***from***, ***to***, ***by*** and ***over***. Here we will categorize prepositions according to type of time reference:

036/2.1 Days (on)

on Sunday(s), on Christmas Day, on her birthday, on January 20th.

This also applies to ***parts*** of the day when they are identified as parts of ***particular*** days: *on Wednesday afternoon, on Christmas morning, on the afternoon of her birthday, on the evening of February 16th*, etc.

Or when there is implicit contrast with the same parts of other days: *on the third night of the attack, on the second morning of the festival, on a hot afternoon in late August,* etc. The usual German equivalent is *an* (Exception: *in der Nacht*).

036/2.2 Parts of the day (in)

in the morning(s), in the afternoon(s), in the evening(s).

For reference to a part of the day as a ***period*** (especially one period of the day in contrast to another), the usual preposition is ***in***: *When I call tomorrow, shall I call in the afternoon or (in) the evening* (dt. *nachmittags/am Nachmittag oder abends/am Abend*)?

An exception is ***at*** *night*: *Bob writes in the morning(s), relaxes in the afternoon(s) and drives a taxi at night; When we go on holiday next weekend, we'll be travelling at night.* In this case there is no article, even if a particular night is meant (as in the second example).

In *the night* (N.B. with article!) also occurs, but never in contrast to other times of day. It emphasizes the idea of 'during or within the period': *Under stress, I often wake up several times in the night.* It is the only option when the meaning is 'during the coming night/during the one just past': *If you get cold in the night there's an extra blanket in the wardrobe; Did you hear that loud noise in the night?*

036/2.3 Weeks, months, seasons, years (in)

In is also the standard preposition for longer spans of time. These can be seasons or calendar periods: *in (the) autumn, in (the) winter, in (the) spring, in January, in July, in 1861, in the coming week.* Or more general time-spans: *in the school holidays, in my childhood, in the Victorian Age, in the present-day, in the past/future,* etc.

⚠ Note that unlike German, English has no articles before the names of months (*in August,* dt. *im August*). With year numerals ***in*** is always used in English, but omitted in German: *Jason worked in Texas in 1984* (dt. *1984 arbeitete Jason in Texas*).

036/2.4 Clock times and points of the day (at)

at 4 pm, at 11.30, at dawn/noon/midnight.

036/2.5 Festivities, events, general time location (at)

At is also used for more general time location, e.g. with festive and religious periods (*at Christmas, at Easter, at Whitsun,* etc.), points and stages (*at the age of three, at that time/stage/point,* etc.), and with events and happenings: *at the party/meeting/concert,* etc. With event expressions like these, ***at*** can be regarded as a double reference to time ***and*** place.

A related use is with mealtimes: *at breakfast (time), at lunch(time), at dinner(time),* etc. Also: *at the weekend.*

Note that 'phases' call forth the 'during' meaning, and normally require ***in***: *in my life/childhood/youth/adolescence,* etc. (see also **036/2.3**). This also applies to the word *age* when it means 'era' or 'period': *in old age, in middle age, in the Elizabethan Age,* etc.

036/2.6 No preposition

No preposition is used with *yesterday, today, tomorrow,* and related expressions: *We saw her today/the day-before-yesterday,* etc. This also applies to expressions with *next, last,* and *this* when speaker-related (i.e. deictic): *We are seeing her tomorrow/tonight/this evening.* In American English, especially in the media, this use is extended to the days of the week and sometimes even dates: *The President met major union leaders Saturday; He visits Princeton University September 12.*

036/2.7 Time periods and their beginning and end

As with all point-time location, ***at*** can be used with expressions referring to the beginning and end of time-spans (*at the start of his career; at the end of our time in Canada*). However, prepositions more specifically expressing (or implying) time-spans are:

- ***from: From*** (dt. *ab*) refers to the beginning of a period, and means 'starting then (at the stated time)'. It usually occurs together with the adverb *onwards* (shortened informally to the particle *on*): *From next week (onwards) we will be living in Spain; From the middle of the film on(wards) I was thoroughly bored; From 1990 the company's success declined rapidly.*
- ***until, till, up to: Until*** (dt. *bis)* means the opposite of *from,* i.e. 'ending then (at the stated time)': *Until 1990 the company was very successful; We lived in France until last year.*
  Till is the less formal version. It does not usually occur at the beginning of sentences: *Let's wait till (until) tomorrow and see if the weather is fine.*
  Another alternative is ***up to***. This particularly stresses the period of time, and/or the end of it. It tends to be used for longer time-spans, and also mainly for past time: *Up to 1990 the company was very successful; Up to now the dog has been very well behaved.*
  Until/till can be used also as conjunctions.
- ***from ... to/till/until:*** The usual way of referring to a stretch of clock or calendar time is with ***from ... to***: *The castle is open to the general public from April to October; Eric was at university from 1993 to 1997.*
  Until/till can replace ***to***, but give slightly more emphasis to the time limit: *You can play in the garden from now until (till) lunchtime; The hotel beach is closed from midnight till dawn.*
- ***between:*** In its literal sense, ***between*** means 'sometime/several times during the time-span': *The police say the woman must have left the house again between midnight and 6 am.*
  But it is often used informally to mean the whole of a time-span, i.e. in the sense of ***from ... to***: *Eric was at university between 1993 and 1997.*
- ***by: By*** also translates German *bis,* but in the sense of *vor* or *spätestens dann*: *They managed to get home by seven o'clock; Applications must be sent in by March 31st.*
  That is, the point of time here indicates a kind of ultimatum or limit, and ***by*** means 'not later than'.
  It is important to distinguish between ***by*** and ***until***. This is sometimes a problem for German speakers, as German *bis* is used for both. ***By*** and ***until*** not only have different foreground meanings, but also relate the action (or state) quite differently to a time-span. Compare: ⚠

(10) a. Sharon was in the office until lunchtime.
b. Sharon was in the office by lunchtime.

(10)a. says that Sharon spent a period of time in the office. That period ended at lunchtime. After this, she was no longer in the office. German: *Bis zum Mittagessen war Sharon die ganze Zeit im Büro*. ***Until*** means 'all the time up to', and therefore goes only with verbs expressing events or states that fill a time-span: *was* in (10)a. can be replaced, for instance, by a verb like *stayed*, but not by one like *arrived.*
(10)b., on the other hand, says that Sharon spent a period of time out of the office. That period ended at some point before lunchtime. After that, she was in the office. German: *Bis zum Mittagessen war Sharon im Büro angekommen*.
By relates to a point of time, and therefore goes only with verbs expressing events or states that can happen ***at*** a particular point. In (10)b. *was* can be replaced, for instance, by a verb like *arrived*, but not by one like *stayed.*

- ***since:*** Like ***from***, ***since*** (dt. *seit*) refers to the beginning of a period. With ***since***, however, it is always a past period. Moreover, ***since*** also implies the end, as it actually regards the time-span from the end point back to the beginning. This is why verbs referring to ***since***-time-spans have to be in the ***perfect***: *Since her arrival in Kuala Lumpur, Hermione had been unhappy; We have lived in California since 1980*. The past perfect here means 'up to ***then***' (*then* = a time implied in the context); the present perfect means 'up to ***now***' (see chapter 10). Note, however, that like ***from***, ***since*** refers to a ***point of time*** and not to a quantity of time. This point of time is the ***start*** of the time-span. For reference to an actual length or quantity of time, we need ***for***, e.g. *for three weeks, for two years*, etc. (see next section). ***Since*** is also used as a ***conjunction*** (see chapter 7).
- ***for:*** As we have just seen, ***for*** is used with an ***amount of time***. Unlike ***since***, it is not associated with any particular tense, and can be used for any time level: *We are staying in Edinburgh for four days; Why don't you just sit down for a few minutes and have a rest?; Last year Mike and Warren went to Kenya for a month*.
The German equivalent, in most cases, is 'zero', i.e. no preposition at all. In informal and regional English the 'zero solution' is also possible, though limited mainly to certain verbs with a durative element in their meanings (like *stay, wait, stand, lie*, etc.): *We waited two hours for the train; I stayed two nights in Blackpool*. Standard English prefers the ***for***-phrase (*I stayed in Blackpool for two nights*).
With the present perfect, ***for***-phrases become *up-to-now*-time-spans: *I've been doing this job for twenty years* (usually implying *I'm still doing it*; see chapter 10).
The equivalent meaning with the past perfect is *up-to-then*: *I had been staying at the Cranfield Hotel for a week*.
⚠ In cases like these, German uses *seit* (*seit 20 Jahren/seit einer Woche*). As a result, German speakers often wrongly transfer this into English as **since 20 years, *since three weeks*, etc. Note that ***since*** is used only with ***points of time***, and ***for*** with ***amounts of time***.
To make this finally clear, let us take an example of each with the same contextual meaning. Supposing I moved to Wales on July 1st. Then I can say on July 28th:

(11) a. I have been in Wales ***for four weeks***. (= an ***amount*** of time)
Ich bin seit 4 Wochen in Wales.
b. I have been in Wales ***since July 1st***. (= a ***point*** of time)
Ich bin seit dem 1. Juli in Wales.

- ***in, during, throughout:*** As we have already seen, ***in*** is the standard preposition for periods of time, and means 'at one or more points between the beginning and end of the time-span'. That is, it is used for general location inside a given ***period***, just as it is used, as a place preposition, for general location inside a given ***space***. A more specific preposition with the same sense is ***during*** (dt. *während*). More exactly, this means 'in the course of' (dt. *im Verlauf von*), and tends to stress the length of the period slightly more: *During our school holidays we were often taken to the seaside.* Or its progression through certain phases: *The mood of the senior staff began to change during the meeting.*
During is typical with events and processes viewed as 'in progress': *During our trip we saw many famous historical buildings; The glass was obviously broken during delivery.*
A second meaning of ***during*** is 'for the whole duration/length of', i.e. 'from beginning to end': *Cinema doors are kept closed during the film.*
Throughout gives added emphasis to this meaning: *Passengers are kindly requested to remain seated throughout the flight.*
Note that ***during*** cannot be used as a conjunction (i.e. to introduce a clause, see chapter 7): **During the film is being shown cinema doors are kept closed.* The equivalent of German *während* in this case is ***while***: *While the film is being shown …*
- ***in/within: In*** is also used to stress the idea of a ***time limit*** ('not later than the end of'): *My workmen have to complete this job in three days.*
Within (dt. *innerhalb*) means the same, but is more emphatic or formal: *We have to pay the bill within a month.*
- ***in = at the end of:*** Finally, ***in*** can also mean ***at the end of*** a particular (quantified) time-span: *We are leaving for America in two weeks.*
In this sense (and ***only*** in this sense!) the word *time* can be added. The time expression itself is then placed in the genitive plural: *We are leaving for America in two weeks' time.*
In some contexts, there may be ambiguity between this meaning and the one discussed just previously, e.g. *They'll get here in 20 minutes* could mean either (12)a. or (12)b.:

(12) a. It won't take them longer than that, and maybe less. (= ***within***)
b. They will appear 20 minutes from now. (= ***at the end of*** that time-span)

If we change the original to *They'll get here in 20 minutes' time*, then the only possible meaning is (12)b.
Note in this connection also the phrases ***in time*** (dt. *rechtzeitig*), and ***on time*** (dt. *pünktlich*).
- ***after, before: After*** (= 'later than'), and ***before*** (= 'earlier than') are straightforward in meaning. Essentially they relate to time points, but may imply periods, e.g. *after mid-*

night may mean 'at any time in the period following midnight', and *before midnight*, similarly, 'at any time in the period preceding it'.

They are used not only as prepositions but also as conjunctions (see chapter 7). Informally, ***before*** is used as an adverb meaning 'in the past up to then/now', e.g. *Had you/ Have you ever seen the man before?*

A further adverb use (applying also to ***after***) is in the contextual meaning 'before this/ that', postmodifying nouns: *Last year we were in Cornwall and the year before in Scotland.* Similarly with *next year* and *the year after*.

- ***over:*** This is used in two time senses: firstly, 'in the course of/during': *Over the last few weeks I've grown very fond of this area; Let's talk about this over lunch in the pub.*

  And secondly, 'throughout': *I'll be away over the coming weekend; Chris and Sid were at Rita's over Christmas.*

  Over is also used as an adverb particle in the sense of 'finished': *Problems with fans got worse when the match was over* (= dt. *vorbei*).

036/2.8 Summary of main time prepositions and their problems

- ***on:*** days and parts of particular days: *on our wedding anniversary, on Friday afternoon, on December 24th.*
- ***in:*** means 'during time periods', and is used
  - with parts of the day (*in the afternoon, in the evening*)
  - with longer time-spans, including weeks, months, years, seasons, etc. (*in the coming week, in March, in 1984, in the winter*)
  - to emphasize time limitation, i.e. 'not later than the end of' (*Don't worry! We'll get there easily in 2 hours*).

  With quantified time-spans it can also mean 'at the end of' (*I am retiring in 6 months*). In this case (and only here) we can add the word *time*, after placing the preceding time expression in the genitive (*I am retiring in 6 months' time*).
- ***at:*** used for general time location. The time reference is regarded as expressing a point or place in time:
  - clock times and points of the day (*at 10 am, at noon*)
  - other kinds of point or stage in time (*at the age of ten, at that time of my life*). Note also *at the weekend.*
  - with festive and religious periods (*at Christmas/Easter/Whitsun*)
  - with events and happenings, including mealtimes (*at the party/meeting/concert, at breakfast/dinner*).
- ***since/for: Since*** refers to a ***point of time*** in the past: *since the beginning of this year.* The point of time is implied as being the start of a time-span. As this is an *up-to-now* or *up-to-then* time-span, the perfect tense is required: *We have not seen him since the beginning of this year.*

  For refers to a length or ***quantity of time***: *Joan is taking a temporary job for two months.* It is compatible with any tense or time level. With the perfect tenses ***for***-phrases become *up-to-now* or *up-to-then* time-spans: *I have lived here/I had lived there for ten years.* ***Since*** is used also as a conjunction (though not ***for*** in the time sense).

- ***by/until:*** Both translate German *bis*, but have very different senses. ***By*** means 'then at the latest' (dt. *bis/vor/spätestens dann*): *Applications must be received by March 31st.*
  As it refers to a point of time, ***by*** goes only with expressions saying that events or states start, happen or finish ***at*** a particular point (e.g. with *arrive* or *finish*, but not with *stay*).
  Until means 'ending then (at the stated time)': *We lived in France until last year.* As the sense of ***until*** is 'all the time up to', it goes only with verbs expressing events or states that fill a time-span (e.g. with *stay, live*, etc., but not with *arrive* or *finish*).
  Many verbal expressions can refer to either time-spans or time points. These can go with both ***by*** and ***until***, but note the contrast in meaning: *By 1990 the company was very successful* (= dt. *spätestens ab diesem Zeitpunkt*); *Until 1990 the company was very successful* (= dt. *bis dahin*).
  Until is used also as a conjunction (though not ***by***).
  during: During means either 'in the course of an event/within a time-span' (*United went into the lead twice during the first half of the game*); or 'for the whole length of a time-span': *Car decks are closed to passengers during the crossing.*
  During cannot be used as a conjunction.

036/3 Prepositions of mixed reference

Usage here is not primarily connected with place or time, although place-related meanings occur.

036/3.1 for

For names the ***intended receiver*** of something (dt. *für*): *This parcel here is for you; Sharon bought a present for Selina; There are two big bones for the dog in the kitchen.*

It is also common with the idea of giving and receiving help: *He held the door open for the lady with the shopping; Could you quickly send this fax for me please?*

A closely related meaning is 'in favour of/supporting/representing': *Is Friedman for or against the company's new sales strategy?; Dolethorpe is the area manager for South Lincolnshire; I'm sure I speak for everybody here when I say how happy we are to see Broadbent retire.*

A third major field of meaning, also related, is ***intention*** in a wider sense, i.e.
purpose: *This machine is for peeling potatoes* (dt. *zu*). Gerunds are common here for describing function, but ordinary nouns also: *We use peat here for fuel* (dt. ... *Torf hier als Brennstoff*); *These root crops are for animal fodder* (dt. ... *als Tierfutter* ...); *This jacket is for work, that one for social occasions* (dt. *für*). Note in this connection the question *What's this for?* (dt. *Wozu ist/dient das?*)

In addition, there are certain idiomatic collocations with specific nouns: *for sale, for rent, for hire* (dt. *zu*).

reason: *She got a fine for dangerous driving/a medal for bravery/awards for her films* (dt. *wegen*). Here too we have idiomatic collocations with specific nouns: *for pleasure, for fun, for love* (dt. *aus*).

Questions with *What for?* are common, especially in informal language in the sense of *Why?*: *What was she fined for?; What did they do that for?*

aim: This is a variant of ***purpose***, but is more specific and worth dealing with separately, as a whole series of specific expressions are involved, particularly with prepositional verbs: *to ask for, to apply for* (dt. *um*); *to pray for* (dt. *für*); *to aim for* (dt. *nach/auf*), *to reach for, to head for, to hunt for* (dt. *nach*), *to hope for* (dt. *auf*), etc. Note also variations with *to go*: *to go for a swim/a walk/a run; to go (somewhere) for water/a paper* (= *to fetch*), etc.

A different, though possibly related, use is with certain expressions of ***quantity***. We have already discussed the common use of ***for*** with quantities of ***time*** (*for three days, for five years*, etc., see also under 036/2.7). But ***for*** appears also with other types of quantity, such as ***price*** (*I bought a watch for ten pounds*), ***distance*** (*We used to walk for miles with our parents*), and amounts of ***event*** (chiefly in sport) that are measured in 'sections': *Willis boxed confidently for five rounds; Agassi was completely dominant for the first two sets.*

Verbs related to price (apart from *buy*) are *to swap sth. for sth, to exchange sth. for sth., to offer s.o. sth. for sth.* (i.e. for a particular price).

036/3.2 with

The basic meaning of ***with*** (dt. *mit*) is 'accompanied by/in the presence of', i.e. it expresses a state of being ***together***: *Bill is with Linda and Jane in the living-room; Bert has gone shopping with Dad.*

And also ***occurring*** together: *The ladder fell over with a loud crash; She said goodbye with a sad smile.*

Other, more specific senses of ***connection*** are derived from this:

- actions or states linked to: *to quarrel/fight/compete/do business with; a relationship/friendship/association/connection/problem with; Be careful with my car!; I was pleased with the results of the test; This book is popular with teenagers; With me it's different* (dt. *Bei mir ist es anders*).
- 'using/by means of': *He cut the rope with a knife; They ate the fish and chips with their fingers.*
- 'having/possessing': *the girl with the green eyes; He stood there with his hands in his pockets; a man with a scar over one eye; a tray with a teapot and cups on it; a cup of coffee with sugar in it; Mary is in bed with a heavy cold.*

  In a slight variation of this, ***with*** commonly follows expressions of 'containing': *Fill the saucepan with water; Stuff the chicken with rice and currants; The stadium was packed with fans of both teams; They loaded the trailer with small furniture; His fingers were stained with nicotine.*

  A further variant is 'including': *With a starter and dessert the meal will cost about £40 per guest; The bag comes with a shoulder strap.*
- 'because of/due to': *to shiver with cold/tremble with fear*, etc.; *red with anger, overcome with emotion, puffed up with pride*, etc. This use occurs with adjectives and verbs. The German equivalent is usually *vor.*

  A meaning variant here is 'due to' in the sense of 'considering': *With Barry in hospital, we have decided not to go on holiday this year; Sarah had a lot to do on Friday, with guests coming for the weekend; With so many members of staff sick, the school had to close for the week.* The construction here is quite distinct from those just discussed: ***with*** + noun +

prepositional phrase/adjective/gerund clause. The gerund is particularly common. A German rendering would be *in Anbetracht der Tatsache, dass …*

And a further variation is 'in the same measure as/in proportion to': *With the approach of noon, the heat grew unbearable; Language skills improve with practice; With increasing material insecurity, people change their consumer habits; Good eyesight declines with age.*

036/3.3 without

This is the opposite of ***with*** (dt. *ohne*), meaning 'unaccompanied by/in the absence of': *Bill came to the party without Linda and Jane; She entered the room without a sound; I started an acting career, but without much success; Eating peas without a fork or spoon is difficult.*

It is followed classically by verbs in the gerund: *She left without saying goodbye.*

Chapter 7 Conjunctions

037 Basic features

Conjunctions are grammatical joining words like *and, or, because, although, when, if,* etc. Their chief function is to join two ***clauses*** together: *Oliver married Sharon* ***because*** *he loved her*. A small number (mainly *and* and *or*) are also used to join ***phrases***: *Scott* ***and*** *Winnie are going to Canada for their holidays*.

Although different in function, ***conjunctions*** are often related in meaning to ***prepositions***, e.g. *although* (conjunction) → *despite* (preposition), *while* (conjunction) → *during* (preposition), *as* (conjunction) → *like* (preposition), etc. Several prepositions, in fact, are themselves used as conjunctions, e.g. *after, before, since, until*. The same applies to *as* and *than* in comparative constructions. Reasons for this close relationship between conjunctions and prepositions will become clear later.

We said above that ***conjunctions*** join clauses. But from the point of view of sentence building they actually join ***sentences***. If we take our example *Oliver married Sharon because he loved her*, and remove the conjunction, we are left with two separate sentences: *Oliver married Sharon. He loved her*. When we join them, they become two clauses of the ***same sentence***. This is the ***grammatical*** effect of the conjunction. It also has a ***semantic*** effect: it relates the two clauses in meaning, or, more specifically, it shows how the second clause (the ***conjunction clause***) is related in meaning to the first (the ***free clause***). Here, the relation is one of ***cause***. In the following there are various possibilities, depending on the conjunction chosen:

(1) a. Sarah went into the bedroom. She had turned on the t.v.
b. ***After/When*** she had turned on the t.v., Sarah went into the bedroom.
c. ***Although*** she had turned on the t.v., Sarah went into the bedroom.

The two separate sentences in (1)a. are converted into two clauses of the same sentence in b. and c. The meaning relation to the free clause varies according to the conjunction used. ***After*** and ***when*** in (1)b. introduce a ***time*** relation, ***although*** in (1)c. a relation of ***concession***, i.e. a certain contradiction. The sentences in (2) also show quite different meaning relations between the two clauses, which are again the result of different conjunctions:

(2) a. Sarah turned on the t.v. ***and*** went into the bedroom.
b. Sarah turned on the t.v. ***but*** went into the bedroom.

In (2)a. the relation is a little like that in (1)b., i.e. a time sequence is suggested: the action in the conjunction clause follows the action in the free clause. This is also the case in (2)b., but there is an additional meaning rather like the one in (1)c. The conjunction, that is, introduces a relation of contradiction.

Conjunctions affect the syntax of the sentence in several ways. The most basic point is that they integrate separate sentences into one sentence. But in addition, they give a certain ***syntactic status*** to the conjunction clause that can determine other aspects of its syntactic behaviour and meaning. Some conjunctions make the conjunction clause 'equal' to the free clause, while others make it 'inferior'. For instance, ***and*** and ***but*** introduce an equal relationship. In this case the conjunction clause is said to be ***co-ordinate*** with the free clause. These conjunctions are therefore called ***co-ordinating*** conjunctions. Sentences with only ***co-ordinate clauses***, as in (2), are traditionally called ***compound sentences***.

The conjunctions in (1), by contrast, make the conjunction clause inferior, or ***subordinate***, to the free clause, and are consequently called ***subordinating*** conjunctions. Sentences with ***subordinate clauses***, as in (1)b. and c., are called ***complex sentences***. In a complex sentence, the free clause is traditionally known as the ***main clause*** (though this is a term which is a little problematic, and should be regarded critically, as we will see later).

We return to clause syntax later in the chapter. The next section deals with individual conjunctions and their meanings.

Individual conjunctions and their meanings 038

038/1 Conjunctions expressing cause (reason)

038/1.1 because

This is the most common and most direct way of expressing cause: *Bella wasn't at work today because she has a heavy cold.*

Questions with *why?* are usually answered by a ***because***-clause, rather than one with any other cause conjunction: *'Why wasn't Bella at work today?' 'Because she has a heavy cold'*. In speech the ***free clause*** (main clause) is usually omitted, as it is here (***free clause ellipsis***). If it is included, it must be the first clause, as in the original example (*Bella wasn't at work today because she has a heavy cold*). This is because known information is given first, a common principle in English and many other languages, and one which generally affects the ***sequence*** of clauses. Beginning with the ***conjunction clause*** is possible if no *why?*-question precedes it. However, this then assumes that the information in the conjunction clause is already known: *Because Bella has a heavy cold (as you know), she wasn't at work today.*

038/1.2 as/since

These translate the German *da* in its causal sense. They are much less forceful than ***because***, and are usually used for things which the listener is already aware of. That is, they assume that the conjunction clause information is already known. This is the case even in second position: *Bella wasn't at work today since/as she has a heavy cold.*

038/1.3 for

For (dt. *denn*) is the weakest of the causal conjunctions. It does not give a direct reason for something, but rather an accompanying circumstance which helps to explain it: *She was disappointed not to find her relatives at home, for she had come a long way to see them* (dt., ... *denn sie war weit gereist/zumal sie weit gereist war, um sie zu sehen*).

For is slightly elevated or literary in style, and is hardly heard in speech. ***For***-clauses ***never*** precede the free clause. They always ***follow*** it (**For she had come a long way to see her relatives, she was disappointed ...*). For this reason, ***for*** is regarded traditionally as a ***co-ordinating*** conjunction (see **038/4**).

038/2 Conjunctions expressing time relations

A point of importance with all time conjunctions is a special rule applying to contexts where they have ***future reference***. According to this ***future time clause rule***, a *will*-form ***cannot*** appear in the conjunction clause. The conjunction clause takes the ***present tense*** (usually the simple form), or ***the present perfect***, depending on meaning. *Will*-forms occur only in the free clause, along with other modal auxiliaries, or the imperative: *When Frank **comes** back next Friday he **will/could/might arrive** on the 10.30 train; When Frank comes back next Friday, please **give** him my regards.*

038/2.1 when/whenever

When expresses German *als* (and *wenn* in its time sense). As a general 'time locator' it is equivalent to the preposition *at*: *When I was young there was far less traffic on the roads (= at that time in my life ...)*. Because of this more general time location, ***when*** can also take on the meaning (in context) of 'slightly after': *When we got to the beach, we had our picnic immediately.* This is particularly the case with future reference: *When we get to the beach we'll have our picnic immediately.* (Note that the German equivalent here is *wenn*, but in its ***time*** sense as the 'future form' of *als*).

Other more specified contextual interpretations of ***when*** are:

- during an action: *When I was lying on the bed, I noticed a movement behind one of the curtains.* More specific conjunctions for this meaning are ***while*** and ***as*** (see below).
- for habits: *When Fred goes to the hairdressers he always has his hair highlighted.* The specific and more emphatic equivalent here is ***whenever*** (dt. *immer, wenn*).

Note: ***When*** is not always used as a conjunction. It is sometimes an ***adverb***: *When does the film start?* (dt. *wann?*); *August is the month when most people are on holiday* (= *during which,* dt. *in dem*). In the first example, ***when*** is an ***interrogative adverb***, and in the second a ***relative adverb*** (rather like a relative pronoun). (see also chapter 14, and under **038/6.5**).

038/2.2 as/while

In its time sense ***as*** links two simultaneous actions, i.e. it expresses one action as happening during or parallel to another: *As I took the glass from my hostess, it slipped out of my hand* (dt. *in dem Augenblick, als ...*); *As Joe was climbing over the fence his trousers were torn by the wire* (dt. *Als Joe gerade dabei war, ...*). Actions expressed in ***as***-clauses tend to be short and localized, in the sense of 'just at that moment/precisely at that stage of the action'.

While, on the other hand, refers to more lengthy processes; *I met Sue while I was shopping* (dt. ... *beim Einkaufen/während ich einkaufte*). Note that *during* is the preposition partner of the conjunction ***while.*** The German equivalent of both ***during*** and ***while*** is *während*, but English *during* can only be used as a preposition (i.e. not *... *during I was shopping*).

Here also a reminder of the ***future time clause rule*** (present tense in the conjunction clause!): *Could you get a large loaf while you're shopping tomorrow, please?* (not: *... *while you will be shopping*).

038/2.3 until/not until, as soon as

We have already encountered ***until*** (***till***) as a preposition. As a conjunction it has the same meaning: *I will wait here until (till) you are ready* (dt. ..., *bis du fertig bist*). Note that here too the ***future time clause rule*** applies when the sentence refers to the future.

Not until is the general English rendering of German *erst als/erst dann, wenn*. The negation is usually attached to the free clause; the ***until***-clause stays positive: *Do not open the door until the train stops* (*Öffnen Sie die Tür erst dann, wenn der Zug anhält*); *She did not return to the house until day broke* (*Sie kehrte erst ins Haus zurück, als der Tag anbrach*). The ***until***-clause usually comes second. In more formal style it can be placed first, but ***until*** must then be preceded by ***not***. In this case, the verb in the free clause requires ***inversion*** (see chapter 5): *Not until day broke did she return to the house.*

As soon as is a ***complex conjunction*** (i.e. consisting of more than one word), corresponding to German *sobald*: *As soon as Barbara arrived in America she began to feel homesick* (dt. *Sobald Barbara/Schon als Barbara in Amerika ankam, ...*). And 2 examples showing the ***future time clause rule***: *As soon as you are ready we will have lunch* (dt. *Sobald du fertig bist ...*); *We can leave as soon as I have finished this little job* (not *... *as soon as I will have finished ...*).

038/2.4 after, before

These are also prepositions. Note that German distinguishes here between the preposition and the conjunction: ***after*** = *nach* (preposition), but *nachdem* (conjunction); ***before*** = *vor* (preposition), but *bevor/ehe* (conjunction).

Again, future reference requires application of the ***future time clause rule:*** *After I get my next wages, I'll pay back what I owe you.* As ***after***-clauses tend to involve the meaning of 'completion', use of the present perfect in the conjunction clause is found here more often than with other time conjunctions: *I would like you to go to the chemist's after you have been to the butcher's* (not **... after you will have been ...*). And also, though less frequently, with ***before***: *You may not go out before you have done your homework.*

⚠ Note that in cases like this, German favours a negative after *bevor/ehe*: *... bevor du deine Hausaufgaben nicht gemacht hast.* However, this is ***not*** possible in English (i.e. ***never*** **... before you have not done your homework*).

The conjunction ***before*** is often used in the 'deadline' sense of the preposition *before*, or, more particularly, *by*: *You must finish the work before dinner is ready* (preposition: *before dinner/by dinnertime*). Informally the expression ***by the time*** (***that***) is often used here as a kind of 'complex conjunction' (with ***that*** normally omitted): *You must finish the work by the time dinner is ready.*

038/2.5 since

This is another case where preposition and conjunction are identical. ***Since*** signals the beginning of a past-present (or past-past) time-span. We will consider the past-present time-span first. As ***since*** refers to the point when the time-span began, it refers to a ***time in the past***, e.g. *since 2005*. In the conjunction use, this ***time in the past*** is represented by an action. The verb expressing it must therefore be in the ***past tense***, e.g. *Since Mrs. Jarvis joined the firm ...* To make the point clearer, we can also add the time reference as an adverbial: *Since Mrs. Jarvis joined the firm in 2005 ...* After this, the time-span follows in the sense of 'up-to-now'. For actions in the time-span we therefore need the ***present perfect***: *Since Mrs. Jarvis joined the firm in 2005, it has been making more profit.* It is ***not*** possible here, however, to use the present perfect in the conjunction clause, i.e. not **Since Mrs. Jarvis has joined ...*

With conjunction ***since*** and an 'up-to-now' time-span, the sequence of tense is therefore ***since*** + ***past tense*** + ***present perfect***.

Note that the German tense equivalent in the conjunction clause is either the perfect or the preterite (i.e. *seit + Perfekt oder Präteritum*): *Seit Mrs. Jarvis zur Firma gekommen ist*, bzw. *kam*.

What has just been discussed is the normal case, i.e. the one where ***since*** refers to the ***beginning*** of the time-span. Sometimes, however, ***since*** may relate to the time-span ***as a whole***. Here the present perfect is required in the conjunction clause as well. The verb must express an action that fills the whole time-span, i.e. the action must have an 'up-to-now' sense: *Since Mrs. Jarvis has been with the firm, it has been making more profit.*

Here, then, the sequence of tense is ***since*** + ***present perfect*** + ***present perfect***.

Note that here the German tense equivalent in the conjunction clause is the present tense (i.e. *seit + Präsens*): *Seit Mrs. Jarvis bei der Firma ist, ...*

Since-time-spans do not always extend to the moment of speaking. Their end-point can also be a point in the past, in the sense of 'up-to-then'. Assume, for instance, that we are discussing events in the past, e.g. what was happening to 'the firm' at some point in

2007, e.g. *In March 2007, profits reached a record level.* For reference to events before and leading up to March 2007, we need the ***past perfect***: *Up to then the export business had been improving steadily since Mrs. Jarvis had joined the firm in 2005.* The sequence of tense here, that is, is ***past perfect*** in both clauses. The German pattern for the conjunction clause would be the same (i.e. *seit + Plusquamperfekt*): *Seit Mrs. Jarvis 2005 zur Firma gekommen war, …*

For further discussion of English perfect tenses and their German equivalents, see chapter 10.

038/3 Conjunctions expressing conditions

These introduce a type of clause generally known as a ***conditional clause***. The major representative is ***if***, and the explanations under **038/3.1** in the following also illustrate general features of conditional clauses and conditional meaning.

038/3.1 if

This translates German *wenn* in the sense of *falls*, and means two things together: firstly, that something is being ***imagined*** as a ***possibility*** ('supposing/assuming that'); and secondly, that it is ***causally linked*** to another action or state that is either also ***imagined***, or ***intended*** ('in the case that'): *If you see Hermione tomorrow, please tell her to get in touch with me; If we don't pay the bill immediately, we won't get a discount; If it rains, the game will probably be cancelled.*

The action in the free clause is expressed: a) as a consequence of the ***if***-clause action; and b) as dependent on it.

Like the time conjunctions, conditional conjunctions make certain verb-form patterns compulsory. Similar to the ***future time clause rule***, the ***conditional clause rule*** rules out *will* in the conjunction clause, but requires *will*, other modal auxiliaries, or the imperative in the free clause (see above examples). However, this is just the ***open condition***, one of three basic conditional clause types. The other two, the ***unreal*** and the ***hypothetical conditions***, have their own distinct meanings and basic tense sequences. Here are all three together:

(3) a. If it rains, the game will probably be cancelled.
(***open condition***, future-referring, neutral to high likelihood: conjunction clause present tense, free clause *will*-form, other modal auxiliaries, or the imperative)
b. If it rained, the game would probably be cancelled.
(***unreal condition***, future- or present-referring, 'theoretical', unlikely or impossible: conjunction clause past tense, free clause *would*-form or other modal-conditional form, e.g. *could, might, should,* etc.)
c. If it had rained, the game would probably have been cancelled.
(***hypothetical condition***, past-referring, impossible: conjunction clause past perfect, *would have*-form, or other modal-conditional perfect form, e.g. *could have, might have, should have,* etc.).

See also chapter 11 for more information on conditional clauses and conditional meaning. ***If*** has other meanings that are non-conditional. These are dealt with further below.

038/3.2 supposing (that)

This 'asks' the listener to imagine a particular situation and its consequences (dt. *angenommen*). Although syntactically a verb form followed by a ***that***-clause, it has become a set expression, especially as ***that*** is normally omitted. A common alternative is the form ***suppose***: *Supposing/suppose your firm goes/went bankrupt. What then?* (dt. *Angenommen, deine Firma macht Pleite. Was dann?*). It is most common in the 'theoretical mode' of the ***unreal*** condition: *Suppose he asked you to come back to him. What would you say?* This can also be expressed as an ***if***-clause (*What would you say if he asked you to come back to him?*), but then the imagined condition is not profiled to quite the same extent.

Supposing/suppose-constructions are informal and often heard in speech. Syntactically, they are not subordinate clauses alone, but actually complete sentences with two clauses: the free clause consisting just of the verb, and the conjunction clause with the (usually omitted) ***that***. The meaning of the whole construction is conditional, however, and tense requirements in the conjunction clause follow the ***conditional clause rule***. The whole construction is usually spoken with the intonation of a question, and generally appears in writing with a question mark (*?*).

038/3.3 unless

Unless translates German *es sei denn/wenn nicht*, and is a way of saying 'except if'. This emphasizes the meaning of the free clause: *We are definitely going to the beach tomorrow, unless the weather is bad* (dt. *..., es sei denn/außer wenn ...*); *Unless his driving improves drastically over the next two weeks, Tim is going to fail the driving test.*

That is, the free clause message is regarded as generally valid, or as most likely. The ***unless***-clause simply weakens or restricts this a little by naming 'opposing' circumstances understood as exceptional. As the two clauses have opposing meanings, there is commonly a negative in one of them, especially in the free clause: *Don't disturb me unless there is an emergency* (dt. *...außer im Notfall*); *Henry doesn't let anyone else drive his car unless he trusts them.*

Unless often has a meaning similar to ***if ... not***, and the two are sometimes interchangeable, e.g. *Don't go to Blackpool unless you like crowds/Don't go to Blackpool if you don't like crowds.* Nevertheless, even with the same meaning, ***unless*** usually makes the condition sound stronger, more restrictive and less probable:

(4) a. Dennis will keep the job if his sales record doesn't fall.
b. Dennis will keep the job unless his sales record falls.

(4)b. makes it sound more likely that the sales record will remain intact and therefore that Dennis will keep the job.

Apart from this, there are several cases where ***unless*** and ***if ... not*** do not correspond at all:

(5) a. I'll be happier if she doesn't stay too long.
(*not* *... unless she stays ...)
b. We would have got to the station in time if we hadn't waited ten minutes for John.
(not *... unless we had waited ...)
c. We wouldn't have got to the station in time if we hadn't taken a taxi.
(not *... unless we had taken ...)
d. We wouldn't have got to the station in time, unless we had taken a taxi.
(not *... if we hadn't taken ...)
e. Let's go into the living-room – unless you'd like to have tea in the garden.
(not *... if you wouldn't like ...)

(5)a. has the same pattern of positive and negative as (4)a., and yet, does ***not*** allow replacement by ***unless***. This is because in (5)a. the free clause action (or state) is a consequence ***only*** of something ***not*** happening, i.e. the condition in the conjunction clause ***must*** be expressed as ***negative***. A 'positive version' with ***unless*** would not make any sense here. For a similar reason, ***unless*** cannot be used in ***hypothetical conditions*** like those in (5)b. and c.; With (5)c. replacement by ***unless*** produces a meaningful sentence, as in (5)d., but then the meaning changes. In contrast to (5)c., (5)d. means *We didn't get to the station in time,* and ***unless*** here means only *except if* and ***not*** *if ... not.*

Finally, (5)e. shows ***unless*** in the function of an ***afterthought condition***, i.e. it introduces an alternative in the sense of 'or maybe (instead)'. This would also be a case for the German *es sei denn*. Here, too, there is no equivalence to ***if ... not***.

038/3.4 in case

This means 'as preparation for a future possibility' (dt. *für den Fall, dass ...*): *Put an apple in your bag in case you feel hungry on the train* (*... für den Fall, dass du im Zug hungrig wirst*); *We decided to head for Dover on the M20, in case there were still queues on the M2* (*... denn es war möglich, dass es sich auf der Autobahn 2 noch staute*). Note, as always, the demands of the ***conditional clause rule***: no *will* or *would* in the conjunction clause!

Note also that ***in case*** does ***not*** mean the same as ***if***. Compare:

(6) a. I'll bake a cake in case Ricardo comes home tomorrow.
b. I'll bake a cake if Ricardo comes home tomorrow.

(6)a. means *I'll bake the cake now (today) because Ricardo might come home tomorrow*. With ***in case***, that is, the free clause action ***precedes*** the conjunction clause action.

(6)b. means *I'll wait for Ricardo to come tomorrow, and if he does, then I'll bake the cake.* With ***if***, the free clause action ***follows*** the conjunction clause action.

038/3.5 providing/provided (that)

In terms of form, this is a similar case to that of ***supposing/suppose (that)*** in **038/3.2** above. Syntactically, however, ***providing/provided (that)*** (dt. *vorausgesetzt, dass ...*) behaves like any regular conjunction, introducing an ordinary conjunction clause attached to an ordinary free clause: *You may use my car, providing/provided (that) you are back here in three hours.*

038/4 Conjunctions expressing addition

These are ***and, but, or,*** and traditionally also ***for***. As explained in the introduction above, they count grammatically as ***co-ordinating conjunctions***: they give both clauses an equal syntactic status.

With ***co-ordinating conjunctions*** the conjunction clause cannot be placed first. The free clause must always precede it, i.e. always *Sarah collects stamps and Bobby plays the piano*, and never **And Bobby plays the piano Sarah collects stamps*. In speech and less formal language, it is true, ***co-ordinating conjunctions*** can begin sentences. Then, however, the corresponding free clause(s) must precede in the sentence(s) before: *She has worked in holiday hotels and variety theatres. And she has also been on television. But she has never appeared in feature films.* Sentences beginning with co-ordinating conjunctions like this have an 'afterthought' character, with an imagined pause or break before them.

Co-ordinating conjunctions also join ***phrases***: *I'll make the sandwiches or the coffee; Mark and Sharon got married at the weekend; After the trip we were tired but happy; Bob drives fast but safely.*

Even ***subordinate clauses*** can be joined by a ***co-ordinating conjunction***: *I didn't answer the door because I was tired and (because) (I) didn't want to get up.* Identical parts of both clauses (e.g. other conjunctions, the same subject, etc.) are usually omitted in the second clause: see also below.

It should be noted that ***for*** is an exception regarding these last two points, i.e. it cannot combine phrases or subordinate clauses. In fact, ***for***-clauses themselves can be co-ordinated: *I didn't answer the door for I was tired and didn't want to get up.* This makes them more like subordinate clauses (see, e.g. *because* in the last example). The use of ***for*** is dealt with above in **038/1.3**.

038/4.1 and

In its basic meaning ***and*** (like dt. *und*) simply adds clauses together: *I've watered the plants and John has fed the cat.* If the subject is the same in each, it is generally omitted in the ***and***-clause: *I've watered the plants and fed the cat.* This means that the subject (*I*) performed both actions.

When more than two clauses are added together in this way, the conjunction itself is used only for the last two. Any preceding clauses are joined by commas: *I've watered the plants, fed the cat, wiped the table and swept the floor.*

As just seen above, ***and*** can join phrases as well as clauses: *We met Derek and Clive in the town; Their faces looked pale and thin.*

Apart from just 'simple addition', ***and*** often stands for further meanings in certain contexts. One of these is ***sequence***: *Chop the onions and fry them in a little butter; We collected our luggage and left the airport; They ran to the water and dived in.* That is, we cannot reverse the order of the clauses here without creating nonsense: **He dived in and ran to the water.* In such cases ***and*** basically means ***and then***.

Other contextual meanings are:

- ***consequence***: *Rodney drove into the garage door and damaged it; The roof's leaking and there's water all over the floor.*
- ***contrast***: *I have lived here for five years and still don't know the town well.* Here, ***and*** has the sense of ***but*** (see below).
- ***purpose***: *Could you run and fetch me the scissors from the bathroom, dear?; Let's go and sit over there by the window.*
  The first verb here is usually one of motion or posture. An exception is *try*: *I must try and improve my English.* These are colloquial (particularly British colloquial) uses. ***And*** tends to replace the *to* of the infinitive, especially after *try*, where the standard form would be *try to* (*improve, …* etc.). Here the ***and***-form is only possible when *try* is in the imperative, or combines with a modal verb. Constructions of the *go and sit* type are rendered in colloquial American English (especially with *go* and *come*) by the infinitive without *to: Let's go sit over there.* The preceding verb of motion (*go, sit,* etc.) must itself be in the infinitive or the imperative form.

There are also set uses of ***and*** with certain phrase-types:

- ***pair intensification (adjectives)***: *old and grey; big and strong; hot and sweaty; dull and boring.* The second intensifies the first by giving a slightly different aspect of the same feature. Note also colloquial combinations with *nice*: *nice and fresh* (dt. *schön frisch*); *nice and hot* (dt. *schön heiß*), etc. Here *nice* has the semantic character of an adverb, but actually cannot be used as one (at least with most ordinary adjectives): **nicely hot, *nicely fresh.* Hence the adjective pair solution.
- ***mixtures of colour or substance (adjectives, nouns)***: *a black-and-white cap; concrete and glass buildings.* This is common with items of food and drink, often in the sense of 'served with': *fish and chips; gin and tonic; steak and ale pie.*
- ***function pairs (nouns)***: *a knife and fork; a bat and ball; a horse and cart.* These are two partners that perform a task together. The article is always omitted before the second noun.
- ***comparative intensification (adjectives)***: *Her face was getting redder and redder* (dt. *immer röter*); *The sky was looking more and more threatening* (dt. *immer bedrohlicher*).

038/4.2 or

Or (dt. ***oder***) adds alternative possibilities: *Are you happy, or is something bothering you?*

Again, repeated elements (like subject and auxiliary verb in the following example) are usually omitted: *We could cook tonight for ourselves, or* (*we could*) *eat in the campsite restaurant.*

As we have already seen, ***or*** can join phrases: *You can have wine, beer, or fruit juice; The camp in the hills can be reached only on foot or by jeep.*

Or is often supported and emphasized by ***either*** (dt. *entweder)*, an adverb used to stress the alternatives. ***Either … or*** functions like a 'double conjunction' in a similar way to ***both … and*** (see under ***Quantifiers***, chapter 3): (*Either*) *We could* (*either*) *cook tonight for ourselves, or eat in the campsite restaurant.*

The position of ***either*** is immediately before the first alternative, which can be thought of in two possible ways: the whole first clause (***either*** in initial position); or just the main verb (***either*** immediately before the main verb).

Either can also be used for more than two alternatives: *You can have either wine, beer, or fruit juice*. However, it is preferred for just two. Here are more examples of ***either … or*** combinations:

(7) a. I'm going to buy either the red boots, or the thick-soled trainers.
Ich werde entweder die roten Stiefel oder die Turnschuhe mit den dicken Sohlen kaufen.
b. Either she lost her purse on the way to the restaurant, or somebody stole it from her coat while we were eating.
Entweder hat sie den Geldbeutel auf dem Weg zum Lokal verloren, oder jemand hat ihn aus ihrer Manteltasche gestohlen, während wir gegessen haben.
c. Either Mrs. Simms or Mr. Dafferty will teach the class while I am away.
Entweder Mrs. Simms oder Mr. Dafferty wird den Unterricht übernehmen, wenn ich nicht da bin.

Although basically optional, ***either*** is nearly always used when the alternatives are whole clauses (as in b.), or subjects of the sentence (as in c.). It is also typical to show that the choice has been narrowed down to two from a larger range of possible alternatives (as could be the case, contextually, in a.).

Like ***and***, ***or*** has further (often derived) meanings in particular contexts and constructions:

- ***part alternatives***: Sometimes the alternatives are not strictly exclusive (i.e. only one or the other). They can often be understood both as single options and as a combination: *They often went to the park or down to the river on Sundays* (= *They did both on different Sundays, i.e. sometimes one thing and sometimes the other*); *Would you like a sandwich or a cup of tea?* (*You can have both if you wish*); *For dessert we have ice-cream, fruit, or fruit juice* (i.e. *we have all three for you to select from*).
- ***inclusive meaning with negatives***: After negatives and verbs implying a negative, the meaning of ***or*** is actually ***and***; *I don't like gin or vodka* (= *I don't like gin and I don't like vodka*); *Tom refuses to wear hats or caps* (i.e. 'both not'). See **038/4.3** for a full discussion of this point.
- ***expressing approximation***: When things are not known precisely, possible examples are given and joined with ***or***: *She went to the kiosk for a newspaper or magazine* (*or something like that*). The phrase *or something* is often added in this sense: *Fraser is a banker or something* (dt. … *oder so etwas*) *in the City*. With quantities and numerals (only!) the phrase is *or so*: *Dahlia is 30 or so* (= *about 30*); *There were ten guests or so at the dinner party*. Similarly, *one or two* and *two or three* mean 'a very small number': *There were only two or three people in the queue*.
- ***re-phrasing***: ***Or*** is used for the addition of a more precise or careful formulation: *Roger is my brother, or rather, my half-brother* (dt. … *oder genauer gesagt* …); *They were so happy together, or at least it seemed like it* (dt. … *oder wenigstens schien es so*).

- ***consequence***: ***Or*** introduces threats, warnings and strong consequences: *You'd better be careful with that knife or you'll hurt someone; Get out of here at once, or I'll call the police!* We could also use *or else* here (dt. *sonst/andernfalls*). The free clause usually contains an imperative or forceful recommendation, and the ***or***-clause the consequence of not following it. The effect is like a negative conditional sentence, e.g. *If you aren't careful with that knife, you'll hurt someone.*

038/4.3 Negatives of and: or, either ... or, neither ... nor

After negated verbs, ***and*** cannot be used to join phrases. In this case, as mentioned briefly in the previous section, ***and*** is replaced by ***or***: *Steven Brewer was not handsome or rich, or even particularly educated* (not **... handsome and rich, and even particularly educated*). ***And*** is allowed to remain only if *not* is repeated before each item: *Steven Brewer was not handsome, not rich, and not even particularly educated.*

Here is an example of ***and***-replacement with nouns: *I hadn't seen Jones or his father for some time.* This treats the two people as separate individuals. However, if they are considered together as a pair, ***and*** is possible (*I hadn't seen Jones and his father* – i.e. the two as a 'duo' – *for some time*).

Or-negatives are also emphasized by the addition of ***either***, especially with nouns: *I hadn't seen either Jones or his father for some time.*

A stylistically more elevated version of this is with a positive verb + ***neither ... nor***: *I had seen neither Jones nor his father for some time* (dt. *Seit einiger Zeit hatte ich weder Jones noch seinen Vater gesehen*). When the two nouns are in subject position, ***neither ... nor*** is the only possibility: *Neither Jones nor his father had been seen for some time* (not **Either Jones or his father had not been seen ...*). Otherwise, ***and*** is possible for the 'duo' meaning (with negated verb, of course): *Jones and his father had not been seen for some time* (suggesting that they had disappeared together).

Neither ... nor can also negate different verbs. In this case ***neither*** cannot begin the sentence, but must follow the subject: *My colleagues neither liked me, nor respected my work* (not **Neither my colleagues liked me, nor ...*). A further rule here is that the two different verbs must have the same subject, i.e. we cannot say **My colleagues neither liked me, nor the boss respected/nor did the boss respect my work.* A more simple way of expressing verb-referring ***neither ... nor***-constructions of this kind is to use simple negation, plus an ***and***-clause containing ***nor/neither*** alone as ***negative adverbs***: *My colleagues didn't like me, and nor (neither) did they respect my work.* Note verb ***inversion*** after ***nor/neither*** (see chapter 5 on adverbs). In this form, the construction will also allow different subjects: *My colleagues didn't like me, and nor (neither) did the boss respect my work.* This version can be replaced by ***not ... either***: *My colleagues didn't like me and the boss didn't respect my work either.*

The various alternatives are summarized in the following examples:

(8) a. I had***n't*** seen Jones ***or*** his father for some time.
b. I had seen ***neither*** Jones ***nor*** his father for some time.
c. ***Neither*** Jones ***nor*** his father had been seen for some time.
d. My colleagues ***neither*** liked me, ***nor*** respected my work.

e. My colleagues did*n't* like me, ***and nor/neither*** did the boss respect my work.
f. My colleagues did*n't* like me and the boss did*n't* respect my work ***either***.

038/4.4 but

With ***but*** (dt. *aber*) the added clause ***contrasts*** with the free clause: *She started the race quite fast, but slowed down a lot after ten minutes; Davis looks poor, but he's actually quite well-off.*

Similarly with phrases: *The children were tired but happy*. There is frequently a positive-negative contrast: *They went to bed early but couldn't sleep*. Note that here too, as with ***and/or***, identical subjects and other parallel parts of the clauses are usually omitted in the second clause.

Like other conjunctions, ***but*** always begins the conjunction clause. German *aber*, by contrast, can take an adverbial position after the verb: *Sie gingen früh ins Bett, konnten aber nicht schlafen*. In English this is not possible (**They went to bed early, couldn't but sleep*).

But can also introduce a conjunction clause that has the ***same meaning*** (or roughly the same meaning) as the free clause. Here the free clause is negative and the conjunction clause positive: *They were not tired, but wide awake*. The ***contrast***-meaning of ***but*** is present here only in the grammar (one clause negative, the other positive); in content the clauses have similar meanings, with the second emphasizing the first. Here, the German equivalent of ***but*** is *sondern*: *Sie waren nicht müde, sondern hellwach.*

A related use, also giving emphasis, is in the construction ***not only ... but also***: *She not only lent him her car, but also gave him money*. The emphasis is reinforced even further by placing ***not only*** at the beginning of the free clause. In this case the ***inversion*** rule must be applied (see also chapter 5): *Not only did she lend him her car, but she also gave him money*. It is stylistically better here to repeat the subject in the conjunction clause (rather than omit it).

038/5 Contrast and contradiction with subordinating conjunctions

But, it should be remembered, is a ***co-ordinating*** conjunction, grammatically speaking. Its meaning, however, is shared by several ***subordinating*** conjunctions:

038/5.1 although/though

Although (dt. *obgleich/obwohl*) makes what is called a ***concession***. That is, it 'admits' that there is something that opposes what is said in the free clause: *Although he was still very young, they made him a director of the firm*. The partner preposition is *despite/in spite of*: *In spite of the fact that he was still very young ...* Alternatives here are ***though*** (a little more common in speech than ***although***), and in its emphatic form, ***even though***: *Even though he was still very young ...* The conjunction clause is slightly less emphasized when it is in second position: *They made him a director of the firm, even though he was still very young*. With ***although*** itself, second position can make the conjunction clause sound almost like an afterthought. It then often expresses doubt or reservation: *They made him a director of the firm, although he was still very young.*

Note that ***though*** also occurs as an ***adverb*** (= *yet, however, nevertheless*), chiefly in final position. It cannot then join sentences, and must follow in a separate sentence: *Tom's been made a director of the firm. He's very young, though.*

038/5.2 whereas, while

Whereas (dt. *während/wo(hin)gegen*) underlines a ***contrast*** between two facts or standpoints: *My wife likes holidays by the sea, whereas I prefer mountains.* Initial position is possible, but then suggests that the information in the conjunction clause is already known.

While is also used for ***whereas***, but is slightly more formal and less emphatic: *My wife likes holidays by the sea, while I prefer mountains.*

Unlike ***whereas***, ***while*** can also have the concessive meaning of ***although***, particularly to show that a view or standpoint is acceptable only to a certain extent: *While we appreciate the difficulties of your financial position, we must insist that you repay the loan in the manner already agreed on.* In this case the conjunction clause always appears in initial position.

038/5.3 even if

This also makes a concession, but underlines the 'nevertheless' character of what is said in the free clause: *Even if Jones is a good player, he's certainly not worth that money.* That is, the content of the conjunction clause, though true, does not make the free clause statement less true. With future or past conditional reference, tenses follow the ***if***-clause rule: *Even if she comes, she won't be able to stay long* (dt. *Auch wenn sie kommt, wird sie nicht ...*); *We wouldn't have got much money for the house, even if we had sold it two years later* (dt. ..., *auch wenn wir es 2 Jahre später verkauft hätten*).

038/5.4 no matter, however, whenever, etc.

Strictly speaking, most of these are adverbs and/or adverbials. But they function also as 'pseudo'-conjunctions and join sentences. Most are forms of ***wh***-words (i.e. interrogative adverbs and pronouns). ***No matter*** (= *It doesn't matter*) is derived from a verb. To function like a conjunction it needs a ***wh***-word following it. ***No matter*** translates German *egal* (*wie, was,* usw.). The ***-ever***-forms of the ***wh***-words usually provide an alternative: *No matter how good Jones is* (*However good Jones is*), *he's not worth that money; No matter when they arrive* (*Whenever they arrive*), *you must be there to meet them* (dt. *Wann immer sie ankommen, ...*); *We always have a good time on holiday, no matter where we go* (*..., wherever we go*; dt. ..., *egal wo wir hingehen*); *No matter what she does* (*Whatever she does*), *she does it perfectly; However* (*no matter how*) *good he is, he's not worth that money.*

Semantically, these also emphasize the 'nevertheless' character of the free clause meaning, as with ***even if*** in **038/5.3**.

038/6 Mixed conjunctions

These are all subordinating conjunctions. In their relation to the free clause, however, the major ones (***that*** and ***whether/if***) differ from those discussed so far. Here the conjunction clause, semantically, has a ***content*** relation to the verb in the free clause. For instance, in *I* *don't know whether he is coming*, the conjunction clause tells us ***what*** the subject of the free clause 'doesn't know'. Similarly in *Whether he is coming (or not) is uncertain* the conjunction clause tells us ***what*** 'is uncertain'. The syntactic features are discussed further below.

038/6.1 that

That (dt. *dass*) is the most important conjunction in English. ***That***-clauses express the content of verbs like, for instance, *say, think, know, hope*, etc.: *We hope that you are well.* These are mainly verbs of ***saying***, ***thinking*** and ***feeling***.

That-clauses also postmodify abstract nouns of this type: *I slowly got the impression that something was wrong; Her feeling that she was being deceived grew stronger in the next few weeks.* (See also chapter 14 on noun postmodification). ***That***-clauses follow adjectives of ***feeling*** and ***thinking***, too: *She was sure that she was being deceived; I am sorry that I kept you waiting; Mrs. Beaston was afraid that she might lose her money.*

In addition, they follow adjectives of ***comment*** (e.g. *nice, awful*) and ***speculation*** (e.g. *possible, likely, sure*) after ***It + be***-constructions (known as ***extraposition***, see below): *It's nice that Jane is coming home for the weekend; It is likely that she'll come by train.*

That-clause ***extraposition*** also occurs with certain kinds of ***comment noun*** (*It was a pity/shame/scandal/disaster*, etc. *that the team lost on Sunday*), and a few verbs, principally *seem, appear* and *happen*: *It seems that Brian failed his test; It happened that a police car was passing the shop just at that moment.* **Extraposition** is usual or compulsory in such cases, as ***that***-clauses are generally avoided in initial position.

Finally, ***that*** as a ***conjunction*** must be carefully distinguished from other uses. For example, ***that*** can be a ***demonstrative determiner*** (*That cat belongs to me*, dt. *jene/r/s*), or a ***relative pronoun*** (*The cat that belongs to me is black and white*, dt. *der/die/das*): see also chapter 14. The German equivalent of *conjunction-**that*** is always *dass*:

(9) a. I didn't like the idea ***that*** we should sell the car. [***conjunction***]
Die Vorstellung, ***dass*** wir das Auto verkaufen sollten, gefiel mir nicht.
b. I didn't like the idea ***that*** my wife had had regarding the car. [***relative pronoun***]
Die Idee, ***die*** meine Frau bezüglich des Autos gehabt hatte, gefiel mir nicht.

038/6.2 Omission of that

In speech and informal language, the conjunction ***that*** is often left out, e.g. *We hope you are well.* This mainly happens with common everyday verbs, such as *think, suppose, say, tell*, etc. It is also very likely in speech when the subject of the conjunction-clause is a pronoun: *Dave said he was coming to the lecture; We thought she looked ill.* It is rare with verbs not normally used in colloquial contexts (e.g. *imply, reply, conclude*, etc.). These are tendencies rather than definite rules, though. There is a large degree of individual collocation, i.e. it is often a case of one particular verb being associated with omission, while another with roughly the same meaning is not. Again, a lot depends on the colloquial or everyday nature of the lexical item.

Individual collocation is also responsible for omission with adjectives. A general tendency is for adjectives to omit ***that*** when they express feelings, and the conjunction-clause is short: *We're happy you could come*. ***That***-omission is found much less with adjectives expressing comment, particularly when extraposition is involved: **It was right/ wrong he did it*.

It is generally rare with nouns, except for one or two set-phrase collocations expressing an emotional reaction or comment (and involving ***extraposition***): *It's a pity/shame John isn't here*.

038/6.3 whether/if

Whether translates German *ob*, and means 'the answer to ***question X***'. ***If*** can be used in the same sense: *I don't know whether/if Fraser is playing this afternoon*.

'Question X' here would be *Is Fraser playing this afternoon?* The ***whether***-clause expresses 'question X' not as an actual question, but in the form of a statement.

Clauses like this are called ***indirect questions*** (see chapter 11 and **038/6.5**). They refer to unknown information, and represent a ***direct question*** ('question X') in its ***indirect speech*** form, i.e. as a statement. ***Whether***-clauses are just one of several indirect question types based on different kinds of ***direct question***. The ***direct question*** underlying a ***whether***-clause is always a ***yes-no***-question (see chapter 8).

As ***whether*** implies choice between (at least) two possibilities, an ***or***-clause is often added: *I don't know whether Fraser or Lyle is playing this afternoon; We can't decide whether to go to Spain or Greece for our holiday*. The added alternative is often just the negative of the first possibility. In this case ***or not*** is added: *I don't know whether Fraser is playing this afternoon or not* (= *... or whether he is not playing*). Alternatively, the ***or not***-phrase can follow the verb phrase, or the conjunction itself: *I don't know whether* (*or not*) *Fraser is playing* (*or not*) *this afternoon* (*or not*).

038/6.4 Special points on whether/if

- ***future reference***: When ***whether/if*** refer to the future, the time-clause (***if***-clause) rule does ***not*** apply. Here, that is, tense choices are the normal ones. If the context requires ***will***, then it must appear even in the conjunction-clause: *I don't know whether/if he'll come by bus or train*.
- ***after nouns***: ***Whether*** can be used also to postmodify nouns. It does not usually do this directly, however. Generally ***as to*** or ***of*** precede it: *We must discuss the question* ***of/as to*** *whether we should leave on Friday, or after the weekend*.
  If is not used as a postmodification in this way (i.e. not **... the question if/of if we should leave ...*).
- ***extraposition***: The ***It + be***-construction is also common with ***whether***-clauses: *It is doubtful whether he'll come on Saturday*. This is often the preferred alternative to having the ***whether***-clause in initial position. Initial position is possible, but less emphatic and slightly more formal: *Whether he'll come on Saturday* (*or not*) *is doubtful*.
  Informally, ***if*** can replace ***whether*** in the extraposition version (*It is doubtful if he'll come ...*), but not in initial position (**If he'll come ...*).
- **if*-restriction after verbs:*** Generally speaking, ***if*** is ***not*** used for ***whether*** after verbs referring to processes of decision-making, explanation, or demonstration, such as *show*,

prove, demonstrate, clarify, choose, discuss, etc. (i.e. not **We have to discuss if we should go ...; *The court must prove if she is guilty ...*). An exception is the verb *decide* itself. Here ***if*** is possible, though ***whether*** is usually preferred (*You must decide if/whether you need the money now or later*).

- **whether or not *and* no matter: *Whether*** can follow ***no matter***: *No matter whether I'm in London or Paris, I'm happy.* Without the second alternative, ***or not*** is compulsory: *No matter whether I'm in London or not, I'm happy.* ***No matter*** can also be omitted, i.e. completely replaced by ***whether ... or not***: *We will have a good time, whether (or not) we have money (or not).* The ***whether***-clause can also be in initial position.

038/6.5 where

Where (dt. ***wo***) expresses a place relation and means 'at the place at which': *They're building a new car-park where the old factory used to be.* Here it is a ***conjunction***. Like *when*, however, ***where*** can also be an ***adverb***: *I don't know where the old factory used to be.* In this case it simply means 'the place at which' (i.e. without the first *at*). This is another case of an ***indirect question***, as with ***whether*** (see **038/6.3**). Note, though, that unlike ***whether*** (which is always a conjunction), ***where*** introduces an ***indirect question*** only as an ***adverb***, i.e. more precisely as an ***interrogative adverb***.

As a ***conjunction***, however, ***where*** does not represent a question. Moreover, ***where***-clauses (unlike those with ***whether*** and ***that***) do not have a 'content' relation to the verb in the free clause. They simply add separate information. In this sense, they are like clauses expressing time, cause, reason and contradiction (see above). This kind of link, as we will see below, is in grammatical terms a typical ***adverbial*** function.

038/6.6 so that

This expresses ***purpose*** (dt. *damit)* and ***consequence/result*** (dt. *so dass*): *The children were standing on the seats, so that they could see the stage better* (dt. ..., *damit sie die Bühne besser sehen konnten*); *It had rained through the roof during the night, so that there were large puddles of water on the floor* (dt. ..., *so dass große Wasserpfützen auf dem Boden waren*). Clauses expressing ***consequence*** like this are also referred to as ***consecutive clauses***. In a particular variation of a consecutive clause ***so*** comes before adjectives and adverbs, and ***that*** follows: *I was so tired that I could hardly stand up; Farrell drove so fast that we were thrown around in our seats.* The German construction is similar: ... *fuhr so schnell, dass wir auf den Sitzen hin- und hergeschleudert wurden.* In this version, ***so*** (both in English and German) is an adverb. ***That*** remains a conjunction.

038/6.7 as/than

These are ***comparative particles*** and were explained fully in chapter 4 on adjectives. Note again that ***surplus*** and ***deficit*** comparison use ***more/less than***, and ***equative*** comparison ***as ... as***.

As/than are used as both prepositions and conjunctions. Here is a short reminder of their ***conjunction*** use:

(10) a. Dave is taller than Mary is.
b. Sue reads more books than Bob does.
c. In restaurants, she always orders more food than she can eat.
d. I have walked just as far as you have.
e. The weather was better in February than it was in March.

A general point about all ***comparative clauses*** is that they are in a sense 'incomplete'. The ***comparative element***, which refers to the ***basis of comparison*** (e.g. *taller, more books, more successful*, etc.), appears only in the free clause, not in the comparative clause. That is, we do not say **Dave is taller than Mary is tall*. The ***comparative element*** is always ***omitted*** from the comparative clause. In (10)a., and e. this is the subject complement (***Cs***), in (10)b. and c. the direct object (***Od***), and in (10)d. the adverbial (***A***).

Furthermore, when the main verb in both clauses is the same, it is usually not repeated in the comparative clause. Instead, it is just represented by the auxiliary, as in (10)d. This is called a ***tag form*** (also ***auxiliary pro-form***, see chapter 8). If there is no auxiliary in the free clause, the ***tag*** is formed by adding *do*, as in (10)b. We could repeat the main verb here (i.e. ... *than Bob reads*), but the ***tag*** version is preferred. An exception is with *have* or *be*, as in (10)a. These function as their own ***tags***, which is why they are repeated in the comparative clause.

An alternative (when main verbs are identical, as here) is to omit the verb phrase entirely. The clause itself then disappears, leaving just the compared phrases: *Dave is taller than Mary; Sue reads more books than Bob; I have walked just as far as you; The weather was better in February than in March.*

038/6.8 Other comparative uses of as

Apart from grammatical comparison, ***as*** is also used for lexical comparison, e.g. following the adjective ***same***: *Blanche studies the same subjects as John (does)*.

Beware! It is not **the same subjects like John*. ⚠

Related uses are: *Do as you wish (= in the way in which ...); As you know, Brandon is leaving the firm next month (= according to what ...)*. In all of these uses, ***as***-clauses are similar semantically to relative clauses, and can often be replaced by them, e.g. *Blanche studies the same subjects that John does*. In colloquial English *like* often replaces ***as*** when actions or behaviour are compared: *She doesn't cook like Mum cooks*. But this is not standard.

In standard English, *like* is only a preposition. The standard version of the last sentence is therefore either *She doesn't cook like Mum*, or *She doesn't cook as Mum cooks*. With ***as***-clauses of this kind, equative comparisons with adjectives are preferred, e.g. ... *as well as Mum cooks/... as badly as Mum cooks*, etc.

As if/as though (dt. *als ob*) mean 'in a manner suggesting': *He looks as if/though he hasn't slept for days*. These are ***speculative manner comparisons***. Like conditions, they can also be unreal or hypothetical, e.g. *He looks as if/though he hadn't slept for days.*

038/6.9 Errors with as/than

German speakers tend to confuse ***as*** and ***than***: **Brenda is taller as I am; *Mike is as tall than Brenda; *Blanche studies the same subjects than John.* ⚠

This is probably because in regional and colloquial German, *wie* stands for both, even though standard German distinguishes as carefully between *wie* and *als* as English does between ***as*** and ***than***.

Another problem is the confusion of ***than*** and ***then***. This is probably due to pronunciation problems, i.e. failing to distinguish between the vowels [æ] and [e]. The speaker wrongly pronounces ***than*** like ***then*** and carries the error over into the spelling.

039 Conjunction clauses and sentence syntax

039/1 Clauses as adverbials
039/2 Clauses as subjects, objects and complements
039/3 Adverbs as subordinators instead of conjunctions
039/4 Further subordination
039/5 Clause reduction to indicate function
039/6 Clauses as parts of phrases
039/7 Comma rules

As we said at the beginning of the chapter, conjunction clauses have two kinds of syntactic relation to the free clause: those introduced by ***co-ordinating*** conjunctions (*and, but, or*) have ***equal syntactic status*** with the free clause. In this case we have a ***compound sentence***: *She dived into the lake and swam to the boat.*

Those introduced by ***subordinating*** conjunctions (such as *because, that, although,* etc.) have an 'inferior' or ***subordinate*** status to that of the free clause. In this case we have a ***complex sentence***: *After she dived into the lake, she swam to the boat.*

Here the conjunction clause (*After she dived into the lake ...*) is the ***subordinate clause***. As pointed out above, the free clause in this case is traditionally known as the ***main clause***. However, we prefer to call this the ***matrix*** (or 'framing') ***clause***, as it provides a kind of 'frame' for the ***subordinate clause***. Technically speaking, the ***subordinate clause*** is actually a part of the ***matrix clause*** and has a ***sentence function*** inside it. In our example, for instance, *After she dived into the lake ...* functions as an ***adverbial*** (***A***):

	Subordinate clause (A)	***Matrix clause (main clause)***
(11)	After she dived into the lake,	she swam to the boat

If the subordinate clause is ***reduced*** to a ***phrase*** with roughly the same meaning (e.g. *after that*), we see clearly that it is an element in the matrix clause, and has the same function (i.e. that of an ***adverbial***):

	A	
(12)	After that,	she swam to the boat.

In (12), the subordinate clause of (11) has been reduced to a ***prepositional phrase*** (*after that*), functioning, like the clause, as an ***adverbial***.

This shows that in the ***complex*** sentence in (11) the ***subordinate clause*** is really included in the ***matrix clause***. However, this poses certain theoretical problems not relevant here. So we will keep to the traditional view shown in (11), and regard the two clauses as separate from each other: the ***matrix clause*** as the higher one, but on its own; and the ***subordinate clause*** as the lower one, and ***not*** included in the matrix. This does not alter the fact that the ***subordinate clause*** has a ***sentence function***. But we will simply see this as a function within the sentence as a whole.

We will now discuss the ***sentence functions*** of subordinate conjunction clauses.

039/1 Clauses as adverbials

Most subordinating conjunctions introduce clauses that function as ***adverbials*** (***A***). In sentence analysis it is usual (though not essential) to add the kind of adverbial meaning to the function classification, i.e. ***time***, ***reason***, ***condition***, and so on.

039/1.1 Clauses of time

Conjunctions involved here are: ***when/whenever***, ***as/while***, ***until/not until***, ***as soon as***, ***after***, ***before***, ***since***:

	Matrix clause	*Subordinate clause (A of time)*
(13)	a. I'll let you know	as soon as I arrive in Manchester.
	Subordinate clause (A of time)	*Matrix clause*
	b. While Mary was painting	she heard a loud noise outside her studio.

039/1.2 Clauses of reason

These are introduced by ***because*** and ***as/since***:

	Matrix clause	*Subordinate clause (A of reason)*
(14)	a. Fred failed the exam	because he didn't prepare for it properly.
	Subordinate clause (A of reason)	*Matrix clause*
	b. As Jill was fast asleep	she did not hear the telephone.

Note that ***for*** is usually regarded as a co-ordinating conjunction (see also **038/1.3** above).

039/1.3 Clauses of condition

Conditional conjunctions are ***if***, ***unless***, ***in case***, ***supposing (that)***, and ***providing/provided (that)***:

	Matrix clause	*Subordinate clause (A of condition)*
(15)	a. You should take cash with you	in case credit cards are not accepted.
	Subordinate clause (A of condition)	*Matrix clause*
	b. If Jill is fast asleep	she will not hear the telephone.

039/1.4 Clauses of contrast, contradiction and concession

Here we have: ***although/though, whereas/while, even if, no matter/however/whenever,*** etc.:

	Matrix clause	***Subordinate clause (A of contrast)***
(16) a.	My husband likes jazz,	whereas I prefer rock music.
	Subordinate clause (A of concession)	***Matrix clause***
b.	Though he felt very tired,	he could not get to sleep.

039/1.5 Clauses of purpose and consequence

The main conjunction here is ***so that:***

	Matrix clause	***Subordinate clause (A of purpose)***
(17) a.	I'll open a window,	so that we'll get some fresh air in here.
	Matrix clause	***Subordinate clause (A of consequence)***
b.	Thick snow had fallen,	so that the game had to be cancelled.

As already mentioned, clauses of consequence, as in (17)b., are also called ***consecutive clauses***. It was also pointed out (see **038/6.6** above) that a slightly different kind of consecutive clause, introduced by ***that*** alone, can follow adjectives and adverbs, with ***so*** preceding them, e.g. *I was so tired that I could hardly stand up*. Here, the clause is an integrated part of the adjective/adverb phrase. Cases like this are dealt with further below.

039/1.6 Clauses of place

Where is the only conjunction expressing a place relation. The usual German rendering is *dort, wo*:

	Subordinate clause (A of place)	***Matrix clause***
(18)	Where the two roads join,	there is a large hotel complex.

Where-clauses can also be parts of noun phrases (*The place where the murder was committed ...*), or ***subject complements*** (*That is where the murder was committed*). And as already mentioned, ***where*** (like ***when***) can occur as an ***interrogative adverb***. All these cases are explained further below.

039/2 Clauses as subjects, objects and complements

A very common sentence function of subordinate conjunction clauses is ***direct object*** (***Od***). The ***subject*** function (***S***) is not quite so frequent, and occurs mainly in the form of ***extraposition*** (***It + be***-construction). It is rare at the beginning of a sentence. Clauses as ***subject complements*** (***Cs***) can follow the verb *be*, and do so mainly when the subject of the matrix clause is an abstract noun, such as *question, problem, hope, trouble, difficulty*, etc. By far the most common conjunction in all these functions is ***that*** (dt. *dass*). Others are ***whether/if***:

039/2.1 Direct object (Od)

	Matrix clause	*Subordinate clause (Od)*
(19) a.	He said	that we should open a window.
	Matrix clause	*Subordinate clause (Od)*
b.	She asked me,	if I knew her husband.

Note also the possibility of ***omitting*** *that*: *He said we should open a window.*

039/2.2 Subject (S)

	Subordinate clause (S)	*Matrix clause*
(20) a.	Whether we'll be here next week	is very uncertain.
	Subordinate clause (S)	*Matrix clause*
b.	That you have to work harder,	is quite obvious.

Sentences like this are possible, but usually extraposition is preferred. In this construction, the pronoun ***It*** begins the clause in the function of a 'dummy subject' (called the ***grammatical subject***, or ***S-gramm.***) and the 'real' (or logical) subject (***S-log.***), i.e. the conjunction clause, is pushed to final position, where it receives more stress:

	Matrix clause		
	(S-gramm.)		*Subordinate clause (S-log.)*
(21) a.	It	is very uncertain	whether we'll be here next week.
b.	It	is quite obvious	that you have to work harder.

039/2.3 Subject complement (Cs)

	Matrix clause	*Subordinate clause (Cs)*
(22)	The problem is	that we won't be here next week.

039/3 Adverbs as subordinators instead of conjunctions

As we have already pointed out, ***when*** and ***where*** are not always conjunctions. They can also introduce subordinate clauses as ***interrogative adverbs*** (see also **038/2.1** and **038/6.5** above). In this case they function inside their own clauses as ***adverbials***:

		Subordinate clause (Od)
		A
(23) a.	I do not know	[***when*** the film starts].
		A
b.	She has not told us	[***where*** she lives].

As previously mentioned, adverb-***when*** is German *wann*. With *wo*, however, German is like English, and does not distinguish between the conjunction and the adverb.

It is important to see that the distinction between conjunctions and adverbs here is not just a formal question, but very much concerned with meaning. In (23) ***when*** and ***where*** belong to the ***content*** of the subordinate clause. That is, they represent missing information in it concerning time and place. Subordinate clauses like this are ***indirect questions*** (or ***interrogative clauses***). They always function in the sentence as ***direct object***, or occasionally as ***subject*** or ***subject complement***. Clauses with ***when/where*** as ***conjunctions***, however, always introduce clauses that are ***adverbial***:

		Subordinate clause (A)
		Conj.
(24)	a. I waved to her	[***when*** I saw her].
	b. There is a park	[***where*** she lives].

Other ***adverb subordinators*** are ***how*** and ***why***: *Why she committed the crime is a mystery; The police did not tell us how they had caught the thieves*. Here too the subordinate clauses are ***interrogative clauses*** functioning in the first example as ***subject*** (***S***), and in the second as ***direct object*** (***Od***). The adverbs function inside their own clauses as ***adverbials*** (***A***).

Note, though, that not all interrogative clauses are introduced by adverb subordinators. ***Whether*** and ***if*** also introduce interrogative clauses, as in (19)b., (20)a., and (21) a. above, but they are always ***conjunctions***. Other interrogative clauses are introduced by ***interrogative pronouns***, like *what* and *who*. There is more on interrogative clauses in chapter 11 and 14.

039/4 Further subordination

Complex sentences often have more than one subordinate clause. When there are two or more inside one another, they are arranged in a kind of hierarchy: the highest acts as the matrix for the second one down, the second for the third one down, and so on. Each clause inside another, that is, has a function relating to its 'owner' above it in the hierarchy:

	Subordinate clause 1. (A)	***Subordinate clause 2. (Od)***	***Subordinate clause 3. (A)***
(25)	[Although we told him	[that he would fail the exam	[if he did not prepare
		Matrix clause	
	properly for it]]], he just did not listen.		

In the same sentence there may be other subordinate clauses, of course, that are not inside the same 'box'. For example, we could add one after the matrix in (25). In addition there may be subordinate clauses which are co-ordinated with each other:

	Subordinate clause 1. (A)	***Co-ordinated subordinate clauses 2a. and 2b. (Od)***
(26)	[Although we told him	[that (he would fail the exam) and (have to re-sit it)
	Subordinate clause 3. (A)	***Matrix clause***
	[if he did not prepare properly for it]]],	he just did not listen to us
	Subordinate clause 4. (A)	
	[while we were talking].	

In (26), ***subordinate clause 4.*** is directly dependent on the ***matrix clause*** in the same way as ***subordinate clause 1***. That is, in terms of the whole sentence hierarchy, ***1.*** and ***4.*** are both on the same level of subordination (i.e. the first level). On the second level we now also have two subordinate clauses, ***2a.*** and ***2b***. These are connected by ***co-ordination*** with *and*. A point to note with ***co-ordinated subordinate clauses*** is that they have the ***same function*** (here ***Od***) in relation to the clause above them. Note also the ***ellipsis*** (= omission) of the conjunction ***that*** and other identical items (*he* and *would*) in the second co-ordinated clause ***2b***. Ellipsis of this kind is usual (though not obligatory) in all co-ordinated clauses that come in second position.

Finally, it is not unusual in English for certain conjunctions to follow each other immediately: *He was told* ***that unless*** *he left the country at once, he would be arrested as an illegal immigrant; In your position, I would leave the country at once,* ***because if*** *you don't, you might be arrested*. This tends to be avoided in German: *Ihm wurde gesagt, dass er als illegaler Einwanderer verhaftet werden würde, wenn er nicht …; An deiner Stelle würde ich das Land sofort verlassen, da du verhaftet werden könntest, wenn du es nicht tust.*

In the English sentences, syntactically speaking, one subordination immediately follows the other:

	Matrix clause	***Sub-clause 1. (A)***	***Sub-clause 2. (A)***
(27)	I would leave the country at once,	[because	[if you don't] you might be arrested].

The structure and function of complex sentences are taken up again in chapter 14.

039/5 Clause reduction to indicate function

As shown in the introduction to this section on syntax, it is possible to replace a subordinate clause by a phrase of similar general meaning. This is an easy way to tell the function, and also the extent, of a sub-clause. Let us come back to the sentence in (25): *Although we told him that he would fail the exam if he did not prepare properly for it, he just did not listen.*

Subordinate clause 1 (*Although → for it*) can be reduced, for example, to *in spite of this*: *In spite of this he just did not listen.*

To make sense, *in spite of this* must replace the whole section of the sentence from *although* to *for it*, i.e. the whole of ***Subordinate clause 1***. This shows us precisely how long the clause is, and what it includes, and does not include. Secondly, as *in spite of this* is a prepositional phrase, and therefore functions as an ***adverbial (A)***, the clause itself must be an ***adverbial***. We can repeat this reduction or replacement operation for the other clauses, e.g. *Although we told him* ***this*** (= *that … for it*), *he just did not listen; Although we told him that he would fail the exam* ***under this condition*** (= *if … for it*), *he just did not listen*. This gives us the extent of the ***Subordinate clauses 2.*** and ***3.***, and also shows their functions, i.e. ***2.*** as ***(Od)*** and ***3.*** as ***(A)***.

039/6 Clauses as parts of phrases

The clauses we have looked at so far have been direct parts of sentences or other clauses. This is ***subordination at sentence level***. Alternatively, clauses can be parts of phrases. This is ***subordination at phrase level***. In this case they do ***not*** have sentence functions like *subject, object, adverbial,* etc., but ***phrase functions***, e.g. ***postmodification*** (in a noun phrase), or ***adjectival complement*** (in an adjective phrase).

We will now look at some typical examples of phrase level subordination with conjunctions. As with sentence subordination, it is ***only*** conjunction clauses that interest us in this chapter. Other types of phrase level subordination (e.g. relative clauses, participle clauses, etc.), are dealt with later (see chapter 14).

039/6.1 Consecutive clauses

A certain type of ***consecutive clause*** (clause of ***consequence***), as mentioned previously (see **038/6.6** above), occurs at phrase level: *Dave was so exhausted that he fell asleep immediately.*

Here we have a ***that***-clause following an adjective. It works in combination with the degree adverb ***so*** before the adjective, and functions within the adjective phrase as ***adjectival complement*** (see also chapter 4 on adjectives).

	Adjective phrase (Cs)	***Adjectival complement***
(28) a. Dave was	[so exhausted	that he fell asleep immediately].
b. She was	[so angry	that she almost threw the glass at him].

The construction also occurs with adverb phrases and noun phrases:

	Adverb phrase (A)	***Adverb complement***
(29) a. I had climbed the stairs	[so quickly	that I was out of breath].
	Noun phrase (Od)	***Postmodification***
b. She had won	[so much money	that she no longer had to work].

With nouns, the ***so*** must relate to a quantifier of some kind.

039/6.2 Clauses of comparison

These are clauses introduced by ***than*** and ***as***. These too are integrated parts of adjective, adverb or noun phrases:

	Adjective phrase (Cs)	
		Adjectival complement
(30) a. She was	[taller	than her husband was].
	Adverb phrase (A)	
		Adverb complement
b. I can't run	[as fast	as you can].
	Noun phrase (Od)	
		Postmodification
c. Our new car uses	[less petrol	than the old one did].

With noun phrases, as in the previous section, the comparison relates to a quantifier.

039/6.3 Other types of conjunction clause in adjective phrases

That-clauses are common with many adjectives:

		Adjective phrase (Cs)	
			Adjectival complement
(31)	a. She was	[certain	that she would be leaving the firm].
		Adjective phrase (Cs)	
			Adjectival complement
	b. I am	[surprised	that the storm didn't damage the house].

The following kinds of adjectives occur particularly often with ***that***-clauses:

- ***adjectives of emotion:*** *happy, sad, sorry, delighted,* etc.
- ***adjectives of comment:*** *great, nice, awful, inconvenient, peculiar, right/wrong, silly,* etc. **Extraposition** is usual here: *It's inconvenient that you're leaving tomorrow.* Note that the ***that***-clause is syntactically ***not*** an adjectival complement in such cases, but the ***logical subject*** of the matrix clause:

	Matrix clause			
	(S-gramm.)		***(Cs)***	***Subordinate clause (S-log.)***
(32)	It	is	inconvenient	[that you're leaving ...]

- ***adjectives of probability and certainty:*** *certain, sure, likely, probable, possible,* etc. ***Extraposition*** common: *It is certain that ...*
- ***adjectives of perception:*** *noticeable, evident, obvious, discernible, apparent,* etc. Only with ***extraposition***: *It is obvious that ...*
- ***adjectives of importance:*** *relevant, important, essential, significant, fundamental,* etc. Only with ***extraposition***: *It is important that ...*
  Where alternatives are implied (mainly after negative forms) ***if/whether*** can also occur: *It's not certain if he's coming; It's unimportant whether we decorate the house now or later.*

039/6.4 Other types of conjunction clause in noun phrases

Here again, ***that***-clauses predominate. As with corresponding verbs, they express the ***content*** of the noun:

	Noun phrase (S)			
		Postmodification		
(33)	a. [The hope	that the government would react]	proved unfounded.	
			Noun phrase (Od)	
				Postmodification
	b. McKinley could not refute		[the charge	that he had cheated his customers].

That-clauses typically postmodify abstract nouns, such as *belief, view, opinion, intention, desire, expectation,* etc. We must emphasize again that this type of ***that***-clause is ***not*** a relative clause, and does ***not*** have the meaning of a relative clause.

It is a ***conjunction***, and translates into German as *dass*.

The only other conjunction that occurs in postmodifying position is ***whether***. This rarely postmodifies the noun directly, though. It is usually preceded by the prepositions *on, about, of* or *as to* (= *concerning*): *I had doubts about/as to whether our firm would survive the crisis; The decision on whether the house should be sold was postponed until the following month*: *We must discuss the question of whether a quieter celebration might not be a better alternative.*

039/7 Comma rules

In German, commas are ***grammatical*** markers of ***subordination*** (*Ich ging ins Bett, weil ich müde war*). In English this is ***not*** so. Commas are used in English mainly to suggest a ***pause*** in speaking. They are an optional style device. If the writer thinks no pause is necessary, there will be no comma. This would normally be the case with the English version of the German example just given: *I went to bed because I was tired.*

In ***initial*** position, however, adverbial clauses generally have commas after them: *Because I was tired, I went to bed.* Initial adverbial clauses tend to express known (or less profiled) information, and there is often a need to mark this off from the new (or more profiled) information in the matrix clause. A comma is particularly important when the subordinate clause is fairly long: *Because I was tired and had been up since the very early morning, I went to bed*. Nevertheless, this is a rule of style and not of grammar.

In second position, adverbial clauses generally have no comma before them: *There was a taxi waiting for us when we landed at the airport.* Commas are normally used here only if the matrix clause is long, and the writer feels the need to mark it off, e.g. *Because of the heavy rain we were hardly able to see anything at all on the ground, as the plane came in to land at the airport*; or if the adverbial clause is more of an afterthought: *Give my regards to Stella, if you see her.* Note that these are all cases where the comma marks what in speech would be a pause for breath, or a change in the tone of voice.

⚠ In contrast to German, English does ***not*** use commas

- before clauses that are ***direct objects (Od)***: *I thought that they were leaving tonight* (not **I thought, that they were …*); *She asked them whether they could deliver the couch the next day* (not **She asked them, whether they could …*);
- generally before clauses that are ***subject complements (Cs)***: *The big question is whether we should invite Stan to the party or not* (not **The big question is, whether we should …*)
- generally after clauses that are ***subjects (S)***: *That he had been drinking heavily was obvious* (not **That he had been drinking heavily, was obvious*);
- before clauses that are ***parts of phrases***: *The banks still held the belief that the government would help them* (not **… the belief, that the government …*); *Thea was not sure if her husband still loved her* (not **Thea was not sure, if her husband …*).
- in ***extraposition***: *It is possible that she missed the train* (not **It is possible, that she missed the train*).

All this can be expressed, rather reduced, in a simple couplet:

Commas are placed as good as never
Before and after ***that*** and ***whether***.

Chapter 8 Verbs: Basic Features, Syntax and Forms

Basic features 040

Verbs are traditionally thought of as words referring to ***actions*** and ***states***. In *Sally brushes her teeth three times a day*, for example, the verb *brushes* is a 'doing-word', as children are often taught. In *Sally likes chocolate*, the verb *likes* is a 'being-word', i.e. it refers to a ***state***, in this case an internal one, a feeling. However, a semantic definition is not enough to distinguish verbs from other word-classes. For example, the term *actions* also refers to 'actions' and the term *states* to 'states', yet both these words are nouns, and not verbs!

The distinctive feature of the verb is that it does ***not*** just name the event as a noun does: it includes features of form that express the action or state ***dynamically***, as it unfolds in time. The form *brushes*, for instance, shows that this is a habit, a repeated action, which happens regularly 'now', in the present time of the reader or listener; the form *brushed* would place the habit in our past, and the form *was brushing* would tell us that we are looking at a single past action as it was occurring. The form of verbs also connects them to the person or thing performing the action. In grammatical terms, that is, verbs ***agree*** with their subjects.

All this stresses the characteristic of verbs as 'performers' that bring actions 'to life', rather than just naming or identifying them. Furthermore, this feature is not lexical, but embedded in the grammatical forms of verbs. It is also reflected on a syntactic level, in sentence function. It is verbs that play the most crucial role in ***creating sentences***: they place the other entities named in a certain basic relationship to one another. Verbs, that is, ***unite*** all the other phrases present into a clause or sentence. This is a function that we call ***predication***, i.e. 'saying something' about the way the other parts of the sentence are related to each other in grammar and meaning. It is this that makes a simple collection of words into the basis of a communicative message, or what is known theoretically as a ***proposition***.

040/1 The verb phrase

Just like any other word-class, verbs form phrases. The ***head*** of a ***verb phrase*** is the ***main verb*** (dt. *Vollverb*), sometimes also called the ***lexical verb***. Any other members of the verb phrase are ***auxiliary verbs*** (dt. *Hilfsverben*).

		verb	*phrase*		
		auxiliary	*auxiliary*	*main verb*	
		↓	↓	↓	
(1)	a. My wife	↓	↓	***feeds***	the dog everyday.
	b. My wife	↓	***has***	***fed***	the dog everyday.
	c. My wife	***should***	***have***	***fed***	the dog everyday.
	d. My wife		***will***	***feed***	the dog everyday.

Verb phrases therefore may consist of just a main verb, as in (1)a., or of a main verb preceded by one or more auxiliaries, as in (1)b., c., and d. Auxiliaries always ***precede*** a main verb. That is, in a verb phrase containing more than one element, the head is always the final element. Note that when there are auxiliaries, the main verb itself is always in the form of an ***infinitive*** (here, *feed*), or a ***participle*** (here the past participle, *fed*). After auxiliaries, that is, the main verb always occurs in a ***non-finite*** form (see **040/2**).

As with other phrases, it is the verb phrase ***as a whole*** that has a functional role in the sentence. This is the function of ***predicator (P)***. Verb phrases have no other sentence function:

		P	
(2)	a. My wife	feeds	the dog everyday.
	b. My wife	has fed	the dog everyday.
	c. My wife	should have fed	the dog everyday.
	d. My wife	will feed	the dog everyday.

In every sentence here, *my wife* is the ***subject (S)***, *the dog* the ***direct object (Od)***, and *everyday* an ***adverbial (A)***. The complete sentence analysis in (2) therefore looks like this:

	S	***P***	***Od***	***A***
(3)	My wife	feeds/has fed/should have fed/will feed	the dog	everyday.

040/2 Verb morphology

The following are basic grammatical categories directly connected with verbs and their forms:

040/2.1 Number and person

Verb phrases like those in (1)–(3) are linked by their grammatical form to the ***subject***. That is, they have specific endings which distinguish the ***person*** of the subject, showing whether it is *I, you, he/she/it/*a full noun, etc. Strictly speaking, two things are shown: firstly, the ***person***, and secondly, its ***number*** (= whether ***singular*** or ***plural***). So in the sentence *My wife feeds the dog everyday*, for instance, we say that the verb is 'in the ***third person singular***'. ***Grammatical agreement*** of this kind between subject and verb is known in modern linguistics as ***concord***. ***Concord*** underlines person ***deixis***, and therefore contributes importantly to the ***deictic orientation*** of a sentence. It also shows the close unity between a verb and its subject. What a verb ***predicates***, or 'claims', is claimed, first and foremost, ***about the subject***. This is shown by the fact that some verbs only need a subject to make a grammatically complete sentence, e.g. *The bus is coming*. Verbs that show ***concord*** are called ***finite*** verb forms (see also under **040/2.3**).

040/2.2 Conjugation

Listing a whole set of person and number forms for a particular verb is known traditionally as ***conjugating*** the verb. In Romance languages such as French or Italian (and especially Latin), ***conjugations*** are complex, and there can be as many as 6 quite different person and number forms. There are also different groups of verbs, each with different conjugations. German is much less complex than this, but conjugating in English is simplest. There is only one major conjugation, and here the endings hardly vary. In most persons there are actually none at all, i.e. just ***zero inflections***. Compare the conjugations of *to run* and its German equivalent *laufen*:

Singular	1st person	I ***run***	ich ***laufe***
	2nd person	you ***run***	du ***läufst***/Sie ***laufen***
	3rd person	he/she/it/full noun ***runs***	er/sie/es usw. ***läuft***
Plural	1st person	we ***run***	wir ***laufen***
	2nd person	you ***run***	Ihr ***lauft***/Sie ***laufen***
	3rd person	they/full nouns ***run***	sie ***laufen***

A bit more of a challenge is the verb *to be*, which is ***irregular*** (as in German and many other languages), and has more varied person markings, at least in the singular:

Singular	1st person	I ***am***	ich ***bin***
	2nd person	you ***are***	du ***bist***/Sie ***sind***
	3rd person	he/she/it/full noun ***is***	er/sie/es usw. ***ist***
Plural	1st person	we ***are***	wir ***sind***
	2nd person	you ***are***	Ihr ***seid***/Sie ***sind***
	3rd person	they/full nouns ***are***	sie ***sind***

There are one or two other verbs that show slight irregularities in their conjugations. These are dealt with later. In general, however, conjugating an English verb is quite straightforward. With exception of *to be*, English verbs distinguish only the 3rd person singular from all the other forms. The 3rd person singular is usually marked just by an *-s*-inflection. All other forms are identical with the ***base***-form, or infinitive (see below).

⚠ Probably because it is an exception, the 3rd person singular *-s* has a tendency to be forgotten: **This train run everyday except on Sunday* (instead of *runs*). It seems that as learners do not have to remember many endings anyway, they end up forgetting the single most important one. Another point of confusion may be that the *-s*-inflection is generally associated in English with plural forms (in nouns, that is), but functions here as a singular marker.

Note that past tenses do not inflect at all. They have the same form in all persons:

Singular	1st person	I ***ran***	ich ***lief***
	2nd person	you ***ran***	du ***liefst***/Sie ***liefen***
	3rd person	he/she/it/full noun ***ran***	er/sie/es usw. ***lief***
Plural	1st person	we ***ran***	wir ***liefen***
	2nd person	you ***ran***	Ihr ***lieft***/Sie ***liefen***
	3rd person	they/full nouns ***ran***	sie ***liefen***

Historical processes are generally responsible for this lack of contrastive inflections in English (see chapter 1). Nevertheless, the principle of ***concord*** still operates, even with ***zero inflections***. We will call this ***notional concord***.

Note that *to be* is an exception here too: it is the only verb that distinguishes person and number in the ***past***:

Singular	1st person	I ***was***	ich ***war***
	2nd person	you ***were***	du ***warst***/Sie ***waren***
	3rd person	he/she/it/full noun ***was***	er/sie/es usw. ***war***
Plural	1st person	we ***were***	wir ***waren***
	2nd person	you ***were***	Ihr ***wart***/Sie ***waren***
	3rd person	they/full nouns ***were***	sie ***waren***

040/2.3 Finite and non-finite verbs

As was said in **040/2.2**, ***finite*** verbs show ***concord***. That is, they are ***conjugated***. Verb forms that are ***not*** conjugated and do ***not*** show concord are ***non-finite*** verbs: these are ***infinitives***, ***gerunds*** and ***participles***. Generally speaking, ***non-finite*** verbs do not appear with grammatical subjects at all; when they do, they have no subject agreement. They are never inflected in any way. Furthermore, the subject cannot usually just be added. It generally has to be introduced in some kind of special syntactic construction. For instance, in *It would be unwise to spend a lot of money*, the subject of the infinitive *to spend* is not present in the sentence, but would normally be implied semantically in the context. It is possible to specify the subject grammatically, but this has to be done by a special *for*-construction: *It would be unwise* ***for him*** *to spend a lot of money*. The form of the infinitive itself, though, remains unchanged.

Although we have been talking about finite and non-finite ***verbs***, we should properly call them finite and non-finite ***verb phrases***. In a sentence or clause, it is the status of the verb phrase ***as a whole*** that interests us. The individual verbs inside a ***finite verb phrase*** vary in status. If there is more than one verb, only the first will be finite and the rest non-finite. The main verb is actually always in a non-finite form when accompanied by auxiliaries: in *My wife has fed the dog*, the main verb is a past participle, and in *My wife will feed the dog*, it is an infinitive. The verb phrases as a whole, of course, are in each case finite.

Finally, it is important to realize that ***all*** sentences must contain ***at least one finite*** verb phrase. In ***simple*** sentences the verb phrase is ***always*** finite.

In ***complex*** sentences, verb phrases in ***subordinate clauses*** can be finite or non-finite, but the ***matrix*** verb phrase must ***always be finite***, as in: *He didn't know whether to admit being drunk (or not).*

	Matrix clause	***Subordinate clause 1. (Od)***	***Subordinate clause 2. (Od)***
(4)	He didn't know	[whether to admit	[being drunk]].
	↑	↑	↑
	finite	***non-finite***	***non-finite***

040/2.4 Tense

Tense markers are inflections and other morphological forms that signal the ***time*** that a verb refers to. More exactly, they signal the ***time sphere***, i.e. ***present***, ***past*** or ***future***. These are ***speaker-related*** categories and are therefore another manifestation of ***deixis*** (= ***time*** or ***temporal deixis***). Typically comparable ***time-deictic adverbs*** are *tomorrow, today,* and *yesterday*. When a speaker's *'tomorrow'* shifts into his *'today'* and then becomes his *'yesterday'*, this is one example of the way in which ***subjective time*** is felt always to be 'moving' from the ***future*** through the individual's ***present*** and into his ***past***. Like all deictic concepts, these are dynamic. They move as the speaker reference-point moves. In this case, it is moving forward through time.

Despite the fact that we (and our languages) commonly divide our subjective experience of time into ***three*** time spheres, English tenses relate ***only*** to the ***present*** and the ***past***. There is ***no*** future tense in English. Traditional grammar often treats ***will*** as the 'future tense'. The major factor in the use of ***will*** is actually not time, however, but other types of meaning (as we will see later). It is therefore wrong to call ***will*** a 'tense form'. There are also several other ways of referring to future time in English, but none of them are tense forms as such.

There are therefore only two main (or ***primary***) tense forms in English: ***present*** (e.g. *she runs*), and ***past*** (e.g. *she ran*). In addition, these each have a ***perfect*** form: the ***present perfect***, e.g. *she has run*, oriented to the present; and the ***past perfect***, e.g. *she had run*, oriented to the past. We will call these ***secondary*** tense forms:

Primary tense	***Present***	she runs
Secondary tense	***Present Perfect***	she has run
Primary tense	***Past***	she ran
Secondary tense	***Past Perfect***	she had run

Note that the progressive forms are missing here. This is because the progressive is ***not*** a tense. It belongs to the category of ***aspect*** (see under **040/2.6** below).

040/2.5 The status of the perfect

It is important to add that perfect forms also appear with modals (*will have run, would have run, must have run,* etc.), as well as in ***non-finite*** forms, such as the infinitive (*to have run*) and the gerund (*having run*). But here, too, they have a ***relative*** character: that is, they are always ***oriented*** to a ***primary tense level*** (often determined by context), and are not independent, as will be seen later in the larger sections on individual tenses (see especially chapters 9 and 10).

A further point is that some modern grammarians see the perfect as an ***aspect***, and not as a tense. This is ***not*** the view taken here, however. For us, the perfect forms are definitely ***tenses***, and ***not*** aspects. The point is explained more fully below in the ***aspect***-section (**040/2.6**).

Finally, we could regard ***zero inflection*** for the perfect as a positive marker showing 'non-perfect'. In this way every verb form would be regarded as marked for ***both*** primary ***and*** secondary tense, as in:

	Primary tense	Secondary tense
she runs	*Present*	*Non-Perfect*
she has run	*Present*	*Perfect*
she ran	*Past*	*Non-Perfect*
she had run	*Past*	*Perfect*

The table in **040/2.4** shows an ordinary, practical way of representing ***primary*** and ***secondary*** tense forms. However, the underlying facts are reflected more exactly in the table here above. In this version, each verb form is marked for ***both*** primary ***and*** secondary tenses, and not just for one of them. *She runs* is now therefore regarded as ***present*** (primary) and ***non-perfect*** (secondary); *She has run* as ***present*** (primary) and ***perfect*** (secondary); *She ran* as ***past*** (primary) and ***non-perfect*** (secondary); and *She had run* as ***past*** (primary) and ***perfect*** (secondary).

One advantage of expressing things in this way is that the relation of finite verbs to tense is made clearer. This version allows us to say that ***finite*** verb phrases in English are ***always*** marked for ***primary*** and ***secondary tense***. ***Non-finite*** verb phrases, on the other hand, are ***never*** marked for ***primary*** tense, but ***can*** be marked for ***secondary*** tense.

A second advantage is that it explains the relation between perfect and non-perfect forms more exactly. Perfect verb forms here are shown to be 'sub-forms' of their primary tenses, i.e. a ***present perfect*** is seen as a form of ***present tense*** and a ***past perfect*** as a form of ***past tense***. This view corresponds to the underlying language facts, as will become clear when we look at the tenses in detail later.

A third advantage is that the table shows how the English verb system is neatly arranged in ***pair relations*** (i.e. ***present/past*** + ***perfect/non-perfect***). As set out immediately below, this pattern also applies to ***aspect*** and ***voice***.

040/2.6 Aspect

The contrast between the ***simple form*** (*she runs*) and the ***progressive form*** (*she is running*) is one of ***aspect***. Unlike tense, ***aspect*** does ***not*** refer to time, but to two different views of an act or event. It tells us whether the event is seen (a) ***as a whole***, from beginning to end, or (b) as ***ongoing***, i.e. in the middle of happening and not yet complete. The general grammatical term for the (a)-meaning is ***perfective***, and for the (b)-meaning ***imperfective***. (Note, however, that the term ***perfective*** has nothing to do with the concept *perfect*, which, as we have just seen, is a tense, and not an aspect).

Aspects combine with all tenses. The contrast between them can in principle be shown in any tense, but the most suitable one in English for this purpose is the past:

Perfective **Simple form**	**Imperfective** **Progressive form**
Event ***whole***, i.e. seen from beginning to end	Event ***ongoing***, i.e. seen as in progress
(a) I ***walked*** across the bridge	(b) I ***was walking*** across the bridge

The easiest way to illustrate basic aspectual meaning is to take an event type with a goal or a limit attached to it (here *across the bridge*). The ***perfective aspect*** (= ***simple form***) expresses the fact that the goal was reached, i.e. the event was completed. The ***imperfective aspect*** (= ***progressive form***) means that at an implied or stated point of time the action was still in the course of occurrence (i.e. in progress). In our examples, therefore, (a) means *I went from one end of the bridge to the other*; (b) means that at a particular point of time (e.g. when my mobile phone rang) *I was on my way across the bridge, but had not yet reached the other end*. This basic meaning of the two aspects is discussed in detail and in various typical contexts in the next chapter on tense and aspect. For the moment we can note that all English finite verbs (and also some non-finite verbs) are marked as being ***perfective*** or ***imperfective***.

German verbs, by contrast, are not. German has no grammatical aspect. Whether perfective or imperfective in meaning, German verbs have the same form. The German equivalent of both (a) and (b) is therefore the same: *Ich ging/lief über die Brücke*. The only way of differentiating in German is to use additional terms, like adverbial expressions, for instance: *Ich lief* ***gerade*** *über die Brücke*. That is, ***imperfective*** meaning in German has to be ***lexicalized*** (= expressed through particular vocabulary items) if clarity is necessary. ⚠

As we will see later, ***imperfective*** meaning usually implies that the ***ongoing*** action is/was ***interrupted***, either by a point of time (e.g. *At ten o'clock I was walking across the bridge*), or by another action (e.g. *I was walking across the bridge when my mobile phone rang*). This is known as the ***framework situation*** (see chapter 9, **044/1.1**).

040/2.7 Tense and aspect tables

As the two aspects occur in every tense, a full ***tense-aspect overview*** must combine the tables in **040/2.5** and **040/2.6**:

Tense		Aspect	
Primary	***Secondary***	***Perfective (Simple)***	***Imperfective (Progressive)***
Present	***Non-perfect***	she runs	she is running
Present	***Perfect***	she has run	she has been running
Past	***Non-perfect***	she ran	she was running
Past	***Perfect***	she had run	she had been running

So far, then, we have three major morphological categories for the verb. Each one requires selection from ***two*** alternatives (known as a ***binary paradigm***). Every finite verb form, that is, is marked for:

- ***primary tense*** (***present/past***)
- ***secondary tense*** (***perfect/non-perfect***)
- ***aspect*** (***simple/progressive***)

The various tense and aspect forms, as well as details of conjugation, are dealt with fully in the later section on ***Tense and Aspect***.

040/2.8 Voice

Our fourth category of verb morphology, also has a ***binary paradigm***, from which all verb forms select one member: ***active*** or ***passive***:

(5) a. Mandy's remark annoyed Roberta. [***active***]
b. Roberta was annoyed by Mandy's remark. [***passive***]

The term ***voice*** means here 'manner of speaking'. Morphologically, ***voice*** shows itself in the verb form. But its main effect is on the construction and meaning of the sentence as a whole. ***Active*** and ***passive*** provide different possibilities of expressing the same content, as shown in (5). Semantically, the ***subject*** of the verb in an ***active*** sentence is the 'doer' of an action (also called the ***actor*** or ***agent***). In a ***passive*** sentence, the ***subject*** is the target, i.e. the 'sufferer/victim', or ***patient*** of an action.

The ***active voice*** is regarded traditionally as the base from which the ***passive*** is formed. The semantic role-change is reflected in the syntactic conversion: that is, the ***active direct object*** becomes the ***passive subject***, and the ***active subject*** goes into a **by**-***phrase*** (= the ***agent-adverbial***) in the ***passive*** sentence. The active verb changes too, i.e. into its ***passive form***: this consists of ***auxiliary*** **be** + ***past participle*** of the main verb:

S *P* *Od*
(6) a. Mandy's remark annoyed Roberta. [***active***]

S *P (passive)* *A*
b. Roberta was annoyed by Mandy's remark. [***passive***]

The ***passive operation*** (or ***passivization***) allows the ***active direct object*** to be placed at the beginning of the sentence, or ***fronted***. Communicatively, this changes the focus from ***agent*** to ***patient***. (5)a. and (6)a. are about 'what Mandy's remark did', whereas (5)b. and (6)b. emphasize Roberta and 'what happened to her', i.e. here how she reacted to Mandy's remark. Passive constructions are used especially when the experience of the ***patient*** is stressed, or when the ***agent*** is unknown, unimportant or impersonal, e.g. *Ten passengers were seriously injured today when their coach overturned on the M6 motorway.*

Note that ***passivization*** is only possible in English with verbs that have ***objects*** (= ***transitive verbs***, see below). Not only direct, but also ***indirect objects (Oi)*** in active sentences can become the subjects of passive sentences. These points are discussed in greater detail in the ***Passive*** section later, see chapter 11.4. For further details on ***passive verb forms***, see **040/5**.

To the three verbal markers for tense and aspect we can now add a fourth, i.e. ***voice***, and say that all finite verbs are marked for:

a. primary tense (present/past),
b. secondary tense (perfect/non-perfect),
c. aspect (simple/progressive), and
d. voice (active/passive).

040/2.9 Tense, aspect and voice with non-finite verbs

Non-finite verbs have an irregular relation to tense and aspect. None are marked for primary tense, but three have ***perfect forms***; the infinitive, additionally, has ***a progressive form***. Here an overview:

	Base Form	***Progressive***	***Perfect***	***Perfect + Progressive***
Infinitive	to run	to be running	to have run	to have been running
Gerund	running		having run	
Present Participle	running		having run (= ***Perfect Participle***)	
Past Participle	run			

As there is no primary tense and only the infinitive has a progressive, it is difficult to apply the binary system shown in the tables in **040/2.5** and **040/2.7** to non-finites. In any case, the base forms are really tenseless. They take their time orientation, as we will see later, from the tense of the next higher finite verb.

With non-finites, tense and aspect forms are therefore best regarded as simple additions to, or transforms of, the base forms.

040/2.10 Mood

This category also signals 'manner of speaking', but in a different sense from ***voice***. ***Mood*** (dt. *Modus*) tells us the general way in which an utterance is meant. Is it, for instance, a ***factual statement*** (= ***indicative*** mood), a ***question*** (= ***interrogative*** mood), a ***command***

(= ***imperative*** mood), or a ***non-factual*** (***unreal***) statement like a wish, a speculation, a hypothesis, or some other kind of imagined circumstance (= ***subjunctive*** mood)? To use a modern linguistic term, ***mood*** deals with the general type of ***speech act*** that an utterance represents.

Modern grammars do not usually treat the imperative and interrogative as mood categories, but as separate phenomena, and we will do the same here. Main discussions of ***mood*** generally focus on the distinction between 'real' and 'unreal', with special reference to the ***subjunctive*** (dt. *Konjunktiv*).

In German, ***subjunctive*** forms play a major role, particularly in the ***conditional***, and in ***indirect*** (***reported***) ***speech***. In English, however, the ***subjunctive*** is more or less 'extinct'. Apart from certain minimal uses, it survives mainly in one or two set phrases expressing wishes and exhortations. Morphologically, the ***present subjunctive*** is identical with the infinitive and the imperative; in regular verbs it is therefore distinct from the ordinary indicative only in the 3rd person singular:

(7) a. Long ***live*** the Queen!
Es lebe die Königin!
b. God ***save*** the King!
Gott behüte den König!
c. So ***be*** it!
So sei es.

A more widespread phenomenon is the use of the form ***were*** for all singular persons in ***unreal conditional clauses*** (see also chapter 11.2):

(8) a. If I were you, I would save more money.
Wenn ich du wäre/An deiner Stelle würde ich mehr sparen.
b. If John were coming to the wedding next week, he would have told us.
Wenn John nächste Woche zur Hochzeit käme, ...
c. I don't know what I'd do if Sally weren't here.
Ich weiß nicht, was ich tun würde, wenn Sally nicht hier wäre.

Were is a 'fossilized' form of the ***past subjunctive*** of *to be* (and is the only example of a past subjunctive left in the language). In the 1st person it is still standard usage, but in the 3rd person it now counts as a little elevated, and is often replaced in speech by *was*.

Occasionally, ***present subjunctive*** forms are found in ***that***-clauses following 'exhortative' verbs, such as *urge, demand, insist, require, suggest, ask*, etc. in ***indirect speech***:

(9) a. I suggest that she ***go*** to a doctor.
Ich schlage vor, dass sie zum Arzt geht.
b. They insisted that we ***stay*** the night.
Sie bestanden darauf, dass wir übernachten sollten.

Note that the ***present subjunctive*** form is used even when the introductory verb is in the ***past*** tense, as in (9)b. Though still used in elevated speech (especially in America), the subjunctive is replaced in most neutral varieties of English either by the ordinary indicative (present or past tense, depending on the tense of the introductory verb), or by the ***modal verb*** *should* (in all tenses):

(10) a. I suggest that she ***goes/should go*** to a doctor.
b. They insisted that we ***stayed/should stay*** the night.

In fact, ***modal verbs*** (***modal*** as the adjective of ***mood***) take over many of the functions of ***mood*** in present-day English: not only *should*, but also *may, might, would*, etc.:

(11) a. Would you like some more tea, dear?
Möchtest du ...?
b. May you have a long life and a happy one!
Mögest du ein langes und glückliches Leben haben!

German also uses modal verbs here, but note that they are actually in their ***subjunctive*** forms. In place of its 'missing' subjunctives, English often uses ***past tense*** forms, e.g. ***would*** (the past form of ***will***) in (11)a. or ***should*** (the past form of ***shall***) in (10). Another typical example is ***could***, the past form of ***can*** (as in *Could you help me, please?*). We will call this phenomenon the ***unreal past tense***, i.e. the past tense form when it is used as a ***subjunctive*** to convey, for example, ***conditional*** meaning. Another use of the ***unreal past*** (where German also uses subjunctives) is for ***backshift*** in ***indirect speech***: *He said he wasn't coming tomorrow* (see chapter 11.3).

Modal verbs are ***auxiliary verbs*** (see next section).

040/2.11 Auxiliary verbs

Auxiliaries (dt. ***Hilfsverben***) cannot stand alone, without a ***main*** verb. Unlike German, English does not allow constructions like **I can French*. A lexical verb must always follow (*I can speak French*). ⚠

On the other hand, main verbs ***need*** auxiliaries. The term ***auxiliary*** means 'helping verb', and main verbs need this help in important grammatical ways: firstly, for ***negation***, and secondly, for ***inversion*** (the turnaround of subject and verb, mainly for questions):

(12) a. Dave can***not*** (ca***n't***) swim.
b. ***Could*** you ***help*** me, please?

All auxiliaries and ***only*** auxiliaries have this ***operator function***. Main verbs cannot take on the operator function alone. If there is ***no*** auxiliary in a particular verb phrase, then a ***special operator auxiliary*** (***do***) must be introduced for negation or inversion to take place:

(13) a. He came home yesterday. → He ***did not*** come home yesterday.

b. She won the race. → ***Did*** she ***win*** the race?

A third point is that when a verb phrase contains auxiliaries, they take on the marking for ***concord*** and ***tense***, and ***not*** the main verb (which then occurs in a ***non-finite*** form) e.g. *Bertha* ***is*** *washing her hair* (***is*** = 3rd pers. sg. present tense).

Auxiliaries can be divided into two general categories according to function: (a) those needed for grammatical operations alone (***grammatical auxiliaries***), and (b) those also with individual semantic content (***modal auxiliaries***).

Grammatical auxiliaries are:

- ***be***, used to form the ***passive*** (*The house was sold for £200,000*), and the ***progressive*** (*Sally is painting the window-frames*);
- ***have***, used to form the ***perfect*** (*She has just finished*);
- ***do***, used as a ***special operator*** for ***inversion*** and ***negatives*** when the verb phrase contains no other auxiliary for the ***operator function*** (*Does Hermione like Indian food?; They don't live in Scotland any more*). A further ***special operator*** case is the role of ***do*** as an ***auxiliary pro-form*** (e.g. *Fred works harder than you do*, see **041/2.7** below). A slightly different function is that of an ***emphasizer***: *We did agree on certain conditions, I think.*

Except for this last use of emphatic ***do***, grammatical auxiliaries perform purely grammatical operations (morphological in the case of ***be*** and ***have***, syntactic and morphological with ***do***). That is, they add no lexical content to the verb phrase.

It should be noted, however, that ***be***, ***have***, and ***do*** can also be main lexical verbs, as in: *I am a teacher; Brenda has three children; We are doing a difficult exercise.* They consequently have the normal range of verb morphology (e.g. tenses, aspects and non-finite forms). Furthermore, they retain these forms as auxiliaries, e.g. *I have* ***been*** *thinking; He must* ***have*** *left; The car* ***is being*** *repaired.* This is what allows particularly ***have*** and ***be*** to slip out of the operator role (always the function of the first auxiliary), and become second or third auxiliaries. When they do this, they must appear in a non-finite form (i.e. infinitive or participle). Without this capability, forms such as passive or perfect progressive would not be possible.

Modal auxiliaries are: ***can***, ***may***, ***shall***, ***will***, ***must***, ***could***, ***should***, ***would***, ***might***, ***ought to***, and one or two others that are discussed fully in chapter 12. They have specific individual meanings that must be carefully distinguished. These meanings are typically associated with ***mood*** and for that reason are called ***modal***. They involve mainly ***obligation***, ***necessity***, ***speculation*** and ***volition*** (= wishing, hoping and wanting). That is, they express ***speech acts*** in the fields of personal attitudes and feelings, personal relations with others, and imagined situations.

Modal auxiliaries have only a ***limited range*** of morphological characteristics: they are the same in all persons, and have no non-finite, perfect or aspect forms. They are therefore always finite (despite zero inflection in all persons) and must always come in ***first position*** in the verb phrase, i.e. before any other auxiliaries.

Syntax: the verb in the sentence 041

It is the verb, as ***predicator***, that determines sentence patterns most strongly. It does this through its ***complementation***, i.e. the parts of the sentence dependent upon the verb, such as objects, subject or object complements, and adverbials. Also, morphological or positional changes in the verb mark changes in sentence-type, e.g. from ***declarative*** (statement) to ***interrogative*** (question) or ***imperative*** (command).

041/1 The verb and its complementation

Verbs ***with objects*** are known as ***transitive*** verbs, those ***without objects*** as ***intransitive*** verbs. Many verbs can only be one or the other. Others can be used ***either*** transitively ***or*** intransitively. For instance, *be* can never be transitive and *make* never intransitive; *cook*, on the other hand, can be either:

(14) a. Turner was a famous painter. [*a famous painter* = ***subject complement, Cs***]
b. Fred makes furniture. [*furniture* = ***direct object, Od***]
c. Father is cooking the lunch. [*the lunch* = ***direct object, Od***]
d. Father is cooking.

The verbs in (14)b. and c. both have ***direct objects***, and are therefore ***transitive***. With *cook* in c., however, we can also leave the object out, and then get (14)d. Here, then, *cook* is ***intransitive***. This is easy to see, as the verb now has no complementation at all. Many verbs do have complementation, however, and are nevertheless intransitive. This is the case with *be* in (14)a. *Be* must always have complementation, i.e. we cannot simply say **Turner was*. Here, complementation consists of a ***subject complement (Cs)***, but an ***adverbial (A)*** after *be* is also possible (*John is at work*). A direct object, however, is not. *Be* is therefore always ***intransitive***. The verb *make*, in (14)b. must likewise always have complementation. But in this case it consists of a ***direct object (Od)***. *Make* is therefore always ***transitive***.

To describe complementation types more carefully, we distinguish between three kinds of ***transitive*** verbs: ***monotransitive***, ***ditransitive***, ***complex transitive***. And two kinds of ***intransitive*** verbs (***complemented*** and ***uncomplemented***).

041/1.1 Monotransitive verbs

These take a ***direct object (Od)***:

	S	***P***	***Od***
(15)	Sharon	wrote	a letter.

041/1.2 Ditransitive verbs

As the name ('*di*-transitive') implies, these take two objects, in the order ***indirect object (Oi)*** + ***direct object (Od)***. They can also be expressed ***monotransitively*** by converting the ***Oi*** into the complement of a ***prepositional phrase*** functioning as ***A*** and following the ***Od***:

		S	***P***	***Oi***	***Od***
(16)	a.	Sharon	wrote	Jane	a letter.
		S	***P***	***Od***	***A***
	b.	Sharon	wrote	a letter	to Jane.

041/1.3 Complex transitive verbs

These also have two elements of complementation: a ***direct object (Od)*** + an ***object complement (Co)***:

	S	***P***	***Od***	***Co***
(17)	Sharon	called	Jane	a fool.

041/1.4 Intransitive verbs

These can be ***uncomplemented*** (= without any complementation), or ***complemented***. If ***complemented***, they are followed by a ***subject complement (Cs)***, or an ***adverbial (A)***:

		S	***P***		
(18)	a.	Sharon	was writing.		[*uncomplemented*]
		S	***P***	***Cs***	
	b.	Sharon	looked	happy.	[*complemented*]
		S	***P***	***A***	
	c.	Ally	lives	in Cornwall.	[*complemented*]

041/1.5 Catenatives and complementation by non-finite clauses

Catenatives, or 'linking verbs' are ***main*** verbs like *want, like, remember*, and many others, which are complemented by ***non-finite*** clauses:

(19) a. Maria wants to apply for another job.
b. Fraser does not remember leaving the pub.
c. We stopped to buy groceries.
d. Bobby hates swimming.

We must emphasize again that ***catenatives*** are ***main*** verbs, ***not*** auxiliaries. This means that the non-finite verbs following them are ***separate*** verb-phrases, and therefore ***separate predicators***. That is, they introduce ***separate clauses***: these are ***subordinate clauses*** just like any finite subordinate clause:

S P Od P Od
(20) a. Maria wants [to get another job].
S P Od P Od
b. Fraser does not remember [leaving the pub].
S P A P Od
c. We stopped [to buy groceries].
S P Od P
d. Bobby hates [swimming].

In each case here, the ***matrix verb*** is a ***catenative***, i.e. followed by a non-finite verb as a separate predicator, and therefore a separate clause, as we have said. Taking (20)a. as an example, let us contrast this pattern with that of an auxiliary:

S P Od
(21) a. Maria will get another job.
S P Od P Od
b. Maria wants [to get another job].

(21)a. gives us the ***auxiliary*** pattern. Here ***will*** is a modal auxiliary: ***will get*** is therefore one verb phrase and one predicator, and there is no subordinate clause. In (21)b., as in (20), we have the case of the ***catenative***, i.e. a ***main*** verb with a non-finite following as a separate predicator. Clause reduction gives a simple test of this. For (21)b. we can say *Maria wants* ***this***. For (21)a., however, we cannot say **Maria will this*, which shows that ***will*** cannot stand alone as a main verb, and is therefore an ***auxiliary***.

For more on non-finite clauses, see chapters 13 and 14.

041/1.6 A note on passives

All the verb types just discussed (i.e. the various kinds of transitive verbs, and the catenatives) have particular relations to the passive voice, which has special effects on sentence patterns in each case. These are dealt with in detail in the later section on the ***passive***.

041/2 The verb and basic sentence operations

041/2.1 Negation

The main instrument of negation is the word ***not***, known as the ***negative particle***. In addition, negation of ***finite verbs*** requires an ***auxiliary*** as an ***operator***. The negative particle is placed inside the verb phrase, ***after*** the ***operator***: *The dog has* ***not*** *been well*. If there are several auxiliaries, the ***first*** is the ***operator***; this is the one followed by the particle ***not***: *You should* ***not*** *have come back*. If there is ***no*** auxiliary in the equivalent positive sentence, ***do*** is introduced as a ***special operator***:

Positive ***Negative***
(22) Bob likes carrots. → Bob does not like carrots.

This is generally called **do-*support*** (dt. *To-Do-Umschreibung*). In speech, ***not*** is normally unstressed, and is then shortened to a ***weak form***, pronounced [nt]. In less formal writing this is also shown in the spelling (***n't***), and the weak form is attached to the operator as an ending (called an ***enclitic***):

(23) Bob doesn't like carrots. [bɒb dʌznt laɪk kærəts]

Non-finite verbs are negated simply by placing the negative particle ***before*** them:

(24) a. To be or not to be.
b. Thank you for not smoking.
c. Not having held a post like this before, she has a few things to learn about not letting people take advantage of her.
d. Terry hates not being able to play football.

There are several special negative forms:

- ***can*** is negated as ***cannot/can't***;
- the weak form negation of ***will*** is ***won't***;
- the weak form negation has an ***alternative*** form: instead of shortening the negative particle, we can ***shorten the operator***, and leave the ***particle full***, e.g. instead of *He isn't*, ***He's not***, instead of *They haven't*, ***They've not***, etc. More information on this is given under **041/2.3**.
- the weak form negation of ***I am*** is ***I'm not***, i.e. there is no enclitic form **I amn't*. In questions, however, the form ***aren't*** is used: *Aren't I getting any soup, then?* (See also **041/2.4** below for negated questions).
  after ***inversion*** (e.g. in ***negated questions***) ***not*** follows the subject if it is not enclitic: *Is John not at home?* (*Isn't John at home?*). With inversion after ***adverbs*** of restriction (see chapter 5, **033/5.7**), the enclitic version is not possible: *Only in that case are you not obliged to call the police* (not **Only in that case aren't you obliged ...*).

Note that even as a main verb, ***be*** never takes **do-*support***: *Mr. Attersley isn't in the office today* (not **Mr. Attersley doesn't be in the office today.*). The main verb ***have*** was used in the same way: *I haven't enough money*. However, direct negation of ***have*** is now rare, and **do-*support*** is preferred: *I don't have enough money*.

A popular general alternative for ***have*** in informal and particularly British English is the form ***have got***. As ***have*** here is an auxiliary, negation is always direct: *I haven't got enough money*.

041/2.2 Negation focus

This concerns the question of what part of the sentence is actually being negated. Negation of the verb generally negates its complementation as well. It may be, however, that negation is intended semantically for just one part of the complementation. For instance, (25)a. may mean (25)b. or c. or d.:

(25) a. Sam didn't play darts on Tuesday night in the pub.
b. Sam played billiards.
c. Sam played darts on Wednesday night.
d. Sam played darts on Tuesday night at Ron's house.

Whatever part of the complementation the speaker intends to negate semantically, negation must ***always be attached to the verb***. We cannot say for (25)b. **Sam played not darts on Tuesday night in the pub*, or for (25)c. **Sam played darts not on Tuesday night ...*, or for (25)d. **Sam played darts on Tuesday night not in the pub*. There is actually no possibility of differentiating in the ordinary negated sentence. The only way to do this would be to use the positive sentence and add a focused ***not*** afterwards, e.g. *Sam played billiards, not darts, on Tuesday in the pub*.

It is only the negative particle which is syntactically bound to the verb in this way. But negation can also be carried out ***lexically***, e.g. by quantifiers, adverbs, and pronouns, sometimes in combination. These are generally much more ***focused*** in their reference:

(26) a. Jamie spoke to ***nobody*** at the party, ***scarcely*** drank ***anything*** and touched ***no*** food.
b. He ***never*** likes parties, and ***rarely*** accepts an invitation to ***one***.

Note that in these cases grammatical negation is ruled out (*... *didn't speak to nobody, didn't scarcely drink anything*).

In complex sentences, negation focus is usually confined to the clause where the negation occurs. This is why, for instance, the two sentences of the sentence pair in (27)a. and b., and (27)c. and d. respectively do ***not*** mean the same:

(27) a. Deidre remembered not returning the book.
b. Deidre did not remember returning the book.
c. Jamie was happy when he didn't see Evelyn at the party.
d. Jamie wasn't happy when he saw Evelyn at the party.

However, there are sentences, usually depending on lexical factors, where a negative in one clause may apply to the other. This is what causes the ambiguity in the following. (28)a. can be interpreted as (28)b. or (28)c.:

(28) a. Jamie didn't walk home because he was drunk.
b. It wasn't because he was drunk that Jamie walked home.
c. Because he was drunk, Jamie didn't walk home.

If a. means b., the matrix negative does not negate the matrix verb, but actually the relation given (*for this reason*) between the two clauses. If a. means c., however, the negative focus is confined to the clause with the negated verb (i.e. the matrix clause).

There are other cases where negation focus remains the same, no matter which clause is negated:

(29) a. Sue did not believe that Roy would turn up on time.
b. Sue believed that Roy would not turn up on time.
c. She didn't want her parents to be present at the graduation ceremony.
d. She wanted her parents not to be present at the graduation ceremony.

In fact, with certain kinds of lexical items, notably verbs of 'thinking' and 'wanting', as here, matrix negation is preferred even if the semantic negation focus is on the subordinate verb phrase. This phenomenon is sometimes called ***transferred negation***.

'Communication' verbs, on the other hand, conform to what we would normally expect. As in (27), that is, negation focus is where the negation actually is. In the following a. contrasts with b., and c. with d.:

(30) a. They told us not to leave the city.
b. They didn't tell us to leave the city.
c. Our teacher did not promise to come to the party.
d. Our teacher promised not to come to the party.

Lexical factors play a major role here.

Finally, there is an important point to note on the negation of ***modal auxiliaries***. Following the ***operator principle*** with grammatical auxiliaries, we expect the attached negative particle quite naturally to negate the ***whole*** verb phrase. However, this is not so with ***modals***. Here the verb phrase is divided: either the modal auxiliary itself is negated (***modal negation focus***); or the main verb is negated (***main verb negation focus***). This depends on the particular modal verb. ***Can***, ***need*** and ***may***, for instance, have ***modal negation focus***, i.e. it is here the modal meaning that is negated. With ***should*** and ***must*** there is ***main verb negation focus***:

(31) a. You cannot/may not play in the street today.
(= no permission, ***modal negation***)
b. We need not go shopping today.
(= no obligation/necessity, ***modal negation***)
c. We shouldn't/mustn't disturb the children.
(= obligation to avoid an act, ***main verb negation***)

This 'division of negation' is caused by the fact that modals have lexical meanings of their own. Verb phrases with modals therefore contain two lexical meanings: that of the modal and that of the main verb. Logically, they cannot both be negated at the same time, as this would lead to a contradiction. In (31)c., for example, *must not disturb*, with ***main verb negation***, means 'there is an obligation', i.e. here not to disturb the children, in German *dürfen nicht* (*die Kinder stören*). If it also had modal negation, *must not disturb* would mean, on the other hand, 'there is ***no obligation***' (i.e. in German *müssen nicht stören*). The two meanings would therefore contradict one another.

041/2.3 Weak forms

First and foremost, ***weak forms*** are a pronunciation phenomenon. Certain vowels (usually short, open and/or rounded ones) in various one-syllable function words, such as *of, that, but, and, a,* etc., are pronounced as a *schwa* [ə] when the words are unstressed, e.g. *a cup of tea* [ə kʌp əv ti:] *and a biscuit* [ənd ə bɪskɪt]. This also applies to auxiliaries like *can* [kæn → kən], *must* [mʌst → məst], *should* [ʃʊd → ʃəd], etc. The person forms of the auxiliaries ***be*** and ***have***, and ***will/would*** are reduced mainly to consonants. These ***weak forms*** are also shown in the spelling as ***enclitics***, and are used in informal types of writing such as letters:

(32)	am	→ 'm	(I am	→ I'm)
	are	→ 're	(you are	→ you're)
	is	→ 's	(she is	→ she's)
	have	→ 've	(I have	→ I've)
	has	→ 's	(she has	→ she's)
	had	→ 'd	(I had	→ I'd)
	will	→ 'll	(I will	→ I'll)

We first came across the phenomenon of ***weak forms*** in section **041/2.1** above on negation. Here the weak form introduced was the ***enclitic*** negative particle ***n't***, as in *He isn't coming*. Note in this case, however, that the auxiliary remains in its full form, i.e. it is the ***particle*** that is shortened. Negation is also possible the other way round, i.e. ***shortened auxiliary + full particle***. The two types are free alternatives (except in the case of *I'm not*, which is the only possibility):

Full auxiliary + shortened particle	***Shortened auxiliary + full particle***
–	I'm not
you aren't	you're not
she isn't	she's not
I haven't	I've not
she hasn't	she's not
I hadn't	I'd not
I won't	I'll not
I wouldn't	I'd not (rare)

Personal pronouns are given just as examples. They represent other persons with the same forms. Generally speaking, the full particle forms on the right are preferred when the particle is emphasized and the speaker wishes to avoid misunderstandings (shortened particles can be 'swallowed' easily in quick speech). The full particle is most common with the forms of ***be*** (and is the only possibility in the first person). It is least common with ***will/would***.

Two final points: firstly, auxiliary weak forms are possible not just with pronouns, but also with full nouns: *These plates've not been washed properly; Mike's a mechanic.* Secondly, auxiliary weak forms cannot be used in questions, i.e. *Have you finished?* (but not * *'Ve you finished?*). ***Enclitic negatives***, however, are possible (*Haven't you finished?*). See also next two sections.

041/2.4 The interrogative

Although none other than Shakespeare's Cleopatra could ask her noble lover *How goes it with my brave Mark Antony?*, such a question is not grammatical in modern English. Nowadays, ***inversion*** is possible ***only*** with ***auxiliary verbs*** (and ***not*** with main verbs). As with negation, **do**-***support*** is necessary if the verb phrase contains no auxiliary. Then ***inversion*** can take place, and the ***declarative*** sentence (= the statement) becomes an ***interrogative*** one (= a question):

	Declarative		*Interrogative*
(33)	a. Carol is coming with us. (***auxiliary*** present)	→	Is Carol coming with us?
	b. The Andersons moved to Detroit. (***no auxiliary*** present)	→	Did the Andersons move to Detroit? (**do**-***support*** necessary)

In functional sentence analysis we should then mark the same predicator twice, as it is 'interrupted' by the subject:

	P	***S***	***P***	***A***
(34)	a. ***Is***	Carol	***coming***	with us?
	P	***S***	***P***	***A***
	b. ***Did***	the Andersons	***move***	to Detroit?

Note that as with negation, main verb ***be*** never takes **do**-***support***: *Are the Andersons in Detroit now?* (not **Do the Andersons be ...?*). With ***have***, on the other hand, **do**-***support*** is now the norm: *Do they have their own house?* (rather than *Have they their own house?*, which is still possible, but rare). Again, with the informal alternative ***have got***, ***have*** is an auxiliary and can undergo inversion just like any other: *Have they got their own house?*

The questions discussed here are ***open*** **yes-no-*questions***. If answered by ***yes***, the equivalent declarative sentence (statement) is affirmed, i.e. said to be true. If answered by ***no***, it is denied, i.e. said to be untrue. Thus the answer ***Yes*** to (34)a. says that 'Carol is coming', and the answer ***No*** that she is ***not*** coming. This may seem obvious, but it is an important basis for discussing other question types below.

041/2.5 The negative interrogative

For this, enclitic ***n't*** is simply added to the operator of the positive question:

	Positive interrogative		*Negative Interrogative*
(35)	a. ***Is*** Carol coming with us?	→	***Isn't*** Carol coming with us?
	b. ***Did*** the Andersons move to Detroit?	→	***Didn't*** the Andersons move to Detroit?
	c. ***Do*** you have to work on Saturday?	→	***Don't*** you have to work on Saturday?

The full form ***not*** is less common and more formal. When used, it follows the subject: ***Is*** *Carol* ***not*** *coming with us?*; ***Did*** *the Andersons* ***not*** *move to Detroit?*; ***Do*** *you* ***not*** *have to work on Saturday?* (See also under **041/2.1**). Note, as already pointed out, that the ***enclitic negative interrogative*** of ***be*** in the 1st person singular is ***Aren't I?*** The full form is ***Am I not?***

Negative interrogatives are ***pro-positive confirmation questions***. Here the speaker thinks that the equivalent ***positive*** declarative sentence is/could be true, but is uncertain and wants it confirmed. For instance, *Isn't Carol coming with us?* may mean 'I believed she was coming, but now I have doubts'. The answer ***Yes*** confirms the questioner's belief. ***No*** confirms the opposite (the equivalent ***negative*** declarative sentence). Answers are normally complemented by ***response tags*** for emphasis (*Yes, she is*/*No, she isn't*, see below under **041/2.7**).

041/2.6 wh-questions

These are quite different from the previous two question types. Firstly, they are not answered by *yes* or *no*. Secondly, they do not begin with the verb, but with a ***wh***-word. ***Wh***-words are ***interrogative pronouns*** (*who, what*), ***interrogative adverbs*** (*when, where, why, how*), and ***interrogative determiners*** (*which, whose*). They ***focus*** the question on a particular part of the sentence, most usually a functional element such as subject, object, adverbial or predicate:

	Od	***P***	***S***	***P***	
(36) a.	***What***	are	you	writing?	
	A	***P***	***S***	***P***	***A***
b.	***When***	did	the Andersons	move	to Detroit?

In other words, the question focuses on what would be the ***same*** functional element in the equivalent ***declarative*** sentence:

	S	***P***	***Od***	
(37) a.	I	am writing	***a treatise on Viking battleships.***	
	S	***P***	***A***	***A***
b.	The Andersons	moved	to Detroit	***last month.***

After the ***wh***-word, inversion takes place just as in the other question types. But there is one exception. When the ***wh***-word refers to the ***subject***, there is ***no inversion***, and therefore ***no do****-support* with present or past simple forms:

	S	***P***	***Od***	
(38) a.	Who	stole	my dog?	(not **Who did steal my dog?*)
	S	***P***	***Od***	
b.	What	is causing	that noise in the car engine?	

Another case for ***no* do-*support*** is reference to the ***subject complement (Cs)*** after ***to be***. However, this is an exception. With other verbs, subject complement reference does require **do-*support***:

		Cs	P	S	P
(39)	a.	Who	is	she?	
	b.	What	did	Roger	become?

It may not be clear at first sight that the interrogative pronoun ***who*** in (39)a. functions as ***subject complement***. It becomes obvious, however, when we turn the question into a statement. We then get, e.g. *She is my sister*, where *my sister* can only be ***subject complement***, and *she* is clearly ***subject***. It is important to recognize that ***inversion*** has taken place here, but without **do-*support***, as the verb ***to be*** is its own operator and requires no auxiliary. In (39)b., in contrast, **do-*support*** is necessary. We cannot say here **What became Roger?*

Negation in **wh-*questions*** follows the ordinary statement pattern:

(40) a. Why haven't you done your homework?
b. Who won't be at the meeting tomorrow?

As with other question types, the ***full*** negative particle must ***follow*** the subject when there is inversion: *Why have you not done your homework?*

A third way in which **wh-*questions*** differ from the other types is that they contain certain ***presuppositions***, i.e. they assume automatically that certain things are true. For instance, (41)a. assumes that (41)b. is true, and (41)c. assumes that (41)d. is true:

(41) a. Why haven't you done your homework?
b. You haven't done your homework.
c. Who stole my dog?
d. Somebody stole my dog.

Among other things, this can be an important pragmatic point in arguments. Accusations made via ***wh***-questions tend to make confrontation sharper. This is because the criticism is not direct. For instance, a remark like *Why can't you just act like a normal adult human being?* places the accusation *You don't act like a normal human being* beyond discussion. The ***wh***-question simply makes this into a fact which is then difficult for the other person to deny.

041/2.7 Auxiliary pro-forms

We have already met ***auxiliary pro-forms*** in comparative clauses (see chapter 4). They were also mentioned in connection with *neither/nor* and *so* in chapter 5, **033/6.8**. An ***auxiliary pro-form*** functions like a 'verb pronoun' and is used to avoid repetition of a full verb which occurs in an immediately preceding clause. It is a form of ***ellipsis***: in the ***pro-form clause***, the full verb is omitted, leaving the auxiliary to stand alone. If there is no auxiliary in the preceding verb phrase, **do-*support*** is necessary, as in questions:

(42) a. Rosie can speak French, but her daughter can't.
b. I liked it and my husband did too.
c. We're enjoying the party and so is everyone else here.

The ***pro-form clause*** may be used by another speaker as a reaction to confirm or disagree with what has just been said:

(43) a. "I'm enjoying this food." "So am I."
b. "My wife loves hiking in the hills." "Mine doesn't."
c. "The weather has been lovely!" "It certainly has."

Pro-form clauses used in this way are called ***response tags***. They are particularly common in answer to questions, reinforcing ***yes*** or ***no***. The subject is nearly always a personal pronoun, unless there is a contrast between two or more separate subjects, as in (44)d.:

(44) a. "Are you leaving already?" "Yes, I am."
b. "Does Mike read much?" "Yes, he does."
c. "Can you come on Wednesday evening?" "No, I can't, unfortunately."
d. "Do Chris and Sue like the seaside?" "Well, Chris does, but Sue doesn't."

041/2.8 Question tags

Pro-form clauses also function as reactions to a preceding statement, showing attention, interest, sympathy, or surprise. In this case, they have the form of a question, and are called ***question tags***. The subject is always a pronoun:

(45) a. "Barbara doesn't like cheese, you know." "Doesn't she?"
(dt. ... „(Ach) nee/(Ach) so/Wirklich?")
b. "No, but she has always eaten yoghurt." "Has she?"
(dt. ... „Ja?/So/Tatsächlich?")
c. "I can't find my glasses." "Can't you? Oh dear!"
(dt. ... „Ach nee!/Wirklich nicht?")

These are what we call ***response question tags***. Their meaning, roughly, is *Oh!* or *Really?*

The ***question tag*** has a more widespread use as a ***semi-interrogative***. In this function, it is 'tacked on' to statements, and shows the speaker's desire for ***confirmation***:

(46) a. Barbara likes cheese, ***doesn't she***?
b. You don't work on Saturdays, ***do you***?

Semi-interrogative question tags mean ... *is it not so?* German equivalents are *nicht/nicht wahr?* and *oder?* Unlike these, though, English ***question tags*** are verbal, and must fit the verb form in the statement clause grammatically.

That is, like any other ***auxiliary pro-form***, they use the ***same auxiliary*** as in the preceding verb phrase, or, if there isn't one, **do-*support***.

An important additional point is the ***positive-negative*** or ***negative-positive*** contrast with the statement clause.

Positive verb ***Negative verb***
(47) a. You***'ll*** be here on time tomorrow, ***won't you***?
Negative verb ***Positive verb***
b. You won't be late, ***will you***?

Question tags of this type are typically spoken with a ***falling tone*** on the auxiliary. This expresses fairly high certainty that the statement clause will be confirmed. A ***rising tone*** is more marked, less frequent and implies less certainty. Other speech intentions may also be involved, such as warning, hope, surprise, request, etc.:

\
(48) a. Barbara likes cheese, ***doesn't she***? [belief that this is probably true]
/
b. Barbara likes cheese, ***doesn't she***? [uncertainty whether an assumption made is actually true]
\
c. You won't be late, ***will you***? [certain of co-operation, but friendly reminder]
/
d. You won't be late, ***will you***? ["Is there a danger of this? I hope not!"]
/
e. You couldn't lend me your car, ***could you***? [request for a favour]

There is also a third pattern, ***positive-positive***, spoken usually with a rising tone:

/
(49) Barbara likes cheese, ***does she***?

The speaker here is either drawing a ***conclusion***, or expressing ***surprise*** about new information or knowledge (dt. *Barbara mag Käse also*). Exclamation expressions like *oh!*, or adverbs such as *so* and *then* often occur in this context.

041/2.9 The imperative

This is the collective name for the ***command*** forms; the imperative is properly speaking a ***mood,*** as was pointed out above. In the modern language, it relates to three grammatical persons: 2nd persons singular and plural and 1st person plural. The major form is the one for the 2nd person, given in (50). This presents no difficulty morphologically: it is the same in singular and plural, and is identical with the ordinary finite 2nd person forms, as also with the infinitive base (i.e. without *to*):

(50) a. Come in!
b. Write this down.
c. Fry the onions in a little margarine.
d. Turn left at the traffic-lights.

Officially, the 2nd person imperative has no overt subject. Nevertheless, in informal language subject pronouns are frequently added as a kind of ***vocative emphasis***:

(51) a. Donald, ***you*** peel the potatoes and Sheila, ***you*** boil the water.
b. ***You*** keep quiet, Richard, and listen carefully.

More formally, emphasis is given by adding *do*:

(52) a. ***Do*** keep quiet! [showing insistence, and perhaps also frustration]
b. ***Do*** take a seat! [showing insistence and a certain generosity in the invitation]

Negative commands are formed with ***don't*** (or more formally, **do not**):

(53) a. ***Do not*** park in front of these gates!
b. ***Don't*** forget my letter!

Commands tend to affect ***actions*** rather than states, as states are not usually under the control of an agent. It is difficult logically to tell someone to 'know' or 'want' something, for example, or to 'become rich' or 'be embarrassed'. Nevertheless, there are states, and in particular ***changes of state***, that can imply action, or some other kind of voluntary control. These can plausibly be made the focus of a command, e.g. *Get changed* (dt. *Zieht euch um*), *Be quiet!* (dt. *Seid ruhig!*), *Have more respect!* (dt. *Zeige mehr Respekt!*).

Be is often found in the imperative when action or ***behaviour*** are involved. In negative commands there is often the sense of a warning about certain feelings or moods that are likely to arise:

(54) a. Be careful! Be prepared for the worst! Be on your guard!
b. ***Don't be*** too optimistic about his offer! ***Do not be*** surprised if he withdraws it tomorrow.
c. ***Don't be*** intimidated by his reputation (i.e. ***resist*** that feeling).

Passives, as in (54)c., are generally rare with the imperative, and progressives too, but they can occur: *Be waiting with the car when I come out of the station*.

There is no special English form for the 1st person plural imperative, as in German: *Gehen wir jetzt! Trinken wir was! Schwimmen wir um die Insel!* This is expressed in English by the 2nd person imperative of the verb ***let***, followed by ***us*** and the ***infinitive base***. German, of course, has a similar alternative form with *lassen*:

(55) a. Let us go! (Let's go!) [Lasst uns gehen!]
b. Let's have a drink. [Lasst uns was trinken!]
c. Let's swim round the island. [Lasst uns eine Runde um die Insel schwimmen!]

The verb ***let***, like German *lassen*, is also used in other persons for imperative-type offers and also for more formal exhortations for which German traditionally uses the subjunctive:

(56) a. Let me just give you a hand with that heavy case.
b. Let Ray help you with the shopping.
c. Don't let us disturb you! [Lassen Sie sich nicht von uns stören!]
d. Let there be light! [Es werde Licht!]

And finally, words of encouragement (especially for learning English grammar), from the Gospel of St. John: *Let not your heart be troubled, neither let it be afraid* (*Euer Herz erschrecke nicht und fürchte sich nicht*, Johannes 14, 27).

It is sometimes said that the 'bare' imperative is not heard a lot in English. This is not true. It is used constantly for instructions, directions, invitations, for giving encouragement (*Keep going! Don't give up!*), warnings, etc. What is true, however, is that imperative use is attached to certain contexts, where the role of 'command-giver' is an accepted part of the particular social situation: that is, when an instruction situation is naturally given or has been established (e.g. in telling people how to do certain things, or giving directions in a list).

However, the imperative is usually avoided when people are asked to do single, individual things. The general, neutrally polite way of doing this is to use a ***request*** (*Could you …, Would you …*, etc., see chapter 12). Bare commands can be softened a little by using ***question tags*** (*will you, could you, would you*): *Be a little quieter, Alex, will you?*; *Pass the butter, please, Gina, could you?*

The question tag for the 1st person plural is *shall we*: *Let's go shopping, shall we?*

041/3 Verbal action types (modes of occurrence)

Modes of occurrence are lexical categories which characterize certain kinds of verbal reference, e.g. to the beginning, middle or end of the action, to processes that are complete or incomplete, to continuous or repeated activities, to states, and so on. These are semantic features, but they are affected by grammar, in particular by aspect, and sometimes by tense. Important for us here are four main ***modes of occurrence***:

041/3.1 Telic events

These are ***goal-directed*** processes, such as *sing a song, read the book, cook a meal, walk to the beach, paint the boat, do the crossword puzzle*, etc. Actions like these have an ***end-point***, a conclusion, generally marked by some kind of verb complementation, e.g. an object or an adverbial. This allows us to think of them as either ***complete*** or ***incomplete***, which is an important effect when they combine with ***aspect***: *Laila painted the boat* means that she ***finished*** the task, but *Laila was painting the boat* tells us that at a particular point of time she was in the middle of the activity, and that at that time she ***had not yet finished***. Or, to take another example: *We were crossing the field when we saw a bull in the far corner, and turned back* means that we did not complete the action *cross the field*. It would not make sense to use the simple form here: **We crossed the field when we saw ...*

The typical ***question*** with ***telic events*** is *How long did it take to ...* (*read the book/do the crossword puzzle*, etc.)?

041/3.2 Non-telic events

These are the ***opposite*** of telic events, i.e. they are ***not limited*** in any way by a given end-point.

We can convert some of the telic events above into ***non-telic*** events by taking away the direct object (*sing a song* → *sing*; *cook a meal* → *cook*). Another way is to change the direct object into an ***unlimited quantity***, e.g. by putting it in the plural: *sing a song* → *sing songs*. Similarly, if we change *walk to the beach* into just *walk*, we get a ***non-telic event***. As there is no goal or limit, a ***non-telic event*** cannot be thought of as 'complete' or 'incomplete'. This means that *John was singing* implies also *John sang*. With the telic version this is not so, i.e. *John was singing a song* does not imply *John sang a song*, just as *We were crossing the field* does not imply *We crossed the field*.

The typical ***question*** with ***non-telic events*** is *For how long did John ...* (*sing/cook/walk*, etc.)?

041/3.3 Point-telic events

These are ***momentary*** events, like *drop, kick, arrive, knock, die*, etc. They represent the ***crossing of a borderline***, and finish in the moment that they begin. Use of the simple form here means that the border is crossed, i.e. the 'goal' or end-point is reached, just as with the ordinary telic events: *The train arrived*.

The progressive can have either of two different effects, depending on verb and context. With *arrive*, for example, ***the mode of occurrence*** changes from point-telic to ***telic***, e.g. *The train was arriving* (= process leading to an end point, but not complete). With verbs like *knock* and *drop*, the change is from point-telic to ***non-telic*** with the idea of ***repetition***, e.g. *Someone was knocking at the door* (= repeatedly, an unspecified number of times).

The typical ***question*** with ***point-telic events*** is *When did John ...* (*arrive/drop the cup*, etc.)?

041/3.4 States

A ***state*** is a ***condition***. It is something that ***is***, and not something that is done, like an event or an action. Typical state verbs are those like *love, hate* and *want*, referring to ***feelings***, *know, believe* and *understand*, referring to conditions of ***mind***, *have* and *own*, referring to ***possession***, and *be* and *live*, referring to ***existence***, ***presence***, and ***relation***. In grammar, these kinds of verbs are called ***stative verbs***, a term we will meet a lot in the next chapter on tense and aspect. The verb *do* (as in *What did X do next?*) ***cannot*** generally be applied to states. The progressive form (*What are you doing?*) is particularly incompatible with states, as it refers to ***processes***, i.e. acts in the course of happening.

042 Forms of verbs

042/1 Verb formation
042/2 Particle verbs
042/3 Formation of non-finite verbs
042/4 Forming progressive and perfect
042/5 Forming the passive

In this section we deal with various points of form not yet mentioned: ***formation*** of verbs, among other things through ***derivation***, and the morphology of tense.

042/1 Verb formation

Like other word-classes, verbs in English have no special or 'universal' form (in contrast to those in German and many other languages, where verbs always have certain endings). But there are many common ***affixes***, often connected with specific kinds of meaning, or with Latin roots. Here a selection:

042/1.1 Suffixes

- *-ate* (= 'affect/operate on'): *complicate, duplicate, regulate, separate, violate*. With mixed meanings: *generate, operate, associate,* etc. Pronunciation distinguishes between verbs [eɪt] and adjectives/nouns [ət], e.g. *to duplicate* [dju:plɪkeɪt], *a duplicate* [dju:plɪkət].
- *-ect* (= 'touch/influence'): *affect, connect, detect, direct, elect, protect, select*. Pronunciation: stress on second syllable: *con'nect, de'tect, pro'tect.*
- *-en* (='become/cause to become'): *deaden, deafen, enliven, redden, sadden*. Derivation particularly from adjectives.
- *-ide* (no special meaning): *collide, confide, decide, divide, provide, reside,* etc. Pronunciation: stress on second syllable: *col'lide, con'fide.*
- *-ify* (='change from one state to another'): *nullify, rectify, simplify, solidify, verify*. Derivation from adjectives and nouns.
- *-ive* (no special meaning): *arrive, contrive, derive, survive*. Pronunciation: stress on second syllable: *con'trive, de'rive.*
- *-ize/-ise* (='treat in a certain way'): *advertize, finalize, monopolize, organize*; (= 'behave in a certain way'): *apologize, compromise, sympathize*; (= 'connected to the senses'): *realize, recognize, sensitize*. The *-ize* spellings are often rendered *-ise* in British English (*realise, advertise,* etc.). Derivation especially from nouns. Pronunciation: stress usually on first syllable, in longer words sometimes on second, but ***never*** on the ending: *'advertize, 'organize, a'pologize, 'realize.*

Other common verb endings (though not all necessarily suffixes in the true sense) are *-ain* (*complain, explain, remain, retain, sustain*), *-ase/-aise/-aze* (*amaze, blaze, braise, daze, erase, gaze, graze, raise*), *-ay/-ey* (*convey, delay, purvey, survey*), *-ly* (*apply, rely, reply, supply*), *-arry* (*carry, hurry, marry, parry*), *-ine* (*combine, incline, refine*).

It is a good idea as a learner to develop a 'feel' for the typical shapes of verbs. This helps a lot in memorizing vocabulary. A particularly good technique with verbs is to learn ***collocations***, i.e. verb + an example of complementation: *apply for a job, refine one's style, complain to the manager, gaze at the stars,* and so on. Generally speaking, not enough attention is paid to verbs in vocabulary work.

042/1.2 Prefixes

It is important to note here that prefixes are almost never pronounced with stress. All the following stress mainly the second syllable (in the case of two-syllable words), or the second or third syllable (in the case of three-syllable words): *de'cline, de'value, discon'nect*:

- *dis-* (= 'negative/reversal'): *disagree, disappear, dislike, disregard, disconnect, dislocate.* With mixed meanings: *discuss, display, distinguish.*
- *un-/de-* (= 'reversal'): *untie, undo, undress, unload, decode, detach, devalue, decline.* Related meaning of 'away': *deprive, detract, depart, depose.*
- *en-/em-* (= 'put into a thing/condition'): *enable, embed, enclose, endanger, entangle.* Occasionally with suffix *-en*: *enlighten, enliven.*
- *ex-* (= 'out/away'): *excite, exclaim, exclude, exhale, exit, expel, explain, explode, expose.*
- *in-/im-* (= as for *en-/em-* 'put into/get into/act on'): *incite, include, inflict, inhale, imply, improve, impose, install, induce, inspect, intend, invite.*
- *pre-* (= 'before'): *precede, predict, preoccupy, prepare, presume, prevent.*
- *com-/con-* (= 'with/together'): *combine, confirm, conflict, conform, comply, consider.* Also *co-/col-/cor-* according to following sound: *co-operate, collate, correspond.*
- *re-* (= 'again'): *repeat, re-tell, rewind, re-live,* etc. Related meaning of 'back' in various senses: *react, rebound, resemble, respond* (= 'reciprocal'); *rebel, refuse, reject, renounce, repress, resist* (= 'against'); *remember, remain, reserve, retain, retard* (= 'keep back'); *recede, reduce, return,* etc.

And here again a pronunciation reminder: the stress is ***never*** placed on the prefix: *disa'gree, dis'play, dis'like, un'tie, de'part.*

042/2 Particle verbs

These are verb phrases formed with ***adverb particles*** or ***prepositions*** (see also chapter 5, **033/1** for verb + adverb particle, and chapter 6, **035**, **036**). Verbs combining with ***adverb particles*** are called ***phrasal verbs***. Those combining with ***prepositions*** are ***prepositional verbs***.

At first sight, the two types are easy to confuse, since adverb particles and prepositions are the ***same*** words used in syntactically different ways. Being able to tell the difference is certainly important, as the two kinds of verbs behave quite differently syntactically. Besides this, it is not just a question of distinguishing between ***prepositional verbs*** and

phrasal verbs, but also between ***prepositional verbs*** and ***prepositional phrases***: in this case, too, there are important syntactic differences, which, moreover, are not just theoretical.

Particles (i.e. ***adverb particles*** and ***prepositions***) are important instruments of word formation. In everyday language many native speakers use just a small number of basic verbs, but by combining them with ***particles*** can produce a wide range of meanings. Verbs like *get* and *take* are good examples, e.g. *get on/off/in/out* (movement), *get over* (e.g. an illness), *get through* (e.g. a difficult day), *get by* (dt. *auskommen*), *get along* (dt. *sich vertragen*), *get across* (*to communicate*), and so on. And with *take*: *take on* (e.g. a big job or task), *take over* (dt. *übernehmen*), *take up* (e.g. start a hobby activity), *take in* (e.g. deceive), etc. Each of these verbs has several other meanings in addition. Those given are just 'samples'.

042/2.1 Phrasal verbs

As we have said, these are combinations of ***verb*** + ***adverb particle***. They can be ***transitive*** or ***intransitive***, and in meaning ***literal*** or ***idiomatic***:

(57) a. Brian took off his coat. [***transitive, literal***]
Brian zog seinen Mantel aus.
b. The plane took off. [***intransitive, idiomatic***]
Das Flugzeug startete/hob ab.
c. Put up your hand if you want to speak. [***transitive, literal***]
Melden Sie sich (per Handzeichen), wenn Sie etwas sagen möchten.
d. Could you put guests up for one night? [***transitive, idiomatic***]
Könntet Ihr Gäste für eine Nacht unterbringen?

Take off in (57)a. and *put up* in (57)c. are ***literal***, i.e. they mean what they say. *Take off* here has the meaning of *take* + the meaning of *off*, and *put up* has the meaning of *put* + the meaning of *up*. In b. and d., however, the meaning of the verb phrase as a whole is more than simply the sum of the two parts. It is semantically metaphorical or figurative, i.e. ***idiomatic***. To discover this meaning, the learner has to ask someone or consult a dictionary.

Not all phrasal verbs are clearly one thing or the other semantically: some are a mixture of both, e.g. *look up* (in the sense of German *nachschlagen*) shows the verb in its literal meaning but the particle in an idiomatic sense. What is important with all phrasal verbs, however, is to learn them as ***units***, and preferably in contexts. One *takes off clothes*, for instance, or *puts* them *on*; one *picks up* one's knife and fork and *puts* them *down* on the table, and so on. That is, particle verbs should not be treated mentally as variants of their 'basic' verbs, but as individual and separate items of vocabulary in their own right. This is reflected syntactically in the fact that the ***particle*** is always marked functionally as ***part of the predicator***:

	S	P	Od	A
(58) a.	Brian	took off	his coat.	
b.	She	looked up	the word	in a dictionary.

A second point is ***word order***. With ***transitive*** phrasal verbs the ***adverb particle*** can be placed ***before*** or ***after*** the direct object. In (58), as in two of the examples in (57), it is before the object. Actually, the preferred position is mainly ***after***. This is in fact ***obligatory*** when the direct object is a ***pronoun***:

		S	***P***	***Od***	***P***	
(59)	a.	Brian	took	***his coat***	off.	
		S	***P***	***Od***	***P***	
	b.	Brian	took	***it***	off.	(not **Brian took off it.*)

With a few verbs (e.g. *to put guests up*), the particle also appears more or less ***always*** in the ***after***-position, i.e. even when the object is a full noun.

Adverb particles are the equivalent of German ***separable prefixes***, e.g. *Er zog seinen Mantel* ***aus***. This explains the ***after***-position in the English word order. It is a relic of the language's old German roots! Note, however, that whereas in German the prefix must go right to the end of the sentence, English particles follow ***only*** the object. They ***precede*** everything else, e.g. adverbials:

(60) Sie ***schlug*** das Wort im Wörterbuch ***nach***.
She ***looked*** the word ***up*** in a dictionary.
(but not **She looked the word in a dictionary up.*)

With intransitive phrasal verbs, therefore, the particle always follows the verb immediately: *The plane took off from Stansted Airport* (not **The plane took from Stansted Airport off*).

042/2.2 Prepositional verbs

In this case the particle is ***not*** an adverb particle, but remains a ***preposition***. Like an adverb particle, however, it also functions syntactically as ***part of the predicator***. A noun always follows as ***direct object***:

		S	***P***	***Od***
(61)	a.	Jess	***waited for***	Tom.
		S	***P***	***Od***
	b.	Maggie	***looked after***	the children.

Note the difference to the ***prepositional phrase***, which is ***adverbial***. Compare

		S	***P***	***Od***	
(62)	a.	Jess	***waited on***	the guests.	[***prepositional verb***: dt. *bediente*]
		S	***P***	***A***	
	b.	Jess	waited	***on the corner***.	[***prepositional phrase***]

The difference in syntax is based on a difference in the meaning of the preposition. In (62)b. ***on*** is used in one of its ordinary, ***literal*** meanings, i.e. here in the sense of German *an*. We can exchange the preposition for others without affecting the meaning of the verb, e.g. *Jess waited by the corner/at the bus stop*, etc. But this will ***not*** work with a ***prepositional verb***.

For instance, if we replace ***on*** by ***with*** in (62)a., we get not only a different meaning of the verb, but also a radical change in the relation of the preposition to the noun phrase. Prepositions of prepositional verbs are ***idiomatic***, i.e. they are bound to that particular verb and do not have their ordinary meaning. This is why they cannot be freely exchanged for other prepositions. Some, like ***on*** in (62)a., are actually meaningless. They function just as a grammatical link to a direct object. Others take on a special meaning which they do not normally have. This may apply to the verb as well, as in *come across* in the sense of *find*, or *get over* in the sense of *recover from*, where the sense is figurative.

Further examples of prepositional verbs are *depend on, ask for, deal with, cater for, wonder at*, etc.

Finally, an important note on syntax: a prepositional verb is always followed in simple active sentences by a noun/pronoun as ***direct object*** (sometimes called the ***prepositional object***). Prepositional verbs, that is, are always ***transitive***. Secondly, the preposition must always ***precede*** the noun. This shows that it is a preposition, and not an adverb particle. We can test the distinction between a ***prepositional verb*** and a ***transitive phrasal verb*** as follows: we simply convert the direct object into a ***pronoun***. An adverb particle must then ***shift*** to the ***after***-position, as in (63)a. A preposition remains in the ***same*** position, as in (63)b.:

(63) a. Jess took ***on*** these new tasks. → Jess took ***them on***.
[particle ***shifts*** = ***adverb particle, phrasal verb***]
b. Jess waited on the guests. → Jess waited ***on them***.
[particle in ***same position*** = ***preposition, prepositional verb***]

German also has prepositional verbs, distinct from prepositional phrases:

(64) a. Fritz ***wartete auf*** einen Baum. [prepositional verb]
b. Fritz wartete ***auf einem Baum***. [prepositional phrase]

Notice, by the way, the difference in case (accusative vs. dative). And also, of course, in meaning: in (64)a. Fritz could only be a dog, in (74)b. definitely a cat.

042/2.3 'Particle conversion' in the prepositional phrase

Certain prepositional phrases can allow ***omission*** of the prepositional complement, e.g. *She got in the car → She got in*. When this happens, the preposition becomes an ***adverb particle***, as it loses the noun after it. Most prepositions expressing ***direction*** (and some also ***place***) can be 'converted' in this way into adverb particles:

(65) a. Sally climbed ***up the diving tower*** and jumped ***off the top board.***

b. Sally climbed ***up*** and jumped ***off***.
[***prepositions*** now become ***adverb particles***]

What the adverb particle means exactly is usually signalled in the physical situation, or in the immediate language context, e.g. *I waved to Jim on the other side of the street, and he came* ***across*** (= *across the street*). The verbs in these cases also undergo a change, i.e. from ordinary verbs of motion to ***intransitive phrasal verbs***.

Adverb particles can be ***deictic*** (= speaker-relative): *Come* ***down****!*; *Get* ***out***! One or two are also common in a 'regional' ***deictic*** sense, especially signalling movement to people's homes or workplaces. ***Over***, for instance, often means 'in an easterly or westerly direction'. ***Up*** and ***down*** have a similar function for *northwards* and *southwards*, or for movements from one (known or assumed) topographical level to another. *By* is another common 'local deictic' particle:

(66) a. Edda and Paul are coming ***over*** for Christmas.
b. Roy went ***down*** to see Terry at the weekend.
c. Why don't you drop ***by*** (e.g. my office) for half an hour tomorrow?

042/2.4 Phrasal-prepositional verbs

As these have both an ***adverb particle*** and a ***preposition***, they are a mixture of phrasal and prepositional verbs. Syntactically, however, they behave like ordinary prepositional verbs: the preposition always comes second, and is followed by a direct object (prepositional object):

	Od	
(67) a. I do not ***put up with***	bad manners.	(= *tolerate*)
	Od	
b. She ***looks down on***	her students.	(dt. *verachten*)
	Od	
c. Conny ***comes out with***	some very funny remarks.	(dt. *von sich geben*)

Other examples are: *look forward to* (dt. *sich freuen auf*), *keep on about* (dt. *sich dauernd über etw. auslassen*), *go over to* (dt. *zu etw. übergehen*) *stick up for* (dt. *für etw. einstehen*), *look out for* (dt. *Ausschau halten nach*), etc. There are a few variants which have a ***noun*** instead of an adverb particle, e.g. *find fault with* (dt. *kritisieren*), *take care of* (dt. *aufpassen auf*), *take issue with* (dt. *mit jemandem streiten*), etc. The German equivalents of phrasal-prepositional verbs are prepositional verbs with a separable prefix, e.g. *herabsehen auf, auskommen mit, abhängen von, einstehen für*, etc.

042/2.5 Complex prepositional verbs

This is another special type of prepositional verb. It is complemented by ***two nouns,*** instead of just one. One of these follows the verb immediately. Then comes the ***preposition,*** and then the second noun. The pattern is therefore ***verb + noun + preposition + noun***: *The police accused* ***Martin*** *of* ***the crime****; We congratulated* ***our son*** *on* ***his success****; Governments are blaming* ***banks*** *for* ***the economic depression***.

Some of these verbs are ***ditransitive,*** i.e. the first noun is an ***indirect,*** the second a ***direct object***. This is the case when the first noun is a person in the semantic role of ***receiver,*** e.g. when the verb refers obviously to an act of communication:

		Oi		***Od***
(68)	a. The police accused	Martin	***of***	the crime.
		Oi		***Od***
	b. We congratulated	our son	***on***	his success.
		Oi		***Od***
	c. Governments are blaming	banks	***for***	the economic depression.

Otherwise, they are ***complex transitive,*** i.e. the first noun is a ***direct object*** and the second is an ***object complement***:

		Od		***Co***
(69)	a. Governments are blaming	the economic depression	***on***	the banks.
		Od		***Co***
	b. The court fined	Ray	***for***	a traffic offence.
		Od		***Co***
	c. The police mistook	me	***for***	someone else.

Most ***complex prepositional verbs*** fall into the first category, i.e. the ***ditransitive*** one. Further examples are: *remind someone of X; ask someone for X; deprive someone of X.* Further examples of ***complex transitive*** are: *regard someone as X; punish someone for X; honour someone for X.*

042/2.6 Particles as prefixes

Some particles occur as verb prefixes, as is generally the case in German: *overtake* (dt. *überholen*), *download* (dt. *herunterladen*), *undertake* (dt. *unternehmen*), *upgrade* (dt. *aufwerten*), *outwit* (dt. *überlisten*), *overlook* (dt. *überblicken/übersehen*).

⚠ English prefixes are never separated from the body of the verb, however, as is the case with certain German prefixes: *He downloaded the programme* (dt. *Er lud das Programm herunter*), not **He loaded down …* As we have seen, the grammatical equivalent of the German separable prefix verb is the phrasal verb.

There are one or two English particle prefix verbs with the same particle as phrasal or prepositional verbs, but different meanings, e.g. *overtake* (*überholen*) and *take over* (*übernehmen*), *overlook* (*überblicken/übersehen*), and *look over* (*herüber-/hinübersehen*, or as a prepositional verb *anschauen, inspizieren*).

Particle prefix verbs are never stressed on the prefix, i.e. in our two-syllable examples always on the second syllable: *over'take, up'grade, out'wit*. Exception: *'download* .

042/3 Formation of non-finite verbs

042/3.1 The infinitive

The base form of the infinitive has two versions, one with and one without ***to***.

In general, only one or the other is grammatically possible in particular constructions. For instance, modal verbs mainly take the infinitive without ***to***: *I will come/must come/should come*, etc. Most catenatives, on the other hand, require the infinitive with ***to***, e.g. *I want to come/remembered to come/persuaded Mary to come*, etc. When we just name a particular verb, we can do this in either form, e.g. ***Be** is a stative verb/**To be** is a stative verb*.

As already shown briefly (see **040/2.9** above), the infinitive has a ***progressive*** form, a ***perfect*** form, and a ***perfect progressive*** form,: *to be running, to have run, to have been running* (formation details under **042/4**).These forms are not exceptional or unusual. When they are used, they are normally obligatory. For example, if I comment on someone's red face, I must say *You seem to have been running* (and not **You seem to have run*). In this situation it is the only way of rendering German *Du scheinst gerannt zu sein*. Aspect differences must be shown in English even in the infinitive.

042/3.2 The -ing-form (gerund and present participle)

To form the present participle (or gerund), one simply adds ***-ing*** to the infinitive, observing the following points of spelling:

- a single final *-**e*** is dropped (*make → making*), except with *be* (*be → being*). Double *-**ee*** is kept (*see → seeing*). This sometimes leads to confusion, e.g. **beeing*, instead of *being.;*
- one-syllable verbs with a short vowel and a single final consonant have the final consonant doubled (*hit → hitting, dig → digging, sip → sipping*);
- final single *-**l*** following a vowel is always doubled (*travel → travelling, instil → instilling, rival → rivalling*), though not in American English (*travel → traveling*);
- two-syllable verbs with a stressed second syllable containing a single vowel and final consonant have the final consonant doubled (*refer → referring, begin → beginning, forget → forgetting*).

There is also a ***perfect*** form of gerunds and present participles, e.g. *having made* (see **042/4** below for details of formation).

German also has a present participle, ending in *-end* (*reisend, sitzend, beginnend*), though it is not used much. The English equivalent, by contrast, is very common. There is no real German gerund, but a rough equivalent is the use of the infinitive as a noun (*das Sitzen, das Reisen, das Sehen*).

042/3.3 The past participle

This is the participle that is used in English and German to form the perfect: *done, gone, parked* (German always with a ***ge***-prefix: *getan, gegangen, geparkt*). With ***regular*** verbs (sometimes called ***weak*** verbs), it is formed by adding ***-d*** or ***-ed*** to the infinitive. Spelling rules affecting the doubling of consonants are similar to those for the ***-ing***-forms (*referred, sipped, travelled,* etc.). German regular (or weak) participles are related in form (replacement of final *-en* by *-t*: *geparkt, gereist,* etc.). The past participles of English regular verbs are all ***identical*** with the ***past tense*** form:

infinitive	***past tense***	***past participle***
walk	walked	walked

As in German, the past participles of ***irregular*** (or ***strong***) verbs belong to a variety of individual sub-types based mainly on phonetic patterns of vowel change (known by the German term *Ablaut*), e.g.:

infinitive	***past tense***	***past participle***
sing	sang	sung
drink	drank	drunk

Other types change the vowel only once, and have identical past tense and past participle forms (e.g. *tell* and *find*). Some retain the infinitive form throughout (e.g. *let, put, burst, hurt*); a few (e.g. *run, come*) change in the past tense, but return to the base vowel in the participle; and there are members of all three groups that additionally inflect the participle with *-en* or *-n*. Some change their final consonants to *-t* or add *-t* as an inflection (e.g. *buy, build, bring, feel, lose, learn*):

infinitive	***past tense***	***past participle***
tell	told	told
find	found	found
put	put	put
run	ran	run
freeze	froze	frozen
grow	grew	grown
give	gave	given
lose	lost	lost
send	sent	sent

All this shows that English and German were once very close cousins, even if in other ways they are now only distantly related.

⚠ Note that, despite having the same sort of past tense morphology, regular and irregular verbs in English and German do not necessarily coincide. A regular verb in English can be irregular in German, and the other way round.

A more detailed list of irregular forms is given in the next chapter.

042/4 Forming progressive and perfect

The ***progressive*** is formed with the auxiliary **be** + ***present participle***. The ***present participle*** represents the main (lexical) verb and is always unchanged. Conjugation, tense and other changes of form are signalled only in the auxiliary. To form, for instance, the present progressive of *go* we take the ***present participle*** (*going*), and add ***be*** before it in the appropriate person and tense form, e.g. *You **are** going, she **is** going,* etc. The same applies to the past progressive: *You **were** going, she **was** going,* etc. Similarly, for the progressive infinitive of *go,* we actually need the infinitive of *be*: ***to be** going;* and with a modal verb, the infinitive without *to,* e.g. *I must **be** going.*

The ***perfect*** is formed with the auxiliary **have** + ***past participle***. Here the same conditions apply. All changes take place in the auxiliary. The participle remains unchanged. For the present perfect of *go,* for example, we take the ***past participle*** (*gone*), and precede it with auxiliary ***have*** in the appropriate person and tense form, e.g. *You **have** gone, he **has** gone;* and in the past perfect: *You **had**/he **had** gone.* For the ***perfect infinitive*** of *go,* we need the infinitive of *have*: ***to have** gone.* And, again, for modals the infinitive without *to,* e.g. *He must **have** gone.*

The ***perfect progressive***, as far as the form itself is concerned, is actually the 'perfect of the progressive', and not the 'progressive of the perfect', as we might expect. That is, for *go,* we need to form the progressive first (**be** + ***present participle*** = *be going*), and then the perfect of auxiliary ***be*** (**have** + ***past participle*** = *have been*), which gives us in total **have** + ***past participle*** of **be** + ***present participle*** of **go** (= *have been going*). Now it is auxiliary ***have*** which signals conjugation, tense, and infinitive forms: *You **have** been going, she **had** been going, **to have** been going, he must **have** been going,* etc.

The ***perfect*** form of the ***present participle*** (sometimes called the ***perfect participle***) is actually the ***present participle form*** of auxiliary ***have*** + ***past participle*** of lexical verb. The ***perfect participle*** of *go,* that is, is ***having** gone.* The same form also functions as a ***perfect gerund***.

042/5 Forming the passive

As shown in **040/2.8** above, the ***passive verb form*** consists of the auxiliary **be** + ***past participle*** of the main (lexical) verb: *This meal **was prepared** by experts.* (Note that German passives use the auxiliary *werden,* not *sein*: *Dieses Essen wurde von Experten zubereitet*).

Here, again, the various tense, aspect and conjugation forms are signalled by the auxiliary alone. The past participle remains unchanged. The ***present progressive passive*** of *prepare,* for example, requires auxiliary **be** (in the appropriate person and tense form) + ***present participle*** of **be** + ***past participle*** of *prepare,* e.g. *The meal **is being prepared**.* And in the past tense: *The meal **was being prepared**.*

The ***perfect passive*** of *prepare* requires auxiliary **have** (likewise in the appropriate person and tense form) + past participle of **be** + ***past participle*** of *prepare,* e.g. *The meal **has been prepared**.* And in the past perfect: *The meal **had been prepared**.* Although a perfect progressive passive is grammatically possible (*The meal had been being prepared*), it is usually avoided for stylistic reasons.

There is a ***passive infinitive*** (*to be prepared*) and a ***perfect passive infinitive*** (*to have been prepared*), also without *to*, as after modal auxiliaries, e.g. *must have been prepared*. However, the progressive passive infinitive (*to be being prepared*) is usually avoided, like the perfect progressive passive.

Present participle and ***gerund passives*** are formed with **being** + ***past participle***: *They could not avoid* ***being arrested*** *during the demonstration.*

Perfect participle and ***perfect gerund passives*** are formed with **having been** + ***past participle***: ***Having been convinced*** *by their arguments, I decided to accept the offer.*

Chapter 9 Verbs: The Present and Past Tenses

Overview 043

As explained in chapter 8 ***tense*** and ***aspect*** are basic morphological features of finite verbs in English. Every finite verb is marked for:

- ***present*** or ***past*** (***primary tense***)
- ***perfect*** or ***non-perfect*** (***secondary tense***)
- ***simple form*** or ***progressive form*** (***aspect***)

An overview table with examples:

	Primary Tense	Secondary Tense	Aspect
Andy eats	***present***	***(non-perfect)***[1]	***simple***
Andy is eating	***present***	***(non-perfect)***[1]	***progressive***
Andy has eaten	***present***	***perfect***	***simple***
Andy has been eating	***present***	***perfect***	***progressive***
Andy ate	***past***	***(non-perfect)***[1]	***simple***
Andy was eating	***past***	***(non-perfect)***[1]	***progressive***
Andy had eaten	***past***	***perfect***	***simple***
Andy had been eating	***past***	***perfect***	***progressive***

Table 1: Morphological features of finite verbs ([1]zero marker)

The zero marker for secondary tense will ***not*** be mentioned when we refer to non-perfect verb forms in the text. Here we will just use the conventional names, e.g. *Andy eats* = ***present simple***, *Andy is eating* = ***present progressive***, etc. Only the positive marker will be referred to in the name, e.g. *Andy has eaten* = ***present perfect simple***, *Andy had been eating* = ***past perfect progressive***, etc.

It is important to stress that we nevertheless have three separate morphological categories here, and that they are always represented in any finite verb form. In each category there is a choice between two alternatives, i.e. the ***paradigm*** is ***binary***. This is not just a question of form, but also one of ***meaning***. ***Primary tense*** creates a ***point of reference*** in one of the ***deictic*** time spheres ***present*** or ***past***. ***Secondary tense***, as we will see later, relates this ***reference point*** to the time of the action (or ***action point***, as we will call it in the following); for example, ***perfect*** = action point before reference point. ***Aspect*** tells us whether we are looking at a ***whole action*** from beginning to end, or at an ***action in progress***, i.e. in the middle of happening.

In this and the following chapter, we will show in detail how these basic meanings are interpreted in specific contexts, i.e. how they are exploited for specific purposes of communication.

044 The primary non-perfect tenses and their aspects

Primary tenses, as we have just said, create points of orientation (***reference points***) in the ***present*** and ***past***. The ***secondary tense*** factor (***perfect/non-perfect***) sets up a ***second*** relation. This is between the ***primary tense reference point*** and the ***action point*** (= the time at which the action takes place). Depending on the particular tenses we use, ***reference point*** and ***action point*** are sometimes the same, and sometimes different. This will become fully clear when we discuss the perfect forms.

What we can say now is that in their ***non-perfect*** forms the ***primary tenses*** show that ***action points*** and ***reference points*** are the ***same***. That is, when I say *Cathy ran/was running*, or *Cathy runs/is running*, the ***action point*** and ***reference point*** are identical in each respective example: ***past*** in the first one, ***present*** in the second one. We can illustrate this in a kind of notation (deriving from Reichenbach, *Elements of Symbolic Logic*, New York 1947). We will call these times **A** (for ***action point***), and **R** (for ***reference point***). The third member of the trio is **S**, for ***speaker time*** (i.e. the time of the utterance, which actually, from the speaker's point of view, is always the ***present***). So if I say *Cathy runs/is running*, **A**, **R**, and **S** are all the same time, i.e. the ***present***. In our notation, they are therefore all together, at one point. We will show this in the formula **A,R,S**. This is the formula for the ***present tense***. *Cathy ran/was running*, on the other hand, has the formula **A,R–S**. This is the formula for the ***past tense***. Here, the dash (–) means a ***before/after*** relation. The formula **A,R–S** for the past tense therefore shows that **A** and **R** are now before **S**. But it also shows that **A** and **R** are still together at one point. This is an important feature of the ***primary non-perfect tenses***.

044/1 The general meaning of the aspects

As was said briefly in the last chapter, the category of aspect gives two different views of an action: the ***simple form*** is ***perfective***, i.e. refers to an action ***as a whole***, from beginning to end; the ***progressive form*** is ***imperfective***, i.e. presents the action as ***ongoing***, or in other words, 'in the middle of happening'.

044/1.1 The framework situation

The ***ongoing*** meaning of the ***progressive*** implies a reference point ***inside*** the action. This may be a point of time actually stated adverbially, or it may be implied in another action which interrupts the ongoing one. For the interrupting action the verb is in the ***simple form***, because it is seen as a whole:

(1) a. At 6 pm we were watching the television news.
b. We were watching the television news when I heard a noise in the kitchen.

The action *watching the television news* forms a kind of 'frame' which the other action (*heard a noise*), or the stated point of time (*6 pm*), penetrates or 'falls' into. This is known as a ***time-frame***, or ***framework situation***. It can be illustrated as follows:

(2)

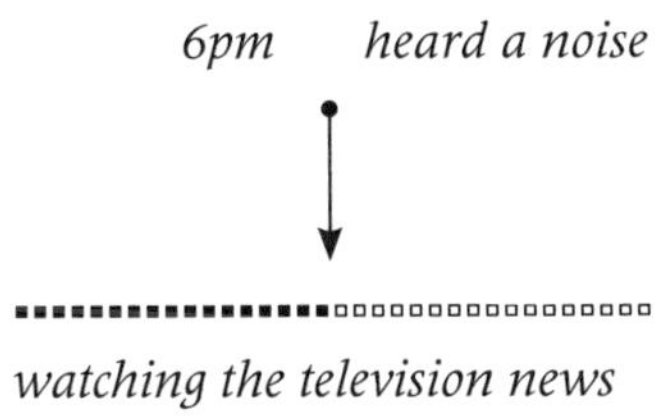

The ***intrusion*** may not cause any real or total interruption. The ***framework action*** could equally continue unhindered. The ***intrusion*** also does not have to be stated explicitly. It may be assumed from the context. But if it cannot be assumed, the progressive will create the expectation that an ***intrusion*** is about to be named. That is, a sentence like *Fred was preparing food* will lead the listener to expect immediate reference to an ***intruding action*** like, for instance, ... *when Gina and the children arrived home*. Without this, the progressive would not make sense, as then a reference point ***inside*** an action would have been implied for no reason. The ***interior reference point***, that is, must be justified by the presence (or 'promise') of an ***intrusion***.

The ***intrusion*** need not literally be a 'point', or momentary action, in the strict sense. It could be a longer time interval or action, e.g. *While Fred was preparing the food, Gina fetched the children from school*. Note, however, that we still have a framework situation here. Even though the intruding action *fetch the children* is not momentary and takes longer to happen than *hear a noise* in (1) and (2), it is nevertheless ***perfective***, i.e. whole and complete. In combination with the ***imperfective*** action *prepare the food*, this leads, as always in such cases, to the ***framework*** interpretation:

(3)

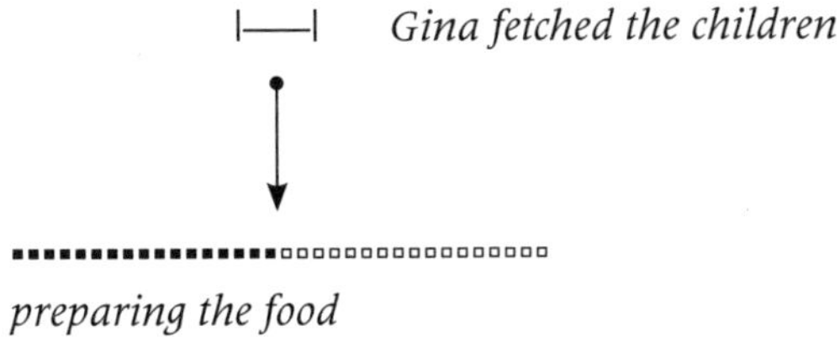

044/1.2 The framework situation and now

The meaning of simple and progressive, and the contrast between them, is easier to demonstrate in the past tense. This is because the simple form cannot be used for single actions in the present tense, except under special circumstances (see below). Nevertheless, basic aspect meaning is ***the same*** in past and present tenses. For example, when a speaker refers to an action actually happening ***now***, i.e. at ***speaker time*** (**S**), the progressive must be used. This is because the action is a ***framework action***, and the point of time ***now*** (**S**) intrudes into it. So we can represent the sentence *Listen, the dog is barking* in the same way as the past progressive in (2) above. The ***intrusion point*** *6 pm* in (2) can be replaced, quite simply, by ***now***:

(4)

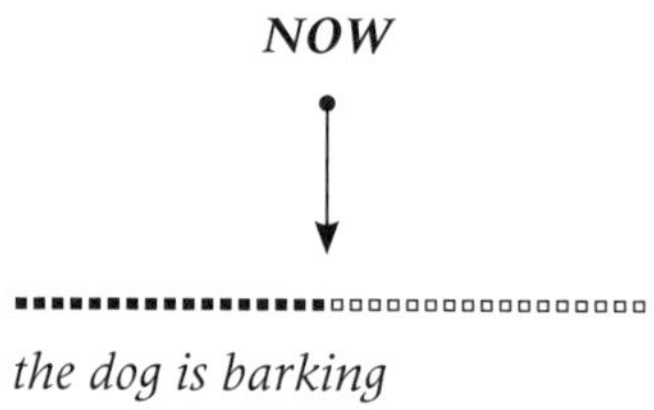

Only the progressive allows us to refer to a point of time ***inside*** an action. This is why there is no alternative to the progressive when we talk about things happening ***now***, at **S**. The ***simple form***, as we have seen, has ***perfective*** meaning, i.e. represents an action as complete. Logically, therefore, it cannot be used for referring to a point of time ***inside*** the action, i.e. during its course. This would be a contradiction: ***now*** says that the action is still going on, whereas the simple form would tell us that the same action was complete. This, to repeat the point, is why ***only the progressive*** can refer to actions happening when the speaker is talking.

Perfective reference to a present action is possible, but allows only one interpretation, i.e. that the action is a ***habit*** – something that happens repeatedly, but is not happening now. (An exception is when the present tense is used to tell a story. See **044/2.5**.)

044/1.3 Framework vs. sequence

Let us return to an example given in the text above: *Fred was preparing food when Gina and the children arrived home.*

This can be illustrated as in the other framework diagrams above, i.e.

(5)

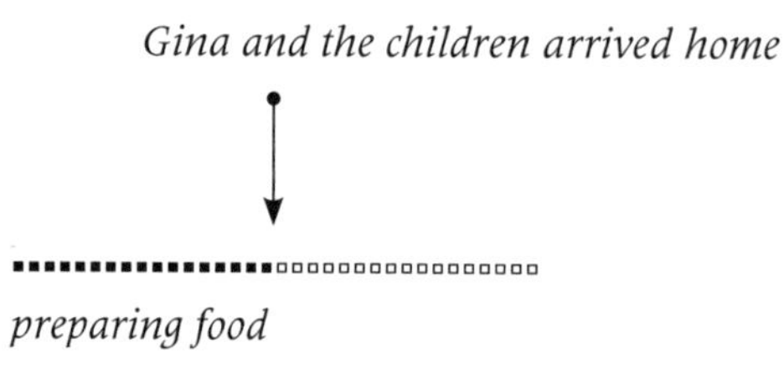

We will now change the sentence into *Fred prepared food when Gina and the children arrived home*. Instead of one progressive and one simple form, we now have two ***simple forms***, and therefore two ***perfective*** actions together.

This changes the nature of their interaction: the framework situation disappears, and the events are interpreted as being in ***sequence***. Moreover their order, or at least the order of their starting points, has reversed: Fred now does not start to prepare the food until ***after*** Gina and the children arrive. This little 'trick' has to do partly with the flexible meaning of the conjunction *when* (*when* + ***progressive*** = *while*/*during*, *when* + ***simple form*** = *after*). But it also illustrates very neatly the basic semantic difference between the two aspects. A simple form accompanying a progressive places one action inside the other. Two simple forms present the actions as external to one another, and so lead to the interpretation of sequence.

Correspondingly, we can say that to describe actions in ***sequence***, we need the ***simple*** form: *Joe washed the cups, cleaned the table and watered the kitchen plants*. Progressives would not make sense here. An action that is followed by another one must be complete, and therefore needs ***perfective*** reference. This applies regardless of the tense used. If this story is told in the present tense (as, for instance, children's stories often are), we still need the simple form: *Joe washes the cups, cleans the table and waters the kitchen plants.*

044/1.4 The progressive in scenic description

On the other hand, several framework actions together add up to a picture of parallel actions happening at the same time; the assumption is that they are all interrupted by the same intrusion: *Your mother and I were sitting on a bench in the park. It was nice weather. The sun was shining, people were sunbathing on the grass, or reading newspapers in the shade of the trees*:

(6)

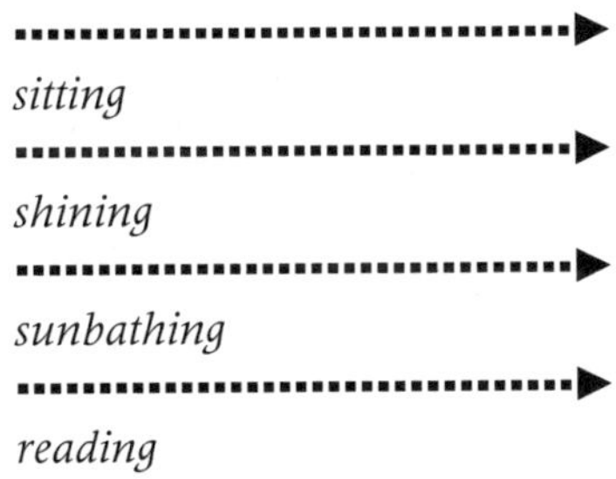

One or more ***perfective*** actions must now intrude into this scene (otherwise the progressives would not be justified), e.g. *Suddenly someone shouted. We looked up*:

(7)

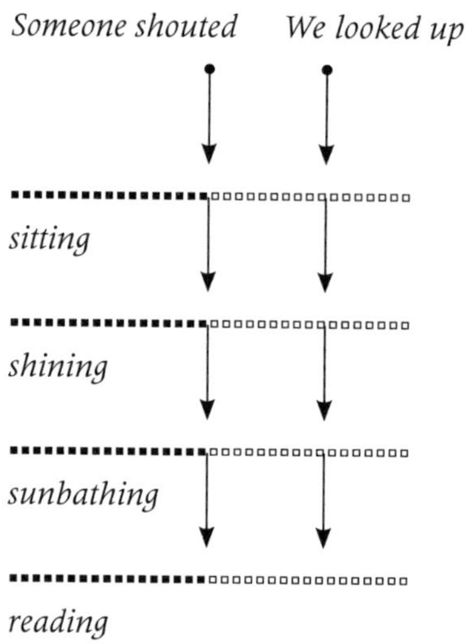

This kind of 'scene-setting' in the ***progressive*** is very common at the beginning of an episode in a story or report. With the first simple forms, a narrative sequence then breaks into the scene, and events happen one after the other: *A young man emerged from the trees on our left, and raced across the grass to the boating pond, about 100 yards in front of us. Four policemen raced after him.*

In a similar way to the scene-setting situation in a story, we assume ***parallel imperfective*** actions when we describe things 'going on' in a picture or photograph: *Look! This photo was taken on a seaside outing in 1934. The figure on the right is Uncle George. He's wearing his famous club tie. And the woman who is standing next to him is Aunt Jane. Young Sam in front of them is holding the new baby, Mildred.*

Note by the way that the present tense is used, even though the actions portrayed are long in the past. For the observer, actions in pictures are going on ***now***, in the 'observer-present'. But the tense is not important. The point is that these are ***imperfective***, ***parallel*** actions, all occurring as part of a ***framework situation***. The ***intrusion*** is the observer's ***now***, the moment of looking. This makes the ***progressive*** obligatory. Even if the past tense is used, it is also obligatory, as here, too, we must assume an ***intrusion point*** (= 'at that point of time when the photo was taken'). Picture description needs the progressive!

In a teaching situation, illustrations are sometimes used to suggest or remind learners of what happens in a story. Here, that is, a picture may stand for a ***perfective action*** in ***sequence***. This requires the ***simple form***. Assume, for instance, a narrative sequence in the present tense: *The boy slips on the muddy river-bank, and falls into the water. A passer-by jumps in and rescues him.*

Let us imagine one illustration for each respective action, i.e. four pictures in all. In the first we see the boy slipping; the second shows him falling into the water; the third is of the passer-by jumping in; and the fourth shows the rescue, perhaps the victim being dragged on to dry land by his rescuer.

This kind of situation has to be handled with care, grammatically. As far as each picture just shows a stage in the story, it stands for a ***simple form***. So I might ask a pupil:

"What ***happens*** in this story first, Sandra? Look at the picture and tell me." The correct answer, despite the fact that Sandra is looking at a picture, is "The boy ***slips*** on the muddy bank", and not **The boy is slipping* ... If, on the other hand, I ask Sandra to describe the picture ***as a picture***, i.e. in isolation, outside its 'memory function', then, of course, the ***progressive*** is necessary: "What ***is happening*** in this picture, Sandra?"

Here, we are back to picture description in its own right, showing a parallel world of (possibly more than one) action, occurring at the ***now***-point (**S**) of the observer. The obvious solution to this ambivalence of pictures as teaching aids is to use different kinds of illustration, if possible, for different functions: the rich-content full picture or photo for practising the progressive, and the simple, abstract matchstick-style illustration for narrative memory support.

Finally, a word of warning on parallel actions. The fact that actions are parallel does ⚠ ***not*** by itself justify the progressive. The English rendering of a German sentence like (8) a. is (8)b.:

(8) a. Während Gina die Kinder von der Schule holte, bereitete Fred das Abendbrot zu.
b. While Gina fetched the children from school, Fred made the evening meal.

The progressive is only correct if the factor ***framework situation*** is involved, as in the variants in (9):

(9) a. When Grandma called, Gina was fetching the children from school, and Fred was preparing the evening meal.
b. While Gina was fetching the children from school, Fred made the evening meal.
c. While Fred was making the evening meal, Gina fetched the children from school.

In (9)a. *fetching* and *preparing* are parallel ***time frames*** and Grandma's call is the ***intrusion*** that occurs during both. In (9)b. only *fetching* is the ***time frame*** and Fred's action is the ***perfective intrusion***. In (9)c. it is the other way round: Gina's action is shorter and is the ***perfective intrusion*** into Fred's imperfective *making* as the ***time frame*** (see also (3) above).

044/1.5 The aspects and modes of occurrence

Perfectivity and ***imperfectivity*** always have the same meanings (= ***whole*** vs. ***ongoing***). However, these have varying ***side-effects*** on the four basic ***modes of occurrence*** (see chapter 8, **041/3**).

With ***telic*** actions (= ***goal-directed*** processes) progressive = ***incomplete*** (*I was going home*), simple form = ***complete*** (*I went home*). A few verbal expressions referring to telic actions can sometimes be used in the simple form with a ***point of time***. This usually means that the action ***started*** at that time. *I went home at 10 o'clock* therefore means *I left (wherever I was)/I set out for home at 10 o'clock.*

Note, therefore, the difference between:

(10) a. I went home at 10 o'clock (= e.g. that's when I left the party).
b. I was going home at 10 o'clock (= I was already on my way at 10 o'clock, i.e. I had already left the party ***before*** 10 o'clock).

- With ***non-telic*** actions the simple form can mean a complete 'unit' of action. This is usually defined by the context. With a ***point of time*** we have the same effect as with telic actions, i.e. the effect of ***beginning***:

(11) a. Our band played at the Black Cat last week (= a whole unit of playing, e.g. an evening).
b. We practised all day yesterday (= a whole unit).
c. When he saw the tiger, Thompson turned and ran (= started to run).

As was said in chapter 8, **041/3**, the ***telic/non-telic*** distinction is reflected in different ***implicational*** relations between respective progressive and simple forms. *I was reading the book* (***telic***) does ***not*** imply *I read the book*, but *We were practising* (***non-telic***) does imply *We practised*. That is, any amount of a ***non-telic*** action is enough for us to be able to say 'It happened'. But we cannot say that a ***telic*** action 'happened', unless it happened completely.

- ***Point-telic actions***, i.e. momentary ones, are affected by the progressive in two possible ways. Some, like *die*, become ordinary ***telic*** actions, i.e. they are converted from a momentary event into a process moving towards a goal: *The sick animal was dying.* Others, such as *kick*, are converted into ***non-telic*** actions, as they take on a meaning of 'unspecified repetition': *The boy was kicking the ball against the garage door.*
- ***States*** are incompatible with the progressive, as the progressive implies an action/process. However, some ***stative verbs*** can take on an action meaning, and appear then in this meaning in the progressive, e.g. *Sonia is having a bath* (= *taking a bath*), see section below on ***stative verbs***.

Modes of occurrence are important. Combined with basic aspect meaning, they lead, as we have seen, to various secondary meanings, e.g. incomplete/complete, durative/momentary, repetitive, 'longer' vs. 'shorter' actions, and so on. Further secondary meanings (e.g. temporariness) can result from other factors of context, as will be seen in the sections following. However, all such meanings are ***derived***. That is, they result from the ***interaction*** of aspect with other semantic factors in particular contexts. They are not part of basic aspect meaning itself.

044/2 The present tense and its aspects

Reference point of the present tense is ***present time***, i.e. the present of the person speaking or writing. It therefore includes ***speaker time***. The present tense means, then, 'valid at the moment of speaking or writing' (or, to use our symbol, valid at **S**). Apart from this, the present tense must be used, under certain circumstances, for future time, and can very occasionally be found in reference to past time. These are exceptions, however, and are discussed in detail below. The usual meaning of the present tense is for reference to ***present time***, as represented in the formula just given: **A,R,S**.

We start this section with a note on form. Then we deal in detail with particular speech intentions and communicative contexts in which the general semantics of the aspects are realized in the present tense.

044/2.1 A note on 3rd person singular, simple form

Apart from the case of *be*, the only real challenge to learners in conjugating the present simple is remembering the 3rd person singular ***-s***. With the great majority of verbs this is the only ending (see also chapter 8, **040/2**). There are some common exceptions, though:

have → has [hæz] do → does [dʌz]
go → goes [gəʊz] say → says [sez]

Note that with ***go*** the irregularity is only in spelling, with ***say*** only in pronunciation, and with *have* and *do* in both.

Apart from these forms there are a few points to note about pronunciation and spelling. The main one is that the same rules apply as with the plural *-s* for nouns, i.e. generally:

- after voiceless consonants, it is pronounced [s]: *speaks* [spi:ks], *eats* [i:ts], *hopes* [həʊps]
- after voiced consonants and vowels, it is pronounced [z]: *lives* [lɪvz], *runs* [rʌnz], *lies* [laɪz]

Exceptions:

- ***-s*** added to verbs ending in the letters ***-se***, ***-ze***, and ***-ge*** is pronounced [ɪz]: *rises* [raɪzɪz], *blazes* [bleɪzɪz], *rages* [reɪdʒɪz]
- ***-es*** (pronounced [ɪz]) is added to verbs ending in the letters ***-s***, ***-z***, ***-ch***, ***-sh*** and ***-x***: *kisses* [kɪsɪz], *buzzes* [bʌzɪz], *catches* [kætʃɪz], *crashes* [kræʃɪz], *hoaxes* [həʊksɪz]
- with verbs ending in the letter ***-y*** following a consonant, the ***-y*** is replaced by ***-ies***, pronounced [ɪz]: *marries* [mærɪz], *dirties* [də:tɪz], *rallies* [rælɪz]

044/2.2 Actions in progress now

As we have seen, these have to be expressed by the ***present progressive***.

There are two ways in which an action can be thought of as in progress. In the first, the action is quite literally going on as the speaker speaks (i.e. at **S**, the moment of speech):

(12) a. "What are you staring at, Sally?" "Hmn? Oh, nothing. I'm just going over something in my mind."
b. "What's Carol doing?" "She's playing with Teddy in the garden."

Because the action is actually in progress, we call this kind of use an ***actual progressive***.

The second variant concerns longer processes that may not be tangibly unfolding at **S**, but are nevertheless regarded as 'ongoing', or in progress in a more general sense:

(13) a. Dad's firm is building a shopping mall in the town centre.
b. By the way, we're rehearsing a new play at school.
c. Maureen is decorating the guest bedroom at the moment, so you will have to sleep on the couch downstairs.
d. Don't throw that paper away! I'm still doing the crossword.

What these statements tell us is that a temporary situation exists, or that some kind of task or process is in the course of development. But they do not mean that the actions themselves are literally being performed at **S**. (13)c., for instance, does not mean that Maureen is necessarily standing on a ladder, paintbrush in hand, at this very moment. Similarly, for (13)b. to be true, the speaker does not actually have to be at school and on stage when the statement is made. This kind of reference to a more abstract sense of being 'in progress' is known as a ***general progressive***.

044/2.3 Habits and general truths

Reference to things that always happen, or are generally valid, requires the ***simple form***. This, in fact, is the most common function of the ***simple form*** in the present tense:

(14) a. Water boils at 100° centigrade.
b. The Mississippi rises in Minnesota and flows almost the length of the USA to the Gulf of Mexico.
c. A grassy footpath leads over the cliffs from Cuckmere Haven to Seaford Head.
d. The planet Mercury orbits the sun in 88 days.

An important variant on general behaviour of this kind is a ***habit***:

(15) a. Fred McClaughlin works for British Petroleum.
b. I never go out on Sundays without my camera.
c. Brenda and her husband eat a lot of Indian food.
d. Birds fly south in winter.
e. The new car runs much more economically.

Habits and general truths are the same kinds of referent. They are both behavioural characteristics, and are similar in nature to states, which are also expressed in the simple form.

⚠ A common error among German-speaking students is the use of the progressive instead of the simple form for habits, e.g. **I'm never going out on Sundays without my camera,* instead of (15)b., or **Birds are flying south in winter,* instead of (15)d.

Having said this, we must point out that there ***are*** cases where the ***progressive*** is used for habits. These are dealt with in the next section.

044/2.4 Habits in the progressive

As we have just seen, habit reference is typically the domain of the simple form. However, there are two exceptions. Firstly, the progressive ***can*** be used to express a tone of annoyance towards a habit or the circumstances around it:

(16) a. Auntie Jane is always moaning about something or other.
b. I'm constantly forgetting people's names.
c. John Cosgrove is forever making rude remarks about our garden.
d. The kids are continually falling into ponds, off bikes or out of trees!
e. My wife's always telling guests to close the gate when they leave the farm.

In a sense this is a kind of 'modal' use, as it expresses an attitude. It is generally only possible with positive (not negative) sentences. Adverbs which underline the meaning of 'tiresome regularity' are necessary, such as *always, constantly,* and *continually* (but never *often, sometimes, everyday,* etc.). It should be emphasized that the use of the progressive here is ***not*** compulsory. It would also be quite grammatical to use the simple form. The progressive merely emphasizes the negative effect.

In our second case, however, the progressive ***must*** be used for habit reference. This is when the habit is a ***temporary*** one:

(17) a. At present we're eating in pubs and restaurants (as the kitchen is being re-decorated).
b. I'm commuting by train at the moment (because my car, which I usually use, is in the garage being repaired).
c. The children are taking fruit and vegetables to school this week (as the harvest festival is on Friday).
d. Bert is reading the *Independent* everyday while we are on holiday (since the *Guardian,* his usual paper, is not available down here).

As indicated in some of the examples, temporary habits often contrast with permanent ones expressed in the simple form.

044/2.5 Use of the present tense in narratives

Stories are typically told in the past tense. Nevertheless, some writers choose the ***present tense,*** probably because it can sometimes shorten the 'distance' between the reader and the action. The following is an example from a novel:

(18) When the food is ready, I go over and wake Chris. He doesn't want to get up. I tell him again. He says no. I grab the bottom of the sleeping bag, give it a mighty tablecloth jerk, and he is out of it, blinking in the pine needles. It takes him a while to figure out what has happened, while I roll up the sleeping bag. (Robert Pirsig, *Zen and the Art of Motorcycle Maintenance,* London 1976, p. 63).

Children's literature, in particular, makes frequent use of the present tense, especially literature for young children, who can be assumed not to know the past tense.

Quite apart from cases like these, though, there are certain kinds of narrative which use ***only*** the present tense. One is the telling of ***jokes***:

(19) It is Christmastime and a nun is standing outside a Glasgow pub. She is holding a collection box, and is collecting for an international children's fund. She is wearing the kind of clothing which nuns usually wear, and presents rather a contrast to the drinkers entering and leaving the pub, most of whom are working-men ...

Riddles and problem-solving tasks presented for entertainment are another example:

(20) A man looks at a photograph of someone, and murmurs to himself, "Brothers and sisters have I none, that man's father is my father's son." Who is the person in the photograph that he is looking at?

And a third kind is a ***media commentary*** which accompanies the broadcast of a public event, such as a ceremony, pageant, or ritual of some kind. A particularly common type is the ***sports commentary***:

(21) a. ... And as the leaders jump the Canal Turn, it's still Twin Oaks who touches down first, half-a-length clear of Team Challenge and Auntie Dot, as they go out into the country on the final circuit.
b. Ballack races down the left wing, crosses squarely and fiercely into the Liverpool box. Drogba, strongly challenged, just gets a foot to it, and it's a wonderful goal that gives Chelsea a surprising lead.
c. A difficult shot to reach, as the lob lands deep, just inside the baseline, but Federer, thrusting back quickly, gets under it just in time and manages a spectacular return that barely clears the net.

Finally, the contents of plays, films and most kinds of written texts are always described or re-told in the ***present tense***. This is so even when the tense of the original is the past (which is mostly the case with fictional texts):

(22) a. Oliver Twist is apprenticed to an undertaker by Mr. Bumble ... The lad then makes his way to London, where he falls in with a group of pickpockets, including the Artful Dodger. Such notorious figures of the London underworld as the greasy Fagin and the violent Bill Sykes exploit Oliver, and kidnap him ... (Abraham H. Lass, *A Student's Guide to 50 British Novels*, New York 1975, p. 100).
b. ... And when Clarissa, played by Meryl Streep, goes to pick up Richard, her gay writer friend to take him to the prize-giving, she finds him still in his dressing-gown. He is obviously slightly deranged, and is destroying his bookshelves. When she asks him what he's doing, he shouts that he needs more light in the room ... She tries to calm him down, but he seems to be in a world of his own ...
c. In Act 3 the heroine is murdered. The murderer escapes, but is later arrested by the police in the home of a friend where he is hiding.

In critical comments and reviews, the details of non-fiction texts are also repeated mainly in the present tense: *The author criticizes the government in line 3, but praises the Prime*

Minister just a few sentences later ...; In the next paragraph the writer describes life on board a 17th century sailing ship; Towards the end of the letter, the tone becomes more formal.

044/2.6 Interplay of aspects in present tense narratives and comments

Most examples just presented in section **044/2.5** show the simple form in its typical 'narrative' use, i.e. to describe actions ***in sequence***. This is why the ***present simple*** is also used in sports commentaries. These, too, are a kind of story told by a narrator. Note again that the sequence meaning is derived from the underlying general meaning of ***perfectivity***, i.e. wholeness/completeness: an action has to be seen as whole for another action to follow it. Progressives would plant us ***inside*** each action (= in the course of its occurrence); sequences, however, require the external, 'complete' view. This is also the reason for the simple forms in comment reference to what writers 'say' in texts: *the author criticizes the government ..., the writer describes life on board ..., the tone becomes more formal ...* (see examples at end of previous section). ***Whole action*** description is necessary here.

It is also possible to adopt an internal view of any particular action, e.g. *The author is criticizing the government ...* This, however, creates a ***framework situation*** and has a different, ***internal*** meaning, e.g. *When the author says X, Y, and Z, he is, in fact, criticizing the government.* Here, the points X,Y and Z fall inside the framework of *criticizing* and tell us that they are internal parts of the process of criticism, i.e. they add up to, or amount to, criticism.

A more concrete ***framework situation*** is the typical '***now***' example in (20): *Who is the person in the photograph that he is looking at* ***at this moment****?* In (19), on the other hand, we have the narrative 'scene-setting' use at the beginning of a story: ... *a nun is standing outside a Glasgow pub. She is holding a collection box, and is collecting for an international children's fund. She is wearing ...* We could then add some ***intrusion points*** as the first steps in the sequence of the story proper: *On his way into the pub, one of the regular customers notices her. He goes up to her, and says, ...:*

(23)

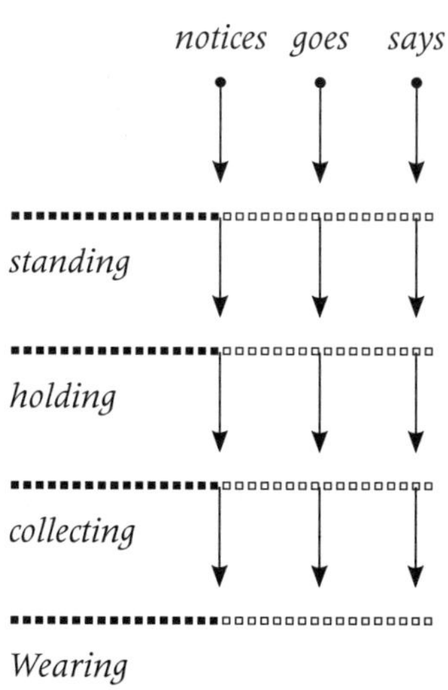

The rest of the joke, by the way, goes: "You need a drop o' whisky, Sister, standing out here in the cold. It's Christmas. Let me bring you out a double." "Never," says the nun primly, "My Mother Superior thinks alcohol is a deadly sin ... Oh, all right. I can see you're kind. The Lord smiles on the generous. Two pounds in the box and a wee drop for me – but in a cup, please, so that it looks like tea." In the pub the man orders a pint of bitter and a double whisky, and then whispers, rather embarrassed, in the barman's ear "... but the whisky in a teacup, if you don't mind." "In a cup!!!" exclaims the barman. "Is that bloody nun still outside?!"

044/2.7 Stative verbs

Certain verbs, like *be, have, seem, think,* etc., are not normally used in the progressive form. These are called ***stative verbs***. Most of them refer to states (see also chapter 8, **041/3.4**), or acts of perception. They can be divided into the following categories of meaning:

- **Sensory perception**: *see, hear, smell, feel, recognize, notice,* etc.
- **Emotion:** *like, dislike, hate, love, want, desire, care, wish,* etc.
- **Thought:** *know, think, understand, assume, suppose, expect, remember, forget, mean, realize, mind, believe, trust, recollect, recall, consider, regard,* etc.
- **Possession:** *have, own, owe, possess, contain, include, belong,* etc.
- **Existence, and relation:** *be, seem, concern, matter, consist, weigh, cost, relate, exist, live,* etc.
- **Appearance and expression:** *seem, appear, look, signify, indicate, show, say, express,* etc.

It should be noted that the lexical fields of stative verbs and the purely semantic idea of a ***state*** (i.e. as an 'inert condition', as described in chapter 8, **041/3.4**) only partly correspond to each other. Various body postures, such as standing, sitting, lying, leaning, hanging, etc., could be regarded by their nature as states. The language 'system', however, sees them as actions, as *hang, lean, lie,* etc., are ordinary dynamic verbs. On the other hand, acts of perception (*see, hear, notice,* etc.) are 'occurrences', i.e. in a sense events or actions, although the verbs referring to them are stative. Another point is that not only perception verbs, but also other statives (*think, like, want, have,* etc.) can be ***transitive***, yet in the general understanding a state is not something that can be 'done to others'. In the final analysis, then, English grammar (and not our semantic understanding) dictates to us what a 'state' is: i.e. something that a stative verb refers to!

044/2.8 Stative verbs with additional action meanings

Some of the ***stative*** verbs just listed have additional ***non-stative*** (or ***dynamic***) meanings. They then express actions, and not states, and can be placed in the progressive form:

- *see:* ***stative***: *Do you see that light down in the valley?* (= *perceive, locate it*)
  dynamic: *Are you seeing Sarah tomorrow?* (= *meeting her*)
  In the sense of *visit, see* has a similar dynamic meaning, e.g. *I'm seeing the doctor this afternoon.*

Note that British English often uses the modal *can* with verbs of perception: *Can you see that light down in the valley?; I can hear a peculiar noise.* There are several particle verbs with *see*, which are only dynamic: *see about, see to* (dt. *sich kümmern um*); *see off* (dt. *verabschieden*), *see out* (dt. *hinausbegleiten*).

- *think:* ***stative***: *What do you think?* (= *What is your opinion?*)
  dynamic: *What are you thinking?* (= *What is going through your mind?*)
  Similar in this respect are *regard, recall, recollect,* and *consider*, all of which can have 'mental activity' meanings, e.g. *I am just considering whether to put out the washing or not* (*reflecting on* ...), or *I am just recalling that scene in the film where the heroine says* ... (*picturing in my mind*).
  Stative *expect/assume* = *think/believe;* ***dynamic*** *expect* = *inwardly wait for* (*I am expecting a phone-call this afternoon*); ***dynamic*** *assume* = German *davon ausgehen.*
  Include, categorized here as a verb of 'possession', can also take on the sense of a mental action: *Were you including us in your remarks?* (= *putting us in this or that category* ...).
  The following can also be ***dynamic***: *understand* (usually in negative = *fail to grasp*), and *forget* (= *not take account of*).
- *have:* ***stative***: *Brian has a bath.* (= *he possesses one in his house*)
  dynamic: *Brian is having a bath.* (= *he is sitting in the bathtub washing himself*)
  The verb *have* is very frequently used like this to mean 'pursuing some kind of activity', e.g. *have a walk* (= *take a walk*); *have something to eat/drink* (= *eat* or *drink something*); *have a swim* (= *swim somewhere for fun*); *have a look* (= *take a look, inspect/examine something*); *have a go* (= *take a turn* or *try something*); *have dinner/breakfast* (= *eat dinner/breakfast*), etc. Almost any noun denoting an act or an occasion for something (a meal, for example) can appear in this kind of dynamic construction with *have*.
- *be:* ***stative***: *Wendy is a bit difficult.* (= *she's a complex character and needs careful handling*)
  dynamic: *Wendy is being a bit difficult.* (= *she is behaving in an uncooperative way)*
  Dynamic meanings also with the following: *weigh* (= *measure the weight of*), and *relate* (German *beziehen auf*).
- *show, indicate, say, express*: ***stative***: *He shows a lot of promise as an actor.* (= *others can see this clearly*)
  dynamic: *He is showing us how well he can act.* (= *deliberately letting us see it*);
  stative: *It says in the paper that three men robbed a bank in the town yesterday* (= *It has been written* ...)
  dynamic: *Quiet everyone! Bob is saying something* (= *he is in the process of speaking*).
  Indicate and *express* are similar to *show* and *say*, respectively.
- *feel:* Progressive and simple forms here mean more or less the same. But the progressive tends to refer to more temporary, 'localized' states, and also to present them as more overt and demonstrable:
  stative: *Fatima doesn't feel well* (= It might be the 'flu)
  dynamic: *Fatima isn't feeling well* (= She's getting car-sick; she must sit in front)
- *look* (= German *aussehen*): This is similar to the case with *feel.* Stative use is always possible; the progressive tends to be restricted to when the sense is more temporary, or due to external influences, e.g. *You're looking good tonight* (Those new clothes make all the difference).

In summary, we can say that there are three types of relation between stative verbs and the progressive:

- A number of statives have an alternative dynamic meaning. They then refer to actions, and can appear in the progressive (e.g. *think, be,* and *have*).
- On the other hand, many statives have no alternative dynamic meaning at all (e.g. *seem, appear, signify, concern, matter, owe, own,* and *possess*). These never appear in the progressive.
- And thirdly, one or two stative verbs like *look* and *feel* can appear in the progressive, but retain their stative meaning (though with more dynamic and temporary overtones).

044/2.9 The present tense in future time clauses and conditionals

We now come to the use of the present tense as a carrier of future meaning.

This function of the present tense is very clearly defined. It involves two types of context. The first is purely grammatical, and concerns what we call a ***sequence-of-tense rule*** in ***future time clauses***. These are future-referring clauses introduced by time conjunctions like *when, after, as soon as, (not) until,* and so on. Here the verb in the ***time clause*** must be in the ***present simple.*** The verb in the ***matrix*** usually has the ***will***-form (or the imperative, or some other modal verb):

(24) a. As soon as we arrive in London, we'll find out what plays are on.
 b. The children will probably be tired when they get back from the zoo.
 c. I'll have a shower before we go down to dinner.

This is also the pattern with ***open conditional clauses***:

(25) a. If you touch me, I'll scream!
 b. Sharon will not be able to play at the squash club, unless she becomes a member first.
 c. If McGrath isn't fit by Saturday, Brookes will have to play in goal.

044/2.10 The present tense with arranged future meaning

The second type of context is with future actions that have been arranged.

Reference to ***arranged future*** events always requires ***present tense***.

(26) a. Brookes is playing in goal on Saturday.
 b. The game starts at 4 o'clock on Saturday afternoon.
 c. We're going on holiday at the end of July. We're staying at a small hotel in St. Ives.
 d. Our train arrives in Cornwall in the early morning.

The two aspects are used for slightly different purposes. The ***simple*** form is generally found with ***inanimate*** subjects (events like parties and films, transport vehicles like buses, boats and planes, etc.). It usually suggests a timetable or programme. With ***animate*** subjects (i.e. people or animals), the ***progressive*** is nearly always used.

Future meaning is dealt with fully in chapter 10.

044/3 The past tense: introduction

Reference point of the past tense is in ***past time***, i.e. any time marked expressly (or implied) as ***before speaker time***, and furthermore ***not including*** speaker time. As represented in our formula, this would be: **A,R–S**. Here, that is, ***reference point*** and ***action point*** are the same, but speaker time is ***later***. How much later is not important. It could be just a second. For instance, if I hear a sudden noise outside the window, I might say, slightly alarmed, "*What was that?*" Or if a conversation partner says something I can't hear properly, I would probably reply, *"I didn't quite catch/understand what you said."* That is, I use the past tense, even though the action is very close to the present.

The major point is this: however close they are to **S** in real time, both **A** and **R** are ***before*** the present: the past tense is therefore ***obligatory***, in particular because **R** is also before **S**. This is what we call ***past focus***. ***Past focus*** requires ***past tense***. But it is also the other way round: ***past tense*** requires ***past focus***. That is, when a past tense is used, listeners assume that a past time is being referred to. This must be clear from the context, either by implication, e.g. *I didn't quite catch what you said* (= *a second ago when you spoke*), or because a ***reference point*** has already been established in the past, i.e. the conversation is already about *yesterday*, or *last week*, *last month*, etc., and this is ***clear to the listener***. This is what we call a ***shared R-context*** (= speaker and listener know that a particular past time is meant).

First of all we discuss past tense ***forms***.

044/4 The past tense: forms

We saw in the last chapter that verbs can have ***regular*** (or ***weak***) past tense forms, or ***irregular*** (or ***strong***) past tense forms. Overall, most verbs are regular. However, it does not seem like this in everyday conversation, as many ***common*** verbs are ***irregular***.

Below we list past tense forms in the conventional way, i.e. together with the infinitive and the past participle, as shown in the last chapter.

044/4.1 Regular

The ending *-**ed*** is added to infinitives ending in a consonant, and -***d*** to infinitives ending in vowels:

infinitive	***past tense***	***past participle***
walk	walked	walked
lie	lied	lied

Pronunciation:

- after voiceless consonants (except [t]) -***ed*** is pronounced [t]: *walked* [wɔ:kt], hoped [həʊpt], *searched* [sə:tʃt]
- after voiced consonants (except [d]) and vowels, -***ed*** is pronounced [d]: *lived* [lɪvd], *lied* [laɪd], *raised* [reɪzd]
- after [t] and [d], -***ed*** is pronounced [ɪd]: *dated* [deɪtɪd], *sided* [saɪdɪd]
- end-consonants in spelling are doubled after short stressed vowels: *dip* → *dipped, prefer* → *preferred*
- in spelling, final **-*y*** after consonants is replaced by **-*ied***, pronounced [ɪd]: *hurry* → *hurried* [hʌrɪd], *carry* → *carried* [kærɪd]

044/4.2 Irregular: all forms identical

infinitive	*past tense*	*past participle*
cut	cut	cut
let	let	let

Also: *put, hit, split, burst, cast, cost, thrust, bet, set, shed, spread, rid, shut, hurt.*
Exception: *beat*:

infinitive	*past tense*	*past participle*
beat	beat	beaten

044/4.3 Irregular: past tense and past participle identical

infinitive	*past tense*	*past participle*
cling	clung	clung
sting	stung	stung

Also: *fling, hang, sing, sling, swing, wring.*

infinitive	*past tense*	*past participle*
bind	bound	bound

Also: *find, grind, wind.*

infinitive	*past tense*	*past participle*
bleed	bled	bled
read	read [red]	read [red]

Also: *breed, feed, speed, lead.*

infinitive	***past tense***	***past participle***
spin	spun	spun
win	won [wʌn]	won
sit	sat	sat
spit	spat	spat
hold	held	held
dig	dug	dug
fight	fought [fɔ:t]	fought
get	got	got
meet	met	met
shine	shone [ʃɒn]	shone
shoot	shot	shot
slide	slid	slid
stick	stuck	stuck
stand	stood	stood

044/4.4 Irregular: past participle in -n/-en, otherwise identical with past tense

infinitive	***past tense***	***past participle***
bear	bore	born (= *geboren*), borne (= *getragen*, poetic)

Also: *swear, tear, wear.*

infinitive	***past tense***	***past participle***
freeze	froze	frozen
break	broke	broken
choose	chose	chosen
speak	spoke	spoken
steal	stole	stolen
weave	wove	woven
bite	bit	bitten
hide	hid	hidden
forget	forgot	forgotten
lie	lay	lain
tread	trod	trodden
wake	woke	woken

044/4.5 Irregular: infinitive, past tense and past participle distinct

infinitive	*past tense*	*past participle*
drink	drank	drunk
shrink	shrank	shrunk

Also: *stink, sink.*

infinitive	*past tense*	*past participle*
ring	rang	rung

Also: *sing, spring.*

infinitive	*past tense*	*past participle*
begin	began	begun
swim	swam	swum

044/4.6 Irregular: infinitive, past tense and past participle distinct, participle in -en or -n

infinitive	*past tense*	*past participle*
drive	drove	driven

Also: *strive, thrive.*

infinitive	*past tense*	*past participle*
ride	rode	ridden
write	wrote	written
stride	strode	stridden
arise	arose	arisen
fly	flew	flown

044/4.7 Irregular: infinitive and past participle identical

infinitive	*past tense*	*past participle*
come	came	come
run	ran	run

044/4.8 Irregular: infinitive and past participle identical, participle in -en or -n

infinitive	*past tense*	*past participle*
blow	blew	blown

Also: *grow, know, throw.*

infinitive	*past tense*	*past participle*
take	took	taken

Also: *shake, forsake.*

infinitive	*past tense*	*past participle*
bid	bade	bidden
give	gave	given
draw	drew	drawn
eat	ate	eaten
fall	fell	fallen
see	saw	seen

044/4.9 Irregular: end-consonant change in past tense and past participle, otherwise all forms identical

infinitive	*past tense*	*past participle*
bend	bent	bent

Also: *lend, send, spend.*

infinitive	*past tense*	*past participle*
build	built	built
have	had	had
make	made	made

044/4.10 Irregular: end-consonant and vowel change, past tense and past participle identical (and pronounced [ɔ:t] following initial sound, e.g. [tɔ:t], [brɔ:t], etc.)

infinitive	*past tense*	*past participle*
teach	taught	taught
bring	brought	brought
catch	caught	caught
seek	sought	sought
think	thought	thought
buy	bought	bought

044/4.11 Irregular: vowel change and end-consonant -d added, past tense and past participle identical

infinitive	*past tense*	*past participle*
sell	sold	sold
tell	told	told
flee	fled	fled
hear	heard [hə:d]	heard
say	said [sed]	said

044/4.12 Irregular: vowel change [i:] → [e] and end-consonant -t added, past tense and past participle identical

infinitive	*past tense*	*past participle*
creep	crept	crept
leap	leapt [lept]	leapt
sleep	slept	slept

Also: *sweep, weep, keep.*

infinitive	*past tense*	*past participle*
feel	felt	felt
dream	dreamt [dremt]/dreamed	dreamt/dreamed
deal	dealt [delt]	dealt

Also: *kneel.*

infinitive	*past tense*	*past participle*
lean	leant [lent]	leant
mean	meant [ment]	meant

044/4.13 Irregular: vowel change [i:] → [e] and consonant change, end-consonant -t added, past tense and past participle identical

infinitive	*past tense*	*past participle*
leave	left	left
cleave	cleft	cleft
lose	lost	lost

044/4.14 Irregular: no vowel change, end-consonant -t added, replaces final -l of a double -ll in spelling, past tense and past participle identical

infinitive	*past tense*	*past participle*
dwell	dwelt	dwelt
spill	spilt/spilled	spilt/spilled
spoil	spoilt/spoiled	spoilt/spoiled

Also: *smell, spell.*

infinitive	*past tense*	*past participle*
burn	burnt/burned	burnt/burned
learn	learnt/learned	learnt/learned

044/4.15 Irregular: regular past tense, irregular past participle

infinitive	*past tense*	*past participle*
mow	mowed	mown
show	showed	shown
sow	sowed	sown
sew	sewed	sewn [N.B. All parts identical in pronunciation to those of *sow*!]
prove	proved	proven
shave	shaved	shaven

044/4.16 Highly irregular forms

infinitive	*past tense*	*past participle*
do	did	done
go	went	gone/been [N.B. *been = gone and returned*]
be	was/were	been

044/4.17 Irregularly spelt forms

infinitive	*past tense*	*past participle*
lay	laid [leɪd]	laid
pay	paid [peɪd]	paid

044/5 The past tense: main interplay of aspects

Aspect rules in the past tense are exactly the same as in the present tense. But there is one significant difference in the consequences of the time effect. In the past, referring to the whole of a single action from beginning to end is a natural option. This is because the point of view is one of ***looking back***. In the present, on the other hand, when action time and speaker time are the same, this kind of ***external*** (***perfective***) view is ***not*** possible: here the speaker is forced to refer to the action as ***ongoing***, as he/she is 'in the middle' of it. In other words, the ***internal*** (***imperfective***) view is the unavoidable consequence of referring to a single action as 'present now'. For this reason, as we have already mentioned, present tense perfective references are naturally interpreted as habits and general truths. (Exceptions, of course, are present tense narratives, and reference to future meaning, see especially **044/2.5–8**).

The normal, neutral way of referring to actions that are past, however, is in the ***simple form***:

(27) a. Trisha visited Sam in hospital yesterday.
b. The two robbers left the shopping mall at 10 am.
c. We went on holiday at the end of July.
d. Our train arrived in Cornwall in the early morning.

Use of the ***progressive*** creates the impression of a ***framework situation***. If no ***intrusion point*** is given immediately, as in (28)a., the question arises as to what it could be. If a time point is present, as in (28)b., the question is why, as an intrusion point, it is contextually significant:

(28) a. Trisha was visiting Sam in hospital yesterday ...

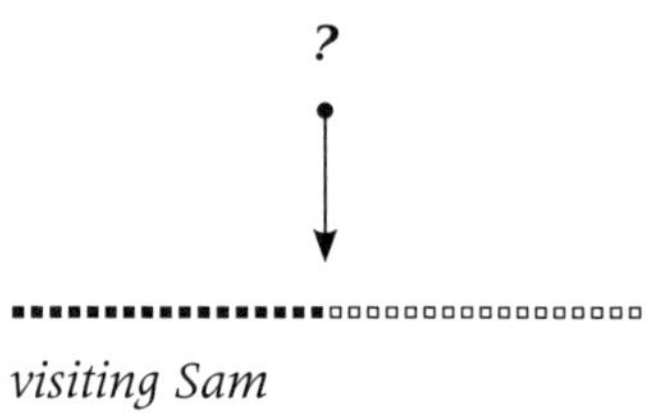

b. The two robbers were leaving the shopping mall at 10 am ...

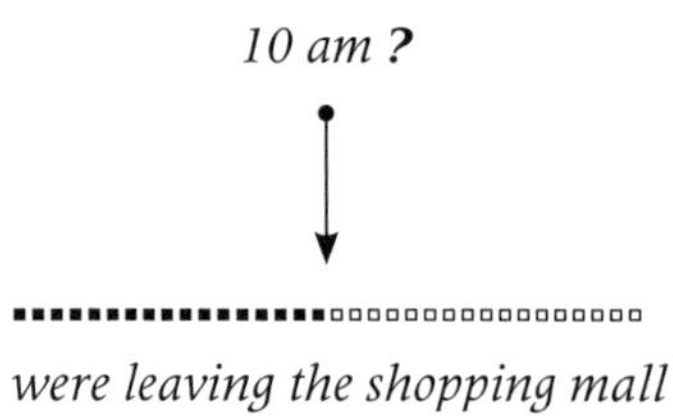

Actions in the ***simple form*** would give us the answers:

(29) a. Trisha was visiting Sam in hospital yesterday, when she met her old friend, Dr. Grant.

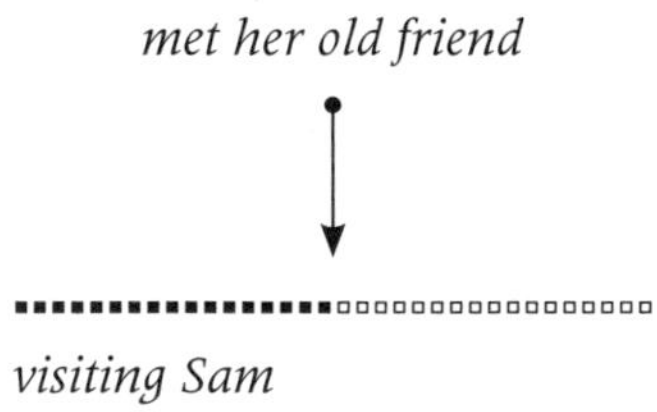

b. The two robbers were leaving the shopping mall at 10 am when they ran into the arms of the police.

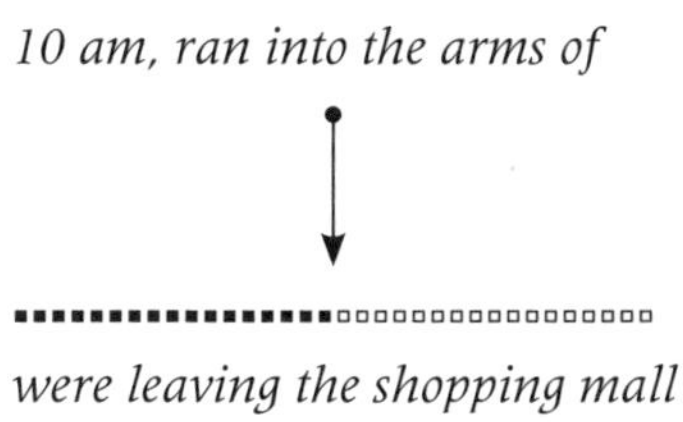

Notice, again, the difference between ***framework situation*** and ***sequence***:

(30) a. What were you doing when the doorbell rang, Mrs. Chunter?

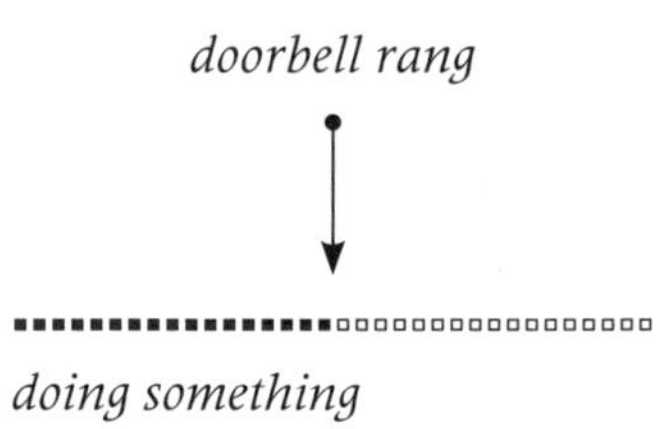

b. What did you do when the doorbell rang, Mrs. Chunter?

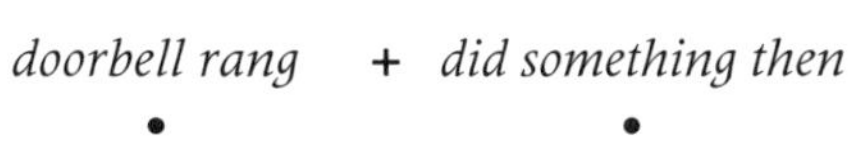

To emphasize the point again, then, events seen ***as a whole*** (= the normal situation) are expressed in the ***simple form***. A particular sign of this ***perfective*** view is the expression of actions in ***sequence***, as in (30)b.

Ongoing events i.e. those in the course of happening at a defined point in the past, require the progressive form. This always implies a ***framework situation*** (= ***imperfective*** view). Actions ***intruding into the framework situation***, on the other hand, are always ***perfective***, and take the simple form. All this can be illustrated using the scene-setting function typical at the beginning of narratives, which makes use of a ***'multiple frame-***

work situation'. This creates a kind of moving picture in which several actions are simultaneously ongoing. Plot elements in sequence (i.e. first steps in the beginning story) then ***intrude*** (see also **044/1.4** above, especially example (7)):

(31) The Morrises were sitting beside the fire. Dolly was reading a book and Fred was attempting to solve a rather difficult crossword puzzle in their daily paper. The dog was snoring peacefully at his feet. Suddenly a loud knock sounded at the front-door. Dolly and Fred both started. "I wonder who that can be so late?" said Dolly hesitantly. Fred laid his paper slowly aside, got up and went into the hall.

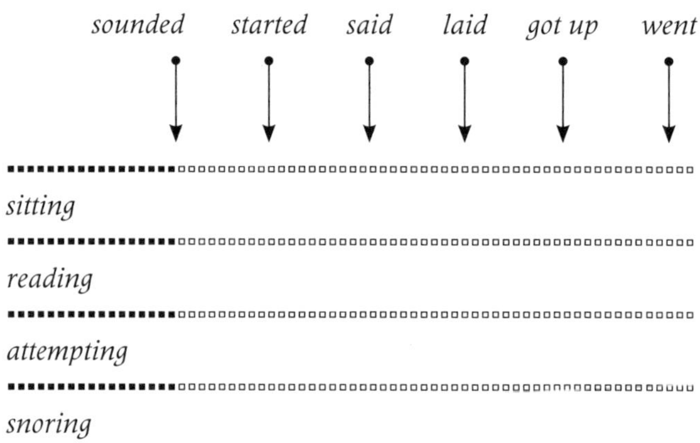

044/6 The past tense: further points on aspect usage

Having discussed the core of aspect meaning in the past tense, we now turn to the finer points of context and one or two border areas of usage. These are the same as in the present tense, and follow the same principles (see also **044/2.2–4**, and **044/2.7–8**.). They concern different ways of regarding an action as 'in progress', reference to habits and states, and the expression of future meaning.

044/6.1 Actual and general progressives

In **044/2.2** we distinguished two ways in which the progressive refers to an action as ongoing: literally (an ***actual progressive***); and in the general sense of being an incomplete, or 'running process', though not necessarily in the course of occurrence at the reference point (a ***general progressive***). Here are past tense examples:

(32) a. I was watching television when the children came in. (***actual progressive***)
b. Mary and George were still modernizing the kitchen when we stayed with them for the weekend. (***general progressive***)

044/6.2 Habits and general truths

General truths are sometimes regarded as 'timeless', but this is misleading. Tense gives them a time-sphere orientation. The present tense says that they are valid at the moment of speech; the past tense that they were valid at some past point of time. The same applies, of course, to habits in the more personal sense. The aspect required (as in the present tense) is the ***simple form***:

(33) a. In Galileo's day, according to the general doctrine, the sun and stars circled the Earth, which occupied the centre of the universe.
b. In those days I worked in the City and travelled to the office everyday by Tube.

As with the present tense, the ***progressive*** is used for two types of habit reference: ***modal***, expressing annoyance, and reference to habits of a ***temporary*** kind:

(34) a. My car was constantly breaking down. I was always getting stranded in some remote corner of the country. (***modal***, 'annoyance' use)
b. At the time Beryl was looking after stray dogs privately. That was before she got a permanent job at the kennels. (***temporary*** habit)

044/6.3 Stative verbs

Stative verbs are subject to the same aspectual principles in any tense (see **044/2.7–044/2.8**). Here are a few past tense examples:

(35) a. Our teachers ***did not realize*** how little we ***understood*** of what they ***thought*** we ***knew***.
b. Nothing ***was*** what it ***appeared*** to be.
c. They ***owned*** a horse in those days, an Arabian filly.
d. Suzie and Eileen ***were*** just ***having*** something to eat, when the phone rang. (***dynamic***, action use of *have*)
e. When we offered to buy the house, we ***were assuming*** that the bank would give us the necessary loan. (***dynamic***, mental action use of ***assume***)

044/6.4 The past tense in future time clauses and conditionals

As a carrier of future meaning in ***future time clauses***, the past tense functions as what is sometimes called a ***future-in-the-past***, i.e. the future viewed from a past reference point:

(36) a. She promised that as soon as they ***arrived*** in London, they ***would find*** out what plays were on.
b. The children ***would*** probably ***be*** tired when they ***got*** back from the zoo, she thought.
c. I said I ***would*** have a shower before we ***went*** down to dinner. (see also example (24) above)

Cases like this nearly always involve ***indirect speech*** (see chapter 11). The ***sequence-of-tense rule*** from a ***present*** perspective requires ***present simple*** in the ***time clause*** and usually a ***will***-form (or some other modal verb) in the ***matrix.*** For the ***future-in-the-past***, these are simply shifted into the past tense, i.e. ***past simple*** in the ***time clause*** and ***would*** (or some other modal past form) in the ***matrix***.

The ***open conditional clause*** can also be shifted back into the past in this way:

(37) a. He explained that Sharon would not be able to play at the squash club, unless she became a member first.
b. The trainer said that if McGrath wasn't fit by Saturday, Brookes would have to play in goal. (see also example (25) above)

This too, then, is an example of ***future-in-the-past***. However, there is also a very different kind of conditional sentence with the ***same*** sequence-of-tense pattern. This is not the result of 'shifting back', and is actually ***not*** a past-referring sentence at all, but ***future-oriented*** from a ***present*** perspective, just like the open conditional sentence:

(38) a. If you ***touched*** me, I'***d*** (***would***) scream!
Wenn du mich berühren würdest, würde ich schreien.
b. Sharon ***would*** not be able to play at the squash club, unless she ***became*** a member first.
Sharon würde nicht im Squash-Club spielen dürfen, bevor sie/wenn sie nicht erst Mitglied werden würde.
c. If McGrath ***wasn't*** fit by Saturday, Brookes ***would*** have to play in goal.
Wenn McGrath bis Samstag nicht fit wäre, müsste Brookes im Tor spielen.

This is the second type of future-referring conditional sentence (after the ***open condition***), often called the ***unreal condition***. It expresses the condition and its outcome as possible, but as more 'theoretical' and less likely than the ***open condition*** does (for more details on conditional meaning, see chapter 11).

044/6.5 The past tense with arranged future meaning

This is another case of a ***future-in-the-past***, i.e. future reference viewed from a past perspective. This type is simply a 'shifted back' version of an ***arranged future*** reference in the ***present tense***:

(39) a. Brookes was playing in goal on the Saturday.
b. The game started at 4 o'clock on the Saturday afternoon.
c. We were going on holiday at the end of July. We were staying at a small hotel in St. Ives.

These sentences could result from indirect speech, but could equally derive from a normal past time perspective in direct speech. An example would be direct future reference in a past tense narrative (future, that is, relative to the reference time of the narrative): *We were training hard for the match against Hurst United. The game started at 4 o'clock on the following Saturday afternoon. Brookes was playing in goal.*

Note again that with arranged future events, the ***simple form*** is used for ***inanimate*** subjects, in particular when the event is part of an official programme or timetable. The progressive is used for people and animals (= ***animate*** subjects).

Chapter 10 Verbs: The Perfect Tenses

045 Introduction

Going back to tense and aspect as a system, we must remember that every finite verb is marked for ***primary tense***, ***secondary tense***, and ***aspect***; and also that all three categories are ***binary paradigms***: ***present*** or ***past*** (primary tense), ***perfect*** or ***non-perfect*** (secondary tense) and ***simple*** or ***progressive*** (aspect). As examples: *has been running* is ***present*** (primary tense), ***perfect*** (secondary tense) and ***progressive*** (aspect); *ran* is ***past*** (primary tense), ***non-perfect*** (secondary tense) and ***simple*** (aspect). And so on.

The important point in this system is that the three categories are ***separate*** from one another, and must be carefully distinguished. Only then can the meaning contrasts ***inside*** a particular category (e.g. ***simple-progressive*** in the ***aspect*** category) be properly explained. This was precisely the approach in the last two chapters.

In this chapter we first of all clarify the general distinction between ***primary tense*** and ***secondary tense***, in preparation for dealing with the main question:

What are the differences between the two members of the ***secondary tense*** category, i.e. between ***perfect*** and ***non-perfect***?

We will approach this question first from the perspective of the ***tense notation*** system introduced at the beginning of chapter 9. As was said, ***primary tense*** locates a ***point of reference*** (**R**) either at the ***speaker-time*** (**S**), or before it.

Expressed in notation form, that is, ***present tense*** = **R,S**, and ***past tense*** = **R–S**. The ***reference point*** (**R**) is not the action point itself, but the immediate perspective from which the action point is viewed. It is necessary to make this distinction between ***reference point*** (**R**) and ***action point*** (**A**) because the two do not always coincide. Take, for instance, a sentence in the past perfect:

(1) Millie had phoned the day before.

What this means is 'the day before the day we are referring to'. That is, the day of the phone-call (the ***action point***) is actually ***before*** another time which the text is oriented to. This 'orientation time' is the ***reference point***. Without it, the use of the past perfect would be ungrammatical. The ***past perfect*** always means 'looking back from a particular point in the past to another point ***before it***'. Here, then, we have the time relation expressed in the notation as **A–R** (= ***action point*** before ***reference point***).

According to our tense system, the verb form *had phoned* in (1) has two tense markers, one for ***primary*** tense (***past***), and one for ***secondary*** tense (***perfect***). The ***past*** gives the relation **R–S**; the ***perfect*** gives the relation **A–R**. This shows us clearly the different functions of ***primary tense*** (relating **S** to **R**), and ***secondary tense*** (relating **R** to **A**). The notation for the verb form *had phoned* as a whole is therefore **A–R–S**.

Note that the other member of the ***secondary tense*** category is the ***non-perfect***. This also relates **R** to **A**, of course, but says that they are the same, i.e. **A,R**. For the ***past non-perfect*** (as, for example, in *Millie phoned*), we therefore have, as a whole, the value **A,R–S**.

The ***present perfect***, like the ***past perfect***, also gives the relation **A–R**. In this case, however, the ***primary*** tense is the ***present*** (= **R,S**). The value for the present perfect as a whole, then, is **A–R,S**.

Here an overview of notation forms for all tenses, so that they can be compared:

	Primary Tense	*Secondary Tense*	Notation	*Aspect*
Andy eats	*present*	*(non-perfect)*	A,R,S	*simple*
Andy is eating	*present*	*(non-perfect)*	A,R,S	*progressive*
Andy has eaten	*present*	*perfect*	A–R,S	*simple*
Andy has been eating	*present*	*perfect*	A–R,S	*progressive*
Andy ate	*past*	*(non-perfect)*	A,R–S	*simple*
Andy was eating	*past*	*(non-perfect)*	A,R–S	*progressive*
Andy had eaten	*past*	*perfect*	A–R–S	*simple*
Andy had been eating	*past*	*perfect*	A–R–S	*progressive*

Note that aspect has no effect on notation forms, i.e. both aspects have the same notation.

The present perfect 046

046/1 Time orientation and general meaning

We have just seen that perfect tenses show an **A–R** relation. The action, that is, is related to a point of time ***after*** its occurrence. In other words, the action is ***not*** seen in the context of the time at which it happened, the ***action point***; instead, it is regarded as a factor of experience at that later time (i.e. at **R**, the ***reference point***). With the ***present perfect***, **R** is at **S**, and the full notation is **A–R,S**, as shown above.

This is a very concise way of expressing the general, basic meaning of the ***present perfect***: the ***present perfect*** expresses a ***past action*** as a ***factor of present experience***.

Consider the following examples:

(2) a. Chris has been working in this office for 5 weeks.
b. I have repaired the heating system.

In the sense of our definition, (2)a. can be interpreted as *Chris now has 5 weeks of work experience in this office,* or *We in this office/the world in general now have (has) 5 weeks' experience of Chris working here.*

The question of exactly ***whose experience*** is meant has to be decided on the basis of the individual context. The general message is 'This experience is now present'. By (2)b. I may mean that the heating system possesses the experience of being repaired, or that I possess the experience of doing it. This is a rather abstract level of meaning. What it signals exactly depends on context and speaker intention. It is these situational factors that give the general meaning its real communicative 'shape'. In the case of (2)b. this could be any of the following:

(3) a. Look at my achievement! I am a success!
b. The heating now works and it'll be warm again.
c. Looking after the heating has always been my job.
d. The job is done, but I can't tell you why it's still cold in here.

These are only typical or probable interpretations. In a real situation the intended message might be a combination of any of them, or something quite different. This underlines the importance of ***contextual meaning*** with the present perfect.

Below (see **046/3–046/5**), we explain typical types of context, and group them in three categories of concrete common usage: the ***continuative perfect***, ***the experiential perfect***, and ***the resultative perfect***. These all represent ***contextual variations of the general meaning***. They are an important basis for a concrete understanding of what the perfect means communicatively. They are also a central factor concerning the choice of ***aspect*** in the perfect, which is not quite the same as in the non-perfect.

A final point to be made in connection with general time-orientation concerns the use of ***time adverbials***. Which ***time adverbials*** are compatible with the present perfect? To answer this, we need to look briefly at the general time relations between adverbials and tense.

046/2 Time orientation, adverbials, and tense

- Some time adverbials are clearly **S**-related (*now, last week*). We will call these ***strongly deictic***.
- Others are **S**-related, but ambiguous. An example is *then,* which is clearly not present-referring, but apart from that could mean either future or past. We will call this type ***weakly deictic***.

- And finally, we have examples like *for three days, all summer, in the afternoon*, etc., which are ***non-deictic***.

Deictic Adverbials can be given a time-notation similar to that of the tenses. For instance, *now* is **R,S**, *last week* **R–S**, *next week* **S–R**, and so on. (The **S–R** value does not apply to tense, as there is no future tense as such. But it is important for adverbials.)

The ***primary tense compatibility rule*** says that **R–S** adverbials can combine only with **R–S** tense, and generally that **R,S** adverbials are compatible only with **R,S** tense. From this it follows that a sentence like **I am doing it yesterday* is wrong, because the tense value **R,S** (*am doing*) clashes with the adverbial value **R–S** (*yesterday*). For the same reason, a present perfect is not compatible with an **R–S** adverbial either (**I have done it yesterday*), since here the primary tense is also **R,S** (i.e. ***present***).

There is also a ***secondary tense compatibility rule***. This has to do with **A–R** relations.

The adverbials concerned are ***time-span*** adverbials with an **A–R** relation in the meaning. This may already be in the adverbial meaning (e.g. *since X*), or it may be required by the context, e.g. when a time-span such as *for three days* is intended to mean *for the last three days*. The rule here is that an **A–R** relation in the adverbial requires an **A–R** relation in the ***secondary tense***, i.e. the verb must be in the ***perfect***.

We can therefore say *I have been in London since June* or *I had been in London since June*, but not **I am in London/I was in London since June*.

German speakers may make mistakes here, as the German equivalents do not use the German perfect: *Ich bin in London seit .../Ich war in London seit ...* ⚠

These points are dealt with in greater detail during discussion of the ***perfect categories*** below.

We will now look at how these basic rules for the present perfect become ***context-specific***.

046/3 Time-span perfects: the continuative

The most concrete use of the present perfect is with a ***past-present time-span***:

(4) a. I've been cooking for over an hour.
b. Mike has been sunbathing in the garden all day.
c. Bengt has been writing a travel guide to Australia since he got back from Melbourne.
d. Phyllis has been teaching at a private school since the beginning of September.

This is called the ***continuative perfect***. It refers to an action which begins in the past and continues to **S**, the moment of speech. In other words, the time meaning is ***up to now***, and the action occurs ***throughout the time-span***. The context usually implies that the action is still going on at **S.**

046/3.1 Time-span and action

What makes this kind of perfect particularly concrete is that it is the only type that permits ***reference to the action time***. This is possible because the action time is identical with the time-span, and **S** is ***part of the time-span***, i.e. its later limit:

(5)

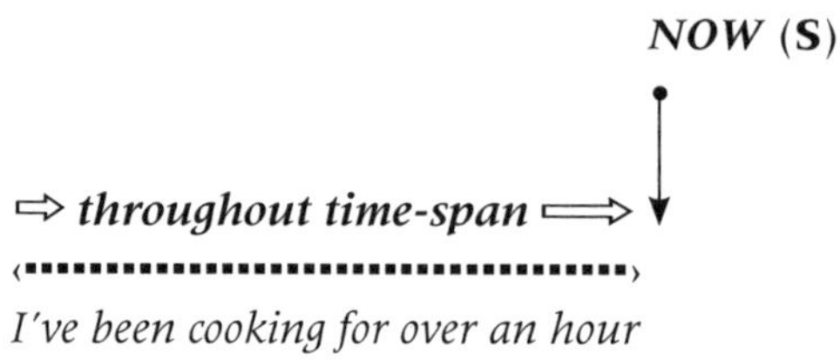

This looks rather like a framework situation (see chapter 9), but it is not one. The difference is that **S** is not an intrusion point. It is not inside the action time, but marks the end of it. This is reflected in the perfect notation **A–R**. The **A–R** relation tells us that we have an 'end view' of the action time. This shows us that ***continuatives*** refer to an ***accumulation*** of action focused on **R**.

What we have here, then, is a particularly concrete variant of the general meaning of the present perfect: ***the presence now of experience of a past action***. The experience of the action in this case is the experience of a ***particular time quantity of it***, see also (2)a. above.

Two interesting points underline this. Firstly, if the time quantity is an exact one, the statement is only true at **S**. For example, *I've been cooking for 40 minutes* is true only when I make the statement. One minute before this, I would have had to say *I've been cooking for 39 minutes*; a minute later I would have to say *I've been cooking for 41 minutes*. Secondly, for ***up to now*** actions ***only*** the present perfect (and no other tense) can be used. The ***continuative perfect*** therefore shows ***general*** present perfect meaning particularly clearly (= 'the possession at **S** of experience of an action before **S**').

046/3.2 Interaction of perfect and time-span

It is important to remember that the time-span is ***not*** part of the tense meaning. The ***up-to-now*** meaning comes either from the ***adverbial*** alone, or from the combination of ***present perfect + adverbial***. There are three types of time adverbial with continuatives:

(6) a. ***non-deictic*** and **R-*neutral***, e.g. *for 40 minutes;*
b. ***non-deictic***, but **A–R**-referring, e.g. *for the **past** 40 minutes;*
c. ***deictic*** and **A–R**-referring, e.g. *for the **last** 40 minutes.*

Type (6)a. can be used with any tense. In combination with a present perfect (*I have been cooking for 40 minutes*) it takes on an ***up-to-now*** meaning.

Type (6)b. can only be used with perfect tenses, because of the 'built-in' **A–R**-reference (see also under **046/2**). With a present perfect it takes on an ***up-to-now*** meaning: *I have been cooking for the past 40 minutes*. With a past perfect, as we will see later, it has an ***up-to-then*** meaning, e.g. *When they arrived, I had been cooking for the past 40 minutes.*

Type (6)c. has an **A–R**-reference, ***and*** an **R,S**-reference. That is, it can only appear with the ***present perfect***.

Finally, a note on the preposition ***for***. As this refers to a ***quantity*** of time (see also chapter 6, **036/2.7**), it underlines the ***throughout*** meaning that is typical of the ***continuative*** perfect: the time-span, that is, is the ***action time***.

And a final reminder: ***since*** must ***never*** be used with a time quantity. The translation of German *seit* with a ***time quantity*** is always ***for***.

046/3.3 Since-structures

These are adverbials that have an **A–R** meaning in the sense of either ***up-to-then*** or ***up-to-now*** (compare (6)b.). With the present perfect (**A–R,S**), the meaning is ***up-to-now*** (owing to the **R,S**-relation of the primary tense, as we have just seen). (4)c. above (*Bengt has been writing a travel guide to Australia since he got back from Melbourne*) can be shown in a diagram like this:

(7)

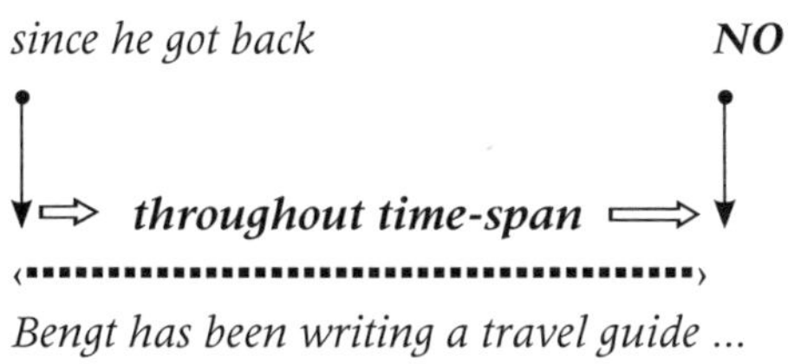

Since and its time structures and their consequences were discussed fully in chapters 6 and 7 (see chapter 6, **036/2.7**, and chapter 7, **038/2.5**). Here are the main points again:

- ***since*** refers to a ***point of time*** and not to a quantity of time;
- this point of time is always the ***start*** of a time-span;
- ***since*** is therefore followed by a time expression (e.g. adverb/noun), or by a verb in the past tense;
- the time-span is always an **A–R** time-span: the verb referring to this must therefore be in the ***perfect***. When **R** is at **S** (**R,S** in our notation), this is the ***present perfect***;
- the sequence of tense is therefore either: ***since*** + ***past tense*** + ***present perfect***; or: ***since*** + ***time expression*** + ***present perfect***.
- it is ***not*** possible to replace the ***past tense*** immediately following ***since*** by a present perfect (i.e. not * ... *since he has got back from Melbourne*).

The reason for the last point is this: the action represents a ***point of time in the past***, shown also by the fact that the verb form could be replaced by an adverbial expression of past time. ***Since*** is therefore followed immediately by a ***past focus*** (=**A,R–S**), making the ***past tense*** necessary.

German speakers often make the mistake of using the present perfect here (i.e. *... *since he has got back from Melbourne*). Reasons for this are:

- German itself can use a perfect here: ... *seit er aus Melbourne zurückgekommen ist.* This has to do with the general use of the German perfect as an English past tense equivalent. The point is discussed later in more detail (see particularly under **046/5.7**, and **046/6.6**).
- ***Since*** is often generally associated in learners' minds with the use of the perfect because of the time-span. But note: first it is the ***starting-point*** of the time-span (past focus!) which follows ***since***; the time-span itself comes after that, in ***second*** place.
- There is also a (not very frequent) use of ***since*** followed directly by the present perfect. This has a different meaning, but is often confused with the normal past tense use (see the next point).

What has just been discussed is the normal case, i.e. the one where ***since*** refers to the ***beginning*** of the time-span. Sometimes, however, ***since*** may relate to the time-span ***as a whole***. Here the present perfect is required in the conjunction clause as well:

(8) Since he ***has been back home***, Bengt has been writing a travel guide to Australia.

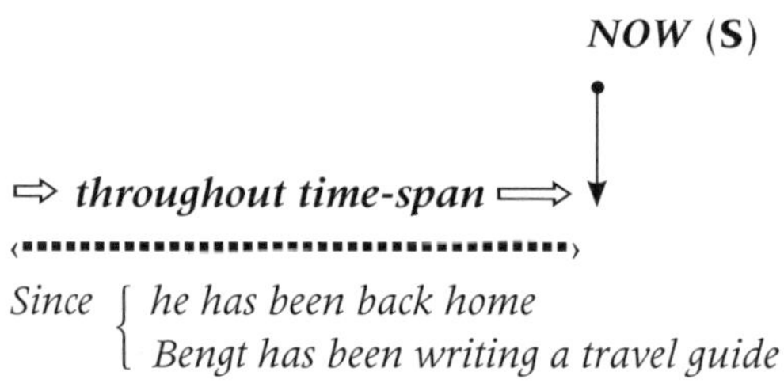

046/3.4 Different forms of continuative, and the aspect question

The preferred choice of aspect with all ***continuatives*** is the ***progressive***. In most cases it is obligatory. It is the progressive which stresses the 'durative', ***throughout*** meaning of the action in relation to the time-span.

To look at things more exactly, though, we need to distinguish between ***actual continuatives*** (like ***actual progressives***), ***general continuatives*** (like ***general progressives***), and a third category, ***habitual continuatives***.

(9) a. I've been cooking dinner for over an hour. (***actual continuative*** = literally in progress).
b. Bengt has been writing a travel guide to Australia since he got back from Melbourne. (***general continuative*** = not literally uninterrupted, but process regarded as continuing throughout the time-span).
c. Phyllis has been teaching at a private school for the last three years. (***habitual continuative*** = habit valid throughout the time-span).

(9)a. and b. are exactly the same as their equivalents in the present or past progressive. ***General continuatives*** normally have a longer time-span than ***actual continuatives***. But apart from that, they are regarded in the same way, i.e. as a ***single action***. This distinguishes both of them from a ***habitual continuative***, as in (9)c., which is not a single action, but a ***repeated*** one. ***General continuatives*** are only possible with ***telic*** actions (*I have been building a shed for 6 months*). With ***non-telic*** actions, continuatives that are obviously not ***actual*** (because of time-span length or other context factors) would normally be understood as ***habitual***: *Sally has been selling houses for the last six months.*

For ***actual*** and ***general continuatives*** with ***telic*** actions (= goal-directed), as in (9)a. and b., the progressive is obligatory. With ***non-telic*** actions it is also usually obligatory: *I've been cooking for over an hour.* Very occasionally, however, a simple form may occur to suggest a certain sense of 'completion', finality, or implication that the action is about to end: *We've waited for over three hours. Let's go now.* This has a strong ***resultative*** meaning (= 'a unit of waiting is complete'), see below under **046/5**.

Habitual continuatives are a special case. The first thing to note is that here, too, the ***progressive*** is the preferred form, as in (9)c. This contrasts with the non-perfect tenses, where the ***simple*** form is necessary (unless the habit is only temporary): *Phyllis teaches at a private school.*

The ***simple*** form, however, is also found in the ***continuative perfect***: *Phyllis has taught at a private school for the last three years.* It is more common here than with ***actual*** and ***general continuatives***, and can also appear with telic actions: *I've cooked the dinner for over 18 months.*

But it also has a resultative, final character. What this means exactly depends on context, e.g. *I've cooked the dinner for over 18 months (and I therefore have the right to continue/the right to stop now,* etc.).

Note that with states, i.e. ***stative*** verbs, the ***simple form*** must always be used, as in other tenses: *Our family has owned this house for 5 generations.*

046/3.5 Negation

When a continuative verb is negated, this does not normally negate the ***action***. Consider the following ***actual continuative*** and its negative:

(10) a. Dicky has been talking on the phone since midday.
b. Dicky has not been talking on the phone since midday.

(10)b. does ***not*** mean that Dicky has not been talking at all. What is negated here, quite simply, is not the action, but the ***time-span***, e.g. *Dicky has been talking on the phone for a long time, but not since midday (only since 1 pm).* If we want to negate the ***action itself***, the ***simple form*** must be used, as in (11)a., which means (11)b.

(11) a. Dicky has not talked on the phone since midday.
b. A phone conversation involving Dicky has not taken place since midday.

This is then no longer a continuative perfect, but an ***experiential perfect*** (see under **046/4** below for full details). The same negation rule applies to ***general continuatives***, i.e. negation of the ***action*** requires the simple form and changes the category of perfect from continuative to ***experiential***.

With ***habitual continuatives*** the case can vary:

(12) a. Dave has not played in the first team for months.
b. Dave has not been playing in the first team for months.

Both are possible in reference to habits and regularities. However, the progressive version (i.e. the negated continuative) is a special case: it would usually point to a ***recent*** change, or a ***temporary break*** in the habit. Otherwise, the ***negative experiential*** as in (12)a. would be used here also.

046/3.6 Continuative meaning in German

⚠ Along with several other European languages, German uses present tense (*das Präsens*) in continuative contexts. A common error is to transfer this into English:

(13) a. Ich sitze seit 9 Uhr hier.
b. *I am sitting here since 9 o'clock.
c. I have been sitting here since 9 o'clock.

The correct equivalent of the German sentence in (13)a. is (13)c., and ***not*** (13)b. The use of the present tense in its non-perfect form is ruled out by the **A–R** character of the time-span. The **A–R** time relation, as explained above and in chapter 8, makes a perfect form necessary in whatever primary tense.

Another way of expressing this (though a less systematic one) is to say: any ***before-*** **S** component in the meaning (here the ***past-present time-span***) rules out the use of a 'straight' (i.e. non-perfect) present tense.

046/4 Time-span perfects: the experiential

Here we have a second, and rather different, use of the present perfect with a ***past-present time-span***. This is the 'perfect of experience', or, as we call it, the ***experiential perfect***, already encountered in its negated form in **046/3.5**. Positive examples are:

(14) a. Harry has never cooked that dish before.
b. I've visited the Frankfurt Book Fair twice.
c. Bengt has written three travel guides to Australia.
d. Have you ever taught at a private school?

This is often less concrete than the continuative, since the time-span is frequently only implied. When this is so, it usually consists of the whole ***up-to-now*** life-span of at least one of the persons or things involved, e.g. in (14)b. *I've visited the Frankfurt book fair twice* ***in my life up to now***; or: *Bengt has written three travel guides to Australia* ***in his life up to now***.

Other adverbs with an ***up-to-now*** meaning that typically occur with ***experientials*** are *so far, ever, never, before,* etc. The time-span may also be limited to a definite period, e.g. *Bengt has written three travel guides to Australia* ***in the past five years***. Details are given below.

046/4.1 Time-span and action

Time-span structures are exactly the same as with the continuative perfect. **S**, that is, is ***part of the time-span***, i.e. its later limit, as all the adverbials just mentioned suggest. However, there is a big difference in the relation of action and time-span. With the ***experiential***, the meaning is not throughout, but ***within*** the time-span:

(15)

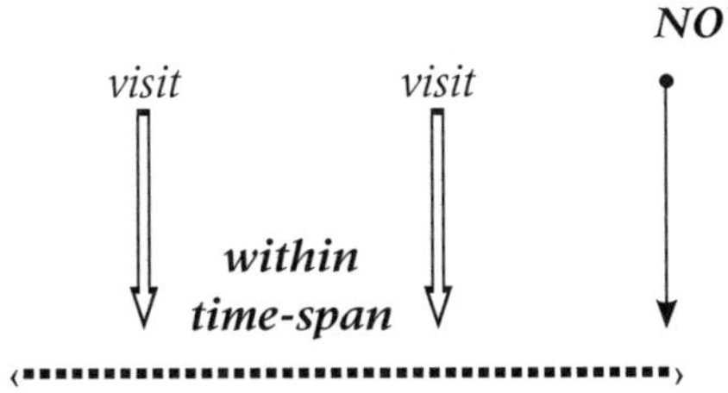

I've visited the Frankfurt Book Fair twice

Unlike the case with the continuative, the time-span here is ***not*** identical with the action time. ***Experiential*** reference is to the ***incidence*** (dt. *Vorkommen*) of the action ***within*** the time-span, i.e. whether it happened at all, and if so, how often. What is similar to the continuative, however, is the reference to an ***accumulation*** of action focused on **R** and **S**, i.e. ***the presence now of experience of a past action***. This is also, then, a clear reflection of the general meaning of the present perfect. Here, the ***accumulation*** is not in the length of the action, but in its numerical incidence. Consequently, ***experientials*** often occur with references to ***frequency*** (*once, twice, several times, often, always, sometimes,* etc.) or other forms of number quantity (*three travel guides, two visits,* etc.).

046/4.2 Types of time-span and their interaction with the perfect

Like the continuative, the ***experiential*** also gets its specific time-span meaning from ***external*** factors. These can be ***up-to-now*** adverbials, as with the continuative; but also various references to number and frequency can imply a ***past-present time-span***:

(16) a. I have often missed the morning train.
b. We have been to that restaurant a lot.
c. Sally has had four dogs (so far).
(See also the examples in (14) above).

The time factor in all examples so far is the 'life-span' type, i.e. meaning 'up to now in the lifetime/existence of things or people mentioned'. These are ***indefinite*** time-spans.

On the other hand, the length of time may be specifically limited (e.g. *in the last three weeks*). These are ***definite*** time-spans:

(17) a. I've had three different jobs in the last ten years.
b. We've been to Brighton this week.
c. Have you seen John today?

For-adverbials (with one or two exceptions) do not occur with ***experientials***, as they stress *throughout* rather than *within*. The usual preposition is *in*, as in (17)a.

Since-structures are also very common, and behave in the same way as with the continuative: *Donna has had no accidents since she bought her new car* (*since she has had her new car*).

Any ***definite*** time-span adverbials follow the same patterns as those with continuatives: that is, they are either quite ***neutral*** (*in ten years*), or **A–R**-referring (*in the past ten years*), or they actually carry the ***up-to-now*** meaning by themselves, e.g. *in the last ten years* (see (6) above).

046/4.3 Aspect and the experiential

Experientials always involve whole actions. This follows logically from the idea of ***incidence***. Saying whether something has happened at all, and if so how often, is reference to a 'complete occasion' of the action. It is underlined by the tendency to use numerals in quantifying the occurrence. The aspect used is therefore the ***simple form***.

046/4.4 Negative experientials

With ***negated experientials*** the time-span is 'filled' with a 'non-action'. This makes them a little like continuatives, especially as *for* can occur in the time-span, which is not the case with ***positive experientials***:

(18) a. I haven't eaten all day.
b. The Tylers have not lived here for 2 years.
c. Dion hasn't made a record since 1991.

Nevertheless, the meaning is clearly ***experiential***, as the reference is to ***incidence within*** a time-span.

The sentences in (18) can be regarded as the ***polar opposites*** of the following continuatives:

(19) a. I have been eating all day.
b. The Tylers have lived here for 2 years.
c. Dion has been making records since 1991.

046/4.5 Interplay of experientials with past tense

Unlike the continuative perfect, the ***experiential*** refers to actions that do ***not*** have an ***up-to-now*** action time. The ***action time***, that is, is ***past***. If the speaker focuses on the action time, therefore, the ***past tense*** is required. Compare:

(20) a. I have spoken to Thelma twice today.
b. I spoke to Thelma on the phone after lunch today, and I spoke to her again when I saw her in the shopping mall at 4 o'clock.

(20)a. and b. could be said at the same time (i.e. at the same **S**) in reference to the ***same*** past events. The difference lies simply in the speaker's perspective.

In (20)a. they are given an ***up-to-now*** time structure (**A–R,S**, present perfect obligatory!). In (19)b. focus is upon the ***action time***, which is ***past*** (**A,R–S**, past tense obligatory!).

In communication, there is frequent interplay (or switching) between the ***experiential perfect*** and the ***past tense***. ***Experiential perfects*** are often used to introduce new topics, events and actions. After that, when further details are mentioned, the focus is usually placed on the circumstances of the action. Reference to the ***action time*** is then either explicit, or implied. This requires the ***past tense***:

(21) a. "***Have*** you (ever) ***been*** to that small Vietnamese restaurant in Grant Street?" "Yes, I ***have***, several times. As a matter of fact, we ***went*** there only ***last week***. The meal ***was*** delicious. I ***had*** duck and Frank ***had*** fish."
b. Briony ***has had*** several holidays in Spain. The ***last one***, I think, ***was*** on the Costa de la Luz. She ***spent*** three weeks near Jerez.

In (21)a. the changeover is obvious when *last week* is mentioned. As already indicated, using an ***adverbial of past time*** automatically requires the ***past tense***. That is, if the adverbial is **A,R–S**, the tense accompanying it must also be **A,R–S**.

This does not have to be an explicit deictic part of the adverbial meaning, as with *last week*. Adverbial **S-*relations*** are usually contextually indicated. Moreover, any ***action-time*** reference is ***past***, obviously, if the action itself is ***past***. It should be noted that this is already ***implied*** in the ***experiential perfect*** itself. Although the chosen time structure is ***up-to-now***, the actions themselves are ***past***. Any reference to their ***action times*** therefore automatically makes the ***past tense*** necessary. This explains the forms *was* and *spent* in (21)b.

046/4.6 Experiential meaning in German

In experiential contexts, German is generally like English, and uses the perfect (*Perfekt*). Sometimes, however, the past tense (*Präteritum*) may also occur. This happens mainly with the verbs *haben* and *sein*, and occasionally with others in more formal and specialized style:

(22) a. Haben Sie ihn heute schon gesehen?
b. Ich habe noch nie Plum Pudding gegessen.
c. Hattest du bisher irgendwelche Schwierigkeiten mit Fluggästen?/Hast du bisher irgendwelche Schwierigkeiten mit Fluggästen gehabt?
d. Warst du jemals in Kanada?/Bist du jemals in Kanada gewesen?
e. Der in Berlin lebende Schriftsteller schrieb außerdem zahlreiche Essays und Kurzgeschichten/... hat außerdem ... geschrieben.

It should be stressed that the English equivalents can only be in the perfect. Again, as with the continuative, it is the **A–R** time-span relation that makes the ***perfect*** necessary for ***experiential*** meaning. The past tense here would be incorrect.

⚠ German speakers occasionally make this mistake because the German perfect and the German past tense are not as sharply distinct in use as they are in English. It should be added, however, that this more commonly leads to problems the other way round: i.e. wrong use of the English perfect when the English past tense is necessary. A more normal mistake for a German speaker would be to use the English present perfect correctly for an experiential introduction, but then to continue using the perfect for further past tense reference:

(23) a. I have been to that restaurant several times before. *In fact, I have been there last week.
b. Briony has had several holidays in Spain. *The last one has been on the Costa de la Luz. *She has spent three weeks near Jerez.

046/4.7 Experiential meaning in colloquial American

In American colloquial English, the ***experiential perfect*** is often replaced by the ***past tense***:

(24)	a. I have played tennis several times this week.	[Standard English]
	I played tennis several times this week.	[colloquial American]
	b. Have you ever been to Spain?	[Standard English]
	Were you ever in/Did you ever go to Spain?	[colloquial American]

Note, however, that this use is not standard, and occurs mainly in informal (and usually spoken) language. It sounds strange to British ears, as it seems to refer to a past time or past circumstances that the listener should already know about, e.g. *Did you ever go to Spain while you were in Europe?* Or: *I played tennis several times earlier this week when I had three days holiday.*

046/5 Non-time-span perfects: the resultative

Our third category of perfect has no time-span at all. Here the present experience of a past event lies simply in a ***state*** that it has left behind. That is, a ***result*** or consequence is present, e.g.:

	action		***present state***
(25)	a. I have washed the car.	→	The car is now washed.
	b. Tom has broken his leg.	→	Tom's leg is now broken.
	c. They have arrived in London.	→	They are now in London.

With ***telic*** and ***point-telic*** action types, the ***state*** referred to is easy to identify when the past participle can function as an adjective (*washed, broken*), as in (25)a. and b. The same is true when there is an adverbial involved as in (25)c. These sentence pairs show particularly clearly that there is a ***logical relation*** between sentences in the ***resultative*** present perfect and those in the present tense. The relation is called ***entailment*** (dt. *lo-*

gische Folgebedeutung): if the ***action-sentence*** is true, then the ***state-sentence*** must also be true. If it is not, the ***action sentence*** is ungrammatical.

The present tense ***entailment*** may not always be as clear as in these examples. Nevertheless, an ***entailment*** of some kind is given with all ***resultatives*** in the ***simple form***, and follows from the fact that the present perfect and the present tense both have an **R,S**-relation. Resultatives in the ***simple form*** are called ***primary resultatives***.

There is a second type of resultative that takes the progressive form:

	action		***present state***
(26)	a. I have been washing the car.	→	That is why my trousers are wet.
	b. Julia has been singing.	→	That is why her voice is hoarse.
	c. We've been decorating the hall.	→	That is why there are paint tins everywhere.

Resultatives of this kind are called ***secondary resultatives***. The principle of ***past action → present state*** is basically the same as with primary resultatives. But there is no strict entailment relation here. This is because of the different nature of the resultative meaning: as shown in the examples, this is basically a ***side-effect***.

Primary and secondary resultatives, then, are both concerned with resulting states, but the types of state are different. This is explained in more detail in the following.

046/5.1 Primary resultatives

With ***primary resultatives***, the resulting state is the ***natural conclusion*** of the action. ***Primary resultatives*** therefore have a tendency to occur mainly with ***telic*** actions. It is also with these that the ***primary resultative*** meaning can be seen most clearly, as above in (25). An end-point, conclusion or goal is part of the mode of occurrence, i.e. built into the action. As the ***simple form*** conveys the meaning of ***completeness***, the resulting state is ***the reaching of that end-point***. This is why there are quite definite ***present tense entailments***, as also seen in (25). Here are some further examples:

	action		***present state (entailment)***
(27)	a. I have repaired your bicycle.	→	The bicycle is now repaired.
	b. Sandra has made some tea.	→	Tea is now made.
	c. We have painted the front door.	→	The door is now painted (a different colour).

When the ***past participle*** can be used as an ***adjective*** like this, the entailment can be expressed directly and unmistakably. But this may not be the case; the entailed state then has to be expressed by paraphrase:

	action		***present state (entailment)***
(28)	a. I have bought muffins for tea.	→	There are muffins for tea.
	b. Jim has sold his car.	→	He no longer possesses one.
	c. We've rung the bell.	→	Our presence here is announced.

In addition to the actual entailed state, there may also be further consequences which the speaker wishes to indicate. These are then contextually implied, e.g.:

Action	*Entailed present state*	*Example of a contextual consequence or other situational meaning*
I have washed the car.	The car is now washed.	So now we can use it for the wedding.
Tom has broken his leg.	Tom's leg is now broken.	He won't be able to play for the next four months at least.
They have arrived in London.	They are now in London.	Let's go and pick them up.

The implied consequence is not part of the verb meaning. Nevertheless, ***primary resultatives*** are very often used to indicate ***additional contextual*** effects like this. In fact, communicatively these may be the main message which the speaker wishes to convey.

Finally, ***primary resultatives*** can also combine with ***non-telic*** modes of occurrence. Although not very common, this happens when there is a need to give the action a ***telic*** character, and show that a completed unit of activity has been 'achieved'. This invariably has an ***additional contextual*** meaning:

Action	*Entailed present state*	*Example of a contextual consequence or other situational meaning*
We have pushed the car.	A unit of *pushing* is now complete.	It still won't start, and its no good pushing anymore.
Paul and Denise have written.	Here is the result of their completed act of communication.	They have a new baby.
Have you tried (e.g. to convince them)?	Is an adequate amount of trying complete?	Can't you do something else to convince them?

046/5.2 Negative primary resultatives

The resulting state here is a negative one:

Action	*Entailed negative present state*	*Example of a contextual consequence or other situational meaning*
I haven't brought the flask of coffee.	The flask of coffee is not here.	We have no hot drink with us.
You haven't done your homework, Beryl.	Your homework is not done.	So please do it now.
We haven't bought any food.	There is no food for supper.	Shall we have a takeaway meal delivered?

046/5.3 Typical primary resultative adverbs: yet, already, just

Yet means 'by this time/by now', and is used in questions and negatives.

In a sense it could be seen as an ***up-to-now*** adverb: *Have you done your homework yet* (= *in the time up to now*)? But it stresses a condition *now* and the fact that the speaker expects a change of state to happen. For this reason we regard perfects with ***yet*** as ***resultatives*** and not experientials. This is underlined by the fact that ***yet*** can also combine with the (***non-perfect***) ***present tense***: *Dora isn't up yet* (= *she's still in bed*).

Already means 'as early as this/now', i.e. it has the sense 'sooner than expected': *I have already bought the bread and the cheese* (*so you only need to buy the other things we need*). ***Already***, that is, expresses the opposite expectation to that of ***yet***. It, too, can appear with the ***present tense***: *John is already in the garden, although Dora hasn't got up yet.*

Just means 'at this moment': *I am just doing my homework*. With the ***perfect*** it suggests a 'fresh' result: *I have just done my homework*. This is often interpreted as meaning 'the very recent past'.

That, however, is a little confusing, as any focus on the past (even the recent past) requires the past tense. All real ***recent past adverbials***, such as *two minutes ago*, or even *just now* (dt. *gerade eben*), can ***only*** appear with the ***past tense***, never with the perfect: *I saw John just now/two minutes ago*, not **I have seen John just now/two minutes ago*.

Note that in colloquial American ***yet***, ***already***, and ***just*** are used with the ***past tense*** (see **046/5.6**).

046/5.4 Primary resultatives as 'news breakers' and their interplay with the past tense

One of the main communicative functions of the present perfect is ***breaking news***, i.e. giving information about the occurrence of new events:

(29) a. An earthquake has occurred in southern California.
b. There has been an accident on the M25 motorway between junctions 4 and 5 in a clockwise direction.
c. Carol and Peter have got married.
d. The actress Belinda Paul has received an award for her performance in the film *Meeting Neighbours*.

The ***present perfect*** is obligatory here, as long as there is ***no focus*** on a ***past time***, i.e. no mention of ***when*** the events happened. However, if the ***action time*** is added, the ***past tense*** must be used:

(30) a. An earthquake occurred late last night in southern California.
b. There was an accident during the rush-hour this morning on the M25 motorway between junctions 4 and 5 in a clockwise direction.
c. Carol and Peter got married yesterday.
d. The actress Belinda Paul received an award for her performance in the film *Meeting Neighbours* at the annual New York Film Gala last night.

After a ***news-breaker perfect*** focus is then usually placed on the ***circumstances*** of the event. Even if no action time is mentioned, it is usually implied, and this makes the past tense obligatory:

(31) a. An earthquake ***has occurred*** in southern California. Residents in the towns of San Juan and Bridley ***were awoken*** by violent tremors in the early hours of this morning.
b. There ***has been*** an accident on the M25 motorway between junctions 4 and 5 in a clockwise direction. A tanker ***ran*** on to the central reservation and ***overturned*** shortly before 9 o'clock. No other vehicle ***was*** involved.
c. Carol and Peter ***have got*** married. The ceremony ***took*** place at a small country church near Sevenoaks, where Peter's mother lives.
d. The actress Belinda Paul ***has received*** an Oscar for her performance in the film *Meeting Neighbours*. On receiving the award she ***said*** ...

This switch from an introductory ***news-breaking perfect*** (= experience now of the past event) to a ***past focus*** with ***past tense*** (what happened ***then***, at the time of the event) is automatic. It happens as soon as the circumstances accompanying the action (e.g. ***when***? ***where***? ***how***? ***who***?) are referred to (see also **046/5.5**).

046/5.5 Implied past focus

To repeat the last statement in the previous section: ***past focus*** occurs immediately when the ***details of the action*** are mentioned:

(32) a. "Bertha has broken her leg." "Oh dear. How did that happen?"
b. "Someone has damaged the car." "Really? Who did that, I wonder?"
c. Jean has been fired. Her boss said her sales-rate was too low.
d. We have sold the flat. A couple from Hertfordshire bought it. They saw the place and signed the contract immediately.

The general rule is that once the perfect has been used to give first information, it cannot be used again, unless there is further reference to other states at **S**.

That is, I can say: *Bertha has broken her leg. She has been taken to a hospital in Farningham* (= focus on where she is ***now***). But I cannot say *Bertha has broken her leg. *She has fallen off a ladder*, because in the second sentence focus must shift to the circumstances of *break her leg*, i.e. the ***past***. Correct version: *She fell off a ladder*. On the other hand, if the falling is mentioned first, it is done in an introductory ***news-breaking perfect***: *Bertha has fallen off a ladder and broken her leg*. The perfect is necessary for *fall* here because there is not yet any past focus.

We therefore have to distinguish carefully between reporting results or effects of an action (***present focus***), and referring to the action itself and its details, which always ***implies past focus***.

Past focus can be implied even without an introductory perfect. The resulting state at **S** can be referred to by a present tense, e.g. *You have a bruise on your arm*. Further details of what led to this state then imply past focus: *Who did that? What happened?* In fact, I might not refer to the bruise at all in words, but just point to it, and then ask the same questions in the past tense. In other words, I do not need to refer to the present state at all if it is obvious to me and the other speaker. In this case the present state is ***presupposed as known***:

(33) a. John: "Who damaged the front gate, Mum?"
b. Mum: "Has it been damaged?"
c. John: "Yes, it has. Someone has almost knocked it off the hinges."
d. Mum: "Show me!" (Shows her). " Goodness me. How did that happen, I wonder?"

John imagines in his first question that Mum already knows the state of the gate. ***Past focus*** is then automatic. However, her reply shows that this ***presupposition*** is ***wrong***. She does not know, and first has to find out what the present state is (***present focus***). John then confirms the present state (***present focus***), Mum also confirms it for herself by looking, and then switches to past focus for the question of who the evil-doer was. Generally speaking, ***wh***-questions always ***imply past focus***.

Action time (and therefore ***past focus***) can be implied in other ways too, for instance through ***place adverbials***:

(34) a. I saw Hopkins on the train this morning (= during the time that I was on the train).
b. Dad met Tom's father at the shops (= during the time that he was shopping).

The past circumstances referred to may also be obvious from the present situation, or known to the speakers from a past situation in which they were involved together. This is a further case where the past time is ***presupposed as known***:

(35) a. Where did you put the wine, Dorothy? (= when you were putting the shopping away this morning).
b. I parked in King Street (= when I parked the car just now to come here).

046/5.6 Primary resultative meaning in colloquial American

As with experiential meaning (see **046/4.7**), the ***primary resultative perfect*** is often replaced by the ***past tense*** in colloquial American:

(36)	a. I have just done my homework.	[Standard English]
	I just did my homework.	[colloquial American]
	b. Mum, Billy has lost another tooth!	[Standard English]
	Mom, Billy lost another tooth!	[colloquial American]
	c. I've already bought the cheese.	[Standard English]
	I already bought the cheese.	[colloquial American]

Again, it should be pointed out that this use is not standard American. To British (or standard American) ears this seems to introduce a past focus that is actually not there.

However, the focus in all such examples is on ***present time***. This is shown quite clearly, for example, by the adverb ***already*** in (36)c.

(See chapter 1 for remarks on non-standard forms).

046/5.7 Problems with primary resultatives for German speakers

⚠ In German, primary resultative meaning is also expressed in the perfect, e.g.: *Bertha hat sich das Bein gebrochen; Ich habe meine Hausaufgaben schon/noch nicht gemacht; Jemand hat das Gartentor beschädigt.*

German speakers therefore have no problems in using the English perfect here. The difficulty is when to stop using it. As the German perfect is used quite freely with past tense meaning, there is a general tendency for German speakers to carry this over into English and use the English perfect also for past tense meaning. As in the case of ***experientials*** (see **046/4.6**, especially example (24) above), the danger is particularly great when introductory ***present*** focus ***switches*** to ***past*** focus, as discussed in **046/5.4** and **046/5.5**. As German could just continue with the perfect here, this is a special 'danger zone' for German speakers:

(37) a. Ein Unfall hat sich auf der Autobahn M25 ... ereignet. Ein Tanklaster ist kurz vor 9 Uhr auf den Mittelstreifen geraten und umgekippt.
... A tanker ***ran*** on to the central reservation and ***overturned*** shortly before 9 o'clock (not *has run ... *has overturned).
b. Carol and Peter haben geheiratet. Die Trauung hat in einer kleinen Kirche auf dem Land nahe Sevenoaks stattgefunden ...
Carol and Peter ***have got*** married. The ceremony ***took*** place at a small country church near Sevenoaks ... (not *has taken place).

This also applies to the other types of ***implied past focus***:

(38) a. Wer hat das gemacht?
Who did that? (not *Who has done ...?)
b. Ich habe heute Hopkins im Zug gesehen.
I saw Hopkins on the train this morning. (not *I have seen ...)
c. Wo hast du (heute morgen nach dem Einkaufen) den Wein hingeräumt, Dorothy?
Where did you put the wine (this morning after shopping), Dorothy? (not *Where have you put ...?)

046/5.8 Secondary resultatives

With ***secondary resultatives***, the resulting state is a ***side-effect*** of the action. In general, the action expresses a ***reason*** for the state: *Julia has been singing (that's why her voice is hoarse); Have you been crying? (Is that why your eyes are red?)*

Secondary resultatives are by far the most common kind of resultative with ***non-telic*** actions. But they are also very common with ***telic*** actions. In this case they say nothing about whether the conclusion of the action has been reached or not. The important point is simply that the ***action itself*** has had a ***side-effect***: *I have been washing the car (that is why my trousers are wet).*

Secondary resultatives always take the ***progressive form***. It is this that stresses the action itself and the fact that the particular state results from the ***ongoing action***.

Here are ***primary*** and ***secondary*** examples in contrast:

	action		*present state*
(39)	a. I have been washing the car.	→	e.g. wet trousers (***secondary***)
	I have washed the car.	→	car washed (***primary***)
	b. We've been decorating the hall.	→	e.g. paint cans everywhere (***secondary***)
	We've decorated the hall	→	hall decorated (***primary***)
	c. Sandra has been making some tea.	→	e.g. tea spilt on the table (***secondary***)
	Sandra has made some tea.	→	tea now made (***primary***)
	d. I have been repairing your bicycle.	→	e.g. oil on my hands (***secondary***)
	I have repaired your bicycle.	→	bicycle now repaired (***primary***)

046/5.9 Secondary resultatives negated

These are not very common but do occur occasionally. Here the state, i.e. the ***side-effect***, results from the fact that an action has ***not*** been taking place. Most usually this involves a habit or repeated action, as in (40)a. and b.:

	action		*present state*
(40)	a. Dad has not been taking his medicine.	→	e.g. that explains why he has stomach ache.
	b. You haven't been watering the plants.	→	e.g. they're dying.
	c. I haven't been attending properly to the. barbecue	→	e.g. the fire needs more fuel.
	d. You haven't been listening.	→	e.g. You can't give me any answers.

046/5.10 Problems with secondary resultatives for German speakers

As there is no progressive in German, the German perfect has only one form. This means that primary and secondary results can only be distinguished according to sense and context. For example, *Ich habe das Auto gewaschen* may mean *That's why I'm wet/tired*, etc. (***secondary***), or it may mean *The car is washed* (***primary***).

The danger in this situation is that German speakers might wrongly use the English present perfect ***simple*** form for the ***secondary*** resultative, i.e. **I've washed the car* for *That's why I'm wet.*

Secondary resultatives are best practised first of all with ***non-telic*** actions, e.g. *I've been cooking (so the windows are open); I've been running (that's why I'm out of breath)*, etc. With a ***non-telic*** action, the ***secondary*** meaning is the most usual resultative one, and the perfect progressive the most natural resultative form. When the connection between perfect progressive and secondary results has been habitualized, this can then be transferred to telic actions.

046/6 The present perfect: concluding points and summary

046/6.1 The three categories and their aspects

The three categories of perfect meaning are:

- ***Continuative Perfect:*** With ***up-to-now time-span***. Action ***throughout*** the time-span.
  Common adverbials: ***for*** *x amount of time*, ***since*** *y point of time*.
  Aspect: ***progressive form***
  Example: *I've been painting this wall for the last three hours.*
- ***Experiential perfect:*** With ***up-to-now time-span***. Action ***within*** the time-span. Time-span may be ***definite*** (e.g. *since last June*) or ***indefinite*** (whole life-span of subject or other entities implied).
  Common adverbials: *ever, never, always, often*, etc. (***indefinite***); ***since*** *y point of time*, ***for*** *x amount of time* (negative only) (***indefinite***). Also numbers of occasions: *once, twice*, etc. (***definite*** and ***indefinite***).
  Aspect: ***simple form***
  Example: *I've never painted this wall; I've painted this wall twice in the last year.*
- ***Resultative perfect:*** No time-span. Action has led to a state, result or consequence in the present. There are two types of ***resultative***.
  - ***Primary resultative***: Mainly with ***telic*** and ***point-telic*** actions. Result or state is the ***logical conclusion*** of the action.
    Common adverbs: *yet, now, already*, etc.
    Aspect: ***simple form***
    Example: *I have washed the car. → The car is now washed.*
  - ***Secondary resultative***: With ***telic*** and ***non-telic*** actions. Result or state is a ***side-effect*** of the action.
    Aspect: ***progressive form***
    Example: *I have been washing the car. → My trousers are wet.*
    Nothing is said here about whether the action was concluded or not.

046/6.2 Some ambiguities between the three categories

Resultative overtones can also be present with ***continuatives*** and ***experientials***. For example, *We've been walking all day* may also carry the message *We're tired*; and *I've never seen that film* may indicate, in context, *I would like to see it*. Nevertheless, whenever an ***up-to-now time-span*** is present or implied, it is the time-span meaning that is most prominent, and makes the category most concrete and easy to grasp. Any resultative overtones are purely contextual. On the other hand, it is important to realize that the time-span perfects can also be used to point to wider consequences in particular situations.

Another slight ambiguity to remember is that ***negated experientials*** with *since-* or *for-*type adverbials are in one way close in meaning to continuatives, and might in a sense be regarded as 'negative continuatives', e.g. *I haven't smoked for three months,* as the time-span is 'filled with a non-action'.

Despite this, though, the experiential meaning is obviously the main meaning: it is the incidence of the event that we are chiefly concerned with in such examples.

046/6.3 The question of 'recency'

It is sometimes said that the present perfect is used particularly for ***recent*** actions, i.e. those close to the moment of speaking. This is often true. In some ways, recency is built into the contextual use of the perfect, e.g. in the ***news-breaking*** use of ***primary resultatives***. In general, news refers to 'fresh' events. This is the case, in fact, with most states at **S**. They usually represent recent changes.

However, recency is not a rule. It is an accompanying meaning of certain contexts. In others it is not present at all. With ***up-to-now*** perfects, for example, the time-span can be of any length, as we have just seen. Another point is that past focus may occur with the very recent past, e.g. as in *two seconds ago*, or *just now*. It should also be noted that certain kinds of ***up-to-now*** time-span adverbials, such as *today, this week,* and even *recently* itself, can actually contain a ***past focus***, and must then occur with the ***past tense***.

Compare:

(41) a. Have you seen her recently?
b. I saw her recently at a conference in Malta.

(41)a. shows a genuine ***experiential*** and covers the entire time-span to **S**. In (41)b., on the other hand, focus on the action time cancels out the up-to-now effect. The time-span is just a larger 'container' for a past point of time. The verb refers to this past point of time. And this would make the present perfect ungrammatical.

046/6.4 The question of the 'pastness' of the action or action time

Learners are sometimes taught that the past tense is used when an action is 'over', and the present perfect is used when an action is 'not over'. This is wrong. ***Resultatives*** and ***experientials*** refer to actions that are ***definitely over***. But they are expressed as ***experience at S***.

It is **S** that is focused on, and not the action time: *I have been to America twice* (*up to now*). As we saw, however, it is also possible to refer to the ***same*** events with ***action time focus***.

Then we need the past tense: *I was in America in 2001 and 2007*. This illustrates that it is not the character of the action itself (e.g. 'past' or 'not yet past') which is important for the tense choice. It is the ***perspective*** chosen by the speaker.

046/6.5 Past tense for present perfect in colloquial American

In colloquial American English the ***experiential*** and the ***primary resultative*** are often replaced by the past tense:

(42) a. I have played tennis several times this week. [English experiential]
I played tennis several times this week. [colloquial American]
b. I have just done my homework. [English primary resultative]
I just did my homework. [colloquial American]

At present this is regarded in American English as sub-standard. It may, however, develop into one of the standard Americanisms in the future.

046/6.6 German-speaker difficulties summarized

⚠ The ***German perfect*** translates both the ***English present perfect*** and the ***English past tense***. That is, it is used for both **A,R–S** (= ***past focus***) and **A–R,S** (= ***present focus*** with ***perfect relation***):

(43)

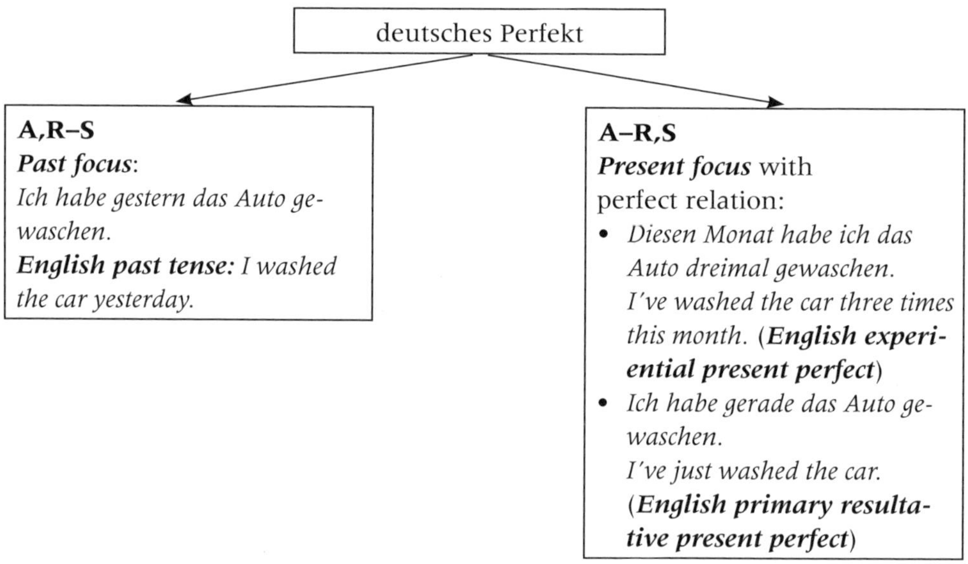

There is thus a tendency for German speakers to transfer the ***past-focus*** use of the ***German perfect*** to English. The English present perfect is then used wrongly with past tense meaning, e.g. **I have washed the car yesterday.*

A first step towards avoiding mistakes of this kind is to remember that the present perfect cannot combine with adverbs of past time. However, in many cases there is no past tense adverb; here, ***past focus*** is just ***implied*** by context, and is more difficult to identify. The following general guidelines can be a help:

- ***Primary resultatives*** and ***experientials*** often just introduce a topic for the first time. After this first reference, ***focus*** usually ***switches*** to the circumstances of ***individual past actions***, and therefore requires ***past tense***.
- When a present state has already been referred to (e.g. either in the present perfect or present tense), ***further reference*** implies ***past focus***: *This burn on my hand? Oh I got that*

from our oven. The same applies when the state is obvious from the situation, and does not need to be mentioned. On seeing an open window, for example, speakers must refer to the act of opening it in the past tense: *Darius probably* ***opened*** *it to let some air in, but I'll close it now.*

- ***Wh***-words (= interrogative adverbs and pronouns) automatically imply ***past focus*** in most cases: *Who did that?; Where did you get that hat?*, etc.
- ***Place adverbials*** usually imply ***action time*** (= ***past focus***): *I got this at the supermarket* (= *when I was at the supermarket*).
- Similarly, ***action time focus*** occurs when there is implied reference to a past situation which speakers and listeners already know about, or once shared with each other: *If you're looking for the milk, I put it in the fridge* (= *when we came back from shopping this morning*).

Two other problems mentioned above:

- ***Continuatives***: here the problem is that German uses a present tense, whereas English definitely requires the present perfect: *Sarah arbeitet seit 3 Jahren in Melbourne = Sarah has been working in Melbourne for 3 years.*
  A simple rule is that a present tense in English can ***never*** refer to an ***up-to-now*** time-span. Adverbial time structures of the **A–R** type always require the perfect.
- ***Secondary resultatives***: as there is no progressive in German, secondary resultatives are not distinct in form from primary resultatives: *Ich habe gekocht* (*deswegen riecht es hier etwas nach Fett*). In English ***secondary resultatives*** require the ***progressive***: *I've been cooking* (*that's why it smells a bit of fat here*).

046/6.7 Present perfect or past tense? Summary

The present perfect is used only in the meanings of the three categories ***continuative***, ***experiential*** or ***resultative***. That is:

- when we refer to an action going on ***throughout*** an ***up-to-now time-span***: *We have been waiting in this queue for three hours.* (***continuative perfect***)
- when we refer to the occurrence of an action a number of times or never ***within*** an ***up-to-now time-span***: *Sharon has played tennis twice this week; Bill and Sue have never had much luck.* (***experiential perfect***)
- when we refer to an action that has led to a ***present result*** or ***consequence***, and we are ***not*** thinking of the action time itself, but of the state ***now*** (i.e. at **S**): *I have fed the dog*, i.e. *the dog is fed* (***primary resultative***); *I have been feeding the dog*, e.g. *that is the reason for the mess on the kitchen floor* (***secondary resultative***). (***resultative perfect***)
  It is ***resultatives*** and ***experientials*** that cause confusion with the past tense. This is because they also refer to actions that are ***past***. Although these actions are definitely ***over***, however, they are related either to an ***up-to-now time-span*** (***experientials***), or directly to a state present ***now*** (***resultatives***). Reference to ***action time*** or ***action circumstances*** makes the past tense obligatory.
  In all, then, any kind of ***past time reference*** requires the ***past tense***. This can be signalled by:

- a ***past time adverbial***: *We moved to this area in 2003/five years ago/last week.*
- an ***adverbial implied by context*** as referring to ***past time***: *She lived in Cornwall at that time/then.*
- an ***adverbial clause implying*** a ***past time***: *I damaged the car-door driving/as I was driving into the garage.*
- a ***past time context*** already ***mentioned*** or being talked about: *We never went to St. Paul's Cathedral* (e.g. *during the holiday in London that we are now talking about*).
- implied reference to an ***earlier*** (***speaker-shared***) ***past time context***: *I saw that film, by the way* (e.g. *as I said I would when we were talking about it last week*); *Where did you put the milk?* (= *when you put it away after using it this morning*).
- Other forms of implied reference to ***action time*** circumstances (see also **046/6.6** above):
  - ***place adverbials***: *I met Tom in the pub* (= *when I was in the pub*);
  - ***interrogative*** adverbs and pronouns: *How did that happen?*
  - reference to the ***cause*** of a present state ***already known*** or indicated: *I hit a tree* (pointing to the bent front wheel of a bicycle).

047 The past perfect

047/1 Time orientation and general meaning

As stated in the introduction, the ***past perfect*** has the notation form **A–R–S**.

The ***primary tense*** relation is **R–S**, i.e. ***past tense***; the ***secondary tense*** relation (as with all perfects) is **A–R** (= ***action time*** before ***reference time***). With the ***present perfect***, the reference time is **S**, i.e. ***now***. With the ***past perfect***, the reference time is ***then***, i.e. a ***past*** point or period of time. This past '***then***' is what the general context must be focused on for the ***past perfect*** to be possible. In other words, before I can use the ***past perfect***, I must already be talking about a ***past context***. Actions further back in the past are then related to this past context. I am therefore looking at those actions from the perspective of this past context (whatever it may be), and relating the actions to the particular '***then***' that I am talking about. This can be done in one of two basic ways:

- in the sense of a ***present-perfect-in-the-past***, e.g. *Sarah had already done her homework then* (= ***past perfect primary resultative***); *At that time we had been living in Toronto for 6 months* (= ***past perfect continuative***);
- in the sense of a ***past-tense-in-the-past***, e.g. *Sarah had seen Tony the day before* (= the day before the day referred to in the particular context).

047/2 The past perfect as present-perfect-in-the-past

This is an exact reflection of present perfect usage. Aspects, meanings and other criteria are exactly the same. Time-spans are ***up-to-then***, instead of ***up-to-now***.

047/2.1 The continuative past perfect

The meaning here is ***throughout*** an ***up-to-then time-span***. The normal aspect is the ***progressive*** form. Example: *I had been cooking for over an hour.* **R** is implied in the surrounding context, expressed in a ***then***-type adverbial such as *at x time,* or reflected in an extra time clause, e.g. *I had been cooking for over an hour at 10 o'clock/when Maria called.*

(44)

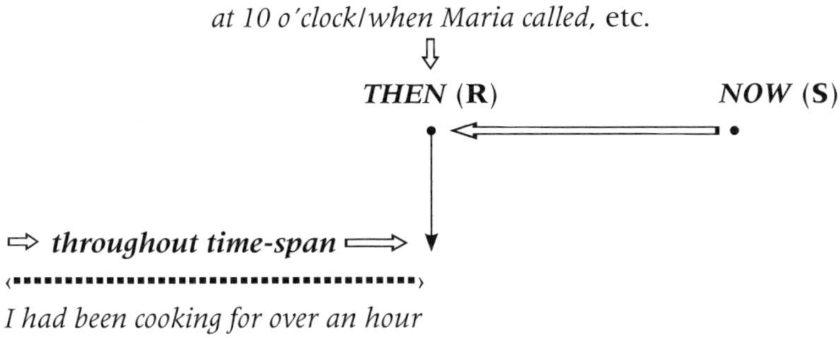

047/2.2 The experiential past perfect

The meaning in this case is ***within*** an ***up-to-then time-span***. The required aspect, as with the experiential present perfect, is the ***simple*** form.

Example: *I had visited the Frankfurt Book Fair twice.* Here, too, **R** can be implied in the surrounding context, or expressed adverbially, e.g. *I had visited the Frankfurt Book Fair twice at that time/up to then.*

(45)

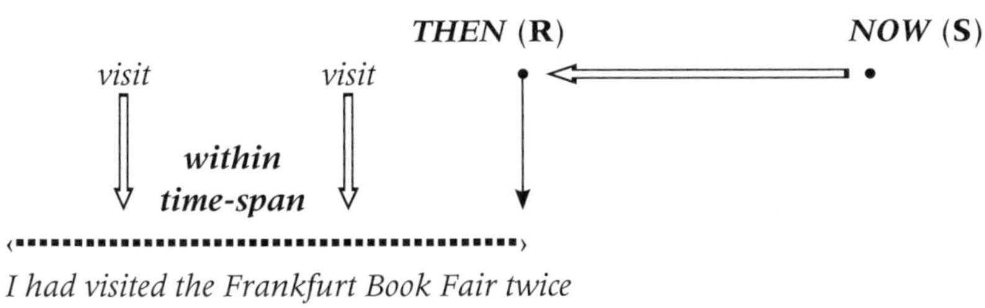

047/2.3 The resultative past perfect

As in the present perfect, ***primary resultative past perfect*** takes the ***simple*** form, and ***secondary resultative past perfect*** takes the ***progressive*** form.

(46) a. As Chris had repaired the heating, it was pleasantly warm again in the room. ***(primary resultative)***

b. As Chris had been repairing the heating, there were tools lying around everywhere in the room. ***(secondary resultative)***

In these examples, **R** is expressed in the past tense of the main clause, but, again, could just be implied by the larger context, or contained in a subordinate clause: *When we got* *back to the hotel, our rooms had been cleaned and the beds made.* Note that, as with the present perfect, the resultating state can be expressed in a non-perfect tense. Here, of course, it is the ***past*** tense:

	action		*resulting past state*
(47)	a. I had washed the car.	→	The car was washed.
	b. I had been washing the car.	→	My trousers were wet.

047/3 The past perfect as past-tense-in-the-past (= pre-past use)

Unlike the present perfect, the ***past perfect*** allows ***focus*** on ***action time***. That is, it functions like the past tense, but in a ***before-then*** or ***pre-past*** sense.

047/3.1 Secondary focus on pre-past action time

Let us return to the sentence in example (1) at the beginning of the chapter:

(48) Millie had phoned the day before.

As we said, this means 'the day before the day we are referring to'. Here, that is, we are ***looking back*** from a particular point in the past (**R**) to another point ***before*** it (**A**). The main focus is still on **R**. However, we have a kind of 'sub-focus' or ***secondary focus*** on the action time. Using the **R**-point as a platform for looking ***further back*** into the past is what we call the ***pre-past*** use of the past perfect. Even a framework situation is possible here, as with the ordinary past tense:

(49) Earlier in the day I had been washing the car when it had started to rain.

Note, though, that this is simply a variant meaning of the same **A–R** time structure as in the 'present perfect' use. That is to say, the **A–R** relation must still be quite clear, with the main focus of the context on **R**. If this is not so, the past perfect cannot be used.

047/3.2 Full focus shift to pre-past action time

To repeat what has just been said: the past perfect cannot be used when there is no clear **A–R** relation. This is shown by the following phenomenon: after looking back into the pre-past, speakers sometimes then stay there, adding more details. When this happens the **R**-focus then shifts completely to that action time, and the speaker 'drifts' into the past tense:

(50) Earlier in the day I ***had been*** washing the car when it ***had started*** to rain. I ***put*** my bucket and sponge back in the garage, but I ***left*** the car outside. I ***wanted*** the rain to wash off the last of the soap suds.

In other words, when the speaker first goes into ***pre-past*** 'mode', the ***past perfect*** is used to signal this. But then the pre-past actions slowly come into the centre of attention.

The need to emphasize the contrast between past and pre-past disappears and the focus changes. The main focus now shifts fully to the pre-past context, and makes it into an ***ordinary past***, i.e. **A,R–S.**

047/3.3 Direct past view vs. intervening R-point

We have just seen how the **A–R** relation disappears to give a ***direct past view*** or focus. That is, there is no longer the idea of looking further back from a standpoint already in the past. The view is now ***direct*** from **S**, without the intervening **R**-point. As already stated, this is an important general difference between the ***past tense*** and the ***past perfect***. Choosing a particular tense means choosing between different perspectives. In the following we see the same actions from these differing perspectives:

(51) a. Sally fed the dog, watered the plants and left the house.
b. Sally left the house. She had fed the dog and (had) watered the plants.

In (51)a. we follow the actions in the order that they happened: first number 1 (*feed*), then number 2 (*water*), and then number 3 (*leave*). Each one, that is, shows the same **A,R–S** relation:

(52)

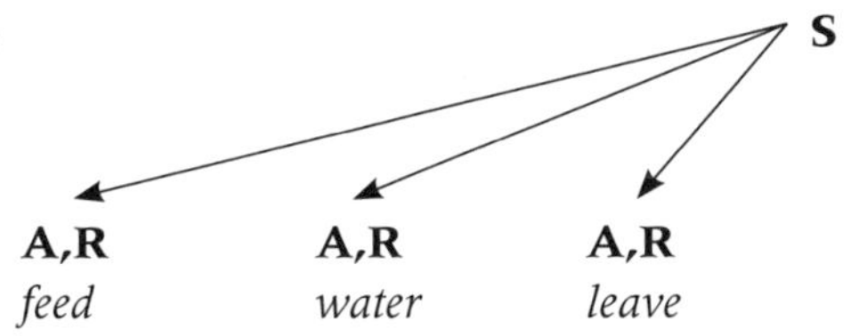

Another way of putting this is to say that each action has its own **R**, i.e. its own point of orientation.

In (51)b. this is not so. Here we see numbers 1 and 2 (*feed/water*) not from their own points of orientation, but from the later perspective of number 3 (*leave*). That is, we choose the standpoint of *leave*, and from it we look further back into the past to *feed* and *water*. In this case, *feed* and *water* do not have their own **R**. They share the same **R** as *leave*:

(53)

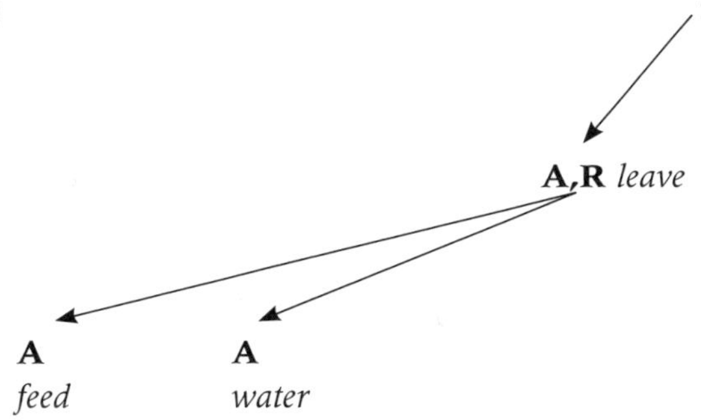

As the arrows in (53) show, the relation of **S** to *feed* and *water* is now ***indirect***, and runs via the **R** of *leave*, i.e. in both cases **A–R–S**. Only *leave* now has a direct relation to **S**, i.e. an **A,R–S** structure.

047/3.4 German speakers and the English past perfect

⚠ In general, the German past perfect (*Plusquamperfekt*) follows the same principles as the English past perfect. But it can also have a direct **A,R–S** meaning. Sometimes German speakers project this use (wrongly) into English. The English past perfect must be used exclusively in the **A–R–S** sense:

(54) a. Ich hatte dir doch vor 5 Wochen schon gesagt, dass ich ein neues Auto kaufen möchte (*Alternative*: Ich sagte dir/ich habe dir gesagt ...).
I ***told*** you 5 weeks ago that I would like to buy a new car (*not* *I had told you ...).
b. Mein Bruder war damals Ingenieur gewesen (*Alternative*: ... war damals Ingenieur/... ist damals Ingenieur gewesen).
At that time my brother was an engineer (*not* *... had been).

In these cases there is ***no pre-past meaning*** involved. German uses past perfects like this (particularly in spoken language) to suggest 'a long time ago' or to indicate that circumstances later changed. This is a kind of 'modal' or emphatic meaning. The time relation itself, however, is **A,R–S**, and in English this requires ***past tense***.

047/4 Some further points of note

047/4.1 Since and the past perfect

As was said in **046/3.3**, ***since***-structures have a 'built-in' **A–R** meaning in the sense of either ***up-to-then*** or ***up-to-now***. With the present perfect the meaning is ***up-to-now*** (**A–R,S**), with the ***past perfect*** it is ***up-to-then*** (**A–R–S**). Or, looking at it the other way round, if the end-point of a ***since***-time-span is in the ***past***, an ***up-to-then*** time structure must be assumed (**A–R–S**), and this makes the ***past perfect*** necessary.

As an example, let us assume focus on *March 2007*, as in *In March 2007, profits reached a record level*. For reference to events before and leading up to March 2007, we then need the ***past perfect***:

(55) Since Mrs. Jarvis ***had joined*** the firm in 2005, the export business ***had been improving*** steadily (*i.e.* ***up-to-then***).

Notice that the ***past perfect*** is used twice here: once for the time-span and once after ***since***. After ***since*** it denotes the beginning of the time-span. This is an example of the ***pre-past*** use (the equivalent in a present perfect context would be the past tense):

(56)

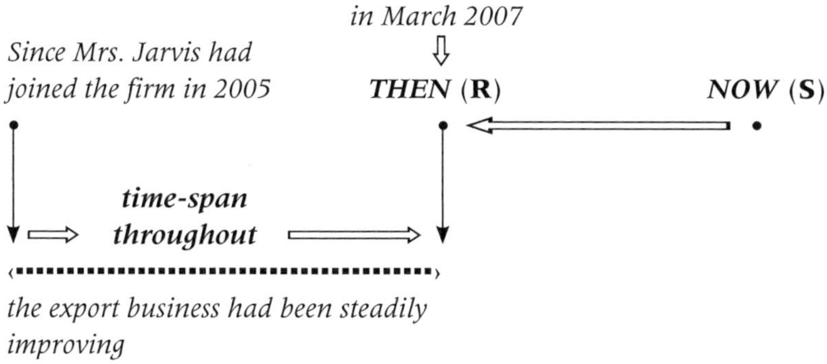

The time-span perfect here is a ***continuative past perfect***. In (57) we have an ***experiential past perfect***:

(57)

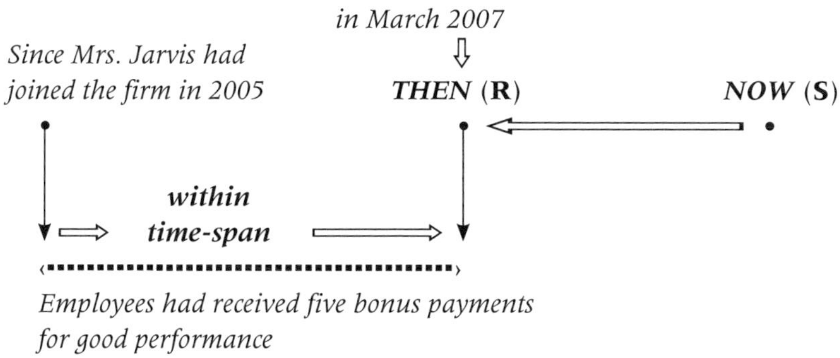

047/4.2 German equivalents of the continuative past perfect

The continuative ***present*** perfect in English is rendered in German by the ***present*** tense (*Präsens*) (see also **046/3.6** above). This corresponds to the use of the German ***past*** tense (*Präteritum*) for the English continuative ***past*** perfect. Compare:

(58) a. Ich ***arbeite*** dort schon seit 5 Jahren. [*deutsches Präsens*]
I ***have been working*** there for 5 years. [continuative ***present*** perfect]
b. Ich ***arbeitete*** dort schon seit 5 Jahren, als ich entlassen wurde. [*deutsches Präteritum*]
I ***had been working*** there for 5 years when I lost my job. [continuative ***past*** perfect]

Alternatively, however, German can also use the past perfect (*Plusquamperfekt*) to express an English past perfect continuative. The German rendering of (58)b., that is, could also be *Ich hatte dort schon seit 5 Jahren gearbeitet, als ich entlassen wurde.*

047/4.3 The past perfect in conditional clauses

The past perfect is obligatory in the ***conditional clause*** of a ***Type III conditional sentence*** (i.e. one referring to the past, with the form *would have* in the matrix clause, see also chapter 11):

(59) If I ***had been*** at the party on Saturday, you would have seen me.

Chapter 11 Verbs: Future and Conditional Meaning, Indirect Speech, the Passive

With future meaning, conditional meaning and indirect speech, we enter the sphere of ***mood*** (i.e. ***modality***). However, this does not mean that we are leaving time and tense behind us. On the contrary, ***future*** and ***conditional meaning*** are strongly connected to considerations of time and tense in several ways. The same is true of ***indirect speech***, which actually shows itself through tense changes.

The point is, though, that time reference itself is ***not*** the major concern of such categories. Instead we are concerned with certain ***speaker attitudes*** that affect the reality or 'factual' status of what is said. And this is the province of ***mood***. Nevertheless, their closeness to tense and time makes it appropriate to deal with such fields immediately after the treatment of tense. This also goes for the ***passive***, although it is the exception here, as it is not a mood. Nevertheless, it has something in common with mood, as it is another field in which the ***perspective of utterance*** is involved.

11.1 Future meaning

Introduction 048

There is no future 'tense' in English. Instead, there are several different ways of referring to future time. In the choice of a particular form, however, time considerations play only a secondary role. Other criteria are much more important, and these are mainly ***modal***.

For example, modal verbs such as *must, might, can* or *should* can all refer to actions in the future (*Sally must/might/can/should come to the meeting tomorrow*); but they are not chosen for that reason. They are selected according to the ***individual modal meaning*** that the speaker wants to express. The same applies to *will* and *be going to*, the verbs that are usually associated most closely with 'expressing' future meaning. First and foremost, these, too, convey specific kinds of modal meaning, connected on the one hand with ***speculation*** and ***prediction***, and on the other with ***intention*** and 'wanting'.

There is also ***non-modal*** future reference, using the present tense, which expresses that something has been arranged.

To repeat, then: we do not use a particular 'future form' because it refers to the future alone, but because we wish to distinguish, for instance, an arranged future event from one that is intended, or a possible or probable event from one that is desired, and so on. Nevertheless, we can, of course apply our ***tense notation*** at least to the time reference itself. This counts then, of course, for all future-referring forms, and is the following: **S–A,R**.

049 The forms of future reference

049/1 The modal future: will

Firstly, some points on usage and form:

- ***Will*** is used nowadays for ***all persons***. In the past, ***shall*** was prescribed for 1st person singular and plural, and ***will*** for the rest. This is no longer the case. ***Shall*** is now reserved for its own special meanings (see under **049/3**).
- In speech and informal language ***will*** is usually shortened to the weak form ***'ll*** when unstressed: *I'll do that for you; Fred'll help with the dishes.*
- The negative weak form is ***won't***: *Fred won't help us.*

049/1.1 Speculation/prediction

Will is used to make predictions, that is, to say that something is possible or probable. This is regarded as a ***subjective*** opinion, and is usually underlined by adverbs or verbal expressions that show the speculative attitude and/or its subjective character:

(1) a. They will deliver the new garden shed tomorrow, I expect.
b. Henry won't arrive until Wednesday (I shouldn't think/perhaps).

Verbs expressing opinions, like *imagine, think, expect, suppose,* etc. are very common as additions. Even if they are not actually present, listeners generally supply them in their minds – or at least a speculative adverb, such as *maybe, perhaps,* etc.

If the added verb is not obviously speculative in meaning (e.g. *think, imagine,* etc., as opposed to *expect, suppose, assume,* and so on), the conditional forms *would/should* are mostly added, e.g. *I should think they will deliver the shed tomorrow.* Note that with the negative equivalent, it is the speculative verb that is negated: *I* ***shouldn't think*** *they will deliver the shed tomorrow.* When the speculative verb (or clause) follows, both verbs are negated: *They **won't deliver** the new garden shed tomorrow, I **don't suppose*** (see also example (1)b. above).

Apart from speculative expressions, ***will*** also requires an ***adverb of future time***, at least in context, or by implication: *It will (probably) rain **soon**; She'll call either **this afternoon** or **this evening**, I should think; He'll certainly be **on the next train*** (= ***when*** *the next train comes*).

049/1.2 Volition: intention, willingness (= requests, offers)

Volition means 'wanting', and is a major field of modal semantics (see chapter 12). ***Will*** has two kinds of ***volitional meaning***: on the one hand ***intention***, and on the other ***willingness*** to do something.

The kind of ***intention*** expressed by ***will*** is the result of a ***spontaneous*** ('on-the-spot') ***decision*** in reaction to another utterance, or to other circumstances which have just arisen in the particular situation:

(2) a. "The Omega hotel is full." "Then we'll try the Rialto. It's next door."
b. "I can't come with you tonight. I'm busy." "OK. I'll go on my own."

This idea of ***spontaneity*** is the major criterion. It is often underlined by the use of adverbials such as *in that case, then*, etc. This general semantic characteristic of ***will*** is important in the contrast with ***going to***.

Closely related to this is the ***spontaneous offer***. This expresses ***willingness*** to do something:

(3) a. "It's a bit cold in here." "I'll close the window."
b. "I can't do all the cooking on my own." "Don't worry, we'll help you."

Offers are also made by addressing ***the listener's*** willingness:

(4) a. "Will you have another glass of wine, Mrs. Morant?" "No, I won't, thank you. I must be leaving."
b. "Won't you sit down, Sarah?" "Yes, I will, thank you."

On the other hand, addressing the listener's ***willingness*** is also a way of making a ***request***:

(5) a. Jean, will you fax Homegate Brothers, please, and tell them the delivery hasn't arrived?
Jean, könnten Sie bitte an die Gebrüder Homegate faxen ...?
b. Will guests kindly queue here for entrance to the restaurant.
Gäste werden gebeten, ...
c. Will you please stop that noise, children!
Könnt ihr bitte mit dem Lärm aufhören, Kinder?!

Although grammatically these are questions, they are regarded basically as disguised commands, and in writing often appear without question marks.

This means also that they are usually reserved for situations where it is acceptable to give instructions or orders. For instance, a request like *Will you pass the bottle, Jack?* is almost an order. It is considered less direct and more polite to use *would*, or other 'distancing' forms. (More on this point in chapter 12 on ***Modality***.)

Note that with ***will*** in ***volitional*** use a time adverbial is not necessary. If no time is mentioned in the context, the reference is usually to the immediate future.

Finally, ***will***-questions may refer to a third person's ***willingness*** to do something. Again, this usually implies a ***request***:

(6) a. Will Tom look after our cat (= is he willing to do this) while we're away?
b. Ask Collins whether he'll (= is willing to) accept a cheque.

049/1.3 Command and request: will in imperative question tags

Will you/won't you are frequently used as ***question tags*** after the ***imperative***. This tends to soften the tone by expressing an appeal for co-operation:

(7) a. Try to get here on time tomorrow, Sally, won't you!
Und versuch bitte morgen pünktlich zu sein, Sally, ja?
b. Don't forget to feed the dog, will you, Charles.
Vergiss bitte nicht, den Hund zu füttern, Charles.

Will you can also be used with positive commands. This sounds a little sharper, emphasizing the speaker's attitude of demand:

(8) a. Just calm down, Meg, will you?
Beruhige dich einfach, Meg.
b. Please stop that noise, children, will you!
Hört doch bitte mit dem Lärm auf, Kinder!

This is a reminder of what was said in the preceding section on the 'command' character of ***will***. It softens the imperative, but is nevertheless more at the 'instruction' end of the request spectrum than other forms. It can be placed, on a scale of directness, between the bare imperative and the ordinary ***will***-question. (9) shows a rising scale of directness from a.–c.:

(9) a. Please stop that noise, children.
b. Please stop that noise, children, will you!
c. Will you please stop that noise, children!

049/1.4 will and future time clauses

We have already met ***future time clauses*** in connection with the present tense (see chapter 9, **044/2.9**). As a reminder, we will deal briefly with them here again, this time from the perspective of ***will***.

Future time clauses are future-referring ***subordinate*** clauses introduced by time conjunctions such as *when, after, before, as soon as, (not) until,* etc. According to the ***sequence-of-tense rule,*** the verb in the ***time clause*** appears only in the ***present tense*** (usually the ***simple*** form, though an obvious framework situation in the future needs the progressive; see below). The ***will***-form occurs only in the ***matrix*** clause (i.e. ***never*** in the time clause):

	Matrix clause	*Subordinate time clause*
(10)	a. We'll call you	as soon as our agent contacts us.
	b. Mary will be surprised	when she sees you.

Will here conveys its usual meanings, i.e. ***volition*** in (10)a. and ***prediction*** in (10)b. The spontaneous meaning does not apply to ***will***-volitives in this case: the volitive here is condition-linked and oriented to the time of the matrix clause.

If, apart from volition or prediction, other meanings are called for, other modals, or the imperative, can be used. In contrast to ***will,*** other modals are also permitted in the subordinate clause:

	Subordinate time clause	*Matrix clause*
(11)	a. When you see her	please give her my regards.
	b. As soon as you can leave	you should contact Paul in Dover.

To summarize, then, the ***sequence-of-tense rule*** prevents the use of ***will*** in the subordinate clause. Note also that ***will*** (and ***never*** the present tense) must be used in the matrix in the case of ***volition*** and ***prediction*** meanings. That is, for (10)a., for example, we ***cannot*** say **We'll call you as soon as our agent will contact us;* and we cannot say **We call you as soon as our agent contacts us.*

049/1.5 will and conditional clauses

As also mentioned in chapter 9, **044/2.9**, ***conditional*** sentences involving ***will*** (usually future-referring) follow exactly the same ***sequence-of-tense rule*** as just explained in **049/1.4**:

	Matrix clause	*Conditional (subordinate) clause*
(12)	a. We'll call you	if our agent contacts us.
	b. We won't call you	unless problems arise.

The ***sequence-of-tense rule*** here is often called the '***if***-clause rule' in traditional grammar, but this is a rather misleading name, since it applies to all ***future time*** sentences, and not just conditional ones. Sentences like those in (12) express ***open conditions*** (see below for more details).

049/1.6 will and present reference

Speculations with ***will*** can refer to ***present*** time:

(13) If the watering-can is not in the shed, it will (almost certainly) be in the garage.

This is the final sign that ***will*** is a modal verb, and that the modal meaning (and not the time reference) is the central factor. The ***notation*** for the time reference of (13) is, in fact, **A,R,S**, as the speaker is referring to the ***present*** position of the watering-can. The ***present tense*** can also replace ***will*** here (though with a loss of speculative modal force):

(14) If the watering-can is not in the shed, it is almost certainly in the garage.

(The structure of the conditional sentence is now changed, and with it also the type of conditional meaning. This different type of condition is explained more fully in **051/4.** below.)

In a slightly different way, the volitional sense of ***will*** can also be seen as ***present-referring***. That is, spontaneous expressions of willingness, offers of help, and requests (see **049/1.2** and **3** above) reflect a speaker-attitude present ***now***, even if the main-verb action is future. In examples like those in (2)–(5) above, therefore, we could say that the modal meaning ***on its own*** has the reading **A,R,S**, although the main verb is ***future***, i.e. **S–A,R.** In other words, verb phrases with ***will*** often have 'double time reference'. With ***will*** this is a little 'theoretical'. But with ***going to*** it is quite concrete (see **049/2.3** below).

049/1.7 will + progressive form

This is sometimes called the **will-*progressive***. More exactly, it is ***will*** in combination with the ***progressive infinitive*** (e.g. *to be doing ...*, see chapter 13).

As in other ***will***-constructions (and after most other modal verbs), the infinitive appears without *to*, e.g. *I **will be waiting** in the airport lounge tomorrow.* Sentences like this refer to a ***framework situation*** in exactly the same way as the ordinary progressive in the present or past tense:

(15) a. I will be waiting in the airport lounge tomorrow, when your flight lands.
Ich werde morgen am Flughafen schon im Empfangsbereich warten, wenn deine Maschine landet.
b. At this time next week you'll be lying on a beach in the Canaries!
Nächste Woche um diese Zeit wirst du an einem Strand auf den Kanaren liegen.

The interplay of aspects here can be illustrated in the kind of time-frame diagram familiar from chapter 9 (see **044/1.1**), where it was applied to aspect in the present and past tenses:

(16)

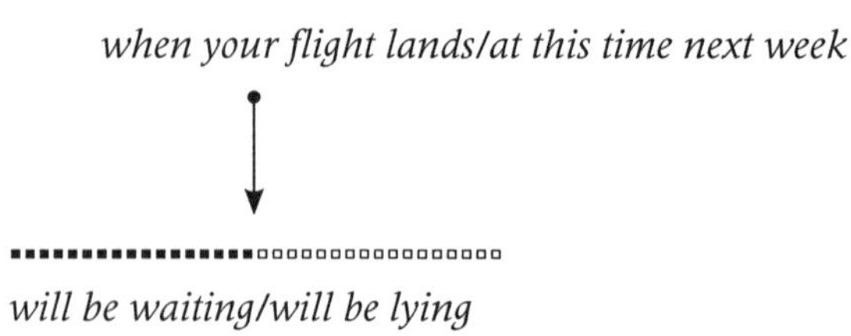

Will-***progressives*** apply to all uses of ***will***, including those with present reference, as in (17)a., (see also **049/1.6**), those in future time sentences, as in (15), and those in conditional sentences, as in (17)b.:

(17) a. The watering-can is in the shed; it will be standing in the far corner by the hose.
b. Even if he arrives early, somebody will be waiting at the airport to meet him.

In (15)a. and (17)b., the framework situations apply to the ***main clauses***. If they apply to the ***sub-clauses***, the ordinary ***present progressive*** is necessary (as ***will*** cannot occur in the sub-clause):

(18) a. If it is raining on our arrival tomorrow, we will take a taxi from the station to the hotel (***not*** *If it will be raining ...).
b. I will do the cooking next week while you're working (***not*** *... while you will be working).

Finally, there is a special use of the **will**-***progressive*** in reference to ***arranged*** future events. This has nothing to do with the ordinary framework meaning, and is explained under **049/4.3** below.

049/2 The modal future: to be going to

For short, we will call this simply the ***going to***-form. Like ***will***, it is used in the meanings of ***speculation/prediction*** and ***volition***. But it has more ***assertive force***, i.e. carries more emphasis. This is shown in fairly specific ways, i.e. the contrasts in usage to ***will*** are usually quite clear and concrete.

049/2.1 Speculation/prediction

Predictions with ***going to*** are stronger than with ***will***. Although the opinion can still be subjective, ***going to*** has a rather more generalized, objective ring than ***will***. It often makes the predicted event seem more or less logically inevitable, and is normally used ***without*** adverbs or verbal expressions showing a degree of certainty or personal opinion (such as *I think, I expect, perhaps, probably*, etc.). A time adverbial is not necessary either. As with ***will*** in ***volitional*** use, reference is generally to the ***immediate*** future if no future time is given in the context (***going to*** is commonly used for warnings of things that are about to happen).

(19) a. According to the weather forecast, it's going to snow this afternoon.
Laut Wetterbericht wird es heute Nachmittag schneien.
b. Watch out! You're going to spill your coffee.
Achtung! Du bist gerade dabei, deinen Kaffee zu verschütten!
c. Our team is going to win on Saturday (I'm sure of it).
Unsere Mannschaft wird am Samstag sicher gewinnen (davon bin ich überzeugt).

Equivalent versions with ***will*** sound more tentative (i.e. less definite). They can frequently be understood as part of conditional sentences: *I reckon it'll snow this afternoon* (*if temperatures stay as low as this*); *Watch out, or you'll spill your coffee* (*if you're not careful*); *Our team will win on Saturday if they stay calm in defence.*

Note that despite its closeness to the present, ***going to*** cannot refer to the present itself. That is, it cannot express a present ***supposition*** as ***will*** can, and could not replace ***will*** in (13) above.

Going to is sometimes found in the prediction sense in conditional sentences: *If James finds out about this, there's going to be trouble*. But it is reserved for emphatic statements, and in general these tend to clash a little with the rather more neutral or tentative nature of an ***if***-clause. The 'natural' partner here is definitely ***will***. Future time clauses, chiefly with *when*, are more common: *Sheila's going to be very tired when she gets home*. Here, too, though, ***will*** is usually favoured unless a need for particular emphasis is felt.

049/2.2 Volition (intentions/decisions)

Going to refers to ***premeditated decisions***, i.e. ones that have been thought about and already made. In this meaning, ***going to*** is the opposite of ***will***. As we have seen, ***will*** expresses spontaneous intentions or decisions. Compare:

(20) a. I'm going to close that window.
b. I'll close that window.

In (20)a. the speaker has been thinking about closing the window and has decided to do so. In (20)b. the decision is made simultaneously with the utterance, i.e. there is no pre-thought. It is a spontaneous reaction to something happening in the situation, e.g. a sudden draught of cold air.

Here are two further examples:

(21) a. "George, I'm going to get the sandwiches." (= "I have already decided to do this.")
"Alright, Martha, then I'll fix the drinks." (= spontaneous offer, as a reaction to Martha's utterance)
b. "We're going to clear up the garden tomorrow." (= a decided plan)
"Oh, I'll help you, then." (= spontaneous offer of help)

049/2.3 going to and double time reference

In **049/1.6** above we said that it is possible to see the modal verb alone as having a different time reference from the main verb. With volitional ***going to*** this factor is much more marked, because what is expressed is the presence (***now***) of a ***plan*** to do something later (i.e. in the future). In other words, there is a ***double time reference***: **A,R,S**, for ***going to*** and **S–A,R** for the main verb following it. This is reflected in the possibility that two different time adverbials (one present-, the other future-referring) can occur at the same time:

(22) We are not going to buy the car now (**A,R,S**) until next year (**S–A,R**).

We will see later that double time reference of this kind can also affect other modal verbs (see chapter 12). But it applies equally to the ***non-modal*** future (see **049/4** below).

049/3 The modal future: shall

Shall is used these days almost exclusively in the 1st person singular and plural. Its use is further restricted, with one or two exceptions, to questions, and also to a narrow band of special meaning. The German equivalent is generally *sollen* (*Soll ich?*/*Sollen wir?*)

049/3.1 Making offers

First-person questions with ***shall*** are commonly used for offers (e.g. of help):

(23) Shall I do your shopping for you while you are ill?
(= Would you like me to ...?)
Soll ich für dich einkaufen, ...?

Shall also functions as the ***question tag*** of ***will*** in first person volitionals:

(24) I'll help you, shall I?

The question tag in this case must be of the ***echo*** type, i.e. the positive-positive pattern (see chapter 8, **041/2.8**).

049/3.2 Making suggestions

Shall-questions are common with ***suggestions*** referring to first-person subjects:

(25) a. Shall we go to the concert tonight? (= let's decide now)
Sollen wir heute Abend ins Konzert gehen?
b. Shall I call you tomorrow?
Soll ich Sie morgen anrufen?

049/3.3 Asking for advice

(26) a. What shall I do? (= please tell me)
Was soll ich tun?
b. Shall we invite the Fergusons or not? (= What do you think?)
Sollen wir ... oder nicht?

049/3.4 Statements of determination or emphasis

Shall is unusual outside questions. Nevertheless, it is still sometimes heard in statements when the speaker wishes to sound determined or emphatic, as with a threat or promise.

The German equivalent in this case is usually with *werden*, or the present tense (not with *sollen*):

(27) a. Give me back my money or I shall complain to the manager!
...., oder ich wende mich an den Filialleiter!
b. I shall be there to help you on Tuesday. Don't worry!
Ich werde am Dienstag da sein, um dir zu helfen, keine Sorge.

049/4 The non-modal future: arrangements

For '***arranged future***' meaning we generally use the ***present tense***, as pointed out in **049/2.8** Exceptionally, ***will*** is also found, or more often, **will +** ***progressive form***. The ***future of arrangement*** treats the future action as a ***fact***, rather than as something just wanted, intended or expected. That is, it gives a statement ***factual*** rather than modal character. If there was a special verb form for expressing this, then that form would be regarded as the 'future tense'. But there is no special form. As with all types of future reference, the ***future of arrangement*** is expressed by forms which also have other meanings. This shows, to repeat the point, that there is ***no*** 'future tense' as such in English.

049/4.1 Present progressive

This is the most common way of referring to an ***arranged future*** action, specifically with ***animate*** subjects (i.e. persons, animals):

(28) a. Sheila is not taking her car to work tomorrow. I'm driving her, as I'm meeting a client in town.
Sheila fährt morgen nicht mit ihrem Auto zur Arbeit. Ich bringe sie hin, da ich einen Kunden in der Stadt treffe.
b. Solomon is not coming to the party next Saturday. He's going to a concert in London with Millie.
Solomon kommt nächsten Samstag nicht zum Fest. Er geht nämlich mit Millie auf ein Konzert nach London.

As the examples show, the German present tense (*Präsens*) is also usual here. But of course German has no aspects and so there is no need to distinguish between the future use of simple and progressive forms. In English, however, this is necessary: ***animate*** subjects almost always appear with the ***progressive***.

⚠ A further point about German is that the *werden*-form is also possible here, e.g. *Sheila wird morgen nicht mit ihrem Auto zur Arbeit fahren*. Note that this ***cannot*** be translated into English by ***will***. ***Will*** is a ***modal*** form, as we have seen (see section **049/1**), and is generally reserved for speculation and volition meanings.

049/4.2 Present simple

This is used especially for ***inanimate*** subjects in 'timetable' or programme-style references:

(29) a. The music festival begins on the first Saturday in May.
b. Their plane lands at 9.30 am local time.
c. The concert lasts three hours, and ends at 11.30 pm.
d. Our boat reaches Dubrovnik on the second day of the cruise.

There are, however, several exceptions to this general tendency. Firstly, the ***progressive*** form is preferred

a) with verbs in the ***passive***
b) usually when the event or its time of occurrence is unscheduled, or goes against an existing plan:

(30) a. The festival is being held in the village hall and the two churches.
b. The lecture is now not taking place until Thursday.

Secondly, use of the simple form is not confined entirely to inanimate subjects. It occasionally occurs also with ***animate*** subjects (i.e. people) when these are regarded as participants in a general timetable plan:

(31) a. The prime minister leaves tomorrow for a tour of the Far East.
b. Polly and Sam arrive tonight and John comes on board tomorrow morning.

These could equally appear with the progressive, however. The simple form adds an elevated stylistic note.

049/4.3 will + progressive form

In speech and informal language the ***present progressive*** is sometimes replaced by the **will**-***progressive***. Compare:

(32) a. Solomon ***is not coming*** to the party next Saturday. He'***s going*** to a concert in London with Millie.
b. Solomon ***will not be coming*** to the party next Saturday. He'***ll be going*** to a concert in London with Millie.

The **will**-***progressive*** in (32)b. means exactly the same as the ***present progressive*** in (32) a., i.e. expresses an ***arrangement***. The **will**-***progressive*** simply sounds a little more tentative, and therefore has the effect of being slightly less direct. Speakers may do this, for example, when they feel that the message is not quite so pleasant, or when they ask a question and wish to make it sound more restrained: *Will you be coming to the party next Saturday* (*by any chance – or have you made other plans?*).

049/4.4 The use of will for arrangements

Apart from the **will**-***progressive*** use just explained, ***will*** does ***not*** normally express arrangements. There are two exceptions to this.

Firstly, with ***stative verbs*** the progressive cannot be used. ***Will*** therefore has to 'take over':

(33) a. Davis will not be at the meeting tomorrow.
b. We will have the goods ready for delivery by next Saturday, Mr. Monroe.

Secondly, ***will*** is seen sometimes in ***formal*** written notices referring to arranged future events:

(34) a. The Queen will receive visitors at 3 pm today.
b. The lecture on public finance will take place at 7 pm in Hall 4.

In ordinary neutral language the present tense would be preferred here: *The Queen is receiving ...; The lecture on public finance takes place ...*

049/5 Past and perfect meanings with future reference

There are also future-referring perfect and past forms to be considered. These are traditionally called the ***future perfect*** and the ***future-in-the-past*** respectively.

049/5.1 The future perfect

This is the form **will have** + ***past participle***, e.g. *will have done*. To put it more exactly, ***will*** combines here with the ***perfect infinitive*** (see also the similar remark on **will-*progressive*** under **049/1.7**, and chapter 13). The ***future perfect*** could be called the 'future version' of the present perfect, i.e. it refers to ***experience of a past event*** which is ***present*** at a ***future*** time. Compare:

(35) a. I have been working here for 28 years. (= **up-to-now**, ***continuative present perfect***)
b. In 2 years' time I will have been working here for 30 years. (= **up-to-'future-then'**, ***continuative future perfect***)

Like the other perfects, the ***future perfect*** has ***experiential*** and ***resultative*** types:

(36) a. After my next visit to Moscow, I will have been to Russia 20 times. (= **up-to-'future-then'**, ***experiential future perfect***)
b. By next Friday the job will have been done. (= **then-*orientation*** alone, no time-span, ***resultative future perfect***)

However, unlike the present perfect (but in common with the past perfect), the ***future perfect*** can take on a 'past' meaning. With the past perfect, we called this the 'past-in-the-past' (or ***pre-past***) use. With the future perfect we could call it ***'past-in-the-future'***:

(37) a. We're putting a new kitchen in the holiday home. We will have installed it fully the weekend before your arrival.
(the weekend before your arrival = a **past-in-the-future adverbial**, i.e. means **past focus** seen from a future point of time)
b. Whenever the flight arrives, airport reception will have been informed at least 20 minutes earlier that the plane is about to land.
(*20 minutes earlier* = a ***past-in-the-future adverbial***)

The German equivalent of the English ***future perfect*** is similar (Futur II, vollendetes Futur), i.e. the form *werden … gemacht haben*, e.g. for (36)a. … *werde ich zwanzigmal in Moskau gewesen sein*; for (36)b. *wird die Arbeit erledigt worden sein*; for (37)a. *Wir werden sie am Wochenende vor eurer Rückkehr schon eingebaut haben*. An exception is the ***continuative*** in (35)b., which is generally not rendered by a German perfect at all (see also chapter 10, **046/3.6**): *In 2 Jahren werde ich seit 20 Jahren hier arbeiten*.

In the terms of our special ***tense notation*** the future perfect in these examples has the reading **S–A–R**. Here we see again the familiar **A–R** structure of perfect forms.

049/5.2 The future perfect as a speculative present perfect or past tense

Will have can refer to the ***present*** in the same way as ***will*** (see **049/1.6**). In this case it functions as a ***speculative present perfect***. In addition, owing to its possibility of ***past focus*** ('past-in-the-future'!), it can also function as a ***speculative past tense***:

(38) a. John will have put the watering-can in the shed (I imagine).
(***speculative present perfect*** = He has probably put it there, i.e. it is probably there)
b. John will have put the watering-can in the shed ***yesterday*** (I imagine).
(***speculative past tense*** = He probably put it there yesterday)

(38)b. could also be used to suggest result, of course (= *the watering-can is probably in the shed*), but leaves other possible meanings equally open (e.g. … *and then he probably locked it and came back into the house*).

The notation readings for *will have put* here are **A–R,S** in (38)a., and **A,R–S** in (38)b.

049/5.3 The future perfect in future time and conditional sentences

Will cannot occur in the sub-clauses of future time and conditional sentences (see **049/1.5**). Here the ***future perfect*** is replaced by the ***present perfect***:

(39) a. If you have lost your way on the moor, contact the nearest ranger-post by mobile phone.
(***not*** *If you will have lost …)
b. When Sue has found the intersection of Broad Street and Hope Avenue, she will almost have reached our apartment.
(***not*** *When Sue will have found …)

Note in this connection that with ***point-telic event verbs*** like *lose* and *find* in these examples (see also chapter 8, **041/3.3**), there is usually little meaning difference between the perfect and the non-perfect forms. This is because ***point-telic event verbs*** refer to an action which is 'over' (i.e. 'complete') immediately when it happens. This factor is especially noticeable in time and conditional clauses like those in (39). *If you have lost ...* in (39)a. could be replaced by *If you lose ...*, and *When Sue has found ...* in (39)b. by *When Sue finds ...*

With other modes of occurrence, for instance ***telic events*** like *do homework* or ***non-telic events*** like *eat*, there is a world of difference. We cannot replace the perfect forms in the following by the non-perfect:

(40) a. When guests have eaten, they must leave the dining-room.
(***not*** *When guests eat ...)
b. If you have done your homework, you can go out, Jimmy.
(***not*** *If you do ...)

049/5.4 The future perfect and the neutralization of the modal and non-modal distinctions

The ***future perfect*** occurs more or less exclusively with ***will***. That is, ***will have*** also expresses ***arrangement***: *At ten o'clock the guests will have eaten and the Christmas show will have started.*

In this case, that is, the distinction between modal and non-modal future meanings is neutralized.

049/5.5 The future-in-the-past

This means looking at a ***future action*** from the point of view of a ***past*** time. It is particularly common in stories told in the past tense. As an illustration, we will start with the opening sentence of a typical story and continue it in the examples in (41). *Robert looked at his watch*:

(41) a. He was attending a meeting in Manchester that evening.
b. His train left at 10.30.
c. He was going to call for a taxi.
d. But then he had another idea. He would walk. This would give him his exercise for the day.
e. When he got to the station, though, he would be a little hot and possibly no longer quite fresh. He would have walked 5 miles.

If Robert thinks these things in his own 'present', he thinks:

(42) a. "I am attending a meeting in Manchester this evening."
(future of ***arrangement, animate subject***: ***present progressive***)
b. "My train leaves at 10.30."
(future of ***arrangement, inanimate subject***: ***present simple***)

c. "I am going to call for a taxi."
(***pre-meditated intention***)

d. "(But I think) I'll walk. This will give me my exercise for the day."
(***spontaneous intention; neutral prediction***)

e. "When I get to the station, though, I will be a little hot and possibly no longer quite fresh. I will have walked 5 miles."
(***future time clause; future perfect***)

Comparing (42) and (41), we see that we can shift all types of future reference back into a past perspective. Note that the last sentence of (41)e. shows a ***future perfect-in-the past*** (see original present-oriented future perfect in (42)e.).

These examples also show that most ***future-in-the-past*** usage has to do – directly or indirectly – with ***reported speech***. This point is taken up in the section on reported speech further below (see 11.3).

Finally, a note on time reference. In all the examples the future action is still in the past, i.e. before **S**. The notation form is therefore **R–A–S**. But the future action may also be at **S**, or even after it (that is, in the 'real' future):

(43) a. Kerry was in a hurry when I saw her yesterday. She was leaving with the children for Barcelona this morning. (**R–A,S**)
b. They would be staying in Barcelona (she said) until the end of next week. (**R–S–A**)

049/6 The basics of future meaning – overview

	Prediction	***Volition***	***Arrangement***
WILL	*Jim will arrive tomorrow, I expect.* – future time adverbial necessary in context – usually adverb or clause showing subjective view, e.g. *I expect/think/suppose, perhaps, if*-clause, etc.	*Now we'll look at page 34.* *It's cold in here. I think I'll close the window.* spontaneous intentions: decisions, offers, requests	***Will*** is **NOT** used to express arrangements, except – with stative verbs occasionally in formal contexts (e.g. announcement notices).
GOING TO	*It is going to rain.* – stronger prediction than with ***will*** – time or other adverbs are optional – if no time adverb is present, reference is usually to immediate events or to present evidence of a future event	It's cold in here. I'm going to close the window. – premeditated intentions: i.e. decisions already reached	***Going to*** is compatible with arrangements, **BUT** does not express them as such.
PRESENT SIMPLE	– **CANNOT** be used in this sense!	– **CANNOT** be used in this sense!	The film begins at 8.30. – timetable reference (usually with ***inanimate*** subject)

	Prediction	*Volition*	*Arrangement*
PRESENT PROGRESSIVE	– **CANNOT** be used in this sense!	Come on Tom, we're leaving! – occasionally used in speech for spontaneous ***will***, in order to show determination (usually in negative social contexts) – otherwise not used in this sense !	Martha is coming tomorrow. – usually ***animate*** subject
***WILL*-PROGRESSIVE**	At this time tomorrow I'll be lying on a beach in the Mediterranean. – necessary for predictions with ***framework situation***	We'll be waiting for you when your train arrives. – necessary for volitional statements with ***framework situation***	We'll be waiting for you when your train arrives. – necessary for future arrangements with ***framework situation***. *I won't be coming tomorrow.* – replaces ***present progressive*** when need is felt for a less direct, more tentative tone

11.2 Conditional meaning

050 Introduction

With ***conditional meaning*** we are entirely in the field of ***mood*** (or ***modality***, as it is often called nowadays). There is therefore no such thing as a 'conditional *tense*'. As the ***conditional*** is a ***modal*** phenomenon, a more accurate label would be 'conditional mood'. Having said this, we must stress three important points.

- Firstly, there is, in fact, not a single 'conditional mood' in English. The ***conditional*** is not a unified phenomenon, but appears in various forms. These are of a morphological, syntactic *and* semantic nature: sometimes all three categories are involved, but at other times only one or two of them.
- Secondly, ***conditional meaning*** is really a particular variation of the larger modal field of ***possibility/speculation***. That is to say, ***conditional forms*** express possibilities, and ***conditional sentences*** make the realization of one possibility dependent on the fulfilment of another, e.g. *If you come early tomorrow, we could have a drink before the film*. This is a ***conditional sentence*** and it includes the ***conditional form*** *could*.
- Thirdly, tense forms and time reference *do* play an important role in creating conditional meaning, even though English has no 'conditional *tense*' as such.

Conditional meaning and conditional forms 051

A lot of conditional meaning involves the modal auxiliaries ***could, would, should*** and ***might***. Consequently, these are often regarded as the 'conditional forms' of English. The term 'conditional form' needs to be used carefully here, however. It is true that these modals often convey conditional meaning. But they can express other meanings too, and cannot then, of course, be called 'conditional'. Furthermore, conditional meaning is often expressed without these forms (conditional sentences, for instance, do not always include conditional forms).

Another point is that the conditional in German does not entirely correspond (in form or content) to what is regarded as conditional in English. For example, German uses the ***subjunctive*** (dt. *Konjunktiv*) for conditional meaning, but this is not possible in English (as English has ***no*** subjunctive). These are all factors which can lead to learner errors of various kinds, and we will look at these factors closely and individually in the following. ⚠

051/1 Concrete points on form

051/1.1 The unreal past

English gets around the problem of having no subjunctive by using the ***past tense*** in a ***modal*** sense. Consider, for instance, the ***conditional sentence***

(44) If I ***came*** to the meeting tomorrow I ***would*** get there very late.
Wenn ich morgen zur Sitzung käme, würde ich dort erst sehr spät eintreffen.

Here the English past tense forms ***came*** and ***would*** (= past tense of ***will***) do not actually refer to the past, but to the future. That is, they are used in a ***modal*** sense to suggest a low level of probability. Note that this is expressed in German by the subjunctive forms ***käme*** and ***würde*** (dt. *Konjunktiv II*). When the English past tense is used modally in this way, we will call it the ***unreal past***.

The ***unreal past*** has other uses too, apart from conditional meaning, for example in ***reported*** (***indirect***) ***speech*** (see **11.3** below).

In conditional sentences, the unreal past refers only to present or future time. 'Subjunctive' reference to ***past*** time requires the ***unreal past perfect***:
*If I **had been** at the meeting yesterday, I would have stated my opinion.*

051/1.2 Modal auxiliaries expressing possibility, and the unreal past

Possibility/probability is a large and important field of modal meaning. We deal with this later in detail, when we look at modal auxiliaries individually (see chapter 12). It is mentioned briefly and generally now, because it is important for ***conditional meaning***, which as we have said, is a kind of 'sub-section' of the modal semantic field ***possibility/ probability***.

Most modal auxiliaries, including *may, will, can, should, must*, etc. express meanings in this field (i.e. they are used for ***speculation***, as we have already seen with *will* and *going to*). Along with many other ordinary main verbs, they can all appear in ***conditional sentences*** (the classical one among these, of course, is ***will***). However, it is only the ***unreal past*** forms ***could*** (from *can*), ***would*** (from *will*), ***should*** (from *shall*), and ***might*** (from *may*) which are traditionally regarded as ***conditional forms***. This is because they express more theoretical, imagined or less likely possibilities than the more open-sounding ordinary ('present') forms. The term ***conditional*** in this sense, then, is to be understood as meaning 'more theoretical' or 'more remote from reality'. And it is reflected in the subjunctive forms of the German equivalents (*würde, könnte*, etc.).

This is a different sense of the term, however, from the one expressed in the label ***conditional sentence***, which means, quite simply, a sentence including a ***conditional clause*** (introduced, for instance, by ***if***). From now on, we will use the term ***conditional*** only in the meaning 'relating to a conditional sentence'. Forms like ***could*** and ***would*** will simply be referred to as 'modal auxiliaries in the unreal past'.

051/1.3 Unreal past of be: were as singular

There is a certain peculiarity of form with the verb ***to be***. In conditional clauses, ***were*** is generally used for the ***unreal past*** in all persons, i.e. also for ***singular***:

(45) If I ***were*** at the meeting tomorrow I ***would*** raise several questions.
Wenn ich morgen an der Sitzung teilnehmen würde, würde ich mehrere Fragen anschneiden.

The singular ***was*** is also heard (mainly for 3rd person), but in general, ***were*** is preferred, in particular for 1st person reference. See also under **051/2.9**, especially example (60), for reference to the form ***were to***.

051/2 Conditional sentences with speculative meaning

The classical ***conditional sentence*** is one containing an **if**-***clause***. This names a ***condition***; the ***matrix clause*** names the ***consequence***, i.e. the result of the condition being fulfilled.

It is customary to identify three main types of ***conditional sentence***:

(46) a. If the heavy rain continues, our cellar will soon be flooded.
Conditional type 1
b. If the heavy rain continued, our cellar would soon be flooded.
Conditional type 2
c. If the heavy rain had continued, our cellar would soon have been flooded.
Conditional type 3

Each has a specific ***syntactic pattern*** ('sequence of tense'), a particular ***time reference*** (present, future, past), and a certain kind of ***'probability'*** meaning. This last point indicates a very important general semantic factor: conditional sentences of these three types express ***speculation***. More exactly, the ***matrix clause*** expresses a ***speculation*** (hence the use of *will/would*), and the ***sub-clause*** a (speculated) ***condition*** on which it depends. The relation between the two is therefore normally ***causal***.

Although these three types are the major ones from a grammatical point of view, however, there are many others. Time references of the two clauses can be varied (e.g. *If the heavy rain had continued, our cellar would no longer exist*). The clauses can be ***volitional***, instead of speculative (*I'll do it if you pay me*); imperatives are common in the matrix (*If he comes, leave!*). In fact, apart from this, ***any*** modal auxiliary can occur in the matrix, and several types also in the **if*-clause*** (*If you can't contact him there, he may be at his mother's*). Furthermore, ***if*** is not the only possible ***conjunction*** in conditionals (others, for instance, are *unless, provided that,* etc.); and even with ***if,*** the conditional meaning may be quite different from the ordinary speculative type, e.g. *If he said that, he was lying;* or *If you tease him he gets very angry;* or (with a question in the matrix) *If you knew he was dishonest, why did you give him money?*

We will consider these types now in detail.

051/2.1 Conditional type 1

This is known as the ***open*** (also ***real*** or ***neutral***) condition. The degree of likelihood ('probability factor') is ***possible*** to ***probable***, depending on context.

The time reference is ***present*** or ***future***.

(47) a. If the heavy rain continues, our cellar will soon be flooded.
Wenn es weiter stark regnet, wird unser Keller bald überschwemmt sein.
b. We will need a replacement in goal on Saturday, if Jones isn't fit by then.
Wir werden am Samstag einen Ersatztorhüter brauchen, wenn Jones bis dahin nicht fit ist.

The sequence of tense (as already mentioned several times) is:

(48) ***Subordinate clause (if-clause)*** ↙ ***Present tense (generally simple form)*** ↘ If the heavy rain continues

Matrix clause ↓ **will-*form*** ↘ our cellar will soon be flooded.

In German the pattern is similar, with *werden* in the matrix and present tense in the sub-clause. Nevertheless, common English errors among German speakers are: firstly, placing ***will*** in the sub-clause, and secondly, leaving it out of the matrix (**If the heavy* *rain will continue, our cellar is soon flooded*). The German pattern is not usually regarded as 'conditional' in German grammar.

051/2.2 Conditional type 2 for theoretical conditions

This syntactic pattern (see (50) below) has ***two*** possible conditional meanings. The first is the ***theoretical*** (also ***unreal***) condition. The degree of likelihood ('probability factor') here is ***slightly possible*** or ***improbable***, depending on context. Time reference is ***present*** or ***future***.

(49) a. If the heavy rain continued, our cellar would soon be flooded.
Wenn es weiter stark regnete (regnen würde), würde unser Keller bald überschwemmt sein (wäre unser Keller bald überschwemmt).
b. We would need a replacement in goal on Saturday, if Jones wasn't fit by then.
Wir würden am Samstag einen Ersatztorhüter brauchen (wir bräuchten ...), wenn Jones bis dahin nicht fit wäre (nicht fit sein sollte).

The sequence of tense here is:

(50)

Subordinate clause **(if-*clause*)** ↓	***Matrix clause*** ↓
Past tense (generally simple form) ↓	**would-*form*** ↓
If the heavy rain continued	our cellar would soon be flooded.

In German this is regarded as *Konditional I* and uses the *past subjunctive* (*Konjunktiv II*). In either clause this can take the form *würde* + infinitive, or alternatively just the main verb in its own past subjunctive form (*wäre, bräuchte*, etc.). The English pattern is much stricter: the ***sub-clause*** definitively needs the ***past tense***, and the ***matrix*** the ***would***-form. There is no alternative as in German.

⚠ German learners consequently tend to make similar errors as with ***Conditional type 1***: firstly, placing ***would*** in the sub-clause, and secondly, leaving it out of the matrix (**If the heavy rain would continue, our cellar was soon flooded*).

051/2.3 Conditional type 2 for hypothetical conditions

This is the second conditional meaning of the ***Conditional type 2*** pattern. Time reference is the same (***present*** or ***future***), but the degree of likelihood ('probability factor') is ***nil***, i.e. ***impossible***. ***Hypothetical*** (or ***closed***) conditions cannot be fulfilled, because the reality of the particular situation is different:

(51) a. If Casey was/were here (which he isn't), he would help us (which he can't).

Wenn Casey hier wäre (was nicht der Fall ist), würde er uns helfen (was jetzt nicht möglich ist).

b. We would have to walk to the wedding next Saturday, if we didn't have your car to transport us.
Wir müssten nächsten Samstag zur Hochzeit laufen (würden laufen müssen), wenn wir dein Auto nicht benutzen könnten.

Whether ***Conditional type 2*** patterns are meant as ***theoretical*** (i.e. still possible), or as ***hypothetical*** (i.e. impossible) depends on context and external situation, of course. The sentences in (49) would also be interpreted as hypothetical if it was clear that the heavy rain (in (49)a.) would not continue, or Jones was fit and ready for action (in (49)b.). Note that the German pattern can also have these two alternative meanings.

Finally, note the ***singular*** use of ***were*** in (51)a. This was explained in **051/1.3** above. In ***Conditional type 2*** patterns, it is often preferred to the ordinary form *was*, especially for ***hypothetical*** meaning. It is nearly always used in the set phrase *If I were you*, which is particularly common when ***advice*** is given: *If I were you, I would take the train* (dt. *An deiner Stelle würde ich mit dem Zug fahren*).

051/2.4 Conditional type 3

This condition is only a ***hypothetical*** (or ***closed***) one. The degree of likelihood ('probability factor') is ***impossible*** here quite simply because of the time reference, which is ***past***. For this reason the pattern is sometimes known as the ***past conditional***:

(52) a. If the heavy rain had continued last month, our cellar would soon have been flooded.
Wenn es den letzten Monat weiter stark geregnet hätte, wäre unser Keller bald überschwemmt gewesen.

b. We would have needed a replacement in goal last Saturday, if Jones hadn't been fit by then.
Wir hätten letzten Samstag einen Ersatztorhüter gebraucht, wenn Jones bis dahin nicht fit gewesen wäre.

The sequence of tense is:

(53)	***Subordinate clause* (if-*clause*)**	***Matrix clause***
	↓	↓
	Past perfect tense (generally simple form)	**would have-*form***
	↓	↓
	If the heavy rain had continued	our cellar would soon have been flooded.

In German this is regarded as *Konditional II* and uses the *past subjunctive perfect* (*Konjunktiv II im Perfekt*). The English **would-have-*form*** is sometimes called the ***conditional perfect***. Its equivalent in the ***if***-clause is the ***unreal past perfect***.

⚠ Again, the danger here among German-speaking learners is that the verb forms in the two clauses (which as always must be strictly kept apart) are mixed up (**If the heavy rained would have continued, our cellar had soon been flooded*).

051/2.5 Summary of types 1–3

We can summarize our three main Conditional types, then, as follows:

- ***Conditional type 1:***
  Syntactic pattern: sub-clause ***present tense*** (simple), matrix ***will***
  Time reference: present or future
  Probability meaning: open (neutral, i.e. possible)
- ***Conditional type 2:***
  Syntactic pattern: sub-clause (***unreal***) ***past tense*** (simple), matrix ***would***
  Time reference: present or future
  Probability meaning: depending on context, either ***theoretical*** (unreal, i.e. slightly possible/improbable), or ***hypothetical*** (closed, i.e. impossible)
- ***Conditional type 3:***
  Syntactic pattern: sub-clause (***unreal***) ***past perfect tense*** (simple), matrix ***would have***
  Time reference: past
  Probability meaning: ***hypothetical*** (closed, i.e. impossible)

General rule-of-thumb: ***will***- and ***would***-forms in matrix clause only, never in ***if***-clause

051/2.6 Varying time references in each clause

In each of the conditional examples just discussed, the time reference was the same for both clauses. It may, however, vary:

(54) a. If he is in town now, he will come to the party tonight.
Conditional type 1 (open), present time + future time
b. If he was in town now, he would come to the party tonight.
Conditional type 2 (theoretical), present time + future time

Notice that we still have the standard sequence of tenses here. The difference between (54) and, say, (47) or (49) above is simply that here in (54) the time reference is not the same for each clause. The ***condition***, that is, relates to ***present*** time, and the ***consequence*** to the ***future***. There is nothing remarkable in this, as it has no effect here on the syntax. However, in the next sections we show that varying time references may lead to different tenses being used from those in the standard types.

051/2.7 Varying time references and tense divergence with Conditional type 1

Conditional type 1 (***open***) allows a considerable amount of tense divergence from the standard. The possible variations and combinations include present perfect and past tense in the ***if***-clause and future perfect (***will have***) in the matrix. Note, however, that the general rule preventing ***will*** in the ***if***-clause is ***never*** contravened:

(55) a. If he ***has*** already ***arrived***, he ***will come*** to the party tonight.
Time reference: present time + future time
Tense sequence: present perfect + ***will***-form
b. If he ***has*** already ***arrived***, he ***will be*** in the café next to the station.
Time reference: present time + present time
Tense sequence: present perfect + ***will***-form
c. If he ***arrived*** yesterday, he ***will come*** to the party tonight.
Time reference: past time + future time
Tense sequence: past tense + ***will***-form
d. If he ***arrived*** yesterday, he ***will be*** in his hotel room now.
Time reference: past time + present time
Tense sequence: past tense + ***will***-form
e. If he ***arrived*** yesterday, he ***will have checked into*** his hotel immediately.
Time reference: past time + past time
Tense sequence: past tense + future perfect (***will have***-form for past speculation)
f. If Joan ***has finished*** the job by next Thursday, she ***will let*** us ***know***.
Time reference: future time + future time
Tense sequence: present perfect + ***will***
g. If we ***save*** £500 a month, we ***will have saved*** £6000 after a year.
Time reference: future time + future time
Tense sequence: present tense + future perfect (***will have***-form as a speculative 'present perfect-in-the-future')

Note that (55)f. has the standard ***type1*** time reference, but a present perfect is used in the ***if***-clause in the meaning of a ***future perfect***. This, again, is because ***will***-forms cannot appear in the ***if***-clause (see also **049/5.3** above and example (39)).

(55)g. also has the standard ***type1*** time reference, but an **A–R** meaning in the matrix requiring ***future perfect***.

051/2.8 Varying time references and tense divergence with Conditional types 2 and 3

There is far less variation possible with ***Conditional types 2*** and ***3***. Past time reference is more constraining. Variants here are usually mixtures of the two types syntactically, with either ***hypothetical*** or ***theoretical*** meaning.

(56) a. If we ***had saved*** more money, we ***would buy*** a house.
Time reference: past time + future time
Tense sequence: past perfect + ***would***-form
b. If we ***had saved*** more money, we ***would have*** enough for a house.
Time reference: past time + present time
Tense sequence: past perfect + ***would***-form
c. If we ***saved*** £500 a month, we ***would have saved*** £6000 after a year.
Time reference: future time + future time
Tense sequence: past tense + conditional perfect (***would have***-form)

(56)c. is the ***theoretical*** version of (55)g. (56)a. and b. are tense pattern mixtures of ***types 2*** and ***3***. Both examples have the same pattern and probability meaning (***hypothetical***), but differing time references in the matrix.

051/2.9 Other speculative modals in conditional sentences

Apart from *will*, other speculative modal auxiliaries can also appear in the matrix:

(57) a. If we arrive at the theatre early, we might get a front-row seat.
b. If we had saved more money, we could have bought a house.
c. If Tony and Jill aren't at home, they may be out with the dog.

Speculative modals cannot generally appear in the ***if***-clause, however. This basic rule applies not only to ***will*** but equally to ***may***, ***might***, ***could***, etc., when these are used in their ***speculative*** senses. That is, we cannot say **If we may arrive at the theatre early …*, or **If we might have saved more money …*, etc., as versions of (57)a. or b.

There are three notable exceptions, however: firstly, ***should***:

(58) a. If you should see Jim, please give him my regards.
Wenn Sie Jim sehen sollten, grüßen Sie ihn bitte von mir.
b. Should you call when we are not available, you may leave a message with our secretary.
Sollten Sie uns zu einer Zeit besuchen, wenn wir nicht anwesend sind, können Sie uns bei unserer Sekretärin eine Nachricht hinterlassen.

Should is used here to underline the ***speculative*** nature of the condition. But it has no other meaning, and could be left out: *If you see Jim …*, and *If you call …* are the ordinary, neutral ways of saying the same thing. More formally, as in (58)b., it can actually replace ***if*** at the beginning of the clause. ***If*** is then omitted entirely, and ***inversion*** of subject and verb takes place. This use of ***should*** occurs particularly when there is an ***imperative*** in the matrix, or some other ***non-speculative*** form (e.g. giving permission, expressing obligation or volition, etc., see under **051/3** below). With a speculative matrix it is usually avoided. It is only used in this sense for ***Conditional type 1***.

A second exception is with ***going to***:

(59) a. If we're not going to get to the theatre in time on foot, we'll just call a taxi.
Wenn sich herausstellt, dass wir nicht rechtzeitig zu Fuß ins Theater kommen, rufen wir einfach ein Taxi.
b. If you're going to feel panic in the caves, we won't go in there.
Wenn du nachher in den Höhlen eine Panikattacke bekommst, gehen wir lieber gar nicht erst hinein.

The meaning of ***if + going to*** here is *if it becomes predictable that* ... That is, the condition is fulfilled ***not*** by the sub-clause actions themselves (here *(not) get to* and *feel*), but by the ***arising of the likelihood*** that they will happen later. The idea is that they should be ***prevented*** by the matrix actions (*call* and *not go*, respectively), which must therefore precede them. This is actually a reversal of the usual sequence of actions in conditional sentences. Normally the action in the ***if***-clause occurs before the matrix action. But this order of events would be illogical and absurd here: **If we don't get to the theatre in time we'll just call a taxi; *If you feel panic in the caves, we won't go in there.*

This usage is also confined mainly to ***Conditional type 1***. It cannot be used with a speculative matrix.

The third case is the slightly dated formula, ***were to***:

(60) a. If you were to see Jim, you would definitely notice the change in him.
Wenn Sie Jim sehen würden, würde Ihnen sicher auffallen ...
b. Were you to call when we were not available, you would be able to leave a message with our secretary.
Sollten (würden) Sie uns (je) zu einer Zeit besuchen, wenn wir nicht anwesend wären, könnten Sie uns bei unserer Sekretärin eine Nachricht hinterlassen.

The meaning and use is the same here as with ***should*** (including the possibility of omitting ***if*** and inverting subject and verb). However, use is confined to ***Conditional type 2***. It is important to note that ***were*** is the same in all persons including singular (*If Sally were to call* ...). The matrix in this case is usually speculative.

For a discussion of individual modal auxiliary meanings, see chapter 12.

051/3 Conditional sentences with non-speculative modal meaning

One or both clauses of conditional sentences may contain a ***non-speculative*** modal component, such as volition, obligation, necessity, advice, a command, etc. This can have an effect on the syntax: a much wider range of forms is then possible.

051/3.1 Non-speculative meaning in the matrix clause

In the following examples, the matrix clauses convey non-speculative meanings. There is a much larger variety of possible forms here than with speculative matrix clauses. The ***if***-clauses themselves still have a speculative nature, i.e. express the possibility that a certain condition may arise. Generally speaking, they must be of ***type 1***, i.e. in the present tense:

(61) a. I'll/I can/I could call a taxi if you need one. (volition/ability)
b. If our guests get tired, they can lie down. (permission)
c. Grandmother must ask for help if the housework and cooking get too much for her. (necessity/obligation)
d. If you run into a thunderstorm, (you should) look for shelter immediately. (advice/necessity/imperative)

(61)a. shows ***will*** in its ***volitional*** meaning. Volitional ***going to*** is also possible. In fact, almost any verb form with a future time sense (e.g. any modal auxiliary, or the imperative, or even ***present progressive***) can occur, depending on the meaning intended:

(62) a. I'm going to leave the firm if they move to Bristol.
b. She's spending her holidays with her parents if Tom doesn't get in touch.
c. If they need financial support, we're going to help them.

What is meant here are plans and arrangements that have already been made ***beforehand***, and will take effect if the particular condition arises.

Sometimes the plan or arrangement factor is simply a 'metaphor' (more or less idiomatic) for other speech intentions, such as threats, promises, resolute reactions, and strong wishes:

(63) a. If you make any more remarks like that, you're leaving.
b. If Sally's flatmates continue the bad behaviour, she's going to move out.
c. If you go to America next year, I'm coming with you!

051/3.2 Non-speculative modal meaning in the if-clause: volition

Volitional meaning is common in ***if***-clauses. This is not to say that speculative meaning entirely disappears. But it is either not expressed in the modal verb at all, or if it is, it is not the only modal meaning. In the volitional sense ***will*** and ***would*** are permissible. Volitional ***going to*** also occurs:

(64) a. If you'll just take a seat for a moment, someone will attend to you immediately.
Wenn Sie sich einen Augenblick setzen möchten …
b. If Rodney would work a bit harder, he would get really good marks at school.
Wenn Rodney sich etwas mehr anstrengen würde …
c. If you're going to misbehave here in the cinema, we'll all be thrown out.
Wenn ihr vorhabt, euch hier im Kino schlecht zu benehmen/Wenn ihr euch hier im Kino (nur) schlecht benehmen wollt/benehmt, werden wir alle rausgeschmissen.

After so much has been said against ***will***- and ***would***-forms in the sub-clause, it may seem strange that they may now (suddenly!) appear there. But this is expressly because they add a different, non-speculative meaning. This use can be paraphrased by *be willing to*, e.g. *If Rodney was willing to work …, If you're willing to take a seat …* As in (64)a., they are often heard as politeness formulas when people are asked to do things. They then have the sense of *please* or *Would you mind?* Their tone is slightly elevated or formal. More neutral alternatives are *If you would like to*, and *If you don't mind*: *If you would like to take/ If you don't mind taking a seat for a moment, someone will attend to you immediately*. Similarly also *wouldn't* in the phrase *If you wouldn't mind* (*If you wouldn't mind taking …*).

Would like frequently occurs in ***if***-clauses in its more literal volitional sense (= dt. *möchten*): *If you would like to come with us on Friday, let us know*. Note that in speech and informal language *would*, like *will*, is generally shortened to *'d*, mainly after personal pronouns: *If you'd like to …*

Without complementation, *would like* in ***if***-clauses is often shortened to just *like*, especially when the ***if***-clause follows the matrix: *You can come with us on Friday, if you like; If you like, we can have a drink beforehand*. This is a very common way of making offers and suggestions.

Note also the use of *won't* in the sense of 'not be willing' or 'refuse to' (possible also in reference to inanimate objects): *If your son won't eat, he'll get sick; If the cases won't fit in the trunk of the car, they'll easily go on the back seat*.

Going to in its ***volitional*** sense means *intend*, as we saw above (**049/2.2**). (64)c. can therefore be paraphrased as *If you intend to misbehave here in the cinema* … It is similar in time relations to the speculative use of ***going to*** in the ***if***-clause (see **2.9** above and example (59)). Compare the following:

(65) a. If Taylor ***leaves*** the firm, we'll start looking for a replacement immediately. (**if**-***clause speculative***)
b. If Taylor's ***going to*** (= intends to) leave the firm, we'll start looking for a replacement immediately. (**if**-***clause volitional***)

In (65)a., the ordinary ***if***-clause version, the search will begin after Taylor has left. In (65)b. it will begin immediately Taylor's ***intention*** to leave is clear, i.e. before he actually does leave.

051/3.3 Other modal meaning in the if-clause

Apart from volition, other modal meanings are also common.

(66) a. If Dave has to work on Saturday, he'll be angry. (obligation)
b. If I can sit just down for a moment, I'll soon feel better. (permission/ability)
c. It would be good if they could phone us before they leave. (ability/possibility).
d. If you must look for shelter up on the moors, you'll find a hut below Kinder Scout. (necessity)

These are not restricted to any particular conditional type. (66)a., b., and d., are ***type 1***, as the present tense forms show, but can also be converted to ***type 2***, e.g. *If Dave had to work on Saturday, he'd be angry*. (66)c. is already ***type 2***, but could be converted to ***type 1***: *It will be good if they can …*

051/3.4 Non-speculative modal meanings in both clauses

It is of course equally possible for both clauses to contain non-speculative meanings:

(67) a. If they can help us, we'll help them. (ability + volition)
b. If you have to fill your tank, look for a petrol station here before 6 pm. (necessity + command)
c. If you'll come this way, you can have a seat while you wait. (volition + ability/permission)
d. If Bella can call us, she should do so immediately when she arrives. (ability + obligation)

These too are possible in all thee conditional types (e.g. If Bella could have called us, she should have done so immediately she arrived – **type 3**).

As pointed out above, non-speculative modals do not mean that the sentence has no speculative meaning at all. In all examples so far, the ***if***-clause itself has a ***basic speculative meaning***: i.e. it proposes a ***possible*** condition, and therefore presents the particular action or state as 'imagined'.

This needs emphasis here, as the next sections deal with conditional sentences which actually do not have this basic speculative meaning.

051/4 False conditionals

False conditionals are those which have no meaning of *condition* (*possibility*) → *fulfilment* → *consequence*. That is, they do ***not*** link possibilities on a ***speculative*** basis. Most of them use the conjunction ***if***, but in various other senses of the word. Some of these are not conditional at all. Others are conditional in a way (***'pseudo-conditionals'***), though it is not the usual (speculative) kind of condition we have been describing so far. One or two other conjunctions are also used in ***'pseudo-conditional'*** senses.

051/4.1 Implicative conditional sentences

The ***if***-clause here expresses a condition: not as a speculation, however, but as an ***assumed*** fact. This is presupposed as true, and the matrix clause comments on it as if it was a ***real*** fact:

(68) a. If Jane tells you that, she is lying.
b. If Fred's version is true, I've misunderstood the situation completely.
c. If Bob really was so successful, we've underestimated him.
d. If I've hurt your feelings, I'm sorry.

These are statements of the logical kind *If x, then y*. The speaker is asserting that ***y*** is automatically the case (i.e. true), if ***x*** is the case (i.e. true). This semantic relation is generally known in logic as ***implication*** or ***entailment***. The typical kind of implication is a comment or judgement, as in the examples. But it may be of a more neutral, defining type, e.g. in: *If something is a triangle, then it has three sides.*

The two clauses very often have the same time reference, indicated either by identical tense forms (e.g. in (68)a.), or at least by the same primary tenses (as in (68)b. and d.). This need not be the case, though, as shown in (68)c.

Will-forms are not usually involved in ***implicative conditionals*** at all.

051/4.2 Conclusive or causal if

In this case, ***if*** means *as, since* or *in view of the fact that*:

(69) a. If you don't like your car, buy a new one.
b. If Rita knew Rick was dishonest, why did she trust him?
c. Of course Barry isn't informed. If he doesn't come to meetings, what does he expect?

The matrix draws a ***logical conclusion***, i.e. *You don't like your car – so buy a new one!*

As in (69)b. and c., this can often take the form of a ***rhetorical question***: i.e. *Rita knew this – so why did she trust him?* Imperatives or modals expressing ability (*... what can he expect?*) and necessity (*... you should/must buy a new one*) are common here. Tense forms are most often the same in each clause.

051/4.3 Habitual if

If here quite simply means *when/whenever*, and links one habit or general truth with another. The association is one of cause, time or consequence, or a mixture of them:

(70) a. If you pour oil on water it floats.
b. If we spend the weekend in London, we always go to a show.
c. If you ask a silly question, you get a silly answer.
d. If you drive fast, you take risks.
e. If you asked her nicely, she usually did you a favour.

The tenses in each clause are the same: usually ***present*** + ***present***, or ***past*** +***past***. ***Will*** can occur in the matrix, but in its ***habitual*** meaning: *If you pour oil on water it will float* (see chapter 12 on modals). Although, again, there is no sense of speculation here, there is still some kind of conditional meaning in many sentences of this type (e.g. (70)a., c., and d.): that is, the ***if***-clause expresses a pre-condition for a consequence in the matrix.

051/4.4 Concessive if

If can also mean *although* or *despite this fact/possibility*:

(71) a. If he's educated, he certainly doesn't show it.
b. Even if he's educated, he doesn't know everything.
c. Even if you run, you won't get to the station in 5 minutes.
d. We're going to climb that mountain even if it kills us.
e. If she said that, she didn't mean it.

The *if*-clauses here are ***adverbial clauses of concession*** (see also chapter 7 on conjunctions). ***If*** and ***even if*** mean the same, but are not completely interchangeable. ***Even if*** lends more emphasis to the restriction, and is nearly always used when there is a future reference (as in (71)c. and d.).

A good paraphrase for both in many cases is with *may ..., but* (dt. *zwar ..., aber*): *He may be educated, but he certainly doesn't show it/he doesn't know everything; She may have said that, but she didn't mean it.* ***Even if*** can also be rendered by ***even though*** when the time reference is past or present, as in (71)b. and e., though not when the reference is future, as in (71)c. and d.

051/4.5 if as whether

If is used as an alternative for ***whether*** in clauses following verbs like *know, ask, wonder, find out,* etc.:

(72) a. Jenny doesn't know if (whether) Martin is teaching tomorrow or not.
b. Have you asked them if (whether) they will help us on Saturday?
c. I wonder if (whether) Brian is going to come to the party tonight.

The German translation of ***if*** here is *ob*. These are ***not*** conditional sentences in any way, and should not be confused with them. Important points to note about this use of ***if*** for ***whether*** are:

- ***if*** is only possible when the clause functions as a ***direct object*** and follows the matrix verb
- ***if*** in this case is followed by ***normal future-referring verb forms***, (i.e. ***will, going to***, or present tense, depending on the particular future meaning involved); that is, ***if***-clause rules do ***not*** apply!
- ***if*** cannot follow a preposition.
- When in doubt, use ***whether***!

051/4.6 whether as a 'pseudo-conditional'

Whether itself has two ***'pseudo-conditional'*** meanings, one in which the sub-clause is ***subject*** (***S***) and one in which it functions as an ***adverbial*** (***A***):

(73) a. Whether we help Christine (or not) will depend on her behaviour. (***S***)
b. Whether we help Christine (or not), she will succeed. (***A***)

Note that these uses (unlike that in **051/4.5**) follow the syntactic ***if***-clause pattern (***no*** *will/would* in the sub-clause!). ***If*** cannot replace ***whether*** in these cases. The German equivalent, again, is *ob*.

051/4.7 in case

The difficult case of ***in case*** was dealt with under individual conjunctions in chapter 7 (see **038/3.4**). Here, again, as a reminder: ***in case*** has a pseudo-conditional meaning quite different from the regular conditional meaning of ***if***. The normal German translation of ***in case*** is *für den Fall, dass …*

(74) a. We'll take sandwiches with us in case we get hungry.
Wir nehmen belegte Brote mit für den Fall, dass wir Hunger kriegen.
b. I've got in some beer too, just in case Harry comes round tonight.
Ich habe noch etwas Bier gekauft, für den Fall, dass Harry heute Abend vorbeikommt.

In case, that is, means 'as preparation for this future possibility'. Note, again, that syntactically ***if***-clause rules apply.

051/5 Speculative conditions: other types and variants

Here we return to the genuine conditional, but in a variety of structures without ***if*** (or without ***if*** in its normal senses). In some cases other conjunctions take its place; in others, conditional structures are used without overtly creating conditional clauses; and in others again, conditional meaning is implied in non-conditional structures.

Note that ***if***-clause rules apply wherever the clause structure is appropriate, i.e. wherever there is a conditional-type sub-clause and a corresponding matrix.

051/5.1 unless

Unless gives a condition under which something will ***not*** happen. It restricts the truth of the main clause, though in the sense of 'except if': that is, the ***probability*** of the main clause action is actually emphasized:

(75) a. We will not stop on the way to Brighton unless we get really tired.
(assumption: we will not get tired and will not stop)
… es sei denn, wir werden wirklich sehr müde.
b. The snow will be good for skiing tomorrow, unless temperatures rise unexpectedly during the night.
(assumption: temperatures will not rise, and skiing will be good)
… es sei denn, es gibt in der Nacht einen unerwarteten Temperaturanstieg.
c. You wouldn't have got us by phone yesterday, unless you had called very early in the morning.
(assumption: you wouldn't have called so early, and therefore would not have contacted us)
… es sei denn, du hättest uns ganz früh am Morgen angerufen.

For details on the relation of ***unless*** to ***if … not***, see also chapter 7, **038/3.3**.

051/5.2 provided that/as long as

These are stronger, more emphatic forms of ***if***, stressing that the condition must be fulfilled. They are most often associated with ***permission*** and ***offers***, as in (76)b. ***Provided*** is often treated as a conjunction on its own, with ***that*** omitted, especially in speech and informal language.

(76) a. We will go to the beach tomorrow provided (that) the weather is good.
(i.e. only on that condition)
..., vorausgesetzt, wir haben gutes Wetter.
b. Joey and Simon can use my car provided that/as long as they pay for the petrol.
..., solange sie das Benzin bezahlen.

A further example of a conjunction-type phrase of this kind is ***on condition that***: *I'll lend her money on condition that she pays it back within one month.*

All of these allow conditional patterns of ***types 2*** and ***3*** as well, of course: *I'd lend her the money on condition that she paid it back within one month; Joey and Simon could have used my car, provided that/as long as they had paid for the petrol.*

051/5.3 supposing/suppose (that)

As with *provided*, this is syntactically a verb form plus ***that***-clause (with ***that*** generally omitted). Meaning and construction are similar to those with verbs like ***imagine*** or ***assume***. That is, the speaker visualizes (imagines) a particular situation or condition and states or asks what the consequences might be (or might have been):

(77) a. Supposing/suppose Bella loses/lost her job. She couldn't possibly still continue to pay for the house.
Angenommen, Bella verliert ihren Arbeitsplatz/würde ihren Arbeitsplatz verlieren/verlöre ihren Arbeitsplatz ...
b. Imagine/supposing you had been driving fast down the motorway when the tyre burst. What would have happened then?
Stell' dir mal vor, du wärst mit hoher Geschwindigkeit auf der Autobahn gefahren, als der Reifen platzte ...

Unlike *provided*, ***suppose/supposing*** cannot be regarded themselves as subordinating conjunctions. This is because they introduce a complete sentence (as is clear from the examples), and not just a subordinate conditional clause. The consequence of the imagined condition must be referred to in a separate sentence (like *What would have happened then?* in (77)b.). Nevertheless, the tense pattern in sentences introduced by ***suppose/supposing*** follows the ***if***-clause rule (i.e. no *will* or *would* in the same clause!).

All three conditional types are common here.

051/5.4 The verb wish and the expression if only

Wish is another verb connected with conditions. In this case the speaker expresses regret that a particular condition remains or remained unfulfilled.

Tenses following ***wish*** are those in ***if***-clauses, i.e. the ***unreal past*** or the ***unreal past perfect***:

(78) a. I wish I knew the answer to that question (but I don't).
b. Sheila wishes John was going to Australia with them (but he isn't).
c. The Robertsons wish they had been at the wedding (but they weren't).

What follows ***wish*** is a ***that***-clause, but usually with ***that*** omitted, as here. Note that the meaning of the sub-clauses in (78) is ***hypothetical*** (i.e. impossible), even with (78)a. and b., which refer to the present and future.

When reference to the present and future is ***theoretical*** (i.e. possible but not likely), both ***past tense*** and ***would***-form occur:

(79) a. I wish you visited us/would visit us more often.
b. Sheila wishes John was/would be more attentive to the children.
c. Mother wishes Tim helped/would help more with the housework.

The ***would***-form in this case is ***volitional***, and underlines the desire for a change of behaviour. Other modals (e.g. *could*) are also possible, depending on meaning, for instance: *I wish you could (= were able to) visit us more often; The Robertsons wish they could have been at the wedding.*

Note, however, that neither the ***will***-form nor the present tense can follow ***wish***. When ***wish*** has an 'open' meaning in the sense of *want/would like*, it takes the infinitive (see also chapter 13): *We wish to congratulate you, Mr. Boyle, on your sales record this year.*

The expression ***if only*** (dt. *wenn ... nur*) can also express strong wishes in the sense of (78) and (79):

(80) a. If only you visited us/would visit us/could visit us more often.
Wenn du uns nur öfter besuchtest/besuchen würdest/könntest.
b. If only John was/would be more attentive to the children.
Wenn John nur aufmerksamer zu den Kindern wäre/sein würde.
c. If only the Robertsons had been/could have been at the wedding.
Wenn die Robertsons nur an der Hochzeit gewesen wären/hätten sein können.

This is a stronger form of wishing, and tends to add a more dramatic note of 'longing'. Unlike *wish*, ***if only*** can be used with present tense (as in the open conditional ***type 1***), or with volitional ***will***:

(81) If only he tries/he will try harder, we'll be happy.

If only-clauses can be used as ***if***-clauses, as in (81), but are more usual alone, as complete sentences, as in (80). ***If only*** is then an adverb phrase (not a conjunction).

051/5.5 The expressions as if, it is time, had better

As if (also ***as though***) is the equivalent of German *als ob*. In its 'open' meaning it is followed by the whole range of tense and modal forms (including *will*), as appropriate. Here, that is, it does not follow ***if***-clause patterns:

(82) a. You talk as if I never come to see you nowadays.
b. He sounds as if he doesn't care.
c. It looks as if Joe will take the job in Australia.

However, it can also be paired with ***theoretical*** and ***hypothetical*** meaning, and is then followed by the tense pattern of ***if***-clauses in ***types 2 and 3***, i.e. ***unreal past*** or ***unreal past perfect***, depending on time reference:

(83) a. You talk as if I never came to see you nowadays.
Du redest, als ob ich euch heutzutage nie besuchen würde.
b. He sounds as if he didn't care.
Er klingt, als ob es ihm egal wäre.
c. She's celebrating as if she had won a million pounds.
Sie feiert, als ob sie eine Million Pfund gewonnen hätte.

The phrase ***it is time*** is a way of saying *should/ought to*, and implies a certain lateness. As ***theoretical*** meaning is involved, the ***unreal past*** is necessary:

(84) a. It is time we were going.
Es ist Zeit, dass wir gehen/Es ist Zeit für uns zu gehen.
b. It is time you went to bed, young Sally!
Es ist Zeit, dass du ins Bett gehst/Zeit für Dich ins Bett zu gehen, kleine Sally!

Finally, the phrase ***had better*** expresses a strong recommendation. It is always used in this form and no other, and is followed by the infinitive. It is mentioned here because it too is a manifestation of an ***unreal past***, with ***theoretical*** meaning, as in an ***if***-clause ***type 2*** pattern:

(85) a. We had better take a taxi.
Wir nehmen lieber ein Taxi.
b. You had better go to bed, young Sally!
Du gehst lieber ins Bett/solltest lieber ins Bett gehen, kleine Sally!

051/5.6 Conditions expressed or implied in phrases and other clause types

Many phrases express or imply conditions:

(86) a. ***In that case*** we'll (we had better) take a taxi.
(If that is the case ...)
b. ***With a bit of luck*** we would have won the game.
(If we had had more luck ...)
c. ***Without George*** we would never have found the missing money.
(If George hadn't been with us ...)
d. The race won't take place ***in these conditions***.
(If conditions are as bad as this ...)

And also other types of clause:

(87) a. ***Do that again*** and you'll be in trouble!
(If you do that again ...)
b. We would give you a lift home, ***but we don't have the car with us.***
(If we had the car with us ...)
c. ***They must decide right now*** or forget the offer.
(If they don't decide right now, they must ...)
d. ***Hearing all his stories***, you'd think he was Casanova.
(If you heard all his stories, you'd think ...)

It is important to stress that conditional meaning is only implied here.

Structurally and semantically the clauses and phrases shown are not actually conditional in nature. They represent conditions 'metaphorically', i.e. rather on a pragmatic level.

11.3 Indirect (reported) speech

Introduction: direct and indirect speech 052

Direct speech is the presentation of spoken words in their original form, i.e. 'from the mouth of the individual speaker'. It normally occurs as part of a larger piece of communication by a 'general speaker', or ***narrator***. Assume, for example, that I am the ***narrator***, the general speaker, and I am talking to you about a person called Chantal. She has been ill, and I tell you the following: *Chantal is much better now. "I'm feeling on top of the world," she said when I saw her this morning for coffee at Dino's.*

In part of my statement to you, I reproduce Chantal's own words: *"I'm feeling on top of the world"*. This is ***direct speech***. You, the listener, feel that Chantal is talking to you directly, although the person actually communicating Chantal's words is not Chantal herself, but me, the ***narrator***. In direct speech, that is, the ***narrator*** simulates original communication by the person whose words are quoted (the ***direct speaker***).

In writing this is signalled by ***speech marks***. These are ***inverted commas*** (i.e "and"), which enclose the ***direct speech*** and mark it off from the rest of the communication.

Another way of telling you what Chantal said is in the mode of what we call ***reporting***. Here, I do not repeat Chantal's own words as if she were speaking herself.

That is, there is ***no*** direct speaker. Everything I say here is presented from ***my*** perspective, that of the ***narrator***: *Chantal is much better now. She said that she was feeling on top of the world when I saw her this morning for coffee at Dino's.*

Chantal's words here are more or less the same. But there are one or two grammatical differences showing that this time she does ***not*** speak directly. What she says is conveyed to you from the ***narrator perspective***, i.e. mine. This is what we call ***indirect*** (or ***reported***) ***speech***.

Although the ***speaker perspective*** stays the same and there is no change in deixis, we tend to regard ***indirect speech*** as a conversion from direct speech. This is because ***indirect speech*** uses certain grammatical forms to signal that this is not the original perspective of the specific individual speaker. The words are the ***narrator's version*** of the original, and the grammar forms show this by signalling a certain distance. German does the same thing, though in a different way. Compare the following English ***direct speech*** sentence with its ***indirect*** versions in English and German:

(88) a. Chantal said: "***I am*** feeling on top of the world." [English ***direct***]
b. Chantal said that ***she was feeling*** on top of the world. [English ***indirect***]
c. Chantal sagte, ***sie fühle*** sich topfit. [German ***indirect***]

The central feature in the change form ***direct*** to ***indirect*** speech lies in the ***verb form***.

The German indirect speech, in (88)c., uses the *present subjunctive* (dt. *Konjunktiv I*). The English version, in (88)b., uses the ***unreal past*** (another case where ***modal tense change*** compensates for the lack of a subjunctive in English!). However, English does ***not always*** use the unreal past for indirect speech; moreover, German does not always use the present subjunctive. That is, converting ***direct*** to ***indirect speech*** is a rather complex matter in both languages, and there is no one-to-one correspondence between the two languages.

⚠ One should therefore never try just to 'translate' ***German indirect speech*** into ***English indirect speech*** (or *vice versa*). This will just not work. The two systems are entirely different.

053 The forms of indirect speech

053/1 Tense regulation in indirect speech
053/2 Other changes in indirect speech
053/3 Reporting verbs in indirect speech
053/4 Questions in indirect speech
053/5 Commands in indirect speech

As we said above, indirect speech forms are normally treated as forms derived from direct speech. This is the best way to show them. The question, then, is: how is ***direct*** speech ***converted*** into ***indirect*** speech? The main changes are the following:

- the ***direct speech*** clause loses its specific ***punctuation***, i.e. inverted commas and any other delimiting punctuation, usually an ordinary comma before or after it (occasionally also a preceding colon);

- as a ***reported clause*** it becomes a regular ***sub-clause*** (typically a ***that***-clause) in the function of ***direct object*** (***Od***);
- the ***subject pronoun*** (and with it ***verb concord***) changes, except when narrator and individual speaker are identical;
- this may result in other ***deictic*** changes, usually in accompanying adverbials;
- under certain circumstances ***tense changes*** take place in the sub-clause; this is known as ***backshift***.

From a learning and teaching point of view, the last point (***tense change***) is the most important and most difficult one.

Finally, it is good to distinguish between two different speech times: first, the time of the ***direct utterance*** (***direct-S***); second, the time of ***reporting*** by the ***narrator*** (***indirect-S***).

053/1 Tense regulation in indirect speech

Tense regulation (i.e. change or no change) affects the tense of the ***verb in the sub-clause*** (or ***reported clause***). It is determined by the tense of the ***reporting verb*** (i.e. the ***matrix verb***). If this is in the ***past tense***, the change from direct to indirect speech leads to a 'backward movement' of tenses in the ***reported clause*** (i.e. the ***sub-clause***). Details on this ***backshift*** are given below.

053/1.1 Reporting verb in present tense

When the ***reporting verb*** is in the ***present tense***, the ***sub-clause tenses*** stay the ***same*** as in the ***direct*** speech, i.e. there is ***no*** backshift. This applies also when the ***reporting verb*** is in the ***present perfect*** or in any ***future*** or ***modal*** form that is ***not*** in the unreal ***past***:

(89) a. Holly says/has said/will say, "***I have*** a heavy cold." [***direct***]
b. Holly says/has said/will say (that) ***she has*** a heavy cold. [***indirect***]

The only changes are in the punctuation (no speech marks or comma before them) and in the subject and verb concord. But the sub-clause tense (here the ***present***) remains unchanged. This applies equally to any sub-clause tense (e.g. past, present perfect, ***will***-form, etc.):

(90) a. Holly says/has said/will say, "***I have had/had*** a heavy cold." [***direct***]
b. Holly says/has said/will say (that) ***she has had/had*** a heavy cold. [***indirect***]

053/1.2 Reporting verb in past tense

When the ***reporting verb*** is in the ***past tense***, the ***sub-clause primary tense*** is ***backshifted***. That is, all ***present tense*** forms become ***past tense*** forms. This also means that a ***sub-clause present perfect***, as in (91)c., is ***backshifted*** to the ***past perfect***, as in (91)d.:

(91) a. Holly said, "***I have*** a heavy cold." [***direct***]
b. Holly said (that) ***she had*** a heavy cold. [***indirect***]
c. Holly said, "I ***have had*** a heavy cold." [***direct***]
d. Holly said (that) she ***had had*** a heavy cold. [***indirect***]

In the same way, ***will*** becomes ***would***, ***can*** becomes ***could*** and ***going to*** also receives a ***past tense*** form:

(92) a. Holly said, "***I will/can/am going to*** buy a car." [***direct***]
b. Holly said (that) ***she would/could/was going to*** buy a car. [***indirect***]

This all happens regardless of the aspect. That is, verbs must be ***backshifted*** not only in the simple form, but also in the ***progressive***:

(93) a. Holly said, "***I am decorating*** the hall at the moment." [***direct***]
b. Holly said (that) ***she was decorating*** the hall at the moment. [***indirect***]

Backshift must also occur when the ***reporting verb*** is in the ***unreal past***, or in the ***past perfect*** (***real*** as well as ***unreal***):

(94) a. If you told the boss you ***were*** ill, he would say you ***were pretending***.
Wenn du dem Chef sagen würdest, du seist krank, würde er sagen, du simulierst.
b. I wish Brian had said that he ***worked*** for a different firm now.
Ich wünsche, Brian hätte gesagt, er arbeite jetzt für eine andere Firma.

053/1.3 Past tense in reporting verb and past tense in direct speech

A ***past tense*** in the original ***direct speech*** very often stays the same (= ***no backshift***!):

(95) a. Holly said, "***I had*** a heavy cold last week." [***direct***]
b. Holly said (that) ***she had*** a heavy cold last week. [***indirect***]
c. Trevor said at the party: "***I was*** in Malibu in May." [***direct***]
d. Trevor said at the party that ***he was*** in Malibu in May. [***indirect***]

But it may also be ***backshifted*** to the ***past perfect***. For instance, (95)b. and d. might be expressed as:

(96) a. Holly said (that) ***she had had*** a heavy cold last week.
b. Trevor said at the party that ***he had been*** in Malibu in May.

Here the narrator's focus of attention is on ***direct-S***, i.e. the occasions when Holly and Trevor were speaking. In (96)b., for instance, the main topic of conversation could be the party itself and the people there. Trevor's stay in Malibu is just a momentary flashback to a ***pre-past time***. That is, we have the typical past perfect use: looking back further into the past from a reference point already in the past (shown in our ***tense notation*** as **A–R–S**). This reference point (**R**), as we have said, is actually ***direct-S***. The **S** in the formula is the ***narrator's*** **S**, i.e. ***indirect-S*** (see chapters 9 and 10 for a full explanation of tense notation).

With a ***direct speech past tense***, therefore, ***backshift*** is in principle ***optional***.

It just depends on the narrator's focus and point of view. However, there are one or two general guidelines to help in the choice (see next section).

053/1.4 Direct speech past tense: optional backshift

In general, past tenses are ***not backshifted***:

- in ***further sub-clauses***, especially time clauses (e.g. with *when*), and especially in reference to one specific occasion: *She said they hadn't bought the house because it was too expensive; Julia told me she had been to the Guggenheim museum when she lived in New York.*
- with the ***progressive***: *The old couple told the police that they were watching television at the time of the break-in.*
- when ***deictic time references*** (*today, yesterday, last week*, etc.) are the ***same*** for narrator and direct speaker: *Dave told me he **visited** Mary on Wednesday (this week);*
- when the narrator otherwise feels there is not much time distance between ***indirect-S*** and ***direct-S***: *Julia said she **bought** the dress at Taylor's* (expressed by the narrator, for instance, not long after Julia says this);
- when ***action-time focus*** is the ***same*** for narrator and direct speaker, as in (95)b. and d., or in the following: *Sue said Tom left for Paris **on May 5th***. Here the narrator focuses on the date of the original action, just as Sue, the direct speaker did. For the narrator, that is, the relation of the action to the ***indirect-S*** is the same as its relation to the ***direct-S*** (i.e. in our notation **A,R–S**).

The last point is probably the most usual reason for ***not*** applying backshift: the focus of both narrator and direct speaker is the same. Staying with this last example for a moment, let us assume now that the narrator focuses his report on Sue, and her condition at the time of the conversation. Sue tells the narrator this in direct speech in (97)a., and the narrator later reports this as (97)b.:

(97) a. Sue: "I am slowly getting used to being without Tom, but it was difficult at first, after he left on May 5th." [***direct***]
b. Sue said she was slowly getting used to being without Tom, but it had been difficult at first, after he had left on May 5th. [***indirect***]

The narrator now uses ***backshift*** in (97)b. in order to differentiate clearly between two ***different*** past times: on the one hand, the time of Tom's departure and Sue's difficulties (***pre-past***); on the other, the (***past***) time of the conversation with Sue, and her feelings then. Sue is in the 'topic foreground' here, and ***primary focus*** is on ***direct-S***.

053/1.5 Backshift with modal verbs and future reference

We have already seen that modal verbs in present tense forms (e.g. ***will, can*** and ***going to***) are also backshifted (see example (92) above). So also with ***may*** (→ ***might***), and ***to be to*** (→ ***was/were to***):

(98) a. Mother said, "You may play in the garden, but you are not to go on the lawn." [***direct***]
b. Mother said (that) they might play in the garden, but were not to go on the lawn. [***indirect***]

In informal and spoken language, however, backshift is frequently not applied when the action is in the future from the narrator's point of view, i.e. in relation to ***indirect-S***: *Sarah said she will/is going to/can come next Saturday.*

This applies also to non-modal future reference: *Sarah said she is coming next Saturday; Bill said the lecture tonight begins at 7 o'clock.*

The effect is to make the statement sound generally more objective and more certain. Any uncertainty, however, requires backshift: *Sarah said (at first) that she would/was going to/could come next Saturday (but now it seems doubtful).*

May in its speculative meaning is usually not backshifted (*Sarah said she may come*), so that the modal differentiation between ***may*** (open possibility) and ***might*** (lower possibility) is still kept (see chapter 12).

Must, which actually has no past tense form itself, can also occur unchanged in past indirect speech: *She said, "I must leave immediately"* (***direct***) → *She said she must leave immediately* (***indirect***). This happens most when the action has a future relation to ***indirect-S***: *She said, "I must work overtime tomorrow"* (***direct***) → *She said she must work overtime tomorrow* (***indirect***).

With a ***past*** relation to ***indirect-S***, there is a tendency to prefer the replacement verb ***have to*** (backshifted), especially when a clear past time adverb is present: *She said she had to work overtime the next day.* This is a tendency only, however, and is also affected by certain meaning differences between the two forms (see chapter 12 for further details on the relation between ***must*** and ***have to***).

Modals already in ***unreal past*** forms (***would, could, should, might, ought to***) in the direct speech do not change. The same applies to all ***unreal past*** tenses in ***conditional type 2*** sentences:

(99) a. Mother said, "You shouldn't go on the lawn." [***direct***]
b. Mother said (that) they shouldn't go on the lawn. [***indirect***]
c. Joanna said, "If Dave was here, he would help you." [***direct***]
d. Joanna said that if Dave was here, he would help us. [***indirect***]

053/2 Other changes in indirect speech

We have already seen that the change from direct to indirect speech also makes changes in ***subject pronouns*** necessary. In addition, ***personal pronouns*** in other functions may be involved, and ***adverbial elements*** often need replacement as well.

All these factors are ***deictic*** (i.e. speaker-related). In ***direct*** speech, ***deixis*** is oriented to the ***direct speaker***. In ***indirect*** speech it is oriented to the ***narrator***. This is what makes the changes necessary. However, none of them are automatic. They are semantic, rather than grammatical, and can depend strongly on context.

053/2.1 Personal pronouns

These change because the same person is referred to differently from the perspective of the narrator. Most common changes are 1st person → 3rd person, 2nd person → 1st person, and 2nd person → 3rd person. This can also mean changes in ***possessive determiners***:

(100) a. Wendy said, "***I*** am tired."
b. Wendy said (that) ***she*** was tired.
c. The chairman told me, "***You*** have 20 minutes for ***your*** presentation."
d. The chairman told me (that) ***I*** had 20 minutes for ***my*** presentation.
e. Jason and Marie said, "***We*** went to America in 1998."
f. Jason and Marie said (that) ***they*** went to America in 1998.

On the other hand, the pronoun may need no change because the person-relation is the ***same*** for the ***narrator*** as for the ***direct-speaker***:

(101) a. I said, "***I*** am hungry."
b. I said (that) ***I*** was hungry.
c. The chairman told me, "***They*** have 20 minutes for the presentation."
d. The chairman told me (that) ***they*** had 20 minutes for the presentation.

Changes are also possible, of course, from a full noun to a pronoun or *vice versa*. Apart from the subject, other functions (object, prepositional complement, etc.) may also be involved:

(102) a. Sally said (to me), "Bill saw ***you*** yesterday in the High Street."
b. Sally said (that) Bill saw ***me*** yesterday in the High Street.
(*said by me to someone else*)
c. The neighbour told me, "***I*** have given the key back to ***your wife***."
d. The neighbour told me (that) ***she*** had given the key back to ***you***.
(*said by me to my wife*)

053/2.2 Time adverbials

There are ***three*** possibilities for adverbial reference to the state or action in a ***reported clause***: direct speech deixis; indirect speech deixis; no deixis. The choice depends on the relation of the ***reporting time*** (***indirect-S***) to the time of the original direct speech (***direct-S***). In the following, (103)a. is a direct speech example, and (103)b., c., and d. give the corresponding reported versions, each of them connected to a different reporting time (i.e. ***indirect-S***):

(103) a. Jim said, "I sold my car ***yesterday***."
b. Jim said (that) he sold his car ***yesterday***.
(*reported on same day*)
c. Jim said he sold his car ***the day before yesterday***.
(*reported the day after Jim's statement*)
d. Jim said he had sold his car ***the day before*** (= the day before the day on which we spoke).
(*reported much later without specific time reference*)

- In (103)b. ***indirect-S*** and ***direct-S*** have the ***same deictic*** reference: deictic adverb ***remains unchanged***.
- In (103)c. ***indirect-S*** and ***direct-S*** have ***different*** deictic references: deictic adverb ***changes*** to one with ***indirect-S-orientation***.
- In (103)d. ***indirect-S*** and ***direct-S*** have ***different*** deictic references: deictic adverb ***changes*** to ***non-deictic adverb*** referring to ***direct-S***.

The last possibility, i.e. the change from ***direct-S-deixis*** to ***non-deictic direct-S-reference***, is very common. The following gives a few examples of equivalents:

(104)	***direct-S-deixis***		***non-deictic direct-S-reference***
	today	→	that day
	now	→	then
	this week	→	that week
	yesterday	→	the day before/the previous day
	two days ago	→	two days before
	tomorrow	→	the next/following day/the day after

053/2.3 Place adverbs and demonstratives

Basically, there are only 2 major deictic place adverbs, ***here*** and ***there***. Noun phrases with ***demonstrative*** determiners (***this/these/that/those***) are also deictic and often involved in adverbial reference. The principles applying here are similar to those with time reference. As the range of expressions is much smaller, however, the case is more simply explained.

(105) a. Jim said, "I arrived here on April 4th."
b. Jim said (that) he arrived here on April 4th.
c. Jim said that he arrived there on April 4th.
d. Jim said that he arrived in New York on April 4th.

(105)b. means the ***narrator*** must be in New York at ***indirect-S***. (105)c. means he must ***not*** be in New York (but somewhere else), while (105)d. leaves the question open.

Demonstratives refer to a speaker's position in relation to another object, person, etc. (see chapter 3). As long as the direct speaker and the narrator are in the ***same*** relation to the object, the same demonstrative can be transferred from the direct to the indirect speech.

(106) a. She said (*holding up a pen*), "I bought this at Carretto's."
b. (*Narrator holds up same pen*): She said (that) she bought this pen at Carretto's.
c. Jane (*pointing to pictures on a gallery wall*): "I don't like those pictures."
d. (*Narrator points to same pictures*): Jane says she doesn't like those pictures.

When the demonstratives ***this/these*** are relevant ***only*** to the ***direct speaker*** (i.e. the ***narrator*** has a completely different distance relation to the particular object), they cannot be transferred to the indirect speech. If the narrator still keeps a 'pointing attitude', ***that/those*** replace them. Most often, however, the deixis is no longer kept: another appropriate determiner is used instead:

(107) a. "We could meet them here, in this café," said Polly.
b. Polly said we could meet them in that café we always go to in Oxford Street.
c. She said (*showing me a pair of socks*), "I bought these socks for you."
d. She said (that) she had bought me some socks (*narrator does not have socks actually present*).

053/3 Reporting verbs in indirect speech

Reporting verbs used so far in the examples have been confined to *say* and *tell*. These are the most common, together with *ask*. *Ask* is a ***verb of enquiry***. Along with one or two others like it, it introduces its own variant of indirect speech: the ***indirect question***. Another sub-category of indirect speech is the ***indirect command***. The reporting verb *tell* also plays a major role here, but there are several others, such as *order, command* and *urge*. These special types of indirect speech are dealt with fully below (see **053/4** and **053/5**).

Returning to ***declaratives*** (i.e. ***statements***) in indirect speech, we must bear in mind that despite the frequency of *say* and *tell*, almost any ***utterance verb*** can take on the role of a ***reporting verb***. This is important in recognizing when indirect speech rules must be applied. Here are a few examples of less obvious reporting verbs:

(108) a. Fred complains that he has not eaten proper hot food for days.
b. Bella joked bitterly that without a job she would now have plenty of time for culture.
c. The police claim that Murdoch hit one of their officers.
d. My wife remarked that men often talked a lot, but said little.

Moreover, indirect speech may not present a reported ***utterance*** at all. It may be just the content of thought or feeling. In this case the ***reporting verb*** will refer to states and actions that are mental or psychological, e.g. *think, suppose, imagine, feel*, etc. Nevertheless, it is still a good idea for grammar purposes to think of the ***reported clause*** as being 'derived' from one in direct speech:

(109) a. Marie believes: "I have been tricked." [***direct***]
b. Marie believes she has been tricked. [***indirect***]
c. Taylor felt: "Fingers and Luigi are taking too long with the safe." [***direct***]
d. Taylor felt that Fingers and Luigi were taking too long with the safe. [***indirect***]

In addition to these general, more semantic points, there are several important syntactic features of ***reporting verbs*** and ***reporting clauses*** that need to be looked at closely.

053/3.1 Transferred negation with mental reporting verbs

With ***think*** and a number of other mental verbs, ***sub-clause negation*** is normally ***transferred*** to the matrix clause with no change of meaning:

(110) a. Cathy doesn't think John looks well.
(= Cathy thinks John doesn't look well.)
b. We didn't think the parking-lot was safe.
(= We thought the parking-lot wasn't safe.)

The transferred version is usually preferred, and is more neutral. The non-transferred alternative, in brackets, emphasizes the matrix clause and the 'thinking perspective' slightly more (which may suggest that the reported clause is not true).

Other common verbs involved in transferred negation are ***believe***, ***expect***, ***imagine***, ***suppose***, and also ***seem***: *Briony doesn't seem to be happy* (= *Briony seems not to be happy*).

With ***suppose*** and ***expect*** non-transfer is rare, e.g. *I don't suppose Travers will accept our offer* (and usually not **I suppose Travers will not accept …*).

When the 'thinking verb' (i.e. the matrix clause) is placed in ***second*** position, as often in speech and informal language, ***both*** verbs are negated: *Travers will **not** accept our offer, I **don't** suppose.*

Another rather peculiar feature in this respect is the use of ***questions tags***. When these refer to the ***sub-clause verb*** they remain ***positive***, even when the negative in the sub-clause has been transferred to the matrix: *I **don't** suppose Travers will accept our offer, **will** he?*

That is, the question tag behaves as if the sub-clause verb was still negative (which semantically speaking it is!).

053/3.2 Reporting verbs in the interrogative

Questions can be formed quite normally with ***reporting verbs***: *Did John say he was coming?*; *Did you think the parking-lot was safe?*

There are two points to note: Firstly, this is ***not*** what is meant by an indirect question! (See below). Secondly, **yes-no-*questions*** like these are quite straightforward. **Wh-*questions***, however, are syntactically more complex and can lead to ambiguity, as shown in the following section.

053/3.3 Transferred interrogative with secondary fronting

In the following example (111)a. is a perfectly normal example of a ***wh***-word in a ***reporting verb question***. But what does the sentence mean? Does it mean (111)b. or (111)c.?

(111) a. When did Celia say she was leaving for Toronto?
b. When did she say this?
c. When is Celia leaving, according to her statement?

Logically, it may seem that the only answer can be (111)b. But this is ***not*** so: the meaning of (111)a. can be either (111)b., or (111)c. In other words, (111)a. is ***ambiguous***. It can be rendered in German either as *Wann sagte Celia, dass sie nach Toronto aufbricht?* (the b.-version); or as *Was hat Celia gesagt, wann sie nach Toronto aufbricht?* (the c.-version). And in fact, the ***normal interpretation*** would be this last one, the c.-version.

Wh-words referring to something ***in the sub-clause*** (here the verb ***leave***) must be placed ***at the beginning*** of the sentence, i.e. actually ***in the matrix clause***, even though they do not refer to it. We call this ***secondary fronting***. There is actually often no other way of constructing the sentence. Here are other examples:

(112) a. Who do you think you are!?
Was glaubst du, wer du bist?!
b. What did Mike say he wanted?
Was hat Mike gesagt, dass er wollte?
c. What kind of present do you suppose Jamie might like most?
Was für ein Geschenk, glaubst du, würde Jamie am besten gefallen?

As we can see from (112), most cases of ***secondary fronting*** are not ambiguous. The ***wh***-word refers only to something in the sub-clause. We could also call this a ***transferred interrogative***. As with ***transferred negation***, explained in **053/3.1** above, what really belongs in the sub-clause is placed in the matrix clause:

A → ***Od***
(113) a. When did Celia say [she was leaving for Toronto]?

Od → ***Od***
b. What did Mike say [he wanted]?

(113) makes the real syntactic and semantic relations clear. The interrogative adverb ***when*** in a. enquires after an ***adverbial*** element complementing *leave*. An answer to the question would show this clearly, e.g. a prepositional phrase like *on Saturday* (*She is leaving on Saturday*). Similarly, the interrogative pronoun ***what*** in b. complements *wanted* as ***direct object***. Again, an answer would make this clear: *He wanted some advice.*

It is therefore good to remember the principle as follows: in **wh-*questions*** with ***reporting verbs***, the ***wh***-element starting the sentence may (and most often does) complement the verb in the ***sub-clause***.

Secondary fronting is not confined to indirect speech. It also occurs frequently in relative clauses (see chapter 14).

053/3.4 Free indirect speech

In ***free indirect speech*** the reporting verbs are missing. This is usually a written phenomenon, involving connected texts, and going beyond the boundary of the single sentence:

(114) a. *Robert said he was now tired of all the fuss and the bright lights.* At first he had enjoyed the publicity, and the feeling of being a celebrity. But now he just wanted to be left alone.
b. *Cynthia tried to imagine what it would be like without her job.* She would have less money, that was true. It was certainly going to be a problem living on her savings and social benefits. On the other hand she would be free to write, and that was what she wanted more than anything.
c. *She thought of Simon, and looked at her watch.* His plane was certainly just coming in to land in Chicago. He would be tired and irritable, as he always was on business trips. She must call him later and say a few soothing words that would calm his nerves before the big meeting took place in the early evening.

Passages in ***free indirect speech*** are typically introduced by sentences in ordinary indirect speech, as in (114)a. and b. (in italics). But they can also be signalled or implied contextually by other means, as in c.

They can be spoken, as in a. More often, however, free indirect speech is used to portray trains of thought and inner processes of 'self-dialogue', as in b. and c. It is common in fictional narrative, dramatizing a character's thoughts and feelings, and presenting them to the reader as a form of 'interior action'. Through this the reader is drawn especially intimately into the particular character's sphere of experience.

053/4 Questions in indirect speech

These are known as ***indirect questions***. As far as punctuation forms, tense and other deictic elements are concerned, they generally follow the same principles as declaratives (i.e. statements). But there are one or two additional points to be made regarding ***word-order***, **do**-***support*** and the basic distinction between **yes-no-*questions*** and **wh-*questions***. There are also certain restrictions affecting ***reporting verbs***.

053/4.1 Contrasts to direct questions

Important general points to note about ***indirect questions*** are that they:

- do not use **do**-***support***,
- have ***no inversion*** or ***question marks***,
- follow declarative word-order,
- place the ***question*** itself in a ***subordinate clause*** (the ***interrogative clause***),
- place the ***question verb*** (***reporting verb***) at the ***beginning*** (whereas in ***direct*** questions the ***question verb*** usually ***follows*** the question).

(115) a. "Have you done your homework, Terry?" Mum asked. [***direct***]
b. Mum asked Terry if he had done his homework. [***indirect***]
c. "Where do you live?" Derek asked Patricia. [***direct***]
d. Derek asked Patricia where she lived. [***indirect***]

As shown in (115), these points apply to both **yes-no-*questions*** and **wh-*questions***. The differences between the two types are explained in the next sections.

053/4.2 yes-no-questions

The ***direct*** question in (115)a. is a **yes-no-*question***. In this case, the ***indirect*** version, shown in (115)b., needs the conjunctions ***if*** or ***whether*** to introduce the ***sub-clause*** with the question (= the ***interrogative clause***).

Here are two further examples:

(116) a. "Can I help you?" I asked a woman customer. [***direct***]
b. I asked a woman customer if I could help her. [***indirect***]
c. "Are you going to Scarborough Fair?" the hippie asked Kate. [***direct***]
d. The hippie asked Kate if she was going to Scarborough Fair. [***indirect***]

053/4.3 wh-questions

These are questions with ***wh***-words (= ***interrogative pronouns*** and ***adverbs***), like the one in (115)c. In the ***indirect*** version, in (115)d., no special conjunction is needed. The ***wh***-word (*where*, an ***interrogative adverb***) itself functions as a kind of 'subordinating element': that is, it introduces the ***interrogative clause***. Here are a few more examples:

(117) a. "***When*** are you leaving?" Kerry asked. [***direct***]
b. Kerry asked ***when*** we were leaving. [***indirect***]
c. "***What***'s the problem?" the flight attendant asked. [***direct***]
d. The flight attendant asked ***what*** the problem was. [***indirect***]
e. "***How*** does this machine work?" asked McCullen. [***direct***]
f. McCullen asked ***how*** the machine worked. [***indirect***]

When and ***how*** are ***interrogative adverbs***, and ***what*** is an ***interrogative pronoun***.

053/4.4 'Question verbs' as reporting verbs

The only ***question verb*** used in our examples so far is ***ask***. This is the most universal, and there are in fact few others. Among these are: *wonder, enquire* (American *inquire*), and *demand/want to know*. All these are occasionally found with ***direct*** questions, but they are much more common with ***indirect***: *I'll enquire whether the next London train goes to Victoria; The lady wanted to know how old the dog was; Sandra wondered where the boy was leading her.*

Direct questions, on the other hand, can occur with many ordinary ***utterance verbs***. A point to note here, though, is that the equivalent ***indirect*** versions need a proper ***verb of enquiry***, such as ***ask, want to know***, etc.:

(118) a. "Where's Kevin!?" ***shouted*** Mr. Sprake. [***direct***]
b. Mr. Sprake ***demanded to know*** where Kevin was. [***indirect***]
c. "What's the problem now?" the flight attendant ***sighed***. [***direct***]
d. The flight attendant ***asked with a sigh*** what the problem was now. [***indirect***]

053/4.5 Indirect questions as implied or 'hidden' questions

These are ***non-reported indirect questions***, i.e. they do ***not*** derive from actual direct questions, and there are ***no*** verbs of enquiry involved. Nevertheless, one can assume a kind of 'theoretical' direct question underlying them, chiefly because of the use of ***wh***-words (including *whether* and *if*). The patterns are those of general indirect speech.

Two semantic kinds of introductory verb are involved. One kind expresses ***communication of knowledge***, including ***explaining*** and ***demonstrating*** ('showing') things:

(119) a. They didn't tell me when their train was arriving.
b. Sandy never explained to Bob why she left him.
c. Have you shown Gaynor how the lawnmower works?
d. Jonah didn't say whether he was coming on Saturday or Sunday.

The second semantic verb-type has to do with ***internal*** states and actions in the form of ***knowledge*** and ***mental awareness***. Adjectives like ***certain*** and ***sure*** are also important here:

(120) a. Terry does not know if the Warrens are at home.
b. We suddenly realized what the problem was.
c. She isn't sure whether she has seen the man before.
d. The colonel could not predict how the enemy would attack.

The 'theoretical' direct question underlying most ***non-reported indirect questions*** can be pointed up by inserting the words *the answer to the question, "…?"* , e.g. *They didn't tell me the answer to the question, "When is your train arriving?"; Have you shown Gaynor the answer to the question, "How does the lawnmower work?"*, and so on.

053/4.6 Indirect requests for instruction and advice

Indirect questions also express requests for advice, instruction, help or suggestion. One form is based on ***shall/should*** and other modals. They can be ***reported***:

(121) a. "What ***shall*** we do?" they asked. [***direct***]
b. They asked what they ***should*** do. [***indirect***]
c. "When ***can*** I come?" I asked. [***direct***]
d. I asked when I ***could*** come. [***indirect***]

Or ***non-reported***:

(122) a. I didn't know where I should wait for them.
(= ... *the answer to the question, "Where shall/should I wait ...?"*)
b. The students hadn't understood what they should do.
(= ... *the answer to the question, "What shall/should we do?"*)

Another form, common mainly with the ***non-reported*** variety, is with the ***infinitive*** following the ***wh***-word:

(123) a. I didn't know ***where to wait*** for them.
... wo ich auf sie warten soll.
b. The students hadn't understood ***what to do***.
... was sie tun sollten.
c. We were not sure exactly (about) ***when to come***.
... wann wir kommen sollten.
d. Daphne can't decide ***whether to take the job***.
... ob sie die Arbeitsstelle annehmen soll(e).

In cases like these, the ***infinitive* + wh*-construction*** is the most common rendering of German *sollen*. In examples like (123)d. only ***whether*** is possible (and ***not*** *if*).

053/4.7 The syntax of indirect questions

The function of an ***interrogative clause*** is chiefly ***direct object*** (***Od***), occasionally also ***subject complement*** (***Cs***):

S P Oi Od S P A
(124) a. The hippie asked Kate [if she was going to Scarborough Fair].
S P Od A S P
b. Kerry asked [when we were leaving].
S P Cs S P Od
c. The problem is [whether she will pass the exam].

Note that the verb ***ask*** is usually ***ditransitive***, i.e. with a personal object in the matrix clause as ***indirect object*** (***Oi***) and the following ***interrogative clause*** as ***direct object*** (***Od***), as in (124)a. However, like other verbs of enquiry it may be ***monotransitive***, i.e. followed directly by the ***interrogative clause***, as in (124)b. Note also that *if/whether* are ***conjunctions*** (and therefore not marked for function); *when/where/how* are ***interrogative adverbs***, and function as ***adverbial*** (***A***).

In (120)c. the ***interrogative clause*** is ***adjectival complement***, that is, part of the ***adjective phrase***, *sure whether she has seen the man before*. The adjective phrase as a whole functions here as ***subject complement*** (***Cs***). This contrasts with a case like that in (124)c., where the interrogative clause itself functions as (***Cs***).

053/4.8 Indirect questions in free indirect speech

These keep the ordinary ***direct question word-order***. Compare a. and b. in the following, assuming they belong together as part of the same text:

(125) a. He wondered where he would find her.
b. Did he have a hope of finding her at all?

Regular indirect questions, as in (125)a. are expressed in sub-clauses, introduced by ***verbs of enquiry*** in the matrix. As ***free indirect speech*** has no utterance verbs, of course, ***free indirect questions*** are expressed in single clauses ***without verbs of enquiry***. To mark them as questions, therefore, the original direct question word-order has to be kept. The direct question underlying (125)b. would be "Do I have a hope of finding her at all?"

053/5 Commands in indirect speech

What is meant here is the ***indirect*** equivalent of a command expressed in ***direct*** speech by the ***imperative***. ***Indirect commands*** are formed by using an appropriate ***verb of command*** (*order, tell,* etc.) followed by an ***object + infinitive construction***. The object is an ***indirect object*** (***Oi***).

053/5.1 Direct to indirect

Most important here is the ***infinitive construction*** in English:

(126) a. "Get out of my garden immediately!" Mrs. Wiggins told the boy. [***direct***]
b. Mrs. Wiggins told the boy to get out of her garden immediately. [***indirect***]
c. "Take the prisoners to Cell-Block H," the captain ordered the sergeant. [***direct***]
d. The captain ordered the sergeant to take the prisoners to Cell-Block H. [***indirect***]

German equivalents use the infinitive as well, but also *sollen* (often depending on the particular ***verb of command***): *Mrs. Wiggins sagte dem Jungen, er solle ihren Garten gefälligst sofort verlassen; Der Hauptmann befahl dem Feldwebel, er solle die Gefangenen in den Zellenblock H bringen/ ..., die Gefangenen in den Zellenblock H zu bringen.*

In modern English only the ***infinitive construction*** is in general use. Variants with *should* are either formal and antiquated, or they do not express a command as such. They are presented briefly below (**053/5.2**) in connection with individual ***verbs of command***.

Note also the use and position of the ***negative*** with the infinitive construction: *Mrs. Wiggins told the boy* ***not*** *to stay in her garden; The police ordered the demonstrators* ***not*** *to enter the city square.*

053/5.2 Verbs of command: order, command, tell

There are certain ***that***-clause alternatives:

(127) a. Mrs. Wiggins told the boy that he ***should/was to/must*** get out of her garden.
b. The captain ordered/commanded that the sergeant ***should take/take*** the prisoners to Cell-Block H.

With ***tell*** in (127)a. ***should*** and ***must*** do not express a command as such, but obligation or strong recommendation. However, they may be used to represent ***indirect commands*** in a more restrained or metaphorical style. The verb ***to be to***, on the other hand, is a regular ***indirect*** way of conveying an order or instruction (see chapter 12 for details on modals).

With ***order/command*** in (127)b. ***should*** does express the command, and not its own modal meaning. That is, it has a purely grammatical, 'subjunctive' function. The alternative is to use the genuine subjunctive form *take* (a 'fossil' not generally heard much nowadays, see chapter 8, **040/2.10**). Both expressions are formal and stylistically marked. Note that with ***that***-clauses the ***indirect object*** disappears.

053/5.3 Verbs of request and recommendation: beg, urge, warn, remind, advise, recommend

Strictly speaking, these are not verbs of command, but in some contexts come close in meaning (as command 'metaphors'). They also take the same ***object + infinitive constructions***. This is much the preferred structure, though variations with ***should*** and the subjunctive are possible with most:

(128) a. She begged me to help the family. [no alternative usual]
b. They urged her to see a doctor.
They urged that she see/should see ...
c. The lifeguard warned us not to swim near the rocks.
... warned us that we should not swim ...
d. My son reminded me to give him the house-key.
... reminded me that I should/was to ...
e. Our neighbours advised/recommended us to go to the police.
... advised/recommended that we go/should go ...

Note that use of a ***that***-clause with the subjunctive, or ***should*** in the same function, correlates here also with the compulsory loss of the ***indirect object***, as in (128)b. and e. (see also *order/command* in **053/5.2**). In c. and d. ***should*** has its own modal meaning (= strong recommendation/obligation), and here the ***indirect object*** is kept. Note that the verb ***warn*** requires ***negation*** of the following infinitive when it means 'warn *against* this action'.

053/5.4 The syntax of indirect commands

Here is an overview of syntactic functions in the ***object + infinitive construction***.

Note that the ***indirect object*** cannot be left out of this construction in English (as it often can in German).

(129) a.
S P Oi Od P A A
Mrs. Wiggins told the boy [to get out of her garden immediately].

b.
S P Oi Od P Oi Od
My son reminded me [to give him the house-key].

c.
S P Oi Od P Od
They urged her [to see a doctor].

11.4 The passive voice

054 Introduction: active and passive voice

Voice was introduced in chapter 8 as our fourth category of ***morphological verb markers***, in addition to those of tense and aspect. As we showed there (chapter 8, **040/2.8**), voice is also a ***binary*** category. That is, there are two members, called ***active*** and ***passive***, and all verbs are in one form or the other.

Voice is not just a morphological category, however, but above all a ***syntactic*** phenomenon affecting ***sentence construction***. This is why we speak not simply of active and passive verb forms, but also of active and passive ***sentences***. A ***passive*** sentence is usually regarded as a purely syntactic variant of an ***active*** sentence. Both, that is, are considered to have the ***same meaning***:

(130) a. Jane met Ronnie at the airport. [***active***]
b. Ronnie was met by Jane at the airport. [***passive***]
c. City will probably beat United this afternoon. [***active***]
d. United will probably be beaten by City this afternoon. [***passive***]

It is true that in (130) the members of each pair (a./b. and c./d.) have the same ***content*** meaning (i.e. the same ***semantic*** meaning). They are not entirely equivalent, however.

The ***communicative*** meanings of active and passive variants are actually ***different***. This results from the change in ***word-order***. Converting an active sentence to a passive makes the ***object of the active*** sentence into the ***subject of the passive*** sentence.

This puts it at the beginning, giving it a certain focus as 'old information', i.e. as something that is already the topic of conversation. In other words, (130)a. is about *Jane*, whereas (130)b. is about *Ronnie*; (130)c. is about *City*, but (130)d. is about *United*. We can express this also in terms of ***agent*** and ***patient***. The ***agent*** is the ***doer*** and the ***patient*** is the ***target*** of an action, i.e. the ***agent*** carries it out, and the ***patient*** 'suffers' it. With an ***agent*** + ***action*** + ***patient*** sentence, speakers generally use the ***active*** version when the ***agent*** is the old information, and the ***passive*** version when the ***patient*** is the old information.

Another specific reason for using the passive is when the ***agent*** is ***unknown*** or ***unimportant***, and the focus of both old and new information is 'what happened to the patient'.

Forming and using the passive 055

055/1 Basic features of active-passive conversion

055/1.1 Transitive and intransitive verbs

In English the passive can be formed ***only*** from ***transitive*** verbs. This is because only an ***active object*** can become a ***passive subject***.

In German this is not so. German can form impersonal, generalized passives from intransitive verbs. Here there is no English equivalent. A paraphrase must be found: ⚠

(131) a. Es wurde viel gelacht und getanzt.
People laughed and danced a lot.
b. Sonntags wurde immer um Punkt 12 Uhr gegessen.
Sunday lunch was always at noon on the dot.
c. Bei uns in der Familie wird wenig ferngesehen.
They (we) don't watch much television in our family.

055/1.2 The passive verb form

This consists of ***auxiliary*** **be** + ***main verb past participle***. The auxiliary is the carrier of tense and aspect, which must correspond to those of the equivalent active sentence:

(132) a. Heavy goods traffic ***does not use*** this road. [***present simple active***]
This road ***is not used*** by heavy goods traffic. [***present simple passive***]
Diese Straße wird nicht für den LKW-Verkehr benutzt.
b. Joe ***was repairing*** the bicycles. [***past progressive active***]
The bicycles ***were being*** repaired by Joe. [***past progressive passive***]
Die Fahrräder wurden (gerade) von Joe repariert.
c. Marie ***will do*** the shopping. [**will**-***form, simple active***]
The shopping ***will be done*** by Marie. [**will**-***form, simple passive***]
Die Einkäufe werden von Marie erledigt (werden).

There are several things to take note of here. Firstly, there must be ***subject concord***, as always. However, in the transition from active to passive the passive subject may differ in number and/or person from the active subject. This is the case, for example, in (132)b., and it can be a source of error for the unwary (**The bicycles was being repaired ...*).

Secondly, the auxiliary in the German passive is not *sein*, but *werden*. This sometimes leads German speakers to form the English passive (wrongly!) with *get*: **The bicycles were getting repaired ...* This kind of error is encouraged by the fact that there are a number of English collocations with **get + *past participle***, e.g. *get married, get hurt, get lost*, etc. Note, however, that these are ***not*** passive constructions, and *get* here is ***not*** an auxiliary, but a ***main verb*** followed by a participle functioning as an ***adjective***.

Finally, ***perfect progressives*** are ***not*** usually put in the passive. Either the active voice is just kept, or other paraphrases are found:

(133) a. Joe has been repairing the bicycles. [***active***]
b. The bicycles have been out of action/under repair. [***passive equivalent***]
(not *The bicycles have been being repaired)
c. We had been painting the boat. [***active***]
d. The boat had been in dry dock, being painted. [***passive equivalent***]
(not *The boat had been being painted)

055/1.3 Other changes

Two other major changes in the construction of passive sentences are syntactic, as we have variously seen already:

- ***active object → passive subject,***
- ***active subject → passive* by*-agent*.**

In an operational diagram, the active-passive transition could therefore be represented as follows (see also chapter 8, **040/2.8**):

S ***P*** ***Od***
(134) a. Marie will do the shopping. [***active***]

S ***P (passive)*** ***A***
b. The shopping will be done by Marie. [***passive***]

Like any prepositional phrase, the **by*-phrase*** functions as an ***adverbial*** (***A***). *Marie*, the **by*-agent***, is syntactically a prepositional complement.

055/1.4 Omission of the by-phrase

The **by*-phrase*** can be omitted when the agent is unknown, unspecified or unimportant. In many cases the unimportance of the agent is already reflected in the choice of the passive rather than the active verb form. That is, the passive is chosen precisely because the agent is not known or the action is not usually thought of as having a specified agent. It would be very unnatural, for instance, to want to specify an agent for the following passives: *Three men were lost when the boat sank; Our roof has not been damaged in the storm; Fortunately, no one was hurt when the car hit the bank of snow.*

On the other hand, there may be an obvious, but ***unidentified*** agent: *The dead man had quite clearly been murdered; Several computers and a printer were stolen.*

Or the agency is ***generalized***, i.e. several or many people are involved, but their identity is not important: *Gold was discovered in the west in the 1880s; Dinner had been finished and the tables had been cleared; Hopefully all Meg's efforts for the church will be rewarded in some way.*

Generalized agency is also very common when responsibility lies with a 'collective' authority: *We weren't informed of the delay until we got to the airport; The hotel rooms have not been properly cleaned; A big party was held in the theatre foyer.*

And finally it is used for 'people in general', in preference often to an active sentence with *one* or *someone* as a subject: *Tickets cannot be purchased on the train; All enquiries should be made at the information desk; I was told that there were no vacancies at the hotel.*

055/2 Transitive verb types and their relation to the passive

So far we have just spoken about the ***objects*** of verbs without saying which kinds of object. This is clarified in detail in the following, along with other features of verb complementation which are also affected by the change from ***active*** to ***passive***. Generally speaking, transitivity disappears from a sentence when it becomes passive. However, this is not always the case.

055/2.1 Monotransitive verbs

The most common kind of transitive verb has just ***one object***, i.e. a ***direct object*** (***Od***). The general condition for an ***active-passive*** conversion is the presence of a ***direct object*** in the ***active*** sentence, which then becomes the ***subject*** of the equivalent ***passive*** sentence, see examples (128), (130), and (132) above.

055/2.2 Complex transitive verbs

These are verbs with ***direct object (Od) + object complement (Co)***. The same rules apply as with monotransitive verbs, but in addition the ***active object complement*** becomes ***passive subject complement***:

S ***P*** ***Od*** ***Co***

(135) a. The shareholders elected Gary chairman. [*active*]

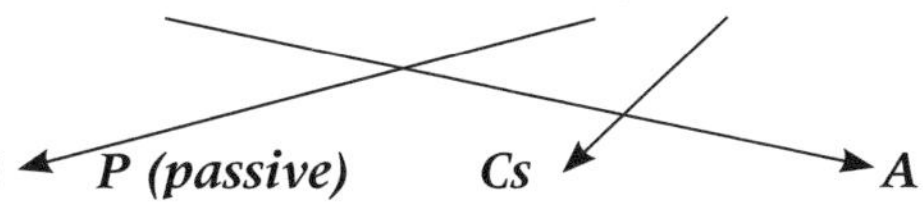

S ***P (passive)*** ***Cs*** ***A***

b. Gary was elected chairman by the shareholders. [*passive*]

S *P* *Od* *Co*
c. The previous owner had painted the doors blue. [*active*]

S *P (passive)* *Cs* *A*
d. The doors had been painted blue by the previous owner. [*passive*]

055/2.3 Ditransitive verbs

These take an ***indirect object (Oi) + direct object (Od)***. With ditransitive verbs there are ***two*** possible passive constructions.

In the first, the same rules apply as with monotransitive, but in addition the ***active indirect object (Oi)*** becomes part of a ***prepositional phrase*** (with ***to*** or ***for***), i.e. ***prepositional complement***. The ***prepositional phrase*** as a whole functions as an ***adverbial (A)***:

S *P* *Oi* *Od*
(136) a. Julia gave Douglas a present. [*active*]

S *P (passive)* *A* *A*
b. A present was given to Douglas by Julia. [*passive*]

In the second type of passive construction, the ***active indirect object (Oi)*** becomes ***passive subject***, and the ***active direct object (Od)*** remains so in the passive sentence:

S *P* *Oi* *Od*
(137) a. Julia gave Douglas a present. [*active*]

S *P (passive)* *Od* *A*
b. Douglas was given a present by Julia. [*passive*]

Here, then, an element of transitivity remains in the passive sentence in the form of a ***passive direct object***.

055/3 Further points on the passive

055/3.1 A note on the past participle

Taken for itself, a past participle expresses the completion of an action, and is often used as an ***adjective*** meaning 'in a state resulting from', e.g. *broken, gone, painted, eaten.*

When the verb is ***transitive***, the participle is therefore naturally ***passive*** in meaning (i.e.'being in a state resulting from a ***suffered*** action'): *a parked car, a painted face, cut glass, bottled beer, fried fish*. Predicative use of the past participle adjective (*The beer is bottled*) is sometimes called the ***statal passive*** (dt. *Zustandspassiv*). An important point to remember here is that both ***real passive*** and ***statal passive*** use the verb *be*. Out of context, therefore, this can lead to ambiguity. Consider:

(138) a. The store is closed at 6 pm.
b. The meal was cooked.
c. The two cars were sold.

The verb *be* here could be understood in German as either *werden* or *sein*, e.g. *Der Laden wird um 18 Uhr geschlossen/Der Laden ist ab18 Uhr geschlossen*. In the first interpretation, of course, an action is carried out at that time ***by*** someone, and in the second the store is ***in*** that state at that time (meaning incidentally that the action leading to it must have been carried out ***before*** that time). This is likely to be more of a problem in comprehension that in active production of the language. And the ambiguity is only there in the ***simple*** form. The ***progressive*** (*The store is being closed*) shows clearly that the ***action*** is meant.

055/3.2 Prepositional verbs in passive constructions

Prepositional verbs are ***transitive*** (see chapter 8, **042/2.2**), and can therefore be used in the ***passive***:

(139) a. The host families ***did not look after*** their guests properly. [***active prepositional verb***]
b. The guests ***were not looked after*** properly by their host families. [***passive prepositional verb***]
c. The police ***decided on*** three strategies. [***active prepositional verb***]
d. Three strategies ***were decided on*** by the police. [***passive prepositional verb***]

What seems a little irregular in this construction is that the preposition is not followed by the noun connected with it. But this is the case quite simply because the noun concerned (*the guests* in b. and *three strategies* in d.) occupies the ***subject position*** in the passive sentence, leaving an 'empty slot' after the preposition. In formal style this is sometimes avoided, and other verbs are chosen for the passive. However, it is quite normal in neutral and less formal varieties of English. Occasionally it is even extended to certain verb-preposition combinations not normally regarded in the active voice as prepositional verbs:

(140) a. My flowerbeds have been ***walked on***!
b. The bed had not been ***slept in*** for weeks.
c. The pool must not be ***dived into***.

In the ***active*** voice these would be ***intransitive*** verbs followed by ***prepositional phrases*** as adverbials of place or direction (e.g. *Somebody has walked on my flowerbeds*). The passive, that is, would not normally be possible. However, for semantic reasons the ***active prepositional complement*** (*my flowerbeds, the bed, the pool*) can also be regarded as having a

patient ('sufferer') role. This gives a certain 'transitive' character to the verb-preposition combination, which then allows a meaningful passive version, with the ***active prepositional complement*** functioning as ***passive subject***.

In this form verb + preposition take on the full character of a prepositional verb.

Phrasal-prepositional verbs are not particularly favoured in the passive, as on the whole they tend to sound rather awkward. But there are one or two that do passivize:

(141) a. Even today, dialect speakers ***are*** often ***looked down on***. (= *regarded as inferior*)
b. Famous filmstars and sports personalities ***are*** frequently ***looked up to*** as role models. (= *regarded as superior*)
c. The old district councils were ***done away with*** in the 1960s. (= *abolished*)

It is similar with certain idiomatic combinations of verb-noun-preposition, verb-verb-preposition, etc. These are rather like phrasal-prepositional verbs and occasionally allow the passive:

(142) a. Small children in Victorian factories ***were*** often ***taken advantage of***. (= *exploited*)
b. While we are away the house ***is being taken care of*** by a property management service. (= *being looked after*)
c. The old district councils ***were got rid of*** in the 1960s. (= *abolished*)

Long sequences ending with a preposition like this are generally felt to be rather awkward, however, and alternatives are often preferred. When a noun is part of the idiom, there is sometimes a stylistic preference for making that noun (where possible) into the passive subject. So, for example, *Advantage was often taken of small children in Victorian factories* might be preferred to the version in (142)a., especially in writing.

We have similar competition between the versions in (143)a. and b. (143)c. is the only possible version with that particular idiom. Many other phrases of this kind are not passivized at all.

(143) a. Teachers ***are*** hardly ever ***paid attention to*** at our school. (informal)
b. ***Attention is*** hardly ever ***paid to*** teachers at our school. (stylistically preferable)
c. ***Allowances*** must ***be made for*** the clumsiness of small children. (***not*** *The clumsiness of small children must be made allowances for.)

055/3.3 Phrasal verbs in passive constructions

Phrasal verbs can be transitive or intransitive (see chapter 8, **042/2.1**). Only the ***transitive*** ones, of course, can be put into the passive:

(144) a. The caretaker of the school always turns the lights off. [***active phrasal verb***]
b. The lights are always turned off by the caretaker of the school. [***passive phrasal verb***]
c. The waitress took my plate away. [***active phrasal verb***]
d. My plate was taken away by the waitress. [***passive phrasal verb***]

The main feature of transitive phrasal verbs is that the adverb particle can come before or after an object noun: this choice is no longer given in the passive, as, again, the ***object noun*** has disappeared and become the ***passive subject***.

055/3.4 Non-finite verbs in the passive form

Non-finite verbs also have passive forms:

(145) a. Jim did not want ***to be beaten*** by the problem. [***passive infinitive***]
b. She claimed ***to have been robbed***. [***passive perfect infinitive***]
c. Lara hates ***being forced*** to do housework. [***passive gerund***]
d. I remember ***having been impressed*** by the new house. [***passive perfect gerund***]
e. ***Being confronted*** with her lie, she was now obliged to tell the truth. [***passive present participle***]
f. ***Having been fired***, I now had no regular income. [***passive perfect participle***]

These are taken up again in chapter 13.

055/3.5 Passive catenatives with the infinitive

Certain ***catenatives*** followed by the infinitive are particularly common in their ***passive*** forms (see also chapter 13):

(146) a. The rock singer ***was reported/said*** to be recovering in an expensive clinic.
b. You ***are expected/requested*** to hand in essays punctually.
c. Terry ***was considered/thought*** to be the best player in the club.
d. Passengers ***were obliged/forced*** to wait for the next train.

To be supposed to is also a 'fossilized' passive form.

Chapter 12 Verbs: Modal Verbs

The term ***modal*** is the adjective from the noun ***mood***, or as modern grammarians often prefer to call it, ***modality***. Modality, as has already been said several times, is concerned with certain ***speaker attitudes*** that affect the reality or 'factual' status of what is said, and in particular how the speaker intends this to be understood. The grammatical expression of modality is carried out mainly by ***modal verbs***. These represent certain broad categories of ***speech intention*** that generally concern the speaker's relationship to others. That is, many of these categories reflect a dimension of language that is social, or ***pragmatic***.

056 Modal verbs: types and forms

We will distinguish between two basic types of ***modals*** according to form: firstly, the traditional ***modal auxiliaries*** like *can* and *must*, which we call the ***primary modals***; and secondly, a variety of other verbal constructions like *going to, have to, be supposed to*, etc., which express modal meanings, but do not have the form of auxiliaries (though they are mainly treated as such). We will refer to these as the ***secondary modals***.

056/1 Primary modals

The ***ten primary modals*** are: ***can, could, will, would, shall, should, may, might, ought, must***. All of them are ***auxiliaries***, and share the following specific and idiosyncratic features:

056/1.1 Restricted morphology

Modal auxiliaries are very restricted morphologically (a feature known traditionally as ***defective***):

- they have no inflections for person or number, i.e. are the same in all persons: *I/we, you, he/she/it/they* ***can/could/must/should***, etc.;
- they have ***no aspect*** distinctions, ***no perfect*** and ***no non-finite*** forms;
- there are ***present/past*** tense distinctions in four cases: ***can/could, will/would, shall/should, may/might***; however, the past tense forms are more frequently used as ***unreal pasts*** to refer to present or future time in a conditional or other modal sense, as was seen extensively, for example, in chapter 11.

- ***must*** and ***ought*** have no 'tense partners': there is no formal past tense of ***must***, and no formal present tense of ***ought***; historically, ***ought*** is a fossilized past tense form of an Old English verb that no longer exists in any other form; ***ought*** is also used mainly as an ***unreal past***.

056/1.2 Auxiliary function

Modal auxiliaries function only as auxiliaries, and can never appear as main verbs (unlike the ***grammatical auxiliaries***, *be, do, have*).

This is not so in German, where we can say things like *Ich kann Französisch, ich will Suppe*, etc. But in English forms like **I can French*, or **I will soup* are not possible. ⚠

Modal auxiliaries are followed only by the ***infinitive*** (unlike the grammatical auxiliaries, which, as a group, combine with all non-finite forms except the gerund). All the ***primary modals***, except for ***ought***, take infinitives ***without* to**.

056/1.3 Lexical-semantic character

Modal auxiliaries are selected for ***semantic*** reasons. That is, their uses are determined by their individual ***lexical*** and ***pragmatic*** meanings. This is another contrast to the grammatical auxiliaries, which are used (except in one minor case) just to perform morphological and syntactic operations. A ***modal auxiliary***, then, is a ***semantic verb in its own right***. This has important effects on ***time reference*** and ***negation***, described in the next two sections.

056/1.4 Double time reference and tense paradox

Following from what has just been said under **056/1.3** is a certain peculiarity of time reference. Because they have their own individual lexis, ***modal auxiliaries*** may create a ***double time reference*** inside a single verb phrase.

This happens when the main verb refers to the future (= action not yet happened), but the auxiliary clearly signifies an attitude present at (**S**), i.e. the moment of utterance. So, for example, in the sentence *Joanna might not arrive until 4 o'clock* the modal ***might*** gives a future meaning to the main verb *arrive*, but refers at the same time to an attitude of speculation present ***now***. We could in fact add ***now*** to the sentence (*Joanna might not arrive until 4 o'clock* ***now***), giving a single verb phrase two time references, which is normally not possible. We will call this phenomenon the ***tense paradox*** of modal verbs.

056/1.5 Negation

When the ***negative particle*** is attached to a ***grammatical auxiliary***, it negates the verb phrase as a whole. This means in effect that the ***action of the main verb*** is negated, as in (1)a.

When the negative particle is attached to a ***modal auxiliary*** there are two possibilities: ***either*** the effect is the same as in (1)a., which is the case in (1)b., ***or*** only the ***modal meaning*** is negated, as in (1)c.:

(1) a. Charlie does ***not swim***.
b. Charlie may ***not swim*** (if the weather's bad). [***speculation***]
c. Charlie ***may not*** swim (I am not going to allow it). [***permission***]

(1)a. and (1)b. are about ***'not swimming'***. (1)c. is about ***'not having permission'*** (i.e. not being allowed) to do something.

In other words, when ***may*** means 'perhaps', ***not*** negates the ***main verb***; when ***may*** means 'have permission', ***not*** negates ***may*** (= no permission). Most modals take only one of the two patterns. These must be learnt individually, as they depend on the particular individual modal meaning. Here are more examples:

(2) a. You ***can't*** swim in that lake.	[no ability, possibility or permission: ***modal meaning negated***]
b. You must***n't swim*** in that lake.	[obligation ***not*** to do something: ***main verb meaning negated***]
c. You should***n't swim*** in that lake.	[recommendation ***not*** to do something: ***main verb meaning negated***]
d. She ***wouldn't*** swim in that lake.	[no possibility, ***modal meaning negated***]

056/2 Secondary modals

In addition to the ten primary modals there are a number of verbs and verb combinations which express similar kinds of modal meaning, but which do not have the same unified grammatical features. In other words, they are ***not***, strictly speaking, ***auxiliaries***.

Most of them are combinations of ***main verbs*** (usually *be* or *have*) and adjectival or verbal expressions. Like all main verbs they have the usual range of tense forms and an infinitive form. They are all followed by the ***infinitive***, usually ***with* to**, and are really ***catenatives*** (i.e. 'linking verbs' introducing non-finite structures). Nevertheless, they are generally regarded as having ***auxiliary*** character: that is, they are treated (because of their meanings) as if they were part of the same verb phrase (and predicator) as their respective main verb. We will call these ***secondary modals***. They are: ***dare, need, have got to, have to, be to, be supposed to, be going to, be able to, be allowed to***.

Several secondary modals have important tasks as ***suppletives***, that is, as ***replacement verbs*** for ***primary modals***, when these, due to their 'defective' character, cannot be used in certain tenses and other forms.

The grammar of the ***secondary modals*** is dealt with below when specific verbs are discussed individually (see particularly under **057/4** and **057/5**).

Modal meanings 057

We will present modal verbs from the viewpoint of meaning, looking at main fields of modality in detail and seeing how they are expressed.
Modal meanings can be divided into two basic categories. Nearly all ***primary modals*** can express both of them.

- The first category is ***potential***, i.e. every kind of factor connected with ***possibility*** and ***speculation***, but also with the ***ability*** or ***tendency*** to act in a particular way.
- The second category is ***volition/compulsion***, i.e. ***desiring*** and ***requesting***, but also imposing one's wishes on others in the form of ***advice***, ***recommendation*** or ***obligation***.

This basic general division can be further differentiated into: a) ***ability/capability***, b) ***speculation***, c) ***direct statements of volition***, d) ***permission/ requests***, e) ***obligation/necessity***.

The category c), ***direct statements of volition***, was dealt with under ***Future Meaning*** in chapter 11, and will not be mentioned again here.

057/1 Ability/capability

Ability is to be understood here in three possible ways:

- firstly, ***personal capability***;
- secondly, ***a tendency for things to happen*** in a particular way;
- thirdly, the possibility of something happening because an ***opportunity for it to happen*** is contained in a given situation.

These are the core meanings of ***can*** and ***could***.

057/1.1 General ability

Here, ***can*** is used for the present tense and ***could*** for the past:

(3) a. Bertie can speak French, but his wife can't speak a word.
b. My son could already read quite well before he started school.
c. I could not swim until I was 15 years old.

In this sense of general ability, ***can*** is only present-referring. It cannot refer to future time. For the future a ***suppletive*** is necessary, i.e. ***be able***:

(4) a. After she has lived in Paris for a year, she'll be able to speak French like a native!
b. If you don't practise everyday, you will never be able to play the piano properly.

In the same way, the future-in-the-past is expressed by ***would be able*** (and ***not*** *could*):

(5) a. After she had lived in Paris for a year, she thought, she would be able to speak French like a native!
b. I was told that if I didn't practise everyday, I would never be able to play the piano properly.

Non-suppletive replacement of ***can/could*** by ***be able*** is generally possible, though the ***primary modal*** is preferred in informal to neutral style when no suppletive is necessary, in particular in the present tense, i.e. *Bertie can speak French* is generally preferred to *Bertie is able to speak French.*

Be able is used, however, when a more formal tone is intended, especially in writing: *As my mother is able to walk only short distances, the hospital should provide transport for her.*

057/1.2 Feasability/opportunity

Can is also used in the sense of something being ***feasible*** or ***practicable***. This applies both to single occasions, and to habits or repeated actions:

(6) a. Mary can get us a newspaper when she goes shopping this afternoon.
b. We can't come to your party tomorrow, as Vanessa is ill.
c. Dave says he can water the plants in our apartment while we're on holiday.

Can here refers to ***future time*** (in contrast to the case in **057/1.1**). It can be replaced by ***be able***, but this then requires the ***will***-form: *Mary will be able* (***not*** **is able*) *to get us a newspaper when she goes shopping this afternoon.*

As in **057/1.1**, ***be able*** is preferred for a more formal tone: *Unfortunately, I will not be able to attend any departmental meetings in the next three weeks.*

057/1.3 Past tense reference to specific occasions

Could is ***not*** used for past reference to *specific* occasions. This requires ***be able***:

(7) a. Although we started late, we ***were able*** to reach the mountain hut by nightfall. (***not*** **... we could reach the hut ...*)
b. Dave ***was able*** to water the plants in our apartment while we were on holiday. (***not*** **... could water the plants ...*)

⚠ On this point there is a contrast to German, where *konnte* is quite normal: ... *konnten wir die Berghütte ... erreichen; Dave konnte die Pflanzen bei uns in der Wohnung gießen* ... Consequently, the incorrect use of ***could*** by German speakers is common here. It is further encouraged by the rather confusing fact that ***could*** is quite permissible in the ***negative*** (and also with verbs of ***perception***, see below):

(8) a. As we started late, we ***could not*** reach the mountain hut by nightfall.
b. Dave ***couldn't*** water the plants in our apartment while we were on holiday, because he was ill.

A common ***could***-replacement in 'achievement' senses, as in (6)a., is the verb ***manage***: *He had been injured, but* ***managed*** *to get fit in time for the big game and* ***was able*** *to play on Saturday.*

057/1.4 can/could + verbs of sensory perception

Ability reference with ***can/could*** is common in British English with verbs of ***sensory perception***. As just indicated in **057/1.3**, the '***could***-ban' with specific past references does not apply here:

(9) a. "Can you see something moving in the bushes over there?" Rachel whispered. I looked closely, but could see nothing.
b. Charles put his ear to the wall: he could hear voices clearly in the other room.
c. I could not taste any sherry in my soup.

057/1.5 Perfect tenses

As modals have no perfect form, ***suppletives*** are necessary for the perfect. For ***can/could***, apart from ***be able***, other lexical verbs like ***manage*** also offer a solution:

(10) a. The weather has been so bad that we haven't been able to go out for weeks.
b. They had always managed to reach London by car in less than 6 hours.

057/1.6 Tendency or habit-potential

This means an ability to have a certain effect, or a tendency to behave in a particular way:

(11) a. It can snow in these hills even in summer.
b. When I was younger I could be awfully moody.
c. As a puppy our dog could get very aggressive when provoked.
d. Stepping on a sea-urchin can give you a nasty wound.

This sense does not allow substitution by ***be able***.

057/1.7 could as unreal past

Could in this sense is the equivalent of German *könnte*, and refers to a theoretically possible (or imagined) ability. Traditionally, this use is regarded as 'conditional' (see last chapter 11), and means the same as ***would be able***:

(12) a. Mary could get us a newspaper when she goes shopping this afternoon.
b. Could you get here by 6 o'clock on Friday? Then we could have something to eat in town before the film starts.

The theoretical quality of the unreal past adds ***distance*** to an utterance; it therefore sounds less direct, and therefore more 'careful' or tentative, than the present tense form ***can***. This makes ***could*** a popular ***social metaphor*** in ***requests*** (see below in **057/4.1**). The question in (11)b., in fact, could be regarded, in context, as a request, though in its basic meaning it is simply a reference to theoretical ability.

When referring to ***general ability*** and ***habit-potential***, ***could*** suggests that the action has not actually happened (whereas ***can*** implies that it has):

(13) a. Jerry could do any kind of work around the house.
b. My girlfriend could easily swim 5 miles.
c. Stepping on a sea-urchin could give you a nasty wound.

057/1.8 could have as hypothetical past

This is the equivalent of German *hätte können*, and refers to a ***hypothetical*** possibility, i.e. an ***unfulfilled one*** in the past (traditionally a 'past conditional'), with the same meaning as ***would have been able***:

(14) a. Mary could have got us a newspaper when she went shopping this afternoon (= she would have been able to buy one, but didn't).
... hätte uns eine Zeitung kaufen können, als sie ...
b. You could have turned left at the traffic lights (= that would have been possible too, though in fact you turned right).
Du hättest an der Ampel links abbiegen können.

057/1.9 could have as theoretical past

This is a second meaning of ***could have***, the equivalent of German *könnte getan haben*, and meaning 'this was possible, but we don't know if it happened':

(15) a. The robbers could have hidden the money in the woods (= they were able to do so, and perhaps they did).
Die Räuber könnten das Geld im Wald versteckt haben.
b. Damien could have spoken to Mike the night before (= he was able to do so, and perhaps he did).
Damien könnte schon in der Nacht zuvor mit Mike gesprochen haben.

Would have been able is ***not*** possible as a replacement in this case. Here, ***could have*** refers to ability or possibility in the sense of ***opportunity***. But it can also imply an attitude of ***speculation*** on likelihood or probability, and therefore has 'half a foot', so to speak, in the next section.

057/2 Speculation

Modals expressing ***likelihood/probability*** generally differ from each other according to levels of ***certainty***. But this is not the only factor. There are also distinctions in speaker attitude or ***speech intention***.

From this point of view, ***speculation*** can be divided into three sub-categories:

- ***prediction*** (giving a forecast of something);
- ***conjecture*** (giving a possibility);
- and ***deduction*** (drawing a conclusion).

Prediction (represented by ***will*** and ***going to***) was dealt with in chapter 11.1 as part of the large field of future and conditional meaning. Here we want to look mainly at the other two sub-categories, ***conjecture*** and ***deduction***. But first a general comparison of the three:

(16) a. Cynthia ***must*** be home by now. [***deduction***]
b. Cynthia ***will*** be home by now, I expect. [***prediction***]
c. Cynthia ***could*** be home by now. [***conjecture***]

All three show the speaker's personal opinion. On a scale of speaker-certainty, (16)a. is the most forceful and (16)c. the least.

But as indicated, the modals also show different kinds of speech intention. (16)b. states a ***belief***. From this point of view it is the most confident. (16)a. is more forceful, but only says that something is ***logical*** on the basis of normal circumstances. However, it may signal that some doubt has arisen as to whether circumstances are, in fact, normal: *Cynthia must be home by now, surely, so why isn't she answering the phone?* This could therefore mean *If she's not home, I have absolutely no explanation why*. (16)c. simply gives ***one possible interpretation*** of the situation while at the same time saying that there are others.

057/2.1 Conjecture: possibilities expressed by could, may, might

Conjecture, then, basically means guessing, i.e. making a speculative statement which leaves room for doubt. ***Could***, ***may*** and ***might*** translate as German *könnte*, but to differing degrees of certainty. The general order from 'most' to 'least' is normally felt to be: ***could – may – might***:

(17) a. The weather could be bad tomorrow.
Morgen kann/könnte schlechtes Wetter sein.
b. The weather may be bad tomorrow.
Morgen könnte schlechtes Wetter sein.
c. The weather might be bad tomorrow.
Morgen könnte eventuell schlechtes Wetter sein.

The differences are relatively slight, as the German translations show. When the modal verb is stressed, they in fact become even less marked, and more interchangeable.

There are three things to note here about ***could***: firstly, it cannot in this case be replaced by *would be able*; secondly, its 'present partner' *can* is not possible in this meaning; and thirdly, ***may*** and ***might*** are generally the preferred forms for conjecture, anyway, especially with personal subjects.

This is because ***could*** is often ambiguous between ***conjecture*** and ***ability*** meanings:

(18) a. They may deliver the new garden shed tomorrow.
b. They might deliver the new garden shed tomorrow.
c. They could deliver the new garden shed tomorrow.

(18)c. can mean, like a. and b., 'It is possible that they will ...'. On the other hand, it could be interpreted in the ***ability*** sense 'They are/would be able/be in a position to ...'.

057/2.2 Negation with could, may, might

It was mentioned above (under **056/1.5**) that negation has varying effects on different modal auxiliaries. This can be seen here with ***may/might*** on the one hand, and ***could*** on the other. With ***may/might, not*** negates the ***main verb***.

With ***could***, however, ***not*** negates the ***modal***. Compare:

(19) a. The dog ***may/might not*** be hungry.
(= It is ***possible*** that the dog ***is not*** hungry.)
Der Hund hat vielleicht keinen Hunger.
b. The dog ***could not*** be hungry.
(= It is ***not possible*** that the dog is hungry.)
Der Hund kann unmöglich Hunger haben.

In the ***negative***, *could* actually passes from the sub-category of conjecture to that of ***deduction***, and expresses the negative of ***must*** (see below).

057/2.3 Open conjecture about the past

This is the field of ***could have/may have/might have***. In ***open conjecture*** the speaker is saying 'It is possible that it happened like this'.

(20) a. After the robbery, the two gangsters ***could have hidden*** the money in the woods (= this was possible).
Die zwei Verbrecher könnten das Geld im Wald versteckt haben.
b. After the robbery, the two gangsters ***may/might have*** hidden the money in the woods (= this was possible).
Die Verbrecher könnten das Geld (vielleicht/möglicherweise) im Wald versteckt haben.

In (20) the meaning is that of the ordinary ***past*** tense (i.e. non-perfect). But the forms can also stand for the ***present perfect*** or ***past perfect***:

(21) a. "Why are David and Jane so late, I wonder?" "They could have/may have/might have got lost." (= It is possible that they have got lost).
... Sie könnten sich verlaufen/verfahren haben.
b. "Dora's eyes were very red yesterday." "Yes, I think she may have been crying." (= She had possibly been crying).
... Sie könnte geweint haben/Möglicherweise hatte sie geweint.

Note again that ***could have*** takes on a different meaning in the ***negative***: *They couldn't have got lost* (dt. *Es ist einfach nicht möglich, dass sie sich verlaufen haben.*), see remarks in the previous section, **057/2.2**, and also in **057/2.5**.

057/2.4 Hypothetical conjecture about the past

In contrast to ***open*** conjecture, ***hypothetical*** conjecture gives an ***imagined alternative*** to the way things actually were. It is always connected with a ***hypothetical condition***:

(22) a. If we hadn't had the map with us, we could have/might have lost our way (= this would have been possible).
Wenn wir die Karte nicht dabei gehabt hätten, hätten wir uns verlaufen können/ hätten wir uns möglicherweise verlaufen.
b. If I hadn't been in London at that time, I might never have met my future wife (= this would possibly never have happened).
Wäre ich damals nicht in London gewesen, wäre ich meiner zukünftigen Frau möglicherweise niemals begegnet.

Note that ***may have*** is ***not*** used for ***hypothetical*** conjecture. And again, ***could have*** takes on a different meaning in the ***negative***: *If I hadn't been in London at that time, I could never have met my future wife* means 'this would never have been possible'. Contrast this with the interpretation of (22)b. In the ***negative***, that is, only ***might have*** (i.e. ***might not have***) is permissible.

057/2.5 Deduction with must

Deduction means ***logical expectation*** or obvious ***conclusion***. The main modal involved here is ***must***:

(23) a. Judging by the size of their house and their five cars, the McAllisters must have quite a lot of money.
Der Größe ihres Hauses und den fünf Autos nach zu urteilen, muss die Familie McAllister recht viel Geld haben.
b. Melanie must be very proud of her achievements.
Melanie muss auf das, was sie erreicht hat, sehr stolz sein.
c. Her boyfriend must see her quite often (= obviously does), as his car is frequently outside the house.
... besucht sie offensichtlich sehr oft, denn ...

These are typical ***conclusions***. However, they are statements on the way things look. They do not necessarily express a belief in fact, but a personal judgement on appearances, and may function communicatively as requests for confirmation: *Melanie must be very proud of her achievements, I suppose.*

The most usual main verbs are statives, in particular *be* and *have*. ***Must*** is widely used in speech and informal language for comments, especially negative ones, involving irony or exaggeration: *You must be joking!; Sally must be mad!; He must weigh a ton!; They must be a bit naïve.*

The ***negative*** is ***cannot/can't/could not/couldn't***:

(24) a. You must be thirsty. [***positive***]
You've just had a litre of water! You can't/couldn't (possibly) be thirsty! [***negative***]
Du kannst unmöglich (noch) Durst haben.
b. Brian must be very happy. [***positive***]
Brian can't/couldn't (possibly) be happy. [***negative***]

Must have is used for ***past*** or ***perfect*** time reference. The negative partner is ***can't have/ couldn't have***:

(25) a. Shazay is ill in bed. She must have caught a cold.
... muss sich erkältet haben.
b. Clonn and Teddie were in the High Street at that time. They must have seen the accident.
... müssen den Unfall miterlebt haben.
c. You can't/couldn't have loved her much if you just let her leave.
Du kannst sie unmöglich so sehr geliebt haben, ...
d. They can't have left the party yet. Look, their car is still outside.
Sie können das Fest noch nicht verlassen haben ...

057/2.6 A note on deduction negatives

We have just seen that a ***negative conclusion*** is expressed by the ***negative*** of ***can/could***. The form ***must not*** is generally not used for this meaning. The reason is not grammatical, but semantic. ***Must not*** usually expresses a ***negative obligation*** or ***prohibition*** (see **057/4.3** below). To avoid ambiguity it is usually reserved only for this meaning.

Nevertheless, in speech one does occasionally hear ***must not*** used for negative conclusion, e.g. *They must not have left the party yet,* instead of the version in (25)d. This sounds awkward, though, and is best avoided in the standard language.

A rather different point concerns ***negated conclusion***, i.e. expressing that a specific conclusion should ***not*** be drawn. This is done with ***need not/needn't*** or through paraphrases such as ***doesn't mean***, often supported by ***necessarily***. Both are generally accompanied by a ***because***-clause:

(26) a. Just because they have 5 cars, it doesn't (necessarily) mean that they're rich.
…, muss es nicht (unbedingt) heißen, dass sie reich sind.
b. Clonn and Teddie needn't necessarily have seen the accident just because they were in the High Street at that time.
… müssen nicht unbedingt den Unfall miterlebt haben, bloß weil sie …

The reason that ***must not*** cannot be used in this case is grammatical. With ***must***, ***not*** negates the ***main verb*** (see **056/1.5** above). This point is especially important for the modal field of ***obligation***, and is taken up again further below (see **057/4.3**).

057/2.7 Expectations with should and ought to

Should and ***ought to*** have the same meaning, and translate German *sollte/müsste/dürfte*. ***Ought*** is the only ***primary*** modal that takes a **to-*infinitive***.

The two verbs also convey an ***expectation*** which the speaker feels is logical or reasonable. Unlike ***must***, however, they do ***not*** express a deduction or conclusion based on past or present evidence. Moreover, they are less forceful, and more tentative. They also keep the same meaning when negated:

(27) a. Shazay was ill last week, but she should be better again now (= it is reasonable to expect this).
… aber sie müsste/sollte/dürfte jetzt wieder gesund sein.
b. This job ought not (oughtn't) to take very long.
c. As it's a weekday, the pool shouldn't be crowded tomorrow.

For acoustic reasons the full form ***ought not*** (stressing ***not***) is preferred to the weak form. ***Shouldn't***, however, is used quite freely. Note that as with *must*, ***not*** here negates the ***main verb***.

Should/ought to are used particularly when the expected situation is not the case, i.e. is apparently contradicted by the facts: *Tom should be back by now. I wonder where he has got to.; There ought to be more people than this in the cinema. Perhaps the film is not so popular after all.*

Past or ***perfect*** time reference is with ***should have/ought to have***:

(28) a. The parcel should have arrived last week. Can you fax Tate, Mary, and ask if it got there?
… sollte letzte Woche angekommen sein …
b. The workmen ought to have finished the job by the end of next week.
… sollten bis Ende nächster Woche mit der Arbeit fertig (geworden) sein.

Note that the last example stands for a future perfect.

Unlike *must have*, ***should have/ought to have*** can stand for a ***hypothetical*** past or perfect reference, i.e. equivalent to German *hätte (nicht) sollen/ nicht dürfen*:

(29) a. It should have been much warmer yesterday. The weather forecast had said we would have a sunny day with cloudless skies!
... hätte gestern viel warmer sein müssen/sollen ...
b. Preparations ought not to have taken so long, but we had only two people to help us.
... hätten nicht so lange dauern sollen, aber ...

057/3 Permission

When we ask others to ***allow*** us to do or have something, we are making a ***request*** (dt. *Bitte*) for ***permission***. Many requests for things, including favours as well as concrete objects, are based on the communicative principle that the ***consent*** of others is necessary before we can get what we want. The first communicative step when we want something is therefore often a ***request for permission***.

057/3.1 Asking for permission: may, could

The general polite and formal way of asking for permission is with ***may***. This is used when the ***permission-seeker*** feels a sense of social distance to the ***addressee*** (the person spoken to), perhaps, for instance, because the addressee is a relative stranger, or somebody of higher social status. But it may also be because the request involves a large favour; in this case it is also heard between people close to each other. The German equivalent is *dürfte(n)*:

(30) a. May I have another piece of cake, please, Mrs. Taylor?
Dürfte ich mir noch ein Stück Kuchen nehmen, Frau Taylor?
b. May I ask you something personal, Dr. James?
Dürfte ich Ihnen eine persönliche Frage stellen, Herr Dr. James?
c. May I borrow your car for the evening, Dudley?
Dürfte ich mir dein Auto für den Abend leihen, Dudley?

May is used mainly in the first person (singular and plural), i.e. when speakers are asking for permission for themselves.

Could is a much more common way of requesting permission. It is less formal than ***may***, but still shows politeness through distance and respect (***unreal past***!). It can be used in any social setting, whether familiar or formal, but in a more formal relationship it is not as defensive as ***may***, and does not suggest any higher social status on the part of the addressee. It is used in all persons (i.e. also for asking on behalf of a third person). The German equivalent, in most cases, is *darf/dürfen* or *könnte(n)*:

(31) a. Could I borrow your camera for a moment (please), Darcey?
Darf ich/Könnte ich kurz deine Kamera haben, Darcey?
b. Could Sarah wear your red dress to the party tonight, Donna?
Darf/könnte Sarah heute Abend dein rotes Kleid zum Fest anziehen, Donna?
c. Could I borrow your car for the evening, Dudley?
Darf/Könnte ich mir dein Auto für den Abend leihen, Dudley?

A common way of increasing the careful or polite character of ***could*** is to introduce it by the phrase *Do you think …?*: *Do you think Sarah could wear your red dress to the party tonight, Donna?*; *Do you think I could borrow your car for the evening, Dudley?*

057/3.2 Asking for permission: can, might

Can is familiar and direct and used when the request is for something small or fairly self-evident. Like ***could*** it is used for 3rd person requests as well:

(32) a. Can we have supper in the garden today, Mum?
Können wir heute im Garten zu Abend essen, Mama?
b. Can Brian borrow your book on butterflies?
Kann Brian dein Buch über Schmetterlinge ausleihen?

Might, the unreal past of ***may***, is occasionally used for permission requests, but is very tentative. It suggests that the request is for something large, or requires special tact, perhaps because of the particular situation, or the addressee's higher social status. For ordinary requests it sounds old-fashioned, or ironic.

(33) a. Might I ask you a question, Lady Blantyre?
Dürfte ich mir erlauben, Ihnen eine Frage zu stellen, Lady B.?
b. Might I make a suggestion, children? What about bed?
Dürfte ich vielleicht einen Vorschlag machen, Kinder? …

057/3.3 Giving and refusing permission

The usual ***modal*** way of ***giving*** (or ***refusing***) permission is with ***can*** (***can't/cannot***):

(34) a. You can use my cello, if you like, Valentine.
Du darfst ruhig mein Cello benutzen, wenn du willst, Valentine.
b. No, Brian can't borrow my book on butterflies. He's got at least three others of mine that he hasn't given back yet!

Short responses, of course, are the most common: *Yes, of course/Yes you can*; *No, I'm afraid not*; *No, she can't, I'm afraid*, etc.

Nowadays, ***may*** is hardly used for giving permission; if it is used, it sounds elevated and a little old-fashioned, especially in a short response (*Yes, you may*; *no, you may not*).

Giving permission without having been asked, as in (34)a., amounts to an offer or a suggestion. ***Could*** is possible here too. The unreal past gives it a more theoretical ('conditional') ring: *You could come next Friday, if you like. We'll be at home then.* Note, however, that it is not normally used in short responses to ***could***-requests: "*Could I drive this evening?*" "*Yes (you can), certainly*" (not **Yes, you could*).

057/3.4 Neutral reference to permission

This is reference simply to whether someone has permission to do something:

(35) a. Bill can't come to the party tonight. His parents won't let him.
b. As children, we couldn't play/weren't allowed to play in the street on Sundays.
c. You can't park/are not allowed to park here without a permit.
Ohne Ausweis darf man hier nicht parken.
d. Sheena can stay out till midnight tonight (her parents have given her special permission as it's her birthday).
Sheena darf heute bis Mitternacht unterwegs sein.
e. Fred and Brenda are allowing their daughter to go/are letting their daughter go to Paris on her own.
Fred und Brenda lassen ihre Tochter allein nach Paris fahren.

The most usual modal verb here is ***can*** (***could*** in the past). ***May*** is old-fashioned (it is used in example (1)c. above for grammatical illustration only!). Note that the suppletive ***to be allowed to*** is used for ***general rules*** only, as in (35)b. and c. It sounds rather 'official' in the personal sphere, but is nevertheless quite common. ***Can*** is a less formal alternative. Otherwise for single occasions ***allow*** is possible only in the active voice, as in (35)e. ***Let*** is also a common alternative, especially in speech and informal language.

057/3.5 Some permission metaphors

There are several common ***pragmatic metaphors*** for permission. One type, for asking permission, is to ask whether the addressee ***objects*** to the intended action. Another type, common for refusing permission, is a direct statement of ***volition***, such as a ***wish*** or preference:

(36) a. Would you mind my (me) closing/if I closed the window?
Hätten Sie etwas dagegen, wenn ich ...?
b. Is it all right if I take the car?
Wäre es in Ordnung/ist es ok, wenn ich ...?
c. (You can play on the beach, but) I don't want you to go in the water today, Lilly.
Du darfst am Strand spielen, aber ich möchte nicht, dass Du heute ins Wasser gehst, Lilly.
d. You can wash the dog in the garden, Gerald, but I'd rather you didn't do it in the bath.
..., aber mir wäre es lieber, du würdest es nicht in der Badewanne machen.

Note that modals (apart from 'conditional' *would*) are not involved here. Volitional statements like those in (36)c. and d. can also be seen as ***directives***, dealt with in the next section.

057/4 Directives

Directives are instructions and orders. They are expressed very directly by the ***imperative***. The command form, though, is generally reserved for fairly specific situations (see chapter 8, **041/2.9**). In general, ***directives*** are phrased either as ***requests***, or as statements of ***obligation***. In both cases ***modal verbs*** are strongly involved.

Whereas ***permission-requests*** are typically in the 1st person (see **057/3.1**, and **057/3.2**), ***directive-requests*** tend to be in the 2nd person. This naturally reflects the difference in communication perspectives; asking for ***permission*** usually focuses on something ***speakers*** want to do themselves; making a ***directive*** generally involves a ***demand***, i.e. something that speakers want their ***addressees*** to do.

057/4.1 Requests: could, would, can

Could is careful, polite, and can be used to both strangers and friends, superiors and equals. If it is introduced by *Do you think...?*, the politeness is increased (see also under **057/3.1**):

(37) a. Excuse me, could you tell me the way to the next Underground station (please)?
b. Could you pass me the soup again, please, Mrs. Wynslop?
c. Do you think you could close the window, please, Sue?

Can is more direct and familiar. It tends to occur mainly in situations where instructions can be expected and the requested action does not take much extra effort, or is all part of the 'expected service':

(38) a. Can you get some washing-powder when you go shopping, Sonia?
b. Can you send a mail to that firm in Amsterdam, please, Jane, and ask when their executive is arriving in Manchester?

Would is similar to ***could*** in politeness, but it assumes that the request will be fulfilled. It therefore often has the 'flavour' of a polite command. It can be used in a familiar relationship, but is favoured especially in formal or public situations. With an appropriate tone of voice, speakers can make ***would***-requests sound quite demanding:

(39) a. Would you follow me, please, ladies and gentlemen?
b. Would you take a seat for a moment, please? The director will see you immediately.
c. Would you stop talking now, please, class!

In public situations, *like to* is sometimes added to soften the tone: *Would you like to take a seat for a moment, please?*

A further variation is ***would you mind + gerund***. This is used for 'bigger', less expected, or more individual tasks; but it is also commonly heard when there is a tone of warning or disapproval:

(40) a. Mrs. Baines is out of the office at the moment. Would you mind calling back later?
b. Would you mind closing the door, please, Tim?
c. Would you mind keeping your voices down, please?

Note that this is a typical field of ***pragmatic metaphor***. The use of ***would*** derives from its volitional meaning; ***would you mind …?*** refers literally to any 'objections' to the intended action which the addressee may have (see also under **057/3.5**); and ***can/could*** basically ask about the addressee's ***ability*** to do something.

057/4.2 Obligation and necessity with must

One of the central meanings of ***must*** is ***obligation***, i.e. being required or expected to do something. It amounts in most cases to a ***command*** or instruction:

(41) a. You must be back home by midnight, Chloe.
b. (My mother says) we must be back home by midnight, Tony.
c. The children can play in the garden, but they must keep off the flower-beds, Dahlia.

Must expresses obligation in a very direct way, almost as a personal demand. It implies that the speaker is the source of the authority, or at least supports it and identifies with it. There may be a strong moral aspect to the obligation, particularly with 1st person reference, as in (41)b., or in the following:

(42) a. We must buy a present for the Herriots this Christmas. We forgot last year.
b. I must visit the Herriots when I'm in California. I promised I would.
c. You must try to be more punctual, Simon. You're always late.

As these examples again show, ***must*** tends to indicate that ***the speaker*** is ***imposing the obligation***. In (42)a. and b. the speaker imposes it on him- or herself.

On the other hand, ***must*** can also refer to a ***necessity*** imposed by external circumstances:

(43) a. You must take a taxi (it's too late to walk and there are no buses).
b. We must go back the way we came (as this is a dead-end).

Very often, there is a mixed meaning of both ***necessity*** and ***obligation***:

(44) a. The children must put on their sweaters (as it's getting cold).
b. Ricky must cut the grass (it is too long).
c. You must tell us by tomorrow if you can't play on Saturday (so that we can find a replacement in time).

The imperative element can also be intended as ***advice, recommendation, warning,*** as an emphasized ***invitation*** or ***offer***, or as a strong ***wish***:

(45) a. Dad must go to the doctor's tomorrow if his leg still hurts.
b. Pauline must be careful riding that horse.
c. You must have one of these chocolates, darling. They're delicious!
d. I just must see that film.

057/4.3 Negation with must

Negatives with ***must*** always negate the ***main verb***:

(46) a. You must not be back later than midnight, Chloe.
Du darfst nicht später als Mitternacht nach Hause kommen, Chloe.
b. The children mustn't go on the flowerbeds.
Die Kinder dürfen die Blumenbeete nicht betreten.

Note that the German equivalent of ***must not*** is ***nicht dürfen***. That is, ***must not*** does ***not*** ⚠ mean *nicht müssen*! The English for *nicht müssen* is *not have to* (see below).

There is a further slight problem with ***nicht dürfen***, as this can also be rendered in English as ***cannot/not be allowed to***. And of course there is a difference between ***must not*** and ***cannot***:

(47) a. You can't park here, Jim (= It isn't allowed).
Du darfst hier nicht parken, Jim (= Es ist nicht erlaubt).
b. You mustn't park here, Jim (= It is forbidden).
Du darfst hier nicht parken, Jim (= Es ist ausdrücklich verboten).

Must not implies a 'command not to', suggesting ***emphatic prevention*** of something, perhaps because it is likely to happen, has already happened, or was allowed in the past.

057/4.4 Obligation and necessity with have to

Obligation can also be expressed by ***have to***, a ***secondary modal***. In certain grammatical contexts, ***have to*** functions as a suppletive for ***must***. But we will deal first with its non-suppletive use.

Have to is generally more neutral and less forceful than ***must***. It does not imply that the obligation or order comes from the speaker, or that the speaker supports it. It is therefore nearly always used for 'speaker-external' rules, especially those of a general, habitual kind:

(48) a. I can't see you on Saturday, as I have to help my mother in the house.
b. Rebecca has to work overtime on 4 days a week (the firm forces her).
c. Because of security checks, we have to be at the airport two hours before the flight leaves.

Outside its suppletive function, ***have to*** tends to be reserved for this objective kind of obligation reference, and cannot replace ***must*** in examples (41)–(45), except possibly (41) b. It is rarely used for advice, recommendation or invitation.

It is also not used for necessity, except in reference to habits and general truths: *When the weather is bad, the farm-workers have to shelter in the barn.* A second exception is when ***have to*** takes on its role as a ***suppletive*** for ***must*** (on this point, see **057/4.5**).

Note that ***have to*** behaves grammatically like a main verb, and takes **do-*support*** in questions and negatives: *"Does Rebecca have to work overtime today?" "No, she doesn't have to work overtime at all this week."* (***not*** **Has Rebecca to work …?; *No, she hasn't to work …*). See **057/4.5** for details on ***have to*** in the negative. Informal British English tends to use the form ***have got to*** for ***have to***. Here, rather confusingly, ***have*** is an auxiliary, and forms questions and negatives ***without*** **do-*support***: *"Has Rebecca got to work overtime today?" "No, she hasn't got to today."*

057/4.5 Negation with have to

Negatives with ***have to*** always negate the ***modal***. That is, if we want to say that there is ***no obligation*** to do something, we use ***not have to*** (as a ***suppletive*** for ***must***, see further below in this section). The German equivalent here is ***nicht müssen***:

(49) a. Paul doesn't have to help me next week (= there is no obligation or necessity to do so).
Paul muss mir nächste Woche nicht helfen.
b. I don't have to be back before midnight (= there is no obligation to be back …).
Ich muss nicht vor Mitternacht zurück sein.
c. As his leg is all right again, Dad doesn't have to go to the doctor's tomorrow (= there is no necessity to do so).
…, muss Papa morgen nicht zum Arzt.

⚠ A common error among German speakers is to render ***nicht müssen*** in English as **must not*. As was pointed out above, ***must not*** does ***not*** negate the ***obligation/necessity*** meaning, but actually ***keeps*** it. Compare:

(50) a. My pupils mustn't read that book (= I forbid them to do so).
Meine Schüler dürfen dieses Buch nicht lesen.
b. My pupils don't have to read that book (= there is no obligation to read it, i.e. they are free to decide whether to read it or not).
Meine Schüler müssen dieses Buch nicht lesen.

Have to takes on a ***suppletive*** function here, as ***must*** itself cannot be semantically negated. Other ***suppletive*** functions of ***have to*** concern the tenses, as shown in the following two sections.

057/4.6 Past and perfect tenses with must and have to

In all perfect and past tense forms, ***must*** is replaced by ***have to***:

(51) a. Since the beginning of the year, all the workers at Gary's firm have had to do more overtime.
... müssen ... mehr Überstunden leisten.
b. When I was at school, we all had to wear school uniform.
... mussten wir alle eine Schuluniform tragen.

There is an exception with ***indirect speech*** in the past tense (see also chapter 11, **053/1.5**).
In this case there is a choice of keeping ***must*** or replacing it by ***had to***: *They told me that I* ***must/had to*** *wear school uniform.*

057/4.7 Future time-orientation with must and have to

With future reference, matters are not quite so clear-cut. On the one hand, there is usually no grammatical need for a tense change, as all main verbs with modals refer to the future anyway: *Natalie must go to the doctor's tomorrow; We must return our books to the library by the end of this week.*

On the other hand, the ***will***-future is often used when conditional or time clauses are involved. For ***must***, this then requires suppletive ***will have to***: *If there's a thunderstorm while you're out this afternoon, you'll have to take cover.* The present form ***must*** is possible here, too (*... you must take cover*), but speakers tend to prefer the ***will***-form when the future necessity arises from a future condition. It gives a more predictive, less forceful quality to the reference, and also puts a little more emphasis on a future ***change of plan***.

Here a few examples for comparison:

(52) a. When the new law comes into force, all drivers must wear seat-belts.
[forceful and definitive, obligation stressed]
..., müssen alle Fahrer Sicherheitsgurte anlegen.
b. When the new law comes into force, all drivers will have to wear seat-belts.
[neutral-predictive, necessity and change of plan in forefront]
..., werden alle Fahrer Sicherheitsgurte anlegen müssen.
c. If the pain continues, Natalie must go to the doctor's tomorrow.
[definitive and forceful recommendation]
..., muss sie morgen zum Arzt gehen.
d. If the pain continues, Natalie will have to go to the doctor's tomorrow.
[less forceful, more a prediction of future necessity]
..., wird sie morgen zum Arzt gehen müssen.

057/4.8 have to and need

The secondary modal ***need*** can be treated grammatically as a main verb (followed by a ***to***-infinitive), or as an auxiliary (followed by an infinitive without ***to***):

(53) a. "Need I call a taxi for Janet?/Do I need to call a taxi for Janet?"
b. "No, you needn't call her a taxi/you don't need to call her a taxi now, as Ron and Doris are taking her home."

Need (dt. *brauchen/müssen*) refers explicitly to ***necessity***.

In the negative ***need*** and ***have to*** are often synonymous. In (53)b., for instance, we could replace ***needn't*** by ***don't have to*** (*You don't have to call …*). This doesn't mean, however, that they are always interchangeable. ***Needn't*** (***not need***) only functions as a ***negative-suppletive*** for ***must*** in the ***necessity*** sense. The ***obligation*** meaning of ***must*** can only be negated by ***not have to***, e.g.

(54) a. Wir müssen dieses Seminar nicht besuchen (es ist nicht unbedingt nötig, weil wir den Inhalt schon kennen).
b. We needn't/don't need/don't have to attend this seminar (as we already know the content).
c. Wir müssen dieses Seminar nicht besuchen (es ist nicht vorgeschrieben).
d. We don't have to attend this seminar (because the rules don't require it).

(54)a. can be rendered in English by (54)b., but (54)c. only by (54)d., i.e. only by the ***not have to***-version. The general and most common ***negative-suppletive*** for ***must*** is therefore ***not have to***.

057/4.9 Duty and advisability with should and ought to

Should/ought to express duty, and correct or recommended behaviour. The German equivalent is *sollte(n)*.

(55) a. John should/ought to stop smoking if he intends to do more sport.
[advice/recommendation]
b. If we want to cross the main road, we should/ought to use the pedestrian crossing.
[moral duty/recommendation]
c. Politicians should/ought to tell the truth.
[moral duty/recommendation]

Note that ***ought*** is the only primary modal that takes a ***to***-infinitive.

Should/ought to are particularly common in situations where the correct behaviour is actually not taking place, or contravention threatens. The examples in (55), for instance, might suggest contexts in which: (for a.) John has no intention to stop smoking, or finds it difficult to give up; (for b.) we are about to cross a busy road without using the crossing; (for c.) politicians have been caught lying.

This contextual suggestion of (threatening) 'non-fulfillment' tends to be even greater with ***ought***, which is a little stronger in emphasis.

In the ***negative, should/ought to*** are like ***must***, in that they negate the ***main verb***. That is they express the duty or recommendation ***not*** to do something. ***Ought to*** is less common than ***should*** in the negative, and then, because of its stronger emphasis, usually takes the ***full form*** (***not***), rather than the weak form (*n't*):

(56) a. John should***n't***/ought ***not*** to smoke (= It is advisable for John ***not*** to smoke).
b. Politicians should***n't***/ought ***not*** to tell lies (= It is their duty/advisable for them ***not*** to tell lies).
c. You should***n't***/ought ***not*** to go out in this weather without a jacket on.

057/4.10 should and ought to in questions

As with any other modal verb, ***yes-no***-questions are grammatically possible with ***should/ought to***. However, they tend to be reserved for writing. Spoken language often avoids putting ***should/ought to*** in initial sentence position as they are difficult to pronounce clearly there, and can easily be misunderstood.

The preferred alternative is an ***indirect question*** type using catenatives such as ***think*** or ***believe***:

(57) a. Do you think I should/ought to take the dog to the vet's?
Sollte ich den Hund vielleicht zum Tierarzt bringen?
b. Don't you think I should/ought to take the dog to the vet's?
Glaubst du nicht, dass ich den Hund zum Tierarzt bringen sollte?
c. Shouldn't I/oughtn't I/ought I not to take the dog to the vet's?
Sollte ich den Hund nicht (lieber) zum Tierarzt bringen?

The direct question version in (57)c. is more appropriate to writing. Weak forms, of course, can be used in informal types of text, such as letters, notes, diaries, etc. Note the position of full-form ***not***. This always ***follows*** the subject pronoun (see also chapter 8, **041/2.1**).

Wh-questions are not affected by tendencies to 'initial position avoidance', as they do not, of course, begin with verbs:

(58) a. When should one plant one's potatoes?
b. What should we always remember before we cross the road, children?
c. Why shouldn't William stay with us?

Ought to is generally not heard so much in questions as ***should***, probably because the syntax is more complicated. Note the position of ***to***, and also of the full form ***not*** (which applies, of course, to any auxiliary): *When ought one to plant ...?; What ought we always to remember ...?; Why ought William not to stay with us/Why oughtn't William to stay with us?*

057/4.11 should have/ought to have and other past reference

These express ***hypothetical*** meaning. That is, they refer to actions which were advisable, or 'a duty', but which were not carried out:

(59) a. You should have asked us for help. It was silly to carry all those bricks on your own.
Du hättest uns um Hilfe bitten sollen ...
b. Christine ought not to have told the children that horror story. They certainly won't be able to sleep now.
Christine hätte den Kindern die Horrorgeschichte nicht erzählen sollen/dürfen ...

⚠ ***Should have*** is sometimes mistakenly used by German speakers as the past tense of ***should***. In the ***directive*** sense, German *sollte(n)* is rendered in English as ***were to/were supposed to*** (see **057/4.17**, and **057/4.18**).

In ***indirect speech, should/ought to*** are used themselves for ***past*** reference (i.e. as ***back-shifted*** forms): *My wife said I should not/ought not to disturb the children so late.* (See also under ***indirect commands*** below and in chapter 11)

057/4.12 should and must

Should is sometimes used as a ***pragmatic metaphor*** for ***must***, especially in more formal and official varieties of English:

(60) a. In the event of an emergency, passengers should proceed to the marked assembly points.
Im Notfall haben sich die Passagiere an die ausgeschilderten Sammelpunkte zu begeben.
b. Teachers should not ask pupils to contact them at the door of the staffroom.
Lehrer dürfen Schüler nicht an die Tür des Lehrerzimmers bestellen.
c. All visitors should notify Reception and sign the visitors' book before entering the College.

Note that ***ought to*** is ***not*** used in this way. The reason for this use of ***should*** is that it represents a more restrained and less direct reference to obligation and duty. It is more friendly than ***must***, as it sounds less stern and absolute.

It is therefore preferred for official directives. But it is also heard in spoken announcements of a less formal kind: *Ladies and gentlemen, you have three hours in Heidelberg. You should be back here on the bus by 5.30 pm.*

057/4.13 The passive with should and must and other directive variants

Official directives (notices, public announcements, official letters, etc.) frequently use ***passive*** constructions (with the passive infinitive) after ***should*** and ***must***, and other directive verbs. This 'cushions' the instructive force, i.e. makes the order less personal and more objective:

(61) a. All applications must be received by November 31st.
b. Payment should be made only by bank transfer or money order.
c. This door should be kept locked at all times.

The cushioning effect of the passive is seen also with several non-modal expressions also common in announcement-style contexts. These are verbs with a *request*-type meaning (*request, require, ask,* etc.). They are frequently supported by adverbs underlining the 'co-operative style' of the instruction. A further point is that the passive has no agent, i.e. the directive source is unmentioned, which again softens the sense of being ordered to do something by a particular authority:

(62) a. Staff are kindly asked not to smoke in the corridors.
b. Diners are politely requested to place their used crockery on the trolleys provided.
c. Guests are courteously advised that parking outside the hotel is illegal and will lead to wheel-clamping.

057/4.14 should in indirect questions and commands

Should functions as the past tense of ***shall*** in indirect speech. This occurs most frequently in indirect questions and commands:

(63) a. The hotel manager asked: "Shall I reserve the room for you?" [***direct***]
b. The hotel manager asked if he should reserve the hotel room for us. [***indirect***]

If ***should*** appears in the original direct speech, it remains unchanged in the indirect version:

(64) a. The hotel manager asked: "Should I reserve the room for you?" [***direct***]
b. The hotel manager asked if he should reserve the hotel room for us. [***indirect***]

A less usual case is the use of ***should*** in ***finite*** indirect commands. These are introduced by ***that***-clauses after verbs such as *tell, order, command, demand, request, urge, recommend, advise, insist,* etc.:

(65) a. We told the hotel manager: "Please reserve the room for us." [***direct***]
b. We told the hotel manager that he should reserve the hotel room for us. [***indirect***]

Most verbs of this kind have no indirect object before the ***that***-clause: *The headmaster urged/recommended/advised that the Smiths should send their son to another school.* (***That***-clauses after catenatives are dealt with in detail in the next chapter).

Should is also used when the reporting verb is in the present tense: *The Smiths are insisting that their son should stay at the school.*

A rather elevated alternative to ***should*** here is the use of the old ***subjunctive*** form (identical with the infinitive): *The headmaster urged that the Smiths send their son ...; The Smiths are insisting that their son stay ...*

The subjunctive construction is possible with all verbs of command except *tell.* Although still popular in America, however, it is not heard much in British English, where the ***should***-version is also regarded as rather formal.

Generally, the most common way of expressing indirect commands is by infinitive or other non-finite clauses: *We told the hotel manager to reserve the room for us; The headmaster urged/advised the Smiths to send their son to another school; The Smiths are insisting on their son staying ...*

For details on the use of non-finite verb forms, see next chapter.

057/4.15 Volitive should with expressions of purpose and intention

This is a very similar phenomenon to the one described in the last section. For this reason it is included here in the ***directive*** section, although the meaning is not strictly directive as such.

There are several types of volitive ***should***. The first means ***purpose***, and is introduced by the conjunction ***so that***:

(66) a. Maureen spoke slowly so that her grandmother should understand what she was saying.
b. Larry used the back entrance to the building so that he shouldn't be seen by anyone.

Should underlines the purpose meaning of the conjunction. Again, this is a slightly antiquated and literary use. A more normal modern rendering would use ***would*** or ***could***. But the reinforcing intention/purpose element of ***should*** is then lost.

In the present tense ***will*** or ***can*** must be used anyway, as ***should*** is confined to past tense contexts: *Maureen is speaking slowly so that her grandmother will/can understand ...; Larry is using the back entrance so that he won't/can't be seen ...*

A second type of ***intention***-conveying ***should*** occurs in ***that***-clauses following verbs of arrangement and plan, such as *agree, arrange, decide, determine, intend, plan*, etc.:

(67) a. They had arranged that their daughter should spend a year studying in America.
b. I did not intend that you should feel sorry for me.

A more neutral alternative in the modern language would be an infinitive structure (see also the next chapter): *They had arranged for their daughter to spend ...; I did not intend you to feel ...*

Should is possible here also in the present tense. Possible replacements are *will/would* or subjunctive forms (*They had arranged that their daughter spend ...; I did not intend that you feel ...*). The subjunctive, however, is avoided nowadays in everyday style.

Finally, ***should*** can appear in ***that***-clauses following ***volitional adjectives*** like *anxious, concerned, desirous, eager*, etc. Subjunctive forms can substitute here too, and with some (though not all) adjectives a ***for ... to*** construction :

(68) a. Jamie's parents were eager that he should study at Oxford.
b. ... were eager that he study ...
c. ... were eager for him to study ...

057/4.16 Declarative commands with will

Declarative commands are instructions or orders given as statements, rather than as requests, imperatives, or as obligation metaphors:

(69) a. Flight crews will proceed immediately to their aircraft when ordered to do so by the duty officer.
b. All nursing staff will report to the sister 10 minutes before the end of their shift.
c. After arrival at Victoria you will take a taxi to the Coach and Horses pub in Westbourne Grove and collect a small package discreetly from the barman, to whom you will identify yourself as 'Mr. Swan'.

Will here, particularly in written instructions, public notices, etc., gives a formal tone of authority that assumes co-operation and compliance. It is restricted to contexts where orders and instructions are not questioned (like the military). A more conciliatory tone would be expressed by ***should***, but this would be a metaphor, and would make the order much less direct.

In speech ***will***-commands are sometimes heard from adult to child, occasionally in a tone of reproach:

(70) a. You can play football in the park later, Derek. You'll do your homework properly first.
b. All right, boys and girls, you have two hours free now. You'll be back here on the bus no later than 5 o'clock.

057/4.17 Declarative commands and reported instructions with to be to

With the secondary modal ***to be to*** (dt. *sollen*) the tone is softer:

(71) a. All nursing staff are to report to the sister 10 minutes before the end of their shift.
b. You are to be back here on the bus no later than 5 o'clock.

Nevertheless, ***to be to*** still has the clear mark of an order or instruction, and shows authority when used to give a direct order, as in (71). But it is also used to report instructions that have come from other sources (i.e. not from the speaker), or, quite simply, arrangements:

(72) a. We are to be back on the bus by 5 at the latest (Mr. Daly says).
b. Armstrong is to leave the company immediately (by order of the board), you know.
c. None of the team are to give interviews before the game (the trainer has decided).
d. You and I were to meet Brangwen and Cliff at the Black Cat café at 9 (= that's what I had arranged with them).

Note that ***to be to*** has another meaning dealt with below (see **057/5.5**).

057/4.18 Reported instructions with to be supposed to

This secondary modal can report instructions or arrangements in the same way as ***to be to***, i.e. quite neutrally: *We're supposed to meet Brangwen and Cliff at the Black Cat café at 9.*

However, it often adds the meaning that instructions or arrangements have already been contravened or look as if they might be:

(73) a. You're supposed to be in bed (= that was the arrangement, and now you're in the kitchen!).
Du solltest im Bett sein ...!
b. Tom and Celia were supposed to be here by 10 o'clock (and it's now 11: Where are they?)
Tom und Celia sollten bis 10 Uhr hier sein ...
c. We're not supposed to be in this park after dark (so I think we'd better leave now).
In diesem Park sollen wir nach Einbruch der Dunkelheit nicht sein ...

To be supposed to has another meaning explained further below (see **057/5.4**).

057/5 Other modal usage

057/5.1 should as a would-equivalent

An older use of ***should*** is as a ***would***-equivalent (i.e. in a 'conditional' sense) with volitional catenatives such as *like, prefer, hate,* etc.: *I should hate to be left alone like that in a strange place* (= *I would hate to be* ...).

It is only used like this in the 1st person. It sounds especially tentative and is now regarded as 'hypercorrect' and a little dated. But it is still commonly found with verbs of thinking (*think, expect, imagine*) in ***speculative*** utterances:

(74) I should think our neighbours are on holiday. I shouldn't imagine that they would have locked up the house otherwise.

Should can also stand for volitive ***would*** in conditional sentences:

(75) With a cold like that I should stay in bed, if I were you.

057/5.2 'Notional' should after adjectives

What might be called a '***notional***' or unreal function of ***should*** occurs after certain kinds of adjectives. These are ***adjectives of comment*** referring to actual circumstances and happenings, and usually saying that the speaker finds something surprising and/or annoying about them. The sentence construction is always ***extraposition*** (***It*** + ***be***) with an adjective + ***that***-clause:

(76) a. It's ***amazing*** that Melanie ***should*** still be here. She told everyone she was going to Rome.
(= She is still here, and I find this amazing.)
b. It's ***odd*** that they ***shouldn't*** remember her birthday. They've never forgotten it before.
(= They have forgotten her birthday and I find this odd.)
c. It's ***upsetting*** that Marvin ***should*** do/***should have done*** so badly in the exam: he seemed to be so well prepared.
(He did so badly and I/we find this upsetting.)

The reference here is to something factual. However, ***should*** makes an ***idea*** out of it, and shows that the speaker is giving a personal opinion or reaction to the very ***notion*** or ***principle*** of what happened.

Should is not obligatory, and can be replaced by ordinary non-modal forms: *It's amazing that Melanie is still here …, It's odd that they haven't remembered/didn't remember her birthday*. But this just comments on the fact as a fact, not as a principle or idea (***notion***).

Note that with past tense and present perfect meaning, ***should have*** can be used, but the ordinary ***should***-form is usually equally acceptable.

057/5.3 should for shall

Should is sometimes used as a more restrained and 'careful' variation of a ***shall***-question:

(77) Should I cut the grass before doing the flowerbeds?
(= Do you want me/advise me to …?)
Soll ich (vielleicht/wohl) das Gras mähen, bevor ich mich um die Blumenbeete kümmere?

057/5.4 The 'rumour' meaning of to be supposed to

Like German *sollen*, ***to be supposed to*** also conveys the meaning of ***rumour/reputation***, or 'that's what people say':

(78) a. Her husband is supposed to be away on business (but I don't believe it, frankly!).
… soll geschäftlich verreist sein …
b. Hello! What a surprise! I thought you were supposed to be in Edinburgh.
… Ich dachte, du solltest in Edinburgh sein.
c. McCrombie and Bishop are supposed to be the fastest wingers in the history of Scottish rugby.
… sollen die schnellsten Außenspieler in der Geschichte des schottischen Rugby sein.

In context ***to be supposed to*** often casts doubt on the truth of 'what people say', though this is not necessarily implied by the verb alone. The verb itself has a 'truth-neutral' meaning.

057/5.5 The 'destiny' meaning of to be to

This also translates into German as *sollen*. In this sense it means 'what is or was destined to happen' in people's lives.

(79) a. Are we ever to meet again?
Will es das Schicksal, dass wir uns je wiedersehen?
b. Annie Gonagle was later to become the world sprint champion over 100 metres.
Später sollte Annie Gonagle Weltmeisterin im 100-Meter-Lauf werden.
c. This was the first time the two stars ever played together in one band, and it was to be the last.
... und es sollte auch das letzte Mal sein.

Chapter 13 Verbs: Non-finite Verbs

Basic features 058

As was said in our introduction to verbs in chapter 8, ***non-finite*** verbs are ***infinitives***, ***gerunds*** and ***participles***. Grammatically, their main general characteristics are these:

- they are ***not*** conjugated forms, i.e. unlike finite verbs they do ***not*** show ***concord*** (= grammatical subject-verb agreement),
- and in any case most frequently appear ***without*** a separate ***subject*** of their own;
- when they do take a ***separate subject***, this cannot usually just be added to the verb, but has to feature as part of a ***special syntactic construction***;
- they form ***verb phrases*** and function as ***predicators*** like any finite verb, but
- as ***predicators*** they can appear ***only*** in ***subordinate*** clauses – that is, they can ***never*** be predicators of matrix clauses.
- with regard to tense and aspect they are ***defective***, i.e. they do not take the full range of forms, and
- usually just appear in their ***base*** (or 'ordinary') ***form***.

13.1 The infinitive

Forms 059

With regard to tense and aspect, there are ***four*** forms of the infinitive:

a. ***the infinitive base form*** ⟶ *to run*
b. ***the progressive infinitive*** ⟶ *to be running*
c. ***the perfect infinitive*** ⟶ *to have run*
d. ***the perfect progressive infinitive*** ⟶ *to have been running*

Expressing this in the same terms as for finite verbs, we would say that the infinitive has ***two tenses***, each with ***two aspects***:

Tense	Aspect	
	Simple	***Progressive***
Base form Non-perfect	to run	to be running
Perfect	to have run	to have been running

Note that there are only ***two tense*** forms, and not four, as with finite verbs. That is, there is no 'past tense infinitive' or 'past perfect infinitive'. This is an example of what is meant when we say that regarding tense and aspect, non-finite verbs are ***defective***.

Certain forms are missing from the 'system', quite simply because they are not necessary. Special tense-marking of non-finite verbs is generally not needed, as their time orientation is usually the same as that of the finite verb closest to them. For example, in *I wanted to go to the party*, it is clear that *to go* refers to the ***past*** because *want* is in the ***past tense***.

There are situations, however, where there is a difference in time orientation between finite and non-finite verb, as in *He seems to have lost his money yesterday afternoon*. The infinitive therefore needs a ***'before'***-form, i.e. the ***perfect infinitive***. However, this one form is enough and stands, according to context, for the past tense, the present perfect, or the past perfect. We come back to this point in detail later (see under **060/9.2**).

Note that verb forms like *must have gone, should have come*, and so on, are strictly speaking cases of ***modal auxiliary + perfect infinitive***.

A further point on form concerns the use of ***to***. There are two variants, one ***with* to** (the **to-*infinitive***), the other ***without***. When we refer to verbs in their infinitive forms, it is customary to use the **to-*infinitive***: *to walk, to run, to stop*, etc. This signals quite clearly that it is the infinitive that we mean, and not some other form of the verb. Where this is clear, however, it is equally correct to leave the ***to*** out: *walk, run, stop*, etc.

In the syntax of a phrase or sentence, however, one or other form is nearly always obligatory. This is usually the **to-*infinitive***, e.g. *I didn't want to come*.

But there are constructions (mainly certain verbs) that must be followed by the ***infinitive without* to**, e.g. *You must come tomorrow*.

060 Infinitive constructions

060/1 The infinitive after verbs

There are many verbs in English that are followed by infinitives, among them, as we have seen, the ***modal auxiliaries*** (generally ***infinitive without* to**):

(1) David ***should get*** some exercise. He ***must lose*** weight.

The vast majority, however, are ordinary ***main verbs*** (generally **to-*infinitive***):

(2) David ***wants to get*** some exercise if he really ***intends to lose*** weight.

Main verbs linked in this way to infinitives (or to other non-finites) are called ***catenatives*** (= 'linking verbs').

Catenatives combine with the infinitive in three different ways. Some are followed ***directly*** by the infinitive (*I learnt to swim at a young age*). Others need an ***object*** before the infinitive (*My mother taught me to swim*). And others follow ***either*** pattern, depending upon meaning: *I wanted to go to university; My parents wanted me to go to university.*

The following sections give details on each of these patterns. Alternative constructions are also indicated. However, they are not necessarily freely interchangeable.

060/1.1 Verb + infinitive

There is ***no object*** between the catenative verb and the infinitive:

(3) a. You forgot to wash your hands.
b. Chantal promised to help Ray with the gardening.
c. Our team did not manage to reach the next round of the Cup.

The verbs in this category follow ***only*** this pattern. That is, an object between catenative and infinitive is ***not*** possible.

This is clear in most cases, as most of these verbs are generally only monotransitive. That is, they take ***one object*** only, and the ***object*** in this case is the ***infinitive clause***. One or two, however, can be ditransitive in simple sentences, and then take ***two objects***, e.g. *promise*, or *refuse*, as in *He promised/refused me help*. Note, however, that with the ***infinitive*** these are ***only monotransitive.*** That is, we cannot say, for instance, **Chantal promised Ray to help him*, or **She refused me to come to the party*.

Common members of this category are: *agree, appear, arrange, attempt* (also gerund), *begin* (also gerund), *care, consent, determine, fail, forget, hesitate, hope, learn, manage, neglect, prepare, promise, propose* (also gerund), *refuse, regret* (also gerund), *remember* (also gerund), *seem, start* (also gerund), *swear, try* (also gerund).

Note that gerund alternatives may change the meaning of the construction (see below in section on ***Gerund***, 13.2., **062/1**).

060/1.2 Verb + object + infinitive

Here there ***must*** be an ***object*** between the catenative verb and the infinitive:

(4) a. The doctors advised Julie to take a long rest.
b. Can you remind me to post this letter tomorrow, Henry?
c. Her grandfather encouraged her to play the piano.

The verbs in this category also follow ***only*** this pattern. It is ***not*** possible in this construction to make such verbs monotransitive. We cannot, for instance, say **The doctor advised/ encouraged to take a long rest.*

Common members of this category are: *advise* (also gerund), *allow* (also gerund), *compel, encourage* (also gerund), *forbid, force, instruct, invite, lead, oblige, order, permit* (also gerund), *persuade, remind, request, show how, teach* (also gerund), *tell, tempt, urge, warn.*

Here again, gerund alternatives may change the meaning of the construction (see below in section on ***Gerund***, 13.2., **062/1**).

060/1.3 Either pattern

With catenatives in this category an object is possible but not obligatory. That is, the pattern is either ***verb + infinitive***, or ***verb + object + infinitive***, depending on the meaning intended:

(5) a. They wanted to go on holiday immediately.
b. They wanted me to go on holiday immediately.
c. We expected to arrive before midnight.
d. We expected our guests to arrive before midnight.

Common members of this category are: *ask, expect, hate, help, intend* (also gerund), *like* (also gerund), *love* (also gerund), *mean* (also gerund), *prefer* (also gerund), *want* (also gerund).

As with preceding categories, gerund alternatives may not be freely interchangeable (see below in section on ***Gerund***).

060/2 The infinitive after verbs: some special cases

060/2.1 The infinitive without to

This is sometimes called the 'bare' infinitive. First and foremost it occurs with ***modal auxiliaries***, as we have already seen:

(6) a. All applicants must pass an entrance exam.
b. My wife can speak seven languages.

Secondly, it occurs with verbs of ***perception*** (such as *feel, hear, notice, see, watch,* etc.), which also take an intervening object (***verb + object + infinitive without*** **to**):

(7) a. We watched the plane land.
b. Three witnesses saw the man steal the watch.

(Verbs of ***perception*** also appear with ***present participles***: see **064/1.9** below).

The verbs *make, let* and *have* (in the senses of 'force', 'allow', and 'cause') follow the same pattern:

(8) a. A sudden noise made us look up.
b. Sue's parents do not let her smoke in the house.
c. I had the hotel porter bring my cases down.

060/2.2 Verbs of knowing and thinking

Certain verbs connected with the semantic fields of ***knowledge*** and ***thought*** take infinitives under certain restricted circumstances. Typical examples are: *assume, believe, consider, feel* (in the sense of *think*), *know, presume, suppose, think, understand,* etc. These are followed by the ***object + infinitive*** pattern, but only when the infinitive is *be*.

(9) a. The boss assumed Arthur to be ill.
b. People believe McCann to be the best salesman in the firm.
c. Wendy considered her relationship with Jeff to be over.

The style is elevated. More neutral and more common with this kind of verb is a ***that***-clause: *The boss assumed that Arthur was .../People believe that McCann is ...*

The infinitive version occurs more often with the catenative in the ***passive*** (especially with a generalized agent):

(10) a. Arthur was assumed to be ill.
b. McCann is believed to be the best salesman in the firm.
c. Wendy's relationship with Jeff was considered (by her) to be over.

060/3 The infinitive after adjectives

Many kinds of adjectives 'attract' the infinitive. It is necessary to group them in semantic categories: this is because ***different types of adjective*** affect the ***meaning relation*** between the infinitive and the adjective (or other elements in the sentence) in ***different ways***. In some cases differences in syntax are also involved.

Most people are familiar with the famous sentence pair coined by the linguist Noam Chomsky: *John is easy to please/John is eager to please.* The relation between *John,* the adjective and the infinitive is very different in each case. Below we explain such phenomena (though without using Chomsky's models of explanation!).

060/3.1 Volitional adjectives

These express ***the subject's willingness or unwillingness*** regarding a particular action, e.g. *eager, hesitant, keen,* etc. They can be paraphrased in a general sense by *want to/not want to*:

(11) a. Barbara is keen to go to university (= wants very much to go ...).
Barbara ist versessen darauf, an die Uni zu gehen.
b. I was hesitant to spend so much money on a jacket (= I didn't really want to spend .../wasn't sure whether I should spend ...).
Ich zögerte, so viel Geld ...

Others of this type are: *prepared, ready, reluctant, unwilling, willing,* and also *quick* and *slow*: *He is sometimes rather quick to criticize his children* (dt. ... *manchmal etwas schnell dabei, ...*).

Note that the ***subject*** of the ***matrix verb*** *be* is also the implied ***subject*** of the ***infinitive***, e.g. for (11)a. *Barbara is keen ..., Barbara will go.*

060/3.2 Emotional-reactive adjectives

These show the subject's emotional reaction to something that has happened or is in the course of happening, e.g. *happy, sad, surprised,* etc. The infinitive refers to the action which causes the feeling:

(12) a. We are very happy to have you here as our guests (= We have you here as our guests and this makes us happy).
b. I was surprised to see her again (= I saw her again and this made me surprised).

Others in the group are: *angry, astonished, delighted, disappointed, disgusted, glad, horrified, relieved, sorry,* etc.

With this group, too, the ***subject*** of the ***matrix verb*** *be* is always the implied ***subject*** of the ***infinitive***, e.g. for (12)b. *I was surprised ..., I saw her again.*

060/3.3 Evaluative adjectives with extraposition

These adjectives are of the '*nice-nasty*' type, and express a ***value judgement*** (dt. *Werturteil*) on some action. They refer mainly to ***behaviour***: *cruel, generous, kind,* etc. The infinitive expresses the action which the speaker is commenting on:

(13) a. To give her so much money was very generous (= Somebody gave her a lot of money and this was generous).
b. It was very generous (of Bob) to give her so much money (= Bob gave her a lot of money and in this respect he was very generous).

Although grammatically possible, beginning the sentence with the infinitive clause, as in (13)a., is usually avoided. This is because there is more emphasis in English on elements ***at the end*** of the sentence. The preferred solution is therefore to place the infinitive clause ***after the adjective***, and open the sentence with an ***It + be***-construction, known as ***extraposition***, as in (13)b.

It is also common (though not obligatory) to mention the 'doer' (i.e. the ***agent***) in an ***of***-phrase, as indicated in the brackets. This relates the speaker's comment also to the responsibility of the 'doer' and not just to the action.

Further examples: *It would be unwise of Dave and Mary to buy such an expensive house; It was rather mean of Ryan to leave you all alone in a strange city; It is a bit silly of us to park on a main road like this.*

More or less any ***evaluative adjective*** can be used in this kind of construction: *foolish, nasty, nice, polite, rude, ridiculous, stupid, wise,* etc.

An alternative to the infinitive in most cases is a ***that***-clause: *It was rather mean that Ryan left you all alone in a strange city.*

Adjectives expressing levels of ***feasibility*** and ***difficulty*** (*possible, difficult, easy,* etc.) also combine with the infinitive in ***extraposition*** constructions: *It is difficult/impossible/not easy to get hot food in this town after 8 pm.*

060/3.4 Evaluative and speculative adjectives in 'false subject' constructions

An alternative to extraposition with ***evaluative*** adjectives is what we will call the ***false subject construction***:

(14) a. Ryan was rather mean to leave you all alone in a strange city.
b. Bob was very generous to give her so much money.
c. Dave and Mary would be unwise to buy such an expensive house.
d. We are silly to park on a main road like this.

Here the ***implied subject*** of the ***infinitive*** appears as the ***subject*** of the ***matrix verb*** *be.* This gives a 'false' impression of the primary, or most important, meaning: the ***adjective*** describes the ***action***, not primarily the person.

In (14)a., for example, it is not really (or at least mainly) Ryan who was 'mean', but what he did. This is shown by the ***extraposition*** version with a ***that***-clause mentioned at the end of **060/3.3**: *It was rather mean that Ryan left you all alone in a strange city*. In (14), then, the ***apparent subject*** of the ***matrix clause*** (*Ryan, Bob, Dave and Mary, we*) is basically just the ***implied subject*** of the ***infinitive***.

False subject constructions are very common also with the ***speculative*** adjectives *certain, likely* and *sure;* with *bound* there is no alternative (as extraposition is ***not*** possible in this case):

(15) a. Gina is certain/likely/sure to win the competition.
(= It is certain/likely/sure that Gina will win ...)
b. Gina is bound to win the competition.
(No extraposition possible, but meaning same as a.)
Gina wird sicher den Wettbewerb gewinnen.

Here the 'falseness' of the subject is much clearer even than in (14), as it is obvious that semantically the adjectives cannot refer to the subject at all, i.e. 'Gina', for instance, could never be 'likely'. And although she could, theoretically, be 'certain' or 'sure', it is clear from the extraposition version that this is ***not*** the intended meaning at all. It is not Gina who is sure/certain, but in fact the ***speaker***.

Therefore (15)a. and b. ***cannot*** be translated into German as *Gina ist sich sicher, dass sie den Wettbewerb gewinnen wird.*

There are false subject constructions in German too, but they are only possible with a very small number of evaluative adjectives, e.g. *Wir waren dumm, dort zu parken,* but not, for example, **Er war gemein, dich allein zu lassen.*

060/3.5 False subjects implying infinitive objects and prepositional complements

False subject constructions are particularly popular when the ***false subject*** is semantically the implied ***direct object*** of the infinitive (i.e. the ***patient*** of the action):

(16) a. Avocados are good to eat.
(= It is good to eat avocados).
b. Simon's new car is lovely to drive.
(= It is lovely to drive Simon's new car).
c. Last season, this team was very exciting to watch.
(= It was very exciting to watch this team last season).

False subjects can also be the implied ***complements*** of ***prepositions***:

(17) a. Brenda is nice to be with, as she is pleasant to talk to.
(= It is nice to be with Brenda, as it is pleasant to talk to her).
b. Professor Donovan's lectures were often amusing to listen to.
(= It was amusing to listen to Professor Donovan's lectures).
c. The pool is not safe to swim in.
(= It is not safe to swim in the pool).

False subjects with implied ***object*** and ***prepositional complement*** meanings appear like this with many ***evaluative adjectives***: *all right, amazing, amusing, awful, bad, exciting, fantastic, good, great, interesting, lovely, nice, pleasant, suitable, terrible, wonderful,* etc.

A particular sub-group are the ***feasibility*** adjectives already mentioned above in connection with ***extraposition*** (see **060/3.3**). These are adjectives expressing degrees of difficulty or possibility: *awkward, difficult, easy, hard, simple,* etc.:

(18) a. The problem was easy to describe but difficult to solve.
Das Problem war leicht zu beschreiben, aber schwer zu lösen.
b. The house is hard to find after dark.
Das Haus ist nach Einbruch der Dunkelheit schwer zu finden.

The adjective *ready,* as in *The food is ready to eat,* also belongs in this sub-group.

As the translations in (18) show, the same type of construction is found here too in German, this time with a rather larger number of adjectives: *Der Wagen ist schön zu fahren/ Das Rad ist schwer zu lenken/Dieses Buch ist spannend zu lesen.* However, the construction is still not as common as in English, e.g. for *This dress is not suitable to wear to a wedding,* we cannot say in German **Dieses Kleid ist nicht passend auf einer Hochzeit zu tragen.*

060/3.6 False subject constructions with noun phrases

Nouns can also be inserted after the adjectives:

(19) a. Brenda is a ***nice girl*** to be with, as she is a ***pleasant person*** to talk to.
b. Sally's house is a ***difficult place*** to find after dark.
c. Chelsea were a very ***exciting team*** to watch last season.

Note that with nouns inserted like this, extraposition is no longer possible: **It was a very exciting team to watch Chelsea last season.*

Some adjectives ***only*** feature in this type of false subject construction (i.e. ***false subject*** = implied infinitive ***object***), when they are ***accompanied by a noun***:

(20) a. A tennis racket is an ***odd present*** to give David.
(not *A tennis racket is odd to give David).
Ein Tennisschläger ist ein seltsames Geschenk für David.
b. That was not the ***right remark*** to make at such a time.
(not *That remark was not right to make ...)

Adjectives in this group such as *peculiar, strange, funny* (= *odd*), *wrong, silly, foolish , stupid, correct,* etc. usually comment on the appropriateness of certain things or behaviour in particular situations.

Finally, certain ***evaluative nouns*** can appear in false subject constructions ***without*** adjectives. Here, ***extraposition*** is possible:

(21) a. Last season Chelsea were ***a pleasure*** to watch.
(= It was a pleasure to watch Chelsea ...)
b. Brenda is a joy to be with.
(= It is ***a joy*** to be with Brenda).
c. These cakes were ***a trouble*** to bake.
(= It was a trouble to bake these cakes).

060/4 Infinitive clauses as shortened relative clauses

Infinitives are sometimes used as noun ***postmodifications*** in the sense of ***relative clauses***:

(22) a. The most famous scientist to teach at Princeton was Einstein.
(The most famous scientist who taught ...)
b. The second horse to finish the race was Red Arrow.
(The second horse that finished ...)
c. Can I get you something to drink, Mary?
(... something that you can drink ...?)

This can be the case only under certain conditions, all of which are illustrated in the examples in (22). The conditions are:

- the particular noun is preceded by a ***superlative adjective***, as in (22)a., or
- the particular noun is preceded by an ***ordinal number***, as in (22)b., or
- the original relative clause contains a ***modal verb***, as in (22)c.

We will now look at these points in detail, paying careful attention not only to the meaning, but also to the implied (or ***underlying***) ***syntactic*** relationship between the infinitive and the noun that it postmodifies (called the ***antecedent noun***).

060/4.1 After superlative adjectives

After ***superlative*** adjectives (*biggest, best, fastest* ...) the ***antecedent noun*** is the implied ***subject*** of the ***infinitive*** following. This corresponds to the fact that in the full relative clause version the ***relative pronoun*** is also the ***subject*** of the relative clause:

(23) a. This was the fastest ship ever to cross the Atlantic.
S *(P)* *P*
(... which (has) ever crossed ...)
b. My uncle once interviewed the greatest cricketer ever to play for Australia, Donald Bradman.
S *(P)* *P*
(... who has ever played ...)
c. The most popular model of car to be sold in the last ten years has been the Tiara Town Liner.
(... which has been sold ...)

The adjectives *last, next* and *only* are also included in this group: *Up to then Anne Bryant had been the only woman in the company to become managing director* (= ... ***who*** *had become* ...); *The next car to park in front of my driveway was a Ford Escort* (= ... ***which*** *parked* ...).

060/4.2 After ordinal numbers

The case is the same after ***ordinal numbers*** (*first, second, third* ...): that is, the antecedent noun is the implied ***subject*** of the infinitive following:

(24) a. The second man to lose his job will be Roscoe.
S *P*
(The second man who will lose ...)
b. I once met the first person to swim the Channel.
S *P*
(... the first person who swam ...)

060/4.3 The infinitive as a modal relative clause

Most infinitives used as relative clauses are ***modal*** in meaning. That is, the ***relative clause*** equivalent contains a ***modal*** verb – usually *should, can/could,* or *must.* The ***antecedent noun*** in this case is very frequently the implied ***direct object*** of the ***infinitive*** following: and accordingly, in the relative clause version, the ***relative pronoun*** is the ***direct object*** of the relative clause verb:

(25) a. If you're interested in motorcycles, the man to see is Bob.
Od S P
(... the man whom you *should* see ...)
b. For the party the girls had bought a lot of things to eat.
Od S P
(... a lot of things that people/guests *could* eat)

As a whole the noun phrases concerned can generally have any sentence function. For instance in (25)a. the noun phrase *the man to see* is ***subject*** of the matrix clause; in (25)b. *a lot of things to eat* is ***direct object*** of the sentence as a whole. The most common function, however, is ***direct object***, often with *have* as matrix verb:

Od
(26) a. This afternoon we have (a great deal of work to do).
Od S P
(... work which we *must* do)
Od
b. Kevin has (an apology to make).
Od S P
(... an apology which he *should/must* make)

But we will return now to the relation between the ***antecedent noun*** and the ***infinitive***. Apart from being direct objects, ***antecedent nouns*** often function as the implied ***complements of prepositions***:

(27) a. We've got a special brush to clean the grill with.
A S P Od
(...with which we *can* clean the grill)
b. You'll find a tray to put the glasses on in the cupboard.
A S P Od
(...on which you *can* put the glasses)

In this case, of course, they are part of an ***adverbial*** (***A***) sentence function, as shown.

Less often, the ***antecedent noun*** has an implied ***subject*** function.

(28) a. I'm looking for a doctor to treat my son's dermatitis.
S ***P***
(... who *will/is able* to treat ...)
b. Maureen has bought a lamp to go on the desk in the corner.
S ***P***
(... which *can* go ...)

060/4.4 Indefinite pronouns with modal relative infinitives

Indefinite pronouns (*something, no-one, anybody*, etc.) have a particular attraction for the infinitive in this ***modal-relative*** meaning:

(29) a. I have nothing to do at the moment.
(... nothing *that* I *can/must* do ...)
b. Is there anything to drink in the house?
(... anything *that* we *can* drink ...?)
c. Incidentally, we have something important to tell you.
(... *that* we *must/ought* to tell you)

Here too we have the implied ***object*** relation of ***antecedent noun*** to infinitive. This is demonstrated clearly in the equivalent relative clauses. As with full nouns, ***prepositional*** relations are also common, and ***subject*** relations can also occur:

(30) a. My daughter at last has someone to play with.
(... someone *with whom* she *can* play)
b. Grandmother has nobody to talk to.
(... nobody *to whom* she *can* talk).
c. We have no-one to drive the car.
(... who *can/is to/will* drive the car).

060/4.5 Some additional points on the modal relative infinitive

In conclusion, there are three points on ***modal relative infinitives*** that need a final word of explanation.

Firstly, some infinitives used in this way imply ***purpose***. For instance, (30)c. might be paraphrased as ... *no-one whose job (purpose) is to drive the car*, and (27)a. as ... *a special brush for cleaning the grill with*. It should be emphasized, however, that these are ***not*** 'purpose' infinitives as such (see under **060/6** below for 'true' infinitives of purpose). The purpose meaning evolves in certain cases here quite simply from the combination of an implied ***ability***-modal (e.g. *can*) and the particular lexical items used e.g. a ***tool*** like a brush, or a ***task*** such as driving a car. Purpose infinitives can be preceded by ***in order to***. This is not permissible in these examples, though: **... a special brush in order to clean the grill with; *... no-one in order to drive the car.*

Another point is a general one regarding the ***implied function*** of the ***antecedent noun*** in relation to the infinitive. How can we tell what the ***implied function*** is? One way is quite simply to give what seems to be a paraphrase that is logical in the context. This is the semantic approach in our paraphrase examples above. Underlying these, however, are more exact ***syntactic*** indications:

- If the ***infinitive verb*** is ***transitive*** and there is nothing else following it, the ***antecedent noun*** is the ***implied direct object*** (e.g. *presents to buy = presents that someone must buy*).
- If the ***infinitive verb*** is followed by a ***preposition*** and ***nothing else***, the ***antecedent noun*** is the implied ***prepositional complement*** (*no one to play with = no-one with whom someone can play*).
  If the infinitive verb is a ***prepositional verb***, of course, the ***antecedent noun*** is a ***prepositional*** (i.e. ***direct***) ***object***: *a moment to look forward to = a moment to* ***which*** (= ***Od***) *someone can look forward.*
- If the ***infinitive verb*** is
  a) ***intransitive*** (*no-one to sing*), or
  b) ***transitive*** with an ***object*** after it (*no-one to sing songs*),
  the ***antecedent noun*** is the ***implied subject*** (*no-one who can sing/no-one who can sing songs*).
- If the ***infinitive verb*** could be ***intransitive*** or ***transitive*** and there is nothing else following it, then syntax and meaning will be ambiguous, as in (31):

(31) a. At the moment we have no-one to drive.
(***transitive*** = no-one that we can drive, i.e. no passengers;
intransitive = no-one who can drive, i.e. no drivers)
b. There will be people to help.
(***transitive*** = people who need help; ***intransitive*** = people who can help).

Thirdly, ***transitive infinitives*** with nothing following, such as *a job to do, a family to support, customers to see, friends to visit,* etc. might at first sight be interpreted as passive in meaning. However, they are not. ***Passive*** meaning must be signalled clearly by the ***passive*** infinitive.

Generally, of course, active and passive verbs mean the same, and this is also true of the infinitive, i.e. *a job to do* and *a job to be done* are equivalent in meaning. However, they are still structurally different and in a sentence can mean rather different things:

(32) a. I have a job to do.
(= a job that I must do)
b. I have a job to be done.
(= a job that must be done by someone else).

That is, in the passive version the agent need not be specified, and might not be identical with the matrix subject. In the active version, the agent (i.e. the implied subject) is always identical with the matrix subject.

Postmodification in the noun phrase is described in detail in chapter 14.

060/5 Infinitive clauses as appositive postmodifications

A further type of noun ***postmodification*** is the ***appositive clause***:

(33) a. The committee did not accept Bradshaw's suggestion to build a new factory.
b. Caroline's intention to marry Olaf displeased her parents.
c. The plan to launch a manned spacecraft so soon is unrealistic.

The infinitives here are ***not*** the same as relative clauses and ***cannot*** be paraphrased by them. Here the infinitive states the ***content*** of what the antecedent noun ***refers to***. That is, it describes the antecedent noun in more detail. In a way, then, we can say that the ***antecedent noun*** and the ***infinitive clause*** mean the ***same thing***. We can express the meaning relation between them as follows:

(34) a. Bradshaw's suggestion was to build a new factory.
b. Caroline's intention was/is to marry Olaf.
c. The plan is to launch a manned spacecraft.

This kind of postmodification is known as an ***appositive postmodification***. It is common also, as we shall see later, with gerunds and *that*-clauses. The antecedent noun is typically an ***abstract noun*** referring to some mental or emotional state or act. (See chapter 14 for information on postmodification).

060/6 Infinitives of purpose

In full form these are expressed by ***in order to***, meaning 'with the purpose of (doing)'.
They are often shortened to the infinitive alone, especially in less formal style:

(35) a. Mavis has gone to the greengrocer's (in order) to buy oranges.
(... with the purpose of buying ...)
b. Inspector Dunway bent down (in order) to look at the footprints more closely.

Purpose infinitives are frequently used to give ***reasons*** for actions:

(36) a. Why has Mavis gone to the greengrocer's? ... (In order) to buy oranges
b. Why did Inspector Dunway bend down? ... (In order) to look at the footprints ...

060/6.1 Subject-subject relation

In order to structures require ***subject-subject*** relations. That is, the ***matrix subject*** must be the implied ***subject*** of the ***infinitive***.

In (35)a. and (36)a., for example, *Mavis* is the subject of both *has gone* and *to buy*. Similarly, in (35)b. and (36)b. *Inspector Dunway* is the ***subject*** of *bent down* and *to look at*.

A full purpose infinitive with ***in order to*** can only be used when there is ***subject identity*** of this kind.

060/6.2 Object-subject relation

On the other hand, ***reduced*** purpose infinitives, i.e. without ***in order***, allow an ***object-subject*** relation:

(37) a. We have hired a builder to repair the roof.
b. Bill called a taxi to take him to the airport.
c. The actor is paying this journalist to write his memoirs.

Here, it is the ***object*** of the ***matrix*** clause that is the implied ***subject*** of the ***infinitive***. In (37)c., for instance, it is the ***actor*** who ***pays***, but the ***journalist*** who ***writes***. These infinitives cannot have ***in order*** added to them. Neither can the infinitive be used alone in this form to answer a ***why***-question. In this case ***subject-subject*** identity is needed and the verbal expression must be changed accordingly, as in (40)b. and d., respectively:

(38) a. "Why did Bill call a taxi?" "*To take him to the airport."
b. "To get to the airport."
c. "Why is the actor paying this journalist?" "*To write his memoirs."
d. "To have his memoirs written."

060/6.3 Purpose meaning in noun postmodification

A ***postmodifying*** infinitive clause may convey a purpose meaning:

(39) a. We can't afford a chef just to cook for us.
b. The firm is developing a spray to kill insects.
c. At all cosmetic stores you can buy creams to remove body hair.

Despite the purpose meaning, however, these are ***not*** purpose infinitives as such, but ***modal relative infinitives***: *... a chef who would ...; ... a spray that can kill ...; ... creams that will/can remove ...*

It is the implied ***ability***-modal (e.g. *can*) and the particular lexical items used which lead in certain cases to the purpose meaning (see also **060/4.5**).

Notice that there may occasionally be ambiguity between ***infinitive clauses*** as ***post-modifiers*** and those functioning as separate purpose clauses. (40)a., for example, can mean either (40)b. or (40)c.:

(40) a. We need a spray to kill insects.
b. We need a spray which can kill insects.
c. We need a spray in order to kill insects (= so that we can kill them).

060/7 Infinitives in indirect questions and indirect commands

This has already been dealt with in chapter 11. Here we will restrict explanation to a few points presented from the perspective of the infinitive.

060/7.1 Indirect questions

Just as a reminder, what we are talking about here are indirect **wh-*questions***, in which infinitives play an important role. The main characteristic is the introduction of the subordinate (***interrogative***) clause by an ***interrogative pronoun*** or ***adverb***, such as *what, who, how*, etc.:

(41) a. I'll ask Julie what to give Ralph for Christmas.
b. I'll ask Julie what I should give Ralph for Christmas.

(41)a. and b. are different versions of the same sentence. As with ***modal relative infinitives*** (see under **060/4.3** above), the infinitive stands for a finite verb phrase containing a ***modal***, in this case usually *should* or *must*. The ***matrix subject*** must be the implied ***subject*** of the ***infinitive*** (i.e. a ***subject-subject*** relation is required). The ***matrix object***, i.e. *Julie* in (41), is an ***indirect object***. The catenative pattern here is obligatory ***verb + object + infinitive***, see **060/1.2** above.

060/7.2 Non-reported indirect questions

A certain type of indirect question does not report an actual utterance, but simply expresses a questioning attitude or a gap in knowledge. It is this type which occurs most frequently with the infinitive:

(42) a. Her boyfriend didn't know what to wear to the wedding.
b. I am just wondering who to invite to my little party.

In this type of meaning the infinitive can also follow appropriate adjectives and nouns. An intervening ***preposition*** is often necessary:

(43) a. We weren't quite sure about where to go for Chinese food.
(= ... where we should go ...)
b. Many students have questions on how to react to discipline problems in class.
(= ... how they should react ...)
c. Are you aware of what to do in the case of an emergency?
(= what you should do ...)

Non-reported indirect questions are not confined to gaps in knowledge. They are also considered to underlie statements on the presence of knowledge, i.e. as 'answers' to actual or implied questions. *We were quite sure about where to go for Chinese food; I'm aware of what to do in the case of an emergency.* (See also chapter 11).

060/7.3 Indirect commands

Like the indirect question type just presented under **060/7.1**, ***indirect commands*** follow the obligatory ***verb + object + infinitive*** pattern (see here also **060/1.2** above). Another similarity is that they too stand for finite verb phrases containing a ***modal***, also usually *should* or *must*, though sometimes *can/could/would*. The difference lies in the ***catenative type***, which here expresses (overtly or by implication) a ***command*** or ***request*** (*ask, tell, request, instruct, urge, command, order, warn*, etc.):

(44) a. The teacher told her pupils to listen carefully.
(... that they should/were to/must listen carefully)
b. The pupils asked their teacher to speak more slowly.
(... if she could/would speak more slowly)

A further difference lies in the syntax. Here the ***matrix object*** is the implied ***subject*** of the ***infinitive*** (i.e. there is an ***object-subject*** relation). The ***object*** itself, though (*her pupils/ their teacher*), is an ***indirect object***, just as before. As we saw in chapter 11 (**055/3.5**, also chapter 12, **057/4.13**) catenatives are often passivized. This happens with command and request verbs particularly when the command source is official or anonymous, and a certain softening of the command is required:

(45) a. Hotel guests are kindly requested not to smoke in the lobby.
b. The children were warned not to swim by the rocks.

Some command types (usually expressing instructions) are very close in meaning to non-reported indirect questions. They contain **wh-*words*** that stand for a knowledge gap and indicate answers to real or imagined questions:

(46) a. The manageress will show you how to operate the till.
b. Mr. Braithwaite was explaining to me where to park.
c. They had not told Wendy who to see at the bank.

Command infinitives can also follow a suitable ***noun***. They then function as an ***appositive postmodification*** (see under **060/5** above):

(47) a. The soldiers received orders to advance on the enemy lines.
b. Mother's instructions not to get dirty in the garden were ignored.

060/8 Consecutive infinitives

These convey a ***result*** or ***consequence***. They are always part of a ***noun phrase***, ***adverb phrase*** or ***adjective phrase*** and are typically associated with the quantifying expressions ***too*** (adverb of degree) and ***enough*** (adverb of degree and quantifier/determiner). Related expressions (e.g. *sufficient, to suffice*, etc.) also occur:

(48) a. Freeman didn't have enough courage to carry out his plan.
(= Freeman had so little courage that he couldn't carry out ...)
Freeman hatte nicht genug Mut, um seinen Plan in die Tat umzusetzen.

b. The children are too excited to sleep.
(= The children are so excited that they can't sleep.)
Die Kinder sind zu aufgeregt, um zu schlafen.

c. The company certainly has sufficient capital to develop further plants abroad.
(The company certainly has so much capital that it can develop ...)
Das Unternehmen verfügt zweifellos über ausreichend Kapital, um weitere Werke im Ausland aufzubauen.

⚠ Note here that German uses the *um ... zu*-construction. In this case, however, it does ***not*** signal a purpose clause, and ***cannot*** be rendered in English by *in order to*, i.e. ***not***, for example, **The children were too excited in order to sleep*, or *Freeman didn't have enough courage in order to carry out his plan*. ***In order to*** can be used ***only*** with ***purpose*** infinitives!

A further point to note is that here, too, the infinitive has a ***modal*** coloration in the ***ability*** sense (= *can/could, be able*).

And finally, the subject relation here is ***subject-subject***, i.e. the ***matrix subject*** is the implied ***subject*** of the ***infinitive*** (see, however, **060/8.6** below).

The following is a more detailed overview of structures involved.

060/8.1 too + adjective/adverb + infinitive

The consequence expressed here is a negative one. An action is prevented by the high level or quantity of a particular feature. The prevented action is expressed by the infinitive:

(49) a. The walls of the house are too thin to keep out traffic noise.
(= ... are so thin that they could not keep out ...)
Die Wände des Hauses sind zu dünn, um Verkehrslärm abzuhalten.

b. We were driving too fast to look at the landscape.
(... were driving so fast that we could not look ...)
Wir fuhren zu schnell, um die Landschaft betrachten zu können.

060/8.2 enough + noun + infinitive

Enough is used here as a quantifier. It means 'as much as required for a particular action or state'. It is more common in the negative and then means 'too little/too few for a particular action':

(50) a. Frank Dwyer is now earning enough money to buy a large house.
(= Frank Dwyer is able to buy a large house because he has the necessary income.)
Frank Dwyer verdient jetzt genug, um ein großes Haus zu kaufen.

b. We had not taken enough water with us to survive for more than ten days.
(We could not survive for more than ten days on the amount of water we had.)
Wir hatten nicht genug Wasser mitgenommen, um länger als 10 Tage überleben zu können.

Enough* + *noun is often alternatively expressed by ***the* + *noun*** (derived from ***the_neces-sary* + *noun***): *Mary had finally summoned the (necessary) courage to leave Stanley and end her marriage; We don't have the (necessary amount of) space to accommodate 20 guests.*

060/8.3 Adjective/adverb + enough + infinitive

Enough is used here as an adverb of degree. Note that (unusually for English) it follows the adjective or adverb it refers to. It can be paraphrased here as 'as much of the feature named as required for a particular state or action'. The negative means 'too little of the necessary feature':

(51) a. Brown is now playing well enough to be picked for the first team.
(... is now playing so well that he can be picked ...)
b. The walls of the house are not thick enough to keep out traffic noise.
(= ... cannot keep out traffic noise because they do not have the necessary thickness)

060/8.4 Verb + enough + infinitive

Enough in this case is either an adverb of degree (when it refers to a verb, as in a.), or it is a quantifier pronoun, as in b.:

(52) a. I hadn't slept enough to feel really refreshed.
b. We have saved quite a bit of money, and now we have enough to buy a small car.

060/8.5 so + adjective/adverb + as + infinitive

This is a more elevated (and slightly dated) way of saying *enough*, or 'to such a level that'. Except in set expressions like the one in c., this construction is not used much nowadays. Preferred alternatives are in brackets:

(53) a. Pauline's mother was so kind as to give us a bed for the night.
(Pauline's mother was kind enough to give us/very kindly gave us a bed for the night.)
b. Colin drove so fast as to scare everyone in the car.
(Colin drove so fast that he scared everyone in the car.)
c. Would you be so kind as to help me?

In direct requests for help, as in c., the expression is still heard, and is very polite. More neutral is *Would you mind ...?*

060/8.6 Subject-object relations and the 'open slot'

All examples so far have had the ***subject-subject*** relation usual for this construction. There are cases, however, where the ***matrix subject*** is the implied ***object*** of the ***infinitive***.

(54) a. My bags were too heavy to carry.
b. The soup was too hot to eat.
c. All luxury goods must be cheap enough to buy.

This case is rather like that of the modal relative infinitive (see **060/4.3** and **5** above). Where the infinitive is ***transitive*** and ***nothing follows it***, the resulting 'open slot' is regarded as implicitly filled by the ***matrix subject***.

The ***passive*** infinitive could be used here too: *My bags were too heavy to be carried; The soup was too hot to be eaten; All luxury goods must be cheap enough to be bought*. However, the passive form is a little clumsy in many cases and is usually avoided. The active infinitive gives a neater solution.

This does not mean, though, that the active infinitive here is really 'passive' in meaning. Passivization is no longer possible when we introduce the ***active subject*** in a ***for***-construction, e.g. *The soup was too hot for us to eat*. This therefore no longer has 'passive' meaning. The ***subject-object*** relation, however, still remains. (The ***for***-construction is dealt with properly below under **060/10.2**).

Just as with modal relatives, the 'open slot' concept extends here also to usage with ***prepositions***. An open slot after prepositions tells us that the ***matrix subject*** is now also the implied ***prepositional complement*** in the infinitive clause:

(55) a. The ice on the pond is too thin to walk on.
b. The water will be too cold to swim in.
c. That light is not bright enough to see by.

060/8.7 The obligatory 'open slot' and common errors connected with it

So far we have taken the correct English sentence as given, and explained how to understand the syntax of the 'open slot' receptively. However, the slot also has to be produced: in other words, it is obligatory with infinitive constructions of the type discussed.

The rule is: If the ***matrix subject*** is identical with the ***object*** or the ***prepositional complement*** of the ***infinitive clause***, then those functions ('slots') ***must*** be left ***empty***.

⚠ The following are common errors:

(56) a. *My bags were too heavy to carry them.
b. *The ice on the pond is too thin to walk on it.
c. *The soup was too hot for me to be eaten.

Note once more that the ***active infinitive*** is always preferred over the passive infinitive, especially in speech, i.e. *My bags were too heavy to carry*, rather than *My bags were too heavy to be carried*.

060/9 The perfect, progressive and passive forms of the infinitive

060/9.1 General time-orientation of the infinitive

It has already been said that non-finite verbs do not usually have to be marked for tense. Generally, they have the same time orientation as their catenatives.

Consider:

(57) a. Sally likes to go to bed early on weekdays.
b. Sally liked to go to bed early on weekdays.
c. Sally would like to go to bed early on weekdays.

To go is ***present***-oriented in (57)a., following ***likes***. It is ***past***-oriented in (57)b., following ***liked***, and it is ***future***-oriented in (57)c., following ***would like***. That is, the orientation corresponds to the time-reference of the main verb.

060/9.2 Contrasting time-orientation of the perfect infinitive

When the infinitive has an ***earlier*** time-reference than that of its accompanying main verb, the ***perfect infinitive*** is necessary:

(58) a. The guests appear to have left yesterday morning.
(= It appears that they left ...)
b. The victim seemed to have met a friend in a pub the night before the murder.
(= It seemed that she had met a friend ...)
c. Sawyer claims to have broken his leg.
(= Sawyer claims that he has broken his leg ...)

In (58)a. the ***perfect infinitive*** stands for a ***finite past tense***, in (58)b. for a ***finite past perfect***, and in (58)c. for a ***finite present perfect***. In other words, the ***perfect infinitive*** functions as the ***infinitive form*** of the ***past tense***, the ***present perfect*** and the ***past perfect***.

It can also stand for a ***future perfect***. Here it is oriented not to the catenative, but to a future point of time indicated by context and adverbials. It then means '***earlier*** than this': *We expect you to have finished the job when we get back from America.*

060/9.3 The progressive infinitive

Progressive and ***base forms*** of the infinitive contrast aspectually in the same way as the progressive and simple forms of finite verbs:

(59) a. The managers expect us to be making tea for them when they get here.
b. The managers expect us to make tea for them when they get here.

Here we have the typical distinction between a ***framework situation*** in (59)a., and a ***whole action*** in (59)b. In a. the action of making tea is expected by the managers to be ***in progress*** already when they arrive, but in b. to start when they arrive. That is, the ***whole***

action meaning of the base infinitive leads to the interpretation of sequence (*arrive* and then *make*).

060/9.4 The perfect progressive infinitive

Like the ordinary perfect infinitive, this can function either as a ***past tense*** or as a ***perfect***, but with ***progressive meaning***, of course:

(60) a. It must be awful to have been lying out there in the cold for hours.
(= ***continuative present perfect*** – 'up-to-now', or ***continuative past perfect*** – 'up-to-then')
b. The pots are clean: someone appears to have been doing the washing-up.
(= ***secondary resultative present perfect***)
c. He claims to have been eating in a restaurant on the Lower East Side at the time of the murder, but the police don't believe him.
(= ***past tense*** use in a ***framework situation***)

060/9.5 The passive infinitive

The ***passive infinitive*** could also be called the 'infinitive form of the passive'. It is formed with **(to) be +** ***past participle*** of ***main verb***: *to be loved, to be seen, to be done,* etc. Use and meaning of the passive are the same as with finite verbs:

(61) a. We intended to be seen and we were seen.
b. Jane wanted to be chosen as a candidate and she was chosen.

And in the following the contrast between ***active*** and ***passive infinitives***:

(62) a. Sam did not expect to be cheated by other shopkeepers.
b. Sam did not expect other shopkeepers to cheat him.

There are two special points to note:

- Firstly, the ***passive*** is ***not*** used in the ***progressive infinitive forms***. For instance, the ***active*** sentence *Jason is believed to have been re-organizing the business* would not normally be turned into its ***passive*** equivalent **The business is believed to have been being re-organized.* Sentences like this are not ungrammatical, and are even heard occasionally. But they are normally avoided for reasons of style. A paraphrase would be preferred, e.g. *The business is believed to have been in the process of re-organization.*
- ⚠ Secondly, in German, the ordinary active infinitive is used in certain cases with passive meaning. However, in English this is ***never*** the case. With English infinitives, ***passive meaning*** can be expressed ***only*** in the ***passive form***:

(63) a. Der Mann ist zu bedauern.
The man is to be pitied.

b. Das zu verkaufende Auto stand in der Einfahrt.
The car that was being sold/was to be sold was parked in the driveway.

060/10 Syntax: sentence functions in and around the infinitive

We have mentioned various individual syntactic points connected with infinitive clause functions, but here we will give a more detailed overview.

060/10.1 The infinitive clause

Infinitives form separate subordinate clauses with their own complementation (i.e. objects, complements, adverbials). In their own clauses they function as ***predicators (P)*** like any finite verb. The infinitive clause, like any other subordinate clause, has a functional relation to its matrix clause. It can function as ***subject (S)***, ***direct object (Od)***, ***adverbial (A)***, ***subject complement (Cs)***, or ***object complement (Co)***:

Od
(64) a. Roberta planned [to fly to London].
A
b. She was flying to London [to see her parents].
Cs
c. Roberta's plan was [to fly to London].
Co
d. Roberta wanted her brother [to fly to London].
S
e. [To see her parents] was Roberta's greatest desire.

We have listed the subject function last here, as it is a little unusual. The preferred form of the sentence in (64)e. would be an ***extraposition***:

S-gramm. ***S-log.***
(65) ***It*** was Roberta's greatest desire [***to see her parents***].

With ***extraposition***, the infinitive clause is pushed to the end of the sentence and replaced at the beginning by an 'empty' ***it***. ***It*** is the ***grammatical subject*** and the ***infinitive clause*** is the ***logical subject*** of the sentence. The syntax of ***extraposition*** was also presented in chapter 7 (**039/2.2**).

Internally, infinitive clauses are analysed like any other, with the infinitive itself, as mentioned above, functioning as ***predicator (P)***. A complete analysis of (64)a. and b., then, looks like this:

S P Od P A
(66) a. Roberta planned [to fly to London].
S P A A P Od
b. She was flying to London [to see her parents].

060/10.2 The subject function inside the infinitive clause

As we have already seen, the ***subject*** of the ***infinitive*** is not ***overt*** (i.e. actually present), but normally ***implied***. It is usually identical with a subject or object in the matrix clause.

When the infinitive follows a ***catenative*** directly, as in (64)a., the ***matrix subject*** is the implied ***infinitive subject***. When the ***matrix verb*** is a ***non-catenative***, this is only the case when the infinitive clause is ***adverbial***, as in (64)b. Otherwise there is ***no*** subject-subject identity, as in (64)c. and e.

When a ***matrix catenative*** has an ***object*** in the matrix clause (i.e. between it and the infinitive clause), this is the implied ***infinitive subject***, as in (64)d.

In all other cases, the ***infinitive subject*** is implied ***semantically*** by context and lexis. In (64)c., for instance, it is clearly *Roberta*, the only person mentioned. In (64)e. there is another personal noun, *her parents*, but this is the direct object of the infinitive. Again, the only possibility remaining for the infinitive subject is Roberta herself.

Changing the lexical items can often change the subject implication. In (67)a. below, for instance, the infinitive subject cannot be inferred from the sentence. It may be Roberta, or it may not. If we want to make this clear, we can make the ***infinitive subject overt***, i.e. state it expressly. This is done with the help of the **for-*construction***, as in (67) b.:

(67) a. It was Roberta's idea to get a dog.
b. It was Roberta's idea ***for Mrs. Penrose*** to get a dog.

The **for-*construction*** is used particularly when the actual infinitive subject is different from what might otherwise be implied. In (64)c., for instance, there can be no doubt that the implied infinitive subject is *Roberta*, as we saw. However, if the plan is about someone else flying to London, the infinitive subject must be overt: *Roberta's plan was* ***for her brother*** *to fly to London.*

Apart from clarifying the infinitive subject, the **for-*construction*** is also used to emphasize the subject personally: *It would be best* ***for me*** *to take my annual holiday in July (as I am needed here in August to arrange the conference).*

Another way of introducing the infinitive subject (already seen above) is with ***of***. This is more restricted, though. It is confined to adjectives which express a 'behaviour' comment on the action: *It was rather nice* ***of Marion*** *to invite me to her party.*

Otherwise, preference is for leaving the subject unstated, as it is normally implied in the social context, e.g. *It's going to be difficult to get there on time*, spoken by one person to another in a car stuck in a traffic queue (= *It's going to be difficult for us to get there on time*).

In addition, finally, there is the generalized reference, where the agent is unknown, unimportant or just 'people in general':

(68) a. It was irresponsible and selfish to leave rubbish in the woods like that.
b. It is dangerous to bathe near the rocks at the eastern end of the beach.

060/10.3 Functions of the infinitive clause with catenatives

We return now to look at the functions of the infinitive clause as a whole.

When the infinitive clause directly follows a ***matrix catenative*** verb, the function of the clause is usually that of ***direct object (Od)***:

		Od
(69)	a. We were hoping	[to arrive before midnight].
		Od
	b. The children didn't manage	[to fly the model aircraft].

After a catenative verb of ***being***, ***seeming*** or ***becoming*** the infinitive clause is ***subject complement (Cs)***. After other verb types it can be an ***adverbial (A)***:

		Cs
(70)	a. Jamie appeared	[to be happy].
		A
	b. We stopped	[to buy food].

The ***adverbial*** here expresses ***purpose***.

Matrix verbs may have their own ***adverbials*** preceding the sub-clause, e.g. *We were hoping* ***desperately*** *to arrive before midnight; We stopped* ***on the way to London*** *to buy food.*

Catenatives like *want* and *like* can be ***complex transitive***. They then take a ***direct object (Od)*** in the ***matrix***, with the infinitive clause as ***object complement (Co)***.

Others, like *tell* and *ask*, are ***ditransitive***. These take an ***indirect object (Oi)*** in the matrix, with the infinitive clause is ***direct object (Od)***:

		Od	***Co***
(71)	a. Billy wanted	Rita	[to marry him].
		Oi	***Od***
	b. Billy asked	Rita	[to marry him].

These are the two major syntactic-functional patterns with the very common construction ***verb + object + infinitive clause***. Which of the two is the right one in a particular case depends on the individual catenative and its meaning.

The following common catenatives are regarded as ***complex transitive***: *compel, encourage, expect, force, hate, help, intend, lead, like, mean, oblige, prefer, tempt; let* and *make* also belong to this group, but take the infinitive without *to*. All these verbs, that is, have the *want*-pattern in (71)a.

The following are considered ***ditransitive***, like *ask* in (71)b.: *advise, allow, forbid, instruct, invite, order, permit, persuade, remind, request, show how, teach, tell, urge, warn*. These refer mainly to acts of ***communication***, placing the following personal object in the ***recipient*** role, the typical role of the indirect object.

060/10.4 Catenatives in the passive

With the infinitive, ***monotransitive catenatives*** cannot be passivized. That is, the infinitive clause cannot become a passive subject: **To swim was learnt by John*. **Extraposition** is ***not*** possible either: **It was promised by Bill and Mandy to feed the dog everyday.*

However, many ***complex transitive*** and all ***ditransitive catenatives*** allow the passive, and in fact are often passivized. This is because in many contexts the verbal meaning is in the foreground, emphasis is on the ***patient*** (i.e. the 'sufferer'), and the agent is unimportant:

(72) a. After that experience, she will never be tempted to get drunk again.
b. I had been asked to go to a party on that evening.
c. The soldiers were ordered to guard the presidential palace.

The passive softens commands and requests (see also chapter 12), and is very common in public announcements: *Passengers are requested to join their vehicles immediately.* All catenative actions involving outside force or communication 'attract' the passive: *You were expected to get here on time; Cynthia was forbidden to enter the shop again; The children have been taught to treat animals kindly.*

Note that there are several ***catenatives*** in the ***complex transitive*** group which do not form passives, e.g. *want, like, prefer, hate.*

All ***ditransitive catenatives*** allow the passive, but note that only the indirect object can become the passive subject, i.e. we cannot say **To enter the shop again was forbidden to Cynthia.*

060/10.5 Infinitive clause functions with adjectives

With ***adjectives*** the infinitive clause is usually ***part*** of the ***adjective phrase***. That is to say, it has no function at sentence level, but merely at phrase level, as an ***adjectival complement***. In the sentence *Barbara is keen to go to university,* and *Helen was sad to leave,* the phrase functions are:

	Head	Adjectival Complement
(73)	keen	to go to university
	sad	to leave

The adjective phrase as a whole functions as the ***subject complement (Cs)*** of the sentence. An analysis of the whole sentence in each case would then be:

	S	P	Cs	P	A
(74) a.	Barbara	is	[keen	[to go	to university]].

	S	P	Cs	P
b.	Helen	was	[sad	[to leave]].

With ***extraposition*** and the **for-*construction*** or adjectival **of-*construction***, the analysis is:

S-gramm ***P*** ***Cs*** ***S-log*** ***S*** ***P*** ***Od*** ***A***
(75) a. It would be [best] [for me to take my holiday in July].
S-gramm ***P*** ***Cs*** ***(S)*** ***S-log*** ***P*** ***Od*** ***A***
b. It was [nice [of Marion]] [to invite me to her party].

The **for-*construction*** is analysed here simply as a subject-indicator inside the infinitive clause.

Note that the syntax of the **of-*construction*** is a little different. This takes account of the fact that *of* partly relates the adjective to the person; it is therefore shown as an adjectival complement. The (S) above *Marion* and the lower arrow indicate her as the implied ***infinitive subject***.

In the sentences *Gina is likely to win the competition, Avocados are good to eat,* and *Brenda is nice to be with* we have ***false subject constructions***. These are analysed as follows:

S-gramm ***P*** ***Cs*** ***S-log*** ***P*** ***Od***
(76) a. Gina is [likely] [to win the competition].
(S) →
S-gramm ***P*** ***Cs*** ***S-log*** ***P***
b. Avocados are [good] [to eat].
(Od) →
S-gramm ***P*** ***Cs*** ***S-log*** ***P*** ***A***
c. Brenda is [nice] [to be with].
(part of A) →

As with extraposition, we have here also ***two subjects***. One is the apparent (***false***) subject, ***S-gramm***, the other the real subject, i.e. the ***infinitive clause, S-log***. What we have shown additionally is where the false subject really belongs: i.e. in (76)a. *Gina* is semantically the implied ***infinitive subject***; in (76)b. *avocados* is the implied ***infinitive direct object***; and in (76)c. *Brenda* is the implied ***prepositional complement*** of *with* (= part of an ***adverbial***) in the ***infinitive clause***.

Finally, we come to ***consecutive infinitives***. These are regular ***adjectival complements*** like those partnering the adjectives in (74). However, where there is an open slot, implied ***direct objects*** and ***prepositional complements*** in the ***infinitive clause*** are also marked accordingly by arrows:

S ***P*** ***Cs*** ***P***
(77) a. My bags were [too heavy [to carry]].
(Od) →
S ***P*** ***Cs*** ***P*** ***A***
b. The water will be [too cold [to swim in]].
(A) →

060/10.6 Infinitive clause functions with nouns

The syntax of the ***infinitive clause*** with ***nouns*** is similar to that of adjectives. That is, the ***infinitive clause*** is usually ***part*** of the ***noun phrase***. It then functions at phrase level as a ***postmodification***, as has already been mentioned several times. In the sentences *I once met the first person to swim the Channel*, and *The man to see is Bob*, the phrase functions are:

		Premodification	***Head***	***Postmodification***
(78)	a.	the first	person	to swim the Channel
	b.	the	man	to see

The noun phrase as a whole functions in the first case as the ***direct object (Od)*** of the sentence, in the second as ***subject (S)*** of the sentence. A full analysis is therefore:

S A P Od P Od
(79) a. I once met [the first person [to swim the Channel]].
S P P Cs
b. [The man [to see]] is Bob.

The postmodifying infinitives have the meanings here of ***relative clauses***. In the first case (with an ordinal number), the ***antecedent noun***, i.e. the head, is the implied ***infinitive subject***. In the second, a ***modal relative infinitive***, the ***antecedent noun*** is the implied ***infinitive direct object***.

Note that we are referring now to functions ***inside*** the noun phrase. As the analysis in (79) shows, these are quite independent of, and have nothing to do with, the ***sentence function*** of the noun phrase ***as a whole***.

Appositive and ***consecutive infinitives*** are also ***postmodifications***:

S P Od P Od
(80) a. [Caroline's intention [to marry Olaf]] displeased her parents.
S P Od P Od
b. We did not have [enough money [to join the tennis club].

Extraposition and ***false subject constructions*** with nouns follow exactly the same patterns as with adjectives. Here the infinitive clauses are ***not*** postmodifications:

S-gramm P Cs S-log P Od
(81) a. It would be [a shame] [to miss the match].
S-gramm P Cs S-log P Od
b. The manager was [a fool] [to sell those players].
S-gramm P Cs S-log P
c. Arsenal are [a pleasure] [to watch].

13.2 The gerund

061 Form, syntax, general meaning
062 Gerund constructions

Form, syntax, general meaning 061

061/1 The subject of a gerund
061/2 The gerund clause as subject
061/3 Tense, aspect and passive with the gerund

The ***gerund*** is an *-ing*-form. It refers to actions or fields of activity. It names them in the same way that a noun does (*swimming, fishing, eating*), and functions syntactically in a sentence like a noun:

(82) a. Swimming is fun. [***subject***]
b. I love fishing. [***direct object***]
c. His favourite pastime was eating. [***subject complement***]

For this reason the gerund is generally regarded as a ***nominal*** *-ing*-form. In this respect it is similar to the infinitive, which also takes on 'nominal' sentence functions like subject and direct object. However, the nominal character of the gerund is even stronger. Unlike the infinitive, the gerund

- is ***only nominal*** and can ***never*** be used as an adverbial,
- can appear as the ***complement*** of a ***preposition*** (*a rod for fishing*),
- can be the first or second element in a ***compound noun*** (*a fishing-rod, shark- fishing*),
- can be preceded by an **s-*genitive*** or a ***possessive determiner*** (*He did not like my fishing right next to him*).

Similar to the infinitive, on the other hand, is the fact that the gerund introduces its own ***subordinate clause***, functions as ***predicator*** inside it, and can have its ***own complementation*** just like any finite verb:

	S	P	Od		
			P	Od	
(83) a.	Monkeys	like	[eating	nuts].	

	S		P		Od	P	Cs
b.	[Taking photographs]					is	my job.

Inside its own clause, that is, the ***gerund*** has a ***verbal*** character. It is only the gerund clause ***as a whole*** that is ***nominal*** in its relation to the rest of the sentence, as (83) shows.

It is important to remember that when we talk about constructions with 'the gerund', we are speaking rather loosely: more exactly, we mean the ***gerund clause***. (The same point applies to the infinitive, too, of course).

061/1 The subject of a gerund

As with the other non-finite verbs, the ***gerund subject*** can be ***general***, or ***implied***. The implication can be in the social situation, the wider context, or, more narrowly, in the rest of the sentence:

(84) a. Jogging is healthy. (***general***)
b. Sitting here on the beach in this high wind isn't very pleasant, is it?
(e.g. ... as we are doing at the moment ...: ***contextually and socially implied***)
c. Spending a few days on the coast will do ***you*** good. (***implied in sentence***)

As with infinitives, the most usual type of subject implication occurs after a ***catenative***: the ***catenative subject*** is then the ***implied subject*** of the ***gerund***:

```
           S        P      Od   P    Od
(85) a. Monkeys  like   [eating nuts].
           (S) ─────────────→
```

When there is divergence between the two subjects, the ***gerund subject*** is made ***explicit***. Traditionally, this is done by placing it as a ***genitive noun*** (or ***possessive determiner***) before the gerund:

(86) a. Tom resented ***Dick's*** playing golf without him.
(= Dick played golf without Tom and Tom resented it.)
b. My boss hates ***my*** getting to work late.
(= I sometimes get to work late and my boss hates it.)

However, the use of genitive and possessive in this way is now seen as rather elevated, and/or a little dated. In ordinary neutral language the ***s***-genitive is replaced by the ***ordinary noun***, and the possessive determiner by the ***object form*** of the ***pronoun***:

(87) a. Tom resented ***Dick*** playing golf without him.
b. My boss hates ***me*** getting to work late.

Genitive/possessive forms still tend to be preferred when the ***gerund*** clause ***begins*** the sentence. In the following many would choose (88)a. and c., rather than (88)b. and d., unless using very informal style:

(88) a. ***Dick's*** playing golf without him annoyed Tom.
b. Dick playing golf without him annoyed Tom.
c. ***My*** getting to work late makes my boss angry.
d. Me getting to work late makes my boss angry.

Finally, in sentence analysis, the added ***gerund subject*** (even though a genitive or an object pronoun) is regarded as ***part of the gerund clause*** and marked ***S***. A full analysis would then look, for example, like this:

S P Od S P Od A
(89) a. Tom resented [Dick('s) playing golf without him].
S P Od S P A A
b. My boss hates [my/me getting to work late].
S S P A A P Od Co
c. [My/me getting to work late] makes my boss angry.

061/2 The gerund clause as subject

We have had several examples so far of gerunds and gerund clauses functioning as the ***subject*** of a sentence, see (82)a., (84)a., (88), (89)c. This is far more common than with the infinitive, where it is usually avoided and turned into an ***extraposition***. But ***extraposition*** is used with the gerund too, especially in speech, to give emphasis:

(90) a. It's great fun swimming in a rough sea.
(= Swimming in a rough sea is great fun.)
b. It was a profound experience reading that novel.
(= Reading that novel was a profound experience.)
c. It might be difficult adjusting to life in a different climate.
(= Adjusting to life in a different climate might be difficult.)

The emphasis comes from the position at the end of the sentence. In English this tends to give new or important information more profile. The syntactic analysis is the same as with the infinitive:

S-gramm. ***S-log.***
(91) ***It*** is great fun [***swimming in a rough sea***].

Gerunds also function frequently as the 'subjects' of abbreviated sentences in the telegram style of public notices: *No camping; Painting in progress; Dumping prohibited.*

061/3 Tense, aspect and passive with the gerund

With regard to tense and aspect, there are ***three*** forms of the ***gerund***:

a. ***the gerund base form*** ⟶ *running*
b. ***the perfect gerund*** ⟶ *having run*
c. ***the perfect progressive gerund*** ⟶ *having been running*

The ***gerund*** therefore has ***two tenses***, but makes an ***aspect distinction*** only in the ***perfect***. In table form:

Tense	Aspect	
	Simple	***Progressive***
Base form ***Non-perfect***	running	
Perfect	having run	having been running

061/3.1 Tense usage

There is often no need to distinguish in usage between the ***base form*** and the ***perfect***. (92)a. and b., for instance, mean the same:

(92) a. They accused Riley of ***stealing*** the watch.
b. They accused Riley of ***having stolen*** the watch.

This is because, depending upon the ***catenative*** used, the ***base form*** itself often suggests a ***past*** meaning in relation to it. In (92)a., for example, ***stealing*** means 'that he had stolen'. As the time-level difference between the ***catenative*** and the ***gerund*** is clear, the perfect gerund form, as in (92)b., is not necessary (though it is a perfectly correct alternative). This ***pastness*** of ***base gerund reference*** has to do with what we describe below as its ***factive*** meaning (see **062/1** and **2**).

061/3.2 Aspect

There are two points to make here.

- Firstly, unlike the infinitive, the gerund has ***no*** *base + progressive form*, such as **being eating*.
- Secondly, despite being an *ing*-form itself, the ***base gerund*** is ***not*** usually used for progressive meaning. Generally, it expresses ***simple form*** meaning, i.e. the ***whole*** of an action. (93)a., that is, means (93)b. Consequently, (93)c. means (93)d.

(93) a. Do you remember running along the river bank to the boathouse?
b. Do you remember that we/how we ran along the river bank to the boathouse?
c. Do you remember running along the river bank to the boathouse when we saw that boy fall into the water?
d. Do you remember that we/how we ran along the river bank to the boathouse when/after we saw the boy fall into the water?

It is important to realize, then, that (93)c. does ***not*** express a framework situation, but a ***sequence*** of actions: *We saw the boy … and then ran to the boathouse* (e.g. *to get help*).

How, then, can a ***framework situation*** be expressed? One solution is to use the ***perfect gerund***, as this does have a ***progressive*** variant. As the ***perfect gerund*** usually has the ***same time reference*** as the base form, its ***progressive*** variant can normally be used as an equivalent for the 'missing base form progressive'. Other possibilities are either to use a ***lexical*** alternative, as in (94)b., or simply to keep the ***finite verb*** form, as in (94)c.

In the following, then, all three express ***the same framework*** situation:

(94) a. Do you remember ***having been running*** along the river bank to the boathouse when we saw that boy fall into the water?
b. Do you remember being ***in the middle of*** running along the river bank to the boathouse when we saw that boy fall into the water?
c. Do you remember that we/how ***we were running*** along the river bank to the boathouse when we saw the boy fall into the water?

The ***simple form*** version of (94)a. (i.e. *having run*), on the other hand, would mean the same as the base form gerund in (93)a. and c.

061/3.3 The passive gerund in the two tenses

There are two ***passive*** forms, one in the ***base form*** and the other in the ***perfect***. There is ***no*** progressive equivalent in either:

(95) a. Jane resents being transferred to another department.
b. Jane resents having been transferred to another department.

Both sentences can mean *Jane resents the fact that she was transferred …* However, they may point to different time levels. (95)a., for instance, could refer to the future (*Jane resents the fact that she is going to be transferred …*). In this case, (95)b. is not equivalent.

061/3.4 The gerund with stative verbs

We said above that the gerund typically refers to actions or fields of activity.
However, states and acts of perception are not excluded:

(96) a. Just being in New York made Gail happy.
b. We suddenly regretted owning such a big car.
c. The boss does not like hearing that sort of remark.

Gerund constructions 062

062/1 The gerund after verbs
062/2 Catenatives: gerund or infinitive according to meaning
062/3 Catenatives: gerund or infinitive according to grammar
062/4 Catenatives: gerund or infinitive with little or no difference
062/5 The gerund after prepositions
062/6 The gerund in noun compounds
062/7 The action nominal

062/1 The gerund after verbs

Just as many ***catenatives*** are followed by the infinitive, so others take the ***gerund***. Some of these take only the gerund (*finish*, for example, as in *I have finished doing my work*). Others can alternatively be followed by ***that***-clauses, e.g. *suggest*: *Sally suggested going to an Indian restaurant for a meal* / *Sally suggested that we (should) go/went to an Indian restaurant for a meal.*

Others again can combine with either ***gerund*** or ***infinitive***, though usually with a difference in meaning: *My wife proposed buying a Japanese car/My wife proposed to buy a Japanese car* (where in the first example *propose* means *suggest* and in the second *intend*).

We look at individual catenatives and their various possible complementations from section **062/1.2** onwards.

062/1.1 A general relation between gerund and catenative meanings

The gerund usually refers to ***facts***. That is, we can render the sentences in (95) and (96) a. and b. as

(97) a. Jane resents the fact that she has been transferred to another department.
b. Just the fact that she was in New York made Gail happy.
c. We suddenly regretted the fact that we owned such a big car.

It is actually impossible to 'resent' or 'regret' something that does not exist or is not a fact. It would be nonsense, for example, to state (97)a. if Jane had not in fact been transferred to another department. Catenatives like these are called ***factive*** verbs. They require the statement in the sub-clause to be true. Otherwise they do not make any sense. This is why they are 'attracted' to gerunds.

Most ***factive*** verbs express a ***mental attitude*** or a ***feeling*** towards something that has happened. The majority of catenatives followed by gerunds are like this. Most typically they are ***retrospective*** acts, i.e. they ***look back*** on a ***gerund act*** that has already happened. Precisely this is where the ***pastness*** of the gerund meaning comes from. The gerund act must be 'in the past' (or at least partly 'in the past') in relation to the catenative attitude.

As a further illustration, we will contrast verbs like *resent* and *regret* with verbs like *think* and *say*. We can say *Jane said/thought that she had been transferred to another department.* But we cannot say **Jane said/thought the fact that she had been transferred to another department.* In other words, whereas *regret* and *resent* are ***factive*** verbs, *say* and *think* are ***non-factive***. In general, ***non-factive*** catenatives are ***not*** used with the ***gerund***: **Jane said/thought being transferred ...*

This is not a definite rule, and there are several exceptions. But it is a general principle that gives a certain guide as to which verbs take the gerund and which do not.

062/1.2 Verbs with the gerund only

These are: *avoid, can't/couldn't help, can't/couldn't stand, can't/couldn't endure, defer, delay, enjoy, entail, excuse, finish, give up, involve, it's no use/no good/ worth/not worth, keep (on), mind, miss, postpone, prevent, put off, resist, risk, save, tolerate*

Examples:

(98) a. We must not delay starting the job any longer.
b. Your headache does not excuse your being rude to everybody.
c. Speculating on the stock-market always involves taking certain risks.
d. Gina liked the hotel, but she missed not having a whole room to herself.
e. If you can give me a stamp it will save me going to the post-office.

There is a special case of gerund use with the verbs *come* and *go*: *go swimming/shopping/hiking/mountain climbing*, etc.; *come dancing/fishing/cycling*, etc. The unusual point here is that the gerund appears after ***intransitive*** verbs in an ***adverbial*** function. Consequently, some grammar writers view the *-ing*-form here as a participle and not as a gerund.

However, we will regard it as a ***gerund***. The point is discussed more fully under ***Participles*** below (see 13.3. **064/3.5**).

062/1.3 Verbs with gerund or that-clause

These are: *admit, anticipate, deny, dread, imagine, recollect, resent (+ the fact that), suggest.*

Examples:

(99) a. We had anticipated winning the competition/... that we would win ...
b. Blackstone denied being drunk at the wheel of his car/... that he had been ...
c. Just imagine lying on the beach now in the hot sun/... that we are lying ...

There are no semantic differences between the two forms with these verbs.

062/1.4 Verbs with gerund or infinitive

These are as follows. The underlined verbs can additionally take a **that**-***clause***:

advise, <u>agree</u>, allow, attempt, bear, begin, <u>consider</u>, continue, <u>decide</u>, go on, hate, intend, like, love, <u>mean</u>, need, permit, prefer, <u>propose</u>, <u>recommend</u>, <u>regret</u>, <u>remember</u>, <u>remind</u>, start, stop, try, <u>understand</u>, want (= be necessary), <u>warn</u>

With these verbs there are three different possibilities for the gerund-infinitive relation:

- The catenative has two different meanings, depending on which form follows (*consider, bear, go on, hate, like, love, mean, prefer, propose, regret, remember, stop, try, understand, want*).
- The syntax (but not the meaning) of the catenative determines the form that follows (*advise, agree, allow, decide, need, permit, recommend, remind, want, warn*).
- There is basically no difference, though there may be certain collocational restrictions (*attempt, begin, dread, continue, intend, start*).

Gerunds and *that*-clauses (where these are possible) are usually semantically equivalent, though there are one or two exceptions. Individual verbs are presented in detail in the sections following.

062/2 Catenatives: gerund or infinitive according to meaning

062/2.1 consider, go on, bear

- **consider**: ***object + infinitive***, but only with certain stative verbs (principally *be, have, mean*). The meaning is then *believe* (*= have an opinion about*) or *regard as*: *At the time people considered her to be the finest actress of the age.*
  The most usual complementation in this meaning is a **that-*clause***: *At the time people considered that she was the finest actress of the age.*
  With the ***gerund*** **consider** means *think about*: *We are considering taking a holiday in Scotland this year.*
  That-*clauses* occur in this meaning too, but with appropriate ***modal*** verbs: *We are considering that we might take a holiday in Scotland this year.*
- **go on**: ***infinitive***, in the meaning *turn to a new action or topic*, or *enter a new phase*: *Having discussed America, the speaker went on to talk about Britain; After years on the London stage, she went on to achieve great success in films.*
  With the ***gerund***, **go on** has the ***factive*** meaning of *continue*: *Everyone thought the scandal would end her career, but she went on attracting large audiences.*
- **bear:** ***gerund***, in the negative form *can't bear*, meaning *can't endure, hate*: *She can't bear people contradicting her* (*= when it happens it makes her very angry*), ***factive***.
  Also related meaning, without modal, but negative and usually figurative: *The boss's remarks at the general meeting don't bear repeating* (i.e. *they shouldn't be repeated, as they were shocking and offensive*). Note here the unusual ***passive*** meaning of the ***gerund*** verb. More is said on this below in **062/2.5**.
  With ***infinitive***, ***non-factive***, suggesting that the action is avoided or prevented, e.g.: *My dog can't bear strangers to touch him* (*and prevents them from doing so if they try*); *I couldn't bear to say goodbye* (*and therefore didn't go to the airport to see them off*).

062/2.2 hate, like, love, prefer

With the ***gerund***, all these verbs are typically ***factive***.

- **hate**, **like**, **love**: ***gerund***, typical with habits, but also with single actions: *We hated staying at that dirty hotel* (*= we stayed at that dirty hotel and hated it*); *John likes smoking cigars* (*= he smokes cigars and likes it*); *Sarah loved spending the summer with the Ellenbogens in New Hampshire* (*= Sarah spent the summer with the Ellenbogens … and loved it*).
  In American English, the ***infinitive*** is preferred in ***habit*** meanings. In British English the infinitive is heard occasionally, but only when there is ***reduced factivity***: *Fred hates to eat fast food* (*and avoids it whenever he can!*); *I like to watch the waves crashing on the rocks at high-tide* (*though I don't get the chance to do so very often*).
  The infinitive generally has a 'theoretical' tone to it (in keeping with its general ***non-factive*** meaning); it is therefore always used with 'conditional' *would*: *We would hate to*

stay at that hotel again (and will avoid it in future); Would you like to come with us on Sunday, Tom?

With the ***infinitive***, *like* has a further, different ***non-factive*** meaning: *I like to be at the station early in the mornings (= I think it advisable/I do it that way because it's a good idea).*

- **prefer:** ***gerund*** for ***factive*** reference in the meaning *like/enjoy more*: *Gary prefers cycling to playing golf (= he does both, but likes the first one better).*

  With the infinitive, *prefer* has a slightly different, ***non-factive*** meaning: *However, last week Gary preferred to play golf (= chose this activity instead); "Why didn't you take the bus?" "We preferred to walk."*

  With *would* (as with *like/hate/love*) *prefer* is also ***non-factive***, and takes the ***infinitive***: *Would you like to come with us on Sunday, Tom, or would you prefer to stay at home?*

062/2.3 remember, regret

With the ***gerund***, these, too, are typically ***factive*** (i.e. act first and *regret/remember* later): *Jill and David regret moving to London (= ... regret the fact that they moved ...); Can you remember posting the letter (= ... remember the fact that you posted ...).*

With the ***infinitive***, ***non-factive*** *remember* and *regret* have different meanings: *Can you remember to post the letter? (= ... keep in mind that you have to ...).*

Regret + infinitive is a set phrase for introducing bad news and is heard more or less only in this context: *I regret to tell you that you have failed the exam.*

062/2.4 mean, propose

With the ***gerund*** these are not obviously factive, and do not have the retrospective view of the typical factive verbs. But this has to do with their lexical nature, which is future-oriented.

In this use *mean* has the sense of *involve/have as a consequence/make necessary*, and *propose* is equivalent to *suggest*: *This job means being available 24 hours a day (... involves being, ..., makes this necessary); I proposed changing trains in Birmingham (... suggested changing ...);* Note that *suggest* and *involve* also take the ***gerund***!

Followed by an ***infinitive***, *mean* and *propose* both mean *intend*: *Marvin meant to upset Sally (= he did it deliberately); I propose to change trains in Birmingham (= that is my plan).*

062/2.5 stop, try, understand, want

With the ***gerund*** *stop* and *understand* are clearly ***factive***, *try* less obviously so.

- **stop:** ***gerund*** in the sense of *cease or discontinue an action*, infinitive in the sense of *purpose* i.e. *stop (one action) in order to do (a different action)*: *Bill has stopped smoking (= ... has ceased/given up); Bill has stopped to smoke* (= Bill has stopped something else, e.g. working, cutting the hedge, in order to smoke). Note in this case that the ***infinitive*** clause is ***adverbial*** in function.
- **try:** ***gerund*** in the sense of *perform the action to get a particular result*: *Chana tried opening a window (= she opened a window – in order, for instance, to get rid of a bad smell).* Although

not retrospective, *try* here is still ***factive*** in the sense that the second action actually happened.

With the ***infinitive*** *try* has its normal meaning, i.e. *attempt, endeavour, to perform an action*: *Chana tried to open a window* (= *the open window was the desired result*).

The difference is highlighted in the following contrast:

(100) a. Jane tried opening a window, but without success.
(The open window did not achieve the desired result.)
b. Jane tried to open a window, but without success.
(She couldn't get the window open.)

- **understand:** ***gerund*** in the meaning *see why/appreciate the reason for*.
  This is classically ***factive***: *I didn't understand Ray quitting his job like that* (= *I didn't understand why* ...).
  With an ***object + infinitive*** (usually of a stative like *be*, or an utterance verb such as *say*), understand means *think/imagine that*: *I understood Ray to be quitting his job* (= *I thought that he was going to* ...).
- **want:** ***gerund*** in the meaning *need* (see also under **062/4.2** below for *need*).
  Want is often used informally (and particularly in speech) for *need*: *The car wants washing; Your hair wants cutting.*
  Note that the syntax here has a certain resemblance to that of ***false subject constructions*** with the infinitive (see 13.1, **060/3.4**). That is, the ***subject*** of the ***matrix clause*** is semantically the ***direct object*** of the ***sub-clause***. This is unusual with the gerund, but occurs sporadically (see also *bear* in **062/2.1** above, and *need* in **062/4.2** below).
  The meaning could also be regarded in this case as ***passive*** (*Your hair needs to be cut*), though in the ***gerund*** construction a passive gerund is actually ***not*** possible (**Your hair wants being cut*).
  The standard meaning of *want* (= *wish/desire*) requires the ***infinitive*** (see 13.1, **060/1.3**).

062/2.6 Factive vs. implicative meaning with gerund and infinitive

We now want to underline a general contrast between gerund and infinitive. First of all, let us go back to what was said in **062/1.1** above: the ***gerund*** most usually refers to actions and states as ***facts*** (or ***'truths'***) which already exist. It is therefore attracted to catenatives which require exactly this, like for instance, *regret*. Catenatives like this are what we have been calling ***factive*** verbs. They have a preference for the gerund because they ***presuppose*** the ***truth of the sub-clause***. This is the case even when they are ***negated***. For instance, *I regret getting drunk* and *I do not regret getting drunk* both ***presuppose*** the statement *I got drunk*. That is, ***negating*** a ***factive*** verb does ***not*** negate the ***sub-clause***.

We will now turn to a different kind of catenative, one that usually combines with the ***infinitive***: *I managed to get drunk*. At first sight *manage* here seems to have the same effect as *regret*: both say *I got drunk*. But there is a significant difference. If we ***negate*** *manage* (*I didn't manage to get drunk*), then I did ***not*** get drunk. That is, ***negating*** this kind of catenative also ***negates the sub-clause***. Here we see that the second action cannot exist without the first. That is, if I did ***not manage*** something, then I ***did not do*** it. Similarly, if I say I 'managed' something, then I mean I 'did it'. The following show the same relation, i.e. the first action ***implies*** the second:

(101) a. Freya happened to meet Beth in the supermarket.
(= Freya met Beth in the supermarket.)
b. We took care to leave the building only after dark.
(= We left the building only after dark.)

Catenatives like *manage, happen* and *take care* are what we call ***implicative*** verbs.

Some verbs can have both ***implicative*** and ***factive*** meanings. When they are ***factive***, they take the ***gerund***; when they are ***implicative***, they take the ***infinitive***:

(102) a. Bert remembered to post the letter.
(***implicative***: He posted it.)
b. Bert remembered posting the letter.
(***factive***: He posted it first and remembered this afterwards.)
c. I didn't like to open the parcel as it was addressed to you.
(***implicative***: I did not open the parcel.)
d. I didn't like opening the parcel as it was addressed to you.
(***factive***: I opened the parcel.)
e. Mary preferred to be treated by Dr. Ives rather than by Dr. Stopes.
(***implicative***: So she wasn't treated by Dr. Stopes.)
f. Mary preferred being treated by Dr. Ives rather than by Dr. Stopes.
(***factive***: She was treated by both, but she liked Dr. Ives better.)

This does not mean that all catenatives taking both gerund and infinitive are necessarily implicative with the infinitive. But it points to one interesting dimension of difference between the two forms.

Other examples of ***implicative*** verbs are: *bother, dare, trouble, fail, forget* and *refuse*. The first three are often used in the ***negative*** for ***negative implications*** (*I didn't bother/dare to phone him*). The second three are used in the ***positive*** for ***negative implications*** (*He forgot/refused to give me the information*).

062/3 Catenatives: gerund or infinitive according to grammar

In these cases there is no meaning difference between gerund and infinitive use. It is the syntactic construction involved that makes one or the other form compulsory.

062/3.1 permit, advise, recommend, allow

If there is an ***object*** (usually personal and indirect) between the catenative and the non-finite clause, the ***infinitive*** is necessary: *Teachers here do not allow pupils to eat in class; The doctors advised Bullymore to lose weight.*

The infinitive stays even when the catenative is passivized (and the object is lost): *Pupils are not allowed (by teachers) to eat in class; Bullymore was advised (by the doctors) to drink plenty of water.*

When there is ***no object*** between the catenative and non-finite clause, i.e. if just the non-finite action alone is meant, the ***gerund*** is necessary: *Teachers here do not allow eating in class; The doctors advised drinking plenty of water.*

Catenative passivization is also possible here. The ***gerund clause*** becomes the ***subject***: *Eating in class is not allowed; Drinking plenty of water was advised.*

⚠ One important consequence of this ***grammatical gerund rule*** is that even in passive sentences like the last examples, it is ***not*** possible to replace the gerund by the infinitive: **To eat in class is not allowed*. This also rules out extrapositions of the kind **It is not allowed to eat in class* or **It is advised/ recommended to drink plenty of water*. German speakers tend to make such errors because of the German pattern *Es ist nicht erlaubt, im Unterricht zu essen*.

062/3.2 warn, agree, decide, remind

This is a different kind of syntactic case. These four verbs can be used with or without prepositions.

As ***prepositional verbs*** they must take the ***gerund***: *My financial advisor has warned me against investing the money in foreign markets; The two partner firms have at last agreed on building new plants in Scotland; They decided on going to the Canary Islands for their holiday; Sitting out here reminds me of being in our old cottage garden in Kent.*

Without prepositions they take the ***infinitive***, or a *that*-clause: *My financial advisor has warned me not to invest …; The two partner firms have at last agreed to build …; They decided to go …*, etc.

062/4 Catenatives: gerund or infinitive with little or no difference

Whether used with gerund or infinitive, the verbs in this group (*attempt, begin, start, dread, continue, intend, need*) show no individual change in meaning. Nor are there any major syntax changes involved:

(103) a. The neighbours began hammering on the wall.
b. The neighbours began to hammer on the wall.
c. We will not attempt climbing Ben Nevis till the summer.
d. We will not attempt to climb Ben Nevis till the summer.

(103)a. and b., and (103)c. and d. are grammatically and semantically interchangeable.

However, there are certain contextual restrictions, mainly determined by the type of action referred to in the non-finite clause. There is a tendency to reserve the ***gerund*** for ***process-like*** actions. (103)a., for instance, suggests more intensity and the prospect of a lengthier activity than the more neutral version in (103)b. Likewise, the ***gerund*** in (103) c. profiles the activity *climb* as a process or 'operation'. For more neutral, 'non-process' contexts the gerund sounds strange, and the ***infinitive*** is preferred: *Don't attempt to climb that tree; The key started to slip out of his hand.*

The ***infinitive*** is also required with most stative verbs and all passives:

(104) a. The children started to be very frightened of the dark.
(not *The children started being very frightened ...)
b. Slowly, we began to understand the problem more clearly.
(not *Slowly we began understanding ...)
c. The British tourist detained in the USA continues to be held in custody.
(not *... continues being held ...)

Two special cases follow.

062/4.1 dread

One or two set phrases with *dread* (*dread to think/dread to imagine*) take the ***infinitive***: *I dread to imagine what might have happened if the burning candle had fallen over* (dt. *Ich wage nicht, daran zu denken, was hätte passieren können, wenn ...*).

Otherwise, the ***gerund*** is used: *Sadie dreaded returning home* (= *... was very afraid about it*); *I dread meeting anyone I might know* (= *I'm very afraid of this happening*).

062/4.2 need

Need can combine with the ***gerund*** in the meaning *this action is necessary.*

The same use and meaning was explained above with *want* (see under **062/2.5**): *The car needs washing; Your hair needs cutting.*

This is another example of an unusual ***false subject construction*** with a ***gerund***, where the ***subject*** of the ***matrix clause*** is semantically the ***direct object*** of the ***sub-clause***. Again, we could regard the meaning here basically as ***passive***. In fact the passive would be used with ***infinitive*** equivalent: *The car needs to be washed.* However, a passive gerund is ***not*** possible (**The car needs being washed*).

062/5 The gerund after prepositions

Prepositions are always associated syntactically with nouns and nominal expressions. As gerund clauses are nominal in character, it is not surprising that we often find gerunds following prepositions.

062/5.1 With prepositions alone

Prepositions especially common on their own with the gerund are: *about, against, by, for, without,* as well as composite prepositional expressions like *instead of, because of, in favour of,* etc.:

(105) a. What about having lunch at Dodson's?
b. The prisoners escaped by climbing over the main wall.

c. Connors left the restaurant without paying his bill.
d. Some teachers were for calling the police, but others were against taking any kind of legal action, and nobody was in favour of telling the press.

The ***subject*** of the gerund can be specified after prepositions in the usual way:

(106) a. What about us (our) having lunch at Dodson's?
b. New staff are not employed without the manager('s) asking the board first.
c. Nearby residents were against the city council('s) building a ring road around the old town.

062/5.2 After prepositions following adjectives and nouns

Gerunds also feature strongly in prepositional phrases following ***adjectives*** (i.e. as part of the adjectival complement) and nouns (i.e. as part of the postmodification). The prepositions here mainly have an idiomatic character:

(107) a. I was a bit wary of showing too much enthusiasm too soon.
b. Jim had great skill in dealing with people, but a nasty habit of being rude to those he didn't like.
c. We were sad about leaving, but were by that time used to saying goodbye.

⚠ Note that ***used to*** (dt. *gewöhnt an*) is an ***adjective + preposition*** and must be followed by the gerund. A common error here is to use an infinitive (**We were used to say goodbye*). This results from confusion with the catenative ***used + infinitive***, as in *I used to read comics*, which is a completely different structure with a different meaning (i.e. 'past habit': dt. *Ich las gerne/viel Comic-Hefte*).

Other common prepositional expressions often followed by the gerund are: *accustomed to, anger at, angry at, angry with someone for doing something, apology for, bad/good at, capable of, congratulations on, difficulty in, fed up with, fond of, guilty of, happy/sorry/sad etc. about, hate/love of, horror of/at, preference for, punishment for, success in, surprise at, tired of*

062/5.3 After prepositional verbs

And finally, gerunds frequently combine with prepositional verbs:

(108) a. They were looking forward to seeing the island again in summer.
b. My wife accuses me of snoring too loudly when I sleep.
c. The police have charged Henrietta with driving dangerously.

Other common 'gerund candidates' are: *agree on, criticize someone for, decide on, forgive someone for, prevent someone from, punish someone for, remind someone of, stop someone from, warn someone about/against.*

062/6 The gerund in noun compounds

The gerund is an important element in noun-formation (see also chapter 2).

062/6.1 Gerund + noun

Here the gerund appears as a ***premodifier***. Many of these compounds are spelt with hyphens, and are then often regarded as 'compound nouns': *swimming-pool, walking-stick, ironing board, gardening gloves,* etc.

The gerund here usually refers to a ***purpose***, e.g. *a pool for swimming* (*in*), *a stick for walking* (*with*), *a board for ironing (on), gloves for gardening,* etc.

A point of pronunciation is that the gerund is stressed but not the head noun:

```
            /                  /
(109) a. swimming-pool    ironing board
            /                  /
      b. walking stick    gardening gloves
```

Gerund premodifiers are no longer verbal in character and have no clausal function as predicator.

062/6.2 Noun + gerund

Here the gerund appears as the ***head noun*** and the ordinary noun as the ***premodifier***. These combinations are usually either spelt with a hyphen, or (in specific cases) written as one word: *water-skiing, windsurfing, beer-brewing, mountain-climbing, snow-boarding, sightseeing, sunbathing.*

The gerund relates to an activity, and the noun premodifier specifies its type more closely. The noun is either the ***potential direct object*** (*brewing beer*), or part of a ***potential adverbial*** (*skiing on water*).

Here, too, the first element is stressed (though in this case, of course, it is not the gerund):

```
           /             /
(110)   water-skiing   beer-brewing
```

062/7 The action nominal

The gerund can be converted syntactically into a full noun with the same meaning.

The full noun version is called the ***action nominal***:

Gerund

(111) a. ***Painting the kitchen*** was a hard job.

↓

Action nominal

b. ***The painting of the kitchen*** was a hard job.

The ***gerund clause*** *painting the kitchen* in (111)a. has become a ***noun phrase*** in (111)b. It has now entirely lost its verbal character. The gerund itself is no longer predicator in a clause, but the ***head*** of a noun phrase. The ***direct object*** in the gerund clause has become part of a postmodifying *of*-phrase.

062/7.1 Meaning and use: emphasis on procedure

The ***action nominal*** focuses on the ***procedure*** or ***performance*** of the action.

The gerund can imply this too, but it does not emphasize it. In (111), for example, a. and b. can mean more or less the same thing. (111)b., however, stresses the ***process*** itself and the nature of the job.

The *action nominal* is also a little more elevated in style. Whereas gerunds tend to be preferred in neutral and informal language, action nominals are generally used when contexts are more ***formal***, especially in ***official declarations*** (e.g. on public notices) which require a tone of authority:

(112) a. The washing of clothes in this pond is prohibited.
b. The feeding of the deer in this park is not allowed.

Gerunds are certainly possible here, but sound less forceful and authoritative (*Washing clothes in this pond is prohibited; Feeding the deer in this park is not allowed*).

062/7.2 Meaning and use: the manner of the action

As the ***action nominal*** gives more profile to procedure, performance and process, it is nearly always preferred for the meaning '***the way in which*** the action took place'. The ***gerund***, on the other hand, is preferred for the meaning '***the fact that*** the action took place':

(113) a. I did not like Faraday('s) training that dog.
(= the fact that he trained it, ***gerund***)
b. I did not like Faraday's training of that dog.
(= the way that he trained it, ***action nominal***).

062/7.3 Syntax: contrasts with gerund

The following table shows the distinctions in syntactic behaviour between gerund and action nominal:

Action nominal	Gerund
Can be preceded by the definite article or any other kind of determiner: *The/this/our training of dogs is a serious matter.*	Cannot be preceded by any kind of determiner ***except*** genitive or possessive: **The training dogs is a serious business.*
Needs a determiner of some kind: **Training of dogs.*	Can occur with no determiner: *Training dogs is a serious business.*

Action nominal	Gerund
Potential direct object part of a post- modifying prepositional phrase with *of*: *the training of dogs.*	Immediately followed by an object: *Training dogs.*
Modification by adjective: *The **serious** training of dogs.*	Modification by adverb: *Training dogs **seriously**.*
Cannot be formed from stative verbs: **The knowing of the problem.*	Can be formed from stative verbs: *Knowing the problem.*
Has no perfect form: **The having trained of dogs.*	Has a perfect form: *Having trained dogs...*

062/7.4 Intransitive verbs

Like gerunds, ***action nominals*** can also be used with ***intransitive*** verbs. There is then no *of*-modification:

(114) a. The driving in London is getting worse and worse.
b. Sally hated the training.

The ***definite article*** here shows clearly that this is an ***action nominal***.

However, as both ***gerunds*** and ***action nominals*** appear with ***genitives*** and ***possessives***, there may be ambiguity. (115)a. may be interpreted as (115)b. or (115)c.:

(115) a. Mother does not like Nigel's driving.
b. Mother does not like the ***fact*** that Nigel drives (i.e. she would prefer someone else to drive – ***gerund*** interpretation).
c. Mother does not like the ***way*** that Nigel drives (i.e. she would prefer him to drive differently – ***action nominal*** interpretation).

13.3 The participles

Form, syntax, general meaning 063

The third kind of non-finite verb we must deal with is the ***participle***. There are two main types: the ***present participle*** and the ***past participle***. To these we could add another one, the ***perfect participle***; but this is essentially just the ***perfect*** form of the ***present participle***, and not really a separate type.

063/1 Uses and functions of participles: an introduction

The ***present participle*** is an *-ing*-form identical with the gerund, and can introduce a subordinate clause in the same way. In meaning and function, however, the participle is very different.

Generally, it presents an action as ***in progress*** or ***ongoing***, and is therefore used to construct the ***progressive form***, as in *I am* ***writing*** *a novel at the moment.* All ***participle clauses*** have an ***adverbial*** function at sentence level.

- ***Present participles*** generally refer to actions in progress ***accompanying*** the matrix action in some way, e.g. ***Taking*** *a deep breath, Ramona began the story; Ted walked in* ***carrying*** *a bunch of flowers.*
  Present participles ***postmodify*** nouns in the sense of ***relative clauses***: *The man* ***standing*** *over there is my uncle* (= *The man who is standing …*). Again the meaning is typically progressive.
  Present participles also ***premodify*** nouns: ***Freezing*** *rain made the roads very dangerous.* This is a feature they share with gerunds, but the meaning relation to the noun is different: the ***participle*** here again has the sense of a ***relative clause*** (*Rain which was freezing …*). But it is also being used like an ***adjective***, firstly because it premodifies, and secondly because ***premodifying participles*** always convert a pure action into a ***characteristic feature*** of the noun.
- In contrast to the present participle, the ***past participle*** refers to a ***state resulting from an action***. It too helps to construct other verb forms. In keeping with its 'resulting state' meaning, these are the ***perfect*** and the ***passive***: *The car was* ***repaired*** *by Suzanne; I have* ***written*** *my novel.*
  Otherwise its functions are identical to those of the present participle, i.e. ***pre***- and ***postmodifying*** nouns in the ***relative clause*** sense (*Fried fish makes a wonderful quick meal; The car parked outside the house was Dawson's*); and introducing ***adverbial clauses*** at sentence level: ***Soaked*** *from the downpour, we took shelter in an old barn.* Here, too, the 'resulting state' meaning is quite clear. Here again, especially in the premodifying position, we see the adjectival ('describing') character of the participle.

Note that we can contrast present and past participles in a general way by saying that ***past participles*** have ***passive*** meaning ('suffering this state'), whereas ***present participles*** have ***active*** meaning ('doing this action').

This adjectival note brings us back to the contrast with the gerund. Comparing the gerund and the participles syntactically to other word-classes (parts of speech), we can say, putting it simply, that ***gerunds*** are like ***nouns***, whereas ***participles*** are like ***adjectives*** and ***adverbs***.

Participle clauses are ***not*** usually determined syntactically by the matrix verb. In contrast to gerund and infinitive, they can appear quite freely with any type of matrix clause. As there is no real link between participle and matrix verb, the matrix verb does ***not*** have real catenative character. Exceptions to this principle are verbs of perception, mentioned again further below.

063/2 The syntax of the participle clause

Like the other non-finites, ***participles*** are ***predicators*** and form ***subordinate clauses***, except when used like adjectives (e.g. as premodifiers). The function of the clauses, as we have seen, is ***adverbial***:

A P Od S P Od

(116) a. [Taking a deep breath], Ramona began the story.

(S)

A P A S P A

b. [Soaked from the downpour], we sheltered in an old barn.

(S)

S P A P Od

c. Ted walked in [carrying a bunch of flowers].

(S)

Here for clarity we have marked all the functions in both clauses. Notice (as indicated by the arrows) that the ***implied subject*** of the ***participle clause*** must be the ***matrix subject***, i.e. in (116) *Ramona, we,* and *Ted.*

Comical effects may occur if this rule is contravened:

(117) a. * Raining heavily, Barbara took a taxi.

b. * Soaked from the downpour, we gave Eli shelter and fresh clothes.

From (117)a. we get the impression that it was *Barbara* who was 'raining heavily'; from (117)b. it seems that *we* were the ones who were 'soaked', although from the sense of the matrix clause it must have been *Eli.*

These are called ***misrelated*** (or 'dangling') ***participles***. In such obvious cases as these they are regarded as grammatical errors. But one or two examples of misrelated participles have become acceptable with certain types of expression, particularly in spoken language. We return to this later (see **064/3.1** and **2** below).

The obvious solution in the case of (117) is to use finite clauses: *It was raining heavily and Barbara took a taxi; Eli was soaked from the downpour, and we gave her ...*

Under certain circumstances, participle clauses may also have their own separate subjects, simply inserted before the participle: *Donna being 8 months pregnant, a long holiday abroad was out of the question.*

These are known traditionally as ***absolute*** participle clauses. However, they are not common outside formal or literary language. A much more common solution is to introduce the subject in a ***with***-construction: *He sat in the car with the engine running; With her coat thrown over her arm, she left the building quickly* (see also **064/3.3** below).

Finally, there are certain constructions in which the ***direct object*** of the ***matrix*** clause is understood as the ***implied participle subject***:

(118) a. We watched our children playing cricket.
(= Our children were playing cricket and we watched them).
b. The hotel manager discovered a guest lying asleep in a flower-bed.
(= A guest was lying asleep in a flower-bed and the hotel manager discovered him/her.)

This kind of construction occurs mainly with verbs of perception (*see, hear, watch,* etc.). Verbs like this link their direct object in a very strong sense with the participle clause and thereby take on the character of catenatives. Here a full analysis, again with ***implied participle subjects*** indicated by arrows.

S P Od A P Od
(119) a. We watched our children [playing cricket].
(S) →
S P Od A P A A
b. The hotel manager discovered a guest [lying asleep in a flower-bed].
(S) →

063/3 Tense, aspect and passive with participles

The ***past participle*** exists alone in the ***base form***. The ***present participle***, on the other hand, has ***three*** tense/aspect forms identical to those of the gerund:

a. ***the past participle base form*** → *painted*
b. ***the present participle base form (progressive)*** → *painting*
c. ***the perfect participle*** → *having painted*
d. ***the progressive perfect participle*** → *having been painting*

Like the gerund, the ***present participle*** therefore has ***two tenses***, but makes an ***aspect distinction*** only in the ***perfect***. That is, the base form has only one aspect. Unlike the gerund base form, however, ***present participle base form*** has ***progressive*** meaning. There is no 'simple form' of the base. In table overview the ***present*** and ***perfect participles*** can be presented like this (compare gerund table 13.2, **061/3**):

Tense	Aspect	
	Simple	Progressive
Base form Non-perfect		painting
Perfect Participle	having painted	having been painting

In addition, there are two ***passive*** forms:

- the ***passive present participle*** → being painted
- the ***passive perfect participle*** → having been painted

These are again identical with those of the gerund, though the ***passive present participle***, like the active form, is ***progressive*** in meaning.

Note that although the ***past participle*** itself has only ***one*** form, this is actually used in constructing the passive and perfect forms of the other participles.

The participles in use 064

064/1 The present participle at sentence level

As we have already seen in the general introduction, present participles typically express actions running parallel to those expressed in the matrix clause. That is, they have an ***ongoing***, or ***progressive***, meaning.

(120) a. The man entered the bank carrying a large leather case.
(= When the man entered the bank, he was carrying ...)
b. Roy sat on a park bench, listening to the birds.
(As he sat there, he was listening ...)
c. The young couple ran across the grass laughing.
(As they ran ... they were laughing.)

German also has a present participle (dt. *Partizip Präsens*), e.g. *tragend, zuhörend, lachend*. But it is not used much and is generally regarded as rather elevated or unnatural. The preferred German solution here is to use finite clauses connected by *und* or other conjunctions: *Roy saß auf einer Parkbank und hörte den Vögeln zu; ein junges Paar rannte* (*lachend*) *über das Gras* (*und lachte*).

This rather general relation of parallel actions to each other usually serves more specific contextual or communicative purposes.

064/1.1 Accompanying actions giving more detail

One typical communicative role of the present participle is to express ***accompanying*** actions which 'fill out', as it were, a more general kind of matrix action or state. This is often a bodily posture (*stand, sit, lie*, etc.) or a general movement (such as *go* or *come*), which participles then fill with more specific detail. As they do so, they often build up a piece-by-piece picture of a complex event:

(121) a. In July we are going to travel through Finland, staying in wooden cabins and lodges, cooking our own food, and enjoying the peace and beauty of idyllic woodlands and lakes.
b. Mehmet comforted the sick camel, patting its haunches, running his hand softly over its head and whispering gentle words of encouragement.
c. Some of the guests stood on the side lawn, drinking tea and chatting, while others sat on the terrace reading or just looking out to sea.

The cumulation here is fairly literary, or at least textual. But participles are used in more neutral, everyday language for the same purpose, i.e. to add information about accompanying actions:

(122) a. The children were on the floor, playing with their toys.
b. Mrs. Higgins is in the kitchen, making tea.
c. Fry then started an argument, shouting at me, and telling me that I was incompetent.

064/1.2 Framework situations

A variation on parallel or accompanying meaning is the ***framework situation*** itself:

(123) a. I burnt my fingers lighting the gas.
(= ... while/as I was lighting ...)
b. Terry broke his leg playing football.
(= ... when he was playing ...)
c. Be careful swimming by those rocks!
(= ... when you are swimming ...)

The framework meaning is underlined by the time conjunctions in the paraphrases. In fact, the conjunctions *while* and *when* can appear with the participle alone, particularly in more formal style: *Terry broke his leg while playing football; Be careful when swimming by those rocks!*

Other conjunctions with ***modal*** overtones can also be used. Note that the framework situation still remains, though:

(124) a. If intending to make duty-free purchases, passengers must show personal identification at the checkout.
b. No one is allowed into the university library unless carrying a student or staff membership card.
c. The waiter stood by the table as if hoping for a tip.
d. Although not planning any immediate trips away, I went into the travel agents' out of curiosity.

064/1.3 Instrumental overtones

Another variation on 'accompaniment' is ***instrumental*** meaning:

(125) a. They reached the mountain top crawling on their hands and knees.
b. We could only paint the ceiling standing on very high ladders.
c. The Indians crossed the marshes walking on stilts.
d. Cathy started to scoop the water out of the boat using her hands.

Instrumental meaning is contextual and lexical. It is a by-product of the accompaniment component, and very often no more than a nuance. Nevertheless, participles are frequently used to suggest this meaning in appropriate contexts. However, they ***cannot*** express instrumentality if there is ***no*** parallel time factor: **We could only accommodate all our guests borrowing chairs from the neighbours;* **We only got rid of the smell re-decorating the room.*

Here, where the two actions are not parallel, we need an overt instrumental marker, i.e. the preposition ***by***, which then converts the *ing*-form into a ***gerund***: *We could only accommodate all our guests* ***by*** *borrowing chairs from the neighbours; We only got rid of the smell* ***by*** *re-decorating the room.*

064/1.4 An idiomatic variation on accompaniment

This is a very specialized and restricted case, where the participle is placed (exceptionally) between the main verb and the rest of its complementation:

(126) a. His daughter came running out of the house to greet him.
(= His daughter came out of the house running, i.e. she was running when she came out of the house.)
Seine Tochter kam aus dem Haus gelaufen ...
b. The child ran crying to its mother.
... rannte weinend zu seiner Mutter.
c. A cyclist went peddling through the pool of water in the road.
... fuhr kräftig in die Pedale tretend durch die Pfütze ...

This position gives stylistic and semantic emphasis to the participle and the manner that it refers to. The more normal, neutral variation is with the participle at the end, e.g. *The child ran to its mother crying.*

064/1.5 The present participle of point-telic verbs

These refer to ***momentary actions*** (see chapter 8, **041/3.3**), such as *knock, start, arrive, die, appear, leave, hit, drop, kick, break,* etc.

In the present participle form they show the same ***mode-of-occurrence*** patterns as in the ***progressive***:

(127) a. When leaving the garage I noticed a peculiar noise in the car engine.
b. Crabbe hurt his hand knocking on Jenny's door.

In (127)a. *leave* is expanded into a ***single telic event***, while in (127)b. *knock* is understood as a ***repeated point-telic event***. These are the two alternative effects of progressive meaning on various ***point-telic*** verbs.

In addition, point-telic verb participles are used to refer to an action immediately preceding or following that of the main verb. The effect is to emphasize that the two acts are strongly linked, often in a causal way:

(128) a. Kicking the ball away angrily, Johnston walked off the field.
b. Standing up suddenly, Frank hit his head on the low lamp.
c. Arriving at the airport in rather a panic, we immediately went to the wrong terminal.
d. Switching on the flashlight, Bugsby examined the lock on the safe.

When the participle clause follows the matrix, the action sequence is reversed, i.e. it is the participle action that follows:

(129) a. The model aeroplane flew into the hedge, breaking off one of its wings.
b. A tennis-ball flew suddenly through the open window, landing in the housemaster's soup.
c. Frank stood up suddenly, hitting his head on the low lamp.

064/1.6 Stative participles with causal meaning

The present participles of ***stative*** verbs have a ***causal*** meaning in adverbial clauses in ***initial*** position:

(130) a. Feeling very tired, we went to bed.
(As we felt tired ...)
b. Wanting to see the world, Sid joined the navy.
(Because he wanted ...)
c. Knowing the painting was a fake, Harry contacted the gallery manager.
(As he knew the painting was a fake, Harry ...)

When they ***follow*** the matrix clause, however, stative participles usually have the same ***temporal-parallel*** meaning as non-stative participles:

(131) a. We went to bed feeling very tired.
(We felt very tired when we went to bed.)
b. Sid joined the Navy wanting to see the world.
(Sid wanted to see the world when he ...)
c. Harry contacted the gallery manager knowing the painting was a fake (Harry knew the painting was a fake when he contacted ...)

As the participle clause here is spoken together with the matrix without a pause, there is no comma between them in writing.

There are one or two exceptions to the pattern just shown in (131). The most prominent is the present participle of *be*, which never shows a temporal-parallel relation to the matrix verb. That is, it keeps its causal meaning, even in the end position. Other stative participles can have the ***option*** of keeping their causal meaning in end position. Where this is the case, they are usually separated from the matrix by intonation and comma:

(132) a. I could not come to the meeting, being ill.
(= …, as I was ill.)
b. Rutherford was obliged to walk home, having no money left for a taxi.
(= …, as he had no money left for a taxi.)
c. The robbers gave themselves up to the police, realizing there was no chance of escape.
(= … as they realized …)

For causal meaning the ***initial*** position is nevertheless the preferred one.

Note that stative participles in ***postmodifying*** position (see below under **064/2.2**) are ***always*** temporal.

064/1.7 Non-stative participles with causal meaning

When they refer to ***habits***, ***non-stative*** participles can also take on causal meaning. They then correspond, of course (like stative participles), to the finite ***simple*** form:

(133) a. Working 16 hours a day for 20 years, Baker had no time to develop any private life.
(= …, as he worked)
b. Grandmother got quite good at crossword puzzles, doing the one in the *Guardian* everyday
(= …, because she did the one …)

064/1.8 The present participle following verbs of sensory perception

The main area of catenative use with the present participle is with verbs of ***sensory perception***, such as *see, hear, smell, feel, recognize, notice, observe, watch,* etc. The syntactic pattern is ***verb + direct object + present participle***:

(134) a. We watched two children feeding the swans on the lake.
b. Mrs. Broughton heard the milkman coming up the garden path.
c. Judy felt the train pulling slowly away from the platform.

Here, essentially, a framework situation is also involved. The act of perception ***intrudes*** into the ***ongoing*** participle action:

(135) a. The two children were feeding swans. We watched them (while they were doing this).
b. The milkman was coming up the garden path when Mrs. Broughton heard him.
c. The train was pulling slowly away from the platform. Judy felt this.

The participle clause, like all those discussed so far, has the function of an ***adverbial***.

064/1.9 Verbs of perception: present participle or infinitive?

Perception verbs can alternatively be followed by the ***infinitive***: or, more precisely, by an ***object + infinitive without* to** (see also 13.2):

(136) a. We watched the two children feed the swans on the lake.
b. Mrs. Broughton heard the milkman come up the garden path.
c. Judy felt the train pull away from the platform.

The difference in meaning between the participle and infinitive is one of ***aspect***. The ***infinitive*** is equivalent to the ***simple form*** and means that the ***whole of the action*** was perceived. In (136)a., that is, the feeding was seen from beginning to end, in b. the milkman was heard on the whole of the garden path from the gate to the front door, and in c. Judy felt the entire 'starting-phase' of the train. The ***participle*** on the other hand, as we would expect from the ***framework*** meaning, expresses that only ***part*** of the ***ongoing*** action was perceived. The contrast can be seen most clearly with ***telic event verbs***, i.e. those referring to ***goal-directed processes*** (see chapter 8, **041/3.**):

(137) a. We saw the dog crossing the road.
(***present participle*** = *action* ***in progress***: The dog was crossing the road when we saw it.)
b. We saw the dog cross the road.
(***infinitive*** = *action* ***complete***: The dog crossed the road; we saw this.)
c. She watched her father making the sandwiches.
(***present participle*** = *action* ***in progress***: Her father was making the sandwiches and she watched him for some time during the process.)
d. She watched her father make the sandwiches.
(***infinitive*** = *action* ***complete***: Her father made the sandwiches and she watched this.)

As a consequence of the ***aspect*** difference, the ***participle*** is preferred when the act of perception focuses on the ***process*** or ***course*** of action, and/or the way in which it is carried out. The ***infinitive*** tends to stress the ***fact*** that something happened.

Note that German uses a completely different construction here, e.g. for (137)a. and b.:

(138) a. Wir sahen, wie der Hund die Straße überquerte.
b. Wir sahen, wie der Hund gerade die Straße überquerte.

There are two important points to remember here. Firstly, German cannot signal progressive meaning grammatically, but can do so lexically. So although (138)a. is the basic translation for both (137)a. and (137)b., the ***progressive*** meaning can be expressed more precisely by adding an adverb like *gerade*, as in (138)b. As we have already seen, this is the standard German way of expressing the finite progressive as well.

Secondly, the German construction should ***never*** be translated literally into English as ⚠ **We saw how the dog crossed/was crossing the road.*

064/1.10 Other catenatives with present participles

Some other verbs also act as ***catenatives*** with ***present participles***, such as *discover, find, leave, catch, keep, get* and *have*. The meaning and syntax are the same as with verbs of perception:

(139) a. Barbara found/discovered the book lying on her desk.
(= the book was lying on Barbara's desk when she found it)
b. I left the children playing in the garden.
(= the children were playing in the garden when I left them)

Only the participle version (***not*** the infinitive) is possible here.

Catch is similar to *find*: *Our neighbours caught a man breaking into their garden shed* (... *haben einen Mann beim Einbrechen in ihren Gartenschuppen gefasst*).

Keep without a personal object takes the ***gerund*** and means *do repeatedly*. With ***object + participle*** it means *force someone/something to continue a particular activity*:

(140) a. Fred kept ringing Susan, but got no reply. [***gerund***]
b. I kept the car engine running while I waited. [***present participle***]

Get/have plus ***object + present participle*** is a slightly colloquial way of saying *cause something/someone to do something*:

(141) a. The doctors will soon get you up and walking again.
b. Jack had that washing-machine working in no time.

Along with one or two other catenatives, *get* can also be followed by the participle ***without*** an object in between (i.e. simply ***verb + present participle***):

(142) a. After the storm we got moving again quickly.
b. Some guests took a seat, but others remained standing.

The syntactic analysis of constructions like those in (140)b., (141) and (142) is discussed in the next section.

064/1.11 Syntax of the present participle after catenatives

As we have already seen, participle clauses typically have an adverbial function. This is also the case, with one or two exceptions, after catenatives. Here, too, participle clauses stand for time clauses in the progressive (see also example (119) above):

S P Od A P Od
(143) a. We saw the dog [crossing the road].
S P Od A P Od
b. Our neighbours caught a man [breaking into their garden shed].

By contrast, ***infinitive clauses*** after perception verbs are ***object complements***:

S P Od Co P Od
(144) a. We saw the dog [cross the road].
S P Od Co P A
b. She heard the milkman [come up the garden path].

The reason for this is that the infinitive clause is not a *when*-clause. The paraphrase here would be *We saw that the dog crossed the road*, or *The dog crossed the road; we saw this*. Semantically, that is, the sub-clause does not give the circumstances under which the perception took place. Instead, it represents an important element of what was actually perceived.

Considerations of this kind also affect one or two participle constructions. Participle clauses following the catenatives *keep*, *get* and *have* are parts of ***causative*** constructions, and function as ***object complements***:

S P Od Co P
(145) a. I kept the car engine [running].
S P Od Co P A
b. Jack had that washing-machine [working] in no time.

Where there is no direct object in the matrix after these verbs, the participle clause functions as ***subject complement***:

S P Cs P A A
(146) a. We got [moving again] quickly.
S P Cs P
b. Other guests remained [standing].

064/1.12 The present participle in the passive

By its nature, the present participle is an active form. The passive equivalent is basically the past participle (see below). Nevertheless, the ***passive present participle*** (form: **being + *past participle***) must be used when the ***ongoing*** character of the action is in the forefront, i.e. when there is obvious reference to a ***framework situation***:

(147) a. The baby makes contented noises when being fed. (= … when it is being fed.)
b. The car caught fire while being repaired. (= … while it was being repaired.)

064/2 The present participle at phrase level

064/2.1 Following adjectives

A small group of adjectives, mainly referring to attitude or disposition, 'attract' the present participle. These are: *bored, busy, content(ed)/ discontented, happy/unhappy, satisfied/ dissatisfied,* and a few of their synonyms.

(148) a. We're very busy preparing for the conference.
b. John is quite happy working for a publisher.
c. Celia was dissatisfied sitting at home all day.
d. Fred is content being a caretaker and technician.

The participle clauses here restrict the sense in which the adjectives apply. Their position is therefore fixed and they are parts of the adjective phrase, functioning as adjectival complements:

S P Cs P A
(149) a. We're [very busy/preparing for the conference].
↑ ↑
{ ***head*** ***adjectival complement***
adjective ***phrase*** }

S P Cs P A A
b. Celia was [dissatisfied/sitting at home all day].
↑ ↑
{ ***head*** ***adjectival complement***
adjective ***phrase*** }

Note that with some of these adjectives prepositions can be inserted, e.g. *John is quite happy* ***about*** *working for a publisher; Celia was dissatisfied* ***with*** *sitting at home all day*. The preposition converts the participle into a ***gerund*** in these cases.

064/2.2 Following nouns

Participle clauses frequently function as ***postmodifiers*** in noun phrases: the sense is that of a reduced or ***shortened relative clause***:

(150) a. The train standing at platform 6 is the Intercity to Sheffield.
(The train which is standing …)
b. The boat hit a log floating in the water.
(… a log which was floating …)

The ***implied participle subject*** in each case is the ***antecedent*** noun, i.e. *the train* in a. and *a log* in b. This is seen clearly when the participle clause is expanded into a ***full relative clause***. The relative pronoun ***which*** is then the subject of the relative clause. A full functional analysis looks like this:

S ***P*** ***A*** ***P*** ***Cs***

(151) a. [The train /standing at platform 6] is the Intercity to Sheffield.

↑ ↑

head ***postmodification***

noun ***phrase***

S ***P*** ***Od*** ***P*** ***A***

b. The boat hit [a log /floating in the water].

↑ ↑

head ***postmodification***

noun ***phrase***

We saw above that not all present participles necessarily correspond to progressive forms. This applies equally to those in postmodifications. Postmodifying participles can also refer to ***habits*** and ***general truths***. They are then equivalent to finite ***simple forms***:

(152) a. The road leading to Draycott is flooded.
(The road which leads …)
b. Many people working in traditional industries lost their jobs.
(Many people who worked …)

The participles of stative verbs are a similar case. They, too, of course, are derived from finite simple forms:

(153) a. The police found boxes containing explosives in the lorry
(… boxes which contained …)
b. Anyone noticing anything suspicious should inform the railway authorities immediately
(Anyone who notices …)

Passive present participles (see **064/1.12**) are also used in postmodifying function: *The suspect being questioned by the police at that moment was McArthur.*

Postmodification is dealt with in full in chapter 14.

064/2.3 Participles following nouns as separate clauses

Not all present participles following nouns are necessarily postmodifications. They may introduce separate ***adverbial clauses***, as in the following:

A theoretical question here is whether the *-ing*-form should not rather be seen as a gerund, as it follows a ***preposition***. On the other hand, the same construction occurs with the past participle, and also when there is no verb at all (i.e. in what are sometimes called ***verbless clauses***): *With the house paid off at last, we are free of debt; He stood there with his hands in his pockets*. This is probably why the *-ing*-form is generally regarded as a ***participle*** (see also **064/6.3** below).

We will keep to this view here, but explain ***with*** as being a kind of 'quasi-conjunction' which introduces the clause as a whole. The case is a little similar to that of ***for*** in the ***for***-construction with infinitives.

064/3.4 Prepositions and conjunctions

The discussion at the end of **064/3.3** shows us an 'exception that proves the rule' – and reminds us of the general principle: ***gerunds*** follow ***prepositions***, whereas ***present participles*** follow ***conjunctions***:

(165) a. On arriving in New York we felt a surge of excitement. (***gerund***)
b. When arriving in New York, we felt a surge of excitement. (***present participle***)

Note here that *before* and *after* can be both prepositions and conjunctions, so that an *ing*-form following them can be regarded as either a gerund or a participle: *Just after/just before arriving in New York we felt a surge of excitement.*

064/3.5 Activities with come and go

Another borderline case, already mentioned in the discussion of the gerund (see 13.2 **062/1.2**), is the use of the *-ing*-form after *come* and *go* in expressions such as *go swimming, come dancing, go shopping, come skiing, go sailing*, etc. The *-ing*-forms here look like participles (as they follow intransitive verbs and are obviously adverbial in function). Unusually, however, they are ***gerunds***. It is actually the meaning that makes this clear: they refer to fields of activity, a typical communicative function of the gerund.

Another point is that the *-ing*-form does not describe the preceding action more closely, i.e. give us details on how it happens. This would be the typical function of a participle (e.g. *He sat in an armchair reading*). Instead, the *-ing*-form in this case gives the ***goal*** or destination of the ***matrix action***: *go shopping* = 'go to a place where shopping is done'; *go swimming* = 'go to a place where swimming is done', etc.

In older phases of English, the gerund character of the *-ing*-form was quite clear from the syntax too, as there was a ***preposition*** before it: to go *a-hunting, a-dancing, a-singing*, etc. This preposition *a* was derived from an earlier use of *on*, meaning *during* or *in the process of* an action (see also modern use, as in (165)a. above). So what looks like a participle in modern English syntax is really a kind of 'fossilized' gerund.

064/3.6 Summary of functional gerund-participle distinctions

Gerund-participle distinctions are reflected first and foremost in their very different sentence and phrase functions. Here a summary overview:

Gerund	*Present participle*
Subject: Swimming is fun ***Direct Object:*** I like swimming ***Subject complement:*** My great hobby is swimming **(*never Adverbial,*** *except in the case of* **go shopping,** *etc.*) ***Premodifier in noun phrases*** *in the sense of a* ***prepositional phrase*** *with* **for:** a swimming-pool; a walking-stick	***Adverbial:*** He sat in a chair reading Feeling tired, I went to bed **(never *Subject or Object, and only rarely Complement*)** ***Pre- and postmodifier in noun phrases*** *in the sense of* ***a relative clause:*** a passing car; the girl standing in the corner

064/4 The perfect participle

Like the other non-finites, the present participle has a perfect form, the ***perfect participle***, used to signal ***past*** or ***perfect*** meaning in relation to the time of the matrix verb. The ***perfect participle*** is identical in form with the ***perfect gerund***. At sentence level it functions in the same way as the present participle, introducing ***adverbial*** clauses:

(166) a. Having done an industrial practical during my university vacations, I had a definite advantage later on the job market.
b. Marlyn did not go to lunch with the rest of the department, having already eaten alone at 12 o'clock.

Unlike the present participle, the ***perfect participle*** cannot be used as a pre- or postmodifier in a noun phrase, i.e. not **She is a student having done an industrial practical* for *She is a student who has done …*

Though also heard in speech, the perfect participle has rather a formal character stylistically.

064/4.1 Tense and time relations

Like its 'partners' in the gerund and infinitive, the ***perfect participle*** can represent either a ***finite past tense*** or a ***finite present perfect***.

Expressed in finite form, the sub-clauses in (166) would both have the ***past perfect***: *As I had done an industrial practical during my university vacations …; … as she had already eaten alone.*

The following examples show ***past tense*** and ***present perfect*** meanings:

(167) a. Having met the directors yesterday, Mr. Mayfield is going to see other members of staff this morning.
(= As he met the directors yesterday, …)
b. I'm giving the annual conference a miss this year, having been to the last four.
(= … as I have been to the last four.)

With the gerund we saw that the meanings of the ordinary form and the perfect form overlap. That is, the ordinary gerund itself can suggest 'pastness'. This is not the case with the present participle, however.

We cannot, for instance, express (167)a. alternatively as **Meeting the directors yesterday* ... This would not make sense, as the present participle always suggests an action parallel or simultaneous with that of the matrix verb.

The distinction between the present and perfect participles is therefore quite clear-cut, and if we wish to express ***'beforeness'***, we ***must*** use the ***perfect participle***.

The only exception to this is with ***point-telic verbs***, which in their ***present participle*** form can express a certain sequence, as in (168)a. (see also **064/1.5** above). There is nevertheless a slight difference between this and the ***perfect participle*** version in (168)b.:

(168) a. Arriving at the airport in rather a panic, we immediately went to the wrong terminal.
b. Having arrived at the airport in rather a panic, we immediately went to the wrong terminal.

The present participle version gives a stronger sense of connection. It suggests that the first action is part of the second action, and 'glides over' into it. The perfect participle, on the other hand, tends rather to separate the events from one another.

064/4.2 Causal meaning

In all the examples given so far, the ***perfect participle*** has ***causal*** meaning.

This is not always the case. Sometimes only the time factor is present:

(169) a. Having climbed the steps to the top of the cliffs, we sat down on the grass to enjoy the sea view.
(= After we had climbed ...)
b. Having settled herself in an armchair, the cat soon fell asleep.
(= After she had settled herself ...)

Nevertheless, ***causal*** overtones are the rule rather than the exception. As the examples in (169) show, they are not always present, and are therefore not part of the base meaning. But in usage, the ***perfect participle*** is preferred for contexts where a ***causal link*** has to be expressed.

This is particularly so when (as with the present participle) a ***separate subject*** is introduced by ***with***: *With Fred having sold the car, the whole family now had to spend weekends at home.*

064/4.3 Aspect

All examples so far have shown the ***perfect participle*** in the ***simple form***. As presented in the participle overview at the beginning of 13.3 (see the table in **063/3** above), the ***perfect participle*** also has a ***progressive*** variant:

(170) a. Having been talking on the phone all morning, I'm rather hoarse.
(= As I have been talking ...)
b. Mrs. Crabbe did not hear the doorbell ring, having been watering her flowers in the garden at the time.
(= ... as she had been watering ...)

The perfect participle does, however, sound rather clumsy in the progressive, and would normally be given a finite rendering.

064/4.4 Passive

It is more popular, by contrast, in the passive:

(171) a. Having been called three times in the night for nothing, I decided not to answer the phone again.
b. Georgina was very careful with her investments, having been disappointed several times by the promise of quick profit.

064/5 The past participle: introduction

As was said in the introduction to the chapter, the ***past participle*** has the ***same grammatical functions*** as the present participle:

- as ***pre***- and ***postmodification*** in noun phrases (*a painted door; a door painted green*) in the sense of relative clauses;
- in ***adverbial clauses*** at sentence level (*Totally exhausted, she collapsed on the sofa*).

The past participle refers to a ***state resulting from an action***. As most past participles are from ***transitive*** verbs, ***past participle*** meaning is generally ***passive***.

064/6 The past participle at sentence level

As with the other participles, the ***implied subject*** of the ***past participle clause*** must be the ***subject*** of the ***matrix clause***. Here, however, the participle refers to a ***state*** that the subject is in, and not an action that it performs. This state ***results*** from an action, but the ***implied subject*** is the ***'sufferer'*** (i.e. the ***patient***) and not the 'doer' (or agent). That is, to repeat the point just made in **064/5**, the past participle has ***passive*** meaning: it can generally be expressed alternatively by a finite passive verb or, frequently, the passive form of the perfect participle:

(172) a. Damaged by the storm, the ships headed for the harbour.
(= Having been damaged, ...; The ships had been damaged ..., and headed ...)
b. Jane collapsed on the sofa, exhausted by all the excitement.
(= ..., having been exhausted ...; Jane had been exhausted by ..., and collapsed ...)

Passive meaning naturally 'attracts' the prepositional *by*-phrase. This, in fact, is the main element of complementation found in ***past participle clauses***. Like this, any other elements are usually also ***adverbial*** (as the passive meaning generally rules out object and complement functions):

A P A S P A
(173) a. [Damaged by the storm], the ships headed for the harbour.
(S)
S P A A P A
b. Jane collapsed on the sofa, [exhausted by all the excitement].
(S)

064/6.1 Accompanying states

Past participle clauses can have ***accompanying*** meaning in the same way as present participle clauses. This is the case, for example, in (172).
It is true that the perfect tense equivalents suggest 'beforeness', but they have ***resultative*** meaning. That is, the ***resulting state*** accompanies the ***matrix action***, giving the manner or circumstances in which it happens. There may also be causal overtones, as partly in (172), but these are lexical and contextual. The following examples, for instance, are related purely to time and manner:

(174) a. We got back from shopping completely drenched by the rain.
b. The new wedding clothes arrived the next day, packed in cardboard boxes.

As with the present participle, conjunctions can be added to make further meanings more precise, e.g.:

(175) a. (If/when) cleaned up and re-decorated, the flat will sell for a higher price.
b. Flowers look best (when) freshly cut.

The conjunctions here are optional, but with more specific meanings (such as various conditional types, concession, contradiction, etc.) they have to be included:

(176) a. Although painted in bright colours, the picture has a rather depressing character.
b. The food will not be acceptable unless cooked by professionals.
c. If intended as a joke, Davidson's remark was in rather bad taste.

064/6.2 The past participle as a 'passive' participle

The past participle can often be understood as a more direct ***'passive'*** participle. Here it shortens a clause in the passive which refers to a ***parallel*** action:

(177) a. Drunk shortly before bedtime, hot chocolate is very soothing.
(= When it is drunk, ...)
b. The cheese was delicious eaten with that garlic pickle.
(= ... when it was eaten ...)
c. The weekend could be very relaxing, spent at a country hotel.
(= ... if it is spent ...)

It should be noted here that the ***past participle*** is equivalent to a finite ***simple form***, i.e. it is the action ***as a whole*** that is meant. This is shown by the paraphrases in (177).

The equivalent of a finite ***passive progressive form*** is the ***passive present participle***. Compare:

(178) a. When questioned by the police, the witness changed her story.
(= when she was questioned ...)
b. When being questioned by the police, the witness changed her story.
(= ... when she was being questioned ...)

The ***present participle*** emphasizes the ***framework situation***, i.e. the meaning of *during* or *while*. When there is no emphasis on this ***ongoing*** meaning, the ***past participle*** is used.

(178)a. means that the witness changed her story as a result of the whole interview. The story may have collapsed after just one question, or after several, but it expresses the process of questioning as a whole event. (178)b. means 'in the course of being questioned'. That is, the witness changed her story in the middle of the interview.

064/6.3 Separate subject introduction by with

Like the other participles, the past participle can have a ***separate*** subject. This can just be inserted before the participle, or, more commonly, introduced by ***with***, which sounds less formal:

(179) a. His hands clasped tightly, Basil listened to the accusations.
b. With his hands clasped tightly, Basil listened to the accusations.
c. Her briefcase under her arm, Jenny dashed for the bus.
d. With her briefcase under her arm, Jenny dashed for the bus.

Here, too, ***with*** is very common when there are ***causal*** overtones:

(180) a. With the fence now repaired, no-one can just walk into our garden.
(= As the fence has now been repaired, ...)
b. With all the tourist facilities closed for the winter, coastal holiday resorts often look very dreary.
(= As all the tourist facilities have been closed, ...)

064/6.4 Past participles following catenatives: causative meaning

There are a few ***catenative constructions*** with the past participle. All have the pattern ***verb + object + past participle***. Those in this section are ***causative***:

- ***have*** and ***get***, meaning ***ask/order/cause to be done***: *Mum and Dad have had the living-room re-decorated* (*... haben das Wohnzimmer neu streichen und tapezieren lassen*); *I must get my hair cut* (*Ich muss mir (endlich) die Haare schneiden lassen*).
- ***have*** and ***get***, meaning ***suffer/experience something negative***: *We've had our car stolen* (= *We've suffered the theft of our car; Jemand hat uns das Auto gestohlen*); *You'll get your new trousers torn if you climb trees in them* (= *You'll suffer torn trousers ...; Du wirst Löcher in der neuen Hose kriegen, ...*). There is a suggestion here that the 'victim' is partly responsible (especially with *get*).
- ***get***, meaning ***manage/complete***: *The firm must get the job done by February* (= *... must manage to complete the job ...; ... muss die Arbeit bis Februar zu Ende bringen/erledigen*); *I got the article written during the vacation* (= *... managed to write it...; Ich schaffte es, den Artikel in den Ferien zu schreiben*).
- ***make*** in the fixed expressions ***make something/oneself heard/understood/felt***: *The music was so loud that we could hardly make our voices heard* (*... so laut, dass wir uns nicht verständigen konnten*); *As I do not speak the language, I cannot make myself understood* (*..., kann ich mich nicht verständigen*); *The new manager's influence was slowly making itself felt* (*Der Einfluss des neuen Abteilungsleiters wurde langsam spürbar*).

064/6.5 Past participles following catenatives: the shortened passive infinitive

Past participle meaning is generally passive. But after the following verbs, the participle quite clearly stands syntactically for a ***shortened passive infinitive***:

- ***volitional verbs*** (mainly *want* and *like*): *We would like the groceries (to be) delivered, please* (*Wir würden die Einkäufe gern liefern lassen*); *Mr.Taylor wants this letter (to be) sent off immediately* (*... will/möchte, dass dieser Brief sofort abgeschickt wird*).
- ***verbs of perception***: *I've never heard the word used in that context* (*... noch nie gehört, wie das Wort in dem Zusammenhang benutzt wurde*); *They saw Manchester United beaten by Barcelona* (*... sahen, wie Manchester United von Barcelona geschlagen wurde*).
  This is the passive form of the active 'perception' construction taking the ***infinitive without* to**, i.e. *We saw Barcelona beat Manchester United.*
  Unlike the normal infinitive, the ***infinitive without* to** has ***no*** passive form, i.e. it is not possible to say **They saw Manchester United be beaten.*
  Here, therefore, the past participle must be used alone.
  Here, too, we can see the ***aspect*** difference (simple form meaning vs. progressive meaning) between the ***past participle*** and the ***present participle*** which was discussed under **064/6.2** above:

(181) a. We saw Manchester United ***beaten*** by Barcelona.
(= We saw the whole match – ***past participle***)
b. We saw Manchester United ***being beaten*** by Barcelona.
(= We saw Manchester United progressing towards defeat/in the course of being beaten – ***present participle***)

064/6.6 Past participles following verbs with no object

Like the present participle, the ***past participle*** follows a small number of verbs without an object (e.g. *remain, get, stay, feel*):

(182) a. Several toys got broken at the children's party.
b. Most of the audience remained seated after the performance.
c. After the meeting Louise felt drained of all her energy.

In constructions like this the participle is a grammatical 'borderline case' between a verb and an adjective. In principle it can be regarded as either. However, we will take the view that it is an adjective. The effect on syntax is seen in the next section.

064/6.7 Syntax of the past participle at sentence level

Unlike clauses with present participles, those with bare infinitives and past participles do not stand for time clauses, and are therefore not adverbial, but function as ***object complements***:

S P Od Co P
(183) a. Mum and Dad have had the living-room [re-decorated].
(S) →

S P Od Co P A
b. We saw Manchester United [beaten by Barcelona]
(S) →

With verbs of perception, this corresponds to the analysis of the active versions with the bare infinitive: *We saw Barcelona beat Manchester United.*

After verbs like *get, stay* and *feel*, as we said in the last section, we will regard the participle as an ***adjective***. As a result, it loses its clausal character and predicator function and becomes a phrase functioning as subject complement:

S P Cs A
(184) a. Several toys got broken at the children's party.
A S P Cs ***(adjective phrase)***
b. After the meeting Louise felt [drained of all her energy].

064/7 The past participle at phrase level

064/7.1 Following nouns

Like the present participle, the past participle can introduce a ***postmodifying*** clause in a noun phrase, also equivalent to a reduced or ***shortened relative clause***. Again, it should be noted that the meaning is passive:

(185) a. The furniture made in this factory is mainly for export.
(The furniture which is/has been made in this factory ...)
b. I do not like the pork-pies sold in the corner-shop.
(... the pork-pies which are sold in the corner-shop)

Implied subject here also is the ***antecedent***, i.e. *the furniture* in a. and *the pork-pies* in b. A full functional analysis of these sentences would be as follows:

```
           S                 P      A            P    A    A
(186) a. [The furniture/made in this factory]  is mainly for export.
          {     ↑              ↑            }
          {    head     postmodification    }
          {    noun          phrase         }

         S     P     Od                  P     A
      b. I do not like [the pork-pies/sold in this shop].
                       {     ↑            ↑          }
                       {    head   postmodification  }
                       {    noun        phrase       }
```

064/7.2 Premodifying nouns

Like the present participle, the past participle also appears as a ***premodifier***:

(187) a. The policemen discovered stolen goods in the man's shed.
(... goods which had been stolen ...)
b. That broken window has still not been replaced.
(That window which was/has been broken ...)
c. Used cars can be unreliable.
(Cars which have been used ...)
d. Stuffed animals adorned the verandah of the hunting-lodge.
(Animals which had been stuffed ...)

As with the present participle, no complementation is possible, and predicator and clause functions are lost. The participle becomes like an ***adjective***, emphasizing a ***feature*** or ***characteristic***. Past participles are even more 'adjective-like' than present participles, in fact: by their nature, they express states.

If an event or process is meant, ***postmodification*** is required, as with the present participle:

(188) a. The goods stolen included watches and jewellery.
b. Any windows broken will be paid for by the insurance company.
c. The vehicle used in the robbery has not yet been traced by the police.
d. All sports kit supplied must be washed and returned to the club after matches.

Although, therefore, both pre- and postmodifying variants are like relative clauses in sense, it is important to distinguish between reference to a ***feature/characteristic*** (= premodifying meaning) and reference to an ***action*** or ***process*** (postmodifying meaning). On *-ed*-adjectives, see also chapter 4, **029/2.3** and **4**.

064/7.3 Predicative use

Another indication that past participles are more adjective-like is that, in contrast to present participles, they can all occur ***predicatively*** as full ***adjectives*** (i.e. in ***subject complement*** function):

(189) a. The goods in the shed are stolen.
b. That window has been broken for a long time.
c. All cars in the showroom are used.
d. The huge birds frightened us, even though they were only stuffed.

Only certain present participles which have become full lexical adjectives can be used in this way, e.g. *thrilling, exciting, boring,* etc. (see **064/2.8** above).

The predicative position of the past participle can lead to ***ambiguity*** with the ***passive***. Out of context, for instance, (190)a. can mean either (190)b. or (190)c.:

(190) a. At 6 pm the shop was shut.
b. *Passive verbal meaning*: The shop was shut by someone at that time.
c. *Adjective state meaning*: The shop was in that state at 6 pm, i.e. somebody had already shut it.

This kind of ambiguity cannot occur in German, as German passives are formed with *werden*: *Um 18 Uhr* ***wurde*** *der Laden geschlossen* (***passive verbal meaning***); *Um 18 Uhr* ***war*** *der Laden geschlossen* (***adjective state meaning***).

Other examples: *The goods were stolen* (= *wurden gestohlen* or *waren gestohlen*); *The meat was cooked* (= *wurde gekocht/zubereitet* or *war gekocht/gar*). Some grammars call the ***adjective state meaning*** the ***statal passive*** (as opposed to the ***actual*** or ***verbal passive***).

064/7.4 The intransitive past participle

The ***adjectival*** use of the ***past participle*** is usually confined to those formed from ***transitive*** verbs. This is naturally so, as the past participle typically expresses a result or state in a ***passive*** sense, and passives are possible only with transitive verbs.

However, there are a few ***intransitive*** past participles used as adjectives:

(191) a. a fallen tree (= a tree which has fallen)
b. a faded colour (= a colour that has faded)
c. an escaped animal (= an animal that has escaped)
d. a retired teacher (= a teacher who has retired)

The meaning here is ***active***. That is, the ***head noun*** is the potential ***subject*** of the action (generally the ***agent***, and never the ***patient***).

Other examples are *advanced, experienced, departed, recovered, well-behaved, outspoken,* etc.

One or two past participles used in this way can only appear ***predicatively*** (i.e. as ***subject complements***), e.g. *gone* and intransitive *finished*: *My car is gone* (= *missing*)!; *I've been busy washing the car, but I'm finished* (*with it*) *now.*

Others can be regarded as transitive or intransitive, e.g. *married, divorced, hardened, softened,* etc. (See also chapter 4, **029/2.3**).

064/7.5 'False' participles and -ed-adjectives

A number of past participle-style adjectives are 'pseudo'-formed. That is, they look as if they come from verbs, but actually do not. These may be:

- ***negative*** forms of real participles: *unexpected, inexperienced, unhurried,* etc. In these cases the positive form comes from a genuine verb, but the negative form does not.
- forms derived from ***nouns***: *talented, skilled, wooded, honeyed,* etc.
  Typical here are ***compound*** forms with an ***adjective*** as the first element: *long-sleeved, large-boned, bad-tempered, full-blooded,* etc. Note, however, that *well* usually occurs here (and not **good*): *well-muscled, well-disposed, well-intentioned.*
  The ***-ed***-meaning here is ***having*** ... (e.g. *long sleeves, good muscles, large bones,* etc.).
- ***full adjectives*** ending in ***-ed*** which are ***not*** participles: *crooked, wicked, naked,* etc. Note that here the ending is pronounced as [ɪd]: [krʊkɪd], [wɪkɪd], [neɪkɪd].
  (See also chapter 4, **029/2.4**).

Chapter 14 Phrase and Clause at Complex Level

This chapter returns to clauses and phrases. It is basically concerned with the clause, firstly as part of the phrase, and secondly at sentence level.

14.1 The complex phrase

065 Introduction

So far we have met ***subordination*** only at ***sentence level*** (see also under **14.2**). However, it can also take place at ***phrase level***. Subordinate clauses are then ***parts of phrases***. Phrases containing clauses are known as ***complex*** phrases, as opposed to ***simple*** phrases, which contain no clauses.

Though it is the ***complex*** phrase that we are essentially concerned with here, certain types of ***simple*** phrase must also be discussed in connection with it, as there is interaction and dependence of various kinds between the two.

066 Postmodification in the noun phrase

The term ***modification*** means 'describing element(s)'. In a noun phrase, the describing elements ***preceding*** the noun are called the ***premodification***. Those ***following*** it form the ***postmodification*** (see also chapter 2.1, **012/1**).

The ***postmodification*** consists either of a ***prepositional phrase*** or a ***clause*** such as a ***relative clause***, ***infinitive clause*** or ***participle clause***. The noun they follow (i.e. the ***head*** of the noun phrase) is called the ***antecedent*** of the postmodification:

		Premodification	***Head*** (= ***antecedent***)	***Postmodification***
(1)	a.	The tall	man	who was sitting by the window
	b.	The tall	man	sitting by the window
	c.	Der große	Mann,	der am Fenster saß

The postmodification in (1)a. is a ***relative clause***, and in (1)b. a ***present participle clause***. They have the same meaning. (1)c. gives the German equivalent.

Note that in German a participle clause cannot appear as a postmodification like this. German participle clauses, where used, have to ***premodify*** the noun: *Der große, am Fenster sitzende Mann*. This, on the other hand, is not possible in English (see also chapter 13).

With regard to general meaning, there are two types of postmodification: ***restrictive*** and ***non-restrictive***.

The usual type is ***restrictive***, and means 'just that one', i.e. it ***identifies*** the ***antecedent***. The usual interpretation of (1)a. and b. would be the ***restrictive*** one, i.e. in the meaning 'only that man' (dt. *der(jenige) Mann, der am Fenster saß*). If I say *The tall man who was sitting by the window stood up*, I am using the postmodification to identify which man I mean.

Notice that English (in contrast to German) ***never*** has a comma between an antecedent and a restrictive postmodification. We will see the reason for this further below.

We will now consider a ***non-restrictive*** interpretation. Here a ***comma*** is needed, both before and after the postmodification:

(2) a. The tall man, who was sitting by the window, stood up.
b. Der große Mann, der (übrigens) am Fenster saß ...

The relation to the antecedent here is different. Here the postmodification is not being used to say which man is meant. The identity of the man must already be clear from the context, as the main message of (2)a. is *The tall man stood up*. The ***relative clause*** here gives ***extra information*** (*The tall man was sitting by the window. He stood up*). It is not needed to identify the antecedent and could be left out without changing his identity, or making the listener wonder who the speaker is talking about. Here are two more examples that make the difference especially clear:

(3) a. The guests, who were sitting in the garden, got wet in the sudden downpour.
b. The guests who were sitting in the garden got wet in the sudden downpour.

(3)a. means ***all*** the guests (*The guests were sitting in the garden, and got wet in the sudden downpour*). (3)b. means only ***some*** of the guests (the ones in the garden, but not those already inside the house, for instance).

The ***commas*** in the non-restrictive variety show two things: firstly, the clause is a ***parenthesis*** (dt. *Einschub*) and interrupts the flow of the main sentence, i.e. in (3)a. *The guests got wet in the sudden downpour*. Secondly, the commas stand (as always) for ***pauses*** in the spoken language. For the parenthesis, the voice is usually lowered and the intonation changes slightly. Restrictive postmodifications, on the other hand, are pronounced as a unit (i.e. in 'one breath') with the antecedent:

(4) a. The guests, who were sitting in the garden, got wet in the sudden downpour.

b. The guests who were sitting in the garden got wet in the sudden downpour.

Restrictive postmodifications are the rule. Non-restrictive postmodifications tend to be the exception. When they occur, it is usually with relative clauses. With other forms of postmodification the non-restrictive type is possible, but rare. Non-restriction is also found mainly in the written language. For explanations on the syntactic analysis of restrictive vs. non-restrictive postmodification, see under **066/1.2** and **1.10** below.

066/1 The relative clause

This is the most general kind of ***finite*** clause that can directly postmodify a noun. A ***relative clause*** is linked to the antecedent by a ***relative pronoun***. The ***relative pronoun*** stands for the ***antecedent***, i.e. is identical with it.

Grammatically, the relative pronoun is a kind of 'subordinator', i.e. it functions rather like a conjunction, joining the clause to a preceding element that it is dependent on. Here, however, that element is the head of a phrase (and not a matrix clause, as in subordination at sentence level). Although it stands for the antecedent, the ***relative pronoun*** is grammatically separate. That is, it introduces its own subordinate clause (= the relative clause), and has its own ***separate function*** inside the clause (see further below for details).

066/1.1 Relative pronouns

As the ***relative pronoun*** refers to the ***antecedent***, the kind of pronoun used must correspond, firstly, to the ***nature of the antecedent***:

- ***who*** is used for persons of both sexes,
- ***which*** is used for things and (usually) animals,
- ***that*** is used for everything (things, persons and animals), but is less formal stylistically; it is particularly colloquial in the ***subject*** function (see below) when used for ***persons***.
- all three pronouns can be ***omitted*** under certain grammatical conditions. This is then known as the ***zero relative pronoun***. It occurs in speech and informal written styles.

Secondly, the kind of pronoun depends on whether the relative clause is ***restrictive*** or ***non-restrictive***:

- ***who*** and ***which*** appear in both ***restrictive*** and ***non-restrictive*** relative clauses;
- ***that*** and the ***zero relative pronoun*** are used only in ***restrictive*** relative clauses.

Thirdly, the choice is affected by the sentence ***function*** of the relative pronoun inside the relative clause.

- ***whom*** is used in formal language as the ***object*** case of ***who***, and appears as ***direct object*** and after ***prepositions***; in neutral language ***whom*** is replaced by the ordinary form ***who*** (except when immediately following prepositions, see under **066/1.3**);
- the ***zero relative pronoun*** also appears in all functions ***except*** subject.

Specific examples of the various pronouns in different sentence functions are given under **066/1.3** below. The next section deals generally with functions in the relative clause.

066/1.2 Sentence functions inside and outside relative clauses

The first thing to point out here is that ordinary sentence functions apply ***inside*** relative clauses, and only inside them. The relative clause itself has ***no direct*** external relation to the larger sentence.

Taken for itself, a relative clause has only a ***phrase function***, i.e. as a ***postmodification*** in a noun phrase. That is, it is part of a noun phrase. It is then the noun phrase ***as a whole*** which has a function in the larger sentence, e.g. as subject, direct object, etc.

For analysis purposes we will separate relative clauses and other postmodification types from their antecedents by a slant (/). We will mark the whole noun phrase by curl brackets, i.e. by {and}:

S S P A P Cs A
(5) a. {The guests /who were sitting in the garden/} got wet in the sudden downpour.
S Od S P P Cs
b. {The car /that I drive/} is very old.
S P Od S P Cs
c. My wife chose {the shoes /that were most expensive/}.
S S P A P Cs A
d. {The guests, /who were sitting in the garden/,} got wet in the sudden downpour.

The kind of phrase analysis illustrated here is not confined to relative clauses. It can be applied to all types of postmodification (see, for instance section **066/3** below), and, moreover, to the complex phrase in general (see **067/1** and **2** below for application to adjective and prepositional phrases).

But to return to our focus on the relative clause: in (5)a.–c. the examples are ***restrictive***, whereas (5)d. is ***non-restrictive***. It is the ***non-restrictive*** version of (5)a.

We represent ***non-restrictive*** relative clauses here in basically the same way as restrictive, i.e. as part of the noun phrase. Only the commas in (5)d. show the difference.

However, it is possible to take a completely different view. According to this perspective, non-restrictives are ***not*** part of the noun phrase, but are quite separate clauses at sentence level:

S S P A P Cs A
(6) The guests [/who were sitting in the garden/] got wet in the sudden downpour.

Here the slants show that the relative clause has an antecedent; the square brackets, on the other hand, indicate that the clause is subordinated at sentence level, i.e. independently of the noun phrase. Which of the two analysis forms one chooses is a matter of opinion. We choose the version in (5)d. The version in (6) is reserved here for sentential relative clauses (see **066/1.10** below).

066/1.3 Possible functions of relative pronouns

Here we show functions of the relative pronoun only, and also which alternative pronouns are possible according to the rules just given in **066/1.1**.

S
(7) a. I know {the man /***who*** won the money/}.
that

Od
b. {The house /***that*** Sharon bought/} needs a lot of repair work.
which
zero (Ø)

Od
c. {The teacher /***whom*** we particularly liked/} was Mrs. Taylor.
who
that
zero (Ø)

Cs
d. Have we forgotten {the person /***who*** Joan once was/}?
that
zero (Ø)

Co
e. {The names /***which*** he called her/} were deeply offensive.
that
zero (Ø)

A
f. I can't remember {the woman /***to whom*** I gave the parcel/}.
A ***A***
that/who(m) ***to***
zero (Ø) ***to***

A
g. I can't remember {the address /***to which*** I sent the parcel/}.
A ***A***
that/which ***to***
zero (Ø) ***to***

With regard to (7)a., 'careful' speakers would usually prefer ***who*** to ***that*** for ***persons*** when the relative pronoun is ***subject***. ***That*** here is particularly colloquial. In other functions, especially ***object***, as in (7)c., it is the other way round in ordinary language, i.e. ***that*** is usually preferred to ***who(m)***.

(7)f. and g. are ***prepositional relative clauses***. The relative pronouns here are parts of prepositional phrases, i.e. strictly speaking ***prepositional complements***, or as we will call them ***prepositional relative pronouns***. The ***prepositional phrase*** as a whole functions as an ***adverbial***.

The most important practical feature here is the ***position of the preposition***. When it occurs before the relative pronoun, the prepositional phrase 'stays together'. However, this is very formal style and is only possible with the pronouns ***whom*** (note the object case!) and ***which***. With ***who***, ***that*** and ***zero*** the preposition is ***postposed***, i.e. it goes to the ***end*** of the relative clause (nowadays the only normal position in speech and less formal language). This leads to what is called a ***discontinuous prepositional phrase***, in which each part is marked for the adverbial function.

066/1.4 A note on indirect objects

Relative pronouns do not usually function as indirect objects. That is, sentences like the following are generally avoided: **I can't remember the woman who/that/(zero)I gave the parcel.* In relative clauses indirect objects are always converted into prepositional phrases, i.e. adverbials: *I can't remember the woman* ***who(m)/that/(zero)*** *I gave the parcel* ***to***.

The reason is that the usual strict sequence of ***predicator + indirect object + direct object*** cannot be kept in the relative clause, as the relative pronoun (i.e. the potential indirect object) has to be at the beginning of the clause. The preposition solution is therefore introduced to avoid contravening the normal sequence principle.

This is similar also with ***wh***-questions, i.e. *Who did you give the parcel to?* and not **Who did you give the parcel?* (See also chapter 1, **003/3.4**).

066/1.5 Omitting the relative pronoun: contact clauses

In speech the relative pronoun is usually omitted where possible. To summarize, this is grammatically allowed

- only in ***restrictive*** relative clauses;
- when the relative pronoun is ***not the subject*** of the relative clause.

Relative clauses with no pronoun are sometimes called ***contact clauses*** or ***shortened relative clauses***. Here the term ***contact clause*** is preferred, as in this book the expression shortened relative clause is applied also to other forms of relative clause reduction, such as participle clauses and prepositional phrases. For us, that is, the ***contact clause*** is only ***one*** example of a ***shortened relative clause***.

The omitted relative pronoun was introduced above as the ***zero relative pronoun***. This is to signal that the 'gap' left behind is something concrete or positive, i.e. it is a 'presence', and among other things should be marked for syntactic function, e.g.:

Od
(8) a. {The watch /***(Ø)*** I gave Sue for her birthday/} is not working.
A ***A***
b. My husband is {the man /***(Ø)*** I am buying the present for/}.

066/1.6 Genitives

The ***genitive*** relative pronoun ***whose*** is syntactically a ***determiner*** and is followed by a noun. It is normally used only for ***personal antecedents***.

S
(9) a. {The player/***whose leg*** was broken/} is back in training.
Der Spieler, dessen Bein gebrochen war ...
A ***A***
b. That was {the woman /***whose daughter*** we gave the first prize to/}.
... die Frau, deren Tochter ...

Occasionally, ***whose*** is found after inanimate antecedents (i.e. those denoting things), e.g. *The police called at the house whose front-door had been damaged*. However, this is usually avoided because ***whose*** is regarded as the genitive of ***who***, which can refer only to people.

Genitives after ***inanimate*** antecedents have their own form, ***of which***:

(10) a. Two old cars, the doors of which had been torn off, stood in the middle of the yard.
b. The house stood at the edge of a high cliff, the face of which fell vertically to the rocky shore about 50 feet below.

Of which is usually preferred, as in the examples, with the 'belonging' noun placed before it (*the doors of which, the face of which*), but the reverse order can sometimes also occur (*of which the doors, of which the face*).

Of which is used mainly in ***non-restrictive*** clauses. In restrictive clauses, it usually sounds clumsy or unnecessarily elaborate in style (e.g. in *The police called at the house the front-door of which/of which the front-door had been damaged*). More common are paraphrases: *The police called at the house where the front-door had been damaged/with the damaged front-door/which had had its front-door damaged*, etc.).

With ***persons*** there is also the form ***of whom***, a parallel to ***of which***, and under certain limited conditions an alternative to ***whose***:

(11) a. Casey, the wife of whom was seeking a divorce, had decided to take a new solicitor.
b. At church I spoke to the choir-leader, the son of whom had also recently joined the choir.

This form is less frequent than ***whose***. Like ***of which***, it can also sound rather awkward stylistically. However, it is possible when the person is ***stressed*** (see also general remarks on ***of***-genitives with persons, in chapter 2.3, **019/1**). ***Of whom*** is used almost exclusively in ***non-restrictive*** clauses.

The constructions ***of which*** and ***of whom*** as in (10) and (11), with the noun preceding, are really no longer relative clauses. Strictly speaking, they belong to the category of ***apposition*** (see later below).

066/1.7 Partitives

These are quantifiers with ***of*** (see especially chapter 2.2, **016/5**, and 2.3, **020/1.2**), and combine with relative pronouns to produce expressions like *half of which, several of whom,* etc.:

(12) a. The four men, two of whom had guns, entered the bank shortly before 9 am.
b. On the riverbank there were crowds of people, many of whom had brought picnics with them.
c. The grass was full of fallen apples, some of which had already turned brown.

Again, these are cases of ***apposition*** (see under **066/4** below).

066/1.8 Relative adverbs

The adverbs ***when, where*** and ***why*** are often used like relative pronouns, and are then called ***relative adverbs***. Functionally they are ***adverbial***. In most cases there are alternatives with ***prepositional relative pronouns***:

A
(13) a. You must visit us on {a day /***when*** we're not busy/}.
on which

A
b. This must be {the road /***where*** the robbery took place/}.
in which

A
c. There is {a good reason /***why*** we dislike him/}.
for which

066/1.9 Relative adverbs: replacement and omission

With expressions of ***place, time, manner***, and ***cause***, there are varied individual possibilities for ***omission***.

When and ***where*** cannot generally be left out, but ***zero*** is possible with the ***prepositional*** versions, e.g. ... *the road the robbery took place in.*

On the other hand, ***why*** is often omitted completely after *reason*, especially in less formal language: *The reason I'm asking about Joe is that I'm worried about him.*

Another possibility with the noun *reason* is to use the relative pronoun ***that*** (instead of *why*): *The reason that I'm asking about Joe...*

Note in this case that the preposition is generally ***omitted*** too. It would be unusual to hear: *(*)The reason I'm asking about Joe for.*

066/1.10 Sentential relative clauses

This is a special type of non-restrictive relative clause: the antecedent here is the ***whole*** of the ***preceding clause***:

(14) a. He called me a liar, which was very insulting.
Er nannte mich einen Lügner, was sehr beleidigend war.
b. The police have blocked off Borough High Street, which will make us rather late.
..., was bedeutet, dass wir recht spät dran sein werden.

The relative pronoun in ***sentential relative clauses*** is always ***which***.

⚠ Note that the German equivalent is *was*. This must ***not*** be rendered in English as *what*, i.e. not **He called me a liar, what was very insulting.*

Note also that as sentential relative clauses are non-restrictive, there must be a ***comma*** before them. The fact that they have a whole clause as an antecedent means that they are subordinate to that clause at sentence level. We therefore show this by square brackets, just as with any other sub-clause. The slants remain to indicate that this is a relative clause (see also section **066/1.2** above):

(15) The police have blocked off Borough High Street, [/which will make us rather late/].

066/2 The relative clause: other phenomena

066/2.1 Postponed relative clauses

Generally speaking, relative clauses should immediately follow their antecedent, so that everything belonging to the noun phrase forms a closed unit. Sometimes, however, it can be more economical to finish the matrix clause first and place the relative clause after it. This happens mainly in speech, and especially when the relative clause is long. The antecedent must still be quite clear, of course:

(16) a. Then a ***woman*** came in ***who said*** she had been stuck in a traffic jam for three hours.
b. They had a ***quarrel*** that evening ***which was*** so loud that the neighbours complained.
c. (*)Dave bought a DVD player in a shop in the High Street which he took back the next day.

A sentence like (16)c., though possible, would probably be avoided, as it could suggest that *shop* or *High Street* are the antecedent of *which* and not *DVD player*, as obviously intended.

066/2.2 Further clauses within a relative clause

As in examples (16)a. and b., relative clauses can contain ***further clauses***:

(17) a. I do not want to sell a car that is old, but still runs well.
b. The workers who went on strike last year just before their firm closed down got what they wanted.
c. Last week I had a customer who complained that she had not been asked if the water temperature was all right while her hair was being washed.

This is basically no different from any other kind of multi-complex clause at sentence level. What should be noted here, however, is that in this case everything belongs ultimately ***inside*** a single ***phrase***, e.g.:

S ***S*** ***P*** ***A*** ***A*** ***A*** ***S***
(18) {The workers /who went on strike last year [just before their firm
P ***P*** ***A*** ***Cs***
closed down]/}were eventually successful.

066/2.3 Secondary fronting

This is a widespread phenomenon which also involves further clauses ***inside*** the relative clause (see previous section). Here, the relative pronoun has a rather odd syntactic status: it does ***not*** have a function in the relative clause itself (i.e. in the immediate ***'matrix'*** part), but in ***one of the sub-clauses***:

(19) a. One thing ***that*** I forgot ***to do*** was post your letter.
Eine Sache, die ich vergessen habe zu tun, war, deinen Brief einzuwerfen.
b. My first book was the one ***that*** I hated ***writing*** most.
Mein erstes Buch war das, das zu schreiben ich am meisten hasste.
c. The police never found the weapon ***that*** the murderer said he ***had used***.
Die Polizei hat nie die Waffe gefunden, von der der Mörder behauptete, er habe davon Gebrauch gemacht.
d. The man ***that*** the police believed ***had held*** up the bank was arrested last week.
Der Mann, von dem die Polizei glaubte, dass er die Bank ausgeraubt hätte, wurde letzte Woche verhaftet.

Although the relative pronoun (***that*** in these examples) ***appears*** to be the object of the relative clause verb (i.e. the ***'matrix'*** verb), it is actually the ***object*** or ***subject*** of the ***subordinate verb***:

S *Od* *S* *P* *Od* *P*
(20) a. {One thing/***that*** I forgot [***to do***]/} was post your letter.

Cs *Od* *S* *P* *Od* *P* *A*
b. My first book was {the one /***that*** I hated [***writing***] most/}.

Od *Od* *S* *P* *Od* *S* *P*
c. The police never found {the weapon /***that*** the murderer said [he ***had used***]/}.

S *S* *S* *P* *Od* *P* *Od*
d. {The man/***that*** the police believed [***had held up*** the bank]/} was arrested last week.

Looking at it from the ***perspective of the sub-clause***, we will call this process ***secondary fronting***: the subject or object of the sub-clause has been 'removed' from it and ***fronted*** (i.e. placed before the matrix) as a relative pronoun.

As the translations in (19) show, the phenomenon is not unknown in German. However, it is generally confined to non-finite verbs, as in (19)a. and b. With finite verbs, as in c. and d. (*had held, had used*) a different German construction is necessary.

Ordinary ***omission*** rules apply also to ***secondary fronting***: that is, ***that*** can be replaced by ***zero*** in every one of these examples, e.g. *My first book was the one I hated writing most.* Interestingly enough, this is possible in (19)d., even though the relative pronoun is the ***subject*** of the ***sub-clause*** and not the object. However, it ***appears*** to be the ***object*** of the relative clause verb (i.e. the matrix verb), and this 'false object function' is enough to make omission possible: *The man the police believed had held up the bank...*

Although syntactically quite complicated, ***secondary fronting*** occurs particularly often in speech. It is also common with **wh-*interrogatives***, as already seen in chapter 11.

066/3 Other types of relative postmodification

The noun phrases in (21) all mean the same:

(21) a. the man who is standing on the corner
b. the man standing on the corner
c. the man on the corner

(21)b. and c., in other words, are ***shortened*** or ***reduced*** forms of (21)a. From the other perspective, we could expand the ***prepositional phrase*** in c. into the ***participle clause*** in b., and this, in turn, into the ***full relative clause*** in (21)a. We therefore regard postmodifications of the types in b. and c. as ***shortened*** or ***reduced*** relative clauses. In speech and other informal language they are a much more common type of ***relative postmodification*** than the relative clause itself. In the following they are discussed individually.

066/3.1 Present participle clauses

Here the ***antecedent*** is the ***implied subject*** of the participle. Apart from this, everything is signalled in the same way as with the relative clause (including, of course, the internal functions of the clause):

```
          S            P       A              P  Cs
(22) a. {The man /standing on the corner/} is  my father.
            S            P        Od               P        Od
     b. Security staff searched  {customers /entering the store/}.
```

Present participles are usually interpreted as ***progressive*** in meaning (e.g. *customers who* ***were entering*** *the store*). In postmodifications, however, they can also refer to ***habits***, and in this case stand for ***simple*** forms: *The road connecting the villages of Ambleside and Tunthwaite has been blocked by snowdrifts* (= *the road which* ***connects*** ...). Similarly, the participles of certain ***stative*** verbs can also occur occasionally as postmodifiers: *A woman found a diamond ring costing more than £ 20,000 on Brighton Pier yesterday.* These also represent ***simple*** forms (= *a diamond ring which cost/costs* ...).

Present participles can appear in the ***passive***. In postmodifications the antecedent is then the implied subject of a ***passive*** action ***in progress***: *The house being renovated in Dean Street belongs to Mrs. Fox.*

066/3.2 Past participle clauses

As past participles have passive meaning, the ***antecedent*** in this case is the ***implied passive subject*** of the participle:

```
          S          P        A       P     Cs
(23) a. {The car /parked by the gate/} is not mine.
           S      P           Od          P       A                A
     b. Police are looking for {two men /seen near the building yesterday/}.
```

The postmodifications here mean, respectively, *the car which has been/was parked* ..., and *two men who were seen* ...

066/3.3 Prepositional phrases

Strictly speaking, the noun phrase is no longer complex when the postmodification contains no verb. However, as we are discussing prepositional phrases which stand for relative clauses, it is appropriate to mention them here too.

```
          S          A          P      Cs
(24) a. {The car /by the gate/} is not mine.
           S     P     Od                A
     b. Fred watched {the woman /across the street/}.
```

It is important to note that not all prepositional phrases represent relative postmodification. For example, in *the children with the ice-creams*, or *the wheels of the bus* expansion into relative clauses is not possible. The meaning here is ***genitive*** (see further below), and not relative.

066/3.4 Infinitive clauses

Infinitive clauses can postmodify nouns in the sense of relative clauses under the following conditions:

Firstly, the noun can be ***premodified*** by a ***superlative*** adjective (including the related adjectives *next, last* and *only*), or by an ***ordinal number*** (*first, second, third,* etc.). The antecedent is the ***implied subject*** of the infinitive:

(25) a. Martin was the next guest to arrive (= the next guest who arrived).
b. Sally is the best journalist ever to work for this paper (= the best journalist who has ever worked ...).

Passive infinitives are also common in this sense: *This is Walter, the largest pig to be bred at Selsey Farm; Sykes was the only man to be rescued from the sinking tanker.*

The second (and much more frequent) case is when the relative clause represented by the infinitive is ***modal*** in meaning (i.e. contains a ***modal*** verb). In this case the antecedent is the ***implied object*** of the infinitive, or the ***implied complement*** of a ***preposition***:

(26) a. I have some important things to say (= things which I must/should/can say).
b. Spain is the place to go to if you want sun (= the place which you should go to ...).

Postmodifying infinitives of this type are very common after ***indefinite pronouns***: *Can I get you something to drink?* (= *something that you can drink*); *We have nothing to do today* (= *nothing that we can/must do*), see also chapter 13.1.

066/3.5 Non-restrictive senses

Non-restrictive postmodification with participles or prepositional phrases is not frequent, but does occur, mainly in press and literary texts:

(27) a. A large otter, basking in the sun on the bank, suddenly roused and shot into the water.
b. The police are looking for Joe Saunders, thought to be hiding somewhere in Manchester.
c. A thousand Everton fans, in London for their team's away match against Spurs, were allowed to camp out in Hyde Park.

066/3.6 Ambiguity between postmodification and separate clauses or phrases

Participles and prepositional phrases following nouns ***may*** or ***may not*** be postmodifications. In (28) two examples are postmodifying, and two others are not, i.e. they are quite ***separate*** from the noun they follow, and have a separate function:

(28) a. We heard someone moving around upstairs.
Wir hörten, wie sich jemand im Obergeschoss bewegte.
b. He washed his car in the street.
Er wusch sein Auto auf der Straße.
c. I've cut down the tree in the front-garden.
Ich habe den Baum im Vorgarten gefällt.
d. You must be careful on the path leading down to the valley.
Auf dem Weg ins Tal hinunter müsst ihr vorsichtig sein.

In (28)c. the prepositional phrase *in the front garden* describes and identifies the *tree*, i.e. it tells us which tree is meant. It is therefore a ***postmodification*** and can be expanded into a ***relative clause***: *the tree which was in the front-garden*. The same applies to the participle clause in (28)d., i.e. ... *the path which leads down into the valley*.

On the other hand, the participle clause in (28)a. and the prepositional phrase in (28) b., are ***not*** postmodifications and cannot be expressed as relative clauses. (28)a. means *We heard someone while he/she was moving around upstairs*, and ***not*** **We heard someone who was moving around upstairs*. The participle clause functions here as an ***adverbial*** in a typical ***perception construction*** (see also chapter 13.3. **064/1.8**). In (28)b. *in the street* refers to *washed*, not *car*, and is likewise a ***separate adverbial***.

To make the point even clearer, we will take examples which are ***ambiguous***. (29)a., for instance, can mean either (29)b., or (29)c.:

(29) a. Selma spoke to the boy in the corner.
b. ... to the boy who was in the corner. [*Question:* ***Which*** boy ...?]
c. It was in the corner that she spoke to the boy. [*Question:* ***Where*** did she speak to the (already identified) boy?]

Similarly, (30)a. can mean either (30)b., or (30)c.:

(30) a. I saw the man talking to Helen.
b. I saw the man who was talking to Helen (but I saw no other man).
[*Question:* ***Which*** man/men did you see? *Answer*: Only the one who was talking to Helen.]
c. I saw the (already identified) man as he was talking to Helen. [*Question:* ***What*** was the man doing when you saw him? *Answer*: He was talking to Helen.]

On these points, see also chapter 13.3, **064/2.3** and **4**.

066/3.7 Confusion of participles with gerunds following nouns

Another point of confusion concerns the ***gerund***. That is, an -***ing***-form following a noun may not be a present participle at all, but a ***gerund***. This affects the meaning, of course. Note the contrast:

(31) a. Mrs. Craythorpe hated guests arriving late.
[***Gerund***: She hated it when guests turned up late.]
b. Mrs. Craythorpe looked after guests arriving late.
[***Participle*** (*postmodifying*): She took care of any guests who arrived late.]

The example in (32)a., on the other hand, is ambiguous. It may mean b. or c.:

(32) a. I didn't remember the man talking to Helen.
b. I didn't remember that the (already identified) man talked to Helen.
[***Gerund interpretation***]
c. I didn't remember the man who was talking to Helen.
[***Postmodifying participle interpretation***]

066/3.8 Adjective phrases as postmodifiers

Sometimes adjective phrases can be postmodifiers, nearly always with an adjectival complement. Restrictive examples are: *a bucket full of water* (= *a bucket that is full of water*); *three features typical of this landscape* (= *three features that are typical* ...); *the person angry with everybody* (= *the person who is angry* ...). The following are non-restrictive:

(33) a. Kelly, red in the face, sat down to get her breath back.
b. The coach, unhappy with his team's performance, stormed out of the arena.
c. I looked at the whisky bottle, half-empty on the sideboard.

Note that if it is a postmodification the adjective phrase must follow the noun immediately. In other positions it functions as an adverbial, even if the meaning appears to be similar:

A
(34) a. [Red in the face], Kelly sat down to get her breath back.
A
b. The coach stormed out of the arena, [unhappy with his team's performance].

There is a difference in meaning between these examples and the postmodifying versions. Here the adjective phrase refers not only to the person, but, more than this, to the ***action as a whole***. It gives a reason for the action, or an accompanying circumstance. This is why it is ***adverbial*** in function.

066/3.9 Nominal relative clauses

These are actually ***not*** relative clauses as such, but do have a connection to relative clauses. As they are often confused with relative clauses, they deserve special mention here. ***Nominal relative clauses*** are introduced by certain ***wh***-words, in particular ***what***, but also ***where***, and one or two others:

(35) a. Charlotte showed me ***what*** her friend had written to her.
(***what*** = the things that ...)
b. ***What*** we need most at the moment is a holiday.
(= The thing that we need ...)
c. Bromley is ***where*** my father worked.
(***where*** = the place where/at which ...)

The ***wh***-word does in fact stand for a relative pronoun, but not alone: as the paraphrases in brackets show, it stands for the ***antecedent*** as well. This is also underlined by the German equivalent *das, was.*

Note that in English, however, *what* cannot be used as an ordinary relative pronoun at all, i.e. we cannot say **that what.*

Clauses like this are 'nominal' in the sense that they function like nouns, e.g. as subjects or objects. The ***wh***-word is known as a ***nominal relative pronoun*** (***what***), or a ***nominal relative adverb*** (***where***). Inside the clause these have their own separate functions:

Od Od
(36) a. Charlotte showed me [***what*** her friend had written to her].
S Od
b. [***What*** we need most at the moment] is a holiday.
Cs A
c. Bromley is [***where*** my father worked].

Who has restricted and informal use as a nominal relative pronoun: *Jimmy Mackinson is who I prefer as a singer*. In neutral and less informal language, a full noun phrase would be preferable: *Jimmy Mackinson is the man (that/who/whom) I prefer as a singer.*

A second meaning of ***nominal relative elements*** is 'any'. Here it is usual to use an ***-ever***-pronoun or -adverb, i.e. ***whatever/wherever*** (though ***what/where*** are still possible): *You can do whatever you like* (= *anything you like*, dt. ... *was auch immer du willst*); *My home is wherever you are* (= *anywhere you are*, dt. ... *überall, wo du bist*).

Who, again, has restricted use here, and only as an object: *You can invite who you like to the party*. In the meaning of 'any' ***whoever*** is preferred: *You can invite whoever you like to the party; I want to see whoever is in charge here* (= *the person who* ...).

Similarly, the general form for things is ***whichever***: *You can choose whichever shoes you like; I'll take whichever of the two papers you have.*

In the sense of 'any', ***whatever*** is also common here: *You can choose whatever shoes you like*. Note that ***whichever*** is used as both a determiner and a pronoun.

The -*ever*-pronouns and -adverbs also occur typically in ***adverbial*** clauses:

(37) a. Whatever Chrissie did, she was always successful.
(= whichever things she did ...)
b. Wherever he went, she was with him, however he treated her.
(= to whichever place he went, ..., in whichever way he treated her)

Strictly speaking, the clauses themselves are not grammatically nominal here. Nevertheless, they are identical in meaning with nominal relative clauses, i.e. their semantic function is the same, and they can be alternatively expressed by nominal constructions, e.g. after prepositions: *Regardless of what Chrissie did ...*; *Regardless of where he went/how he treated her*, etc.

066/4 Appositive postmodification

This kind of postmodification expresses the antecedent ***in other words***, i.e. gives an ***equivalent*** in terms of content. It has two basic forms:

- firstly, postmodification by an equivalent noun phrase (*Mr. Rhys, the village baker, delivers bread to people's homes*);
- secondly, postmodification by prepositional phrase and/or some kind of clause (*His hopes of winning the race were frustrated; My plan to take an early train came to nothing*).

In both cases the ***equivalence*** can be shown by making a separate sentence in which antecedent and postmodification are joined by the verb ***be***, with the postmodification then becoming ***subject complement (Cs)***: *Mr. Rhys is the village baker; My plan was to take an early train.*

066/4.1 Apposition: postmodification by noun phrase

Here, one noun phrase postmodifies another:

(38) a. David Purglass, our local MP, is retiring next year.
b. The school caretaker, Mr. Blayne, has a flat in the school building.

Traditionally, the two noun phrases are said to be ***in apposition*** to one another (literally meaning 'placed side-by-side'). We will regard this, however, as being a variant of ordinary postmodification.

(38) shows three things that are typical of ***apposition***. First, one of the nouns is a ***proper noun*** (i.e. a name). Second, the postmodification is ***non-restrictive***. Third, the postmodification gives information on the ***antecedent's identity***. None of these necessarily apply, however:

(39) a. The school caretaker, a former plumber, has a flat in the school building.
b. The pop band Cruise Raiders have disbanded.

In (39)a. there is no name or any other identifying function involved. The second noun just gives ***further information*** on the antecedent. Other examples: *The vicar, an expert on local art, showed me his collection of paintings; My brother, a great storyteller, told us all about his adventures in Africa.*

In (39)b. we do have an identifying function, as the apposition noun is again a name: unlike those in (38), however, it is in this case ***restrictive***. Other examples: *my cousin Dan, the writer Paul Auster, the musical Cats, the Japanese island Hokkaido.*

The antecedent can also be a common noun referring, for instance, to some kind of general concept or category, of which the apposition noun is a member or an example, e.g. *the species dog; the conjunction when; the item cheese; the number 4; a letter A; the term "foul".*

Apposition is in some ways similar to a relative clause: *The school caretaker, whose name is Mr. Blayne/who is a former plumber, …; The vicar, who is an expert on local art, …*

The similarity is confined, though, to relative clauses with the verb *be*, showing ***equivalence***. Furthermore, many cases of apposition cannot be expanded into relative clauses without changing the meaning slightly. For instance, expressing (38)a. as *David Purglass, who is our local MP, …* suggests that the listener already knows David Purglass, whereas the original does not.

Non-restrictive apposition has a particularly irregular relation to relative-clause-expansion. We cannot say *The writer whose name is Paul Auster …* without giving the impression that we are talking about the name rather than the person; the same applies to something like *The item that is called cheese*, which would not usually be regarded as equivalent to the apposition version. We therefore treat apposition as a distinct category, quite different from relative postmodification.

066/4.2 Other elements in the apposition phrase

Sometimes the apposition expresses a quantity or part-quantity of the antecedent. It can then consist of a quantifying pronoun or partitive expression, usually with a postmodification of its own:

(40) a. A group of Birmingham fans, all carrying sticks or bottles, attacked rival supporters outside the ground before the game.
b. A few hundred demonstrators, most of them peaceful, had gathered in the main square.

Here, too, there is a relation to relative clauses: *Several Birmingham fans, all of whom were carrying sticks or bottles, …; A few hundred demonstrators, most of whom were peaceful, …*

Another kind of part-relation picks out certain items or members of the antecedent category for emphasis or exemplification. Here the apposition is introduced by focussing adverbial expressions, like *for example, especially, specifically*, etc. Occasionally these may even follow the apposition noun:

(41) a. The recession has drastically affected many low-income families, ***particularly*** those with only one wage-earner.
b. Certain important sections of the working community, ***such as*** nurses and social workers, are habitually paid low wages.
c. A lot of outdoor workers, those employed in the building trade, ***for instance***, face short-time pay in the winter.

Here, too, the apposition noun is frequently a pronoun, such as *that/those*, or a prop-form with *one/ones*.

Other kinds of introducing expression show that the apposition is an explanation, an alternative expression, or a more exact way of referring to the antecedent:

(42) a. Two pupils, ***namely/that is to say***, Guy Robinson and Cheryl Peters, are getting prizes this term for outstanding performance.
b. The worst department head is Truckfield, ***in other words/that is***, my boss.

Apart from these types, adverbials of a more general kind can also be included in the apposition phrase, even as further clauses:

(43) a. Smithson, ***at that time*** a sailor, had no fixed address in London.
b. At the moment they're having lunch with 2 Americans, ***probably*** friends of Paul's.
c. She married a Scotsman, a confidence trickster, ***as it turned out***.

Apposition of this type belongs to written rather than spoken style. It is common in press and literary texts.

066/4.3 Appositive clauses

We now pass from apposition by noun phrase to apposition by ***clause***. The majority of ***appositive clauses*** are ***restrictive*** (unlike noun phrases in apposition).

The ***restrictive appositive clause*** occurs widely throughout all styles of the language, also in speech. It has two common characteristics. Firstly, it typically postmodifies an ***abstract noun*** such as *fact, belief, hope, possibility, idea, intention*, etc. Secondly, although not nouns, the clause types involved have 'nominal' character: infinitives, gerunds (in this case after the preposition ***of***), and finite clauses with ***that*** (i.e. ***that***-clauses):

(44) a. Roger did not keep his ***promise to visit*** us at Christmas.
b. Arsenal's ***hopes of winning*** the Championship were finally destroyed by the defeat in Liverpool.
c. The ***possibility that*** the supply ship would arrive before nightfall now seemed remote.

Note that in ***that***-clauses the word ***that*** is a ***conjunction*** (and ***not*** a relative pronoun!). A ***restrictive appositive clause*** says what the antecedent ***consists of***, i.e. specifies its 'substance'. There is no similarity here at all with relative postmodification. In fact, relative postmodification and the ***restrictive appositive clause*** are regarded as two contrasting types.

066/4.4 Non-restrictive clause apposition

Most appositive clauses like those discussed in **066/4.3** can also appear in ***non-restrictive*** versions, though these are not common:

(45) a. Roger did not keep his promise, to visit us at Christmas.
b. Arsenal's hopes, i.e. of winning the Championship, were finally destroyed by the defeat in Liverpool.
c. Our belief, that the supply ship would arrive before nightfall, was now proven wrong.

The meaning here is one of explanation in the sense of *that is/that is to say/i.e.*, and this would normally be added, as in (45)b., especially in the case of ***preposition + gerund***.

However, ***gerund clauses*** often occur ***without*** *of*. These are always ***non-restrictive***:

(46) My main form of exercise, jogging in the park, keeps me fairly fit.

Gerunds of this type also feature frequently as ***antecedents***, so that in fact we can turn the order in (46) around. This brings us back to the ***noun phrase*** form of apposition, as presented under **066/4.1** and **2**:

(47) Jogging in the park, my main form of exercise, keeps me fairly fit.

Other clause types also occur as ***antecedents***, though less commonly than gerunds, and generally more often in written rather than in spoken styles:

(48) a. She just said that she was ill, a rather weak excuse.
b. To climb the mountain by the northern route, Colin's idea incidentally, would have been sheer madness.
c. I wondered whether Barnes could actually do the job, a question which seemed to interest no-one else.

066/5 Genitive postmodification

The *of*-genitive forms a prepositional phrase. Unlike the typical prepositional phrase, however, it is ***not*** an example of relative postmodification (see **066/3.3**). Generally speaking, postmodifying *of*-genitives are in a category of their own.

An exception is when *of* is used in an ***appositive*** sense, as seen in **066/4.3**. Here it occurs with a gerund, i.e. a ***clause***. There is also ***phrase apposition*** with *of*, dealt with below. It is included here (rather than in the last section) for overview reasons. The following summarizes the *of*-meanings presented in chapter 2.

066/5.1 Possession in a literal sense

Of here means 'possessed by' or 'belonging to'. The ***possessing*** noun is typically inanimate and is the ***prepositional complement***: *the garage of the house, a leg of the table*. The ***belonging*** noun is often a ***part*** of the ***possessing*** noun. Variants are: locations and spatial areas (*the West End of London, the bank of the river, the end of the chain*); and members of categories (*a type of hammer, a sort of sausage*).

066/5.2 Constitutive meaning

In this case the genitive tells us what something consists of, comprises, or contains. Here it is usually the ***antecedent*** which is the ***possessing*** noun:

- ***consisting of***: *a family of four, a panel of judges, a beam of white light.*
  Materials and colours belong here: *a dress of red satin, tools of stone, eyes of blue, a heart of gold.*
  An abstract variant is ***media content/portrayal***: *a map of the city, the photo of Diana, rumours of Bowlby's resignation, the story of her life.*
- ***possessing in the sense of 'characterized by'***: *a man of charm, a field of controversy, a matter of importance, a child of eight, a mother of four*, etc.
- ***caused by/resulting from***: *the horrors of war, the pleasure of your company, the dangers of alcohol, the fear of unemployment, a smile of satisfaction, the effects of the recession.*
- ***equivalent to (appositive* of*-phrases)***: *the city of Canterbury, a speed of 120 miles per hour, a height of ten feet, the game of snooker, the age of eleven, the issue of unemployment.*
  Here the first noun refers to a general entity or category, which the ***of***-noun belongs to, or specifies more closely.
- ***purpose***: Found especially in institutional names and titles: *a court of law, the Faculty of Science, the Society of Authors, a place of worship, the Department of Trade, the Ministry of Labour.*
- ***containing***: *a bag of sweets, a book of stamps, a pack of cards, the museum of modern art.*
  Depending on context, many expressions of this type can be seen as ***partitives*** (see following point). The emphasis is then on the second noun.
- ***measures and partitives:***
  Here the ***belonging*** noun is a ***measurement***: *a pint of beer, two pounds of potatoes*. In this case the first noun and the preposition are seen as ***premodifying*** the second noun.
  Partitives are a similar case. These may have ***grammatical quantifiers*** (*some of the people, most of the children*), ***whole numerals*** (*two of the horses*), ***fractions*** (*half of the money*), or ***lexical quantifiers*** (*a cup of tea, a plate of chips*).
  Measuring expressions can also be the other way round, with the ***measurement*** as ***prepositional complement***: *a walk of five minutes, a flight of ten hours*. In other words, the order of belonging and possessing is reversed. It is now the ***antecedent*** that is the ***possessing*** noun.

066/5.3 of-genitives with verb-related nouns

With nouns related to verbs, an accompanying genitive may express the original ***subject*** or ***object*** of the particular verb: *the arrival of the Queen* (***subject*** = *The Queen arrived*); *her dislike of crowds* (***object*** = *She disliked crowds*). (See also chapter 2).

066/5.4 with as a genitive

The preposition ***with*** may also express genitive meaning (see chapter 6, **036/3.2**), and belongs then in the category of ***genitive postmodification***: *the man with the red tie; a house with a red door; the bottle with the water in it.*

066/6 Multiple postmodification

Nouns often have more than one postmodification. We then speak of ***multiple postmodification***. As an illustration we will take the most common example, which consists of two postmodifications. These refer to their antecedents in one of two ways.

- Firstly, they can be ***parallel*** (or ***co-ordinate***): *the woman in the big house who has the fierce the dog*. In this case each postmodification refers to the ***same antecedent***, i.e. *woman*.
- The second possibility is that they are structured ***in sequence***. Here the two postmodifications have ***different*** (or partly different) ***antecedents***, as in *the student of English from Tokyo*.

The first refers to the ***head noun alone***. The second refers to the ***head noun plus first postmodification***. We call this ***sequential*** postmodification.

066/6.1 Parallel postmodification

Parallel postmodifications are ***co-ordinate***, i.e. not arranged in any hierarchy. They are therefore ***independent*** of each other:

(49) a. Danny, who is a keen golfer and (who) loves sailing, is a games teacher.
b. The woman in the red armchair wearing the monkey costume seems a bit sad.
c. The man with the false beard talking to the barman is my colleague.

In diagram form (i.e. with brackets) the pattern looks like this:

(50) a. {Danny, /who is a keen golfer/ and /loves sailing/,} is a games teacher.
b. {The woman /in the red armchair/ /wearing the monkey costume/} seems a bit sad.
c. {The man /with the false beard/ /talking to the barman/} is my colleague.

Parallel postmodifications must be either ***both restrictive***, or ***both non-restrictive***. As they are independent, each opens and closes with its own separate slant. The independence is clearest in meaning and grammar when both postmodifications are ***non-restrictive***, as in

(49)/(50)a. We could leave one or both out. Or we could reverse the order: *Danny, who loves sailing and (who) is a keen golfer ...*

In (49)/(50)b. the two postmodifications are ***restrictive***. That is, both define the woman's identity. Nevertheless, each postmodification identifies the antecedent ***separately*** and for itself (assuming, of course, that there is only one woman wearing a monkey costume, and only one in the armchair): *the woman in the red armchair ...; the woman wearing the monkey costume ...* Here, too, the order can be reversed: *the woman wearing the monkey costume in the red armchair...*

Order reversal is not always a reliable test, however, as it may not be possible for other structural reasons. Reversing the order in (49)/(50)c., for example, creates a change of antecedent, or at least leads to ambiguity: *The man talking to the barman with the false beard* would usually mean that the false beard belonged to the barman.

The need for clarity, and in particular the desire to ***avoid ambiguity***, make the generally preferred order ***phrase before clause***. Despite their independence, the two postmodifications are then usually easier to understand, even if there is no obvious ambiguity (see also under **066/6.4** below).

When both are prepositional phrases, flexibility is often greater. For example, *the man with the false beard at the bar* and *the man at the bar with the false beard* can be taken to mean the same. Nevertheless, shifting the postmodifications around here too can change one of the antecedents, e.g. in *the dog on the long leash with the old woman* and *the dog with the old woman on the long leash.*

066/6.2 Sequential postmodification

Here, the ***antecedent*** of the ***second*** postmodification is the ***head noun + first postmodification*** together:

(51) a. A collector of antiques from Birmingham has been arrested.
b. The man next door, who is a keen swimmer, is building a pool in his garden.

And with brackets:

(52) a. {A collector /of antiques /from Birmingham//} has been arrested.
b. {The man /next door, /who is a keen swimmer//,} is building a pool in his garden.

The fact that there is no closing slant after the first postmodification shows that this is a ***sequential*** relation. *From Birmingham* postmodifies *a collector of antiques,* and the relative clause in (52)b. postmodifies *the man next door.*

Sequential patterns must consist of two ***restrictive postmodifications***, as in (51)/(52)a., or a ***restrictive*** followed by a ***non-restrictive*** one, as in the b. examples. (Note that two ***restrictive*** postmodifications can also be ***parallel***, see examples (49)/(50)b. above).

066/6.3 Parallel and sequential postmodification in contrast

Here are two examples for contrast:

(53) a. {The woman /in the big house/ /with the fierce dog/} is on holiday. [***parallel***]
b. {A student /of English/ from Tokyo//} has joined our course. [***sequential***]

The distinction is shown by the different slant positions in (53)a. and b. In the ***parallel*** example in (53)a. both postmodifications identify the ***same antecedent***, i.e. in both cases the head noun *woman*; in other words, they do this ***separately*** (*the woman in the big house* and *the woman with the fierce dog*), and are enclosed by their own separate slants.

In ***sequential*** postmodification there is a kind of cumulative or 'snowball' effect: the head noun in (53)b., *student*, is firstly postmodified by *of English*. Then, in a second step, *student of English* is postmodified by *from Tokyo*. Both postmodifications have a fixed position, as each ***antecedent*** is ***different*** (*student* in the first case, and *student of English* in the second). The slant positions show this relation. The first postmodification is not closed by its own slant until the end of the sequence. That is, the second postmodification starts before the first has closed. This indicates that the second one also postmodifies the first.

With many single sentences it may not be clear whether the second postmodification refers to the ***head noun alone*** or to the ***head noun + first postmodification***. The meaning must then be decided by the larger context and the speaker's intention. In (53)a., for instance, we are assuming a context that allows the speaker to define *woman* by ***either*** of the two postmodifying phrases. However, this may not be given. Imagine as a counter-example four women living in four houses, two of which are big and two small; in addition there are two fierce dogs, one in a big house and the other in a small house. The speaker must then firstly identify *woman* by *in the big house*, and then *woman in the big house* by *with the fierce dog*. The two postmodifications are then ***sequential***. As so often in English, syntax here is dependent on the intended meaning, a fact also made clear in section **066/6.4**.

066/6.4 Order of postmodifications

In sequential relations, obviously, the order is fixed by meaning. Where this is unclear, or where the relations are parallel, general order principles are as follows:

- ***restrictive before non-restrictive***: *The company's decision to build a new factory, taken yesterday, was no surprise.*
- ***phrases before clauses***: *The company's decision yesterday to build a new factory …*
- ***non-finite before finite***: *Persons wishing to log in who have forgotten their password …*
- ***clarity of meaning/avoidance of ambiguity***: *The man in Newport Road with the German girlfriend* (= *The man lives in Newport Road and has a German girlfriend*); *The man with the German girlfriend in Newport Road* (= *The man has a German girlfriend and she lives in Newport Road*).
  Using the second example in the sense of the first one is possible, but would usually be avoided because of the ambiguity (see also above under **066/6.1**).

- ***closeness of connection to antecedent***: This principle applies when all the others do not. It concerns postmodifications with the same structures, especially ***prepositional phrases***: *A collector of antiques from Birmingham.*
  The preposition ***of*** creates a particularly strong bond, i.e. here we cannot say **A collector from Birmingham of antiques.* ***Of***-phrases are generally fixed in position (leading to ***sequential*** relations with the second postmodification). This is partly due to the semantic closeness of the *belonging* relation. But in examples like the one above it also has to do with an 'implied verb' in the noun (= *someone who collects* ...). ***Of*** connects this to a potential object (*antiques*), or to some other grammatical complement. Other prepositions can express the connection too, e.g. *a dealer in silk in Tashkent* (not **a dealer in Tashkent in silk*); *a glance at the letter during my lunchbreak* (not **a glance during my lunchbreak at the letter*).
  In many further cases the order is not so strict and may depend upon the emphasis given by the speaker. Neutral expression, however, tends to prefer 'complements first': *her focus on her career at that time* (rather than (*) *her focus at that time on her career*); *my journey to Scotland in the summer* (rather than (*) *my journey in the summer to Scotland*); *a long wait for the bus in Atlanta* (rather than (*) *a long wait in Atlanta for the bus*).

066/6.5 Further postmodification

Further postmodifications are possible, but more than three are unusual. The same principles apply:

(54) a. {A collector /of antiques/from Birmingham/who stole a valuable painting///} has been sentenced to a year in prison.
[***sequential***]
b. {The man /in the black suit/ /with the false beard/ /talking to the barman/} is my colleague.
[***parallel***]

Note, again, that single slants show ***sequential*** relations; they open successive postmodifications which do not close until the end of the sequence. In (54)a. the relative clause postmodifies *a collector of antiques from Birmingham*, the phrase *from Birmingham* postmodifies *a collector of antiques* and *of antiques* postmodifies *collector*. The whole series is then closed at the end by three slants corresponding to the three opening slants.

Parallel postmodifications, in (54)b., close separately, as described above. This indicates that each one postmodifies the ***same antecedent***, i.e. the ***head noun***: *the man in the black suit, the man with the false beard, the man talking to the barman*. Here each postmodification is closed by its own slant.

Mixtures of parallel and sequential relations are also possible here. Sequential, as already explained, must come first:

(55) a. {The man /in the black suit/with the false beard///talking to the barman/} is my colleague.
[***sequential + parallel***]

b. {The man /in the black suit/with the false beard//talking to the barman//} is my colleague.
[***sequential + parallel sequential***]

c. {A painting /by Constable/worth nearly £8m//that had been removed from the National Gallery for cleaning //} has been stolen from storage.
[***sequential + parallel sequential***]

(55)a. and b. are alternative interpretations of (54)b.

In (55)a. *with the false beard* postmodifies *the man in the black suit*. That is, the relation here is ***sequential***, as shown by the first two slants after *beard*, which close the first two postmodifications (*in the black suit* and *with the false beard*) together. The third slant here opens an independent and ***parallel*** postmodification of the ***head noun*** *man*. This is a mixture, then, of two separate noun phrases, either of which could identify the ***same man*** independently, i.e. *the man in the black suit with the false beard*, and *the man talking to the barman*.

The version in (55)b. also presents the first two postmodifications as ***sequential***: with the difference, however, that only the second closes after *beard*. The first, *in the black suit*, remains open until after *barman*. This means that *talking to the barman* and *with the false beard* each postmodify *the man in the black suit* in a ***sequential*** relation. To each other, however they have a ***parallel*** relation: *the man in the black suit with the false beard*, and *the man in the black suit talking to the barman*.

(55)c. shows a similar structure to (55)b. The parallel sequences here are: *a painting by Constable that had been removed …*, and *a painting by Constable worth nearly £8m*.

Complex adjective and prepositional phrases 067

067/1 The complex adjective phrase
067/2 The complex prepositional phrase

067/1 The complex adjective phrase

A ***complex adjective phrase*** is one with a ***clause*** as ***adjectival complement***. For instance, in the sentence *I was sure that Jane would help us* there is a complex adjective phrase: *sure that Jane would help us*. In the sentence it functions as ***subject complement (Cs)***:

	S	*P*	*Cs*	*S*	*P*	*Od*
(56)	I	was	{sure	/that Jane	would help	us/}.

As with noun phrases, we have marked off the adjective phrase here by curl brackets, {}, and the adjectival complement by slants, //.

Inside the adjective phrase, the functions are as follows:

	Head	*Adjectival Complement*
(57)	sure	that Jane would help us

As was said in chapter 4, ***adjectival complements*** are similar syntactically to postmodifications in noun phrases. They tell us what the adjective applies to, i.e. how and in what respect it is to be understood. Typical clause types in this function are ***that***-clauses and ***infinitive*** clauses, as well as ***comparative*** and ***consecutive*** clauses. ***Wh***-clauses can also occur.

067/1.1 that-clauses

Adjectives referring to feelings and other mental states (knowledge, speculation, supposition, etc.) typically have ***that***-clauses as complements: *We were not unhappy/aware/certain that our guests had already left.*

With adjectives of ***emotion***, the ***that***-clause expresses the ***cause*** of the feeling; or, to put it another way, the adjective conveys a ***reaction*** to the fact expressed in the ***that***-clause. Other 'mental state' adjectives express knowledge or understanding of what is referred to in the ***that***-clause.

067/1.2 wh-clauses

Adjectives relating to knowledge of facts (*sure, certain, clear,* etc.) can also have ***wh***-clauses as complements. These express ***indirect questions*** (= ***interrogative clauses***): *I wasn't sure where I had put my key; The guests were not certain why they had been invited.*

Prepositions are often inserted between the adjective and the rest of the complement: *The guests were not certain about why they had been invited* (see below under ***Prepositions***).

067/1.3 Comparative clauses

Comparative phrases and ***clauses*** are those introduced by the ***comparative particles***. These are ***as*** (for ***equative*** comparison) and ***than*** (for ***surplus*** and ***deficit*** comparison, see chapter 4, **031/4–6**). Comparative phrases are without verbs, e.g. *as John* in (58)a. When a verb is added, as in (58)b., we have a ***comparative clause***:

(58) a. I'm not as successful as John.
b. I'm not as successful as John is.
c. I'm less successful than John is.
d. I'm more successful than I expected.
e. Today the sun seems hotter than it did yesterday.

Note that ***periphrastic*** comparatives (i.e. with *more, less, as*) have ***premodification*** of the adjective as well as ***complementation***:

	Premodification	*Head*	*Adjectival Complement*
(59)	a. less	successful	than John is
	b. more	successful	than I expected

A full sentence analysis looks like this:

	S P	***Cs***	***S P***
(60)	I am	{less successful /than	John is/}.

Note the use of ***auxiliary pro-forms*** in examples like (58)e. (see also chapter 4, **031/6.4**, and chapter 8, **040/2.11**).

067/1.4 Infinitive clauses

Infinitives occur as adjectival complements with:

- ***volitional*** adjectives: *She was unwilling to forgive him.*
- ***emotional-reactive*** adjectives: *I am delighted to be here.*
- adjectives in ***consecutive constructions***: *They were too tired to go on.* (See chapter 13.1, **060/8** and **067/1.5** below.)

There are certain cases where infinitives following adjectives are ***not*** part of the adjective phrase:

- in ***extraposition***: *It is easy to do this exercise.* Here the infinitive clause is the ***logical subject*** of the sentence, and therefore separate from the adjective: *To do this exercise is easy.*
- in ***false subject constructions***: *This exercise is easy to do.* Here the infinitive is also part of the ***logical subject*** of the sentence: *To do this exercise is easy.*

For details on adjectives followed by infinitives, see chapter 13.1, **060/3**.

067/1.5 Consecutive clauses

These are ***infinitive clauses*** which follow adjectives modified by ***too*** and ***enough***: *He wasn't old enough to drive a car.*

They may also be ***that***-clauses, where the adjective is premodified by ***so***: *I was so tired that I could hardly stand.*

Consecutive clauses describe ***consequences***: *I could hardly stand (because I was so tired).*

067/1.6 Present participles

These are not common as adjectival complements, but occur typically after the adjective *busy*, and some others with a similar meaning, such as *occupied, preoccupied, active*, etc.: *Jane was busy doing her homework.*

Sentence functions are similar to those in other cases of clause complementation:

	S	***P***	***Cs***	***P***	***Od***
(61)	Jane	was	{busy/	doing	her homework/}.

067/1.7 Preposition + clause

As we saw in chapter 4, **030/3.1**, ***prepositional phrases*** often occur as adjectival complements. The preposition meaning is usually idiomatic (*good at, interested in, bored with*). Prepositions following adjectives like this are themselves often followed by ***clauses***. These are generally of three kinds:

- The most common is the ***gerund***, e.g. *good at playing chess, interested in learning French, bored with watching television*. The adjective in such cases generally expresses either an ***attitude*** towards the activity, or the ***ability*** to perform it.
- Then there is the ***indirect question***, in either finite or non-finite form: *The branch manager was uncertain about how he should tell his staff/about how to tell his staff the bad news.* An example of this type was given in **067/1.2** above.
- Finally, we have the ***nominal relative clause*** (see **066/3.9** above): *Yvonne was not interested in what the other guests were saying.*

To be exact, the clauses here are part of the prepositional phrase, i.e. they really belong in section **067/2** on ***complex prepositional phrases***. They must be mentioned here too, though, as it is the adjective that determines the preposition, and therefore forms a larger semantic and grammatical unit with it.

067/1.8 Further subordination within the complement clause

Like postmodifying clauses in noun phrases (and just like any clause at sentence level), ***adjectival complement clauses*** can have further sub-clauses inside them:

```
         S P Cs           S    P    Od A      S  P  A
(62) a. I am  {sure /that Jane will help us  [when she gets home]/}.
           S   P Cs              P        A         A              S
     b. Delia was  {unwilling /to stay at the meeting  [until the final decision
           P-pass
        was taken]/}.
```

067/1.9 More than one adjectival complement

Just as noun phrases may have more than one postmodifier, so adjective phrases may have ***more than one complement***:

(63) a. They were {blue /in the face /with cold//}.
b. She was {so happy /with the present /that she almost cried//}.
c. Tommy is {more interested /in the relationship/ than Gina//}.
d. They are always {too busy /having a good time/ to notice the children//}.

Technically, (63)a. and c. are not complex phrases, as they contain no clauses. But as was pointed out at the beginning of the chapter, there are many points here where a thorough treatment needs to consider simple and complex phrases in their relations with each other.

In contrast to multiple postmodification in the noun phrase, ***multiple adjectival complements*** are always ***sequential***. In other words, the ***second complement*** in each of the examples refers not just to the head (i.e. the adjective alone), but to the ***head + first complement*** together. This applies even when the order of the two complements can be reversed, which is often the case with comparatives, e.g. *Tommy is more interested than Gina in the relationship*. This is simply an example of ***postponement*** (see **066/2.1** above, and also chapter 4, **031/6.6**). Despite this, the comparison is understood as referring to *interested in the relationship* and not just to *interested*.

067/2 The complex prepositional phrase

A lot has already been said about verbs and clauses following prepositions (see **067/1.7** above, and particularly chapter 13, **062/5**). This section will give just a brief reminder of the syntax and list a selection of examples by way of summary.

In the ***complex*** prepositional phrase, the ***prepositional complement*** is a ***clause***:

	Head	***Prepositional Complement***
(64)	a. by	climbing through a window
	b. of	when we should sell the house
	c. about	what McBride has done

Note that these are the three structural clause types mentioned above in **067/1.7**: the ***gerund***, as in a., the ***interrogative clause***, in b., and the ***nominal relative clause*** in c. In sentences they look like this:

S P A A P A
(65) a. The burglar got into the house {by /climbing through a window/}.
S A S P Od P Cs
b. {The question /{of /when we should sell the house/}/} is a difficult one.
S P Cs Od S P
c. We are not {very enthusiastic/ {about /what McBride has done/}}.

(65)b. and c. clearly show how the prepositional phrase is a phrase in its own right inside other phrases.

For instance, in (65)b. we have a noun phrase as subject, *the question of when we should sell the house*, placed inside the first set of curl brackets{}. The head, *question*, is then postmodified by the phrase in the first set of slants //. As this is a prepositional phrase, *of when we should sell the house*, it is also placed inside its own curl brackets{}. Finally, the second set of slants // show the ***prepositional complement***, consisting of the interrogative clause *when we should sell the house*. In (65)a. the prepositional phrase is a direct part of the sentence, and therefore has a sentence function, i.e. ***adverbial***.

14.2 Aspects of the complex sentence

068 Forms and functions

Here we return to the general level of the sentence, and give an overview of complex sentence structures from a functional perspective. Various aspects of sentence analysis presented so far individually are brought together here in summary form. This is not just to be understood analytically, however. Awareness of complex sentence syntax is a necessary basis for using structural patterns competently when speaking or writing.

068 Forms and functions

068/1 Clauses as subject (S)

As subjects are generally noun phrases, clauses in this function are regarded as 'nominal' in character. This has no further consequences analytically. But the term is often used in other grammars.

068/1.1 Finite clauses

Finite sub-clauses (in all functions) must be introduced by ***conjunctions, interrogative pronouns/adverbs/determiners*** (i.e. ***wh***-words), or ***nominal relative pronouns*** (also ***wh***-words, like *what, whoever*, etc.). That is, they need what we generally call a ***subordinating element***.

S
(66) a. [Whether Christine will be at the party] is not quite clear at the moment.
S
b. [That Roger will be at the party] is fairly certain.
S
c. [What I need most now] is a drink.

Sentences like (66)c., where a nominal relative clause is used for emphasis, are called ***pseudo-cleft*** sentences (see also below under **068/7.5**). They are the most common form of finite subject clause. Subject clauses like those in (66)a. and b. are usually avoided in speech and ordinary neutral language. The need is usually felt, especially in spoken language, to give them more emphasis by using ***extraposition*** (see also below), e.g.: *It is fairly certain that Roger will be at the party.*

068/1.2 Non-finite clauses

The typical non-finite clause form in the subject function is the ***gerund***, as in (67)a. ***Infinitives***, as in (67)b., are not common. ***Extraposition*** is preferred here, too, for the reason just given in **068/1.1**.

S
(67) a. [Going to the theatre] is one of my favourite hobbies.
S
b. [To take the cross-country route in this weather] would be foolish.

The preferred ***extraposition*** version of (67)b. is *It would be foolish to take the cross-country route in this weather.*

Note that participle clauses can never function as subject. Another point is that non-finite clauses do not generally appear with a subordinating element, i.e. we do not say, for instance, **That going to the theatre* ..., or **That to take the cross-country route* ... An exception is the ***interrogative clause***, which needs a ***wh***-word: *How to get into the building unseen was a problem.*

A final point is that non-finite verbs do not occur in nominal relative clauses, i.e. not **What to need is a drink.*

068/2 Clauses as direct object (Od)

Here, too, we have a typical 'nominal' function of a clause (see also preceding section).

068/2.1 Finite clauses

The same applies here as in **068/1**, except that the conjunction ***that*** can be omitted. In object clauses, ***if*** (in the sense of German *ob*) can also replace ***whether*** in less formal usage:

Od
(68) a. I do not know [whether/if Christine will be at the party].
Od
b. I think [that Roger will be at the party].
Od
c. The teacher liked [what most of her pupils had written].

Omission of ***that*** in (68)b. produces *I think Roger will be at the party* (the usual version in speech).

068/2.2 Non-finite clauses

Both ***gerunds*** and ***infinitives*** (but, again, ***never*** participles) are very common as direct objects:

		Od
(69) a. We would like		[to come to the party].
	Od	
b. I love	[going to the theatre].	
		Od
c. They regretted		[having invested all their money in that company].

Otherwise, the same applies as stated in **068/1**. The only kind of ***subordinating element*** found with non-finite clauses is a ***wh***-word in ***interrogative clauses***: *She had not decided whether to come.* Non-finite clauses are automatically subordinate and therefore need no grammatical marker of subordination as finite clauses do.

Note again, as a reminder, that nominal relative clauses cannot be non-finite.

068/2.3 Object clauses in ditransitive constructions

The matrix verbs in the preceding sections are monotransitive. Object clauses may also follow ***ditransitive*** matrix verbs:

	Oi	***Od***
(70) a. We told	the boy	[that he had got the job].
b. She asked	us	[if/whether we could help her].

The direct object can also be an ***infinitive clause***:

	Oi	***Od***
(71) a. We told	the boy	[to start the job the next day].
b. She asked	us	[to help her].

This is one variant of the ***'object + infinitive' construction***. For the other, see section **068/4** below.

Other verbs of this kind are *allow, convince, forbid, instruct, invite, order, permit, persuade, recommend, remind, request, show how, teach, urge, warn,* etc. (See chapter 13.1, **060/10.3**.) These all express acts of communication ('giving or sending a message'), which involve a ***recipient***. This is the ***indirect object*** in the matrix clause. The ***infinitive clause*** is then the ***direct object***.

068/3 Clauses as subject complement (Cs)

Since nouns (as well as adjectives) can be subject complements, clauses in this function are also often regarded as 'nominal'.

068/3.1 Finite clauses

Here again, ***that***-clauses predominate. But we also have ***interrogative clauses***, as in (72)b., and ***nominal relative clauses***, as in (72)c. The usual matrix verb is *be*:

(72) a. The problem is [that Roger will be at the party]. (*Cs*)
b. The question is [why the luggage was left unattended]. (*Cs*)
c. The person responsible is [whoever was in charge of the luggage]. (*Cs*)

068/3.2 Non-finite clauses

The 'nominal' character of the subject complement means that all ***-ing***-forms in this function are ***gerunds*** (and ***never*** present participles). Again the usual matrix verb is *be*, and with infinitives also *seem* and *appear*. ***Interrogative clauses*** with the infinitive also feature here, as in (73)b.:

(73) a. My most enjoyable pastime is [going to the theatre]. (*Cs*)
b. The question was [how to get in touch with the owners]. (*Cs*)
c. Betty's illness seems [to have affected the whole family]. (*Cs*)

The ordinary verbs of 'becoming' followed by subject complements in simple sentences do not occur with clausal subject complements. Two special verbs that do, however, are *come* and *turn out*: *Going to the theatre came to be my most enjoyable pastime*; *The project turned out to be a disaster*. The infinitive clauses here both function as subject complements.

068/4 Clauses as object complement (Co)

With one exception (see **068/4.5**), only ***infinitive*** clauses can function as ***object complements***. They follow catenatives which are ***complex transitive***, i.e. those which take a ***direct object*** in the matrix clause. This is the second variant of the ***'object + infinitive'*** construction (see also chapter 13.1, **060/10.3**, and **068/2.3** above). Whether the object following the matrix verb is a ***direct object*** depends on the meaning relation between object and verb. The catenatives involved fall roughly into four categories of meaning.

068/4.1 Volitional verbs

These are verbs of 'wanting':

	Od	*Co*
(74) a. We do not want	Roger	[to come to our party].
b. The firm expects	me	[to work on Saturdays].
c. Jane encouraged	Sue	[to apply for the job].

Others are: *intend, like, mean, need, prefer, require, tempt,* etc. *Let* and *help* can also be placed in this group. *Let* takes the infinitive ***without*** *to*, and *help* sometimes also, especially in informal language: *She let me borrow her car; Kerry helped me (to) paint the garden fence.*

The verb *expect* means here 'demand something of someone'. In its other meaning (= 'anticipate'), it is categorized under **068/4.3** below. The semantic difference does not affect the syntactic function.

068/4.2 Causative verbs

	Od	*Co*
(75) a. A cow on the road caused	the car	[to swerve].
b. Bad weather at sea forced	us	[to return to harbour].
c. The trainer makes	his team	[run 20 miles every week].

Others are: *compel, lead, oblige,* etc. Note that *make*, like *let* in the volitional category, takes the infinitive ***without*** *to*.

A further expression like these is *to have someone do something* (= dt. *veranlassen, dass jemand etwas macht*): *I had the supermarket deliver my groceries* (dt. *Ich ließ mir die Lebensmittel vom Supermarkt liefern*).

068/4.3 Mental verbs

These are verbs of knowing and thinking:

	Od	*Co*
(76) a. I consider	Jackson	[to be the best candidate].
b. She expected	Brian	[to arrive two days later].

Expect here means 'anticipate'. It is the only verb in the group which can appear freely with any infinitive verb. The others are confined to *be* (see also chapter 13, **060/2.2**): *assume, believe, feel* (in the sense of *think*), *know, presume, suppose, think, understand,* etc.

068/4.4 Verbs of perception

These are verbs like *see, hear* and *feel*. They take an infinitive ***without*** *to*:

		Od	***Co***
(77)	a. We saw	the man	[swim across the river].
	b. She heard	someone	[come up the stairs].

Note that verbs of perception also appear with the ***present participle***, e.g. *We saw the man swimming across the river.* This means *We saw the man as he was swimming* ... (i.e. in the process of swimming/in the middle of the action), whereas the infinitive version in (77) a. means the whole action from beginning to end (*The man swam across the river. We saw this.*). Similarly, (77)b. means *Someone came up the stairs* (i.e. *from bottom to top*), *and she heard this.*

Apart from the distinction in meaning, there is also a difference in functional analysis. The ***present participle*** clause is regarded as an ***adverbial*** and ***not*** as an object complement (see below under **068/5.2**, and also chapter 13, **064/1.8–9**). Note that (rather more rarely) perception verbs also occur with the ***past participle*** (see chapter 13.3, **064/6.5** below).

068/4.5 Exception: object + past participle clause

A few complex transitive catenatives can take a ***past participle clause*** as an object complement. Typical examples are *get, have,* and *make* in idiomatic or semi-idiomatic constructions like *to have/get something done, to make oneself heard*, etc. Others are ***volitional*** and ***perception*** verbs in ***shortened passive infinitive*** constructions: *Mary would like the walls painted pink; I've rarely heard the song sung as badly as that*:

		Od	***Co***
(78)	a. Jim is going to have	his hair	[cut short].
	b. Mary would like	the walls	[painted pink].

On constructions like this, see also chapter 13.3, **064/6.4** and **5**.

068/5 Clauses as adverbials (A)

The ***adverbial*** function has the largest variety of structures and meanings. These are reflected particularly in the range of conjunctions used. With finite clauses especially, it is the ***conjunction*** that specifies function and individual meaning. On the point of meaning, it is usual in sentence analysis, as we said in chapter 7, to state the semantic type of adverbial clause involved in a particular case.

This is good as a practical guide, but it is not an essential part of the grammatical analysis. Semantic categories of adverbial are in any case often not clearly defined. They tend to be 'fuzzy' at the edges, and shade over into one another. But we will keep to the tradition and name the main meaning categories. The list does not claim to be complete, but it gives the most important semantic types as an orientation.

068/5.1 Clauses of time

(79) a. Gary was very tired *A* [when he got home].

b. *A* [Before I left the house] I closed all the windows.

c. We were caught in a thunderstorm *A* [(while) crossing the moors].

d. The filmstar was arrested *A* {on/arriving at Heathrow/}.

Examples like (79)d. are not quite legitimate in this section, of course, as the ***adverbial*** here consists of a phrase and not a clause. This is the reason for the curl brackets and slants. The ***gerund clause*** functions inside the ***prepositional phrase*** as ***prepositional complement*** (see 14.1, **067/2** above). Nevertheless, it is included as a typical example of the way gerund clauses 'participate' in adverbials, i.e. accompanied by prepositions. Gerund clauses cannot function as adverbials on their own.

This contrasts with the ***present participle***, which always functions, as in (79)c., as an ***adverbial*** at sentence level. Conjunctions, as in the brackets, may appear with participles, especially in written language, to express the meaning more precisely. The time meaning of a present participle clause comes from its basic semantic function: expressing a ***parallel*** action. This sense is always present, although it may not necessarily be in the foreground contextually (see following section).

Other common ***time conjunctions*** are: ***whenever, as, (not) until, as soon as, after, since***.

068/5.2 Clauses of manner and circumstance

Present participle clauses can also be understood as clauses of ***manner***, as in (80)a., and ***manner/circumstance***, as in (80)b. (80)c., also a typical adverbial of ***manner***, is another example of a prepositional phrase with the gerund:

(80) a. Beryl sat on the sofa *A* [staring at the television].

b. I noticed Jamie *A* [talking to an older woman at a corner table].

c. Our guests left *A* {without /saying goodbye/}.

We could see the participle clauses here also as clauses of ***time***: they tell us that an action happened at the same time as the matrix action. But they also do more. In (80)a. the participle clause expresses ***how*** Beryl sat on the sofa.

This is a typical case where a general verb of posture or movement in the matrix clause is 'filled out' semantically with more textual detail by the participle clause (see also 13.3, **064/1.1**).

Other examples of ***accompanying actions*** with a ***manner*** meaning are: *Smiling sadly, Blake left the room; "Help!" they shouted, waving at us frantically from their boat.* And with the ***past participle***: *She came to the party dressed entirely in pink.*

(80)b. shows the typical construction after a verb of perception. Here the accompanying action gives rather the circumstances under which the matrix action takes place (*How/in what situation was Jamie observed?*).

068/5.3 Clauses of place

Place relations are generally expressed by finite clauses introduced by the conjunction ***where*** (occasionally also by its compound ***wherever***). In addition, ***time*** clauses are sometimes also used as 'metaphors' for ***place***:

		A
(81)	a. Yellow patches of grass remained	[where the tents had stood].
	b. Tell our guests that they can sleep	[wherever they like].

A
c. [Until it reaches the farm], the path is just a mud track.

A
d. The river gets wider [after it leaves the village].

068/5.4 Clauses of reason

With finite clauses, conjunctions used here are ***because, as*** and ***since***.

Present participles of ***stative verbs*** are used in a ***causal*** sense, and the ***perfect participle*** can also have ***causal*** overtones:

		A
(82)	a. We're a little bad-tempered	[because we're hungry].
	b. I'll pay for all the drinks	[as you bought the food].

A
c. [Realizing the bather was in difficulties], we called the coastguard.

A
d. [Having slept badly the night before], they felt very tired.

068/5.5 Clauses of purpose

With finite clauses the general conjunction is ***so that***.

The ***infinitive*** also conveys ***purpose***, either alone or with ***in order*** before it. A third possibility is the ***infinitive*** with ***so as*** preceding it:

		A
(83)	a. Jim gave the children money	[so that they could buy food].
	b. We went for a walk	[(in order) to get some fresh air].
	c. Joanna moved back to Leeds	[so as to be near her mother].

Note that ***so as*** means 'with this purpose/intention in mind'. It generally means that the intended outcome is an emphasized side-effect or special purpose, and is found especially with negative intentions. For example, in *I used scissors to cut the paper* ***so as*** *to avoid tearing it,* we could express both purposes by the simple infinitive, but only the ***second*** one by ***so as*** (= *I used scissors because I wanted to avoid tearing the paper*).

068/5.6 Clauses of condition

Only finite structures are used here. Conjunctions are ***if, unless, in case, supposing (that),*** and ***providing/provided (that)***. Note also the inverted form with ***should*** in c., which means the same as ***if***. And note further, as a reminder, that ***in case*** does ***not*** mean the same as ***if*** (see also chapter 7, **038/3.4**)!

(84) a. [If you come to the party] (*A*) you will meet Joan.
b. You will not meet Joan [unless you come to the party] (*A*).
c. [Should you have any difficulties] (*A*), you can contact us at any time.

068/5.7 Clauses of consequence (consecutive clauses)

Apart from introducing clauses of purpose, the conjunction ***so that*** is used also in ***consecutive clauses***, which express a ***consequence***. Note that this kind of result is ***not*** a purpose or an aim, but simply an unintended effect (***so that*** = dt. *so dass* ...).

(85)a. is 'classical'. (85)b.-c. are syntactic variants commented on below:

(85) a. Most of the guests began leaving early, [so that by midnight only three of us were left] (*A*).
b. Most of the guests began leaving early, [so by midnight only three of us were left].
c. She so loves gold [that she would die for it] (*A*).
d. She loves gold {so passionately/that she would die for it/}.

Several things must be said here, both about syntax and practical grammar.

Firstly, (85)b. is the most common ***informal*** way of saying (85)a. Here the complex conjunction ***so that*** is reduced to ***so*** alone. Opinions vary as to whether this is acceptable in more formal and written English. Traditionally, ***so*** is not a conjunction, but an adverb, and cannot therefore be used to join clauses in this way. The solution, according to this view, is to add ***and***: ... *and so by midnight only three of us were left*. However, acceptability is changing, and many would now regard (85)b. as perfectly standard. Our recommendation is still to avoid this use of ***so*** in formal or 'careful' style.

In (85)c. ***so*** is not part of the conjunction, but an ***adverb of degree***. It functions here as a separate ***adverbial***. Its use like this, i.e. to modify a verb directly, is slightly elevated stylistically. In this use, ***so*** can only occur in this position, before the main verb. The use of ***that*** on its own to introduce an ***adverbial*** clause is an exception, and works only with a corresponding 'partner' adverb of degree in the matrix.

A more common and comfortable alternative to this is (85)d., where, again, as in (79) d. and (80)c., we have a ***phrase*** as the ***adverbial***, and not a clause. This is an ***adverb phrase*** with the same pattern as the adjective phrase type in 14.2, **067/1.5** above. The ***that***-clause is consecutive, but functions as an adverb complement (analogous to an adjectival complement, see also chapter 5, **033/2**).

We will now come back to the point made at the beginning of the section: as ***so that*** is also used for purpose clauses, there can sometimes be confusion or ambiguity. (86)a. is ***ambiguous*** between ***purpose*** and ***consequence***. (86)b. gives the ***consequence*** (= ***consecutive***) interpretation, (86)c. the ***purpose*** interpretation. Note that the distinction is reflected in two different German conjunctions:

(86) a. The garage repaired the car quickly, so that we were able to continue our journey the very next day.
b. … with the result that we were able to continue …
(*dt.* …, so dass …)
c. … with the aim of making it possible for us to continue …
(*dt.* …, damit …)

Finally, ***non-finite clauses*** can also occasionally have consecutive meaning:

(87) a. The cat suddenly jumped on to the table, [knocking over a cup of tea]. (*A*)
b. The Davidsons returned home [to find their house burgled]. (*A*)

Present participle clauses like the one in (87)a. are usually those of ***point-telic*** verbs, and suggest sequence (see also chapter 13.3, **064/1.5**). It would not be wrong to regard clauses like this as time clauses. But the foreground meaning, ***consequence***, is explained better if we categorize this instance as ***consecutive***.

An ***infinitive*** clause can be used consecutively, as in (87)b., when it refers to something negative revealed unexpectedly at the close of an action of movement or change: *Mr. Brasenose turned the corner to see a fire engine outside his shop; I went into the garden to discover that the rain had completely flooded the lawn.*

068/5.8 Clauses of concession and contrast

These express a contradiction to the matrix clause. There are two types:

- The clause of ***concession*** means 'in spite of this', and lends a sense of ***'nevertheless'*** to the matrix. Chief conjunctions here are ***although/though***.
- The other type is the clause of ***contrast***, with ***whereas/while***.

A special variant of the clause of ***concession*** is one with an -***ever***-pronoun or -adverb, as in (88)c.:

A
(88) a. [Although/though I don't like Cheevers personally], he's important to me as a business partner.

A
b. I like cricket, [whereas my brother prefers tennis].

A
c. [Wherever you go in August], you'll find the beaches crowded.

Other conjunctions introducing ***concession*** clauses are ***even if*** and ***even though***.

Contrast meaning is the meaning of opposites. ***Whereas/while*** are typically used for this, as in (88)b. However, in more formal style they can also have ***concession*** meaning and could replace ***although/though*** in (88)a. The ***concession*** variant with -***ever***-pronouns and -adverbs (***however/whatever/ whenever***, etc.), as illustrated in (88)c., has a partly conditional overtone (= *under any condition*) and is sometimes called ***conditional-concessive***. The sub-clause means *If you go to any place in August …*

068/5.9 Clauses of comparison/similarity

Clauses of ***comparison*** at phrase level have to do with ***grammatical comparison***, for instance with ***comparatives*** of adjectives or adverbs, e.g. *Bill works harder than John does* (see also chapter 4, **031/6** and **8**, as well as 14.1, **067/1.3** above).

But there is a different type of ***comparison clause*** at sentence level. This expresses a ***semantic similarity*** between itself and the matrix clause. It is usually either a ***comment*** on the content of the matrix, or a reference to a parallel act or state. Conjunctions are ***as***, ***as if*** and ***as though***. As they often refer to something imagined by the speaker, hypothetical meaning and conditional forms are common:

A
(89) a. [As Mr. Symons has told you], the firm is developing strong business links to Asian companies.

A
b. He ate the bread and cheese [as if he hadn't had a good meal for weeks].

A
c. She treats me [as though I didn't exist].

068/6 Examples of sentence analysis

In this short section we give a few examples of how complex sentences can be analysed as a whole according to the functional system presented so far.

068/6.1 Sentence level functions of clauses

Here we just analyse the functions of sub-clauses in sentences, and nothing else. There are no examples of subordination at phrase level.

Od ***A*** ***Od***
(90) a. We thought [Brian would help us [if we did not manage [to finish
Od
[repairing the car on our own]]]].
Cs ***Od*** ***A***
b. Sally appears [to regret [being nasty to Tom [before she had heard
Od
[where he had been]]]].
A ***Od*** ***Od***
c. [As soon as I discovered [that I had failed the exam]], I decided [to practise
A
more syntax in future [whenever I had the opportunity]].

068/6.2 Sentence and phrase level functions of clauses

In this case we also analyse just the functions of sub-clauses. This time, though, some of them are subordinated at phrase level. This is shown by enclosing complex phrases in curl brackets {}, and the clauses inside them in slants //.

Od ***A*** ***Od***
(91) a. I hate [people disturbing me [when I am trying [to show private pupils
Od
[how to analyse {the sentences /that they have been given for homework/}]]]].
A ***Co***
b. [Although Roger was {sure /the Blackstones would let him [use their car
A ***Co***
[while he was staying with them]]/}], he did not want them [to feel {an obligation /to do so/}].
A
c. [When the head waiter became {aware /that {the customer /wearing the dark suit/} had left the restaurant {without /paying his bill/}/}]
Od ***Od***
he began [to wonder [whether this might not be {the escaped criminal /that the London police were looking for/}]].

068/6.3 Analysis of all functions

We will now take the examples in (91) and show ***all*** the functions, i.e. also those ***inside*** the individual clauses:

S P Od S P Od A S P Od P Oi
(92) a. I hate [people disturbing me [when I am trying [to show private pupils
Od A P Od Od S P-pass A
[how to analyse {the sentences /that they have been given for homework/}]]]].
A S P Cs S P Od Co P Od
b. [Although Roger was {sure /the Blackstones would let him [use their car
A S P A S P Od Co P
[while he was staying with them]]/}], he did not want them [to feel
Od P Od
{an obligation /to do this/}].
A S P Cs S P Od
c. [When the head waiter became {aware /that {the customer /wearing the dark
P Od A P Od S P
suit/} had left the restaurant {without /paying his bill/}/}] he began
Od P Od S P Cs Od S
[to wonder [whether this might not be {the escaped criminal /that the London
P
police were looking for/}]].

068/7 Analysing special clause and sentence types

This section looks at the syntax of certain common sentence and clause types that are irregular in their construction, or present some other kind of analytical difficulty. Some will be familiar from previous discussion. Others are mentioned here for the first time.

068/7.1 Existential sentences

These begin with a ***there + be***-construction. It is known as an ***existential*** construction because it tells us that something/someone 'exists'. ***There*** is an ***existential pronoun***, and stands for German *es*:

(93) a. There was a bible on the bedside-table (= A bible on the bedside-table 'existed').
Es lag eine Bibel auf dem Nachttisch.
b. There are two men standing outside our gate (= Two men standing outside our gate 'exist').
Es sind/stehen zwei Männer vor unserem Gartentor.

This is a ***postponement device*** similar in syntax to extraposition (see **068/7.2**). Existential ***there*** is used to introduce new information (usually, though not always, expressed by an ***indefinite*** noun phrase).

English sentences do not usually begin with new information. This is preferred in second or third place in the sentence. However, if the phrase referring to the new information functions as the ***subject*** of the sentence, then it should come first. We have, therefore, a dilemma. The solution is to use the ***there + be***-construction. This ***postpones*** the real subject (***S-log.***) to a later sentence position, and ***there*** takes its place at the beginning as an 'empty' or grammatical subject (***S-gramm.***). The rest of the sentence can be treated as a postmodification of the 'existing' noun phrase:

	S-gramm.	*P*	*S-log.*
(94) a.	There	was	{a bible /on the bedside-table/}.
b.	There	are	{two men /standing outside our gate/}.

Note that the verb-form conforms here to the ***number*** (singular or plural) of the ***S-log. phrase***.

In contrast to the German equivalent, the English existential construction generally uses ***only*** the verb ***be*** in the matrix. Sometimes other verbs denoting existence, occurrence or position can be found in literary language, e.g. *There stood an ancient oak-tree at the gateway to the plantation*. However, this sounds not only elevated in style, but slightly old-fashioned, and would not be heard or seen in ordinary neutral language.

A common mistake among German speakers is to shift a present participle, as in (94) b., into the matrix to make a single progressive form, i.e. **There are standing two men outside our gate*. ⚠

068/7.2 Extraposition

This is also a ***postponement*** device, mostly in the form of an ***It + be***-construction. Here, a ***clause*** is postponed, and not a phrase (as with existential sentences). The clause (generally a ***that***-clause or an ***infinitive*** clause) is the ***S-log.***, and the 'empty' or 'dummy' ***it*** is the ***S-gramm.***:

	S-gramm.	*P*	*Cs*	*S-log.*
(95) a.	It	was	difficult	[to follow the lecture].
b.	It	is	nice	[that you'll be home for Christmas].

The gerund also occurs. Examples that spring to mind are particularly the idiomatic phrases with *worth, no good/no use*. Other kinds of action comment are also found with the gerund, especially in speech:

	S-gramm.	*P*	*Cs*	*S-log.*
(96) a.	It	is	pleasant	[sitting here in the sunshine].
b.	It	is	worth	[seeing that film].

We have so far called ***extraposition*** an ***It + be***-construction. This is the main form, but it is not the only one. ***Extraposition*** can occur with certain other verbs too:

	S-gramm.	*P*	*Od*	*S-log.*
(97) a.	It	worried	us	[that Christine had lost her job].
b.	It	happened		[that Julie saw Brian at the party].
c.	It	surprised	Julie	[to see Brian at the party].

The verbs are principally: those expressing reactions and feelings (e.g. *worry, annoy, surprise, move*); verbs meaning *happen* or *seem* (*It turned out/seemed that the painting was a fake*); verbs in the ***passive*** expressing a mental or communicative act in a general, anonymous or impersonal way: *It was decided/suggested/assumed/thought/revealed that about a hundred jobs at the firm would be lost.*

Finally, extraposition occurs also with clauses functioning as ***direct object***. In this case, ***it*** is the ***grammatical direct object*** and the clause is the ***logical direct object***:

	S	*P*	*Od-gramm.*	*Co*	*Od-log.*
(98)	a. Bernadette	thought	it	difficult	[to follow the lecture].
	b. Strong winds	made	it	dangerous	[to climb the cliff].

068/7.3 Cleft sentences

These are common devices for emphasis. They also involve ***postponement***. The ***cleft sentence*** (dt. *Spaltsatz*) is similar on the surface to extraposition, as it is also an ***It + be***-construction. In the ***cleft sentence***, however, the second clause is a ***relative clause***. The ***antecedent*** is stressed: *It was CLAIRE that/who got the second prize last night in the pub quiz.*

Cleft sentences can pick out various elements in a sentence for emphasis, including even adverbials and complements. In (99) the first example is the ordinary neutral sentence. The rest are cleft sentences emphasizing different parts of the original. Possible contextual reasons for the emphasis are shown by the contrast examples in brackets:

(99) a. Claire got the second prize last night in the pub quiz.
b. It was Claire that/who got the second prize last night in the pub quiz.
(… ***not*** Felicity …)
c. It was the second prize that Claire got last night in the pub quiz.
(… ***not*** the first prize …)
d. It was last night that Claire got the second prize in the pub quiz.
(… ***not*** the night before …)
e. It was in the pub quiz that Claire got the second prize last night.
(… ***not*** in the darts competition …)

The syntax is as follows:

S P Cs *S P* *Od* *A* *A*
(100) a. It was {Claire /that got the second prize last night in the pub quiz/}.
S P Cs *Od* *S P* *A* *A*
b. It was {the second prize /that Claire got last night in the pub quiz/}.

Note that there are two contrasts to the extraposition construction: the pronoun ***it*** here is the regular and only subject of the matrix; secondly, the ***second clause*** in a ***cleft sentence*** (unlike the second clause in extraposition) belongs to the ***subject complement***. In extraposition, the second clause is the logical subject, and can replace the grammatical subject ***it*** at the beginning of the sentence.

On this basis we can distinguish the two constructions:

(101) a. ***It*** was your idea ***that we should get married.***
That we should get married was your idea. (= ***Extraposition***)
b. It was your idea that I rejected.
*That I rejected was your idea. (= ***Cleft sentence***)

It is only necessary to distinguish, of course, when the sub-clause in each is introduced by ***that***. And as a reminder: ***that*** is a ***conjunction*** in ***extraposition***, but a ***relative pronoun*** in a ***cleft sentence***.

068/7.4 A note on the relative clause in cleft sentences

Note that the function of the ***relative pronoun*** is the same as the function of its ***antecedent*** in the ***original neutral sentence***: in (100)b., for instance, the relative pronoun is ***direct object***. This can be explained from the internal syntax of the relative clause, of course. But going back to (99)a. we can see that the antecedent in the cleft sentence version, *the second prize*, is also the ***original direct object*** in the neutral version. This is another way of saying what the cleft sentence does: i.e. it focuses on certain elements in certain functions in the original. In (99)b. this is the ***subject***, *Claire*, in (99)c. the ***direct object***, *the second prize*, and in d. and e. the ***adverbials*** *last night* and *in the pub quiz*.

This last point, however, brings us to one of several 'irregularities' (or exceptions) shown by the relative clause in a cleft sentence.

Normal relative clauses allow only nouns as antecedents. In ***cleft relative clauses***, however, the antecedent may be a ***prepositional phrase***, as in (99)e.

Furthermore, prepositional phrases cannot normally function as subject complements. In this case, however, they do.

A third irregularity is the fact that the relative clause, although restrictive, does ***not define*** or ***identify*** the ***antecedent***. In (100), for instance, *Claire* and *the second prize* identify themselves, and do not need any defining postmodification. Nevertheless, a ***cleft relative clause*** does identify something. But the question is, what? The answer becomes clear when we express the cleft-sentence as an ordinary one, taking its antecedent now as the new subject and keeping the relative clause as it is. There is now an 'antecedent gap' which we need to fill. Doing this in a way that keeps the sense of the original, we get (102)b. from (102)a. and (102)d. from (102)c.:

(102) a. It was Claire that got the second prize.
b. Claire was the person that got the second prize.
c. It was the second prize that Claire got.
d. The second prize was the prize that Claire got.

In b. and d. the relative clause has become a regular one that now defines its antecedent normally. The new antecedent refers simply to a larger category which the subject (= the old antecedent) is a member of. The answer to our question, then, is this: a ***cleft relative clause*** defines (in sense) a 'missing antecedent'. This stands for a more general category of things or persons which the ***cleft antecedent*** belongs to.

068/7.5 Pseudo-cleft sentences

These are related to cleft sentences, but instead of relative clauses they contain ***nominal relative clauses*** (see also **068/7.6**). The most common nominal relative element is ***what***, but others also occur:

(103) a. A cup of tea is what I need right now.
b. Where I'd like to be at the moment is in Hawaii.
c. What children want most at Christmas is snow.
d. August is when most Europeans go on holiday.

Here, as with cleft sentences, two clauses are made out of one for purposes of emphasis:

I need a cup of tea right now ⟶ *A cup of tea is what I need right now;*
Most Europeans go on holiday in August ⟶ *August is when ...*

Emphasis is generally on ***things*** (rather than persons), and is placed on the ***subject*** or ***object*** of the base sentence (less frequently, on the ***adverbial***, as in b. and d., and sometimes even on the verb phrase and the action, as explained further below).

In the ***pseudo-cleft sentence***, the ***emphasized element*** is the ***phrase in the matrix clause***, which functions as subject or subject complement (see example (103)).

The most common pseudo-cleft sentences are with ***what***, with the sub-clause more frequently as ***subject***, as in (102)c. The other ***wh***-clauses tend to be more common as ***subject complement***. A full analysis looks like this:

S Od S P A A P Cs
(104) a. [What children want most at Christmas] is snow.
S P Cs A S P A
b. August is [when most Europeans go on holiday].

Note that like ordinary relative pronouns and adverbs, ***nominal relative pronouns*** and ***adverbs*** have a function ***inside their own clauses***, e.g. in (103)a. ***what*** is the ***direct object*** of *want*. Their function is the same as the ***original function*** of the emphasized element in the ***base sentence***:

S ***P*** ***Od***

(105) a. Selina's coldness bothers me.

S ***S*** ***P*** ***Od*** ***Cs***

b. [What bothers me] is Selina's coldness.

S ***P*** ***Od***

c. I hate Selina's coldness.

S ***Od*** ***S*** ***P*** ***P*** ***Cs***

d. [What I hate] is Selina's coldness.

A speciality with the ***pseudo-cleft*** construction is that it can also focus on the ***verb phrase***. In this case, ***do*** is used in the sub-clause as a ***verbal pro-form***, and an ***infinitive*** occurs (with or – usually – without *to*) in the matrix clause: *What most Europeans* ***do*** *in August is* ***go*** *on holiday.*

The infinitive is also used when there is a past tense in the sub-clause: *What most people* ***did*** *for a holiday last year was* ***stay*** *at home.*

When there is a ***progressive form*** in the sub-clause, this is reflected in the matrix as a ***gerund***: *What most people* ***are doing*** *for a holiday this year is* ***staying*** *at home.*

A ***perfect*** in the sub-clause appears in the matrix either as an ordinary ***infinitive***, or as a ***past participle***: *What you****'ve done*** *is* ***(to) ruin*** *my business/is* ***ruined*** *my business.*

Function analysis is as follows:

S ***Od*** ***S*** ***P*** ***A*** ***A*** ***P*** ***Cs*** ***P*** ***A***

(106) a. [What most people did for a holiday last year] was [stay at home].

S ***Od*** ***S*** ***P*** ***A*** ***A*** ***P*** ***Cs*** ***P*** ***A***

b. [What most people are doing for a holiday this year] is [staying at home].

Verb-phrase emphasis is common in speech, but less so in more formal and written language.

Finally, it can be said that the pseudo-cleft sentence has more emotional emphasis than the cleft sentence and is heard more often. It is not quite so flexible syntactically, however, and as we have said, tends to be applied mainly to inanimate subjects or objects in the base sentence. Reference to persons is possible in some cases. This requires the pronoun ***who***: *Mrs. Simmonds was who I meant.*

However, ***who*** sounds awkward as a nominal relative pronoun, and is generally avoided (see also 14.1, **066/3.9**). The normal solution is to use an ordinary noun phrase with a relative clause: *Mrs. Simmonds was the woman (that/who/whom) I meant.*

068/7.6 Nominal relative clauses

We have just been discussing ***nominal relative clauses*** in pseudo-cleft sentences. But they occur in other sentence types too:

S P Od Od S P
(107) a. I don't like [what Ralph has written].
S P Od S P-pass A
b. The police have recovered [what was stolen from the gallery].
S Od S P A P Od
c. [What the critics say] never bothers Ralph.
S P Od A S P A Od S P Od
d. Maureen hated [where she went to school] and [whoever taught her].

It should be remembered that the ***-ever***-pronouns and -adverbs have the meaning 'any'. Apart from featuring in the classical 'nominal' clauses (i.e. those functioning as subject, object or complement), they also occur in ***adverbial*** clauses: *She is popular wherever she sings; Whatever he does, he makes grave mistakes; Whoever you see, give them my regards.*

Finally, a point on ***prepositions***: nominal relative pronouns can complement prepositions in the same way as ordinary relative pronouns. With a nominal relative pronoun, the preposition ***must*** be postposed (i.e. placed at the end of the clause, or at least after the verb):

Od A S P A
(108) a. The government is partly financing [what we're working on].
(... the project that we're working on)
S Od S P
b. [Whoever she was waiting for] didn't turn up.
(The person that she was waiting for ...)

In brackets, for comparison, are ordinary relative clauses with the same meaning. Note that in (108)a. the pronoun is part of a ***prepositional phrase***, and is therefore part of an ***adverbial*** function. In (108)b. it is a ***prepositional object***, i.e. ***Od*** of the prepositional verb *wait for*.

068/7.7 Interrogative clauses

Interrogative clauses, as a reminder, are ***indirect questions***. These and their syntax were dealt with in detail in chapter 11.3, **053/4**. They are briefly mentioned again here, as they are sometimes confused with nominal relative clauses. The reason for this is that both use ***wh***-words, and both, actually, are 'nominal' in function:

(109) a. I repeated what my colleagues had said at the meeting.
(***what*** = ... *the things which* ...)
b. I wondered what my colleagues had said at the meeting.
(***what*** = ... *which things* ...)

Replacement by the phrase *the things which* in (109)a. shows that ***what*** stands for the sequence ***antecedent + relative pronoun***, and is therefore a ***nominal relative pronoun***. In

(109)b. *which* in the phrase *which things* can only be a ***question word*** (here an ***interrogative determiner***). This makes it clear that in b. a mental question was being asked. So in b. we have an ***interrogative clause***. The difference is also shown, of course, in the clear semantic distinction between the two matrix verbs (i.e. *wonder* means to 'ask oneself', whereas *repeat* presupposes knowledge).

With interrogative clauses the matrix verb (or its complementation) usually refers to the presence, absence or communication of knowledge, e.g. *I asked/knew/was told what my colleagues had said*. In many cases, in fact, we can re-phrase an ***interrogative clause*** as a ***direct question***, and then add the words *the answer to the question* before it, e.g. *I asked/knew/was told* **the answer to the question** *"What did my colleagues say?"*

There may be ambiguity. The sentence in (110)a. could mean (at least out of context) either (110)b. or (110)c. But our '*thing*-test' will distinguish the two meanings:

(110) a. The teacher asked Simon what she had asked Chris.
b. The teacher asked Simon the same question that she had asked Chris.
[... *the thing which* ... = ***nominal relative clause***]
c. The teacher asked Simon, "What did I ask Chris?"
[... *which thing* ... = ***interrogative clause***]